Simply Psychology

To Sebastian with love from his grandpa

Simply Psychology

Third Edition

Michael W. Eysenck

Psychology Press
Taylor & Francis Group

HOVE AND NEW YORK

Published 2013 by Psychology Press
27 Church Road, Hove, East Sussex, BN3 2FA

Simultaneously published in the USA and Canada
by Psychology Press
711 Third Avenue, New York, NY 10017

www.psypress.com

Psychology Press is an imprint of the Taylor & Francis Group, an informa business

© 2013 by Psychology Press

British Library Cataloguing in Publication Data
A catalogue record for this book is available from the British Library

Library of Congress Cataloging-in-Publication Data
Eysenck, Michael W.
    Simply psychology / Michael W. Eysenck. — 3rd ed.
      p. cm.
    Includes bibliographical references and index.
    ISBN 978–1–84872–102–9 (softcover)
  1. Psychology.   I. Title.

BF121.E97 2012
150—dc23   2012033157

ISBN 978–1–84872–102–9

Typeset in India by Newgen Imaging Systems (P) Ltd
Printed and bound in Slovenia.

Contents

About the author   *vii*
Preface   *ix*

1   Introduction   2
2   Methods of investigation   16

Part 1   **Biological approach**   **33**
3   Biological bases of behaviour   34
4   Stress   50
5   Emotion   68
6   Aggression   84

Part 2   **Behaviourist approach**   **101**
7   Conditioning and learning   102

Part 3   **Developmental approach**   **119**
8   Cognitive development   120
9   Language development   136
10 Moral development   150
11 Sex and gender   164

Part 4   **Social approach**   **179**
12 Attachment and deprivation   180
13 Prejudice and discrimination   196
14 Pro-social behaviour   212
15 Social influence   228
16 Social perception and attraction   246

Part 5   **Individual differences**   **261**
17 Intelligence   262
18 Personality   278
19 The self-concept   296

Part 6   **Cognitive approach**   **311**
20 Visual perception   312
21 Memory   328
22 Problem solving and creativity   348

Part 7   **Effective learning**   **363**
23 Effective studying and learning   364

Glossary   381
References   391
Index   423

About the author

Michael W. Eysenck is one of the best-known psychologists in Europe. He is Professorial Fellow at Roehampton University and Emeritus Professor at Royal Holloway, University of London. He is especially interested in cognitive psychology (about which he has written several books) and most of his research focuses on the role of cognitive factors in anxiety within normal and clinical populations.

He has published 43 books. His previous textbooks published by Psychology Press include *Psychology for AS Level (5th Edn)* (2012), *Psychology for A2 Level* (2009), *A2 Psychology: Key Topics (2nd Edn)* (2006), *Psychology: An International Perspective* (2004), *Psychology: A Student's Handbook (6th Edn)* (with Mark Keane) (2010), *Fundamentals of Psychology* (2009), *Fundamentals of Cognition (2nd Edn)* (2012), *Perspectives on Psychology* (1994), and *Individual Differences: Normal and Abnormal* (1994). He has also written several articles on topics within the AS Psychology specification for the journal *Psychology Review*, and has given talks at numerous A-level conferences.

In his spare time, Michael Eysenck enjoys travelling, tennis, walking, and an occasional game of golf. He is a keen supporter of Manchester United Football Club.

Preface

There has been a dramatic increase in the number of students of psychology in recent years. This increase has happened at all levels, and includes GCSE, AS level, A2 level, and university degree courses. In addition, there are many more students of nursing, education, business studies, and so on, who study psychology as part of their courses. It is my hope that this book will be of use to all students who are starting to study psychology.

There are two main approaches to writing a simple introduction to psychology. One is to leave out everything that is hard or challenging; this is what might be called the "filleted" approach. The other is to present a more rounded account of modern psychology in a simple and accessible way. I have done my best to follow the second approach. Whether I have succeeded is for the readers of this book to decide.

This is the third edition of *Simply Psychology*. I have retained the structure of the second edition. However, nearly all of the chapters have been extensively updated, and some of them are very different from the previous edition.

In my opinion, psychology is the most interesting subject you can study. An important part of my intention in this chapter (and the entire book) is to convince you of that. Media coverage often makes it look as if psychologists only succeed in discovering things everyone has always known. I may be biased, but I feel very strongly that this state of affairs tells us more about the media than about psychology. Hopefully, as you read this chapter and the rest of the book, you will find yourself agreeing with me that psychological research goes well beyond the obvious. Indeed, it is full of important insights into human behaviour that can (and already have) benefited society greatly.

What could be more interesting or important than achieving an understanding of our fellow human beings? Enjoy psychology!!!

Introduction

1

What is psychology?

What is psychology? It is amazingly wide ranging. Here are just a few examples. Some psychologists are involved in treating mental disorders and use many techniques not dreamt of by Sigmund Freud. There are also forensic psychologists who engage in offender profiling and tracking down serial killers and other criminals. Other psychologists make use of brain scanners, with their research producing the brightly coloured pictures of brain activity found in magazines. Still other psychologists (known as health psychologists) are hard at work trying to persuade us to adopt healthier lifestyles with less smoking and drinking and more physical exercise.

What is the science of psychology actually about?

What is the common element in the varied activities of psychologists? Probably the most frequent definition of psychology is that it is the scientific study of behaviour. However, this definition is too limited, because most psychologists try to understand *why* people behave in certain ways. To achieve that understanding, we must consider *internal* processes and motives. Thus, we arrive at the following definition:

> Psychology is a science in which behavioural and other evidence (e.g., individuals' reports of their thoughts and feelings; patterns of brain activation) is used to understand the internal processes leading people (and members of other species) to behave as they do.

As you read this book, you may be bewildered (hopefully not *too* bewildered!) by the numerous approaches psychologists have adopted in their attempts to understand human behaviour. These approaches exist because our behaviour is jointly determined by several factors including the following:

- The specific stimuli presented to us
- Our recent experiences (e.g., being stuck in a traffic jam)
- Our genetic endowment
- Our physiological system
- Our cognitive system (our perceptions, thoughts, and memories)
- The social environment

- The cultural environment
- Our previous life experiences (including those of childhood)
- Our personal characteristics (including intelligence, personality, and mental health)

We can see that our behaviour is determined by many factors by considering "road rage" as a concrete example. This is a phenomenon in which motorists become uncontrollably angry and threaten physical violence to motorists who have frustrated them.

How can we understand the behaviour of a man exhibiting road rage? His behaviour may depend partly on the genes he has inherited, which may have led him to develop a very aggressive personality. It may depend in part on his childhood experiences, for example, the presence of violence in the family. It may depend in part on the man's clinical history. He may, for example, have a history of psychopathic or antisocial behaviour. It may depend on his thoughts and feelings (e.g., the other motorist reminds him of someone he despises). It may depend on the man's physiological state. For example, his internal bodily state may be highly aroused and agitated because he is already late for an important appointment or has a very stressful job. Finally, his behaviour may depend on cultural factors—expressing one's anger by physically attacking someone is more unacceptable in some cultures than others.

The take-home message is that there is no *single* "correct" interpretation of the man's road rage. Probably several of the factors just discussed contributed to his behaviour. Thus, the scope of psychology needs to be very broad if we are to understand human behaviour. More generally, psychology is a multidisciplinary science that has been enriched by physiologists, neuroscientists, sociologists, biologists, biochemists, anthropologists, and others.

How useful is psychology?

Most people think psychology is a fascinating subject (which it is!). We are all interested in trying to understand ourselves and other people, and that is the central goal of psychology. However, there is more controversy concerning the usefulness of psychology. Sceptics argue that psychology tells us what we already know (the science of the bleeding obvious!). They also argue that laboratory findings don't generalise to everyday life because laboratory research is so artificial. Finally, sceptics claim most psychological research is trivial (e.g., rats running through mazes).

The strengths and limitations of laboratory research are discussed in Chapter 2. However, it is worth emphasising here that the greatest strength of laboratory research is that it allows us to study behaviour under well-controlled conditions. As a result, we can identify some determinants of behaviour much more clearly than would be possible through simply observing people in everyday life. The advantages of experimental control typically outweigh the disadvantages of artificiality.

Perhaps the greatest criticism made by those knowing little about psychology is that it is "just common sense". There are two major problems with that criticism. First, common sense doesn't form a coherent set of assumptions about behaviour. Consider the commonsensical views contained

Why is common sense of limited usefulness?

in proverbs. Several pairs of proverbs express opposite meanings to each other. For example, "Absence makes the heart grow fonder" can be contrasted with "Out of sight, out of mind", and "Many hands make light work" is the opposite of "Too many cooks spoil the broth". Since common sense involves such incompatible views, it can't be used as a sound basis for understanding human behaviour.

Second, the notion that psychology is just common sense can be disproved by considering research in psychology in which the findings differed greatly from what most people would have predicted. A well-known example is Stanley Milgram's (1974) work on obedience to authority (see Chapter 15). In essence, participants were told to administer electric shocks of increasing intensity to a middle-aged man with a heart condition. At 180 volts, the man shouted out, "I can't stand the pain!" By 270 volts, the man produced only an agonised scream.

Common sense can be contradictory: "Look before you leap" vs. "He who hesitates is Lost".

If you had been a participant in this research, would you have been willing to give the maximum (and potentially deadly) 450-volt shock? Milgram found that everyone denied they personally would do such a thing. Psychiatrists predicted that only one person in a thousand would go on to the 450-volt stage. In fact, about 65% of Milgram's participants gave the maximum shock—650 times as many people as the experts had predicted!

Milgram's findings were totally unexpected, and provided us with fresh insights into human behaviour. By the way, I should point out that no shocks were actually administered, but the participants didn't know this when taking part in the experiment.

Below is a short quiz so you can see for yourself whether the findings in psychology are obvious. Many of the items are based on those used by Furnham (1988). For each item, decide whether you think it is true or false:

Psychology quiz	
1. Flashbulb memories (i.e., vivid memories for dramatic world events like 9/11) are exceptionally accurate and long-lived.	TRUE/FALSE
2. In making decisions, committees tend to be more conservative than individuals.	TRUE/FALSE
3. In small amounts, alcohol is a stimulant.	TRUE/FALSE
4. Physically attractive adults have better social skills and physical health than unattractive ones	TRUE/FALSE
5. Very intelligent children tend to be less strong physically than those of average intelligence.	TRUE/FALSE

6. Patients with amnesia have very poor long-term memory but can still acquire many skills such as learning the piano.	TRUE/FALSE
7. People's behaviour in most situations depends far more on their personality than on the situation itself.	TRUE/FALSE
8. A schizophrenic is someone with a split personality.	TRUE/FALSE

The correct answer is "False" to most of the questions. However, the correct answer is "True" to questions 4 and 6. Unless you already know a lot about psychology, you probably had several wrong answers—thus, psychology is *not* simply common sense!

Hindsight bias

When is hindsight bias involved?

We have seen that it is wrong to assume that findings in psychology merely confirm common sense. Why, then, do so many people claim that most findings in psychology are unsurprising or obvious? In other words, why do they argue, "I knew it all along"? The answer was discovered by Fischhoff and Beyth (1975) in research to which we now turn.

Fischhoff and Beyth (1975) asked American students to estimate the probability of various outcomes on the eve of President Nixon's trips to China and Russia. After the trips were over, the students performed the same tasks but were told to ignore their knowledge of what had actually happened. In spite of these instructions, participants with the benefit of hindsight gave events that had actually happened a much higher probability than they did beforehand. Thus, the students couldn't stop themselves using their knowledge of what had happened. This tendency to be wise after the event is **hindsight bias**.

Hindsight bias occurs in part because information about what has *actually* happened alters the memory for what had been *expected* ahead of the event (Hardt et al., 2010). This helps to explain why it is very hard to prevent hindsight bias. Pohl and Hell (1996) found that warning participants in advance about hindsight bias didn't reduce the bias at all. The stubborn persistence of hindsight bias is a problem for teachers of psychology because it produces students who are unimpressed by most findings in psychology!

Findings: Simple and complex

In spite of the existence of hindsight bias, it must be admitted that some findings in psychology are actually obvious. For example, you won't be surprised to hear that practice has beneficial effects on long-term memory.

So far I have only provided you with a *simple* finding relating to the effects of practice. The findings are much less obvious when we consider more *complex* issues. Suppose you need to remember material from a textbook for a test next week. Is it better to spend nearly all your time studying the material or to spend some time studying the material but most of it testing how much you can remember? Most people think the former strategy is better. However, the evidence indicates the latter is superior (Karpicke et al., 2009; see Chapter 23).

KEY TERM

Hindsight bias: the tendency to be wise after the event using the benefit of hindsight.

In sum, simple findings in psychology are often fairly obvious. However, that is rarely the case with more complex findings, which are generally hard for non-psychologists to predict or to explain.

Cross-cultural psychology

The overwhelming majority of psychological research has been on people from Western, Educated, Industrialised, Rich, and Democratic (WEIRD) societies (Henrich et al., 2010). Detailed figures were provided by Arnett (2008), who considered research in the top psychology journals for the years 2003–2007. Of the participants, 96% were from WEIRD societies (68% from the United States alone). Of the first authors, 99% were from WEIRD societies (73% from the United States). These figures occurred even though only 12% of the world's population belongs to WEIRD societies (5% to the United States).

Why is it is important to study cross-cultural differences?

Does the narrow focus of most psychological research matter? In essence, it wouldn't matter if the findings obtained in American studies were the same as those obtained elsewhere in the world. However, it would matter if there were substantial differences in behaviour in different countries.

The above issue has been addressed by researchers within **cross-cultural psychology**. These researchers compare different cultures (a **culture** exists when a given population has shared beliefs, attitudes, and practices). Note that on this definition there are several cultures *within* countries such as the United States or United Kingdom.

As people and cultures are so diverse psychologists must take care not to overgeneralise their findings to everyone without sufficient evidence.

Unsurprisingly, the evidence indicates large differences in attitudes and behaviour across cultures and countries (see Henrich et al., 2010, for a review). As Westen (1996, p. 679) pointed out, "By twentieth century Western standards, nearly every human who has ever lived outside the contemporary West is lazy, passive, and lacking in industriousness. In contrast, by the standards of most cultures in human history, most Westerns are self-centered and frenetic." Since those living in WEIRD societies aren't remotely representative of the world's population as a whole, it is ill-advised to generalise from them to the rest of mankind.

There are also important differences between inhabitants of the United States and other Western societies (Henrich et al., 2010). Within Western industrialised countries, Lipset (1996) found Americans were most inclined to see the world in absolute moral terms, were the least class conscious, were the most patriotic, had the highest income inequality rate, and were among the most optimistic.

We will be discussing cross-cultural differences in several aspects of human behaviour. Examples include attachment behaviour (Chapter 12), pro-social behaviour (Chapter 14), personality (Chapter 18), and the self-concept (Chapter 19).

KEY TERMS

Cross-cultural psychology: the systematic study of similarities in and differences between cultures around the world.

Culture: the values, beliefs, and practices shared by members of a given society.

Individualism vs. collectivism

It has often been argued (e.g., Hofstede, 1980) that we should distinguish between individualistic and collectivistic cultures. **Individualistic cultures** emphasise independence, personal responsibility, and each person's uniqueness. In contrast, **collectivistic cultures** emphasise interdependence, sharing of responsibility, and group membership.

Hofstede (1980) carried out a study on IBM employees in 52 countries. The United States and United Kingdom scored very high on individualism, whereas Ecuador, Venezuela, and several Far East countries scored low.

There are various limitations with Hofstede's approach. First, he assumed that individualism and collectivism are *opposites* of each other. In fact, however, they are essentially *independent* of each other (Triandis et al., 1993).

Second, the concepts of individualism and collectivism are very broad. As A.P. Fiske (2002, p. 83) pointed out, "IND [individualism] amalgamates Thomas Paine, Vincent van Gogh, Mahatma Gandhi, Michael Jordan, Hugh Hefner, and Adolf Hitler into one category!"

Third, what is true at the level of a culture isn't necessarily true at the level of individuals within that culture. Triandis et al. (2001) found that only 60% of those living in individualistic cultures had individualistic beliefs, and only 60% of those in collectivistic cultures had collectivistic beliefs.

Cultural influences: Fixed or flexible?

It is often assumed our culture has a fixed and constant impact on us. However, that assumption is incorrect. Cultural influences affect us most when we are in situations making culture-relevant information easily accessible. For example, you may identify more with your own culture when you hear the national anthem than at other times.

Hong et al. (1997) showed the flexibility of cultural influences in a study on Westernised Chinese students in Hong Kong. Participants were shown pictures strongly related to the American culture (e.g., the American flag; Marilyn Monroe) or the Chinese culture (e.g., a Chinese dragon; the Great Wall). After that, they interpreted an ambiguous picture. Those exposed to symbols of American culture favoured an individualistic interpretation. In contrast, those exposed to symbols of Chinese culture favoured a collectivistic interpretation.

Conclusions

People's behaviour is strongly influenced by the culture to which they belong. As a result, we need to be cautious about assuming that findings obtained in American or European studies (where most psychological research takes place) are applicable elsewhere in the world.

We also need to be cautious about assuming that some cultures are superior to others. Western psychologists have an unfortunate tendency to refer to non-Western cultures as "undeveloped", "under-developed", or "primitive". According to Owusu-Bempah and Howitt (1994, p. 165), it would be more accurate to say that all cultures are highly developed in some ways: "[There is] a materially advanced but spiritually bankrupt culture in the West; a spiritually developed and relatively socially stagnant culture in the East, and a developed social consciousness, but relatively undeveloped material culture in Africa."

KEY TERMS

Individualistic cultures: cultures (mainly in Western societies) in which the emphasis is on personal responsibility rather than on group needs; see **collectivistic cultures.**

Collectivistic cultures: cultures (such as many in the Far East) in which the emphasis is on group solidarity rather than on individual responsibility.

There is a tendency for one culture to judge another as being "undeveloped" or "primitive".

Why is psychology important?

Psychology has various unique advantages over all other academic subjects. Most people are very interested in other people. They want to understand them better, and to develop deep and fulfilling relationships with them. They also want to develop a fuller understanding of themselves in the hope this will allow them to cope better with their lives.

Another major reason why psychology is important is because it has numerous applications to everyday life. Applications of special importance can be found in clinical psychology and health psychology. We will consider both briefly.

Clinical psychology

Mental disorders cause untold human misery to tens of millions of people around the world. As we will see, psychology has contributed enormously to the treatment of mental disorders.

Sigmund Freud and beyond

The towering figure in clinical psychology is Sigmund Freud (1846–1939). He developed psychoanalysis, which can be regarded as the first "talking cure". Freud argued that individuals experiencing traumatic events in childhood (e.g., sexual abuse) repress their memories for those events by forcing them into the unconscious (see Chapter 21). Crucial to the success of therapy is allowing patients to gain access to their repressed feelings and thoughts, with the goal being to provide them with insight into the true nature of their problems.

The retrieval of repressed memories can be facilitated by free association or dream analysis. In free association, patients are asked to respond rapidly to emotion words (e.g., "mother") presented to them with the first ideas that come to mind. Freud regarded dream analysis as important because he argued that people's deep-seated feelings and concerns influence their dreams. People's reports of their dreams are typically fairly innocuous but psychoanalysis can reveal the hidden meanings contained in them.

Sigmund Freud (1856–1939), the founder of psychoanalysis.

Why has Freud had an enormous influence? First, psychoanalysis was the first systematic treatment for mental disorders based on psychological principles. Second, Freud argued correctly that childhood experiences influence adult behaviour and personality (see Chapter 18). Third, Freud argued that unconscious processes and motives related to repressed memories partly determine our behaviour. There is convincing evidence that unconscious processes are important (see Chapter 20). Fourth, Freud hugely expanded the scope of psychology. He argued that psychology is relevant to virtually all human behaviour, whereas before him the focus was on topics such as simple learning and associations of ideas.

Many forms of psychological therapy have been developed since Sigmund Freud introduced psychoanalysis over 100 years ago. Of particular importance is cognitive-behavioural therapy. Unsurprisingly, this form of therapy focuses on cognitive factors (i.e., changing patients' negative views about themselves and their lives). It also focuses on behavioural factors (i.e., changing patients' undesirable patterns of behaviour into desirable ones).

The overall evidence reveals fairly small differences in the effectiveness of different forms of therapy. Matt and Navarro (1997) found in a thorough review that 75% of patients receiving therapy based on psychological principles improved more than the average untreated control patient. Thus, most forms of therapy are at least moderately effective. However, cognitive-behavioural therapy is often the most effective type of treatment and psychoanalysis tends to be the least effective. Psychoanalysis has limited effectiveness because it focuses excessively on *childhood* experiences and tends to de-emphasise adult patients' *current* social and interpersonal problems.

Depression and anxiety

The most common mental disorders are depression or mood disorders and anxiety disorders, and so we will focus on them. Between 5% and 8% of the European population suffers from clinical depression during any given year (Andlin-Sobocki et al., 2005) and the figure is 12% for anxiety disorders (Andlin-Sobocki & Wittchen, 2005). Overall, 75 million Europeans suffer from anxiety and/or depression in any given year.

Apart from the cost in human misery, there are very large financial costs as well. The total annual cost of mental disorders within Europe is 240 billion euros (about £220 billion or $320 billion) when account is taken of lost workdays and productivity loss.

What would happen if all Europeans suffering from anxiety or depression received psychological therapy? It isn't possible to give a precise answer. However, it is indisputable that tens of millions of patients would benefit from such therapy every year. In addition, the cost savings would run into tens of billions of pounds.

Social phobia

So far I have focused on the *general* benefits of clinical psychology. I will conclude this section by considering one disorder in more detail (see Eysenck, 2009a, for a fuller account). **Social phobia** is a disorder in which the individual experiences severe anxiety in many social situations. Indeed, the anxiety is so great that social phobics often avoid social situations to reduce their level of anxiety. We will see how treatment for this disorder has improved recently.

KEY TERM

Social phobia: a mental disorder in which the patient experiences very high levels of anxiety in social situations which often cause him/her to avoid such situations.

According to Clark and Wells (1995), social phobics exaggerate how threatening social situations actually are. In technical terms, they have an **interpretive bias** (the tendency to interpret ambiguous situations in excessively negative ways). It is reasonable to assume that social phobia could be treated successfully by reducing (or eliminating) that interpretive bias.

Exposure therapy has proved moderately successful with social phobia. Exposure therapy (discussed in Chapter 7) involves exposing the patient to feared social situations for lengthy periods of time. It initially creates intense anxiety, but this anxiety typically reduces substantially over time. Exposure therapy allows social phobics to realise that social situations are less threatening than they had previously thought, thus reducing their interpretive bias.

Why is exposure therapy only moderately effective? Social phobics undergoing exposure therapy often engage in safety-seeking behaviours (e.g., avoiding eye contact; "melting into the background") to avoid being negatively evaluated by others. As a result, many social phobics maintain their interpretive bias because they believe their safety-seeking behaviours prevent social disasters.

Suppose that social phobics were instructed to avoid safety-seeking behaviours in social situations. This should allow them to obtain more *accurate* feedback about the impression they make on other people. Exposure therapy + avoidance of safety-seeking behaviours should eliminate interpretive bias. Thus, this form of cognitive-behavioural therapy should be more effective than exposure therapy on its own.

Clark et al. (2006) obtained strong support for the above prediction. Exposure therapy + avoidance of safety-seeking behaviours benefited 84% of patients compared to 42% receiving exposure therapy on its own and 0% for control patients. Thus, treatment for social phobia has improved as a result of having a clearer understanding of the disorder.

Health psychology

The number of people in England and Wales dying from heart disease was 68,000 fewer in 2000 than 1981 (Ünal et al., 2005). This reduction produced a total gain of about 925,415 life years. There are two main ways we might explain this reduction in mortality from heart disease. First, there have been substantial advances in medicine. These advances include the development of more precise and effective surgical interventions, increased use of aspirin to prevent heart attacks, treatment for hypertension, and the use of statins (drugs that reduce cholesterol).

Second, there have been changes in lifestyle. Some of these changes are clearly beneficial (e.g., reductions in smoking) but others have adverse effects (e.g., increased obesity; decreased physical activity). Lifestyle changes involve altering behaviour and so fall within psychology.

Here is a question based on the above information. What percentage of the reduced mortality from heart disease is due to medical advances and what percentage to lifestyle changes? The answer may surprise you. Ünal et al. (2005) found that 79% of the gain in life years was due to lifestyle changes and only 21% to medical interventions!

What is the relevance of the above study to psychology? Lifestyle changes involve changing behaviour, and the experts in devising ways of changing

KEY TERM

Interpretive bias:
negative biased or distorted interpretations of ambiguous stimuli and/or situations.

behaviour are ... psychologists. More specifically, many health psychologists focus on interventions to produce beneficial lifestyle changes. The lifestyle change having by far the greatest impact on reduced mortality from heart disease was a reduction in the number of people smoking. Almost 45% of the total gain in life years from lifestyle changes and medical interventions was attributable to a reduction in smoking.

Viswesvaran and Schmidt (1992) reviewed 633 smoking cessation studies. The annual success rate achieved by health psychologists was 30% with multi-component packages (e.g., basic counselling; information on the health effects of smoking; social skills training). This compared to only 6% for smokers receiving no treatment. If all 10 million smokers in the UK received multi-component smoking cessation packages from health psychologists, this could produce a gain of 24 *million* life years!

Healthy diet

One area in which health psychologists have an increasing role to play is that of healthy eating. There has been a dramatic increase in obesity throughout most of the Western world in recent times. Indeed, we might say that obesity is a very large problem. Since obesity can increase the likelihood of many serious diseases (e.g., diabetes) and can shorten life, it is important to find ways to persuade people to have a healthy diet.

Researchers have used implementation intentions to encourage people to eat more healthily. Implementation intentions are action plans that specify where, when, and how someone is going to achieve a certain goal (see Chapter 23). With respect to healthy eating, an example of an implementation intention would be as follows: "If I am at home and I want to have some dessert after dinner, then I will make myself a fruit salad" (Adriaanse, Vinkers et al., 2011).

Many researchers have compared the effectiveness in promoting a healthy diet of implementation intentions against vague intentions such as "I want to eat more fruit." Adriaanse, Vinkers et al. (2011) reviewed the relevant studies. Implementation intentions were much more effective than vague intentions in increasing healthy eating and decreasing unhealthy eating.

Why are implementation intentions so effective? They create "instant habits" in which the desired behaviour is produced fairly effortlessly when the individual finds himself/herself in the appropriate situation or situations. As a result, those using implementation intentions can eat healthily without requiring high motivation or thinking about their eating behaviour.

Health psychologists have an increasing role to play, helping people change their lifestyle e.g., to eat more healthily.

Organisation of this book

Several approaches have been taken to the study of human behaviour. The organisation of this book is based on the major approaches to psychology.

For example, social psychologists focus on our interactions with others, psychophysiologists study how the physiological system relates to behaviour, and developmental psychologists consider children's behaviour and how it develops over time.

There are six main parts to this book: biological approach; behaviourist approach; developmental approach; social approach; individual differences approach; and cognitive approach (see the figure below). Note, however, that most topics covered are of relevance to more than one approach. What I have done in such cases is to assign each chapter to the approach of most direct relevance.

Finally, there is a chapter on effective learning. This provides a practical account of what you can do to improve your study skills and ensure you benefit as much as possible from reading this book.

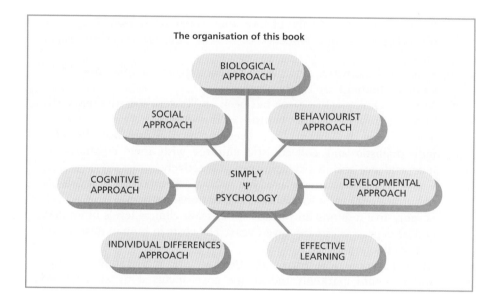

The organisation of this book

Useful features

The following features of this book are designed to make it as useful as possible:

1. Psychologists often use words in ways differing from their everyday usage, which can be confusing. Accordingly, key terms are highlighted, with their definitions given in the margin alongside.
2. A Glossary at the end of the book lists all these key terms in alphabetical order.
3. The text is punctuated with Evaluation boxes consisting of positive (+) and negative (−) points.
4. There are essay questions at the end of nearly every chapter to focus your mind on important issues.

Chapter summary

- Psychology is a science that involves trying to understand people's behaviour.
- Behaviour is jointly determined by numerous factors. These include the current stimuli, recent and childhood experiences, genetic factors, physiological factors, cognitive factors, social factors, cultural factors, personality, and intelligence.
- Critics argue that most laboratory research is artificial. However, such research has the substantial advantage of allowing us to identify many of the determinants of behaviour.
- Critics claim that psychology is merely common sense. However, there is no coherent commonsensical account of human behaviour. In addition, many (or even most) of the findings in psychology are *not* obvious.
- People often mistakenly believe that findings in psychology are obvious because of a tendency to be wise after the event (hindsight bias).
- Most of the obvious findings in psychology are simple ones. More complex findings are rarely obvious.
- Most psychological research has been on Western societies markedly different from most other cultures in the world.
- There is an important (but oversimplified) distinction between individualistic and collectivistic cultures with their emphasis on independence and interdependence, respectively.
- Cultural influences aren't fixed but instead depend on the accessibility of culture-relevant information (e.g., national anthem).
- Seventy-five millions Europeans suffer from clinical levels of anxiety and/or depression in any given year. The costs in human misery and lost production are enormous.
- Most psychological forms of therapy are moderately effective and so could markedly reduce the costs incurred by anxiety and depression.
- Developments in our understanding of social phobia have increased the effectiveness of therapy for that disorder.
- Most of the reduction in deaths from heart disease in recent years is due to lifestyle changes rather than medical advances. Health psychologists have expertise in producing lifestyle changes (e.g., persuading smokers to quit; eating more healthily).
- The chapters of this book are organised into six approaches to psychology: biological; behaviourist; developmental; social; individual differences; and cognitive.
- Useful features of the book include the following: definitions of key terms; a Glossary; Evaluation sections; essay questions; and self-assessment questions.

Further reading

- Colman, A. (1999). *What is psychology? (3rd ed.)*. London: Routledge. Andrew Colman's book provides a very readable introduction to psychology for those with little background knowledge of the subject.

- Eysenck, M.W. (2009). *Fundamentals of psychology*. Hove, UK: Psychology Press. Chapter 1 of this textbook contains a longer introduction to psychology than the one presented in this chapter.

- Furnham, A. (1988). *Lay theories: Everyday understanding of problems in the social sciences*. Oxford, UK: Pergamon. Adrian Furnham discusses a formidable amount of evidence on the limitations of commonsensical views of psychology.

- Henrich, J., Heine, S.J., & Norenza yan, A. (2010). The weirdest people in the world. *Behavioural and Brain Sciences*, *33*, 61–83. This article contains convincing evidence that the cultures studied in most psychological research are very unrepresentative of the world's cultures.

Essay questions

1. What is psychology? What are some of the main factors studied by psychologists in the attempt to understand behaviour?

2. "Psychology is just common sense." Discuss.

3. Why is it important for psychologists to study many different cultures?

4. Discuss some of the contributions that psychology has made to society.

Suppose you wanted to carry out research to increase your understanding of human behaviour. For example, you might be interested in the issue of whether watching violence on television tends to make people more aggressive. How do you think you might go about studying that issue? How many different approaches could you use? Which approach do you think would be most useful? Why do you think that?

Methods of investigation

In this chapter, we will consider the main ways psychologists carry out research into human behaviour. Much of this research has its starting point in some theory. Theories provide general explanations or accounts of certain findings or data. They also generate various **hypotheses** (predictions or expectations about factors influencing certain behaviour based on the theory). For example, someone might put forward a theory claiming that some people are generally more sociable or friendly than others. Here are some of the hypotheses this theory might generate: sociable people smile more at other people; sociable people talk more; sociable people will agree more with the views of others.

Psychologists spend much time collecting behavioural data. Data are collected to test various hypotheses. Most people assume this data collection involves proper laboratory experiments, and it is true there have been literally millions of laboratory experiments in psychology. However, as we will see, psychologists use several methods of investigation, each providing useful information about human behaviour.

As you read about the various methods of investigation in psychology, you may find yourself wondering which methods are the best. In fact, it is more useful to compare psychologists' methods used to the clubs used by golf players. The driver isn't a better or worse club than the putter, it is simply used for a different purpose. In similar fashion, each method of investigation used by psychologists is very useful for testing some hypotheses but of little use when testing other hypotheses.

Experimental method

The experimental method is used more often than any other method in psychological research. Use of the **experimental method** involves a generally high level of *control* over the experimental situation. Whatever aspect of the situation is of primary interest is manipulated systematically to observe the effects on behaviour. The experimental method can be used for laboratory experiments in controlled conditions or for field experiments in more naturalistic conditions.

Most laboratory research starts with the experimenter thinking of an **experimental hypothesis**. This is simply a prediction or expectation of what

What variables does an experimental hypothesis usually refer to?

will happen in a given situation. An example of an experimental hypothesis is that loud noise disrupts people's ability to carry out a task such as learning the information in a chapter of an introductory psychology textbook.

As with most experimental hypotheses, the one just mentioned predicts that some aspect of the situation (the presence of loud noise) affects the participants' behaviour (learning of the information). This is generally expressed more technically. The experimental hypothesis refers to an **independent variable** (some aspect of the situation manipulated or altered by the experimenter). In our example, the presence or absence of loud noise is the independent variable.

The experimental hypothesis also refers to a **dependent variable** (some aspect of the participants' behaviour). In our example, a measure of learning (e.g., a comprehension test) would be used to assess the dependent variable. In a nutshell, most experimental hypotheses predict that a given independent variable will have a specified effect on the dependent variable.

Psychologists using the experimental method hope to show the independent variable *causes* certain effects on behaviour. There has been much controversy (which we will avoid here!) about whether it is possible to show that some manipulation of the environment has *caused* the participants' behaviour to change. At the very least, however, use of the experimental method can provide suggestive evidence about causality.

The experimental hypothesis consists of the predicted effect of the independent variable on the dependent variable. There is also the null hypothesis. The **null hypothesis** states that the independent variable will have *no* effect on the dependent variable. In our example, the null hypothesis would be that loud noise has no effect on learning. The goal of most laboratory studies is to decide whether the findings obtained fit better with the experimental hypothesis or with the null hypothesis.

It might seem easy to carry out a study to test the experimental hypothesis that loud noise disrupts learning. However, various problems need to be avoided. First, we must decide how to manipulate the independent variable. In our example, we want to use loud noise, so we have to decide exactly how loud the noise should be. If it is extremely loud, it might damage the hearing of our participants and so be totally unacceptable. If it is fairly soft, it is unlikely to have any effect. It is also likely to make a difference whether the noise is meaningful (e.g., music or speech) or meaningless (e.g., the noise of a road drill).

Second, we must decide how to measure the dependent variable. We could ask our participants various questions to measure their understanding of the material in the chapter. However, we need to select questions so they are neither too easy nor too hard.

The experimental method is limited in application. Consider the factors influencing our current behaviour (see Chapter 1). The immediate situation is one such factor, and its effects can easily be studied by using the experimental method. However, our behaviour is also influenced by our personality, by our intelligence, by our childhood, and so on. Alas, none of these factors can be turned into an independent variable for the purposes of a laboratory experiment.

Confounding variables

Another issue to consider is whether our experiment contains any confounding variables. **Confounding variables** are variables mistakenly manipulated along

---

KEY TERMS

Independent variable: some aspect of the experimental situation that the experimenter manipulates in order to test a given **experimental hypothesis.**

Dependent variable: some aspect of the participants' behaviour that is measured in an experiment.

Null hypothesis: prediction that the independent variable will have no effect on the dependent variable.

Confounding variables: variables not of interest to the experimenter that are mistakenly manipulated along with the **independent variable.**

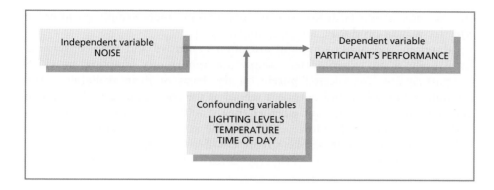

with the independent variable. Suppose one group of participants receives no noise and reads the chapter at midday, whereas the other group receives loud noise and reads the chapter at midnight. If the latter group learns less well than the former group, we wouldn't know whether this was because of the loud noise or because they learned late in the evening when tired. In this example, time of day is a confounding variable.

How do we avoid having any confounding variables? One approach is to turn confounding variables into controlled variables by holding their value constant and not allowing them to vary. Suppose we want to study the effects of noise on learning and are concerned time of day may have an effect. We could make time of day into a controlled variable by testing all our participants at a particular time of day (e.g., late morning). If we did that, time of day couldn't distort our findings. Alternatively, we could simply test our participants at random times of day while checking that there were no systematic time-of-day differences between the two groups (noise vs. no noise).

Selecting participants

Most psychological experiments use fewer than 100 participants. However, experimenters generally want their findings to apply to a much larger group. Typically, the participants used in an experiment consist of a **sample** drawn from some larger **population** (e.g., college students; 16-year-olds). Since we want the findings from a sample to be true of the population, those included in the sample must be a **representative sample** of the population.

In terms of our example, we might study the effects of loud noise on learning in students preparing for the GCSE in psychology. The best way to obtain a representative sample from that population would be to use **random sampling**. We could obtain lists of names from the various Examination Boards of all students due to sit GCSE psychology in a given year. Participants would then be selected at random from these lists. This could be done by picking names out of a hat or by sticking a pin repeatedly into the lists. However, these approaches wouldn't guarantee a truly representative sample because many of those invited to take part would probably refuse.

Another way to obtain a representative sample is by using **quota sampling**. Suppose 70% of GCSE psychology students are female, and 40% of all GCSE psychology students live in the north of England. We could select our sample to ensure 70% were female and 40% lived in the north of England. If we

KEY TERMS

Sample: the participants actually used in a study drawn from some larger **population**.

Population: a large collection of individuals from whom the sample used in a study is drawn.

Representative sample: a **sample** of participants that is chosen to be typical or representative of the **population** from which it is drawn.

Random sampling: selecting the individuals for a sample from a population in a random way.

Quota sampling: selecting a **sample** from a **population** in such a way that those selected are similar to it in certain respects (e.g., proportion of females).

When selecting participants for an experimental study, what should we do?

take account of several features of the population, quota sampling can be an effective way of producing a representative sample.

Random and quota sampling are often expensive and time-consuming. As a result, many experimenters simply use **opportunity sampling**, in which the participants are selected purely on the basis of their availability. For example, you might stand outside a school at the end of the school day. You ask everyone who comes out whether they would take part in a study. This is the easiest approach. However, it has the serious disadvantage that the participants may be nothing like a representative sample.

Standardised procedures

It is very important for the experimenter to ensure every participant in a given condition is treated in the same way. In other words, standardised procedures need to be used. For example, consider the instructions given to participants. The experimenter should write them down to make sure all participants receive the same instructions.

We also need to use standardised procedures for the collection of data from the participants. Suppose we want to assess the effects of loud noise on learning from a book chapter. We could ask participants to write down everything they can remember from the chapter. However, it would be very hard to compare the memory performance of different participants with any precision. A standardised procedure would be to ask all participants the same 20 questions relating to the chapter. Each participant then obtains a score between 0 and 20.

It is harder than you might imagine to ensure that procedures are standardised. Most experiments can be thought of as social encounters between the experimenter and the participant. It is natural to behave differently with different people, but experimenters should avoid doing this.

Rosenthal (1966) studied ways in which experimenters fall short of standardised procedures. Male experimenters were more pleasant, friendly, honest, encouraging, and relaxed when the participant was female rather than male. As Rosenthal (1966) concluded, "Male and female subjects [participants] may, psychologically, simply not be in the same experiment at all."

The study by Rosenthal (1966) is an example of an experimenter effect. An **experimenter effect** consists of unintended effects experimenters have on participants' behaviour (Ambady & Rosenthal, 1996). Such effects can be found even when the participants are animals. An early example of the experimenter effect involved a horse known as Clever Hans. This horse was apparently able to count, tapping its hoof the appropriate number of times when asked simple mathematical questions.

The psychologist Oskar Pfungst was sceptical about Clever Hans' talent. He found the experimenter unconsciously made slight movements when the horse had tapped out the correct answer. All Clever Hans was doing was using these movements as the cue to stop tapping!

Artificiality of the experiment

It is often argued that laboratory research based on the experimental method is *artificial*. Of particular concern is the issue of **ecological validity** (the extent to which research findings can be applied to the real world). Here we will consider two ways experiments can be artificial.

KEY TERMS

Opportunity sampling: selecting a **sample** of participants simply because they happen to be available.

Experimenter effect: unintended influences of the experimenter's behaviour on the behaviour of the participants in an experiment.

Ecological validity: the extent to which research findings are applicable to everyday settings and generalise to other locations, times, and measures.

First, participants in experiments are aware they are being observed by the experimenter, and this can influence their behaviour. A consequence of being observed is that participants may try to work out the experimenter's hypothesis. As a result, participants are influenced by **demand characteristics,** which are "the totality of cues which convey an experimental hypothesis to the subjects" (Orne, 1962).

Orne (1962) found that participants were willing to spend several hours adding numbers on random number sheets and then tearing up each completed sheet! This happened because the participants interpreted the experiment as a test of endurance.

Second, the experimenter's behaviour affects the participant's behaviour but the participant's behaviour generally doesn't influence the experimenter's behaviour. Wachtel (1973) referred to the **implacable experimenter.** He pointed out that in everyday life we often try to persuade other people to behave in certain ways. Psychological research is in danger of providing an oversimplified view focusing on the individual's *response* to situations but not allowing him/her to change the situation or the experimenter's behaviour.

Experimental designs

If we wish to compare two groups exposed to different independent variables, we need to make sure the two groups don't differ in any other important way. This general rule is important when it comes to selecting participants for an experiment. Suppose in a study on learning that all the least intelligent participants receive loud noise, and all the most intelligent ones receive no noise. We wouldn't know whether it was the loud noise or the intelligence level of the participants that caused poor performance in that group.

There are three main types of experimental design:

* **Independent design:** Each participant is included in only one group.
* **Matched participants design:** Each participant is included in only one group. However, each participant in one group is *matched* with one in the other group for some relevant factor (e.g., ability; sex; age).
* **Repeated measures design:** Each participant is included in both groups, so there are exactly the same participants in each group.

With the independent design, the most common way of deciding which participants go into which group is by **randomisation.** In our example, this could involve using a random process such as coin tossing to decide whether any given participant is exposed to loud noise or no noise. With randomisation, it is possible (although improbable) that all the most intelligent participants will be selected for the same group. However, what typically happens is that the participants in the two groups are similar in terms of intelligence, age, and so on.

With the matched participants design, we use information about the participants to decide the group into which each participant should be put. In our example, we might have information about the participants' intelligence

What is an experiment in which each participant is selected for only one group known as?

KEY TERMS

Demand characteristics: cues that are used by participants to try to guess the nature of the study or to work out what the experiment is about.

Implacable experimenter: the typical laboratory situation in which the experimenter's behaviour is uninfluenced by the participant's behaviour.

Independent design: an experimental design in which each participant is included in only one group.

Matched participants design: an experimental design in which the participants in each of two groups are matched in terms of some relevant factor or factors (e.g., intelligence; sex).

Repeated measures design: an experimental design in which each participant appears in both groups.

Randomisation: placing participants into groups on some random basis (e.g., coin tossing).

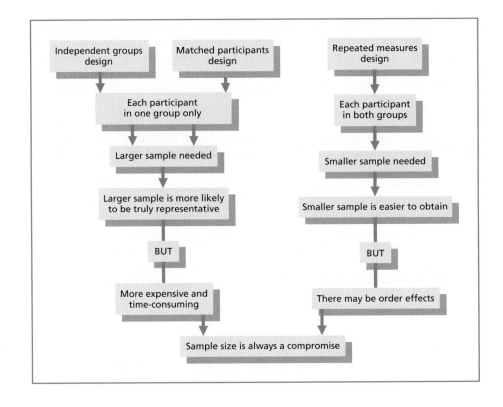

levels. We could then use that information to ensure everyone in one group is matched with someone in the other group on intelligence.

With the repeated measures design, every participant is in both groups. In our example, each participant would learn the chapter in loud noise and also learn it in no noise. This design means we don't have to worry about the participants in one group being cleverer than those in the other group.

Issues with repeated measures design

The main problem with the repeated measures design is that there may well be order effects. Participants' experiences during the experiment may well change them in various ways. For example, they may perform *better* when they are tested on the second occasion because they have previously gained useful knowledge about the experiment or the task. However, they may perform *worse* on the second occasion because they are tired or bored.

It would be difficult to use a repeated measures design in our example. Participants are certain to show better learning of the chapter the second time they read it, regardless of whether or not they are exposed to loud noise.

Suppose we use a repeated measures design in which all participants first learn the chapter in loud noise and then learn it in no noise. The participants would show better learning in no noise simply because of order effects. A better procedure would be to have half the participants learn the chapter first in loud noise and then in no noise, while the other half learn the chapter in no noise and then again in loud noise. In that way, any order effects would be balanced out. This is **counterbalancing**, and it helps to prevent order effects from distorting the findings.

What are field experiments?

Replication

When a psychologist reports the findings from an experiment, he/she hopes other psychologists will be able to obtain similar findings. This is known as **replication**, meaning the experimental findings can be repeated by others. How can researchers maximise the chances of replication? First, the way in which the experiment was carried out should be reported in detail so that others can understand exactly what happened. Second, standardised procedures need to be used. Third, it is important to avoid confounding variables.

Field experiments

Laboratory and field experiments both involve use of the experimental method. However, **field experiments** are carried out in more natural settings and the participants generally don't realise they are taking part in an experiment. This typically makes field experiments less artificial than laboratory experiments, and reduces problems such as experimenter effects and demand characteristics.

We can see the usefulness of field experiments by considering two examples. Shotland and Straw (1976) arranged for a man and a woman to stage an argument and a fight fairly close to a number of bystanders. In one condition, the woman screamed, "I don't know you." In a second condition, she screamed, "I don't know why I married you."

When the bystanders thought the fight involved strangers, 65% of them intervened compared to only 19% when they thought it involved a married couple. Thus, people were much less inclined to lend a helping hand when it was a "lovers' quarrel".

Field experiments can have practical value. Gueguen et al. (2010) were interested in the issue of how doctors can increase patients' adherence to the prescribed medication. Some patients were touched on the forearm for 1–2 seconds by the doctor, whereas others were not. Those who were touched took significantly more of their pills than those who weren't. Thus, a very simple gesture by the doctor can have a beneficial effect on patients.

> **KEY TERMS**
>
> **Counterbalancing:** this is used with the repeated measures design; each condition is equally likely to be used first or second with the participants.
>
> **Replication:** repeating the findings of a study using the same design and procedures.
>
> **Field experiments:** experiments carried out in real-world situations using the **experimental method**.

Limitations

There are various limitations with field experiments. First, it can be hard to have good experimental control in the real world. Second, it is not easy to obtain detailed information from participants in field experiments without them becoming aware they are in an experiment. Note that in the above examples of field experiments, the dependent variable was simple (e.g., intervention: yes or no?; number of pills taken). Third, ethical research in psychology typically involves obtaining voluntary informed consent from participants beforehand. This is rarely possible with field experiments.

One of the limitations of field experiments is that it can be hard to have good experimental control in the real world.

OVERALL EVALUATION

➕ Laboratory studies permit good experimental control and so may allow us to identify some of the causes of certain forms of behaviour. However, such control is often less with field experiments.

➕ The findings from laboratory and field experiments can usually be replicated or repeated by other experimenters.

➕ All the main types of experimental design (independent design; matched participants design; repeated measures design) are suitable when used appropriately.

➖ The experimental method can't be used to assess the impact of several major factors influencing our behaviour (e.g., our personality; our childhood; our genes).

➖ It is important not to be carried away with the notion that psychology involves the experimental approach to the exclusion of almost everything else (David Scott, personal communication). As we will see shortly, there are other important approaches within psychology.

➖ Participants in laboratory studies often don't behave naturally because they are being observed by strangers in an artificial situation. There are also potential problems from demand characteristics and the implacable experimenter. However, experimenter effects and demand characteristics are usually less (or absent) in field experiments.

➖ The findings from laboratory studies often differ from what is found in everyday life; this is the issue of ecological validity. However, ecological validity is often high with field experiments.

Other methods

The experimental method is used much more often than any other in psychology. However, researchers also use numerous other methods, and we will consider some in this section.

Observational studies

Observational studies resemble field experiments in that behaviour is observed in the real world. However, there is an important difference—with observational studies, the experimenter exerts no control over the situation but simply observes people's behaviour as they go about their daily lives. This generally makes it hard to interpret the findings from observational studies.

Watching children interact in a playground is an example of an observational study. It might be predicted that girls would tend to interact more cooperatively than boys, whereas boys would tend to interact more aggressively than girls.

Two or more observers could record the number of cooperative and aggressive actions by boys and girls to test the above hypotheses. It could be very demanding to do this non-stop for an hour or so. Accordingly, researchers often use time-sampling in which they record observations only part of the time. For example, they might observe the children's behaviour for 10 minutes, have a 5-minute break, observe for 10 more minutes, and so on.

Two related problems can arise in observational studies. First, different observers may have different ideas about the meaning of the different categories of behaviour they are looking for. One observer may regard a gentle tap as aggressive behaviour whereas another observer may not. It is, therefore, desirable to use very clear definitions of the behaviour to be measured.

Second, even though the existence of clear definitions of the various categories of behaviour to be recorded is a great advantage, it may not prevent all problems. For example, some observers may fail to spot pieces of behaviour through a lack of attention. We can see whether two observers produce similar judgements. This is done by calculating **inter-observer reliability**. The closer the agreement between the observers, the greater is the inter-observer reliability.

Cross-sectional and longitudinal studies

Suppose we wanted to explore the effects of age on memory. More specifically, we decide to consider two types of memory (see Chapter 21):

What are longitudinal studies?

1. *episodic memory* (memory for events occurring at a given time in a given place);
2. *semantic memory* (knowledge about the world).

The easiest approach would be to use the **cross-sectional method**, in which *different* age groups are tested at the same point in time. An alternative approach is to use the **longitudinal method**. In studies using this method, the *same* group of individuals is tested at two or more points in time.

You might imagine that the apparent effects of age on memory would be similar regardless of the method used. In fact, that *isn't* the case. Rönnlund et al. (2005) compared the effects of age on memory using both methods. With the cross-sectional method, there was a substantial decrease in episodic memory during the years between 35 and 60. In contrast, episodic memory was stable across the years 35 to 60 using the longitudinal method.

The two methods also produced different findings for semantic memory. With the cross-sectional approach, semantic memory was stable from 35 to 60, whereas it increased over the same years with the longitudinal approach.

How can we explain the different findings produced by the two approaches? There is a problem with the cross-sectional method because younger people on average have a higher level of educational attainment than older ones. Thus, it is unclear whether younger people perform well on memory tests because they are young or because they are well-educated.

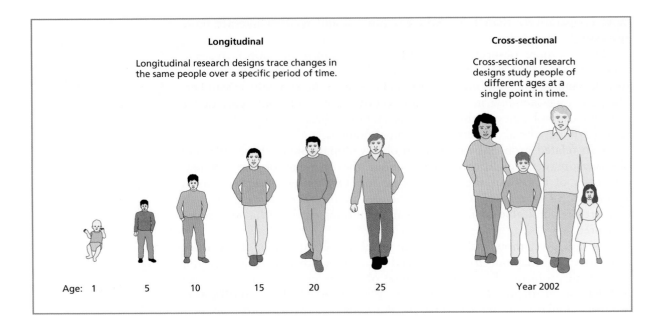

Longitudinal

Longitudinal research designs trace changes in the same people over a specific period of time.

Cross-sectional

Cross-sectional research designs study people of different ages at a single point in time.

Age: 1   5   10   15   20   25   Year 2002

Rönnlund et al. (2005) removed the confounding effect of educational attainment with the cross-sectional method. Their findings resembled much more closely those obtained with the longitudinal method. Thus, aging (at least up to the age of 60) has very few negative effects on episodic and semantic memory.

The longitudinal method is generally preferable because the *same* individuals are studied at each point in time. That eliminates or minimises effects stemming from age-related changes in educational attainment. In view of the superiority of longitudinal studies, you might wonder why there are far more cross-sectional studies. The main reason is that such studies are much less time-consuming and expensive to carry out.

Correlational studies

Suppose we wanted to test the hypothesis that watching violence on television leads to aggressive behaviour (see Chapter 6). We could do this by obtaining two kinds of information from numerous children:

1. the amount of violent television they watched;
2. the extent to which they behaved aggressively in various situations.

If the hypothesis is correct, we would expect children who have seen the most violence on television to be the most aggressive. This hypothesis could be tested by looking for a **correlation** or association between watching violent programmes and being aggressive. The closer the link between these two variables, the higher is the correlation or association.

The key limitation with correlational studies is that it is very hard to interpret the findings. In our example, an association or correlation between television violence watched and aggressive behaviour would be consistent with the hypothesis. Alternatively, however, aggressive children may choose to watch more violent programmes than those who are less aggressive.

KEY TERM

Correlation: an association between two dependent variables or responses produced by participants.

There is a third possibility. Children in disadvantaged families may watch more television of all kinds than those in non-disadvantaged families, and their deprived circumstances may also make them behave aggressively. If so, the number of violent television programmes watched would *not* be the cause of children's aggressive behaviour.

In view of the limitations of correlational studies, why do experimenters carry them out? First, many hypotheses can't be tested directly using the experimental method. For example, the hypothesis that smoking causes several physical diseases can't be tested by forcing some people to smoke and forcing others not to smoke! However, we can examine associations or correlations between the number of cigarettes smoked and the probability of suffering from various diseases.

Second, we can obtain large amounts of data on several variables in a correlational study much more rapidly than could be done with experimental designs. For example, use of questionnaires would permit an experimenter to study the associations or correlations between aggressive behaviour and numerous activities (e.g., watching violent films in the cinema; reading violent books; being frustrated at work or at home).

Case studies

There are often good reasons why it isn't possible to use a large number of participants in a study. A busy clinician or therapist may find the behaviour of a patient very revealing. However, she/he may not have the time to collect information from other patients with the same problem. In such circumstances, it can be very useful to carry out a **case study**, in which one or two individuals are studied in great detail.

A famous case study was carried out by Sigmund Freud on Little Hans, a boy with an extreme fear of horses. According to Freud, Little Hans was sexually attracted to his mother. However, he was very frightened he would be punished for this by his father. Horses resembled his father in that their black muzzles and blinkers looked like his moustache and glasses. As a result, Little Hans transferred or displaced his fear of his father onto horses.

Freud's analysis in this case was incorrect. On Freud's account, Hans should have had a strong fear reaction every time he saw a horse. In fact, he only showed strong fear when he saw a horse pulling a cart at high speed. Little Hans' fear of horses started after he saw a serious accident involving a horse and cart moving at high speed. It was probably this that made him fearful of horses.

Other case studies have proved much more revealing. For example, there is Henry Molaison (HM), a patient with amnesia causing severe memory problems who died in 2008. His memory was so poor that HM "does not know where he lives, who cares for him, or where he ate his last meal" (Corkin, 1984, p. 255).

It would be easy (but wrong!) to conclude that HM simply had very impaired long-term memory. Surprisingly, his ability to learn (and remember) motor skills was essentially intact. For example, he became very good at mirror tracing (tracing patterns in a mirror).

Research on HM indicated that the notion that there is only a single long-term memory system is wrong (see Chapter 21). More specifically, there is an important distinction between memory involving conscious recollection (e.g., where do you live?) and memory that doesn't require conscious recollection (e.g., performing motor skills).

A positive correlation: The taller the player, the higher the score.

A negative correlation: The more time spent playing computer games, the less time spent studying.

No correlation: Where there is no relationship, variables are uncorrelated.

KEY TERM

Case study: the intensive study of one or two individuals.

EVALUATION

➕ Case studies provide rich information that can be used to develop our theoretical understanding.

➕ Case studies can show that a given theory is wrong. For example, HM showed that previous views on long-term memory were oversimplified.

➖ What is true of a particular individual may not be true of other people. Thus, it can be dangerous to draw general conclusions from the case study of one person. In the case of HM, however, other amnesic patients were found to have similar patterns of memory impairment.

➖ Case studies (e.g., those of Freud) often involve the use of lengthy, fairly unstructured interviews. The evidence from such interviews can be excessively influenced by the interviewer's views.

Ethical issues

There are more major ethical issues associated with research in psychology than in most other scientific disciplines. There are various reasons for this. First, all psychological studies involve living creatures (whether human or non-human), and their right to be treated caringly can be infringed by an unprincipled or careless researcher.

Second, the findings of psychological research may reveal unpleasant or unacceptable facts about human nature or about certain groups within society. This is especially true of socially sensitive research. This was defined by Sieber and Stanley (1988, p. 49) as "studies in which there are potential social consequences or implications either directly for the participants in research or the class of individuals represented by the research".

Socially sensitive research can pose risks for many people in addition to those directly involved as participants. Consider, for example, a researcher who asks the question, "Are there racial differences in intelligence?", and decides to answer it by carrying out a study. This can produce risks for members of the racial groups to which the participants belong.

Simply asking the question about racial differences in intelligence immediately raises ethical issues. It is likely that the researcher assumes there are racial differences in intelligence and that these differences are important. These assumptions are ethically dubious (and almost certainly incorrect as well). Studying racial differences in intelligence is unhelpful and can be very damaging.

Third, psychological research may lead to the discovery of powerful techniques that can be used for purposes of social control. It would obviously be dangerous if such techniques were to be exploited by dictators or others seeking to exert undue influence on society.

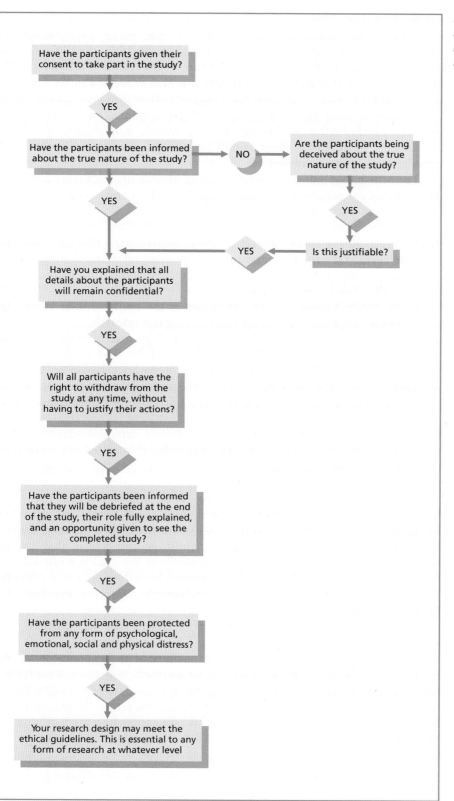

Ethical guidelines that should be addressed by psychologists and students of psychology.

For ethical experimentation, what is it necessary to make sure of?

General principles

The British Psychological Society (BPS) is the major organisation for professional psychologists in the United Kingdom. In 1990, the BPS published its *Ethical Principles for Conducting Research with Human Participants*. The key to carrying out research in an ethical way was expressed in the following way in the *Principles*: "The essential principle is that the investigation should be considered from the standpoint of all participants; foreseeable threats to their psychological well-being, health, values, and dignity should be eliminated." Thus, every effort should be made to ensure participants don't experience pain, stress, or distress.

The British Psychological Society updates its code of ethics every few years. The most recent version was published in 2009. This version emphasised the importance of four major ethical principles:

1. *Respect*: Researchers should respect individual, cultural, and role differences. Of crucial importance is the need for researchers to obtain voluntary informed consent from participants having told them in detail what the experiment involves.
2. *Competence*: Researchers should recognise the limits of their knowledge and experience when planning and carrying out research.
3. *Responsibility*: Researchers should consider all research from the standpoint of research participants. Participants should be told clearly they can withdraw from the experiment at any time without providing a reason. There should also be a debriefing at the end of the experiment. At this debriefing, participants should be given fairly detailed information about the nature of the research.
4. *Integrity*: Researchers should strive to be honest, fair, and accurate in their interactions with participants. For example, they shouldn't exaggerate their professional qualifications.

There are two final issues to discuss. First, ethical research involves a balance between means and ends, which involves a *cost–benefit analysis*. Thus, we should pay some attention to the *value* of research when deciding whether it is ethically acceptable. For example, most people believe that causing suffering to animals is easier to justify ethically if the goal is to find a cure for some serious human illness rather than merely to develop a new cosmetic. However, it can be hard to predict costs and benefits *before* an experiment has been carried out.

Second, there is the acceptability of deceiving the participants. It is obviously important to avoid deception because participants can't give voluntary informed consent if important aspects of the experiment are not revealed. However, deception is sometimes justified. It is more acceptable if the effects of the deception aren't damaging. It is also easier to justify the use of deception in studies that are important in scientific terms. Finally, deception is more justifiable when there are no other, deception-free ways of studying an issue.

Chapter summary

- An experimental hypothesis is a prediction of what will happen in a given experiment. More specifically, it refers to the predicted effect of an independent variable on a dependent variable.

- Confounding variables should be avoided when using the experimental method. This can be done by controlling as many variables as possible.

- Participants should form a representative sample from some population. This can be done by random or quota sampling.

- When using the experimental method, it is important to use standardised procedures and to try to achieve ecological validity.

- Within the experimental method, there are independent designs, repeated measures designs, and matched participants designs.

- Repeated measures designs produce unwanted order effects. These can be handled by counterbalancing.

- Field experiments have the advantage that observations can be made without participants' knowledge. The disadvantage of such experiments is that there is often fairly poor experimental control.

- Observational studies can be very informative. However, they have the disadvantage of a lack of experimental control and there can be issues about the reliability of the measures taken.

- Cross-sectional studies involve various groups studied at a single point in time, whereas longitudinal studies involve one group studied several times. Longitudinal studies are preferable because all the findings are based on the same group of individuals.

- Correlational studies involve comparing two measures of behaviour from the same participants. The findings are generally hard to interpret because correlations reveal associations but don't indicate what has caused any given behaviour.

- Case studies involve investigating one or two individuals in detail. It is often hard to generalise from such a limited sample.

- Socially sensitive research raises ethical issues because of its potentially damaging effects on many people not directly tested in the research.

- Ethical research is based on respect, competence, responsibility, and integrity.

- When deciding whether a proposed piece of research is ethically acceptable, consideration should be paid to its likely value: this involves carrying out a cost–benefit analysis.

Further reading

- British Psychological Society Ethics Committee (2009). *Code of ethics and conduct*. Leicester: British Psychological Society. This excellent document covers all of the most important ethical issues that psychological researchers encounter.

- Coolican, H. (2009). *Research methods and statistics in psychology (5th ed.)*. London: Hodder Education. Most of the topics discussed in this chapter are dealt with in a clear fashion in this textbook by Hugh Coolican.

- Dyer, C. (2006). *Research in psychology: A practical guide to methods and statistics*. Oxford, UK: Blackwell. A wide range of research methods is dealt with in detail in this textbook.

Essay questions

1. What are the main methods of investigation available to psychologists? What are the advantages of these methods? What are their disadvantages?

2. What is the experimental method? Why has it been used so often in psychological research?

3. What are the main features of ethical research? Why is it important for experiments to be ethical?

Part 1

Biological approach

Biological psychology (often shortened to biopsychology) is an important approach. It has been defined as "the study of behaviour and experience in terms of genetics, evolution, and physiology, especially the physiology of the nervous system" (Kalat, 1998, p. 1). More generally, the biological approach to psychology focuses on the ways in which our behaviour is influenced by the body and the brain. Of major importance, much of our behaviour is influenced by the genes we have inherited from our parents.

Chapter 3 • Biological bases of behaviour

We will consider key issues in biopsychology such as the role of genetic factors in explaining behaviour and the organisation of the brain.

Chapter 4 • Stress

We will discuss the causes of stress and the nature of stress including a focus on its physiological aspects with which we are all familiar.

Chapter 5 • Emotion

The nature of emotion is discussed including a consideration of the physiological effects associated with emotional experience.

Chapter 6 • Aggression

The causes of aggression (including the role of genetic factors) are considered, as are ways in which aggression can be reduced.

It is obvious that our behaviour is strongly influenced by our body and by our brain. That is the starting point of the biological approach to psychology. This approach also involves considering whether our behaviour is determined more by environmental factors (e.g., our friends; our experiences; our culture) or by genetic factors (i.e., the genetic make-up we have inherited). Do you think that genetic factors have an important influence on our behaviour?

Centuries ago, phrenologists claimed that it is possible to understand how the brain works by feeling the bumps in the skull. That approach didn't work very well (to put it mildly!). What kinds of measuring instruments do you think could be used to shed light on the mysteries of how the brain works? The phrenologists assumed that each part of the brain had its own special function. Do you think they were right to make this assumption? How could we decide?

Biological bases of behaviour

3

Psychology is linked to other disciplines such as sociology, biology (including related disciplines such as physiology, biochemistry, and genetics). However, it was only after the publication of the book *The Origin of Species* by Charles Darwin that the relevance of biology to psychology became accepted. Before its publication in 1859, people had assumed only human beings had minds, thus making us radically different from other species. The notion that human beings have evolved from other species meant this inflated view of the importance of the human species had to be reassessed.

Darwin was a biologist rather than a psychologist. However, his theory of evolution has had *four* major effects on psychology. First, psychologists began to develop theories of human psychology from the biological perspective. The most famous psychologist to do so was Sigmund Freud. His emphasis on the sex drive in humans would have been almost unthinkable in the days before Darwin.

Second, one lesson from Darwin's theory of evolution was that the study of *non-human* species could be of great value to understanding human behaviour. This led to the development of animal or comparative psychology. It is known as comparative psychology because it involves *comparing* the behaviour of other species with that of humans.

Third, Darwin argued that heredity is important in the development of a species, and that offspring tend to be like their parents. These ideas led psychologists to explore the role of heredity in influencing human behaviour. They also led to renewed interest in the issue of the relative importance of heredity and environment (the nature–nurture debate) in influencing human behaviour.

Fourth, Darwin focused on *variation* among the members of a species. According to his notion of survival of the fittest, evolution favours those members of a species best equipped to live in a given environment. These ideas led to an interest in individual differences and to the study of intelligence and personality (see Chapters 17 and 18).

Evolutionary psychology

Darwin's theory of evolution has recently had a major impact on psychology with the development of evolutionary psychology. **Evolutionary psychology** is built on

Charles Darwin (1809–1882). Darwin's theory of evolution led psychologists to focus on individual differences, genetic influences on behaviour, and the relevance of biology to psychology.

the assumption that the process of evolution has served to shape our minds and behaviour as well as our bodies. As a result, most of our behaviour is adaptive, meaning it is well suited to the environment in which we find ourselves.

Evolutionary psychology has been used to explain why people are willing to behave unselfishly at real cost to themselves (see Chapter 14). Suppose you were faced with the agonising choice of deciding which member of your family you would provide with life-saving assistance. According to evolutionary psychology, you should choose a family member sharing many genes with you (e.g., mother; brother) rather than someone sharing fewer genes (e.g., uncle; great-aunt). That is exactly what Korchmaros and Kenny (2001) found.

The evolutionary psychology approach is thought-provoking. However, it has proved controversial (Confer et al., 2010). Why is evolutionary psychology controversial? It focuses too much on biological determinants of our behaviour while de-emphasising the importance of social and cultural factors.

The brain

Whole books have been written about the biological bases of behaviour, so it will only be possible to deal with a few selected topics in this chapter. Our main focus will be on the brain, which influences behaviour far more than does any other biological structure.

We all know the brain is crucially important for perception, attention, learning, memory, thinking, and problem solving. However, it is also of vital importance for emotion, motivation, and almost all of the other factors determining behaviour. Before we start to discuss the brain, however, we will consider the issue of the impact of heredity on behaviour. This relates to the discipline of genetics.

Inborn characteristics

Human beings differ from each other in endless ways. Some are tall and thin, whereas others are short and fat. Some are intelligent and hard-working, whereas others are unintelligent and poorly motivated.

At the most general level, there are only two possible sources of individual differences: heredity (or nature) and environment (or nurture). In other words, people may differ because of differences in what they have inherited or because of differences in the environment or experiences they have had. Realistically, most individual differences in behaviour are likely to depend on heredity *and* environment.

The nature–nurture issue is concerned with the relative importance of heredity and environment. This issue is dealt with at various places in this book. Examples include individual differences in aggression (Chapter 6), intelligence (Chapter 17), and personality (Chapter 18).

Twin studies

The best method for addressing the nature–nurture issue is by means of twin studies. **Monozygotic twins** (or identical twins) derive from the same fertilised ovum or egg and so share 100% of their genes. **Dizygotic twins** (or fraternal twins) derive from two different fertilised ova or eggs and so share on average 50% of their genes.

If individual differences in some behaviour or personal characteristic (e.g., intelligence) depend in part on genetic factors, identical twins should be more alike than fraternal twins with respect to that behaviour or personal characteristic. In contrast, if environmental factors are all-important, identical twins should be no more alike than fraternal twins.

The evidence indicates strongly that heredity and environment are both important in producing individual differences in numerous characteristics and forms of behaviour. What is surprising is the very wide range of individual differences influenced by genetic factors. For example, Alford et al. (2005) reported a twin study on political attitudes and ideology. Genetic factors accounted for 30% of individual differences in political attitudes and ideology.

The discussion so far has implied that the effects of heredity and environment on behaviour are entirely separate. That is generally *not* the case. Plomin (1990) identified *three* ways an individual's genetic endowment influences his/her environment. Below these three ways are discussed with reference to individual differences in intelligence:

Children of high genetic ability tend to read more books than those of lower genetic ability; this is an example of active covariation.

1. *Active covariation*: This occurs when children of differing genetic ability look for situations reinforcing their genetic differences. For example, children of high genetic ability read far more books than those of lower genetic ability and also receive several more years of education.
2. *Passive covariation*: This occurs when parents of high genetic ability provide a more stimulating environment than parents of lower genetic ability.
3. *Reactive covariation*: This occurs when an individual's genetically influenced behaviour influences how he/she is treated by other people. For example, adults are more likely to discuss complex issues with children of high genetic ability than those of low genetic ability.

What can be concluded from Plomin's analysis? In essence, genetic factors can influence individual differences in intelligence in two ways. First, there is a *direct* genetic influence on intelligence. Second, there is an *indirect* genetic influence on intelligence—genetic factors help to determine the environment in which an individual finds himself/herself, and this environment then influences his/her intelligence.

Common misunderstandings

There are two common misunderstandings about twin research. First, it is sometimes assumed twin studies provide information only about the impact of genetic factors. That is incorrect. Twin studies also provide an estimate of the importance of environmental factors. Indeed, they permit the identification of two types of environmental influence:

1. Shared environmental influences are those within families that make children resemble each other.
2. Non-shared environmental influences are those unique to any given individual.

Second, it is often assumed that the impact of genetic factors on individual differences (e.g., in intelligence) is fixed and unchanging. This is completely

Does the nervous system comprise one, two, or several smaller systems?

wrong. The impact of genetic factors is assessed within a given population and may vary dramatically from one population to another.

We can address the above point by considering genetic influences on intelligence. Suppose we considered a population in which everyone had precisely the same environment. Within that population, individual differences in intelligence would depend solely on genetic factors. In contrast, environmental factors would be hugely important in societies in which some children receive several years of education whereas others received no education at all.

Findings

We saw in the study by Alford et al. (2005) that genetic factors accounted for 30% of individual differences in political attitudes and ideology. Alford et al. also provided estimates of environmental effects. Non-shared environment influences accounted for just over 50% of individual differences in political attitudes and shared environmental influences for just over 15%. Thus, the unique environmental experiences an individual has are much more important than shared family experiences in determining his/her political attitudes.

Twin studies sometimes produce surprising findings concerning the impact of environmental influences. For example, consider the hypothesis favoured by Freud (and many other theorists) that children's personality is determined in large measure by the family environment provided by their parents. According to this hypothesis, adults' personality should depend substantially on shared environmental influences.

The above hypothesis has received very little support. Shared environmental influences contribute practically nothing to individual differences in most major personality factors (Plomin et al., 1997). About 40% of individual differences are due to genetic factors and up to 60% are due to non-shared environmental influences (Plomin et al., 1997) (see Chapter 18).

Evidence that the role of genetic factors varies from population to population was reported by Brace (1996). Genetic factors were of minor importance in influencing individual differences in intelligence among people living in American urban ghettos. However, they were much more important among those living in affluent, white American suburbs. Within the latter population, the great majority enjoyed favourable environmental conditions, and so there was little scope for environmental differences to influence intelligence.

Nervous system

The nervous system contains all the nerve cells in the body (see below). As we will see, the various parts of the nervous system are specialised for different functions. The nervous system is made up of between 15 and 20 billion neurons (nerve cells) and a much larger number of glia (small cells fulfilling various functions). The nervous system is divided into two main sub-systems:

- **Central nervous system:** This consists of the brain and the spinal cord; it is protected by bone and fluid circulating around it.
- **Peripheral nervous system:** This consists of all the other nerve cells in the body. It is divided into the somatic nervous system (concerned with

KEY TERMS

Central nervous system: the brain and spinal cord; it is protected by bone and cerebrospinal fluid.

Peripheral nervous system: it consists of all the nerve cells in the body not located within the **central nervous system**; it is divided into the **somatic nervous system** and the **autonomic nervous system**.

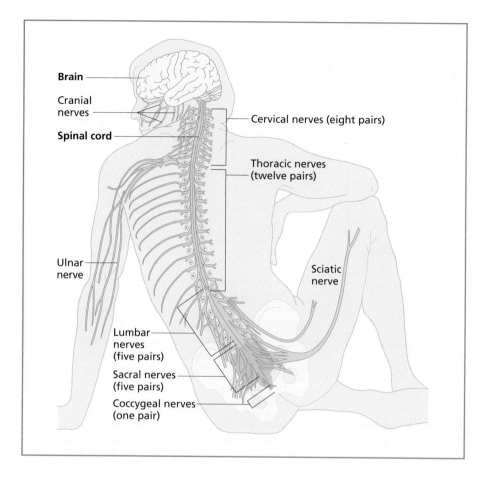

Labels on figure:
- **Brain**
- Cranial nerves
- **Spinal cord**
- Cervical nerves (eight pairs)
- Thoracic nerves (twelve pairs)
- Ulnar nerve
- Sciatic nerve
- Lumbar nerves (five pairs)
- Sacral nerves (five pairs)
- Coccygeal nerves (one pair)

voluntary movements of skeletal muscles) and the autonomic nervous system (concerned with involuntary movements of non-skeletal muscles such as those of the heart).

Peripheral nervous system

Since there is detailed coverage of the brain shortly, we will focus here on the peripheral nervous system. It consists of all the nerve cells in the body not contained within the central nervous system.

The peripheral nervous system divides into two parts: the somatic nervous system and the autonomic nervous system. The somatic nervous system is concerned with interactions with the external environment, whereas the autonomic nervous system is concerned with the body's internal environment.

The **somatic nervous system** consists in part of nerves carrying signals from the eyes, ears, skeletal muscles, and the skin to the central nervous system (see the figures overleaf). It also consists of nerves carrying signals from the central nervous system to the skeletal muscles, skin, and so on.

As mentioned already, the **autonomic nervous system** controls the movement of non-skeletal muscles. The organs within the control of the

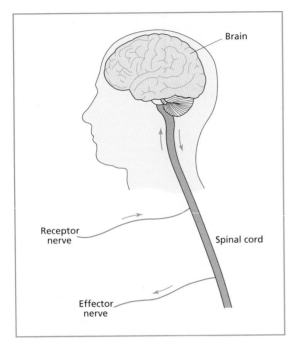

Receptor nerves transmit information to the brain via the spinal cord. Instructions from the brain are sent via the effector nerves.

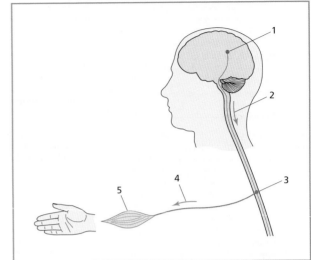

The somatic nervous system: What happens when you decide to move your fingers. (1) The decision arises in the brain; (2) is transmitted via the spinal cord; (3) transfers to another nerve (or series of nerves); (4) the instruction is transmitted to the skeletal muscles; (5) the muscles contract or relax, moving the fingers.

autonomic nervous system include the heart, lungs, eyes, stomach, and the blood vessels of internal organs. The autonomic nervous system is divided into the sympathetic nervous system and the parasympathetic nervous system.

The **sympathetic nervous system** is called into play in situations needing arousal and energy. It produces increased heart rate, reduced activity within the stomach, pupil dilation or expansion, and relaxation of the bronchi of the lungs. These changes prepare us for fight or flight.

The **parasympathetic nervous system** is involved when the body tries to save energy. The effects of activity in the parasympathetic nervous system are the opposite of those of activity in the sympathetic nervous system. The parasympathetic nervous system produces decreased heart rate, increased activity within the stomach, pupil contraction, and constriction of the bronchi of the lungs.

The sympathetic nervous system and the parasympathetic nervous system are both important. For example, consider the case of someone having excessive activity of the sympathetic nervous system but very little activity of the parasympathetic nervous system. He/she would probably be a highly stressed individual who found life very demanding.

> **KEY TERMS**
>
> **Sympathetic nervous system:** the part of the **autonomic nervous system** that produces arousal and energy (e.g., via increased heart rate).
>
> **Parasympathetic nervous system:** the part of the **autonomic nervous system** that is involved in reducing arousal and conserving energy (e.g., by reducing heart rate).

Brain organisation

The first point to be made about the brain is its complexity. It has proved easier to study the structure of the brain than to understand the functions or purposes of its various parts. If scientists open up the skull or cut sections of the brain and put them under slides, they can obtain some idea of the ways in which the brain is structured. It is harder to know what is going on inside the living brain. However, technological advances have allowed us to assess brain functions by watching it in action (see below).

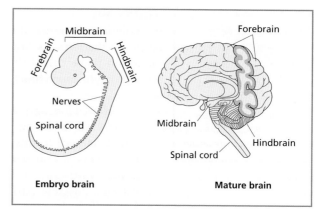

Embryo brain   Mature brain

At the most general level, the brain can be divided into three main regions: forebrain; midbrain; and hindbrain (see the figure below). Note that these terms refer to locations in an embryo's brain and don't indicate clearly the relative positions of the different brain regions in an adult.

Forebrain

This is easily the most important division of the brain. It is located towards the top and the front of the brain. It consists of four parts:

- **Cerebrum**: This contains 70% of all the neurons in the central nervous system. It plays a major role in thinking, use of language, and other cognitive skills (discussed later).
- **Limbic system**: One main part of this system (the amygdala) is involved in several emotional states (see Chapter 5). Another main part (the hippocampus) is of importance in learning and memory.
- **Thalamus**: The main function of the thalamus is as a relay station that passes information on to higher brain centres. It is also involved in wakefulness and sleep.
- **Hypothalamus**: This structure serves various purposes including the control of autonomic functions such as body temperature, hunger, and thirst. It is also involved in the control of sexual behaviour and reactions to stress.

Midbrain

The **midbrain** has various important functions. First, parts of it are involved in vision and hearing, although most perceptual processes occur in the forebrain. Second, some parts of the midbrain are used in movement control. Third, the midbrain contains the reticular activating system, although parts of that system extend into the hindbrain. The reticular activating system is involved in the regulation of sleep, arousal, and wakefulness, in part through its influence on heart rate and breathing rate.

KEY TERMS

Cerebrum: a part of the forebrain crucially involved in thinking and language.

Limbic system: a brain system consisting of the amygdala, the hippocampus, and septal areas, all of which are involved in emotional processing.

Thalamus: a part of the forebrain that is involved in wakefulness and sleep.

Hypothalamus: a part of the forebrain that is involved in controlling body temperature, hunger, thirst, and sexual behaviour.

Midbrain: the middle part of the brain; it is involved in vision, hearing, and the control of movement.

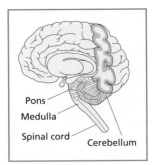

Hindbrain

In evolutionary terms, the **hindbrain** is a very old part of the brain (see the figure on the left). Its brain structures resemble those of reptiles, leading the hindbrain to be called the "reptilian brain". It consists of three parts, each serving one or more functions:

- *Medulla oblongata*: This is part of the reticular activating system, and is involved in the control of breathing, digestion, and swallowing. As a result, damage to this structure can cause death.
- *Pons*: This is also part of the reticular activating system, being involved in the control of consciousness. It acts as a relay station passing messages between different parts of the brain.
- *Cerebellum*: Its main functions are the fine control of balance and bodily coordination. Information about "overlearned" skills such as riding a bicycle or typing is stored in the cerebellum.

Cerebral cortex

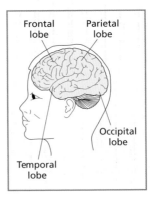

The **cerebral cortex** is the outer layer of the cerebrum within the forebrain. It is only two millimetres deep, but has huge importance in terms of our ability to perceive, think, remember, and use language. We can divide the cerebral cortex up in two main ways:

1. The cerebral cortex within each hemisphere consists of four lobes or areas known as the frontal, parietal, temporal, and occipital (see the figure on the left). The frontal lobe is at the front of the brain and the occipital lobe is at the back of the brain. The other two lobes are in the middle of the brain, with the parietal lobe at the top and the temporal lobe below it.
2. The entire brain (including the cerebral cortex) is divided into two hemispheres: the left and right cerebral hemispheres.

Four lobes

As we saw earlier, the cerebral cortex is divided into four lobes. These lobes differ in terms of what they do. Sternberg (1995, p. 93) provided a summary of their functions: "Higher thought processes, such as abstract reasoning and motor processing, occur in the frontal lobe, somatosensory processing (sensations in the skin and muscles of the body) in the parietal lobe, auditory processing in the temporal lobe, and visual processing in the occipital lobe."

The frontal lobe (especially the area known as the prefrontal lobe) is of central importance with respect to most complex forms of thinking. Consider brain-damaged patients who have suffered extensive damage to the frontal lobe. Such patients often have problems with planning, organising, monitoring their own behaviour, and initiating behaviour (Baddeley, 2007).

The frontal lobe contains the primary motor cortex. This is involved in the planning and control of movements. Far more of the primary motor cortex is

KEY TERMS

Hindbrain: the "reptilian brain", concerned with breathing, digestion, swallowing, the fine control of balance, and the control of consciousness.

Cerebral cortex: the outer layer of the **cerebrum**; it is involved in perception, thinking, and language.

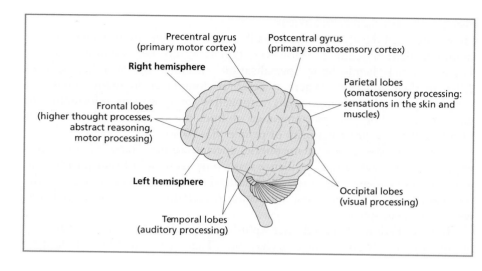

What are the lobes of the cerebral cortex known as?

devoted to those parts of the body involved in making very precise movements (e.g., the fingers) than to those that do not (e.g., the toes).

The parietal lobe contains the primary somatosensory cortex. This area receives information from various senses about temperature, pain, and pressure. Those parts of the body most represented in the primary motor cortex also tend to be well represented in the primary somatosensory cortex.

The temporal lobe is involved in auditory processing. The most important form of this processing is speech perception. Within the temporal lobe, some parts respond most to certain kinds of sound (e.g., those high or low in pitch). In addition, much of our knowledge of the meanings of words and concepts is stored in the temporal lobe. For example, consider patients suffering from **semantic dementia**, a condition involving widespread loss of information about word meanings. They almost invariably have damage within the temporal lobe (Patterson et al., 2007).

The occipital lobe is mainly concerned with visual processing. Nerve fibres from the right side of each eye go to the left occipital lobe, whereas those from the left side go to the right occipital lobe (see the figure on the right). If you are struck on the back of the head close to the occipital area, you will see "stars".

The occipital area plays a key role in vision. However, the temporal and parietal lobes are also involved. As much as 50% of the entire cerebral cortex is devoted to visual processing.

From what has been said so far, you may have the impression that each brain area is specialised for a given function. In fact, that is only the case to a limited extent. The performance of a moderately complex task is typically associated with extensive activation across large areas of the cerebral cortex (Eysenck & Keane, 2010).

> **KEY TERM**
>
> **Semantic dementia:** a condition caused by brain damage in which the patient experiences considerable problems in accessing word meanings.

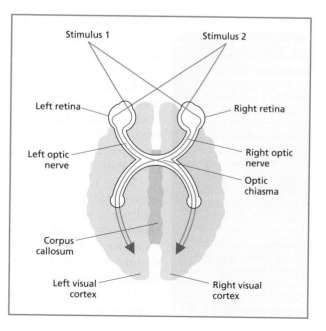

What does hemispheric specialisation mean?

Hemispheric specialisation

I have discussed the cerebral cortex as if its two hemispheres or halves are very similar in their functioning. However, that is by no means entirely correct. There is much **hemispheric specialisation**, meaning the two hemispheres differ in their functions. There is cerebral dominance in many situations, with one hemisphere being mainly responsible for processing information in that situation. For example, language abilities are based mainly in the left hemisphere in the great majority of people (85–90%).

How are split-brain patients defined?

How can we assess hemispheric specialisation? Some of the most important (and interesting) evidence has come from **split-brain patients**. In most of these patients, the corpus callosum (the major connection between the two hemispheres) has been cut surgically to contain severe epileptic seizures within one hemisphere.

It is sometimes believed that split-brain patients have great difficulty in functioning effectively in everyday life. That is *not* the case. Indeed, it wasn't realised initially that cutting the corpus callosum caused them any problems. Split-brain patients ensure environmental information reaches both hemispheres by moving their eyes around. Impaired performance in these patients is produced by presenting visual stimuli briefly to only one hemisphere so the information isn't available to the other one.

Findings

Levy et al. (1972) showed split-brain patients faces in which the left half of one person's face was presented next to the right half of another person's face. The situation was set up so that information about the right half of the picture went to the left hemisphere and information about the left half went to the right hemisphere.

The patients were asked to say what they had seen. They generally reported seeing the right half of the picture. However, when using their fingers to point to what they saw, most patients pointed to the left half of the picture. These findings suggest that language is mainly based in the left hemisphere. In contrast, the spatial processing involved in pointing to something depends far more on the right hemisphere.

Roger Sperry and his colleagues carried out other similar research. In one study, a picture of an object was presented briefly to the right hemisphere. Split-brain patients couldn't name the object, because the right hemisphere has very poor language abilities (see the figure on the next page). After that, the patients put their left hands behind a screen to decide which of the objects hidden there corresponded to the picture. Most of the patients could do this because of the good ability of the right hemisphere to process spatial information.

There has been controversy as to whether split-brain patients have two consciousnesses (one in each hemisphere) or only a single consciousness. The evidence is not clear-cut. However, consider what split-brain patients say very shortly after having had an operation to cut through the corpus callosum. None has ever reported feeling their experience of themselves has changed dramatically because they now have two selves or consciousnesses (Colvin & Gazzaniga, 2007).

Other research has suggested that split-brain patients may have two consciousnesses. Baynes and Gazzaniga (2000) discussed the case of VJ. Her

> **KEY TERMS**
>
> **Hemispheric specialisation:** each hemisphere or half of the brain carries out its own specific functions to some extent; however, the two hemispheres coordinate their activities most of the time.
>
> **Split-brain patients:** individuals in whom the corpus callosum connecting the two halves of the brain has been severed; direct communication between the two hemispheres is not possible.

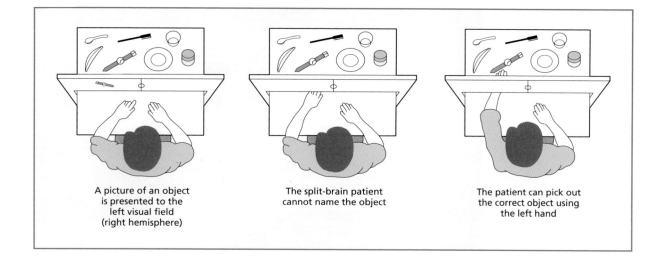

A picture of an object is presented to the left visual field (right hemisphere)

The split-brain patient cannot name the object

The patient can pick out the correct object using the left hand

writing is controlled by the right hemisphere, whereas her speech is controlled by the left hemisphere. She was visibly upset by the independent control of her right and left hands. For example, she was discomfited when she observed her left hand (controlled by the right hemisphere) writing fluently to stimuli that couldn't be seen by the left hemisphere.

In spite of such evidence, Gazzaniga et al. (2009) argued persuasively that split-brain patients have only a *single* conscious system. This system is based in the left hemisphere, and is known as the interpreter. It "seeks explanations for internal and external events in order to produce appropriate response behaviours" (Gazzaniga et al., 2009, p. 465). A major reason why the left hemisphere is likely to be dominant is that language abilities are centred in that hemisphere.

In contrast, the right hemisphere engages in various low-level processing activities and probably lacks its own consciousness. That makes sense because there could be numerous conflicts between the two hemispheres if both had their own consciousness.

Ways of studying the brain

Dramatic technological advances in recent years mean we now have many ways of obtaining detailed information about what the brain is doing when we perform numerous tasks. We can work out *where* and *when* in the brain activity occurs.

Numerous techniques are available for studying brain activity. These techniques vary in terms of how precisely they identify *where* brain activity occurs (spatial resolution) and *when* it occurs (temporal resolution). Here we will focus on two major techniques: functional magnetic resonance imaging (fMRI) and event-related potentials (ERPs).

fMRI involves making use of scanners containing a very large magnet weighing up to 11 tons (see the photo overleaf). What is measured in fMRI is based on assessing brain areas with an accumulation of oxygenated red blood cells suggestive of activity in those areas. Technically, this is the BOLD

Does functional magnetic resonance imaging have poor or good spatial and/ or temporal resolution?

The magnetic resonance imaging (MRI) scanner has proved an extremely valuable source of data in psychology.

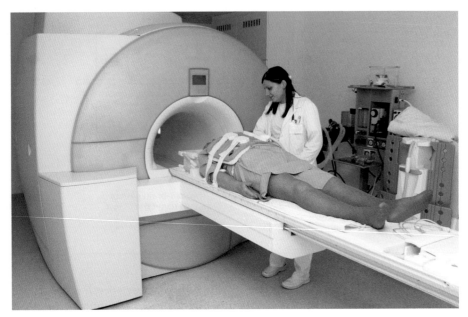

(blood oxygen-level-dependent contrast) signal. Changes in the BOLD signal produced by increased neural activity take some time, so the temporal resolution of fMRI is about 2 or 3 seconds. However, its spatial resolution is very good (approximately 1 millimetre).

Event-related potentials (ERPs) provide a valuable way of measuring brain activity. What happens is that a stimulus is presented several times, and scalp electrodes are used to obtain recordings of brain activity on each trial. Then information from all the recordings is averaged. Why is this done? There is so much brain activity going on all the time that it can be hard to detect the effects of stimulus processing on brain-wave activity. Several trials are needed to distinguish genuine effects of stimulation from background brain activity.

The greatest strength of ERPs is that they provide extremely precise information about the time course of brain activity. Indeed, they can often indicate when a given process occurred to within a few milliseconds. However, ERPs provide only a very approximate indication of the brain regions activated.

Findings

I will briefly consider three lines of research in which the assessment of brain activity has helped to resolve theoretical controversies and other issues. First, we will consider visual perception (see Chapter 20). It would be easy to imagine that all aspects of visual processing take place in the same brain area. As we are about to see, that is not the case at all.

Zeki (1993) argued that the processing of different kinds of information about visual stimuli takes place in widely distributed brain areas. The evidence from brain-imaging studies strongly supports this argument (see Eysenck & Keane, 2010). More specifically, colour, form, and motion are processed in separate parts of the visual cortex.

Additional evidence comes from brain-damaged patients. Patients with damage to a brain area associated with colour processing often have little or no colour perception combined with fairly intact motion perception and reasonable form perception (Bouvier & Engel, 2006). Patients with damage to a brain area associated with motion perception can perceive stationary objects fairly normally but not moving ones (Zihl et al., 1983).

Second, there is the issue of whether visual imagery involves the same processes as visual perception. Kosslyn (1994) argued that the same processes are involved, whereas Pylyshyn (2000) disagreed, claiming instead that imagery involves abstract forms of thinking.

Numerous studies have considered the brain areas activated during visual imagery and visual perception. Of major importance, brain areas involved in the early stages of visual processing are also often activated during visual imagery (Kosslyn & Thompson, 2003). This strongly suggests that perception and imagery involve similar processes. This conclusion is strengthened by the further finding that visual imagery involves *two-thirds* of the brain areas associated with visual perception (Kosslyn, 1994).

Third, suppose we ask people to attend to only one of two simultaneously presented visual or auditory stimuli or messages. How thoroughly is the unattended information processed? Theorists disagreed about the correct answer to that question.

Studies using event-related potentials (ERPs) have shown convincingly that unattended stimuli receive less processing than attended ones with both visual and auditory stimuli. Martinez et al. (1999) found the ERPs to attended visual stimuli were greater than those to unattended ones shortly after presentation.

Coch et al. (2005) asked listeners to attend to one of two auditory messages to detect targets. ERPs 100 ms after target presentation were greater when it was presented on the attended message than the unattended one. This suggests there was more processing of attended than of unattended targets.

EVALUATION

➕ Various techniques for studying the brain (and research on brain-damaged patients) have shed much light on when (and where) in the brain cognitive processes occur.

➕ This approach has proved increasingly successful in clarifying major theoretical issues in cognitive psychology.

➖ It has often been assumed that each brain region is *specialised* for a different function. That is an oversimplification—performance of any given task is typically associated with activity in several different brain regions at the same time.

Chapter summary

- Darwin's theory of evolution led psychologists to focus on individual differences, genetic influences on behaviour, and the relevance of biology to psychology.
- Twin studies provide an effective way of addressing the nature–nurture issue. Such studies indicate that genetic factors often play an important role in influencing individual differences in behaviour.
- There are various ways an individual's genetic endowment influences his/her behaviour. These include active covariation, passive covariation, and reactive covariation.
- The nervous system consists of the central nervous system and the peripheral nervous system. The latter is divided into the somatic nervous system and the autonomic nervous system.
- The autonomic nervous system controls the heart, lungs, eyes, stomach, and the blood vessels of the internal organs. It is divided into the sympathetic nervous and the parasympathetic nervous system.
- The brain can be divided into three main regions: forebrain; midbrain; and hindbrain.
- The forebrain consists of cerebrum (used in thinking), the limbic system (involved in aggression, fear, learning, and memory), the thalamus (a relay station), and the hypothalamus (used in the control of several autonomic functions).
- The midbrain is of relevance to the control of movement, sleep, arousal, and wakefulness.
- The hindbrain consists of the medulla oblongata, the pons, and the cerebellum.
- The cerebral cortex consists of the frontal lobe (front of the brain), the occipital lobe (back of the brain), the parietal lobe (top of the brain), and the temporal lobe (lower part of the brain). The frontal lobe is especially involved in complex cognitive activities and the occipital lobe is specialised for visual processing.
- The cerebral cortex shows some hemispheric specialisation. Language abilities are typically centred in the left hemisphere whereas most spatial processing occurs in the right hemisphere.
- Research on split-brain patients suggests we have a single consciousness based in the left hemisphere.
- Various techniques for studying the brain in action have shown when and where various cognitive processes occur.

Further reading

- Confer, J.C., Easton, J.A., Fleischman, D.S., Goetz, C.D., Lewis, D.M.G., Perilloux, C., & Buss, D.M. (2010). Evolutionary psychology: Controversies, questions, prospects, and limitations. *American Psychologist*, *65*, 110–126. This article contains an evaluation of the strengths and limitations of evolutionary psychology.

- Eysenck, M.W. (2012). *Fundamentals of cognition (2nd ed.)*. Hove, UK: Psychology Press. Chapter 1 of this textbook contains a detailed account of the main techniques for studying the brain in action.

- Pinel, J.P.J. (2009). *Biopsychology (8th ed.)*. Boston: Allyn & Bacon. This textbook provides accessible coverage of the topics covered in this chapter.

Essay questions

1. In what ways has Darwin's theory of evolution influenced the development of psychology?

2. What are the main areas of the cerebral cortex? What are the main functions of each area?

3. What evidence is there for hemispheric specialisation?

4. Describe some methods used to study the brain. How useful are these methods?

We all know the feeling of being stressed. Indeed, it is claimed that ours is the "age of stress" given the 24/7 nature of our society. However, our ancestors had to contend with major epidemics, short life expectancy, poverty, and an almost complete absence of holidays.

Taking the above into account, it might seem reasonable to conclude that stress levels are much the same as they used to be. However, it is popularly believed that people today are more anxious and stressed than people in the past. What is your opinion?

The term "stress" is often used rather vaguely. What do you think are the main signs of stress? In your everyday life, what are the main factors causing you to feel stressed? How do you try to cope with the stress you experience? How successful are these attempts to cope with stress?

Stress

4

We will consider definitions of stress. Before doing so, we need to distinguish between "stressor" and "stress". A stressor refers to any situation that creates stress, and stress refers to our *reactions* to a stressor.

What is stress? According to Colman (2001, p. 711), stress is "the psychological and physical strain or tension generated by physical, emotional, social, economic, or occupational circumstances, events, or experiences that are difficult to manage or endure".

What causes stress? The most obvious answer is that stress is something that happens to us when we are exposed to a stressor such as a forthcoming exam or heavy traffic that prevents us from arriving on time for an important meeting. However, this approach is limited in two ways. First, it assumes we are *passive* and simply allow the environment to have an impact on us.

Second, it ignores the fact that our response to any given situation depends on our abilities and personalities as well as on the situation itself. For example, someone taking their first driving lesson typically finds driving very stressful and demanding, whereas experienced drivers generally do not. In addition, someone who is very socially anxious finds being ignored by others more stressful than does someone who isn't socially anxious.

A much better approach to stress is to regard it as the result of the *interaction* between an individual and his/her environment. More specifically, stress occurs when the perceived demands of a situation *exceed* the individual's perceived ability to handle those demands. Driving is stressful for learner drivers because they have limited ability to meet the demands of handling a car in traffic. Driving isn't stressful for experienced drivers because they are confident their ability will allow them to cope with most driving situations.

What effects are associated with stress? There are four major kinds of effects: physiological; emotional; cognitive; and behavioural (see the figure overleaf). The physiological effects (which are the most complex ones) are discussed in the next section. The emotional effects can be assessed by self-report questionnaires in which individuals answer questions about their mental and/or physical state (see Chapter 5).

With what effects is the stressed state associated?

The various negative effects of stress and anxiety on the cognitive system are discussed by Eysenck et al. (2007). Finally, the behavioural effects of occupational stress are considered by Ross and Altmaier (1994).

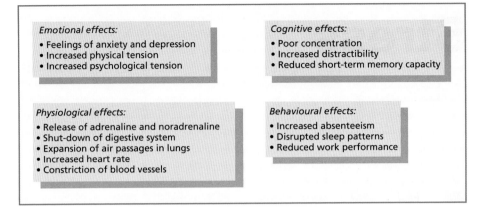

Emotional effects:
• Feelings of anxiety and depression
• Increased physical tension
• Increased psychological tension

Cognitive effects:
• Poor concentration
• Increased distractibility
• Reduced short-term memory capacity

Physiological effects:
• Release of adrenaline and noradrenaline
• Shut-down of digestive system
• Expansion of air passages in lungs
• Increased heart rate
• Constriction of blood vessels

Behavioural effects:
• Increased absenteeism
• Disrupted sleep patterns
• Reduced work performance

Are stress levels increasing?

Twenge (2000) analysed levels of trait anxiety (a personality dimension concerned with the tendency to experience much anxiety) among American children and college students. The average score for both groups was much higher in recent times than several decades ago. She concluded that, "The average American child in the 1980s reported more anxiety than child psychiatric patients in the 1950s" (Twenge, 2000, p. 1007). This suggests we live in a world becoming ever more stressed.

Even more dramatic findings were reported by Twenge et al. (2010). They compared the scores of American college students on the Minnesota Multiphasic Personality Inventory (MMPI) over the decades between 1938 and 2007. The MMPI assesses psychiatric symptoms, and Twenge et al.'s findings revealed a substantial increase in such symptoms over the years. Indeed, Twenge et al. concluded as follows: "Five times as many now score above common cutoffs for psychopathology [mental illness]" (p. 145). Of direct relevance to stress, there were large increases in symptoms of depression, anxiety, and tension.

Why are stress levels rising? Twenge et al. (2010) argued that many young people nowadays belong to "Generation Me". In other words, they are more focused on materialism and status than previous generations but less focused on social connectedness with others.

Physiology of stress

What does the general adaptation syndrome consist of?

How does our body respond to stressors? The first systematic answer was provided by Hans Selye (1950). He found that most hospital patients showed a similar pattern of bodily response, which he called the general adaptation syndrome. This consisted of three stages:

1. *Alarm reaction stage*: A strong physiological stress response making the individual ready for fight or flight.
2. *Resistance*: The physiological efforts to deal with the stressor that started in the alarm reaction stage are at full capacity. This is followed by attempts at more cautious use of the body's resources.

3. *Exhaustion*: The physiological systems used during the previous stages become ineffective and stress-related diseases (e.g., high blood pressure; heart disease) become more likely. In extreme cases, there is shrinkage of parts of the body's immune system (e.g., the spleen and thymus) and bleeding stomach ulcers.

How are adrenaline and noradrenaline related to stress?

Selye's (1950) research has had a major impact on stress research. His notion that there are various stages in the body's physiological response when stressed remains influential. In addition, he identified correctly several physiological stress responses. However, his theoretical approach was oversimplified.

In addition, Selye assumed wrongly that the physiological stress responses are very similar regardless of the stressor. In fact, stressors varying in the degree of fear, anger, and uncertainty they create produce different patterns of physiological response (Mason, 1975).

Two physiological systems

There is now general agreement that stress involves an immediate shock response followed by a countershock response. The first or shock response depends mainly on the sympathetic adrenal medullary (SAM) system. In contrast, the second or countershock response involves the hypothalamic-pituitary-adrenocortical (HPA) axis (see the figure overleaf). Selye (1950) focused mostly on the HPA system and somewhat neglected the SAM system.

We know there are two systems because stressors sometimes have different effects on the two systems. For example, Schommer et al. (2003) used the stressor of repeatedly requiring people to give a speech and perform a mental arithmetic task in front of an audience. With repetition, the SAM system continued to respond strongly, but there was a substantial reduction in HPA activation. However, the two systems do *not* operate in total independence of each other, each system has various effects on the other.

Sympathetic adrenal medullary (SAM) system

The initial response to shock involves the sympathetic adrenal medullary (SAM) system. Activity in the sympathetic branch of the autonomic nervous system (see Chapter 3) stimulates the adrenal medulla. This causes the release of the hormones **adrenaline** and **noradrenaline**. These hormones lead to increased arousal of the sympathetic nervous system and reduced activity in the parasympathetic nervous system.

Heightened activity of the SAM system prepares us for "fight or flight". More specifically, there are the following effects: an increase in energy; increased alertness; increased blood flow to the muscles; increased heart and respiration rate; and reduced activity in the digestive system. There is also increased release of clotting factors into the bloodstream to reduce blood loss in the event of injury.

Finally, note that SAM activity is not *only* associated with stress. We often perceive heightened activity in the SAM as indicating we are stressed. However, we sometimes interpret such activity as meaning we are excited or stimulated.

KEY TERMS

Adrenaline: this hormone produces increased arousal within the **sympathetic nervous system**.

Noradrenaline: a hormone that produces increased arousal within the **sympathetic nervous system**.

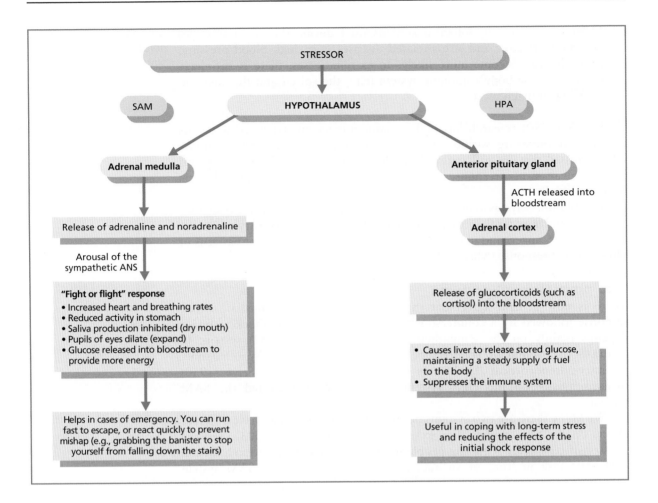

Hypothalamic-pituitary-adrenocortical (HPA) axis

If someone is exposed to a stressor for several hours, activity within the sympathetic adrenal medullary system increasingly uses up bodily resources. This leads to a countershock response designed to minimise damage. This countershock response involves the hypothalamic-pituitary-adrenocortical (HPA) axis. The details of its functioning are discussed below.

The anterior pituitary gland releases several hormones, the most important of which is **adrenocorticotrophic hormone** (**ACTH**). ACTH stimulates the adrenal cortex, which produces **cortisol**. It is often called the "stress hormone" because excess amounts are found in the urine of stressed individuals.

What stressors have the greatest effects on the HPA axis? Dickerson and Kemeny (2004) reviewed 208 laboratory studies. Uncontrollable tasks associated with social-evaluative threat produced the highest levels of cortisol, the greatest ACTH changes, and the longest recovery time.

Cortisol and the other glucocorticoids are useful because they permit maintenance of a steady supply of fuel. They also help to elevate or stabilise blood glucose concentrations, mobilise protein reserves, and conserve salts and water. Individuals without adrenal glands can't produce the normal amounts of glucocorticoids and have to be given additional quantities of glucocorticoids to survive when stressed (Tyrell & Baxter, 1981).

The glucocorticoids also have negative effects. The immune system protects the body against intruders such as viruses and bacteria, and glucocorticoids suppress the immune system. They also have an anti-inflammatory action, slowing the rate at which wounds heal.

In sum, the beneficial effects of HPA activity are achieved at considerable cost, and the HPA can't continue indefinitely at an elevated level of activity. If the adrenal cortex stops producing glucocorticoids, this eliminates the ability to maintain blood glucose concentrations at the appropriate level.

Causes of stress

There are many causes of stress. First, some individuals are more vulnerable than others to experiencing stress because of their personality. Second, severe negative life events and hassles often make us stressed. Third, those with jobs are exposed to many workplace stressors. We will discuss these three types of causes in turn.

Personality

What kinds of people are most vulnerable to stress? In what follows, we will consider two answers to that question.

Type A personality

Two cardiologists (Meyer Friedman and Ray Rosenman) identified the Type A personality in 1959. Individuals with the **Type A personality** exhibit "extremes of competitive achievement striving, hostility, aggressiveness, and a sense of time urgency, evidenced by vigorous voice" (Matthews, 1988, p. 373). In contrast, Type B individuals are more relaxed and less competitive. Friedman and Rosenman's (1959) key prediction was that individuals with the Type A personality are more likely than those with the Type B personality to suffer from coronary heart disease.

Rosenman et al. (1975) reported striking findings. Of nearly 3200 men having no symptoms of coronary heart disease at the start of the study, Type As were nearly twice as likely as Type Bs to have developed coronary heart disease over the following 8½ years.

The above study was limited because it wasn't clear *which* aspect of the Type A personality was most associated with heart disease. Matthews et al. (1977) reanalysed the data from that study and found the hostility component of Type A was of most importance. Support for the importance of hostility was discussed by Chida and Steptoe (2009). There were harmful effects of hostility and anger on symptoms of coronary heart disease (especially in men).

There have been several studies in which interventions have been used to reduce Type A behaviour in patients after a heart attack. These interventions have often been successful in reducing the probability of future heart attacks (Bennett, 1994).

In sum, the Type A personality (especially the hostility component) is associated with stress and coronary heart disease. However, note that the relationship between Type A and coronary heart disease is rather small (Myrtek, 2001).

KEY TERM

Type A personality: a personality type characterised by impatience, competitiveness, time pressure, and hostility.

Type D personality

Denollet (2005) argued that individuals having the Type D (distressed) personality are most susceptible to stress. The **Type D personality** consists of two aspects:

1. high negative affectivity or neuroticism (frequent experience of anxiety, depression, and other negative emotional states; see Chapter 18);
2. high social inhibition (inhibited behaviour in social situations).

Type D individuals are highly stressed and have poor mental health (many symptoms of depression, anxiety, and posttraumatic stress disorder) (Mols & Denollet, 2010). They also report more work-related stress, days absent from work, and burnout. Finally, they have poor physical health.

Denollet (2005) reported findings from people aged between 40 and 70. Only 19% of people in the general population had the Type D personality. However, among those with hypertension (high blood pressure), the figure was 54%, and it was 27% among coronary patients. Type D individuals were also at much greater risk than non-Type D ones for posttraumatic stress disorder, reduced lifespan, and cancer. For example, 27% of cardiac patients with Type D personality died over a 10-year period compared to only 7% of the others.

In sum, Type D individuals are often highly stressed and this impairs their physical and psychological well-being. However, some findings are less impressive than they seem for two reasons. First, individuals high in negative affectivity or neuroticism exaggerate the seriousness of their symptoms (Eysenck, 1997). It is thus possible that Type D individuals may be less ill and stressed than they claim. Second, it is often hard to establish causality. Poor mental or physical health may increase the probability of someone having a Type D personality rather than a Type D personality triggering poor mental or physical health.

Hassles and life events

We can draw a distinction between hassles and life events. Hassles are the minor challenges and interruptions (e.g., arguing with a friend) of everyday life. On average, people experience at least one hassle on about 40% of days (Almeida, 2005). In contrast, **life events** are often major negative events or occurrences (e.g., death of a loved one) causing high levels of stress.

Hassles

DeLongis et al. (1988) considered the effects of hassles (e.g., losing things; concerns about weight) and uplifts (e.g., good weather; relations with friends). The frequency and intensity of hassles were both associated with impaired overall health. However, uplifts had little impact on health.

Stone et al. (1987) considered the hassles and desirable events experienced by participants developing a respiratory illness during the 10 days before its onset. They experienced more hassles and fewer desirable events during that period than control participants who didn't develop a respiratory illness.

The effects of daily hassles depend in part on individuals' experience of major life events. The number of psychiatric symptoms reported by students experiencing major life events was greater if they also had substantial numbers of daily hassles (Johnson & Sherman, 1997).

KEY TERMS

Type D personality: a type of personality that is characterised by high negative affectivity and social inhibition.

Life events: these are major events (mostly having negative consequences) that create high levels of stress, often over a long period of time.

Life events

Early research on life events was carried out by Holmes and Rahe (1967). They developed the Social Readjustment Rating Scale on which people indicate which out of 43 life events have happened to them over a period of time (usually 6 or 12 months). These life events are assigned a value based on their likely impact. Here are various life events taken from this scale with their associated life change units in brackets:

Death of a spouse (100)
Divorce (73)
Marital separation (65)
Prison (63)
Death of a close family member (63)
Change in eating habits (15)
Holiday (13)
Minor violations of the law (11)

Why are holidays treated as stressful life events? According to Holmes and Rahe (1967), any *change* in our lives (whether desirable or not) can be stressful.

What types of life event does the Social Readjustment Rating Scale measure?

Holidays are included in the Social Readjustment Rating Scale because, even though they are enjoyable, they involve a change in our life, which can be stressful.

Findings

Rahe et al. (1970) studied 2500 male US naval personnel. The total number of life changes units was calculated based on the number and severity of life events experienced over the previous 6 months. There was a small (but significant) association between the total life change unit score and the incidence of illness.

Rahe and Arthur (1977) provided support for Rahe et al.'s (1970) findings. Various psychological illnesses, athletic injuries, physical illness, and even traffic accidents occurred more often when life change units were high.

Individuals experiencing more than 300 life change units over a 1-year period are at increased risk for many physical and mental illnesses (Martin, 1989). These illnesses include heart attacks, diabetes, TB, asthma, anxiety, and depression.

Sbarra et al. (2011) carried out a major review on the effects of divorce on mortality based on studies involving a total of 6½ million people. Divorced people tended to die earlier than those who remained married, and this was especially the case among men and younger adults. Two of the factors responsible were changes in health behaviours and long-lasting psychological distress.

Individuals differ in terms of how affected they are by negative life events. Kendler et al. (2004) considered the effects of experiencing several severe life events on the chances of developing major depression. Individuals high in neuroticism (a personality dimension associated with negative emotional states) were *four* times as likely as those low in neuroticism to develop major depression following severe life events.

Workplace stressors

Tens of millions of people spend 1500–2000 hours a year at work, doing jobs that may be very demanding or boring. As a result, the workplace is a major source of stress. What is it about the workplace environment that causes stress? Several factors are involved, but two are of special importance:

1. low job control (especially combined with high job demands);
2. effort–reward imbalance (work rewards are low relative to the effort required).

Low job control leads to several stress-related outcomes. Spector et al. (1988) found it was associated with frustration, anxiety, headaches, stomach upsets, and visits to the doctor. Marmot et al. (1997) and Bosma et al. (1998) reported dramatic findings from a long-term study on over 9000 British civil servants. Workers on the lowest employment grades were *four* times more likely to die of a heart attack than those on the most senior grade. They were also more likely to suffer from cancer, strokes, and gastrointestinal disorders.

The above differences probably occurred because those in the lower positions had much less control over their work than those in the higher positions. However, perhaps those resistant to the effects of stress are more likely to rise to senior job positions.

Kuper et al. (2002) studied effort–reward imbalance among over 10,000 civil servants followed up for 11 years. Effort–reward imbalance was associated with several outcomes suggestive of high levels of stress: non-fatal heart attacks; fatal heart attacks; poor physical functioning; and poor mental functioning. Clinicians in surgery with effort–reward imbalance were *six* times more likely than those without to report the symptoms of burnout (Klein et al., 2010).

Why does effort–reward imbalance cause health problems? Smith et al. (2005) found that such imbalance caused high levels of anger. This anger in turn led to cardiovascular disease.

In sum, low job control and effort–reward imbalance are very stressful. However, two points need to be made. First, workplace stress can be created in other ways (e.g., job lacks variety; job isn't valued by society; job doesn't provide the opportunity to socialise) (Warr, 1996).

Second, we know there are *associations* between poor job control and stress outcomes and between effort–reward imbalance and stress outcomes. Such evidence doesn't prove that the job factors *caused* the stress outcomes.

Technostress

The dramatic increase in the use of computers in the workplace has had profound effects on the lives of tens of millions of workers. Many of the changes stemming from this technological revolution have been very beneficial. For example, messages and documents can be sent instantly anywhere in the world via the use of email. However, there is a cost to be paid in the form of technostress. **Technostress** is the anxiety and stress workers experience when they cope unsuccessfully with the rapid pace of technological change and the increased workload associated with it.

We can see more clearly what is involved in technostress by considering some of the items used by Wang et al. (2008) to assess it:

- I am forced by this technology to do more work than I can handle.
- I have to spend a lot of time everyday reading an overwhelming amount of email messages.

KEY TERM

Technostress: the anxiety and stress caused by difficulties in coping with technological advances (especially in computing).

- I feel my personal life has been invaded by this technology.
- I do not know enough about this technology to handle my job satisfactorily.

Wang et al. (2008) wondered which kinds of organisation were associated with higher and lower levels of technostress. In a study on Chinese workers, they identified two major factors. First, there is power centralisation. Technostress was higher in very centralised companies than in those less centralised. This happened because workers were excluded from involvement in major decisions (e.g., on possible technological changes). Second, there is the organisational culture of innovation. Technostress was higher in companies emphasising innovation.

In sum, technostress is an increasingly important source of work stress in most countries. There are several ways this trend could be reversed. For example, workers should feel involved in decisions that might involve them in having to deal with complex technological changes. In addition, companies should ensure that workers have adequate training in computer-based skills so they can cope more effectively at work.

How does stress cause illness?

We have seen that there is good evidence that stress can increase the chances of someone becoming ill. There are two major ways stress might cause illness:

1. *Directly* by reducing the body's ability to fight illness (e.g., damaging the immune system).
2. *Indirectly* by leading the stressed individual to adopt an unhealthy lifestyle (e.g., smoking; excessive drinking).

Direct route

It is often thought that stress causes illness by impairing the **immune system** (a system of cells in the body that fights disease). Cells in the immune system have receptors for various hormones and neurotransmitters involved in the stress response. These cells may help to explain how stress influences the functioning of the immune system.

Before proceeding, we need to distinguish between natural immunity and specific immunity. Cells involved in natural immunity are all-purpose cells that have rapid effects. In contrast, cells involved in specific immunity are much more limited in their effects and take longer to work.

Segerstrom and Miller (2004) pointed out that it wouldn't make any sense if humans were designed so that even short-term stress impaired the functioning of the immune system. They reviewed the relevant research and produced the following conclusions:

- Short-lived stressors (e.g., public speaking) produce *increased* natural immunity.
- The stress created by loss of a spouse reduces natural immunity.

KEY TERM

Immune system: a system of cells in the body that is involved in fighting disease.

- Stress caused by disasters produces a small increase in natural and specific immunity.
- Life events are associated with reductions in natural and specific immunity *only* in individuals over 55 years or age.

Indirect route

Lifestyle has a major impact on illness and lifespan via the indirect route. Breslow and Enstrom (1980) considered seven health behaviours: not smoking; having breakfast each day; having no more than two alcoholic drinks a day; taking regular exercise; sleeping 7–8 hours a night; not eating between meals; and being no more than 10% overweight.

Individuals practising all seven health behaviours had only 23% of the mortality of those practising fewer than three in a follow-up 9½ years later. Schoenborn (1993) found that the strongest predictors of lifespan were not smoking, taking physical exercise, and regular breakfast eating.

Stressed individuals have somewhat less healthy lifestyles than non-stressed ones. Stressed individuals smoke more, drink more alcohol, take less exercise, and sleep less than non-stressed ones (Cohen & Williamson, 1991). Siegrist and Rodel (2006) reviewed the evidence from 46 studies. High levels of work stress were associated with being overweight and with heavy alcohol consumption by men.

Stress can lead to an unhealthy lifestyle.

Mainous et al. (2010) found that life stress was associated with hardening of the arteries. This occurred in part because stressed individuals smoked more, had a higher caloric intake, and had a less active lifestyle.

In sum, the effects of stressors on the immune system depend on the nature and duration of the stressor. Two additional points need to be made. First, immune system functioning in most stressed individuals is within the normal range (Bachen et al., 1997). This suggests that stress often has small effects on physical health. Second, the immune system is very complex. As a result, it is unwise to claim that stress impairs immune system functioning simply because it affects certain small parts of that system.

Stressed individuals drink more alcohol and smoke more than non-stressed ones.

Methods for reducing stress

We have considered stress and the factors that produce it. How do we handle and resolve stress in our everyday lives? Several methods are effective, and we consider some of them below.

Stress inoculation training

As discussed earlier, millions of people suffer from work-related stress. This stress causes substantial human misery and prevents people from working effectively. An increasing number of companies now use stress management interventions to reduce work-related stress.

What are the main phases in stress inoculation training?

One of the most popular interventions was developed by Meichenbaum (1985). It is known as stress inoculation training and reduces stress whether work-related or not. It involves three main phases:

1. *Assessment*: The therapist discusses the nature of the problem with the individual, and asks his/her views on how to eliminate it.
2. *Stress-reduction techniques*: The individual learns various techniques for reducing stress such as relaxation and self-instruction by using coping self-statements. Examples include "If I keep calm, I can handle this situation" and "Stop worrying because it's pointless."
3. *Application and follow-through*: The individual imagines using the stress-reduction techniques learned in the second phase in difficult situations. After that, he/she uses the techniques in real-life situations.

Findings

Stress inoculation training has various beneficial effects. Keogh et al. (2006) used an intervention closely resembling stress inoculation training on 15- and 16-year-olds a few weeks before important examinations. The intervention significantly improved their examination performance. It also improved the students' mental health by reducing their negative thoughts and attitudes about their ability to cope successfully with the examinations.

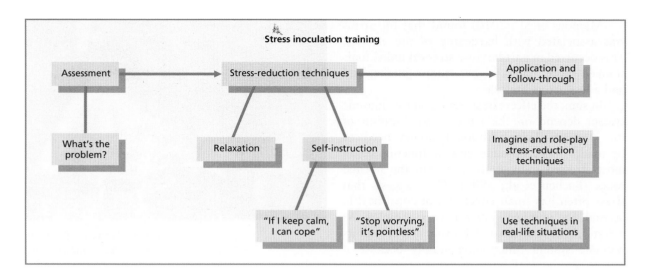

We can assess the effectiveness of stress inoculation training with self-report measures of stress. With such measures, however, individuals may exaggerate training's beneficial effects. An alternative approach is to assess cortisol levels—remember, cortisol is the "stress hormone". Gaab et al. (2003) exposed participants to a stressful situation. Some had received stress inoculation training beforehand. Participants who had received stress inoculation training had significantly smaller cortisol responses in the stressful situation than did controls. They also appraised the situation as less stressful and showed more competence in dealing with it.

EVALUATION

➕ Stress inoculation training reduces stress levels with both long-term and short-lasting stressors.

➕ Stress inoculation training reduces stress significantly whether stress is assessed by self-report measures or cortisol responses.

➕ Stress inoculation training can protect individuals from the negative effects of *future* stressors. This is valuable because "prevention is better than cure".

➖ There are several components to stress inoculation training. As a result, it is often hard to know *which* components are most responsible for reducing stress levels.

➖ It is improbable that *all* the beneficial effects of stress inoculation training on reducing stress are due to *specific* ingredients or components of the training provided. *General* factors common to most interventions (e.g., therapist warmth; alliance between therapist and client) are probably also important (Stevens et al., 2000).

Coping strategies

Much research has been devoted to coping. It can be defined as "efforts to prevent or diminish threat, harm, and loss, or to reduce associated distress" (Carver & Connor-Smith, 2010, p. 685).

Several theorists (e.g., Monat & Lazarus, 1991) have distinguished between problem-focused coping and emotion-focused coping. **Problem-focused coping** involves the use of thoughts or actions to act directly on a *stressful situation* (e.g., seeking information; purposeful or direct action; decision making, planning).

In contrast, **emotion-focused coping** involves using thoughts or actions to act directly on the *emotional state* experienced in a stressful situation. It can involve distraction, avoidance of the situation, seeking social support, emotional control, distancing (detaching oneself from the situation), positive reappraisal of the situation, and relaxation.

Do you think problem-focused or emotion-focused coping is the more effective strategy? You probably chose problem-focused coping because in Western societies it is thought desirable to *confront* stressful situations. An alternative viewpoint is the goodness-of-fit hypothesis (Zakowski et al., 2001). According to this hypothesis, it is preferable to use problem-focused coping when the stressor is controllable but emotion-focused coping when the stressor is uncontrollable.

Avoidance-oriented strategy

Findings

There is support for both of the above viewpoints. Penley et al. (2002) reviewed several studies concerned with coping strategies and health-related outcomes. Problem-focused coping was *positively* associated with physical and psychological health outcomes. In contrast, several forms of emotion-focused coping (e.g., distancing; avoidance; wishful thinking) were all *negatively* associated with the same outcomes.

Some support for the goodness-of-fit hypothesis was reported by Zakowski et al. (2001). Participants were more likely to use problem-focused coping when the stressor was perceived as controllable rather than uncontrollable. However, emotion-focused coping was used more often when the stressor was perceived as uncontrollable.

Zakowski et al. (2001) found the effects of emotion-focused coping on behavioural and self-report measures of stress were as predicted by the goodness-of-fit hypothesis—this form of coping was more effective with an uncontrollable stressor. However, the effects of problem-focused coping on stress did *not* vary as a function of stressor controllability, which is inconsistent with the hypothesis.

Forsythe and Compas (1987) studied the effectiveness of problem-focused and emotion-focused coping when dealing with major life events. The findings were as predicted by the goodness-of-fit hypothesis. Individuals had fewer psychological symptoms when problem-focused coping was used with controllable events and emotion-focused coping with uncontrollable events.

> **KEY TERMS**
>
> **Problem-focused coping:** a general strategy for dealing with stressful situations in which attempts are made to act directly on the source of the stress.
>
> **Emotion-focused coping:** a general strategy for dealing with stressful situations in which the individual concerned attempts to reduce his/her negative emotional state.

EVALUATION

➕ Problem-focused coping and emotion-focused coping are both generally applicable across numerous stressful situations.

➕ Many findings can be accounted for on the goodness-of-fit hypothesis. As predicted, stressed individuals tend to use problem-focused coping with controllable stressors and emotion-focused coping with uncontrollable ones.

➖ Problem-focused and emotion-focused coping aren't entirely separate. For example, as Skinner et al. (2003, p. 227) pointed out, "Making a plan not only guides problem solving but also calms emotion."

➖ In spite of the importance of problem-focused and emotion-focused coping, individuals often use other coping strategies. Examples are rumination (e.g., self-blame; worry) and helplessness (e.g., inaction; passivity) (Skinner et al., 2003).

➖ It is often hard to assess the effectiveness of problem-focused coping because it can produce a mixture of positive *and* negative outcomes. Wu et al. (1993) found doctors who accepted responsibility for their own mistakes made constructive changes to their work habits (a positive outcome). However, they also experienced more distress (a negative outcome).

➖ The coping strategies used by individuals in real-life situations may differ from those they claim to use on questionnaires.

Social support

It has often been argued that social support reduces stress. What is social support? Schaefer et al. (1981) argued that the term has two rather different meanings:

1. *Social network*: the number of people available to provide support (*quantity* of social support).
2. *Perceived support*: the strength of social support that can be provided by these individuals (*quality* of social support). In most research, this is how social support is defined.

Schaefer et al. (1981) discussed evidence showing that perceived support was positively related to health and well-being. In contrast, social network was unrelated to well-being. It was sometimes *negatively* related to well-being because it is very time-consuming and demanding to maintain a large social network.

General findings

Perceived support is often effective in reducing stress. For example, Brown and Harris (1978) studied women who had recently experienced a serious life event. Of those women who didn't have an intimate friend, 37% became depressed against only 10% of those who did.

House et al. (1988) found in a review that individuals with a high level of social support had much lower mortality rates than those with poor social support. Zhang et al. (2007) found in an older sample with diabetes that the risk of death over a 6-year follow-up period was 55% less among those with the highest levels of social support than those with the lowest levels.

How does social support reduce mortality? It is associated with beneficial effects on physiological systems. Uchino et al. (1996) reported across numerous studies that blood pressure was lower in individuals with good social support. Individuals with good social support also had stronger immune system functioning. Uchino (2006) carried out a further review. He discovered that social support was associated with positive changes in cardiovascular, neuroendocrine, and immune system function.

Social support doesn't *always* have beneficial effects. Bolger and Amarel (2007) studied the effects of social support on female students told they would have to give a speech. There were three groups:

1. students who received visible social support (i.e., it was obvious they were receiving it);
2. students who received invisible social support (i.e., they weren't consciously aware of receiving it);
3. students receiving no social support.

The amount of distress experienced was least in the group receiving invisible social support and greatest in the group receiving visible social support. Why was visible social support less effective than no social support? It made the participants feel ineffective because they were reliant on another person for help.

Social support sometimes makes depressed individuals feel more depressed. According to Ibarra-Rovillard and Kuiper (2011), this happens when social support undermines their basic psychological needs. For example, if depressed people have friends who adopt an over-controlling approach, this can cause them to feel that they are losing control of their lives.

Women are more likely to use the "tend-and-befriend" response to stress than the "fight-or-flight" response more often used by men.

Gender differences

Luckow et al. (1998) reviewed 26 studies on gender differences in seeking and using social support. Women sought social support more than men in 25 of these studies. Taylor et al. (2000) developed a theory based in part on this gender difference. They argued that men generally respond to stressful situations with a "fight-or-flight" response, whereas women respond with a "tend-and-befriend" response. Thus, women respond to stressors by protecting and looking after their children (the tend response) and by actively seeking social support from others (the befriend response).

Turton and Campbell (2005) used a questionnaire-based approach to identify the four factors of fight, flight, tend, and befriend. As predicted, females were more likely than males to report using tend-and-befriend strategies in stressful situations.

EVALUATION

⊕ High levels of perceived support are associated with various beneficial effects on physical health, mental health, and mortality.

⊕ One of the main ways social support has beneficial effects is by influencing the functioning of the cardiovascular and immune systems.

⊕ Women make more use of social support than men because they have a preference for the tend-and-befriend response.

⊖ There is an alternative way of accounting for associations between social support and outcomes such as reduced stress and improved physical health. Perhaps individuals who are often stressed and/or in poor physical health have less social support than others. Thus, the causal sequence may sometimes be in the *opposite* direction to the one usually assumed!

⊖ The common assumption that social support *always* has beneficial effects is wrong (e.g., Bolger & Amarel, 2007; Ibarra-Rovillard & Kuiper, 2011). Little is known about the reasons for adverse effects of social support on well-being.

Chapter summary

- Selye argued that the stress response consisted of a three-stage general adaptation syndrome.
- It is now thought that the stress response consists of an initial shock response followed by a countershock response involving the HPA axis.
- The Type A personality is slightly associated with coronary heart disease.
- The Type D personality is moderately associated with stress, high blood pressure, heart attacks, and reduced longevity.
- Severe life events and hassles are both associated with a range of stress-related symptoms.

- Two of the most damaging workplace stressors are low job control and effort–reward imbalance.
- Technostress is an increasingly common form of workplace stress.
- Stress can cause physical illness by impairing the immune system (direct route) or by leading to an unhealthy lifestyle (indirect route).
- Stress inoculation training reduces stress via techniques such as relaxation and coping self-statements.
- Problem-focused coping is often more effective than emotion-focused coping in reducing stress. However, emotion-focused coping can be more effective when stressors are perceived as uncontrollable.
- Social support is used more often by females than by males. It generally reduces stress. However, it can have negative effects if perceived as undermining the individual's basic psychological needs.

Further reading

- Contrada, R.J., & Baum, A. (Eds.) (2011). *The handbook of stress science*. New York: Springer. This edited book contains chapters by leading experts in various areas of stress research including biological, psychological, and social approaches.
- Eysenck, M.W. (2009). *Fundamentals of psychology*. Hove, UK: Psychology Press. Chapter 4 of this textbook contains detailed coverage of stress research.
- Folkman, S., & Moskowitz, J.T. (2004). Coping: Pitfalls and promise. *Annual Review of Psychology*, *55*, 745–774. The authors provide an overview of coping research together with an evaluation of theoretical approaches.
- Segerstrom, S.C., & Miller, G.E. (2004). Psychological stress and the human immune system: A meta-analytic study of 30 years of inquiry. *Psychological Bulletin*, *130*, 601–630. Hundreds of studies on the effects of stress on the immune system are reviewed in this thought-provoking article.

Essay questions

1. What are the effects of stress on physiological processes? How do these effects change over time?

2. What are the most important factors that cause stress? What personality types are most susceptible to stress?

3. Describe some of the main ways people try to cope with stress. How effective are these strategies?

4. It is often claimed that stress can help to cause various physical illnesses. Discuss whether the relevant evidence provides convincing support for this claim.

Sometimes you probably find it hard to tell whether you are experiencing a weak emotion or no emotion at all. How could you decide which it is? There are several emotions including sadness, happiness, anxiety, and anger. In your experience, does each of these emotions seem to differ in terms of the kinds of physiological activities associated with it?

You probably feel anxious or depressed some of the time. Do you wish that you could be free of these emotions? If not, in what ways do you think that such negative emotions serve useful functions in your life?

Emotion

Most (or even all!) of the really important events in our lives are associated with high levels of emotion. When we embark on a new relationship we feel excited, when we pass major exams we feel elated, when we fail to achieve a major goal we feel depressed, and so on. Thus, emotions play a central role in our lives.

How can we define "emotion"? According to Colman (2001, p. 241), emotion is "any short-term evaluative, affective, intentional, psychological state". There are various ways we can tell that someone is experiencing a given emotional state:

1. Typical facial expressions are associated with most emotions (e.g., a smile is associated with happiness).
2. There are certain physiological patterns of activity involving the autonomic nervous system and the brain (see Chapter 3).
3. There are subjective feeling states.
4. An individual's behaviour can help to reveal their current emotional state.

We can consider the concrete example of fear to clarify matters. When someone is fearful, they typically have the following facial expression: the eyebrows are raised and close together, the eyes are open wider than usual, the lips are pulled back, and there is tension in the lower lip.

Fear is also associated with a substantial increase in the activity of the autonomic nervous system (e.g., a faster heart rate and sweating). Individuals in a state of fear use adjectives such as "nervous", "frightened", and "scared to death" to describe their feelings. Finally, someone who is fearful may run away from (or avoid) whatever is making them fearful.

Emotions vs. moods

It is important to distinguish between emotion and mood. What are the main differences? First, **moods** typically last much longer than emotions. Second, moods are less intense than emotions: we attend to our emotional states, whereas moods simply provide a background to our everyday activities. Third, the reasons for being in a given mood are often unclear, whereas emotions are generally produced by a specific event (e.g., being insulted).

It is important to note that being in an emotional state often produces a mood change. In addition, moods can give rise to emotions. As a result, the distinction between emotions and mood states is often somewhat blurred.

Females vs. males

Are females more emotional than males?

It is often assumed that females are more emotional than males. Most of the evidence supports this assumption. For example, it was found across 37 cultures that women reported more intense emotions than men, and that these emotions lasted longer and were expressed more directly (Brody & Hall, 2008). However, that isn't true of all emotions. Men are just as likely as women to report experiencing emotions such as contempt, loneliness, pride, excitement, and guilt (Brody & Hall, 2008).

It is also often assumed that females are more sensitive than males to others' emotional states. Supporting evidence comes from Hoffmann et al. (2010), who asked men and women to recognise the emotions shown in facial expressions. Women performed this task better than men when the facial emotions were subtle.

Why do males and females differ in these ways? In most cultures, males are expected to be independent and competitive, whereas females are expected to be cooperative and helpful (see Chapter 11). The ability to express and to recognise emotions is probably more important for those trained to be cooperative than for those trained to be independent.

How useful are emotions?

It is popularly believed that negative emotions such as anxiety and depression are useless and undesirable. That belief is understandable for various reasons. First, very few people actively *want* to become anxious or depressed. Second, emotions often disrupt our current activities and behaviour. Third, as Keltner and Gross (1999, pp. 467–468) pointed out, emotions "generally lack the logic, rationality, and principled orderliness of reason and other cognitive processes".

In spite of the above arguments, the dominant view nowadays is that all emotions are useful and serve valuable functions. For example, fear or anxiety is associated with selective attention to threat-related stimuli, and rapid detection of danger can be life-saving in threatening environments (Eysenck, 1992). In addition, the increased physiological activity associated with fear and anxiety is useful because it prepares the individual for fight or flight.

Lee et al. (2006) discovered another advantage associated with anxiety. Individuals rated as highly anxious by their teachers at the age of 13 were 6 times less likely than those rated as non-anxious to die before the age of 25. Why is this? Anxious individuals are more cautious and so less likely to take risks.

What useful functions are served by sadness or depression? According to Andrews and Thomson (2009), depression can help individuals to find solutions to complex problems in their lives. It does this most importantly by causing the depressed individual to ruminate (think carefully) about the problem. In addition, depression reduces the motivation to engage in distracting activities.

Oatley and Johnson-Laird (1987) argued that emotions lead individuals to pursue the goal having the greatest survival or other value in the current situation. For example, happiness encourages us to continue with the current goal. In contrast, sadness leads us to abandon our current (unachievable) goal and to conserve energy so we can pursue a more realistic goal. Anxiety motivates us to deal with threats to the achievement of some important goal.

You may still be unconvinced that negative emotions are useful. If so, consider the following attempt by Levenson (1999, p. 496) to bridge the gap between the emotions-are-useful and the emotions-are-disruptive positions:

> Viewed from the perspective of what we were trying to accomplish prior to the emotion taking hold, the subsequent emotional behaviour may appear chaotic and disorganised. But, viewed from the perspective of the survival of the organism, the emotional behaviour represents an elegant, adaptive, and highly organised state of affairs.

How many emotions are there?

The question "How many emotions are there?" sounds easy. Alas, there is little agreement on the answer, in part because the question is somewhat ambiguous. When answering it, we can focus on the number and nature of *basic* emotions (mostly shared with other species) or we can also include *complex* emotions (e.g., shame; guilt) derived from the basis ones. In either case, the boundary between one emotion and another is often fuzzy. Indeed, we sometimes find it hard to decide which emotion we are experiencing!

In what follows, we consider mostly the basic emotions. In doing so, we focus on three main kinds of evidence: (1) facial expressions; (2) self-reports; and (3) brain systems.

Facial expressions

We all display a wide range of facial expressions, and it seems reasonable to assume that each of our basic emotions has its own distinctive expression. Ekman et al. (1972) reviewed the evidence and concluded that observers can reliably detect six emotions in faces: happiness, surprise, anger, sadness, fear, and disgust combined with contempt.

Most of the studies considered by Ekman et al. (1972) were carried out in the United States. Would similar findings be obtained elsewhere in the world? Ekman et al. (1987) asked observers from 10 different countries including Turkey, Greece, Sumatra, and Japan to judge the emotions displayed in 18 faces. There was a high level of agreement across cultures, suggesting the six emotions identified by Ekman et al. (1972) are universal.

In most research, individuals whose faces are photographed are told to produce the facial expressions characteristic of various emotions. This is a rather artificial approach, and it is possible that those individuals fail to

Facial expressions associated with emotion are generally recognised across cultures, suggesting that the expressive aspect of emotion is innate.

experience the relevant emotions. However, reassurance was provided by Levenson et al. (1990). Individuals who posed with different facial expressions reported experiencing the expected emotional states.

An important limitation with Ekman's approach is that some emotions are *not* associated with a readily identifiable emotional expression. For example, consider love and jealousy. They are both generally regarded as emotions. However, they are missing from Ekman's list because neither is associated with a unique facial expression.

There is another limitation with using facial expressions to assess individuals' emotional states. There is much evidence that people can have emotions in the absence of any obvious facial expressions (Matsumoto, 2009). It is also possible for people to produce "emotional" facial expressions without experiencing any emotion (Matsumoto, 2009).

Self-report approach

We have seen there is evidence for the existence of six basic emotions from studies on facial expression. However, a more complex picture emerges when we consider research in which emotional states are assessed by self-report questionnaires. Such questionnaires typically consist of numerous adjectives (e.g., sad, lonely, happy, irritable), and participants indicate which ones describe their current feelings.

The Positive and Negative Affect Schedule (PANAS-X; Watson & Clark, 1994) is an example of a self-report questionnaire. It assesses 11 emotions or moods (fear, sadness, hostility, guilt, shyness, fatigue, surprise, joviality, self-assurance, attentiveness, and serenity).

A problem with self-report questionnaires such as the PANAS-X is that some of the scales used to measure the various mood states are highly associated with each other. This suggests they are measuring similar mood states that aren't really clearly different from each other. Watson and Clark (1992) argued that the evidence was consistent with a hierarchical model (see the figure below). In this model, there are several correlated (but distinguishable) emotional states at the lower level. At the upper level, there are two broad and independent factors called negative affect and positive affect. All emotional or mood states can be related to the two-dimensional structure formed by negative and positive affect.

What are the limitations of the self-report approach? First, individuals' self-reported emotions may be distorted. For example, someone may be unwilling to admit how anxious or depressed they are in a given situation. Second,

A two-level hierarchical model of emotion.

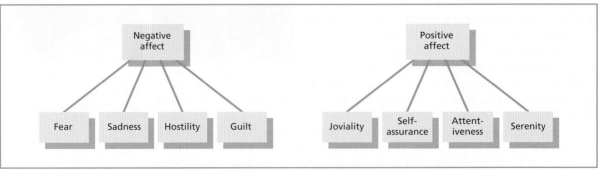

self-report measures rely on language, but language may not adequately capture the full richness of emotional experience (Robinson, 2009).

Brain systems

Panksepp (2000, 2007) argued that several core emotional systems are located within subcortical regions of the brain including the limbic system and the midbrain. According to him, the brain circuitry associated with specific emotions is very similar across numerous species of mammals (including the human species). Panksepp (2000) identified seven basic emotional systems centred within the brain:

According to the hierarchical model of emotions, what is measured by self-report assessment of any specific emotion?

- Seeking/expectancy
- Rage/anger
- Fear/anxiety
- Lust/sexuality
- Care/nurturance
- Panic/separation
- Play/joy

We can compare the above list with the one proposed by Ekman et al. (1972; discussed above). The good news is that three of the emotions identified by Ekman et al. (anger; fear; and happiness) are rather similar to emotions suggested by Panksepp (2000, 2007). The bad news is that there is otherwise practically no overlap! For example, Ekman et al. also identified surprise, sadness, and disgust, all of which are missing from Panksepp's list.

There is further discussion of the relationship between emotions and brain systems later in the chapter. To anticipate a little, Panksepp (2000, 2007) exaggerated the extent to which there is a *separate* brain system associated with each emotion. What is more likely is that general brain systems are involved when an individual experiences a fairly wide range of emotional states (Lindquist et al., 2012).

Conclusions

The evidence discussed above indicates that it is not clear how many basic emotions we possess. The approach based on facial expressions and that based on brain systems differ only slightly in the proposed number of emotions (six vs. seven, respectively), but there is only modest overlap in the specific emotions identified.

In contrast, the self-report approach suggests that emotional or mood states should be thought of in hierarchical terms. Within the hierarchy, there are two major emotions at the higher level and several more specific ones at the lower level.

The approach based on brain systems is the most dubious. As mentioned above, many experts strongly doubt whether each emotion has its own brain system. The approach based on facial expressions is reasonably effective at identifying some of the major emotions. However, it is limited by the fact that some universally accepted emotions (e.g., love) are missing from Ekman's list.

The self-report approach probably provides the most adequate account of the number and nature of basic emotions. The reason is that in principle it is based on our conscious emotional experience, which is of central importance

to the study of emotion. However, some of our emotional experience may be hard or impossible to express using language.

It is encouraging that there is reasonable overlap between the emotional states identified by facial expressions and by self-report. More specifically, both approaches identify sadness and fear, and the emotion of anger based on facial expressions is very similar to the emotion of hostility stemming from the self-report approach. The emotion of happiness based on facial expressions clearly overlaps substantially with the positive affect dimension identified by the self-report approach.

Admittedly, other emotions are found on only one list. For example, surprise and disgust are emotions based on the evidence of facial expressions. Guilt, joviality, self-assurance, attentiveness, and serenity are emotions based on self-report data.

Psychological theories of emotion

There is a bewildering variety of theories of emotion. Some theorists have viewed emotion mainly from a physiological perspective. However, other theorists emphasise the cognitive processes associated with emotion. Still other theorists have provided an overall account of the relationships among the cognitive, physiological, and behavioural systems.

In this section we focus on approaches in which the main emphasis is on cognitive processes. However, physiological processes are sometimes considered as well.

James–Lange theory

The first major theory of emotion was put forward independently by William James in the United States and Carl Lange in Denmark in the mid-1980s. For obvious reasons it became known as the James–Lange theory. According to this theory, the following stages are involved in producing emotion (Dalgleish, 2009):

According to the James–Lange theory, how are bodily changes and emotions related?

1. There is an emotional stimulus (e.g., a car coming rapidly towards you).
2. This perception produces bodily changes (e.g., arousal in the autonomic nervous system).
3. Feedback from the bodily changes to the brain leads to the experience of emotion (e.g., fear or anxiety).

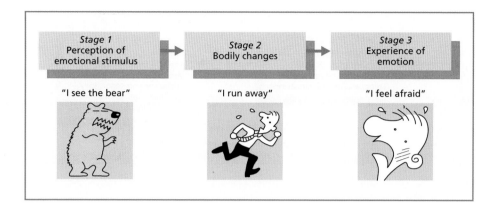

The essence of this approach was expressed by James (1890, p. 451): "If we fancy some strong emotion, and then try to abstract from our consciousness of it all the feelings of its bodily symptoms, we find we have nothing left behind." In other words, our emotions are essentially our experience of our bodily symptoms.

James gave the following example of the predicted sequence of events: "I see a bear, I run away, I feel afraid" (see the figure above). This runs counter to the more commonsensical sequence: "I see a bear, I feel afraid, I run away."

Findings

Patients with spinal cord injury have dramatically reduced awareness of their own bodily arousal. According to the James–Lange theory, such patients should experience a large reduction in the intensity of emotional experience. Hohmann (1966) obtained the predicted findings, with one patient saying, "Sometimes I act angry when I see some injustice … but it just doesn't have the heat to it that it used to."

However, most later research found that patients with spinal cord injury experience as much emotion as healthy controls (Deady et al., 2010). They also report that their current emotional experiences are at least as great as prior to injury (Cobos et al., 2004). Thus, feedback from bodily changes is *not* needed for emotion to be experienced.

A central assumption of the James–Lange theory is that every emotion is associated with its own specific pattern of physiological activity. For example, the autonomic nervous system (see Chapter 3) is activated during the experience of most emotions. As a result, we might expect to find emotion-specific patterns of autonomic responding.

Stephens et al. (2010) assessed autonomic responses (e.g., heart rate variability) while participants listened to emotional music or emotional movies. There was limited evidence of emotion-specific patterns. However, there was also considerable overlap in the pattern of autonomic responding across emotions. Thus, the existence of several different emotions can't be explained with reference to different patterns of autonomic responding from one emotion to another.

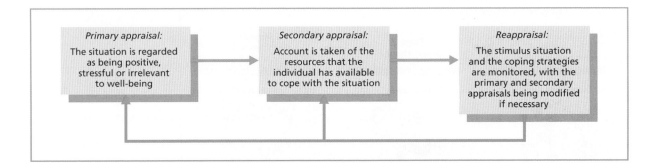

Appraisal theory

What does cognitive appraisal consist of?

Many theorists (e.g., Lazarus, 1982) have argued for the importance of cognitive appraisal in determining *which* emotion we experience in any given situation (Scherer & Ellsworth, 2009). What is **cognitive appraisal**? It is the evaluation or judgement we make about situations relevant to our goals, concerns, and well-being. It typically involves top-down processing based on knowledge and previous experience of similar situations. There are three forms of appraisal: primary appraisal; secondary appraisal; and reappraisal (see the figure above).

Appraisal theorists argue that the emotion we experience depends upon how we interpret the current situation. For example, consider guilt. According to Smith and Lazarus (1993), we experience guilt when the situation is related to our personal commitments, our goals are blocked, and we blame ourselves for what has happened. In contrast, we experience anger when the situation is related to our personal commitments, our goals are blocked, and we blame the other person for what has happened.

Smith and Kirby (2001) argued that cognitive appraisal can occur below the level of conscious awareness based on activation of memories (involving automatic processes). This leads to the improbable hypothesis that stimuli we can't see consciously might nevertheless trigger an emotional state. Research on this hypothesis is discussed below.

Findings

Most research has used short stories in which participants are asked to identify with the central character. The appraisal of any given situation is manipulated across stories to observe the effects on emotional experience. One story used by Smith and Lazarus (1993) involved a student who had performed poorly in an examination. Participants reported he would experience anger when he put the blame on the unhelpful teaching assistants. However, guilt was more common when the student blamed himself (e.g., for doing work at the last minute).

Subsequent research has indicated that any given emotion can be produced via several different combinations of appraisals. Kuppens et al. (2003) studied four appraisals (goal obstacle; other accountability: someone else is to blame; unfairness; and control) thought to be relevant to the experience of anger. Participants described recently experienced unpleasant situations in which one of the four appraisals was present or absent.

None of the four appraisal components was *essential* for the experience of anger. Thus, for example, some participants felt angry without the appraisal of unfairness or the presence of a goal obstacle.

> **KEY TERM**
>
> **Cognitive appraisal:** the individual's interpretation of the current situation; it helps to determine the nature and intensity of his/her emotional experience. It also helps the individual to decide whether he/she has the resources to cope with the situation.

Evidence that stimuli that aren't consciously perceived can cause an emotional state was reported by Chartrand et al. (2006). They presented positive (e.g., music; friends); negative (e.g., war; cancer) or neutral (e.g., building; plant) words repeatedly below the level of conscious awareness. Participants receiving the negative words reported a more negative mood state than those receiving the positive words.

Additional evidence that emotional experiences can be triggered by stimuli that are not perceived consciously has come from research on brain-damaged patients. Of particular importance is a phenomenon known as **affective blindsight**. This is the ability to discriminate between emotional stimuli in the absence of conscious perception of these stimuli.

Pegna et al. (2005) studied a 52-year-old man who was cortically blind. He showed activation of the amygdala (a part of the brain centrally involved in emotion) to faces displaying various emotions. In one experiment, he was shown happy and angry faces he couldn't perceive consciously. In spite of that, he reported the emotion correctly on 59% of the trials.

According to appraisal theory, appraisals cause emotional states rather than emotional states causing appraisals. However, most research has shown only an *association* between appraisals and emotion and so doesn't directly address the issue of causality. Some appraisals may occur *after* a given emotion has been experienced and may be used to justify that emotion.

In one study (Berndsen & Manstead, 2007), participants received various scenarios and rated their level of personal responsibility and guilt. The amount of guilt experienced seemed to determine appraisal (personal responsibility), whereas appraisal theories predict the causality should be in the other direction.

EVALUATION

➕ Appraisal is often of great importance in influencing emotional experience.

➕ Appraisal processes not only determine *whether* we experience emotion but also influence *which* emotion is experienced.

➖ The links between appraisals and specific emotions are flexible and not especially strong.

➖ While it is assumed that appraisal causes emotional experience, it is likely the causality is sometimes in the opposite direction.

Emotion regulation and cognitive reappraisal

Research on appraisal can be seen within the broader perspective of emotion regulation. **Emotion regulation** is "a deliberate, effortful process that seeks to override people's spontaneous emotional responses" (Koole, 2009, p. 6). The basic notion is that we spend much of our time using various emotion-regulation strategies to reduce negative emotional states or to turn them into positive ones.

One of the most effective emotion-regulation strategies is cognitive reappraisal. Suppose an individual's cognitive appraisal of a situation causes him/her to experience a negative emotional state. According to appraisal theory, it should be possible to change that emotional state by cognitive reappraisal, in which the situation is reinterpreted in a more positive way. Other emotion-regulation strategies include controlled breathing, progressive muscle relaxation, stress-induced eating, and distraction.

Findings

Augustine and Hemenover (2009) reviewed numerous studies and found that cognitive reappraisal was a very effective strategy for reducing negative emotion. Recent brain-imaging studies have served to clarify *how* cognitive reappraisal influences emotional states. Ochsner and Gross (2008) reviewed brain-imaging studies in which the emphasis was on two types of reappraisal strategy:

1. *Reinterpretation*: this involves changing the meaning of the context in which a stimulus is presented (e.g., imagining a gruesome picture has been faked).
2. *Distancing*: this involves taking a detached, third-person perspective.

Regardless of which strategy was used, parts of the brain (e.g., prefrontal cortex) involved in cognitive control and in complex cognitive processing were consistently activated. In addition, reappraisal strategies designed to reduce negative emotional states produced reduced activation in the amygdala (which is strongly associated with emotion).

What do the above findings mean? In essence, cognitive processes within the prefrontal cortex improve mood state by leading to reduced activity in brain areas (e.g., amygdala) associated with emotion.

Some individuals show emotion dysregulation—deficits in the ability to use effective emotion-regulation strategies. It is reasonable to predict that individuals having psychiatric symptoms (e.g., anxiety; depression) will tend to exhibit emotion dysregulation. Bradley et al. (2011) obtained strong support for this prediction, especially in individuals suffering from depression.

EVALUATION

➕ Cognitive reappraisal is generally an effective way of reducing negative emotional states and/or enhancing positive ones.

➕ Effective cognitive control involves using cognitive control mechanisms in the prefrontal cortex to reduce activation in emotion-relevant brain regions (e.g., amygdala).

➖ Much remains to be discovered about the precise ways in which cognitive processes in the prefrontal cortex enhance our emotional states.

Brain system or brain systems?

I mentioned earlier that there has been controversy concerning the relationship between our emotions and the brain. On one hand, locationists (e.g., Panksepp, 2000, 2007) assume each emotion is associated with its own brain system centred in a particular location or region of the brain. On the other hand, other theorists (e.g., Lindquist et al., 2012) argue that very similar brain regions are associated with all emotions, and so the locationists' main assumption is simply incorrect.

How can we identify the brain circuits associated with any given emotion? One way is via electrical stimulation in subcortical brain areas. Specific locations within the brain are stimulated by passing a weak electric current through microelectrodes inserted into the brain. The individual concerned simply reports his/her experience.

The effects of such stimulation can be dramatic. Olds and Milner (1954) applied electrical stimulation within the medial forebrain bundle of rats. They discovered it formed part of a reward/pleasure system. Indeed, rats would press a lever more than 6000 times an hour to receive stimulation in that area.

Heath (1964) carried out similar experiments on humans, mostly using patients with mental disorders. He identified a reward/pleasure centre closely resembling the one found in rats. Some individuals stimulated in that area reported that it resembled intense sexual orgasm.

Human research has identified other brain areas associated with a given emotion. For example, Bejjani et al. (1999) applied electrical stimulation to the subcortical areas of a 65-year-old woman with Parkinson's disease. This produced acute sadness and depression (e.g., "I don't want to live any more, I'm disgusted with life"). When the stimulation stopped, her symptoms of depression disappeared within 90 seconds.

Shapira et al. (2006) applied electrical stimulation to a 52-year-old man with obsessive-compulsive disorder in a subcortical area close to the one stimulated by Bejjani et al. (1999). He felt flushed and fearful and said he was having a panic attack. All these symptoms stopped immediately following the end of stimulation.

In sum, there are several fascinating studies in which the brains of individuals have been stimulated. These studies seem to support a locationist position. However, there are good ethical reasons why such studies have been carried out only rarely. As a result, it isn't possible to draw any strong conclusions from such research.

Locationist theory

Various locationist theories have been suggested over the years. However, as Lindquist et al. (2012) pointed out, the most popular of such theories is as follows (see the figure overleaf). It is assumed that fear is especially associated with the amygdala, disgust with the insula, anger with the orbitofrontal cortex, and sadness with the anterior cingulate cortex.

Findings

Research on emotion has probably focused more on the role of the amygdala than on any other part of the brain. The **amygdala** is a small part of the brain

KEY TERM

Amygdala: a small, almond-shaped part of the brain buried deep within the temporal lobe; it is associated with several emotional states (e.g., fear).

The brain regions associated with emotion categories according to the most popular locationist hypotheses of brain–emotion correspondence from four different angles. Fear: amygdala (yellow); disgust (green); anger: orbitofrontal cortex (rust); sadness: anterior cingulate cortex (blue). From Lindquist et al. (2012).

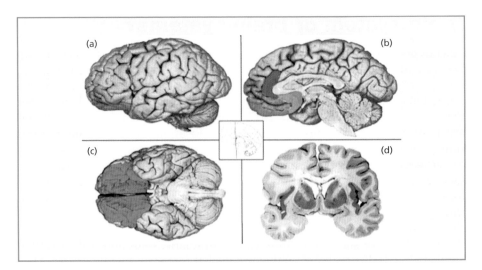

Image of the amygdala, a structure that forms part of the limbic system and that is activated in many emotional states.

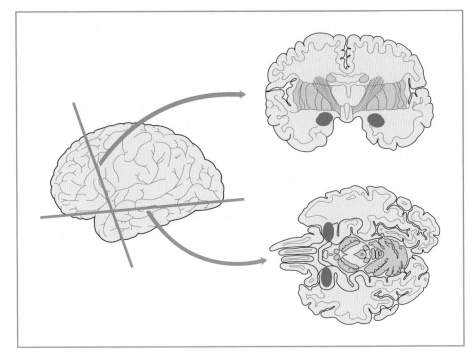

located within the temporal lobe (see the figure above). It plays a key role in emotion. However, the notion that the amygdala is specifically associated with fear rather than other emotions has received mixed support.

Support for the above notion was reported by Feinstein et al. (2011) in a study on S.M., a 44-year-old woman who had suffered severe damage to the amygdala. She experienced practically no fear when exposed to scary movie clips, snakes, or spiders. Even when held up at knife point, she remained calm and didn't feel afraid. However, her emotional reactions were normal when shown movie clips designed to elicit happiness, disgust, or anger.

Evidence inconsistent with the locationist position was reported by Pegna et al. (2005) in a study mentioned earlier. They studied a man who couldn't consciously perceive faces. He was presented with happy, angry, fearful, and neutral faces. There was greater activation of the amygdala to *all* types of emotional faces than to neutral ones.

The most thorough attempt to test the locationist theory was reported by Lindquist et al. (2012). They reviewed research in which patterns of brain activation were assessed for the emotions of anger, sadness, fear, disgust, and happiness. The predictions from the locationist position were straightforward. Amygdala activation should have been observed more often in the presence of fear than any other emotion. In similar fashion, insula activation should have been closely associated with the emotion of disgust, orbitofrontal activation with anger, and activation of the anterior cingulate cortex with sadness.

What did Lindquist et al. (2012) find? First, the amygdala and orbitofrontal cortex were fairly consistently activated in response to emotional experience, but activation was less often found in the insula or anterior cingulate cortex.

Second, of most theoretical importance, there was very little evidence of any selective association between specific emotions and specific brain areas. In other words, any given brain area was about as likely to be activated in the presence of any of the five emotions studied. These findings suggest that rather similar processes underlie all the major emotions.

Functions of brain areas

We have seen that there is little support for the locationist theory. However, the brain areas identified within the theory (i.e., amygdala; insula; orbitofrontal cortex; and anterior cingulate cortex) are all of general importance to emotion. Accordingly, we will consider the role that each area plays in producing emotional experience.

What exactly is the function of the amygdala? According to Sander (2009), it responds to stimuli of immediate *relevance* to the individual. Since our emotional experiences (positive and negative) are generally triggered by relevant stimuli, that makes sense of the finding that amygdala activation is associated with all five emotions studied by Lindquist et al. (2012).

What is the function of the orbitofrontal cortex? One of its main functions is to assess the reward or punishment value of stimuli. As such, it is of relevance to a wide range of positive and negative emotional states.

What is the function of the anterior cingulate cortex? It is more accurate to talk of several functions rather than one. However, this brain area seems to be involved in evaluating whether the individuals goals are being achieved. The outcome of this evaluation can then trigger positive emotions (if the goals are being met) or negative emotions (if they aren't being met).

What is the function of the insula? Lindquist et al. (2012) suggested it is involved in producing awareness of the individual's bodily sensations. As such, it plays a role in a range of different emotional experiences.

We have seen that we can't really explain the existence of several different emotions with reference to different brain systems. How, then, can we account for the diversity of our emotional experience?

Lindquist et al. (2012) answered the above question by focusing on other findings of theirs I haven't discussed so far. They found that brain

What is the function of the amygdala?

areas involved in attentional processes, language, and long-term memory were consistently activated regardless of the emotion being experienced. This suggests the cognitive system plays a major role in determining whether we experience, say, sadness or anger. As argued by appraisal theorists (e.g., Lazarus, 1982; see earlier in the chapter), our emotions are mostly influenced by how the cognitive system interprets and makes sense of our experiences.

Chapter summary

- Emotions are generally associated with certain facial expressions, patterns of activation in the body and brain, subjective feeling states, and forms of behaviour.
- Women tend to be more emotional than men and are more sensitive to others' emotional states.
- All emotional states (even negative ones such as anxiety and depression) fulfil useful functions.
- Self-report data suggest that there are two independent emotion factors (negative affect and positive affect) together with several more specific emotional states.
- There are brain circuits associated with different emotions, but the amygdala is of central importance to most emotions.
- The James–Lange theory exaggerates the extent to which our emotions reflect our experience of bodily symptoms and de-emphasises cognitive processes.
- According to appraisal theory, how we interpret the current situation determines which emotion we experience.
- Emotional states can be produced by stimuli presented below the level of conscious awareness.
- Cognitive reappraisal is an effective emotion-regulation strategy. Individuals with emotion dysregulation tend to have more psychiatric symptoms than other people.
- Studies involving electrical stimulation have suggested that certain brain areas may be associated strongly with a given emotion.
- Locationist theories of emotion assume that fear is associated with the amygdala, disgust with the insula, anger with the orbitofrontal cortex, and sadness with the anterior cingulate cortex. However, the evidence indicates that all four areas are associated with a wide range of emotions rather than being specific to one.
- The amygdala is associated with deciding whether a current stimulus is of immediate relevance and the insula is involved in producing awareness of bodily sensations. The orbitofrontal cortex is involved in assessing the reward or punishment value of stimuli, and the anterior cingulate cortex with evaluating whether goals are being met.

- Areas of the brain concerned with cognitive processes relating to attention, language, and memory are activated during the experience of several different emotional states. Such findings suggest that cognitive processes are important in determining which specific emotion we experience in a given situation.

Further reading

- Fox, E. (2008). *Emotion science: Cognitive and neuroscientific approaches to understanding human emotions*. London: Palgrave Macmillan. Elaine Fox's book provides excellent coverage of contemporary approaches to emotion.

- Izard, C.E. (2009). Emotion theory and research: Highlights, unanswered questions, and emerging issues. *Annual Review of Psychology, 60*, 1–25. Key issues relating to the major emotional states are explored in this review article.

- Power, M.J., & Dalgleish, T. (2008). *Cognition and emotion: From order to disorder (2nd ed.)*. Hove, UK: Psychology Press. There is a thorough discussion of cognitive approaches to emotion in this excellent book by Mick Power and Tim Dalgleish.

- Sander, D., & Scherer, K.R. (2009) (Eds.). *The Oxford companion to emotion and the affective sciences*. Oxford: Oxford University Press. This volume edited by David Sander and Klaus Scherer contains numerous short articles on most of the major topics relating to emotion.

Essay questions

1. What is emotion? How can it be measured?

2. How many emotions are there? Discuss with reference to the relevant research.

3. Describe briefly *two* theories of emotion. What are the strengths and limitations of these theories?

4. What has been learned about emotion by studying patterns of brain activity?

Aggression can take many forms ranging between physical violence and talking in hostile terms about others. You have probably had the misfortune to meet some people who seemed very aggressive and difficult to handle. Thankfully, most people aren't like that.

What do you think it is that causes some people to be aggressive whereas others are gentle and unaggressive? Is it a question of personality, or the experiences people have had? Are men generally more aggressive than women? Are the media to blame? What advice would you give to parents who were concerned about their aggressive child?

Aggression

6

What exactly is aggression? **Aggression** is

> any behavior directed toward another individual that is carried out with
> the intent to cause harm. In addition, the perpetrator must believe that the
> behavior will harm the target and that the target is motivated to avoid the
> behavior.
>
> (Bushman & Anderson, 2001, p. 274)

Note that the harm has to be *deliberate*. Someone who slips on the ice and crashes into someone by accident may cause harm but isn't behaving aggressively. Note also that the victim must want to avoid harm. Whipping a masochist who derives sexual pleasure from the activity isn't aggressive behaviour.

Psychologists argue there is an important distinction between reactive aggression and proactive aggression (Scarpa et al., 2010; Tuvblad et al., 2009). **Reactive aggression** (also known as hostile aggression) is an angry response to a perceived provocation. In contrast, **proactive aggression** (also known as instrumental aggression) is an act planned deliberately beforehand to achieve a particular goal. In essence, the distinction is between *hot*-tempered aggression (reactive) and *cold*-tempered aggression (proactive).

Bushman and Anderson (2001) argued that the above distinction is oversimplified because aggressive behaviour often involves deliberate planning as well as anger. However, the distinction *is* important because the involvement of anger is much greater with reactive aggression than with proactive aggression.

There is another important distinction between direct and indirect aggression. Direct aggression involves the use of physical force (e.g., shoving; punching). In contrast, indirect aggression involves more subtle techniques (e.g., gossiping; spreading false stories) (Kistner et al., 2010).

Historical and cultural factors

Members of the human race often behave aggressively and violently. There have been 15,000 wars in the last 5600 years (almost 2.7 wars per year). It is often assumed that most human societies are becoming increasingly aggressive. For example, the twentieth century witnessed numerous appalling tragedies such as the holocaust, genocide in Rwanda, and the slaughter of millions of Russians in the Stalinist era.

In spite of the above evidence, Stephen Pinker (2011) argued that human violence has *declined* substantially (especially in Western societies). Suppose we consider the rate at which people were killed in typical tribal societies of the past. If that rate had been as great in the twentieth century, two billion people would have been killed rather than the actual figure of 100 million.

Why has violence declined? One reason is because huge increases in longevity mean that life isn't cheap in the way it was when life expectancy was only 30 years or so. Another reason is that changes in society mean that the great majority of people are much more likely to obtain their goals in life by being cooperative rather than by being aggressive and violent.

Cultural differences

There are cultural differences in the problems posed by aggression and violence. McGuire (2008) discussed the 2002 murder rate in numerous countries. It was almost 47 per 100,000 people in South Africa, 13 in Russia, and 5.6 in the United States. In contrast, it was only 2 in the United Kingdom and Poland.

Bonta (1997) discussed 25 societies in which violence scarcely exists. For example, consider the Chewong people living in the mountains of the Malay Peninsula. Their language has no words for fighting, aggression, or warfare. Then there is the Zapotec society based in southern Mexico. This society is especially peaceful even though most other groups in the same general area often engage in fighting.

Why are some societies so much less aggressive and violent than others? According to Bonta (1997), 23 of the 25 peaceful societies he studied strongly believe in the advantages of cooperation and the disadvantages of competition. More generally, **social norms** (cultural expectations concerning appropriate behaviour) are important. For example, social norms in the United States encourage individuals to be competitive and go-getting. This may (at least in part) explain the high levels of aggression found in that society.

Other factors

We have just seen that levels of aggression and violence depend in part on historical and cultural factors. However, numerous other factors are also important. Below we consider the major factors that jointly determine how aggressive any given individual will be.

According to the frustration–aggression hypothesis, what is the relationship between frustration and aggression?

Situational factors

Aggression is much more likely in some situations than in others. Think of occasions when you have behaved aggressively. Many probably involved *frustrating* situations. According to the frustration-aggression hypothesis (Dollard et al., 1939), there are close links between frustration and aggression (see the figure on the next page). More specifically, "The occurrence of aggression always presupposes frustration ... Frustration produces instigations to a number of different types of responses, one of which is an instigation to some form of aggression" (Miller, 1941, pp. 337–338).

KEY TERM

Social norms: agreed standards of behaviour within a group (e.g., family; organisations).

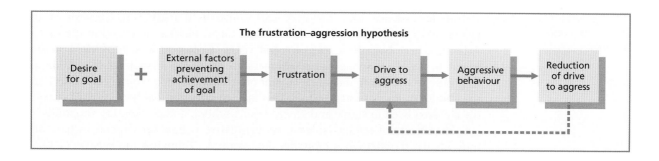

The frustration–aggression hypothesis

Desire for goal **+** External factors preventing achievement of goal → Frustration → Drive to aggress → Aggressive behaviour → Reduction of drive to aggress

Dollard et al. (1939) tested the frustration-aggression hypothesis by asking participants to imagine their reactions in various frustrating situations. In one situation, they were waiting for a bus but the bus driver went past without stopping. Most participants reported that such frustrating situations would make them feel angry.

The frustration-aggression hypothesis is oversimplified in various ways. First, we need to distinguish between frustration *justified* by some reason (e.g., the bus is out of service) and frustration that is *unjustified*. Unjustified frustration produces much more anger and aggression than justified frustration (Pastore, 1952). Second, as we will see, anger and aggression can be caused by factors involving little or no frustration.

In what follows, we will consider situational factors that can lead to aggression. Three such factors are media violence, violent video games, and the family environment. However, aggression can also be caused by more subtle situational factors (e.g., having a friend spread malicious rumours about you) not directly involving violence at all.

Media violence

The average 16-year-old in Western society has seen 13,000 violent murders on television. It is reasonable to assume this must influence her/his behaviour. As we would expect, children who have watched the most television violence tend to be the most aggressive. However, it is hard to interpret this finding (Gunter, 2008). It may be that watching violent programmes causes aggressive behaviour. Alternatively, naturally aggressive children may choose to watch more violent programmes than non-aggressive children. Finally, there may be some truth in both of these interpretations.

Findings

Leyens et al. (1975) considered the causality issue. There was a special Movie Week at a school for juvenile delinquents in Belgium. During this week, some delinquents saw only violent films, whereas others saw only non-violent films. Physical and verbal aggression increased among boys who saw the violent films, but not among those who saw the non-violent ones. However, the effects of the violent films were much stronger shortly after watching them than later on.

Does watching violence on television make people more aggressive?

Does media violence have short- and/or long-term effects?

Media violence doesn't always lead to increased aggression. Charlton et al. (1998) studied aggression in children living on St. Helena, an island in the south Atlantic where Napoleon spent his last years. Television was introduced to the island in 1994, allowing the researchers to assess its impact on the children. Exposure to television (including violent programmes) had *no* observable effect on the children's levels of aggression. This lack of effect probably occurred because the children lived in stable and secure home, school, and community situations.

The effects of media violence on aggressive behaviour depend in part on individual differences in personality. For example, Zillmann and Weaver (1997) showed films containing scenes of gratuitous violence to male participants. Only those high in psychoticism (a personality dimension involving coldness and hostility) showed greater acceptance of violence as an acceptable way of resolving conflicts after watching the films.

Wood et al. (1991) reviewed many studies concerned with the effects of media violence on aggression in children and adolescents. Exposure to media violence led to more aggressive behaviour towards strangers, classmates, and friends shortly after exposure to violent programmes or movies. However, the long-term effects were much smaller.

Comstock and Paik (1991) conducted a very thorough review of research on the effects of media violence. They identified five factors that increased the effects of media violence on aggression:

1. Violent behaviour is presented as an efficient way of getting what you want.
2. The violent person is portrayed as similar to the viewer.
3. Violent behaviour is presented naturalistically.
4. The victim's suffering isn't shown.
5. The viewer is emotionally excited while watching the violent behaviour.

EVALUATION

➕ There is substantial evidence that media violence is associated with (and sometimes causes) aggressive behaviour.

➕ Factors influencing the effects of media violence on aggression (e.g., similarity of violent person to the viewer; extent to which the victim's suffering is shown) have been identified.

➖ There is relatively little evidence of long-term effects of media violence on aggressive behaviour.

➖ Most studies have failed to show that media violence is the *cause* of aggressive behaviour.

Violent video games

There has been a substantial increase in the amount of time young people (especially boys) devote to playing violent video games. It is generally assumed that players of such games are likely to become more aggressive as a result. The evidence supports that assumption. Anderson et al. (2010) combined the findings from numerous studies. Exposure to video game violence was associated with aggressive behaviour, aggressive thoughts, aggressive emotion, and physiological arousal. These findings held in both Eastern and Western cultures, and were little affected by age or by sex.

The above findings only indicate an *association* between the amount of time spent playing violent video games and various measures of aggression. This association may occur because playing such games causes violence or because individuals with aggressive personalities are more likely to play violent video games. The above issue can be addressed by long-term or longitudinal studies in which participants are followed up over time. Barlett et al. (2007) studied the changes occurring when people engaged in increased play of violent video games. This increased play caused progressive increases in aggression and hostility.

Evidence supports the assumption that players of violent video games are likely to become aggressive as a result.

We have seen that violent video games influence individuals' thoughts or cognitions, emotion, and physiological arousal as well as aggressive behaviour. However, the *cognitive* effects are probably of special importance. This was tested by Bushman and Anderson (2002), who exposed participants to violent video games (e.g., *Mortal Kombat*) or non-violent ones (e.g., *3D Pinball*).

After playing violent video games, the participants read ambiguous stories in which it was unclear what the main character would do next. In one story, the main character has a minor traffic accident after braking at traffic lights. He then walks towards the other driver. Participants who had played violent video games expected the main character to feel angrier and to behave more aggressively than those who had played the non-violent games.

Cognitive factors

We all possess a huge amount of interconnected information stored away in long-term memory. For example, we know (perhaps from bitter experience) that drunk individuals are more likely than sober ones to engage in aggressive behaviour. What effect does such knowledge have on us? Subra et al. (2010) presented alcohol-related photos (e.g., vodka bottle) to participants subliminally (below the level of conscious awareness). This caused them to behave more aggressively towards the experimenter than did other participants exposed to subliminal neutral photos.

Early evidence that the knowledge we possess can influence aggressive behaviour was reported in a classic study by Berkowitz and LePage (1967). Male students received electric shocks from another student who was a confederate working for the experimenter. They were then given the chance to give electric shocks to the confederate. In one condition, a revolver and shotgun were close to the shock machine. In another condition, nothing was placed nearby.

What did Berkowitz and LePage (1967) find? The presence of the guns increased by 30% the number of shocks given. This is known as the **weapons effect**.

Why does the weapons effect occur? As Anderson et al. (1998) found, seeing a weapon increases the accessibility of aggression-related thoughts

KEY TERM

Weapons effect: an increase in aggression produced by the sight of a weapon (e.g., gun).

Just seeing a weapon increases the accessibility of aggression-related thoughts, which can lead to aggressive behaviour.

What is the name of the pattern within families in which aggressive behaviour by one family member is matched or exceeded by another family member?

(e.g., assault; destroy; torture). Such thoughts can lead to aggressive behaviour. In the words of Berkowitz (1968, p. 22), "The finger pulls the trigger, but the trigger may also be pulling the finger."

Family processes

Patterson (1982) argued that children's aggressiveness depends very much on family processes. He claimed that what is important is the functioning of the family as a whole rather than simply the behaviour of the child or its parents.

The importance of the family was confirmed by Patterson et al. (1989), who observed the interaction patterns of families in their homes. There was a typical pattern of escalating aggression in the families of aggressive children:

1. The child behaves aggressively (e.g., refusing to do what his/her mother requested).
2. The mother responds aggressively (e.g., shouting angrily at her child).
3. The child reacts in a more aggressive and hostile way (e.g., shouting back loudly at his mother).
4. The mother responds more aggressively than before (e.g., hitting her son).

The above pattern of behaviour forms a **coercive cycle**—a small increase in aggression by the parent or child is matched or exceeded by the other person's aggressive behaviour. According to Patterson et al. (1989), most aggressive behaviour displayed by parents and their children in aggressive families is an attempt to stop the other person being aggressive to them. However, these attempts often serve to provoke further aggression.

Patterson et al. (1989) argued that the aggressive behaviour displayed by children trapped in a coercive cycle can cause rejection by their peers (children of the same age). That can lead to deviant behaviour and delinquency. Aggressive adolescents are more likely than non-aggressive ones to join a gang when they are 13 or 14 years of age This is followed by becoming involved in deviant behaviour with friends at the age of 16 or 17 and then violence by the age of 18 or 19 (Dishion et al., 2010).

EVALUATION

➕ Family processes play an important role in producing aggressive children.

➕ Coercive cycles are found in many aggressive families.

➕ Children may behave aggressively to attract attention from parents who would otherwise ignore them.

➖ The finding that there are many families in which parents and children are both very aggressive may not depend entirely on coercive cycles. As we will see shortly, individual differences in aggressive behaviour depend in part on genetic factors. Thus, children may be aggressive because they have inherited genes for aggression from their parents.

KEY TERM

Coercive cycle: a pattern of behaviour within families in which aggression by one family member produces an aggressive response that leads to an escalation in aggression.

Social learning

Bandura (e.g., 1973; see Chapters 10 and 18) put forward social learning theory, according to which most learning takes place in a social context. He argued that much aggressive behaviour is learned as a result of the particular experiences a child has had. Observational learning is of great importance. It involves watching the behaviour of others and then imitating it.

The essence of the social learning approach to aggression was expressed by Bandura (1973, p. 5): "The specific forms that aggressive behavior takes, the frequency with which it is expressed, the situations in which it is displayed, and the specific targets selected for attack are largely determined by social learning factors."

Two main predictions stem from social learning theory. First, the behaviour produced by individuals who have watched someone behaving aggressively will resemble the behaviour they have observed. For example, if a character in a television programme stares angrily when frustrated, we would expect viewers to copy this angry stare rather than exhibiting other kinds of aggressive behaviour.

Second, we would expect observers to show a greater tendency to imitate a given character's behaviour if it is rewarded than if it is punished. As we will see, there is support for both predictions.

Findings

Bandura et al. (1963) tested an early version of social learning theory in experiments involving a Bobo doll. The doll is inflatable and has a weighted base causing it to bounce back when punched. Bandura et al. showed young child one of two films. One film showed a female adult model behaving aggressively towards the Bobo doll. The other film showed the adult model behaving non-aggressively towards it. As Bandura et al. (1963) predicted, those children who saw the model behave aggressively were much more likely to attack the Bobo doll.

There are some limitations with the above research. Much of the aggressive behaviour Bandura observed was play-fighting rather than real aggression. In

Adult "model" and children attack the Bobo doll.

addition, the fact that the Bobo doll bounces back up when knocked down gives it novelty value. Children unfamiliar with the Bobo doll were *five* times more likely to imitate aggressive behaviour against it than those who had played with it before (Cumberbatch, 1990).

Direct vs. indirect aggression

As we saw earlier, there is an important distinction between direct aggression (e.g., violent behaviour) and indirect aggression (e.g., spreading rumours). According to social learning theory, observing direct aggression should trigger direct aggression in the observer, whereas observing indirect aggression should trigger indirect aggression.

Coyne et al. (2004) presented children aged between 11 and 14 with videos showing direct or indirect aggression. Both forms of aggression led to aggressive behaviour in the children. However, viewing direct aggression led to more directly aggressive responses whereas viewing indirect aggression produced more indirectly aggressive responses.

Rewarded vs. punished behaviour

According to social learning theory, individuals imitate the behaviour of other people when it is rewarded but won't imitate punished behaviour. Bandura (1965) tested these hypotheses using the Bobo doll. Children were much more likely to copy the adult model's aggressive behaviour when it was rewarded than when it was punished (the model was warned not to be aggressive in future).

Carnagey and Anderson (2005) explored the effects of reward and punishment with violent video games. Young people played one of three versions of a video game involving racing cars. In one version, violence was always rewarded, in another version violence was always punished, and the third version was non-violent. Measures were taken of the participants' hostile emotion, aggressive thoughts, and aggressive behaviour.

What did Carnagey and Anderson (2005) find? As expected, the video game in which violence was rewarded led to increased hostile emotion, aggressive thinking, and aggressive behaviour. In contrast, punishing violent behaviour led to increased hostile emotion. However, it didn't increase aggressive thinking or aggressive behaviour.

EVALUATION

➕ There is convincing evidence that aggressive behaviour often depends on observational learning.

➕ Aggressive behaviour is much more likely to be imitated if it is seen to be rewarded rather than punished.

➕ As predicted, the type of aggressive behaviour shown by children tends to resemble the type of aggressive behaviour they have observed (e.g., Coyne et al., 2004).

➖ Bandura overestimated the extent to which children imitate the behaviour of models. For example, children often imitate aggressive behaviour towards a Bobo doll. However, they are much less likely to imitate aggressive behaviour towards another child.

⊖ The social learning approach de-emphasises the role of cognitive processes and biological factors (see below) in influencing aggressive behaviour.

Biological approach

So far we have considered some of the major *external* (or environmental) influences on aggressive behaviour. However, *internal* influences are also important. According to the biological approach, some individuals inherit genes making them more likely than other individuals to be highly aggressive. It has also been argued that the tendency for males to be more aggressive than females is largely due to biological factors. For example, males have higher levels of the sex hormone **testosterone**, and this may help to explain their greater aggressiveness.

Does the evidence suggest that males are physically and/or psychologically more aggressive than females?

Findings

We can carry out twin studies to decide whether human aggression is influenced by genetic factors. In such studies, we compare identical or monozygotic twins (sharing 100% of their genes) with fraternal or dizygotic twins (sharing 50% of their genes). If identical twins are more similar in aggression levels than fraternal twins, genetic factors probably play a role in determining aggression.

Miles and Carey (1997) considered the data from numerous twin studies. Up to 50% of individual differences in aggression were due to genetic factors, with the figure increasing during adolescence compared to childhood.

Similar findings were reported by Tuvblad et al. (2009) in a twin study in which they distinguished between reactive or hot-tempered aggression and proactive or cold-tempered aggression. At the age of 9 or 10, 26% of individual differences in reactive aggression were due to genetic factors, and the figure for proactive aggression was 32%. These figures increased to about 50% for both forms of aggression in twins aged 11–14.

Sex differences

It is widely believed that males are more aggressive than females. Is this belief true? It certainly is if we focus on extreme violence. Brehm et al. (1999) considered figures produced by the US Department of Justice. In 1996, 90% of murderers in the United States were male. A similar gender imbalance is found in most other societies.

Gender differences are less pronounced for other forms of aggression. Eagly and Steffen (1986) found in a review that sex differences were smaller for verbal and other psychological forms of aggression than for physical aggression. Indeed, there is evidence that adolescent girls engage in more indirect aggression than adolescent boys (Bjorkqvist et al., 1992).

Kistner et al. (2010) studied children between the ages of 9 and 11. The boys exhibited more direct or physical aggression than the girls at all ages.

KEY TERM

Testosterone: a hormone that is present in much greater quantities in males than in females; it has been linked to aggressive and sexual behaviour.

In contrast, it was only by the age of 11 that girls resorted to more indirect aggression than boys.

Are males *always* more physically aggressive than females? Bettencourt and Miller (1996) combined the findings from numerous studies and argued the answer is "No". Men typically behaved more aggressively than women in neutral or ambiguous situations. However, sex differences in aggression were much smaller when people were frustrated, threatened, or insulted.

The greater physical aggression shown by men than women may depend in part on their higher levels of the sex hormone testosterone. Cohen-Kettenis and van Goozen (1997) studied transsexuals undergoing hormone treatment in order to change sex. Female-to-male transsexuals were given high dosages of testosterone, whereas male-to-female transsexuals were given female hormones and deprived of male hormones.

As predicted by the biological approach, female-to-male transsexuals showed *increased* aggression during hormone treatment. In contrast, male-to-female transsexuals showed *lowered* levels of aggression.

Why does testosterone lead to increased aggression? Mehta and Beer (2009) addressed this issue in a study in which participants were exposed to social provocation. As expected, individuals with high levels of testosterone responded more aggressively to this provocation. Of most interest, testosterone led to reduced activity in brain areas associated with impulse control and self-regulation. Thus, testosterone reduces the tendency to inhibit aggressive behaviour when angry.

EVALUATION

➕ Twin studies indicate that genetic factors are important in producing individual differences in aggressive behaviour.

➕ The male sex hormone testosterone is associated with increased levels of aggression; increased levels of testosterone lead to increased aggression.

➕ High levels of testosterone are associated with reduced impulse control and self-regulation.

➖ Sex differences in aggression (especially indirect aggression) are smaller than expected by those favouring the biological approach.

➖ Much remains to be discovered about the ways biological factors combine with environmental factors to produce aggressive behaviour.

General aggression model

Which theoretical approach to aggression is the most adequate? As we have seen, many factors play some role in aggression. That led Anderson et al. (1996) and Anderson and Bushman (2002) to put forward a general aggression model based on these factors (see the figure below). Their model consists of four stages:

According to the general aggression model, can situational cues and individual differences produce negative affect, arousal, and/or negative cognitions?

- *Stage 1*: At this stage, the key variables are situational cues (e.g., weapons present) and individual differences (e.g., aggressive personality).
- *Stage 2*: What happens at Stage 1 causes various effects at Stage 2. These include affect (e.g., hostile feelings), arousal (e.g., activation of the autonomic nervous system), and cognitions (e.g., hostile thoughts).
- *Stage 3*: What happens at Stage 2 leads to appraisal processes (e.g., interpretation of the situation; possible coping strategies; consequences of behaving aggressively).
- *Stage 4*: Depending on the outcome of the appraisal processes at Stage 3, the individual decides whether to behave aggressively or non-aggressively.

Findings

The general aggression model combines elements of several previous theories. As a result, some findings discussed already are consistent with the model's predictions. One example is the weapons effect. Another example is research on violent video games. Playing such games has the predicted effects on affect, physiological arousal, and cognitions (Anderson et al., 2010).

According to the model, personality influences aggressive behaviour. Support for this prediction was reported by Hines and Saudino (2008) in a study on intimate partner aggression. Men and women high in neuroticism (a personality dimension relating to experiencing negative emotions; see Chapter

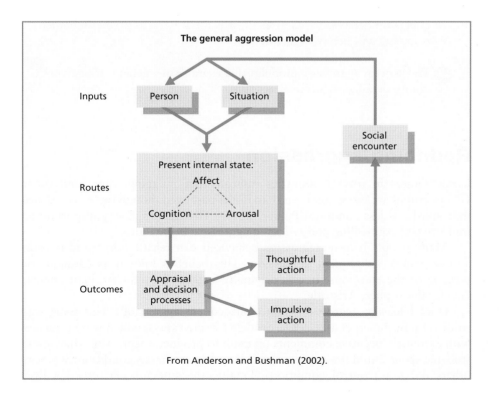

The general aggression model

Inputs — Person, Situation

Routes — Present internal state: Affect, Cognition, Arousal; Social encounter

Outcomes — Appraisal and decision processes; Thoughtful action; Impulsive action

From Anderson and Bushman (2002).

18) showed more aggression towards their intimate partner than did those low in neuroticism.

A major prediction of the model is that the way the current situation is interpreted by someone during Stage 3 determines whether they will behave aggressively. There is plentiful support for this prediction. De Castro et al. (2002) reviewed studies involving social interactions between the participant and someone of the same age. Participants who interpreted the other person's behaviour as indicating hostile intent were more aggressive than those who did not.

Bègue et al. (2010) asked participants to decide whether ambiguous behaviour (e.g., "She cut him off in traffic") was intentional or accidental. Participants who had consumed a lot of alcohol interpreted more behaviours as intentional than did those who hadn't had any alcohol. This helps to explain why people who are drunk are typically more aggressive.

EVALUATION

➕ The general aggression model is more comprehensive in scope than previous theories of aggression.

➕ Aggressive behaviour is determined in part by individual differences in personality.

➕ Appraisal processes including interpretation of the situation have the predicted effects on aggressive behaviour.

➖ Negative affect, arousal, and negative cognitions all have complex effects on behaviour. As a result, it is often hard to predict whether someone will behave aggressively.

➖ The general aggression model provides more of a general framework than a detailed theoretical account.

Reducing aggression

Crime figures in several countries indicate that mugging, rape, and other violent crimes are more common than in the past even though there is evidence that murder is less common (Pinker, 2011). That makes it very important to find ways of controlling and reducing aggressive behaviour.

Many people believe aggressive behaviour can release anger and tension and so reduce subsequent aggression. This belief is known as **catharsis** or purging of the emotions. It was originally suggested by the brilliant ancient Greek philosopher, Aristotle.

Does releasing aggression reduce subsequent aggression? This issue was studied by Bushman et al. (1999). Students wrote essays, which were returned with extremely negative comments on them to produce anger. After that, some students spent 2 minutes hitting a punching bag (catharsis condition) whereas others did not (control condition). Finally, the students performed a task

KEY TERM

Catharsis: the notion that behaving aggressively can cause a release of negative emotions such as anger and frustration and thus reduce subsequent aggression.

against a competitor, after which they decided the intensity of electric shock the competitor should receive. Students in the catharsis condition (hitting the punching bag) behaved *more* aggressively than those in the control condition.

In what follows, we will consider briefly two major approaches to reducing aggression in children and adolescents. First, the children themselves can be the focus of interventions. Second, the parents of aggressive children can receive training or therapy.

Child-based interventions

Wilson et al. (2003) reviewed studies in which children had received intervention programmes to reduce aggression. They discovered that nearly all interventions had some beneficial effects. However, two of the most effective forms of intervention were social competence training and behavioural interventions.

Social competence training consisted of various specific features. For example, it could involve training in communication skills, conflict resolution, self-statements (e.g., "I must remain calm"); and empathy (understanding other people's feelings).

Aggressive children and adolescents generally show little empathy (de Wied et al., 2010), which helps to explain why they attack other people. Zahavi and Asher (1978) told aggressive adolescents that aggression often hurts other people, makes them unhappy, and causes resentment. This led to increased empathy and a large reduction in aggressive behaviour.

There are various behavioural interventions. One of the most common involves providing reward or reinforcement when children behave in helpful, non-aggressive ways (Parke & Slaby, 1983). There is also the time-out technique. Children who behave aggressively are prevented from continuing with a pleasurable activity such as playing with toys by being sent to their room.

In the time-out technique, what happens to children who behave aggressively?

Another way of removing rewards is the incompatible-response technique. It is based on the assumption that children often behave aggressively to gain the reward of receiving adult attention. With this technique, children's aggressive behaviour is ignored (to remove attentional reward) but their helpful behaviour is rewarded. This technique has been found to produce substantial reductions in aggression (Slaby & Crowley, 1977).

Parent training: Eliminating coercive cycles

According to Patterson et al. (1992), we can reduce children's aggressiveness by considering the pattern of interactions within the family. In many families, as we have seen, there are coercive cycles in which family members behave aggressively to try to reduce the aggressive behaviour of another family member. Such a cycle often leads to even more aggression and distress within the family. Some of the steps involved in eliminating such coercive cycles are as follows:

1. Describe the nature of the coercive cycle to parents and explain its disadvantages (e.g., escalation of aggression).
2. Emphasise to parents that they should not give in when their child behaves aggressively.
3. Instruct parents not to respond aggressively when their child is being aggressive.

4. Set up a system in which the child is rewarded for reasonable behaviour but loses rewards for unacceptable or aggressive behaviour.
5. Look out for the signs of positive or desirable behaviour. Display real warmth and affection when such signs are detected to encourage such behaviour.

Lundahl et al. (2006) reviewed studies in which parent training was used in the attempt to reduce children's disruptive behaviour. Overall, there were small to moderate beneficial effects at the end of training, and some of these effects remained at follow-up. These findings indicate the crucial role played by parents in influencing the level of aggressive behaviour exhibited by their offspring.

Chapter summary

- There is an important distinction between reactive aggression (triggered by anger) and proactive aggression (triggered by the desire to obtain some desired outcome).
- There is also an important distinction between direct or physical aggression and indirect aggression that involves more subtle techniques (e.g., spreading rumours).
- There is evidence that there is less violence in Western cultures now than was the case in the past.
- Societies having very little aggression and violence have social norms emphasising cooperation with others and the disadvantages of competition.
- Media violence often has short-term effects on children's aggression, but the long-term effects are small or non-existent.
- Playing violent video games leads to aggressive behaviour, thoughts, and emotion as well as heightened physiological arousal in both Western and Eastern cultures.
- Very aggressive children often come from families in which there is a coercive cycle involving an escalation of aggression between children and parents.
- Individual differences in reactive and proactive aggression depend in part on genetic factors.
- Males tend to exhibit more direct aggression than females. Males have higher levels of testosterone than females, and this is associated with reduced impulse control.
- According to the general aggression model, personality and the interpretation of situations both influence aggressive behaviour.
- Children's aggressive behaviour can be reduced by social competence training and behavioural interventions (e.g., time-out technique).
- Parent training can reduce the coercive cycle within families.

Further reading

- Anderson, C.A., Ihori, N., Bushman, B.J., Rothstein, H.R., Shibuya, A., Swing, E.L. et al. (2010). Violent video game effects on aggression, empathy, and prosocial behaviour in Eastern and Western countries: A meta-analytic review. *Psychological Bulletin*, *136*, 151–173. The authors show how the general aggression model can be tested by considering research on the effects of violent video games from across the world.

- Archer, J. (2009). Does sexual selection explain human sex differences in aggression? *Behavioural and Brain Sciences*, *32*, 249–311. John Archer argues that sex differences in aggression depend mainly on biological factors in our evolutionary history.

- Bentley, E. (2009). Aggression. In M.W. Eysenck (Ed.), *A2 level psychology*. Hove, UK: Psychology Press. In this chapter, Evie Bentley covers the topic of aggression in a comprehensive way.

- Hogg, M.A., & Vaughan, G.M. (2011). *Social psychology (6th ed.)*. New York: Prentice Hall. Chapter 12 of this textbook is devoted to theory and research on aggression.

Essay questions

1. What are the effects of watching media violence and of playing violent video games?

2. What are the key assumptions of the social learning approach to aggression? Discuss its main strengths and weaknesses.

3. To what extent can we understand aggression from the biological approach?

4. It is very important to try to reduce children's aggressive behaviour. What approaches would you recommend to produce non-aggressive children?

Part 2

Behaviourist approach

About 100 years ago, some American psychologists known as the behaviourists argued that the central focus of psychology should be on behaviour because behaviour is reasonably objective and observable. This approach led them to de-emphasise the role of internal processes (e.g., thinking) in influencing behaviour.

The behaviourists argued that most human learning involves what they called conditioning, in which behaviour becomes increasingly dependent on stimuli in the environment. It is often possible to control someone's behaviour by offering them a reward for learning to behave in certain ways. For example, children can be persuaded to run errands if they are paid for doing so.

Chapter 7 • Conditioning and learning

We will discuss the extent to which simple principles of conditioning can explain the complexities of human learning.

Human beings spend most of their time learning about the world, about themselves, and about other people. Some of them spend a lot of time trying to learn enough to pass examinations (see Chapter 23). Most of these are examples of complex learning. However, we also engage in much simpler forms of learning such as learning to salivate when a meal is put on the table and learning what to do by observing others. Some of these forms of learning closely resemble those found in other species.

How many different kinds of learning do you think there are? What determines whether you learn rapidly or slowly?

Conditioning and learning

7

Compared to any other species, we are extremely good at learning. In view of its obvious importance, the study of learning has always been of central concern to psychologists. Historically, the rise of behaviourism in the United States under John Watson (1913) was of major significance. **Behaviourism** was based on the assumption that psychology should study behaviour rather than internal thoughts and feelings.

The behaviourists also assumed that most learning involves conditioning (discussed below). More specifically, they assumed that all learning (even complex forms of learning) could be understood in terms of fairly simple principles.

We will start by considering research on conditioning. After that, we will discuss other kinds of learning ignored by the behaviourists. One example is observational learning, which involves imitating others' behaviour in social situations.

John Watson (1878–1958) believed that psychology should study behaviour rather than thoughts and feelings (behaviourism).

Classical conditioning

Imagine you visit your dentist. As you lie down on the reclining chair, you start to feel frightened. *Why* are you frightened *before* the dentist has caused you any pain? The sights and sounds of the dentist's surgery lead you to *expect* that you are shortly going to be in pain. In other words, you have formed an *association* between the neutral stimuli of the surgery and the painful stimuli involved in drilling. Such associations are of crucial importance in **classical conditioning**. In essence, the fear created by drilling in the past is now triggered by the neutral stimuli of the surgery.

Textbook writers nearly always focus on unpleasant everyday examples of classical conditioning (I've just been guilty of that myself!). However, there are also pleasant examples. Most middle-aged people have especially positive feelings for music that was popular when they were teenagers. Associations are formed between the music and various exciting kinds of stimuli encountered during adolescence.

Findings

The best-known example of classical conditioning comes from Ivan Pavlov's (1849–1936) research on dogs. Dogs (and other animals) salivate when food

Ivan Pavlov and his staff demonstrating classical conditioning on a dog.

is put in their mouths. In technical terms, what we have here is an **unconditioned reflex**—this consists of an unlearned reaction (**unconditioned response**) to a stimulus (**unconditioned stimulus**). In Pavlov's work, food in the mouth was the unconditioned stimulus and salivation was the unconditioned response.

Pavlov trained dogs to salivate to other stimuli that were *not* naturally associated with salivation (see the figure below). In some of his studies, he presented a tone (the training stimulus) just before food on several occasions so that the tone signalled that food would be arriving shortly. Finally, he presented the same tone (the test stimulus) on its own without any food following. The dog salivated to the tone.

The example above illustrates a type of learning known as a **conditioned reflex**. What happens is that a previously neutral stimulus (**conditioned stimulus**) is associated with the unconditioned stimulus and the **conditioned response** (learned response to the conditioned stimulus). In the example, the tone is the conditioned stimulus, the sight of food is the unconditioned stimulus, and salivation is the conditioned response (see the figure below).

Pavlov discovered various features of classical conditioning. One example is generalisation. The conditioned response of salivation was greatest when the tone presented on its own was the same as the one previously presented just before food. However, a smaller amount of salivation was

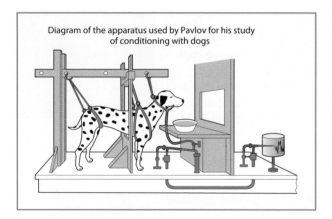

Diagram of the apparatus used by Pavlov for his study of conditioning with dogs

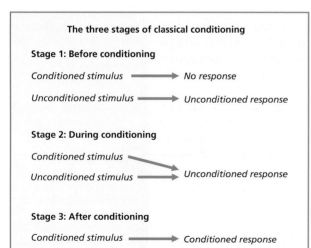

The three stages of classical conditioning

Stage 1: Before conditioning

Conditioned stimulus ⟶ No response

Unconditioned stimulus ⟶ Unconditioned response

Stage 2: During conditioning

Conditioned stimulus

Unconditioned stimulus ⟶ Unconditioned response

Stage 3: After conditioning

Conditioned stimulus ⟶ Conditioned response

KEY TERMS

Unconditioned reflex: a well-established association between an **unconditioned stimulus** and an **unconditioned response**.

Unconditioned response: the well-established reaction (e.g., salivation) to a given **unconditioned stimulus** (e.g., food) in an **unconditioned reflex**.

Unconditioned stimulus: the stimulus that produces a well-established **unconditioned response** in an **unconditioned reflex**.

Conditioned reflex: the new association between a **conditioned stimulus** and an **unconditioned stimulus** that produces a **conditioned response**.

Conditioned stimulus: a neutral stimulus that is paired with an **unconditioned stimulus** to produce classical conditioning.

Conditioned response: the new response that is produced as a result of **classical conditioning**.

obtained when a different tone was used. Generalisation refers to the finding that the strength of the conditioned response (i.e., salivation) depends on the *similarity* between the test stimulus and the previous training stimulus.

When does experimental extinction occur?

Pavlov also discovered the phenomenon of discrimination. Suppose a given tone is paired several times with the sight of food. The dog learns to salivate to the tone. Then another tone is presented on its own. This tone produces a smaller amount of salivation than the first one through generalisation. After that, the first tone is paired with food several more times, but the second tone is never paired with food. Salivation to the first tone increases whereas that to the second tone decreases. In other words, the dog learns to *discriminate* between the two tones.

There is another key feature of classical conditioning. When Pavlov presented the tone on its own several times, there was less and less salivation. Thus, the repeated presentation of the unconditioned stimulus in the absence of the unconditioned response stops the conditioned response. This is known as **extinction**.

When extinction occurs, that does *not* mean the dog or other animal has lost the relevant conditioned reflex. Animals brought back into the experimental situation after extinction produce some salivation in response to the tone. This is known as **spontaneous recovery**. It shows that the salivary response to the tone was *inhibited* (rather than lost) during extinction.

Explanations

Conditioning occurs because the conditioned stimulus (e.g., a tone) allows the dog or other animal to *predict* that the unconditioned stimulus (e.g., food) is about to be presented. The tone provides a clear indication that food is about to arrive. As a result, it produces an effect (i.e., salivation) similar to that produced by the food itself. Experimental extinction occurs when the tone no longer predicts the arrival of food.

Suppose we reversed the order of the two stimuli, with the conditioned stimulus *following* the unconditioned one (i.e., backward conditioning). In these circumstances, the conditioned stimulus couldn't predict the arrival of the unconditioned stimulus. As expected, there is little or no backward conditioning.

Kamin (1969) found that conditioning depends on expectation. Rats in the experimental group received light paired with electric shock and learned to react with fear and avoidance when the light came on. Rats in the control group had no training. Then both groups received a series of trials with a light–tone combination followed by shock. Finally, both groups of animals received only the tone. The control group responded with fear to the tone on its own but the experimental animals did not.

What is going on here? The experimental animals learned initially that light predicted shock. As a result, they subsequently ignored the fact that the tone also predicted shock. The experimental animals showed the **blocking effect**— conditioning to one stimulus (i.e., tone) was blocked by prior conditioning to a different stimulus (i.e., light). In contrast, the control animals learned that tone predicted shock because they hadn't previously learned something different. Various explanations have been offered for blocking (Shanks, 2010). However, attentional processes are crucial. Animals pay little attention to any

KEY TERMS

Extinction: the elimination of a response when it is not followed by reward (**operant conditioning**) or by the **unconditioned stimulus** (classical conditioning).

Spontaneous recovery: the re-emergence of responses over time in **classical conditioning** after **extinction**.

Blocking effect: the lack of a **conditioned response** to a **conditioned stimulus** if another **conditioned stimulus** already predicts the onset of the **unconditioned stimulus**.

given conditioned stimulus if another conditioned stimulus already predicts the arrival of the unconditioned stimulus (Mackintosh, 1975).

Ecological perspective

In most classical conditioning research, the relationship between the conditioned and unconditioned stimuli is *arbitrary*. For example, consider Pavlov's research on dogs. There is no obvious reason for pairing a tone with the sight of food. What are the chances that an animal living in the wild will often encounter the same arbitrary conditioned stimulus immediately before a given unconditioned stimulus? The answer is slim or none.

What is going on? Some psychologists (e.g., Domjan, 2005) adopt an ecological approach, according to which conditioning is fastest when learning is of most benefit to animals in their natural environment. For example, animals should rapidly learn to avoid poisonous foods, as was found by Garcia et al. (1966). Rats were given saccharine-flavoured water followed by a drug causing intestinal illness several hours later. The rats only needed to be sick *once* to learn to avoid drinking the water thereafter. This shows the effectiveness of classical conditioning when relevant to survival.

How does classical conditioning happen in the natural environment? Domjan (2005) argued that the conditioned and unconditioned stimuli are typically different features of the *same* object. Domjan discussed findings from experiments on male Japanese quail in which the conditioned stimulus was the stuffed head of a female quail and the unconditioned stimulus was access to a live female. In these circumstances, classical conditioning was very strong. Indeed, it was so strong the male quail often grabbed the stuffed head and tried to copulate with it!

Classical conditioning can be useful because the presentation of the conditioned stimulus gives the animal time to prepare to cope effectively with the unconditioned stimulus. We can see this in Pavlov's research. Conditioning causing the animal to salivate before food arrived enhanced digestion by secreting digestive hormones and enzymes before the food reached the gut.

There are many other examples of the usefulness of classical conditioning. For example, male blue gourami fish that copulated after exposure to a sexually conditioned stimulus produced 10 times as many offspring as occurred in the absence of the conditioned stimulus (Hollis et al., 1997). The finding that classical conditioning can enhance reproductive success indicates its importance.

Exposure therapy

Conditioning principles have been applied to patients suffering from mental disorders. Many individuals suffer from **phobias** (extreme fears of certain objects or stimuli). Common examples include snake phobia, spider phobia, and social phobia (great fear of social situations; see Chapter 1). According to the behaviourist account, phobias develop when the conditioned or phobic stimulus (e.g., social situations) is associated with a painful or aversive stimulus causing fear.

There is mixed support for the behaviourist account. Hackmann et al. (2000) found that 96% of social phobics remembered experiencing a socially traumatic event. For example, they were harshly criticised in public or couldn't stop blushing on a social occasion. In contrast, Menzies and Clarke

(1993) found only 2% of children with water phobia remembered a direct conditioning experience involving water.

If phobias are acquired through classical conditioning, then presumably they can be eliminated through extinction. In other words, if the phobic or conditioned stimulus is presented repeatedly *without* any aversive consequences, the fear associated with that stimulus should gradually diminish. This line of thinking led to the development of exposure therapy. In **exposure therapy**, phobic individuals are exposed to the feared object or situation (often gradually increasing its threateningness) for lengthy periods of time until their anxiety level reduces.

Exposure therapy has proved very effective in the treatment of most phobias (Choy et al., 2007). Theoretically, this is supposed to be due to reduced strength (and finally extinction) of the conditioned fear response. However, *cognitive* processes are also involved. For example, Vögele et al. (2010) found that social phobics showed a considerable reduction in symptoms following exposure therapy. Recovery was triggered by patients perceiving themselves to have more control over themselves and their emotions. This is important because conditioning theorists typically ignore the role of *cognitive beliefs* in making exposure therapy effective.

EVALUATION

➕ All the main phenomena of classical conditioning have been shown many times.

➕ Classical conditioning often has important biological value (e.g., taste aversion). It allows animals to prepare themselves for the arrival of the unconditioned stimulus.

➕ Exposure therapy, which has proved successful in the treatment of phobias, apparently involves the process of extinction.

➖ Classical conditioning is of limited value in explaining human learning, in part because we possess language. For example, we can produce immediate extinction in humans by telling them the unconditioned stimulus won't be presented again (Davey, 1983).

➖ Much learning in non-human species doesn't involve classical conditioning. As we will see shortly, operant conditioning and observational learning are also important.

➖ The effectiveness of exposure therapy in treating phobias often involves processes (e.g., cognitive ones) ignored by conditioning theorists.

Operant conditioning

In everyday life, people are often persuaded to behave in certain ways by the offer of some reward. For example, young children are well behaved in return for sweets and students try hard on tests to obtain good marks. These are

KEY TERM

Exposure therapy: a form of treatment in which clients are repeatedly exposed to stimuli or situations they fear greatly.

This photo from 1964 shows B. F. Skinner with a rat in a Skinner box.

merely two examples of operant conditioning. **Operant conditioning** is a form of learning in which behaviour is controlled by rewards (also called positive reinforcers) and by unpleasant or aversive stimuli.

Much of operant conditioning is based on the **law of reinforcement**. According to this law, the probability of a given response occurring increases if it is followed by a reward or reinforcer. However, the probability decreases if it is followed by negative or aversive consequences.

The best-known example of operant conditioning comes from research by Burrhus Fred Skinner (1904–1990). He placed a hungry rat in a small box (often called a Skinner box) containing a lever. When the rat pressed the lever, a food pellet appeared. The rat learned that food could be obtained by lever pressing, and so pressed the lever more and more often. This is a clear example of the law of reinforcement. Not surprisingly, the effects of a reward are greater if it is provided shortly after the response has been made rather than if it is delayed.

There are two types of positive reinforcers or rewards: primary reinforcers and secondary reinforcers. **Primary reinforcers** are stimuli needed for survival (e.g., food, water, sleep, air). **Secondary reinforcers** are stimuli that are rewarding because we have learned to associate them with primary reinforcers (e.g., money, praise, attention).

Schedules of reinforcement

It seems reasonable that we keep doing things that are rewarding and stop doing things that aren't rewarding. However, Skinner (1938) found some complexities in operant conditioning. Simple *continuous* reinforcement, in which the reinforcer or reward is given after every response, is rare in everyday life. This led Skinner to consider what happens with *partial* reinforcement in which only some responses are rewarded. He identified four main schedules of reinforcement:

- *Fixed ratio*: Every *n*th (e.g., fifth) response is rewarded. Workers who receive extra money for achieving certain targets are on this schedule.
- *Variable ratio*: On average, every *n*th response is rewarded but the actual gap between two rewards may be very small or fairly large. This schedule is found in fishing and gambling.

- *Fixed interval*: The first response produced after a given interval of time (e.g., 60 seconds) is rewarded. Workers who are paid regularly every week are on this schedule—they receive a reward after a given interval of time but don't need to produce a specific response.
- *Variable interval*: On average, the first response produced after a given interval of time is rewarded. However, the actual interval is mostly shorter or longer than this. Self-employed workers whose customers make payments at irregular times are rewarded at variable intervals (Gross, 1996). However, they don't have to produce a specific response.

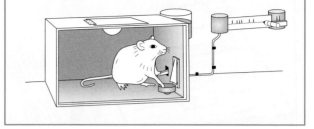

Skinner box for rats, showing chart recording of lever pressing. On the chart, each vertical line represents a single press on the lever.

We might expect continuous reinforcement to produce better conditioning than partial reinforcement. In fact, the opposite is the case— it leads to the *lowest* rate of responding because only a single response is needed to produce each reward. In contrast, the variable schedules (especially variable ratio) lead to very fast rates of responding because they create high levels of motivation. This helps to explain why gamblers find it hard to stop their addiction.

What about extinction (the cessation of responding in the absence of reward)? Those schedules of reinforcement associated with the best conditioning also show the most resistance to extinction. Thus, rats trained on the variable ratio schedule keep responding without reward longer than rats on any other schedule. In contrast, rats trained with continuous reinforcement stop responding the soonest.

Although gamblers have no idea when or if they will receive a payout, they continue to play. This is an example of the most successful reinforcement schedule—variable ratio reinforcement.

One reason continuous reinforcement leads to rapid extinction is because there is a very obvious shift from reward being provided on every trial to reward not being provided at all. Animals trained on the variable schedules are used to reward being provided infrequently and irregularly. As a result, it takes much longer for them to realise they are no longer going to be rewarded for responding.

Shaping

In operant conditioning, the required response has to be made *before* it can be reinforced. How, then, can we condition an animal to produce a complex response it wouldn't produce naturally? The answer is to use **shaping**, in which the animal's behaviour moves towards the desired response through successive approximations.

Suppose we wanted to teach pigeons to play table tennis. Initially, they would be rewarded for touching the table tennis ball. Over time, their actions need increasingly to resemble those involved in playing table tennis to be rewarded. In this way, Skinner persuaded pigeons to play a basic form of table tennis!

KEY TERM

Shaping: a form of operant conditioning in which behaviour is changed slowly in the desired direction by requiring responses to become more and more like the wanted response in order for reward to be given.

"Well, I simply trained them to give me fish by pressing this over and over again."

Instinctive influences

Skinner assumed that virtually *any* response can be conditioned in *any* stimulus situation. This assumption is known as **equipotentiality**, but it is incorrect. In fact, animals' behaviour typically resembles their natural or instinctive behaviour. For example, it would be very hard (or impossible) to train an animal to run away from food to obtain a food reward.

Breland and Breland (1961) trained pigs to insert wooden coins into a piggy bank for reward. The pigs rapidly learned to do this. Much more interestingly, the pigs started to perform slower and slower until eventually they weren't getting enough to eat.

What had happened to the pigs? Over time, each pig started picking up the coin but then repeatedly dropped it on the floor. The pig would "root it [turn it up with its snout], drop it again, root it along the way, pick it up, toss it in the air, drop it, root is some more, and so on" (Breland & Breland, 1961, p. 683). The pig's behaviour increasingly reflected its natural food-getting behaviours. In the words of Breland and Breland, the pigs showed "instinctive drift", and this can't easily be explained in conditioning terms.

Theoretical perspectives

What is learned in operant conditioning? According to Skinner, reinforcement or reward strengthens the association between the stimulus (e.g., the inside of the Skinner box) and the reinforced response (e.g., lever press). In contrast, Tolman (1959) proposed a more *cognitive* theory according to which animals learn much more than implied by Skinner's views. He argued that operant conditioning involves learning a **means–end relationship**—the knowledge that a given response will produce a certain outcome.

Evidence that animals learn means–end relationships was reported by Dickinson and Dawson (1987). Some rats were trained to press a lever to receive sugar water, whereas others learned to press a lever for dry food pellets. After that, the rats were deprived of food or water. Finally, all the rats were tested under extinction conditions in which no reward was provided.

The key findings involved the thirsty rats. Those previously reinforced with sugar water produced far more lever presses in extinction than those reinforced with dry food pellets. The rats used their knowledge of the expected reinforcer to decide how worthwhile it was to press the lever.

More evidence that animals don't simply learn to produce reinforced responses was reported by Gaffan et al. (1983). Rats in a T-shaped maze decided whether to turn left or right. Suppose a rat turns left and finds food at the end of that arm of the maze. According to conditioning principles, the rat has been rewarded for turning left and so should turn left on the next trial. In the rat's natural environment, however, it is generally *not* sensible to return to a place from which food has just been removed. Gaffan et al. found that rats early in training *avoided* the arm of the T-shaped maze in which they had previously found food.

In sum, animals do *not* simply learn mechanically that certain responses are rewarded as implied by Skinner. What they actually acquire is *knowledge* about the situation, and this knowledge determines their actions.

Punishment

So far we have considered the effects of positive reinforcers or rewards on performance. However, operant conditioning can also involve unpleasant or aversive stimuli (e.g., electric shocks). Humans and other species learn to decrease their exposure to aversive stimuli just as they learn to increase their exposure to rewards.

What is the form of conditioning in which a response is followed by an aversive stimulus?

Operant conditioning in which a response is followed by an aversive or unpleasant stimulus is **positive punishment**. If the aversive stimulus occurs shortly after the response, it reduces the likelihood that that response will be produced thereafter. The effects of the aversive stimulus are much less if there is a long delay between the response and the aversive stimulus.

There is also **negative punishment**, in which a positive reinforcer or reward is removed following a given response. For example, a child who starts throwing food on the floor may have the food removed from her/him. The typical effect of negative punishment is to reduce the probability that the punished response will be produced. Another form of negative punishment is the **time-out technique** in which a child is removed from a situation in which he/she has been behaving badly.

Findings

Positive punishment has various unwanted effects. In a review, Gershoff (2002) found that punishment typically produced immediate compliance with the parents' wishes. However, it was associated with aggressive and antisocial behaviour in childhood and adulthood, and with impaired mental health (e.g., depression). It was also associated with a tendency for punished children to abuse their own children or spouse in adulthood.

Gershoff et al. (2010) considered the effects of various forms of punishment administered by mothers to their children in six countries (China; India; Italy; Kenya; Philippines; and Thailand). The findings were broadly similar in all countries. Physical punishment and yelling were associated with greater child aggression, and physical punishment and the time-out technique were associated with greater child anxiety.

Rortvedt and Miltenberger (1994) found that negative punishment in the form of the time-out technique improved children's behaviour. It achieved this while avoiding the negative effects associated with positive punishment. However, Gershoff et al. (2010) in a cross-cultural study found that the time-out technique increased children's anxiety levels.

Avoidance learning

Nearly all drivers stop at traffic lights because of the possibility of aversive consequences (e.g., having an accident; trouble with the police) if they do not. This is a situation in which no aversive stimulus is presented if suitable action is taken, and is an example of **avoidance learning**. Many aversive stimuli

KEY TERMS

Positive punishment: a form of operant conditioning in which the probability of a response is reduced by following it with an unpleasant or aversive stimulus; sometimes known simply as punishment.

Negative punishment: a form of operant conditioning in which the probability of a response being produced is reduced by following it with the removal of a positive reinforcer or reward.

Time-out technique: a form of negative punishment in which undesirable behaviour (e.g., aggression) is reduced by removing the individual from the situation in which he/she has been aggressive.

Avoidance learning: a form of operant conditioning in which an appropriate avoidance response prevents presentation of an unpleasant or aversive stimulus.

What is the name of the therapy in which patients are given tokens for behaving appropriately, which can then be used to obtain rewards?

(**negative reinforcers**) strengthen any response that stops the aversive stimulus being presented.

In experiments on avoidance learning there is typically an initial warning stimulus. This is followed by an aversive stimulus unless the participant makes a given avoidance response. For example, consider a study by Solomon and Wynne (1953). Dogs were placed in a two-compartment apparatus. A change in the lighting was the warning signal that an aversive stimulus (a strong electric shock) was about to be presented. This stimulus could be avoided by jumping into the other compartment. Most dogs received a few shocks early in the experiment. After that, however, they generally avoided shocks for the remaining hundreds of trials.

How can we account for avoidance learning? The avoidance response is rewarded or reinforced by fear reduction (Mowrer, 1947). In addition, participants acquire two beliefs (Lovibond, 2006):

• After the warning stimulus, the unconditioned stimulus (shock) will be presented;
• After performing a given response, the unconditioned stimulus will be omitted.

Declercq and de Houwer (2011) carried out an experiment on avoidance learning with human participants. Questioning of the participants revealed they had acquired those two beliefs.

Token economy

It is now time to consider real-world applications of positive reinforcement. These include the training of circus animals, persuading people to work long hours in return for payment, and raising academic standards by praising students who perform well. Here we will briefly consider the token economy, a form of therapy based on operant conditioning.

The essence of the **token economy** is that individuals are given tokens (e.g., poker chips) in return for behaving in appropriate ways (e.g., maintaining personal hygiene). These tokens are then exchanged for rewards. Token economies have often been used with patients living in hospitals or other institutions. This is partly because the successful use of token economies requires detailed information about the individual's behaviour.

In a classic study, Ayllon and Azrin (1968) used a token economy with hospitalised female schizophrenic patients. They were given tokens for making their own beds, combing their hair, and other desirable actions. The tokens were exchanged for pleasant activities (e.g., seeing a movie; having an extra visit to the canteen). This token economy was very successful, with the number of chores performed each day by the patients increasing from 5 to 40.

Impressive findings were reported by Silverman et al. (2004) in a study in which the token economy was used with cocaine users who had proved extremely hard to treat. Some patients were offered up to $3480 (about £2000) in vouchers for remaining cocaine free over a 39-week period, whereas other patients received no incentive. Of those given a high incentive, 45% managed to remain abstinent for at least 4 weeks compared to 0% of those with no incentive.

KEY TERMS

Negative reinforcers: unpleasant or aversive stimuli that serve to strengthen any responses that prevent these stimuli from being presented.

Token economy: a form of therapy based on operant conditioning in which tokens are given to patients when they produce desirable behaviour; these tokens can then be exchanged for rewards.

It is generally hard to monitor people's behaviour when they are out in the everyday world. However, De Fulio et al. (2009) did so in a study on cocaine dependence. The participants were given jobs involving data entry. Those in the token economy condition were rewarded for abstinence from cocaine with continuous employment on full pay. However, they suffered a temporary pay cut if they had cocaine in their urine samples. The control participants were simply given jobs regardless of whether they were drug-free.

What did De Fulio et al. (2009) find? Over a period of 1 year, the token economy participants had cocaine-free urine samples on 79% of occasions. The comparable figure for the controls was only 51%.

What are the strengths and limitations of operant conditioning?

EVALUATION

➕ Operant conditioning is often very effective. The behaviour of humans and other species can be controlled by clever use of reinforcement (e.g., the training of circus animals).

➕ Positive and negative punishment have been used to improve children's behaviour.

➕ Operant conditioning (e.g., token economy) has reduced the symptoms of patients with mental disorders.

➖ Skinner minimised the role of *internal* factors (e.g., goals; beliefs). As Bandura (1977, p. 27) pointed out, "If actions were determined solely by external rewards and punishments, people would behave like weather vanes, constantly shifting in radically different directions to conform to the whims of others." In fact, we often pursue our long-term goals rather then being influenced by the immediate situation.

➖ Operant conditioning is more about influencing people's *behaviour* than about *learning* in the broad sense. Suppose I offered you £1 every time you said, "The Earth is flat". You might (especially if short of money!) say it hundreds of times, so the reward would have influenced your behaviour. However, I doubt whether it would affect your learning or knowledge so you actually believed that the Earth is flat.

➖ In real life, we don't learn mostly to perform rewarded responses as proposed by Skinner. Instead, we learn a huge amount simply by *observing* others' behaviour (discussed shortly).

➖ Skinner's notion of equipotentiality is incorrect, in part because it de-emphasises the importance of instinctive behaviour.

Observational learning

Albert Bandura agreed with Skinner that learning typically involves rewards. However, he argued convincingly that much learning in everyday life doesn't involve operant conditioning. We often don't need to produce rewarded responses for learning to occur. Bandura emphasised that we learn a huge amount by observing someone else's behaviour (a model)—this is **observational learning**. In sum, Bandura was much more willing than Skinner to accept that *cognitive* processes are of major importance in learning.

Why is observational learning so important to humans? According to Bandura (1977, p. 12), "Psychological theories have traditionally assumed that learning can occur only by performing responses and experiencing their effects. In actuality, virtually all learning phenomena resulting from direct experience occur on a vicarious [second-hand] basis by observing other people's behaviour and its consequences for them."

Observational learning is typically much more efficient than learning (e.g., operant conditioning) that involves actually experiencing a given situation. In the course of a single day, you can observe the behaviour of numerous people in hundreds of situations (e.g., by watching television). In contrast, it would be very hard (or impossible) to put yourself in all of those situations in a short period of time. It can also be safer to observe the fate of others engaging in dangerous actions than to perform the same actions yourself!

Note that observational learning is *not* the same as imitation learning. If you observed someone whose behaviour was followed by punishment it is very unlikely that you would imitate their behaviour.

Various conditions are needed for high levels of observational learning to occur (Bandura, 1977). First, participants must pay attention to the model's behaviour. Second, participants must store away information about that behaviour in long-term memory. Third, participants must have the ability to perform the behaviour they have observed. Fourth, participants need to be motivated to perform the learned behaviour (e.g., by expecting to be rewarded).

The above conditions indicate some of the reasons why there are often large individual differences in observational learning. For example, individuals whose attention and memory are poor will generally exhibit less observational learning than those whose attention and memory are good. Bandura (1986) extended his earlier ideas in his social cognitive theory. According to this theory, individual differences in observational learning depend in part on the individual's cognitive ability.

KEY TERM

Observational learning: learning based on watching the behaviour of others and copying behaviour that is rewarded and not copying punished behaviour.

Findings

There is plentiful evidence of observational learning. Examples are to be found with respect to moral development (Chapter 10) and acquisition of gender roles (Chapter 11). A famous example of observational learning comes from Bandura et al. (1963). It involved a large Bobo doll heavily weighted at the bottom so it bounces back when punched. Young children displayed much more aggressive behaviour towards the Bobo doll when they had previously observed an adult punching it (see Chapter 6).

Is observational learning as effective as learning based on actually performing the behaviour in question? Blandin and Proteau (2000) addressed that issue. Participants performed a timing task under one of three conditions: (1) prior observational learning; (2) prior physical practice; and (3) no prior experience.

Observational learning and prior physical practice led to comparable levels of performance significantly higher than those shown by participants with no prior experience. In addition, those in the observational learning condition developed error correction mechanisms at least as effective as those of participants in the physical practice condition.

Observational learning (even by infants) can be more subtle than assumed by Bandura. Gergely et al. (2002) trained 14-month-old infants to turn on a light. All the infants observed the adult model use her forehead to touch the light and turn it on. There were two conditions:

1. The model's hands were on the table so the infants could see she had *deliberately* chosen to use her forehead rather than her hands.
2. The model had her hands under the table wrapped in a blanket.

The above apparently small change had a dramatic effect on the results. When the model's hands were free, 69% of the infants copied her behaviour by using their forehead rather than their hands to put on the light (see the figure below). In contrast, when the model's hands weren't free, only 21% of the infants copied her behaviour, choosing instead to use their hands.

The findings of Gergely et al. (2002) indicate that infants do *not* necessarily imitate actions that are successful or rewarded. They avoided imitating the model's actions when they believed she had only used her forehead because her hands weren't free.

Why do some children exhibit more observational learning than others? Bandura assumed the answer depended on children's particular experiences. Such experiences are important but are only part of the story. Fenstermacher and Saudino (2007) considered observational learning in identical and fraternal twins. Identical twins share 100% of their genes whereas fraternal twins share only 50%. If genetic factors are important, identical twins should be much more similar than fraternal twins in observational learning. That is precisely what was found.

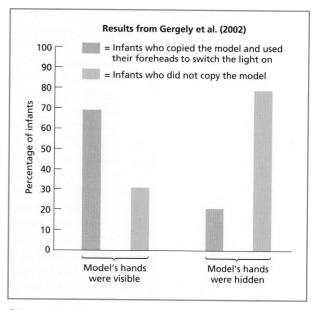

Observational learning in infants is strongly influenced by the context.

EVALUATION

➕ Observational learning occurs very often in children and adults. Indeed, it probably occurs more often than operant conditioning.

➕ Observational learning can have powerful effects on subsequent behaviour comparable in size to learning based on actual performance (e.g., Blandin & Proteau, 2000).

➖ Observational learning can be more complex than assumed by Bandura. Even infants can take account of factors such as the model's intention and situational constraints on her/his behaviour (Gergely et al., 2002).

➖ Observational learning depends more on the individual's interpretation of the situation than assumed by Bandura. Suppose you observe a fellow student receiving a prize for winning a race in athletics. If you aren't interested in athletics, you might conclude that the other student has been wasting his/her time and so not feel tempted to imitate him/her.

➖ Many individual differences in observational learning depend on the factors identified by Bandura. However, genetic factors also influence observational learning and imitation (Fenstermacher & Saudino, 2007).

Chapter summary

- Classical conditioning involves learning to *predict* that a neutral stimulus will be followed shortly by a pleasant or unpleasant stimulus.
- Classical conditioning has great survival value (e.g., taste aversion).
- Exposure therapy (based on classical conditioning) is an effective treatment for various phobias.
- A variable ratio schedule of reinforcement (as found in gambling and fishing) is associated with the fastest rate of responding and the greatest resistance to extinction.
- Operant conditioning involves learning means–end relationships (i.e., a given response produces a certain outcome).
- Positive and negative punishment are both effective. However, the former produces more unwanted side effects.
- Operant conditioning has proved effective when used to treat patients by means of token economies.
- Skinner's approach is much better suited to situations in which we respond to immediate rewards and punishments than to situations in which we pursue long-term goals.

- Observational learning is very common in everyday life. It is typically more efficient than operant conditioning.
- Observational learning doesn't simply involve imitation. It depends on the observer's knowledge and interpretation of the situation.
- Observational learning depends in part on genetic factors.

Further reading

- Domjan, M. (2010). *The principles of learning and behaviour (6th ed.).* Belmont, CA: Wadsworth. This textbook contains very thorough and up-to-date information on all the approaches to learning discussed in this chapter.

- Eysenck, M.W. (2009). *Fundamentals of psychology.* Hove: Psychology Press. Chapter 7 in this textbook discusses in detail the topics dealt with in this chapter.

- Mazur, J.E. (2005). *Learning and behaviour (6th ed.).* New York: Pearson Education. James Mazur covers theory and research on conditioning and observational learning in this textbook.

Essay questions

1. What is involved in classical conditioning? Discuss examples showing its importance in real life.

2. Describe the various types of operant conditioning.

3. How did Skinner explain operant conditioning? What are the limitations with his explanation?

4. What are the main factors influencing observational learning?

Part 3

Developmental approach

Developmental psychology is concerned with the psychological changes occurring during the time between birth and adulthood. However, our primary focus will be on infancy and childhood, because that is the period of time during which the most dramatic changes in development are to be found. Developmental psychology (as Sigmund Freud was one of the first psychologists to realise) is of crucial importance to an understanding of adult behaviour.

The study of children's development is fascinating. This book is dedicated to Sebastian, who was born in May 2012. His parents are my daughter Fleur and her husband Simon, and everyone in the family is looking forward excitedly to watching every stage of his development.

Chapter 8 • Cognitive development

We will consider how and why most young children show rapid development in their ability to think and reason.

Chapter 9 • Language development

The mysterious issue of how it is that most young children acquire language at astonishing speed is addressed at length.

Chapter 10 • Moral development

The processes that allow children to develop an increasingly sophisticated understanding of moral values are discussed.

Chapter 11 • Sex and gender

We will consider how children from a surprisingly young age have a clear sense of being male or female and of the cultural expectations associated with being male or female.

When you look at infants and young children, it is clear that their ability to think and reason is much less than that of older children and adults. This is due in large measure to the fact that they have less knowledge at their disposal. It is also possible that the ways they see and think about the world are very different from ours. For example, when my children were very young, they thought you could tell someone's age by knowing how tall they were! That is an understandable error given that most 5-year-old children are taller than most 4-year-old children, who in turn are taller than most 3-year-olds. What is your best guess as to what goes on in the minds of young children?

Cognitive development

8

Children change and develop in almost every way in the years between infancy and adolescence. However, some of the most dramatic changes take place in terms of cognitive development. Of those who have tried to understand the mysteries of cognitive development, Jean Piaget has been easily the most influential. As a result, his theoretical approach is discussed at length. Lev Vygotsky's theoretical approach is then discussed briefly before we consider a more recent approach.

Finally, we turn to the development of children's ability to understand what other people are thinking and feeling. This ability is of fundamental importance if children are to communicate effectively with other people.

Piaget's theory

Jean Piaget (1896–1980) is the most famous developmental psychologist of all time. He was mainly interested in how children learn to adapt to the world around them. Piaget argued that this process of adaptation occurs as a result of constant interactions between the child and the outside world.

Adaptation depends crucially on two processes:

Developmental psychologist Jean Piaget, c. 1975.

- **Accommodation:** The individual adjusts to the outside world by changing his/her cognitive organisation.
- **Assimilation:** The individual adjusts his/her interpretation of the outside world to fit his/her existing cognitive organisation.

The clearest example of the dominance of accommodation over assimilation is imitation. In imitation, the individual simply copies someone else's actions and contributes nothing from his/her previous knowledge. In contrast, assimilation dominates accommodation in play, with reality being interpreted according to the individual's whim (e.g., a stick is used as a gun).

The individual needs to maintain a stable internal state (equilibrium) in a complex and changing environment. When a child can't understand its experience in terms of its existing knowledge, there is a conflict between what *actually* happens and what the child *expected* to happen. This creates an unpleasant state of disequilibrium. This leads to a

An example of the dominance in play of assimilation over accommodation— pretending that a hairbrush is a microphone.

process of **equilibration,** in which the child uses accommodation and assimilation to restore a state of equilibrium.

We can identify two extreme positions with respect to the changes occurring during cognitive development. At one extreme, the amount of knowledge possessed by children increases considerably, but there are no dramatic changes in *how* they think. At the other extreme, the ways of thinking found in later childhood differ profoundly from those of early childhood.

Piaget identified himself with the latter position, believing there are fundamental differences in cognition among children of different ages. This led him to argue that children pass through a series of stages of cognitive development, each of which is very different from the others.

According to Piaget's stage theory, children's cognitive development goes through four stages (see the figure below). We will consider them in turn.

1. Sensori-motor stage

This stage lasts from birth to about 2 years of age. It is the stage of intelligence in action, since the infant acquires much knowledge by moving around his/her environment. The key achievement of this stage is **object permanence.** This allows the child to be aware of the existence of objects when they aren't visible. Early in the sensori-motor stage, the infant has no awareness of the continued existence of objects; it is literally a case of "out of sight, out of mind".

2. Pre-operational stage

This key stage lasts between the ages of 2 and 7. Thinking during this stage is dominated by *perception*. This often leads to error, because things aren't

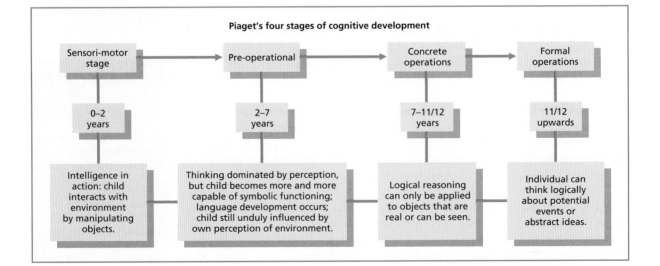

Piaget's four stages of cognitive development

Sensori-motor stage	Pre-operational	Concrete operations	Formal operations
0–2 years	2–7 years	7–11/12 years	11/12 upwards
Intelligence in action: child interacts with environment by manipulating objects.	Thinking dominated by perception, but child becomes more and more capable of symbolic functioning; language development occurs; child still unduly influenced by own perception of environment.	Logical reasoning can only be applied to objects that are real or can be seen.	Individual can think logically about potential events or abstract ideas.

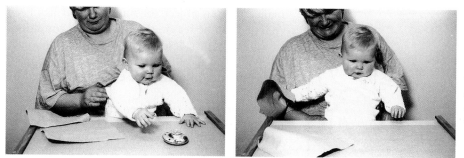

In the left-hand picture, the baby is reaching for a toy he can see. In the right-hand one, he searches in the same place for it although it is hidden under the paper on his right.

always the way they look. Piaget argued that children in the pre-operational stage often pay attention to only part of a given situation: this is called **centration**.

How centration produces errors has been shown in studies of conservation. **Conservation** refers to an understanding that certain aspects of an object remain the same in spite of various changes to one or more of its dimensions.

In his classic studies on conservation of quantity, Piaget gave children two glasses of the same size and shape containing the same quantity of liquid (see the figure on the right). When the child agreed there was the same quantity of liquid in both glasses, all the liquid from one glass was poured into a glass that was taller and thinner.

Pre-operational children failed to show conservation. They argued there was more liquid in the new container ("because it's higher") or that there was more liquid in the original glass ("because it's wider"). In either case, the child centred (focused) on only one dimension (height or width).

According to Piaget, pre-operational children also lack **reversibility**, which is the ability to

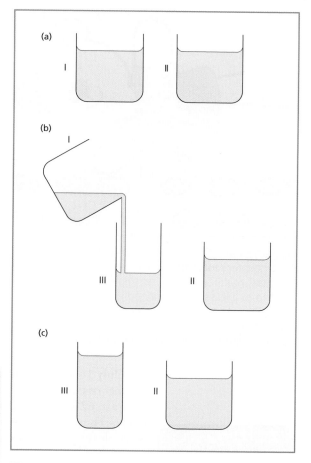

Piaget's study on conservation of quantity. (a) Children agreed that I and II both contained the same quantity of liquid, but when I's liquid was poured into a taller, thinner glass (b and c), the pre-operational children argued that the quantities differed.

KEY TERMS

Centration: in Piaget's theory, the tendency of young children to attend to only part of the information available in a given situation.

Conservation: in Piaget's theorising, the child's understanding that various aspects of an object may remain constant even though other aspects are transformed or changed considerably.

Reversibility: in Piaget's theory, the ability to undo mentally (reverse) some operation that has been carried out (e.g., changing an object's shape).

McGarrigle and Donaldson found that when an experimenter rearranged one of a pair of rows of counters, relatively few 6-year-old children thought that the two rows still contained the same number of counters. However, when "naughty teddy" appeared to mess up the counters accidentally, most children said that the number in the rows was still the same.

realise that an object (or number) that has been changed can be restored to its original condition. In the study just described, reversibility involves knowing that the effect of pouring the liquid from one container into another could be reversed by pouring it back.

Piaget argued that when children acquire the notion of reversibility, they should be able to succeed on most conservation tasks. However, critics of Piaget argue that performance on conservation tasks also depends on *experience* and *cultural factors*.

There is support for the critics. Price-Williams et al. (1969) studied children of Mexican potters. These children showed conservation of volume at an early age when a ball of clay was stretched into an oblong shape, something with which they were familiar from everyday life. However, the same children were much slower to show conservation of volume when the task was a less familiar one.

Other critics claimed that young children can perform much better on conservation tasks than Piaget suggested if the conservation task is changed in various ways. McGarrigle and Donaldson (1974) argued that pre-operational children presented with a conservation task assume the experimenter *intends* to change the amount of liquid or other substance. This assumption biases them against showing conservation.

McGarrigle and Donaldson (1974) tested the above notion on a number of conservation tasks. Six-year-old children were presented with two rows of counters and all agreed there were equal numbers of counters in each row. Then the experimenter deliberately messed up one of the rows or a "naughty" teddy bear did the same in an apparently accidental way.

Only 16% of the children showed conservation (arguing there were the same number of counters in each row) when the experimenter moved the counters. In contrast, 62% showed conservation when the counters were moved by naughty teddy. Thus, children's ability to show conservation can be greatly reduced when the experimenter changes the situation in a deliberate or planned way.

Egocentrism

Pre-operational children also show egocentrism. **Egocentrism** involves children assuming that how they see the world is the same as how other people see it. One of Piaget's tasks to study egocentrism was the three mountains task. Children were presented with a three-dimensional model of an imaginary scene consisting of three mountains. They looked at the scene from one angle (e.g., position A) and a doll was placed at a different location. Then the children were shown pictures of the three mountains from perspectives B, C, or D, and asked to choose the one showing the scene as it appeared to the doll.

What did Piaget find? Four-year-old children chose the picture that was the same as their own view of the scene. The child's assumption that what the doll could see was exactly the same as what he/she could see is an example of egocentrism. Piaget found that it was only when children reached the age of 7 or 8 that they selected the correct picture.

The three mountains task, which was used by Piaget to illustrate egocentrism in children.

Hughes (1975) argued that children perform poorly on the three mountains task because it doesn't relate to their experience. He tested this argument by using a simpler and more realistic situation. There were two walls in the shape of a cross, two policemen dolls, and a boy doll. Children between the ages of 3½ and 5 tried to hide the boy doll so neither of the policemen could see him. About 90% of the children succeeded even though they themselves could still see the boy doll. Thus, they managed to avoid egocentrism at a very young age.

3. Concrete operations stage

According to Piaget, this stage lasts between the ages of 7 and 11 or 12. The main advance shown by children in the concrete operations stage over pre-operational children is that thinking becomes much less dependent on perception. This involves **decentration**, which involves the child being able to spread his/her attention over several features of a problem and relate those features to each other. This is in marked contrast to the limited attentional focus or centration shown by younger children.

An experimental situation used to show how Piaget overstated the amount of egocentrism shown by young children.

Underlying the above advance is the development of various logical and mathematical operations. These operations include the actions indicated by common symbols such as +, −, ÷, ×, > (more than), and < (less than). The most important aspect of such operations is reversibility (discussed earlier), in which the effects of a change can be cancelled out by imagining the reverse change. Thus, for example, we can turn 9 into 14 by adding 5, and we can return to 9 by subtracting 5 from 14.

Piaget stressed that cognitive operations are usually organised into a system or structure (termed a **group** by Piaget). For example, an

KEY TERMS

Decentration: in Piaget's theorising, the ability to focus on several aspects of a problem at once and make coherent sense of them.

Group: in Piaget's theorising, the structure that is formed from the organisation of various related cognitive processes or operations.

operation such as "greater than" should be considered jointly with "less than". Children haven't fully grasped the meaning of "A is greater than B" unless they realise that this statement means the same as "B is less than A".

The main limitation of children in the concrete operations stage is that their thinking is limited to *concrete* situations based fairly directly on their own experiences. The ability to escape from the limitations of immediate reality into the realm of abstract ideas is one that is found only in the fourth (and final) stage of cognitive development.

4. Formal operations stage

Children from the age of 11 or 12 enter the stage of formal operations. In this stage they develop the ability to think in terms of possible (rather than simply actual) states of the world. Thus, individuals in the stage of formal operations can manipulate ideas to a far greater extent than those in the concrete operations stage. In essence, they can think about thinking and have developed the ability to manage their own minds.

Piaget admitted that most adolescents don't attain the stage of formal operations across all complex cognitive tasks. There is actually much variability in their performance which depends on their interests and aptitudes.

Findings

Describe children in the stage of formal operations.

Low and Hollis (2003) explored formal operations. They used the third eye problem in which children indicated where on the human body they would put a third eye and why.

Children aged between 6 and 12 produced very limited answers that involved putting the third eye on the forehead. In contrast, most adults produced useful suggestions (e.g., putting the third eye at the back of the head so the person could see behind them). Only the adults' answers showed the ability to think of possible states of the world they had not experienced directly (i.e., formal operations).

In another condition, children were instructed to put the third eye so they could see more. With these more specific instructions, 12-year-old children (who allegedly have attained the stage of formal operations) produced useful and imaginative answers. For example, they suggested putting the third eye on the back of the hand or in the mouth (so they could see what they were eating). Younger children still failed to produce imaginative answers because they hadn't attained the stage of formal operations.

Bradmetz (1999) assessed formal operational thinking in 62 15-year-olds using various Piagetian tasks. Only *one* participant showed substantial evidence of formal operational thought! In addition, those participants performing relatively well on the tasks had higher IQs than those who performed poorly.

Two conclusions can be drawn from these findings. First, the cognitive abilities associated with formal thought resemble those assessed by traditional intelligence tests. Second, there are very large individual differences in intelligence (see Chapter 17), and there are also large individual differences in the ability to engage in formal operational thinking. This helps to explain why most adults never fully attain the formal operational stage.

EVALUATION

➕ Piaget's theory was an ambitious attempt to explain how children move from being irrational and illogical to being rational and logical.

➕ The notions that children learn certain basic operations (e.g., reversibility), and that these operations then allow them to solve numerous problems, are valuable ones.

➖ Stage theories such as Piaget's *overestimate* the differences between stages but *underestimate* the differences within stages. Cognitive development doesn't occur in the neat stepwise way assumed by Piaget.

➖ Piaget *underestimated* the cognitive abilities of young children but *overestimated* those of adolescents and adults.

➖ Piaget told us *what* cognitive development involves but not *why* or *how* this development occurs. According to Siegler and Munakata (1993), there appears to be a "miraculous transition" from one developmental stage to the next.

Vygotsky's theory

Piaget emphasised the notion that children acquire knowledge through *self-discovery*. In contrast, the Russian psychologist Lev Vygotsky (1896–1934) argued that *social* factors are crucial in influencing cognitive development. Within his approach, the child is an apprentice who learns directly from social interaction and from communication with older children having knowledge he/she lacks.

According to Vygotsky, when do children learn best?

According to Vygotsky, children's learning can be made most effective by taking account of the **zone of proximal development**. This is the gap between what children can achieve on their own and what they can achieve with the assistance of others.

There are two basic aspects of the zone of proximal development. First, children apparently lacking certain skills when tested on their own may perform more effectively in the social context of someone having the necessary knowledge. Second, when a given child's level of understanding is moderately challenged, he/she is most likely to acquire new knowledge rapidly and without a sense of failure.

Vygotsky emphasised the importance of language in cognitive development. In young children, language and thought develop in parallel and have very little impact on each other. After that, however, children use the speech of others and talking to themselves to assist their thinking and problem solving. By the age of 7, egocentric speech (i.e., speaking without paying attention to anyone else present) gives way to inner speech. This inner speech is of direct benefit to thinking.

KEY TERM

Zone of proximal development: in Vygotsky's theory, the gap between the child's current problem-solving ability and his/her potential ability.

Findings

Moss (1992) reviewed studies on mothers' use of the zone of proximal development. There were three main aspects to the mothers' strategies. First, the mother instructed her child in new skills the child couldn't perform on its own. Second, the mother encouraged her child to maintain useful problem-solving tactics it had shown spontaneously. Third, the mother persuaded the child to discard immature and inappropriate forms of behaviour.

The above strategies were generally successful in promoting children's effective learning. Conner et al. (1997) found the strategies used by fathers to encourage their children on problem-solving and language tasks were as effective as those used by mothers.

Vygotsky's notion that inner speech assists children in their thinking has received support. Children using the most inner speech performed difficult tasks better than those making little use of inner speech (Jones, 2007). Vygotsky argued that private speech becomes more internal as children's level of performance improves. Berk (1994) discussed a study in which 4- and 5-year-old children made Lego™ models in three sessions. As predicted by Vygotsky, the children's speech became increasingly internalised from session to session as their model-making performance improved.

Benigno et al. (2011) studied children of 4 and 5 years as they practised a planning task across several sessions. A small number of the children showed sharp improvements in performance. These improvements were preceded by increased internal speech, which may have indicated the children were grappling actively with the task.

Vygotsky assumed children don't produce egocentric or private audible speech after the age of 7. However, Girbau (2002) found contrary evidence in a study in which children of 8 and 10 played in pairs with a Lego™ construction set. Egocentric speech was found in both age groups and was more common in the older group.

EVALUATION

➕ Vygotsky correctly attached considerable importance to the social environment in promoting cognitive development

➕ As Vygotsky predicted, inner speech helps the problem-solving activities of young children, perhaps because it is associated with an active grappling with the problem.

➖ Vygotsky failed to develop a systematic theory of cognitive development.

➖ Vygotsky didn't specify clearly what kinds of social interaction are most beneficial for learning (e.g., general encouragement vs. specific instructions).

Overlapping waves model

Of central interest to Piaget was to understand the cognitive changes occurring in children as they develop. However, the experimental approach he adopted was poorly suited to achieving that goal! Piaget compared the cognitive abilities of children of different ages at a given point in time. As a result, he couldn't observe cognitive changes as they occurred.

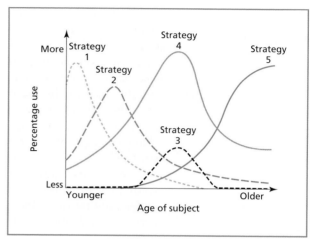

Siegler's overlapping waves model.

In this section, we consider the approach of Robert Siegler. He developed an experimental approach shedding much light on the nature of cognitive change. More specifically, he devised the **microgenetic method**, in which children perform the same cognitive task repeatedly over a short period of time.

Siegler (1998) put forward an overlapping waves model. Its key assumption is that children at any given time typically have various strategies or ways of thinking about a problem. As a result, they exhibit considerable *variability* in strategy use (see the figure above). This assumption is very different from Piaget's view that children at any given stage of development should show reasonable *consistency* in their cognitive processes.

What processes lead to improved strategy selection by children? According to the model, children acquire increasingly detailed knowledge by taking account of the speed and accuracy of problem solution with each strategy. This allows them to select the best strategy more often and to learn that a strategy that is generally effective may not be so for all types of problems.

Findings

Children are remarkably variable in their strategy use across numerous problems (Siegler, 2007). This is so even when the same problem is presented on two occasions close in time. Siegler and Shrager (1984) with preschool children and Siegler and McGilly (1989) with older children found about one-third changed strategies in such circumstances. Most of these changes weren't the result of learning because they involved shift from a more advanced to a less advanced strategy.

It could be argued that variable strategy use is of little interest because it merely reflects a lack of intellectual ability. That is *not* the case. Children who initially use several strategies with a given type of problem generally learn *faster* than those who only use one or two. This happens because it is easier to replace a dominant (but ineffective) strategy when children have access to several other strategies (Siegler, 2007).

Siegler and Jenkins (1989) studied how children learn new strategies. They gave 4- and 5-year-olds the task of solving addition problems such as 3 + 8 = ? One of the most effective strategies used by young children is the count-on strategy—start with the larger number and count on from that point. In the example, start with 8 and count 9, 10, 11.

According to Siegler, what does cognitive development involve?

> **KEY TERM**
>
> **Microgenetic method:** an approach to studying children's changes in cognitive strategies by means of short-term longitudinal studies.

None of the children in the study by Siegler and Jenkins (1989) used this strategy initially. With extensive practice, however, nearly all the children discovered the count-on strategy. Typically, the children took much longer than usual on the problem just before their first use of the new strategy. This suggests they were thinking carefully about the best strategy to use.

As predicted by the overlapping waves theory, the children continued to use other strategies much of the time after discovering the count-on strategy. However, they used the count-on strategy much more often following challenging problems (e.g., 2 + 26) that were very hard to solve with other strategies.

There was a final interesting finding from Siegler and Jenkins's (1989) study. Several children who used the count-on strategy had little conscious understanding of it. Indeed, some even denied using the strategy in spite of very clear videotape evidence! Thus, implicit knowledge (knowledge without conscious awareness) can guide children's choice of strategy.

Are the rapid strategy changes found with use of the microgenetic method similar to those shown by children in their everyday lives? This issue was addressed by Siegler and Svetina (2002), who studied problem solving in 6- and 7-year-olds. There were striking similarities between the patterns of change produced by the microgenetic method and by the natural environment.

EVALUATION

⊕ The microgenetic method is very useful for identifying the details of cognitive change.

⊕ The substantial variability in strategy use shown by individual children is predicted by the overlapping waves model, but is inconsistent with previous theories (including Piaget's).

⊕ Much of cognitive development depends on *competition* among various cognitive strategies.

⊖ The model can't easily be applied to learning on tasks that don't involve clearly defined strategies.

⊖ Much remains to be discovered about how children discover new strategies and how to speed up such discovery.

Theory of mind

A crucial difference between most 5-year-olds and 2- or 3-year-olds is that the former understand that other people's beliefs about the world may differ from their own. This is really important. Social communication is extremely limited if a child assumes everyone else has the same beliefs. Indeed, children lacking a theory of mind typically find it very hard to make friends and to enter successfully into group situations.

Research in this area revolves around the notion of **theory of mind**, which "conveys the idea of understanding social interaction by attributing beliefs, desires, intentions, and emotions to people" (Astington & Jenkins, 1999, p. 1311). In other words, children and adults possessing theory of mind are "mind readers" who can understand what other people are thinking and feeling. Having a theory of mind helps to make humans more intelligent than any other species.

One of the main ways theory of mind has been assessed is by using false-belief tasks. For example, Wimmer and Perner (1983) used models to present children with the following story. A boy called Maxi puts some chocolates in a blue cupboard. While he is out of the room, his mother moves the chocolate to a green cupboard. The children indicated where Maxi would look for the chocolate when he returned to the room.

Most 4-year-olds argued mistakenly that Maxi would look in the green cupboard. This indicates an absence of theory of mind; these children simply assumed that Maxi's beliefs were the same as their own. In contrast, most 5-year-olds produced the right answer.

How do children acquire theory of mind? One possibility is that theory of mind depends on the development of *general* cognitive abilities such as language, planning, and attentional control (Samson & Apperly, 2010). Some of these cognitive abilities involve **executive processes** (processes that organise and coordinate cognitive functioning).

Another possibility is that theory of mind involves a *specific* ability to infer the mental states of others. According to Baron-Cohen (1995), this ability is absent in children suffering from autism. **Autism** is a serious condition involving very poor social interaction (e.g., a failure to develop peer relationships; preference for solitary activities) and impaired communication (e.g., reluctance to maintain a conversation). It makes sense that autistic children have very poor communication skills if they can't work out what others are thinking and feeling.

Baron-Cohen (1995) argued that an important specific ability lacking in autistic children is a shared attention mechanism. This mechanism involves the ability to combine information about your direction of gaze with that of someone else to decide whether you are both attending to the same object. This mechanism is useful in leading to theory of mind (e.g., "Mummy sees the toy").

Findings

It has generally been assumed that theory of mind develops at about the age of 4. Wellman et al. (2001) reviewed numerous studies carried out in seven countries including the United Kingdom, the United States, Japan, and Korea. Most 3-year-olds performed poorly on false-belief tasks, whereas a substantial majority of 5-year-olds produced the correct answers.

In spite of the above findings, even infants possess *some* aspects of theory of mind. O'Neill (1996) had 2-year-old children watch an attractive toy being placed on a high shelf in the presence or absence of their parent. After that, the children asked their parent to let them have the toy. Those children whose parent had been absent previously were much more likely to name the toy and to gesture towards it than were those whose parent had been present.

At what age do children develop a theory of mind?

KEY TERMS

Theory of mind: the understanding by children and adults that other people may have different beliefs, emotions, and intentions than their own.

Executive processes: processes that are involved in coordinating an individual's cognitive functioning when performing tasks.

Autism: a severe disorder involving very poor communication skills, deficient social and language development, and repetitive behaviour.

Thus, even 2-year-olds have some awareness of the knowledge possessed by others.

Several general cognitive abilities underlie theory of mind in healthy children. Mutter et al. (2006) found in young children that theory-of-mind performance depended on working memory capacity (ability to combine processing and storage) and on the strength of inhibitory processes. Inhibitory processes are important because solving false-belief tasks involves inhibiting the tendency to interpret what is going on from your own perspective.

Another general cognitive ability important in the development of theory of mind is language. Supporting evidence was reported by Ketelaars et al. (2010). They found language ability at one point in time predicted children's theory-of-mind performance later on.

We saw earlier that even infants possess some aspects of theory of mind. At the other extreme, adults sometimes have problems with theory-of-mind tasks. Lin et al. (2010) gave adults the task of using their theory of mind to work out a speaker's intentions. Their performance suffered when they performed an attentionally demanding secondary task at the same time.

What should we conclude from the good performance of infants on some theory-of-mind tasks and the imperfect performance of adults on other theory-of-mind tasks? Theory of mind consists of several kinds of knowledge, some of which are much easier than others to acquire (Samson & Apperly, 2010).

Autism

We turn now to autism. There is overwhelming evidence that autistic children have great difficulties with theory of mind. For example, Baron-Cohen et al. (1985) gave 4-year-old children as well as autistic children with a mental age of at least 4 a false-belief problem. More than 80% of the non-autistic children but only 20% of the autistic children solved the problem.

The failure of autistic children to show theory of mind depends heavily on deficient general cognitive abilities. In a study by Pellicano (2010), 4-year-old autistic children were assessed for various executive functions (e.g., inhibitory control). They were also assessed for **central coherence**, which is the ability to use all the information when interpreting a situation. The improvement in theory-of-mind performance between the ages of 4 and 7 was predicted by executive functioning and central coherence at the age of 4.

There is support for the view that autistic children have problems with shared attention. Baron-Cohen et al. (1995) found most young children know that if someone looks at one out of four blocks of chocolate, that is the one he/she wants. As predicted, autistic children didn't realise that was the case.

KEY TERM

Central coherence: the ability to interpret information taking account of the context; being able to "see the big picture".

EVALUATION

⊕ The development of a theory of mind is very important in allowing children to communicate with other people.

⊕ Some of the cognitive abilities (e.g., executive functions; language; central coherence) needed for the development of theory of mind have been identified.

⊕ Many of the problems experienced by autistic children occur because they typically lack a theory of mind. The enormous difficulties they experience provide strong evidence of the importance to children of having a theory of mind.

⊕ One reason why autistic children don't have a theory of mind is because they often lack a shared attention mechanism.

⊖ It has often been assumed that theory of mind is a *single* ability. In fact, however, it probably consists of various different abilities.

⊖ Producing the correct answer on false-belief tasks involves more than simply possessing a theory of mind. It also involves having the necessary motivation and processing resources (Samson & Apperly, 2010).

Chapter summary

- Piaget argued that adaptation to the environment requires accommodation and assimilation.
- Piaget identified four stages of development: (1) sensori-motor (intelligence in action); (2) pre-operational (thinking dominated by perception); (3) concrete operations (cognitive systems can be applied to the real world); and (4) formal operations (cognitive systems can also be applied to possible worlds; thinking about thinking).
- Piaget exaggerated the importance of general cognitive operations and minimised the importance of specific learning experiences. He also underestimated children's cognitive skills and described rather than explained the stages of cognitive development.
- Vygotsky argued that children are apprentices who learn directly from social interaction.
- Children's learning is enhanced by strategies based on the zone of proximal development.
- There is support for Vygotsky's claim that children use inner speech to guide their thinking.

- Siegler developed the microgenetic method in which children perform the same cognitive task repeatedly over a fairly short period of time.
- Children often start using the best strategy on a task without understanding it and sometimes even deny having used it.
- Siegler found that children exhibit much variability in strategy use. They develop improved strategy use by taking account of the speed and accuracy of problem solution with each strategy.
- A theory of mind (ability to "mind read") typically develops at about the age of 4, although some aspects are often present at an earlier age.
- Autistic children lack a theory of mind. This occurs because they have impaired executive functioning, a poor ability to use all available information, and problems with shared attention.

Further reading

- Berk, L.E. (2009). *Child development (9th ed.)*. Boston: Allyn & Bacon. Laura Berk provides good coverage of research and theory on language acquisition in this best-selling textbook.

- Defeyter, M.A. (2011). Cognitive development. In A. Slater & G. Bremner (Eds.), *An introduction to developmental psychology (2nd ed.)*. Chichester, UK: Wiley-Blackwell. This chapter provides an overview of major approaches to cognitive development.

- Eysenck, M.W. (2009). Cognition and development. In M.W. Eysenck (Ed.), *A2 level psychology*. Hove, UK: Psychology Press. Major topics in cognitive development are discussed in detail.

Essay questions

1. Describe Piaget's stage theory of cognitive development. What are the main strengths and limitations of this theory?

2. What were Vygotsky's main contributions to our understanding of cognitive development?

3. Describe Siegler's overlapping waves model. In what ways is it an improvement on Piaget's approach?

4. What is theory of mind? Why do most children develop a theory of mind but some do not?

Language is of great importance to the human species. Indeed, it may well be the most important difference between us and other species. Normal life is impossible for anyone who doesn't have a reasonable ability to understand and to use language, because it is central to education and the work environment. In addition, making (and keeping) friends involves effective communication, most of which depends directly on language.

Mastering language is a complex skill, but nearly all children do so with apparent ease. Moreover, they do so at a very young age before their other cognitive abilities (e.g., thinking; reasoning) are well developed. How do you think they manage to do this?

Several attempts have been made to teach language to chimpanzees over the years. From what you know about chimpanzees, would you guess that any of these attempts have been successful?

Language development

We will start by defining the word "language". According to Sternberg (1995), it is "an organised means of combining words in order to communicate." Parrots say certain words (e.g., "Who's a pretty boy?"), but they aren't using language in the true sense. What they say isn't organised, nor does it involve combining words to pass on a message to others.

How can language be defined?

Several theorists have tried to identify criteria for defining language so we can distinguish between language and non-language. For example, Hockett (1960) suggested various criteria including the following:

- *Semanticity*: The words or other units must have meaning.
- *Arbitrariness*: There is an arbitrary connection between the form or sound of the word and its meaning.
- *Displacement*: Language can be produced in the absence of the object being described.
- *Prevarication*: Language involves the ability to tell lies and jokes.
- *Productivity*: There is an essentially infinite number of different ideas that can be communicated.

One of the most remarkable achievements of young children is the apparently breathtaking speed with which they acquire language as defined by the above criteria. From the age of about 18 months onwards, children learn 10 or more new words every day. By the time they are 2 years old, most children use language to communicate hundreds of messages.

By the age of 5, children who may not even have started at school have mastered most of the grammatical rules of their native language. What is especially impressive is that very few parents formally teach their children the rules of grammar. Indeed, most parents aren't consciously aware of these rules! Thus, young children simply "pick up" the complex rules of grammar with little formal or direct teaching.

In what follows, we will first describe the various stages of language development. After that, we will return to the fascinating issue of how children acquire something as complex as language so quickly and apparently effortlessly. Finally, we will consider attempts to teach language to chimpanzees. There has been much controversy concerning the success (or otherwise) of such attempts.

Stages of language development

It is important to distinguish between **receptive language** (language comprehension) and **productive language** (language expression or speaking). Our central focus will be on productive language, but there are close links between productive and receptive language.

Children (as well as adults) have better receptive than productive language. We would underestimate children's language skills if we assumed their speech reflects all their knowledge of language.

Children acquire *four* kinds of knowledge about language:

1. **Phonology:** the sound system of a language.
2. **Semantics:** the meanings conveyed by words and sentences.
3. **Syntax:** the set of grammatical rules indicating how words may (and may not) be combined to make sentences.
4. **Pragmatics:** the principles determining how language should fit the context (e.g., speak slowly and clearly to a foreigner).

It used to be assumed that children learn about language in the order listed above. However, as we will see, that is an oversimplification. Of particular importance, children acquire knowledge of grammar at the same time as knowledge of words and their meanings.

Initial stages

Infants engage in vocalisation from a very early age. The early babbling of infants up to 6 months of age is similar in all parts of the world. By about 8 months of age, however, infants' vocalisations show signs of the language they have heard. Indeed, adults can sometimes guess accurately from their babbling whether infants have been exposed to French, Chinese, Arabic, or English (De Boysson-Bardies et al., 1984).

Up until the age of 18 months, infants are limited to single-word utterances (although they may be trying to convey much more than their short utterances would suggest). Almost two-thirds of the words used by infants are nouns referring to objects or people that interest them. Words are sometimes used to cover more objects than they should (over-extension) as when my younger daughter referred to every man as "Daddy".

The second stage of language development starts at 18 months. It is the **telegraphic period**, during which children's speech is abbreviated like a telegram. More specifically, content words such as nouns and verbs are included but function words (e.g., *a, the, and*), pronouns, and prepositions are omitted. Even though children at this stage are mostly limited to two-word utterances, they can still communicate numerous meanings. For example, "Daddy chair" may mean "I want to sit in Daddy's chair", "Daddy

Infants engage in vocalisation from a very early age. Here, a baby boy (Sebastian) smiles at the face of his mother (Fleur), and responds to baby talk. At this age, vocalisations are the same in all parts of the world but by 8 months of age infants show signs of the language they have heard.

is sitting in his chair", or "Daddy, sit in your chair!"

At about 24 months, most children start producing utterances that are three words or longer. From 36 months on, children start using complete sentences and exhibit an increasingly accurate knowledge of grammar.

Vocabulary and grammar

Children's language develops considerably between 2 and 5 years of age. For example, the maximum sentence length increases from 4 morphemes (units of meaning) at 24 months to 8 at 30 months (Fenson et al., 1994). Children gradually acquire various **grammatical morphemes** (modifiers that alter meaning). Examples of grammatical morphemes are prepositions, prefixes, and suffixes (e.g., *in*; *on*; plural *–s*; and *the*).

Nearly all children learn the various grammatical morphemes in the same order. They start with simple ones (e.g., including *in* and *on* in sentences). After that, they learn more complex ones (e.g., reducing *they are* to *they're*).

Do children imitate adults' speech or do they learn grammatical rules? Children (especially young ones) often imitate adults' speech. However, evidence they don't merely imitate comes from their grammatical errors. For example, a child will say, "The dog runned away", which adults are unlikely to do. The child makes that mistake because he/she is applying the rule that the past tense of a verb is usually formed by adding *–ed* to the present tense. However, the fact that children are applying grammatical rules doesn't necessarily mean they are consciously aware of those rules.

Using a grammatical rule in situations in which it doesn't apply is known as **over-regularisation**. Evidence that over-regularisation doesn't occur simply because children imitate other children was reported by Berko (1958). Children were shown two pictures of an imaginary animal or bird. They were told, "This is a wug. Now there are two …" (see the figure on the right). Even young children produced the regular plural form "wugs" despite not having heard the word before.

This is a wug

Now there is another one.
There are two of them.
There are two _____.

It used to be thought that young children acquired vocabulary *before* grammar. However, that is *not* the case. Dixon and Marchman (2007) found children aged 16–30 months acquired vocabulary and grammar at the same time. Dionne et al. (2003) assessed vocabulary and grammar in children at the ages of 2 and 3. Vocabulary at age 2 predicted grammar at age 3, and grammar at age 2 predicted vocabulary at age 3. Such findings strongly suggest the processes underlying vocabulary and grammar development are similar.

In sum, the great majority of young children show massive advances in language between the ages of about 18 and 36 months. Their vocabulary expands by hundreds or thousands of words, their sentences become much longer and more complete, and what they say is increasingly grammatical.

KEY TERMS

Grammatical morphemes: prepositions, prefixes, suffixes, and so on that help to indicate the grammatical structure of sentences.

Over-regularisation: this is a language error in which a grammatical rule is applied to situations in which it isn't relevant.

Theories of language development

Now is the time to consider explanations of the seemingly amazing speed with which young children acquire language. Many theories have been proposed. However, most can be categorised as inside-out theories or outside-in theories. Inside-out theorists (e.g., Chomsky; Pinker) argue that language development depends heavily on innate factors and only modestly on the child's own experience. In contrast, outside-in theorists (e.g., Bruner; Tomasello) argue that language experience and other environmental influences are of central importance in language acquisition.

Inside-out theories

Explain the language acquisition device.

Noam Chomsky (1965) argued that the spoken language to which children are exposed is too limited on its own to allow them to develop language with the speed they display. He claimed humans possess a language acquisition device consisting of innate knowledge of grammatical structure.

Chomsky (1986) later replaced the notion of a language acquisition device with the idea of a Universal Grammar common to all languages. It consists of various **linguistic universals** (features common to nearly every language). Examples of linguistic universals are word order and the distinction between nouns and verbs. In English, the typical word order is subject-verb-object (e.g., "The man kicked the ball").

According to Chomsky, children's learning of language doesn't depend solely on the language acquisition device. Children also require some exposure to (and experience with) the language environment provided by their parents and other people to develop language. Such experience determines *which* specific language any given child will learn.

Pinker (1989) was broadly sympathetic to Chomsky's approach. However, he argued that exposure to language is more important than admitted by Chomsky. According to Pinker, children use "semantic bootstrapping" to allocate words to their appropriate word class.

Suppose a young child hears the sentence, "William is throwing a stone", while watching a boy carrying out that action. The child will realise from his/her observations that "William" is the actor, "stone" is the object acted on, and "is throwing" is the action. The child then uses its innate knowledge of word categories to work out that "William" is the subject of the sentence, "stone" is the object, and "is throwing" is the verb.

Bickerton (1984) was influenced by Chomsky's views, which led him to put forward the language bioprogram hypothesis. According to this hypothesis, children will *create* their own grammar even if they aren't exposed to a proper language during their early years.

KEY TERM

Linguistic universals: features (e.g., preferred word orders; the distinction between nouns and verbs) that are found in the great majority of the world's languages.

Findings

Chomsky argued that word order was a linguistic universal. We can test this by considering the preferred word order in numerous languages. Greenberg (1963) did precisely this. The English order (i.e., subject-verb-object) was the norm in 35% of those languages, with a further 44% using the subject-object-verb order. Overall, the subject preceded the object in 98% of those languages.

Why does the subject nearly always precede the object? The subject is the word or phrase a sentence is about, whereas the object is the person or thing acted upon by the verb. The central importance of the subject within the sentence means it is entirely appropriate for it to precede the object.

We turn now to Bickerton's language bioprogram hypothesis. Some of the strongest support comes from the study of pidgin languages. These are new, primitive languages created when two or more groups of people having different native languages are in contact.

Pinker (1984) discussed research on labourers from China, Japan, Korea, Puerto Rico, Portugal, and the Philippines taken to the sugar plantations of Hawaii about 100 years ago. These labourers developed a pidgin language that was very simple and lacked most grammatical structure. Here is an example: "Me cape buy, me check make", which means "He bought my coffee; he made me out a cheque". The offspring of these labourers developed Hawaiian Creole, which is a proper language and fully grammatical.

A limitation with the above evidence is that we don't know the extent to which the development of Hawaiian Creole depended on the labourers' prior exposure to language. Clearer evidence that language can develop in groups almost completely lacking in exposure to a developed language was reported by Senghas et al. (2004). They studied deaf Nicaraguan children at special schools in which attempts were made to teach them Spanish.

In spite of the fact that most of the attempts to teach these deaf children Spanish were unsuccessful, they did manage to acquire language. They developed a new system of gestures that expanded into a basic sign language passed on to successive groups of children who joined the school. Since their Nicaraguan Sign Language bore very little relation to Spanish or the gestures made by hearing children, it appears to be a genuinely new language owing remarkably little to other languages.

What do the above findings mean? They certainly suggest that humans have a strong innate motivation to acquire language (including grammatical rules) and to communicate with others. That is as predicted on Bickerton's language bioprogram hypothesis. However, the findings don't provide strong support for the notion of a language acquisition device.

Conclusions

Chomsky's views have been very influential. However, there is much scepticism about their correctness (Christiansen & Chater, 2008, 2009; Gervain & Mehler, 2010). There are two main reasons for this scepticism. First, the linguistic input to which young children are exposed is much richer than Chomsky believed (Reali & Christiansen, 2005; Weizman & Snow, 2001). For example, mothers and other adults use child-directed speech when speaking to young children. **Child-directed speech** involves very short, simple sentences, a slow rate of speaking, use of a restricted vocabulary, and extra stress on key words (Dockrell & Messer, 1999).

Second, the world's languages differ much more from each other than assumed by Chomsky. It is true that the main European languages are all very similar. However, large differences appear when all the world's 6000 to 8000 languages are considered. Evans and Levinson (2009, p. 429) did precisely that and concluded: "There are vanishingly few universals of language in the direct sense that all languages exhibit them. Instead, diversity can be found at almost every level of linguistic organisation."

EVALUATION

➕ Inside-out theories potentially explain why nearly all children master their native language very rapidly.

➕ Chomsky's theory receives some support from the finding that children can develop a new language even with very limited exposure to a developed language.

➕ Bickerton's (1984) language bioprogram hypothesis has been supported by research on the development of Nicaraguan Sign Language.

➖ The world's languages differ much more than claimed by Chomsky, making it improbable that there is a universal grammar.

➖ Chomsky drastically underestimated the ways in which parents tailor their use of language to assist language learning by their children (see below).

➖ Children's ability to develop a new language probably depends on innate motivation to communicate rather than the possession of an innate grammar.

Outside-in theories

Outside-in theorists (e.g., Tomasello, 2005) emphasise the central role of experience in allowing young children to acquire language. In essence, outside-in theorists argue that the language input to which young children are exposed is sufficient for language acquisition. This is in sharp contrast to Chomsky's views.

Probably the most important environmental factor in children's language learning is the guidance provided by the mother, father and/or caregiver. As we have seen, when parents talk to their young children, they use very short, simple sentences (child-directed speech). However, the length and complexity of what parents say to their child gradually increase as the child's own use of language develops.

Of importance, parents use sentences slightly longer and more complex than those produced by their child (Bohannon & Warren-Leubecker, 1989). **Expansions** consist of fuller and more grammatical versions of what the child has just said. For example, a child might say, "Cat out", with its mother responding, "The cat wants to go out".

KEY TERM

Expansions: utterances of adults that consist of fuller and more accurate versions of what a child has just said.

Saxton (1997) argued that many expansions provide children with an immediate *contrast* between their own incorrect speech and the correct version. For example, a child may say, "He shooted bird!", to which the adult might reply, "He shot the bird!"

How does child-directed speech help children acquire language skills?

We have seen that there is much evidence for child-directed speech. The take-home message is that most parents are "in tune" with their child's current language abilities when they speak to him/her.

According to Tomasello (2005), children's language development depends on their cognitive understanding of the scenes or events they experience in their everyday lives. As a result, children's learning of specific language skills (e.g., grammar) tends to be *gradual*. In addition, young children's limited cognitive ability means that their early use of language often consists of imitating or copying what they have heard.

Findings

Rowe (2008) identified several features of child-directed speech (e.g., more talking; using a greater variety of words). The children of parents who used much child-directed speech showed more rapid language development than other children. In addition, children's language development was faster when the parents had high socioeconomic status (high income; well-educated). These parents made more use of child-directed speech, and also had greater knowledge of child development.

Some evidence suggests child-directed speech isn't essential for normal language development. Schieffelin (1990) studied the Kaluli of New Guinea. Adults talk to children as if they were adults, but Kaluli children develop language at about the normal rate. However, cultures in which child-directed speech is little used may provide different kinds of assistance to children learning language. Ochs and Schieffelin (1995) argued that children in such cultures become involved in social and communal activities that promote shared understanding and language development.

Matthews et al. (2005) provided evidence that children learn grammar fairly slowly. They presented 2- and 3-year-old children with short sentences in which the words were in an ungrammatical subject-object-verb order (e.g., "Bear elephant tugged"). The children in their own speech often copied the ungrammatical word order they had heard when they weren't familiar with the verb in the sentence. However, they rarely spoke ungrammatically when they were very familiar with the verb.

The above findings indicate that using the correct grammatical order is a *gradual* process. It starts with familiar verbs several months before being used with unfamiliar verbs. This is exactly what we would expect to find if children's language development is closely linked to their specific language experience.

Bannard et al. (2009) found that children's speech for the first 2 years after they started to speak was remarkably limited. For example, the children used a small set of familiar verbs and often repeated back what they had just heard. These findings suggest the children's limited cognitive abilities restricted their initial ability to use language.

EVALUATION

➕ Children's language acquisition benefits substantially from exposure to child-directed speech, because it is carefully tailored to young children's needs.

➕ Children's limited cognitive abilities mean that language acquisition is initially gradual and reliant on copying the language they hear.

➖ It is important to find out more about language acquisition in children who apparently have little exposure to child-directed speech.

➖ More needs to be discovered about the processes that allow young children to move from imitative speech to more creative speech.

Animal language

According to Skinner, how does language develop?

There are two main reasons why it is important to study language in other species. First, there is a theoretical controversy concerning the possibility of other species acquiring language. Some theorists (e.g., Chomsky) argue that language is unique to the human species, whereas others (e.g., Skinner) deny this. According to Chomsky, the human species is the only one with a language acquisition device, and so it would be impossible for any other species to develop language. In contrast, Skinner argued there is nothing special about language. As a result, there is no reason why language couldn't be acquired by other species.

Second, studying language in other species leads us to consider precisely what we mean by language. As we will see, chimpanzees provide an interesting test case. They can clearly acquire some features of language but not all of them. That makes it really difficult to decide whether they possess language.

There is one final point to make before we proceed to discuss the relevant evidence on chimpanzees. Their vocal tracts are very different from those of humans and so they can't produce the same sounds as humans. As a result, research has focused on teaching chimpanzees to produce language in other ways (e.g., using sign language).

Findings

Allen and Beatrice Gardner (1969) claimed to have taught American Sign Language to a 1-year-old female chimpanzee called Washoe. After 4 years

"He says the downturn in world trade is adversely affecting banana supply, and warrants a reduction in interest rates".

of training, she knew 132 signs and could arrange them in novel ways. For example, when she saw a swan, she signed "water bird". There was also a suggestion that she had grasped basic aspects of grammar, for example, she signed "tickle me" much more often than "me tickle".

Terrace et al. (1979) disputed the Gardners' claim that Washoe had acquired language. They analysed Washoe's behaviour as revealed in a movie about her. She generally merely *imitated* the signs that had just been made by her teacher, which doesn't suggest she understood grammar.

In addition, many of the signs Washoe learned are the same as gestures occurring naturally in chimpanzees. These included "tickle" (signed by tickling) and "scratch" (signed by scratching). This is not genuine language; as indicated at the start of the chapter, language involves *arbitrary* (rather than direct) relationships between words and their meanings.

With training, what aspects of language can chimpanzees learn to produce?

Bonobos

Washoe was a common chimpanzee and it is often assumed that bonobo chimpanzees are more intelligent. As a result, Savage-Rumbaugh et al. (1986) studied a male bonobo called Kanzi. Kanzi was taught using a keyboard containing geometric symbols known as lexigrams.

In 17 months, Kanzi learned to understand nearly 60 of these lexigrams and could produce nearly 50 by pointing to relevant ones. His comprehension skills were especially good. Kanzi responded correctly to 109 words on a speech comprehension test and behaved appropriately to 105 utterances (e.g., "Kanzi go get me a knife").

Kanzi's language learning was greater than that of Washoe. For example, he could distinguish between "Put the pine needles in your ball" and "Can you put the ball on the pine needles?" However, he differed from young children in

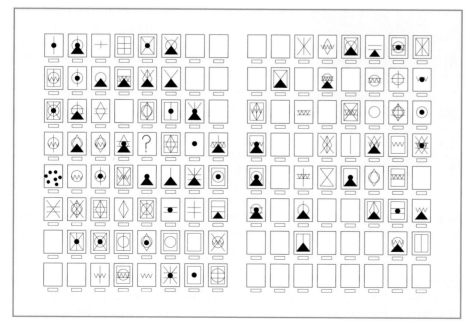

The arrangement of lexigrams on a keyboard. Blank spaces were non-functioning keys, or displayed photographs of trainers.

that the length of his utterances didn't increase much over time. Indeed, most of his utterances consisted of a single lexigram.

Kanzi communicates by pointing at lexigrams. However, his pointing is often accompanied by sounds. Taglialatela et al. (2003) obtained evidence that Kanzi's sounds resembled "saying" the relevant words but in a very high pitch and in a distorted fashion.

Further impressive findings have been obtained from another bonobo called Panbanisha (Brakke & Savage-Rumbaugh, 1995, 1996). She has spent her entire life in captivity receiving training in the use of language. She uses a specially designed keypad with about 400 lexigrams on it. When she presses a sequence of keys, a computer translates the sequence into a synthetic voice. Panbanisha learned 3000 words by the age of 14 years and is very good at combining symbols grammatically. Examples include "Please can I have an iced coffee?" and "I'm thinking about eating something."

Limitations

The findings discussed so far indicate that chimpanzees can acquire several aspects of language. However, there are several important ways in which language learning in chimpanzees falls well short of that in children (Harley, 2010). For example, chimpanzees rarely ask questions, they communicate almost exclusively about the here-and-now, and they can't identify ungrammatical sentences. In contrast, young children are always asking questions, they can talk about absent objects and people, and they have some ability to distinguish between grammatical and ungrammatical sentences.

Sue Savage-Rumbaugh holds a board displaying lexigrams that Kanzi uses to communicate with her.

The crucial issue (and a controversial one) is to identify precisely what it is that chimpanzees have managed to learn. For example, Kanzi has learned to produce, "You give me a banana". It may seem as if this indicates a sophisticated knowledge of language and grammatical rules. However, as Harley (2010, p. 47) pointed out, it may simply indicate that "he's learned to press the right keys in the right order to get a banana". In other words, perhaps Kanzi has learned by operant conditioning (see Chapter 7) that a given sequence of responses is followed by reward.

Lyn (2007) reported some relevant findings from Kanzi and Panbanisha, both of whom understand English at the level of a 2½-old child. An analysis of their errors suggested they had a fairly complex understanding of language including an ability to think in terms of conceptual categories. However, other evidence reported by Lyn suggested Kanzi and Panbanisha have little grasp of grammar.

In sum, it is a mistake to demand a "Yes" or "No" answer to the question of whether chimpanzees can acquire language. What seems to be the case is that they can acquire many aspects of language but that their language learning falls substantially below that of even young children.

EVALUATION

➕ Chimpanzees (especially bonobos) have learned hundreds of words in the form of signs or lexigrams. This achievement satisfies some of the criteria for language put forward by Hockett (1960) and discussed at the start of the chapter (e.g., semanticity, arbitrariness, and prevarication or lying).

➕ Chimpanzees have some understanding of the signs and lexigrams they use.

➖ Chimpanzees show little evidence of productivity, and they rarely refer to objects that haven't been seen for some time (displacement).

➖ It is likely that much of what is learned by chimpanzees is due to operant conditioning rather than a true understanding of language.

➖ Chimpanzees produce spontaneous utterances much less often than young children, and their utterances tend to be very short.

➖ As Chomsky (quoted in Atkinson et al., 1993) pointed out, "If an animal had a capacity as biologically advantageous as language but somehow hadn't used it until now, it would be an evolutionary miracle, like finding an island of humans who could be taught to fly."

Chapter summary

- Various criteria for language have been suggested. They include semanticity, arbitrariness, displacement, prevarication, and productivity.
- Children have better receptive than productive language. Productive language starts with one-word utterances. This is followed by the telegraphic period in which the emphasis is on content words.
- Children sometimes imitate adults' speech, but they also acquire grammatical rules.
- Chomsky argued that humans possess a language acquisition device and that there are language universals. Neither of these assumptions

is correct and the world's languages are much more diverse than assumed by Chomsky.

- According to the language bioprogram hypothesis, children will create a grammar even if exposed to very little language. There is support for this hypothesis in research on deaf Nicaraguan children, which reveals the strong human motivation to communicate.
- Outside-in theorists argue that child-directed speech (tailored to children's needs) plays a vital role in language acquisition.
- According to outside-in theorists, children's acquisition of language depends in part on their cognitive understanding of their everyday experiences. This leads to the prediction (which has research support) that children should acquire language in a gradual fashion.
- Research on chimpanzees is of relevance to the issue of whether there is something special and specifically human about language.
- Bonobo chimpanzees can acquire large vocabularies and can communicate numerous messages.
- The communications of chimpanzees are much more limited than those of young children. For example, there are fewer references to the past or future, there are few long utterances, and there is little evidence that chimpanzees possess grammatical knowledge.

Further reading

- Berk, L.E. (2009). *Child development (9th ed.)*. Boston: Allyn & Bacon. Laura Berk provides good coverage of research and theory on language acquisition in this best-selling textbook.

- Harley, T.A. (2010). *Talking the talk: Language, psychology and science*. Hove, UK: Psychology Press. Chapters 2 and 3 of this excellent textbook by Trevor Harley discuss language in children and animals.

- Hill, H.M. & Kuczaj, S.A. (2011). The development of language. In A. Slater & G. Bremner (Eds.), *An introduction to developmental psychology (2nd ed.)*. Chichester, UK: Wiley-Blackwell. The authors discuss up-to-date research on children's acquisition of language.

- Mitani, J. (1995). Kanzi: The ape at the brink of the human mind. *Scientific American*, 6, 272. This article discusses research on Kanzi's language abilities in an accessible way.

Essay questions

1. Describe the early stages of language development. What are the main changes that occur?

2. Identify some of the main assumptions of inside-out theories. How successful have such theories been?

3. What environmental influences facilitate children's acquisition of language?

4. Describe research on animal language. Does it show that other species can learn language?

As children grow up, most of them show considerable moral development. For example, they come to a greater understanding of the difference between right and wrong. In addition, their behaviour becomes increasingly influenced by moral values, and they experience guilt and shame when they fail to live up to reasonable moral standards.

What causes children to exhibit moral development during the course of their childhood? Does it depend mainly on their parents, or does it depend more on learning from other children? Do children behave in a moral way because they are imitating the behaviour of others?

Moral development

10

This chapter deals with the changes in morality occurring as children grow up into adults. What do we mean by "morality"? It "implies a set of principles or ideals that help the individual to distinguish right from wrong, and to act on this distinction" (Shaffer, 1993).

Why is morality important? One key reason is that society can't work properly unless there is general agreement on what is right and what is wrong. There will always be some moral issues (e.g., animal experiments; nuclear weapons) on which people within a given society will have very different views. However, if there were controversy about all major moral issues, society would become chaotic.

Human morality has three major components (see the figure below):

What are the main components of morality?

1. *Cognitive*: How we think about moral issues and decide what is right and wrong. This component is concerned with moral reasoning.
2. *Emotional*: The feelings (e.g., guilt; pride) associated with moral thoughts and behaviour.
3. *Behavioural*: The extent to which we behave honourably or lie, steal, and cheat.

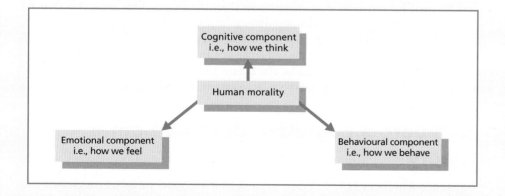

Consistency of human morality?

It might be thought that any given individual would show *consistency* among the three components of morality. For example, someone who has high moral standards with respect to the cognitive component would also have high moral standards with the emotional and behavioural components. In fact, however, there are often large discrepancies between components.

Walker (2004) reviewed research on the relationship between moral reasoning (the cognitive component) and moral action (the behavioural component). On average, individual differences in moral reasoning accounted for only 10% of the variation in moral action. Thus, there was very little consistency between moral reasoning and moral behaviour.

Why do the various components of human morality show relatively little consistency? One reason is that many people have a high level of moral reasoning (cognitive component) but behave in ways they know are wrong when faced with temptation (behavioural component). For example, someone who believes strongly that stealing is wrong may say nothing when given far too much change when buying something in a shop.

Teper et al. (2011) argued that the opposite can also happen. In other words, people sometimes behave in a *more* moral way than they thought they would. In their study, participants had the opportunity to cheat on a maths task. In practice, they cheated less often than they had anticipated. Why was this? The participants displayed more emotional arousal when given the chance to cheat than when they merely considered what they would do in that situation. Thus, emotional arousal acted as a "brake" on their temptation to cheat.

Rest of the chapter

In what follows, we will discuss two major theories of moral development. As we will see, these theories focus mostly on only one of the three components, namely, the cognitive component. In general, research on moral development has focused far more on that component than the others. One reason is that it is generally easier to assess the cognitive component. However, the emotional and behavioural components are at least as important in real life.

After that, we will consider the influence of parents and by peers (other children of the same age). Not surprisingly, the extent to which children and adolescents exhibit moral behaviour depends to a large extent on both parents and peers.

Kohlberg's cognitive-developmental theory

Lawrence Kohlberg (1927–1987) argued that we need to focus on children's cognitive structures to understand their moral development. He assumed that moral reasoning often continues to develop through adolescence and early adulthood.

Kohlberg (e.g., 1963) presented his participants with a series of moral dilemmas. Each dilemma required them to decide whether it is preferable to uphold some law or other moral principle or to reject the moral principle in favour of some basic human need. Here is one of the moral dilemmas he used:

At which level or stage in Kohlberg's theory do children have a punishment-and-obedience orientation?

> In Europe, a woman was dying of cancer. One drug might save her, a form of radium that a druggist in the same town had recently discovered. The druggist was charging 2000 dollars, ten times what the drug cost him to make. The sick woman's husband, Heinz, went to everyone he knew to borrow the money, but he could only get together about half of what it cost. He told the druggist that his wife was dying and asked him to sell it cheaper or let him pay later. But the druggist said "No". The husband got desperate and broke into the man's store to steal the drug for his wife.

The moral principle in this dilemma is that stealing is wrong. However, it was the good motive of wanting to help his sick wife that led Heinz to steal the drug. It is precisely because there are powerful arguments for and against stealing the drug that there is a moral dilemma.

Kohlberg (1966, 1981) used evidence from such moral dilemmas to develop his cognitive-developmental theory. He assumed that all children follow the same sequence of stages in their moral development. Within his theory, there are three levels of moral development with two stages at each level (see the figure below):

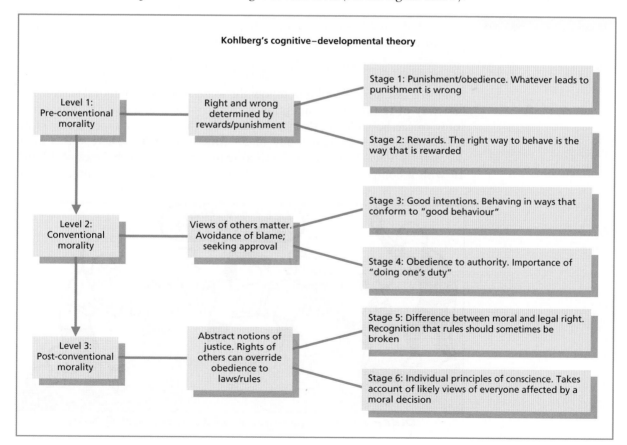

Kohlberg's cognitive–developmental theory

Level 1: Pre-conventional morality → Right and wrong determined by rewards/punishment
- Stage 1: Punishment/obedience. Whatever leads to punishment is wrong
- Stage 2: Rewards. The right way to behave is the way that is rewarded

Level 2: Conventional morality → Views of others matter. Avoidance of blame; seeking approval
- Stage 3: Good intentions. Behaving in ways that conform to "good behaviour"
- Stage 4: Obedience to authority. Importance of "doing one's duty"

Level 3: Post-conventional morality → Abstract notions of justice. Rights of others can override obedience to laws/rules
- Stage 5: Difference between moral and legal right. Recognition that rules should sometimes be broken
- Stage 6: Individual principles of conscience. Takes account of likely views of everyone affected by a moral decision

- *Level 1*: **pre-conventional morality**. What is regarded as right and wrong is determined by the rewards or punishments that are likely to follow rather than by moral issues. Stage 1 of this level is based on a *punishment-and-obedience orientation*. Stealing is wrong because it involves disobeying authority and leads to punishment. Stage 2 of this level is based on the notion that the right way to behave is the way that is rewarded. There is more attention to the needs of others than in Stage 1, but mainly on the basis that if you help others they will help you.
- *Level 2*: **conventional morality**. The views and needs of others are much more important at Level 2 than they were at Level 1. At Level 2, children are very concerned to have others' approval for their actions and to avoid being blamed for behaving wrongly. At Stage 3, the emphasis is on having good intentions and on behaving in ways conforming to most people's ideas of good behaviour. At Stage 4, children believe it is important to do one's duty and to obey the laws or rules of those in authority.
- *Level 3*: **post-conventional morality**. At Level 3, people recognise that the laws or rules of authority figures should sometimes be broken. Abstract notions about justice and the need to treat others with respect can override the need to obey laws and rules. At Stage 5, there is a growing recognition that what is morally right may differ from what is legally right. Finally, at Stage 6, the individual takes into account the likely views of everyone who will be affected by a moral decision. Kohlberg (1981) described this as a kind of "moral musical chairs". In practice, it is rare for anyone to operate most of the time at Stage 6.

Findings

Kohlberg assumed all children follow the same sequences of moral stages. The best way of testing this assumption is to carry out a longitudinal (long-term) study to see how children's moral reasoning changes over time. Colby et al. (1983) reported a 20-year study of 58 American males. There was a large decrease in Stage 1 and Stage 2 moral reasoning between the ages of 10 and 16 with a compensatory increase in Stage 3 and Stage 4 reasoning over the

Older children recognise that rules are flexible.

same time period (see the figure on the right). Most impressively for Kohlberg's theory, all the participants progressed through the moral stages in the predicted sequence.

Other research suggests that shifts in moral development can be from a higher to a lower stage rather than the expected upward direction. Patenaude et al. (2003) found 13% of medical students showed a decline in moral development during their first 3 years at medical school. They speculated this might be due to the structure of medical education.

Is moral development basically the same across most cultures? Snarey (1985) addressed this issue in a review of 44 studies from 26 cultures. People in nearly all these cultures went through the stages of moral development identified by Kohlberg in the same order. There was little evidence that individuals skipped any stage or that they returned to an earlier stage of moral development.

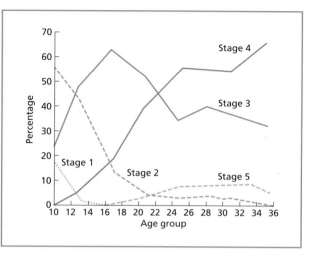

Kohlberg's moral stages studied longitudinally over a 20-year period encompassing ages 10 to 36.

However, Snarey (1985) found more evidence of Stage 5 reasoning in Western cultures than most rural or village cultures. This difference doesn't mean the moral reasoning of those living in Western cultures is superior. Rather, it reflects the individualistic emphasis of most Western cultures (e.g., the greater value attached to human life).

More evidence there are minor cultural differences in moral reasoning was reported by Rochat et al. (2009) in 3- to 5-year-olds living in very diverse cultures. The 3-year-old children in all cultures focused on maximising their own gain. However, there was a greater emphasis on fairness and avoiding being selfish among 5-year-olds in small-scale urban and traditional societies than those in Western cultures. This is consistent with the emphasis on group or collective values in the former societies.

Does an individual's level of moral reasoning predict his/her behaviour? It generally does to some extent. Kohlberg (1975) compared cheating behaviour among students at different levels of moral reasoning. As many as 70% of those at the pre-conventional level of morality cheated, compared to only 15% at the post-conventional level. Students at the conventional level came in the middle (see the figure on the right).

Stams et al. (2006) reviewed numerous studies on moral reasoning in juvenile delinquents, whose behaviour often fails to adhere to moral values. They were at a much lower stage of moral reasoning than other adolescents.

Kohlberg assumed certain kinds of general cognitive development must occur before an individual can advance a stage in his/her moral

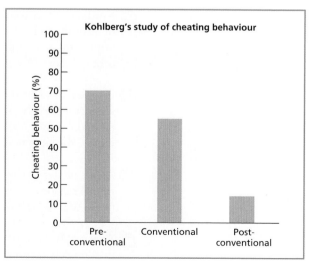

reasoning. For example, those whose moral reasoning is at Stage 5 make use of abstract principles (e.g., of justice), which presumably requires them to be good at abstract thinking. Tomlinson-Keasey and Keasey (1974) found girls of 11 or 12 who showed Stage 5 moral reasoning were good at abstract thinking generally. However, some girls could think abstractly but failed to show Stage 5 moral reasoning. Thus, the ability to think abstractly is a necessary (but not sufficient) requirement for someone to attain Stage 5 or post-conventional morality.

Kohlberg focused very much on the cognitive processes involved in morality. In so doing, he minimised the role of emotional processes. Consider a study by Greene et al. (2004) involving very emotional moral dilemmas. In one of the dilemmas, you, your baby, and some of your townspeople are hiding from enemy soldiers who have been ordered to kill everyone in the town. Your baby will make a lot of noise and lead to all of you being killed unless you smother him to death.

What should you do when confronted by the above dilemma? The participants responded slowly, and their decisions varied. The most important findings related to patterns of brain activity. Brain areas associated with emotion showed increased activity, as did brain areas associated with deliberate cognitive processes. Participants faced a conflict between their emotional response (i.e., the baby must be saved) and their cognitive response (i.e., as many lives as possible must be saved). Thus, their decision did *not* depend solely on cognitive processes and knowledge.

EVALUATION

➕ Kohlberg identified the major stages of moral reasoning.

➕ Children of nearly all cultures work through the stages of moral reasoning in the order predicted by Kohlberg.

➕ Certain kinds of general cognitive development must occur before a child can proceed to the next stage of moral development.

➖ Kohlberg de-emphasised the emotional and behavioural components of morality. This can be seen in his view that justice is the most important principle in moral development. This led to a neglect of other factors (e.g., sympathy; courage).

➖ People's level of moral reasoning is often higher with the imaginary scenarios used by Kohlberg than the moral dilemmas of everyday life (Walker et al., 1995). This is because "It's a lot easier to be moral when you have nothing to lose" (Walker et al., 1995, pp. 381–382).

➖ As discussed at the beginning of this chapter, an individual's level of moral reasoning sometimes predicts his/her moral behaviour poorly (e.g., Walker, 2004).

➖ As we will see shortly, Kohlberg paid insufficient attention to gender differences in morality.

Gilligan's theory

According to Gilligan, which moralities do girls and boys develop?

Carol Gilligan (1977, 1982) disliked what she regarded as the sexist bias of Kohlberg's approach. Kohlberg initially based his theory on interviews with male participants only, and so bias may have been introduced. In addition, Gilligan argued that Kohlberg's assessment of moral development was gender-biased, since most women were classified at Stage 3 of moral development, whereas men were at Stage 4.

In her own theorising, Gilligan argued that females proceed through *three* levels of moral development. At the first level, the emphasis is on survival of the self, which is essentially a selfish perspective. At the second level, an association develops between self-sacrifice and goodness. This assists girls to find their place within society. At the third level, females develop an understanding of themselves and the consequences of their actions.

Kohlberg received criticism for showing a male bias in research.

Gilligan (1982) argued that boys develop the **morality of justice**, in which the focus is on the use of laws and moral principles. In contrast, girls develop the **morality of care**, in which the focus is on human well-being and compassion for others. According to Gilligan, Kohlberg showed sexist bias by regarding the morality of justice as superior to the morality of care. More generally, Gilligan argued that theories of moral reasoning should accord equal importance to the two types of morality.

Where do these gender differences in moral reasoning come from? Gilligan and Wiggins (1987) argued they have their origins in early childhood. Women are the main caregivers in most societies, and girls learn the morality of care through their strong attachment to their mother. Boys are less attached to their mother. They tend to identify with their father, who is often perceived as an authority figure. This identification process leads boys to develop the morality of justice.

Findings

It is hard to test Gilligan's views on the origins of moral orientation. However, Benenson et al. (1998) conducted a relevant study. As predicted, young girls were more attached to their mothers than were young boys. Girls remained closer to their mothers and had more mutual eye contact with them. However, these findings don't really show that girls identify more strongly than boys with their mothers.

Jaffee and Hyde (2000) reviewed numerous studies of moral reasoning. Overall, there was a very small tendency for males to show more justice reasoning. There was a slightly larger (but still small) tendency for females to show more caring reasoning than males.

Schwartz and Rubel (2005) explored related issues in a cross-cultural study involving 70 countries. The importance of 10 basic values to men and women was assessed. The value of most relevance to care orientation was benevolence,

> **KEY TERMS**
>
> **Morality of justice:** this is a form of morality in which the individual emphasises the importance of laws and of moral principles when deciding what is morally acceptable.
>
> **Morality of care:** this is a form of morality in which the individual emphasises the importance of compassion and human well-being when deciding what is morally acceptable.

Girls learn the morality of care through their strong attachment to their mother.

which relates to the preservation and enhancement of other people's welfare. As predicted by Gilligan's theory, women regarded benevolence as slightly more important than men.

The two values in the study by Schwartz and Rubel (2005) most relevant to justice orientation were self-direction (independent thought and choice of action) and universalism (understanding, tolerance, and protection for the welfare of all). Men regarded self-direction as slightly more important than women, but they rated universalism as slightly less important than women.

In spite of the above findings, there are some interesting cultural differences. Skoe (1998) found as predicted by Gilligan that Canadian and American women between the ages of 17 and 26 showed more complex care-based understanding than men. However, there was no gender difference in care-based understanding in Norway, a culture emphasising gender equality in the workplace and in society generally.

Fumagalli et al. (2010) reported a large gender difference in moral reasoning with personal moral dilemmas requiring very emotional decisions. One problem involved a runaway trolley on a track that was going to kill five workmen. The only way to save their lives was to push a stranger over a bridge. The stranger would be killed but the workmen would survive.

What would you do in the above situation? Fumagalli et al. (2010) found men were more likely than women to decide to sacrifice the stranger because it would save four lives. That decision involves controlled cognitive processes, whereas the opposite decision (i.e., not to push the stranger over the bridge) is based on more emotional factors. These gender differences seem reasonably consistent with Gilligan's notion that males focus on justice whereas females focus on care and avoiding harming other people.

EVALUATION

⊕ As Gilligan claimed, Kohlberg exaggerated the importance of the morality of justice and minimised that of the morality of care.

⊕ There is evidence that boys have a more advanced morality of justice whereas girls have a more advanced morality of care.

⊕ Some gender differences in basic values relevant to morality have been found in numerous cultures and are mostly consistent with Gilligan's theory.

⊖ Gender differences in type of morality are typically very small.

⊖ Gilligan emphasised the cognitive component of morality at the expense of the behavioural and emotional components.

Parents, peers, and moral development

It is of theoretical and practical importance to identify the ways in which children's moral development is influenced by the people they know. The strongest influences typically come from the child's parents and his/her **peers** (children of the same age). In this section, we will consider briefly the impact parents have on their children's moral development, followed by a discussion of the role of peers.

Parents

Kelley and Power (1992) carried out several observational studies of American families. They were especially interested in how children regarded (and reacted to) various kinds of bad behaviour. They found there was much similarity between the children's reactions and those of their parents (especially the mother).

The child's early stages of moral development depend very much on its parents. Hoffman (1970) identified three major styles used by parents in the moral development of their children:

Which is the most effective of Hoffman's parenting styles for children's moral development?

1. *Induction*: Explaining why a given action is wrong, with special emphasis on its effects on other people.
2. *Power assertion*: Using spanking, removal of privileges, and harsh words to exert power over a child.
3. *Love withdrawal*: Withholding attention or love when a child behaves badly.

Brody and Shaffer (1982) reviewed studies on parental style and moral development (see the figure overleaf). Induction improved moral development in 86% of the studies. In contrast, power assertion improved moral development in only 18% and love withdrawal in 42% of the studies.

KEY TERM

Peers: children of approximately the same age as a given child.

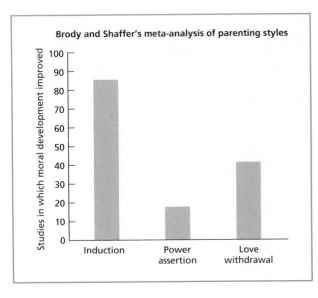

As power assertion had a negative effect on moral development in 82% of the studies, it is a very ineffective parenting style. Power assertion produces children who are aggressive and don't care about others (Zahn-Waxler et al., 1979).

Why is induction so effective? Hoffman (2001) argued it is a direct way in which parental standards can be communicated to their children. Ideally, children should be in a state of mild emotional arousal while parental induction is occurring. This increases the probability that children will continue to follow parental demands even when they aren't being observed.

Another important factor is mutually responsive orientation between mother and child. Mutually responsive orientation "is a positive, mutually binding, and mutually cooperative relationship" (Kochanska et al., 2008). Kochanska et al. (2008) found that mutually responsive orientation during the first 2 years of life strongly predicted moral behaviour at 52 months.

Why is mutually responsive orientation so important? One reason is because strong emotional bonds between mother and child increase the probability that the child will accept the mother's moral guidance. In addition, mutually responsive orientation was associated with low levels of maternal power assertion. As we saw earlier, parental power assertion has negative effects on children's moral development.

Peers

At what age are children especially influenced by peer pressure to behave antisocially?

The views of their peers often have a strong effect on children's thinking and behaviour, and this is perhaps particularly the case late in childhood and adolescence. Berndt (1979) asked children and adolescents aged 9 to 18 how likely it was they would give in to peer pressure if their friends suggested carrying out various forms of antisocial behaviour. Children of all ages were influenced by peer pressure, and this was especially the case with 15-year-olds.

Kandel (1973) found that marijuana use in adolescents depended far more on their friends than their parents. She studied marijuana use in adolescents whose parents and best friend did (or did not) use drugs. When the parents used marijuana but the best friend did not, only 17% of the adolescents smoked marijuana. In contrast, 56% of the adolescents smoked marijuana if their best friend did.

Dishion and Owen (2002) explored peer effects on substance abuse in more detail in adolescence and early adulthood. Having deviant friends increased the probability of substance abuse. In addition, however, engaging in substance abuse increased the probability of selecting deviant friends.

Schlaefli et al. (1985) considered the effects of peers on moral reasoning. They reviewed studies in which children discussed moral issues in peer groups in intensive programmes lasting between 3 and 12 weeks. There were typically substantial beneficial changes in moral development. Children initially low in

moral reasoning often showed changes similar to those found over 4 or 5 years of normal development.

More evidence that peers can have beneficial effects on moral reasoning was reported by Schonert-Reichl (1999) in a study on early adolescents aged between 10 and 13. Adolescents who had the greatest number of close friends had more advanced moral reasoning than those with relatively few close friends.

In sum, friends have strong effects on moral development and behaviour in children and adolescents. Whether these effects are positive or negative depends on the prevailing culture, the moral values of the friends, and various other factors.

Chapter summary

- Morality can be divided into cognitive, emotional, and behavioural components.
- There are often discrepancies among the three components of morality. Individuals often behave in ways they know are wrong. Conversely, people's behaviour can be more moral than they anticipated because of the emotional arousal they experience when faced by temptation.
- Kohlberg argued that moral development always proceeds in order through three levels: pre-conventional morality; conventional morality; and post-conventional or principled morality. His views have been supported in several cross-cultural studies.

- Kohlberg focused on the cognitive component of morality and de-emphasised the emotional and behavioural components.
- Gilligan argued that males develop a morality of justice whereas females develop a morality of care. This is only the case in a limited way. Males and females typically focus on both justice and the well-being of others in their moral decision making.
- Children's moral development is helped by a parenting style based on induction. In contrast, parental power assertion has negative effects.
- Mutually responsive orientation between mother and child leads to faster moral development in children.
- Peers can have a negative influence on moral behaviour (e.g., substance abuse) among adolescents.
- Adolescents who have a large number of close friends tend to have superior moral reasoning to other adolescents.

Further reading

- Berk, L.E. (2009). *Child development (9th ed.).* Boston: Allyn & Bacon. Laura Berk discusses some of the main approaches to children's moral development in this textbook.

- Eysenck, M.W. (2009). Cognitive development. In M.W. Eysenck (Ed.), *A2 level psychology*. Hove, UK: Psychology Press. A section of this chapter is devoted to the development of moral reasoning.

- Hart, D., Watson, N., Dar, A., & Atkins, R. (2011). Prosocial tendencies, antisocial behaviour, and moral development in childhood. In A. Slater & G. Bremner (Eds), *An introduction to developmental psychology (2nd ed.).* Chichester, UK: Wiley-Blackwell. Factors that aid or hinder moral development are discussed in this chapter.

Essay questions

1. What are the major components of morality? How consistently are these components related to each other?
2. Describe (and evaluate) Kohlberg's theory of moral development.
3. To what extent are there gender differences in morality?
4. Discuss the impact of parents and peers on children's moral development.

An issue of constant interest and fascination to most people concerns the differences between boys/men and girls/women. Are all the differences commonly assumed to exist between the sexes in their behaviour, abilities, and attitudes genuine or do many of them merely reflect stereotypical views?

Why do most boys and girls prefer the company of other children of the same sex? Why do boys and girls differ so much in their preferred toys? Are these differences between boys and girls due more to heredity (nature) or to environment (nurture)? These questions (and several others) are addressed in this chapter and some answers are suggested.

Sex and gender

11

When a baby is born, a key question everyone asks is, "Is it a boy or a girl?" Afterwards, how it is treated by its parents and by other people is influenced by its sex. The growing child's thoughts about itself (and its place in the world) increasingly depend on whether it is male or female. For example, most children label themselves and others accurately as male or female by the age of 2. By the age of 3, almost two-thirds of children prefer to play with children of the same sex (La Freniere et al., 1984).

From the age of 3 or 4, children have fairly fixed beliefs about the activities (e.g., housekeeping) and occupations (e.g., doctor, nurse) appropriate for males and females. These are known as **sex-role stereotypes**.

Some of the terms we will be using are as follows:

- Sex and gender: Sex refers to biological differences between boys and girls, whereas gender includes socially determined differences between them. Increasingly, however, gender is also used to refer to biological differences.
- **Gender identity**: This is an individual's awareness of being male or female.
- **Sex-typed behaviour**: This is behaviour consistent with the sex-role stereotypes within a given culture. In other words, it is the behaviour *expected* of a boy or girl.

Sex-typed behaviour typically starts at a young age. The evidence was reviewed by Martin and Ruble (2009). They found that many children were exhibiting such behaviour by around 24 months of age.

Gender identity

Egan and Perry (2001) pointed out there is more to gender identity than simply being aware that one is male or female. It also involves feeling one is a typical member of one's sex, feeling content with one's own biologically determined sex, and experiencing pressure from parents and peers (children of the same age) to conform to sex-role stereotypes.

Egan and Perry (2001) assessed the above feelings in children aged between 10 and 14. Boys had much higher scores than girls on feeling oneself

What is an individual's awareness of being male or female known as?

to be typical of one's sex, on feeling content with one's biological sex, and on experiencing pressure from others to conform to sex-role stereotypes. Thus, it is regarded as more important by children and by society at large (at least in Western cultures) for boys to conform to stereotypical views.

We have already seen that most girls prefer to play with girls and most boys prefer to play with boys. This gender segregation is present throughout childhood from about the age of 3 onwards. What causes this gender segregation? Children are motivated to develop their sense of gender identity, and can do so by playing with children of their own sex. In addition, children increasingly prefer to engage in sex-typed behaviour. This is easier to do in the company of other children of the same sex.

Observed sex differences

There are numerous sex-role stereotypes in most societies. As we have seen, even very young children start to conform to sex-role stereotypes. However, some ideas about sex-typed behaviour are (thankfully!) in steep decline. Few people accept that men should go out to work and have little to do with looking after the home and children, whereas women should stay at home caring for the children.

Some sex-role stereotypes relate to aspects of intelligence and personality. For example, it is often assumed that boys have superior spatial ability whereas girls have superior verbal ability. It is also assumed that girls have more anxious personalities than boys, and that boys are more aggressive than girls.

There has been much controversy concerning the validity of the above assumptions. For example, John Gray (1992) in his best-selling book *Men are from Mars, women are from Venus* argued that there are substantial sex differences. In contrast, Hyde (2005, p. 590) put forward the **gender similarities hypothesis**, according to which "males and females are alike on most – but not all – psychological variables".

Findings

What (if any) sex differences are there in aspects of intelligence? Hyde (2005) reviewed the evidence thoroughly. There was a very small tendency for girls to exhibit superior verbal abilities to boys. This sex difference was most obvious among children having poor verbal abilities. For example, Wheldall and Limbrick (2010) found almost *twice* as many boys as girls were poor readers. More generally, girls on average have slightly higher verbal abilities than boys and also greater academic achievement (Berk, 2006).

Hyde (2005) also found there was a small tendency for boys to outperform girls in mathematics, and this difference increased with age. Else-Quest et al. (2010) reviewed evidence from 69 countries. Overall, there was a very small tendency for boys to perform better than girls in mathematics. However, there was considerable variability from country to country. As expected, this sex difference was greatest in those countries in which men make nearly all the decisions and girls have fewer opportunities than boys.

Spatial ability

Hyde (2005) reported a consistent tendency for males to outperform females on tests of spatial ability. One of the most-used tests of spatial ability is

KEY TERM

Gender similarities hypothesis: the notion that there are only small differences between males and females with respect to the great majority of psychological variables (e.g., abilities; personality).

mental rotation, in which people imagine what would happen if an object were rotated. In a cross-cultural study involving 53 countries (Lippa et al., 2010), males did better than females in every country on mental rotation tasks.

KEY TERM

Mental rotation: a task used to assess spatial ability which involves imagining what would happen if the orientation of an object in space were altered.

There are undoubtedly various reasons for the above sex difference. However, the fact that males spend much more of their time than females playing video games is relevant (Terlecki & Newcombe, 2005). The notion that gender differences in experience on spatial tasks are important is supported by findings showing that training in spatial skills benefits females as much as males (Liu et al., 2008).

How can we explain the gender difference in mental rotation ability? It has been argued that the findings are consistent with a hunter-gatherer theory (Silverman et al., 2007). According to this theory, men in our ancestral past went out hunting and needed expert spatial skills to find their way back home. In contrast, women historically needed different spatial skills to gather plant resources. As predicted on this theory, women in 35 out of the 40 countries studied by Silverman et al. scored higher than men on memory for object locations (useful for gathering plants).

Social factors partly explain the gender difference in mental rotation. When a female gender stereotype was activated, males performed much better than females at mental rotation (Ortner & Sieverding, 2008). However, when a male gender stereotype was activated, there was no gender effect. Thus, female performance is often inhibited by the stereotypical view that females have inferior spatial ability to males.

Cherney (2008) assessed the effects of 4 hours of practice with computer games on mental rotation. Performance improved substantially on two tests of mental rotation even after this limited amount of practice. Of most importance here, the performance improvement was significantly greater for female participants than for male ones. Thus, exposure to appropriate forms of practice can reduce (or eliminate) gender differences in mental rotation.

Personality

What about sex differences in personality? Else-Quest et al. (2006) reviewed numerous studies on sex differences in children's personality. Girls scored higher than boys on effortful control, especially its dimensions of perceptual sensitivity and inhibitory control. Boys scored higher than girls on surgency (similar to extraversion), especially its dimensions of activity and high-intensity pleasure. However, these sex differences were fairly modest in size.

Schmitt et al. (2008) carried out a cross-cultural study on adult personality in 55 countries. Overall, there was a small tendency for women to be higher than men in extraversion, agreeableness, conscientiousness, and neuroticism (tendency to experience negative emotions). Of interest, these sex differences were *larger* in societies in which both sexes have reasonably equal access to education, knowledge, and economic wealth. Schmitt et al. argued that this happened because genuine sex differences in personality are more likely to be suppressed in societies with substantial constraints on women.

Theories of gender development

It is well-known that most children exhibit much sex-typed behaviour in their everyday lives. However, it has proved hard to identify the factors responsible for them acquiring such behaviour. What we will be doing is to consider some of the major theories in this area. Most of them focus on environmental factors such as the influence of the parents. However, some theorists emphasise biological factors, and we will conclude this section with a discussion of the biological approach.

Social cognitive theory

According to social cognitive theory, what does the development of gender-role behaviour involve?

In order to understand social cognitive theory, it is useful to start with an earlier theory from which it developed—social learning theory. According to social learning theory (e.g., Bandura, 1977), gender development occurs as a result of children's experiences. Children learn to behave in ways that are rewarded and to avoid behaving in ways that are punished. Since society has expectations about how boys and girls should behave, the operation of socially delivered rewards and punishments produces sex-typed behaviour. For example, parents encourage girls but not boys to play with dolls, whereas the opposite is the case with guns.

Bussey and Bandura (1999) in their social cognitive theory identified three forms of learning promoting gender development:

1. **Observational learning** or modelling: The child imitates those aspects of others' behaviour he/she believes will increase feelings of mastery. Imitation is more likely when the model is of the same sex as the child.
2. **Direct tuition**: Other people teach the child about gender identity (its awareness of being a boy or girl) and sex-typed behaviour.
3. **Enactive experience**: The child learns about sex-typed behaviour by discovering the outcomes (positive or negative) resulting from its actions.

KEY TERMS

Observational learning: learning based on watching the behaviour of others and copying behaviour that is rewarded and not copying punished behaviour.

Direct tuition: one way of increasing a child's **gender identity** and **sex-typed behaviour** by being instructed by other people.

Enactive experience: this involves the child learning which behaviours are expected of his/her gender within any given culture as a result of being rewarded or punished for behaving in different ways.

Findings

Observational learning was studied by Perry and Bussey (1979). Children of 8 or 9 watched male and female adult models choose between sex-neutral activities (e.g., selecting an apple or a pear). Afterwards, the children generally made the same choices as the same-sex model. Thus, observational learning may be important in gender development. However, Barkley et al. (1977) in an earlier review found children had a significant bias in favour of the same-sexed model in only 18 out of 81 studies.

Young children are exposed to numerous examples of sex-typed behaviour through the media (e.g., television; films). They are also exposed to sex-typed behaviour through video games, which are played by a substantial majority of children in several countries. Dill and Thill (2007) found many sex stereotypes are present in video games. For example, 33% of the male characters in video games behave in an extremely masculine way, and 62% of the female characters are "visions of beauty". In addition, more male than female characters are aggressive (83% vs. 62%, respectively).

Many studies have looked at the effects of direct tuition on gender development. Fagot and Leinbach (1989) found parents encouraged sex-typed behaviour and discouraged sex-inappropriate behaviour in their children before the age of 2. For example, girls were rewarded for playing with dolls and discouraged from climbing trees. Those parents making most use of direct tuition had children who behaved in the most sex-typed way.

Much of the evidence provides only modest support for the role of direct tuition. Golombok and Hines (2002) found in a review there was only a slight tendency for parents to encourage sex-typed behaviours and discourage sex-inappropriate ones. The review also revealed that boys and girls receive equal parental warmth, encouragement of achievement, discipline, and interaction.

It follows from social cognitive theory that children's beliefs and behaviour should be influenced by their parents' beliefs and behaviour. There is much supporting evidence. For example, Tenenbaum and Leaper (2002) found a small tendency for parents with traditional views about gender to have children with greater gender-typed beliefs about themselves.

Parents with non-traditional beliefs have children with few gender-typed beliefs about themselves. Children whose mothers were unmarried had less gender-typed knowledge than children whose mothers were married (Hupp et al., 2010). This occurred because unmarried mothers were more likely than married ones to behave in what are regarded as traditional masculine ways.

Finally, there is enactive experience, in which the reactions of others to a child's behaviour are positive or negative. For example, a child may be praised by other children for choosing to play with sex-typed toys. Kowalski (2007) studied the negative reactions of kindergarten children when a child played with a toy regarded as inappropriate. These reactions included ridicule, correction (e.g., "give that girl puppet to a girl"), and negating the child's gender identity (e.g., "Jeff is a girl"). Most children's behaviour was influenced by these positive and negative reactions.

EVALUATION

➕ Social cognitive theory correctly emphasises the social context in which gender development takes place.

➕ Factors such as observational learning, direct tuition, and enactive experience all contribute to gender development. However, their effects are sometimes fairly modest.

➖ The theory focuses mainly on children's learning of *specific* forms of behaviour. However, as we will see shortly, children also engage in *general* learning (e.g., acquiring organised beliefs about their own gender).

➖ The theory assumes that children are relatively *passive* individuals whose behaviour is strongly influenced by being rewarded and punished. There is insufficient emphasis on children's *active* contributions to their own gender development.

According to self-socialisation theory, when do children acquire gender schemas of their own sex and of the opposite sex?

Self-socialisation theory

Self-socialisation theory (e.g., Martin et al., 2004) developed out of gender schema theory (Martin & Halverson, 1987). The overarching assumption is that children acquire much *knowledge* about gender, and this knowledge strongly influences their beliefs and behaviour. Of central importance is the notion of gender identity ("I am a boy" or "I am a girl"), which is acquired at a very young age. This provides children with a major social identity.

As time goes by, children learn more detailed gender-relevant knowledge. For example, they acquire **gender schemas** consisting of organised beliefs about suitable activities and behaviour for each sex. Martin et al. (1990) argued that the development of gender schemas goes through three stages:

1. Children learn specific information associated with each gender (e.g., boys play with guns; girls play with dolls).
2. Children from 4 or 5 start linking together the different kinds of information they possess about their own gender to form more complex gender schemas. This is done *only* with respect to their own gender.
3. Children from the age of 8 form complex gender schemas of the opposite sex as well as their own.

Schema-consistent activities

Schema-inconsistent activities

What does self-socialisation theory add to social cognitive theory? According to social cognitive theory, one way young children learn sex-typed behaviour is by observing (and then copying) the behaviour of same-sex models. For this to happen, however, children must know what sex they are—they need to have acquired gender identity.

More generally, the knowledge about gender (gender identity; gender schemas) acquired by young children is crucial to gender development and to making sense of their environment. The advantage of self-socialisation theory is that it emphasises the role played by such knowledge.

Findings

Martin et al. (1990) obtained evidence that children's development of gender schemas proceeds through the three stages they had identified. Children received a description of someone of unspecified sex who had a specific sex-typed characteristic (e.g., worked as a nurse). The children were then asked to predict other characteristics the person was likely to possess.

Martin et al. (1990) found that younger children performed poorly on this task because they hadn't reached stage 2 in the development of gender schemas. Somewhat older children performed better when the gender-linked characteristic was appropriate to their own gender because they were more

KEY TERM

Gender schemas: organised knowledge stored in long-term memory in the form of numerous beliefs about the forms of behaviour that are appropriate for each sex.

Boys and girls tend to prefer different toys—is this nature or nurture?

likely to have reached stage 2. Children aged 8 or more had reached stage 3 and so performed well regardless of whether the gender-linked characteristic was appropriate to their own gender.

According to self-socialisation theory, much sex-typed behaviour is influenced by gender identity. Since children show sex-typed behaviour at an early age (often by 2 years), it follows that basic gender identity should also develop early. There is much support for this prediction (Martin & Ruble, 2009). For example, Zosuls et al. (2009) found that 68% of children (especially girls) used gender labels (e.g., "boys"; "girl") by 21 months of age.

Gender identity and sex-typed behaviour

Another prediction from the theory is that children who have acquired gender identity should show more sex-typed behaviour than those who have not. This prediction was also supported in the study by Zosuls et al. (2009). Boys who used gender labels were more likely than other boys to play with trucks rather than dolls, whereas the opposite was the case for girls.

Trautner et al. (2005) provided mixed support for the same prediction. They studied children over a 5-year period from kindergarten onwards. Boys' gender knowledge predicted the extent to which they *preferred* sex-typed toys and activities (e.g., trucks; car washing). It also predicted their *avoidance* of toys and activities associated with girls (e.g., dolls; cooking). Of interest, girls' gender knowledge was much less predictive of their preferred (and avoided) toys and activities, perhaps because they perceived that boys' toys and activities are generally more highly regarded.

The studies by Zosuls et al. (2009) and by Trautner et al. (2005) showed that gender knowledge is associated with sex-typed behaviour. However, that doesn't prove the former helps to cause the latter. A more direct approach involves *manipulating* the gender labels given to objects. Bradbard et al. (1986) presented boys and girls with gender-neutral objects such as burglar alarms and pizza cutters. They were told that some were "boy" objects whereas others were "girl" objects. Finally, the children's object preferences were assessed.

What did Bradbard et al. (1986) find? First, children spent much more time playing with objects they had been told were appropriate to their gender. Second, even a week later, the children remembered whether any given object was a "boy" or a "girl" object.

Subsequent research has confirmed Bradbard et al.'s (1986) findings (Martin & Ruble, 2009). However, the impact of gender labels on object preferences is generally greater for boys than for girls. This probably happens because children believe boys' toys are more exciting than girls' toys.

EVALUATION

➕ The assumption that even young children are actively involved in making sense of the world based on their schema-based knowledge is plausible and supported by much evidence.

➕ Children's knowledge in the form of gender identity and gender schemas often influences their actions (e.g., sex-typed behaviour).

➖ The association between gender identity and behaviour is often not very strong. As Bussey and Bandura (1999, p. 679) pointed out, "Children do not categorize themselves as 'I am a girl' or 'I am a boy' and act in accordance with that schema across situations."

➖ The extent to which children show sex-typed behaviour doesn't depend *only* on gender knowledge. It also depends on the accessibility of that knowledge, and the attractiveness of objects.

➖ The theory de-emphasises the role of social factors in gender development.

Biological theories

There are various biological differences between boys and girls, some of which are more obvious than others. For example, there are hormonal differences between the sexes at a very early stage of development. The male sex hormone testosterone is present in greater amounts in male than female foetuses from about 6 weeks, whereas the opposite is the case for the female sex hormone oestrogen (see Durkin, 1995). These hormonal differences may play a role in gender development.

It is very hard to disentangle the effects of biological and social factors in influencing gender development. The reason is that there are systematic biological *and* social differences between boys and girls. In principle, the best approach would be to study individuals who are biologically boys but treated as girls or biological girls treated as boys. Approximations to this approach are discussed below.

Findings

There is a rare condition in which children are biologically male, but their external genitals appear female and they are treated as girls. At puberty, they develop male genitals and start to look like ordinary adolescent males. Several such cases have been studied in the Dominican Republic where they are known as *Guevedoces* (penis at 12).

Imperato-McGinley et al. (1974) studied the Batista family in the Dominican Republic. Four of the sons were *Guevedoces* and all were raised as girls during childhood, and thought of themselves as females. In spite of that, they all adjusted to the male role in adolescence. According to Gross (1996, p. 584), "They have all taken on male roles, do men's jobs, have married women and are accepted as men."

Zhu and Imperato-McGinley (2008) reported on a larger sample of 18 males with the same condition. They reported that 17 of them (94%) managed successfully to change their gender identity from female to male. This change occurred on average at the age of 16.

In sum, the findings discussed in this section indicate that gender identity doesn't *always* depend on social factors. In spite of being treated as females throughout childhood, the great majority of *Guevedoces* are able to develop a male gender identity in adolescence.

Congenital adrenal hyperplasia

There is another condition known as **congenital adrenal hyperplasia**. This is a genetic disease in which the foetus is exposed to high levels of male sex hormones. What generally happens is that steps are taken to normalise these hormonal levels at birth. While this disease can affect boys and girls, most research has focused on girls. Why is this? The reason is that in girls there is a *conflict* between their social experiences (i.e., being reared as a girl) and their early high exposure to male sex hormones. As a result, we can establish which factor has more impact on behaviour.

Berenbaum and Beltry (2011) reviewed the evidence concerning girls with congenital adrenal hyperplasia. Their behaviour is influenced by their exposure to male sex hormones. For example, they play more than other girls with boys' toys and less with girls' toys. When they grow up, women with congenital adrenal hyperplasia are more likely than other women to choose male-dominant professions (30% vs. 13%) (Frisén et al., 2009). They are also more likely to like rough sports (74% vs. 50%), and to have a non-heterosexual orientation (19% vs. 2%).

Why do girls and women with congenital adrenal hyperplasia behave more like boys and men than most girls and women? The obvious answer is that it is due to their prenatal exposure to male sex hormones. In other words, biological factors can have a substantial impact on gender identity.

An alternative explanation is that the parents of females with congenital adrenal hyperplasia encourage them to have male-type interests and behaviour. However, the evidence does *not* support this explanation. Pasterski et al. (2005) studied children between the ages of 3 and 10. Parents encouraged their daughters with congenital adrenal hyperplasia to play with girls' toys. Indeed, they provided more positive feedback than parents of normal girls when their daughters played with girls' toys.

KEY TERM

Congenital adrenal hyperplasia: an inherited disorder of the adrenal gland causing the levels of male sex hormones in foetuses of both sexes to be unusually high.

EVALUATION

➕ Most of the evidence indicates that biological factors play a role in gender development.

➕ It is hard to provide a social or environmental interpretation of the male interests and behaviour of girls and women with congenital adrenal hyperplasia.

➖ The participants in most of the research have been individuals with very rare conditions. This makes it difficult to know whether the findings apply to the general population.

➖ The biological approach can't account for the impact of social factors on gender development or for cross-cultural differences. For example Wood and Eagly (2002) studied 181 non-industrialised cultures. Men were dominant in 67% of those cultures, women were dominant in 3%, and neither sex was dominant in the remaining 30%. These cross-cultural differences are almost certainly due to environmental influences rather than biological ones.

Masculinity and femininity

It has sometimes been assumed that masculine qualities (based on an instrumental or achieving role) and feminine qualities (based on an expressive or communal role) are mutually exclusive. In other words, any given individual possesses *either* masculine qualities *or* feminine ones.

It has also often been assumed that men are most likely to be psychologically well-adjusted if they possess mainly masculine qualities whereas women should possess mainly feminine qualities. According to this congruence model, individuals who develop characteristics typically associated with the opposite sex are likely to develop an insecure and confused gender identity.

Bem (e.g., 1985) disagreed with both of these assumptions. She argued that it is perfectly possible for someone to possess the main masculine *and* the main feminine characteristics. Such a person would be assertive and independent much of the time, but would also be caring and supportive as and when appropriate. **Androgyny** describes someone who has both masculine and feminine characteristics.

Bem (1985) argued that androgynous individuals would have greater psychological well-being than individuals showing traditional sex-role behaviour. Androgynous individuals have the advantage of being able to handle situations flexibly, using the masculine or feminine side of their personalities as appropriate.

Other theorists (e.g., Adams & Sherer, 1985) put forward the masculinity model. According to this model, society values distinctively masculine qualities (e.g., assertiveness) more than feminine qualities. As a result, individuals

KEY TERM

Androgyny: used to describe an individual who possesses a mixture or combination of masculine and feminine characteristics.

(whether male or female) are likely to have greater psychological well-being if they possess many masculine qualities.

What is Bem's term for those who are high on both masculinity and femininity?

How can we assess masculinity, femininity, and androgyny? One of the most-used measures is the Personal Attributes Questionnaire (Spence et al., 1974), which contains masculine and feminine trait terms. Individuals are assigned to four categories:

* *Androgynous*: high on masculinity; high on femininity.
* *Masculine sex-typed*: high on masculinity; low on femininity.
* *Feminine sex-typed*: low on masculinity; high on femininity.
* *Undifferentiated*: low on masculinity; low on femininity.

Findings

There is some support for all three models (congruence; androgyny; masculinity). However, most of the support for the masculinity model was obtained several years ago. For example, Whitley (1985) found that males and females with masculine characteristics were less likely to suffer from depression. Adams and Sherer (1985) found generally superior psychological adjustment in males and females high in masculinity.

Bassoff and Glass (1982) reviewed 26 studies on mental health. Androgynous individuals on average had better mental health than those high in femininity. However, the mental health of androgynous individuals was no better than that of individuals high in masculinity. Thus, it seemed that high masculinity rather than androgyny itself was important for mental health.

Why was the possession of masculine characteristics so beneficial for psychological well-being? An important part of the answer was suggested in research by Williams and Best (1990). They asked students in 14 countries to describe their "current self" and their "ideal self". Men and women both included more masculine than feminine characteristics in their ideal self than in their current self. Thus, masculine characteristics were previously regarded more highly than feminine ones.

More recent research has provided support for the androgyny model, suggesting we now live in a less masculine-dominated world. Cheng (2005) studied students coping with stressful situations during their first 3 months at university. She found that appropriate coping strategies were used most often by androgynous students.

What are the effects of androgyny on mental health? Lefkowitz and Zeldow (2006) found that high masculinity and high femininity were both associated with good mental health. Those high in both masculinity and femininity (androgynous individuals) had the greatest mental health. In similar fashion, Flett et al. (2009) found that depressed patients tended to have low levels of both masculinity and femininity.

Finally, there is limited support for the congruence model in the area of sexual attraction. Udry and Chantala (2004) studied adolescents, arguing that they would be attracted to members of the opposite sex whose personalities differed considerably from their own. In other words, "exotic is erotic". Udry and Chantala found that couples were most likely to have sex (and to do so earlier in the relationship) when the boy was high in masculinity and the girl was high in femininity.

EVALUATION

⊕ As Bem (1974) claimed, many people are androgynous. For example, Spence and Helmreich (1978) found that 30% of American students fell into that category.

⊕ Bem's androgyny model has become increasingly relevant as traditional ideas about male superiority are consigned to the dustbin of history. For example, androgynous individuals nowadays have superior psychological well-being to other people.

⊖ More needs to be done to work out when the congruence model predicts behaviour better than the androgyny model.

⊖ Most research has been carried out in Western societies. Conceptions of masculinity and femininity may well be rather different in non-Western societies.

Chapter summary

- Sex-role stereotypes provide an increasingly oversimplified view of gender differences.
- Girls have slightly greater verbal ability than boys, but lower mathematical and spatial ability.
- Women on average are higher than men in extraversion, agreeableness, conscientiousness, and neuroticism.
- According to social cognitive theory, gender development depends on observational learning, direct tuition, and enactive experience (positive or negative outcomes).
- Social cognitive theory de-emphasises the acquisition of gender knowledge and children's active engagement in gender development.
- According to self-socialisation theory, young children acquire detailed gender knowledge (e.g., gender identity; gender schemas).
- Gender knowledge predicts the extent to which children exhibit sex-typed behaviour.
- Sex-typed behaviour also depends on situational demands and toy attractiveness.
- Most biological males who are reared as females until adolescence adjust successfully to the male role.
- Girls exposed to high levels of male sex hormones in the womb are more likely than other girls to have a non-heterosexual orientation and to pursue male-dominant professions.
- Biological theories fail to account for the impact of social and cultural factors on gender development.
- It is often assumed that masculine qualities involve an instrumental or achieving role whereas feminine qualities involve an expressive

or communal role. However, androgynous individuals combine masculine and feminine qualities.

- Early research indicated that masculinity was associated with the greatest psychological and physical well-being. However, recent research suggests that androgyny is associated with the greatest well-being.

Further reading

- Bem, S.L. (1993). *The lenses of gender: Transforming the debate on sexual inequality*. New Haven: Yale University Press. Sandra Bem provides a coherent overview of her influential views on androgyny.

- Berenbaum, S.A., & Beltry, A.M. (2011). Sexual differentiation of human behaviour: Effects of prenatal and pubertal organisational hormones. *Frontiers in Neuroendocrinology*, *32*, 183–200. The authors review and evaluate research on biological factors influencing gender development.

- Hyde, J.S. (2005). The gender similarities hypothesis. *American Psychologist*, *60*, 581–592. In this review, Janet Hyde claims that most research indicates that gender differences are much smaller than is often supposed.

- Martin, C.L., & Ruble, D.N. (2009). Patterns of gender development. *Annual Review of Psychology*, *61*, 353–381. This chapter provides a good overview of theory and research in the area of gender development.

Essay questions

1. Describe the biological approach to understanding gender development. How successful has this approach been?

2. In what ways do boys and girls think and behave similarly? In what ways do they think and behave differently?

3. Compare and contrast the social cognitive and self-socialisation theories of gender development.

4. "Androgynous individuals have superior mental health to non-androgynous individuals." Discuss.

Part 4

Social approach

This section is devoted to social psychology, which is, "The scientific investigation of how the thoughts, feelings and behaviour of individuals are influenced by the actual, imagined or implied presence of others" (Hogg & Vaughan, 2005, p. 655).

You may have noticed that you can run faster when competing with a friend than when alone—this means your performance has been affected by the presence of another person. You may have laughed at a joke because your friends did even though you didn't really understand it. Thus, others can influence our behaviour even though no-one asked you to behave differently.

Chapter 12 • Attachment and deprivation

The vital importance of loving attachments to young children (and the potentially devastating effects of being deprived of such attachments) are discussed.

Chapter 13 • Prejudice and discrimination

The reasons why some people are prejudiced against other groups are discussed, together with practical suggestions for reducing prejudice.

Chapter 14 • Pro-social behaviour

Some of the reasons why we often help other people (but sometimes fail to!) are discussed in this chapter.

Chapter 15 • Social influence

The surprising extent to which most of us conform to the behaviour of others and obey authority is shown and reasons why social influence is so strong are identified.

Chapter 16 • Social perception and attraction

Reasons why we find some people more attractive than others are discussed as are how we decide what motivates other people to behave in the ways they do.

Most infants develop a close attachment to their mother and this plays a major role in their emotional development. There are various reasons why this might happen. Do you think that this attachment happens naturally or does it depend on the nature of the interactions between mother and infant? The attachments that a child forms with its parents can be disrupted by events such as day care and divorce. What factors do you think might determine whether children are able to cope successfully with such events?

Attachment and deprivation

12

Infants rapidly start to learn about other people and the world in which they live. Some of the most important aspects of this early learning are in the area of emotion. In this chapter, we will focus on factors influencing children's emotional development. This will include a consideration of the factors helping such development. It will also include some of the factors (e.g., separation; parental divorce) that make it harder for children to develop close bonds with other people.

Attachment

A key feature of emotional development is attachment. Attachment is "a close emotional relationship between two persons, characterised by mutual affection and a desire to maintain proximity [closeness]" (Shaffer, 1993).

In the great majority of cases, the main attachment of the infant is to its mother. However, strong attachments can be formed to other people with whom the infant has regular contact. Weston and Main (1981) found among 44 infants that 12 were securely attached to both parents, 11 were securely attached only to their mothers, and 10 were securely attached only to their fathers. The importance of the first attachment that infants form in early childhood is that it sets the scene for their lifelong social and emotional involvement with others.

Bowlby (1969, 1988) argued that the development of attachment involves five phases:

1. The infant responds in a similar way to everyone.
2. At around 5 months, the infant starts to *discriminate* among other people (e.g., smiling mainly at his/her mother).
3. At around 7 months, the infant remains close to his/her mother or caregiver. He/she shows "separation protest" by becoming upset when the mother leaves.
4. From the age of 3 years, the child takes account of the caregiver's needs.
5. From the age of 5 years, the child has an internal representation of the child–caregiver relationships. As a result, the attachment remains strong even when the child doesn't see the caregiver for some time.

According to Ainsworth, most American infants exhibit which type of attachment to their mothers?

Attachment types

If we are to achieve a full understanding of the attachment between mother and child, we need to have valid ways of measuring it. Ainsworth and Bell (1970) developed the Strange Situation test. The infant (typically about 12 months old) is observed during eight short episodes. Some of the time the infant is with its mother whereas at other times it is with its mother and a stranger, just with a stranger, or entirely on its own.

The child's reactions to the stranger, to separation from the mother, and especially to being reunited with its mother, are all recorded in the Strange Situation test. These reactions allow the infant's attachment to its mother to be assigned to one of three categories:

1. **Secure attachment:** The infant is distressed by the mother's absence, but rapidly returns to contentment after the mother's return, immediately seeking contact with her. There is a clear difference in reaction to the mother and to the stranger. About 70% of American infants show secure attachment.
2. **Resistant attachment:** The infant is insecure in the presence of the mother, becomes very distressed and resists contact when she returns, and is wary of the stranger. About 10% of American infants are resistant.
3. **Avoidant attachment:** The infant doesn't seek contact with the mother, shows little distress when separated from her, and avoids contact with her when she returns. The infant treats the stranger similarly to the mother. About 20% of American infants are avoidant.

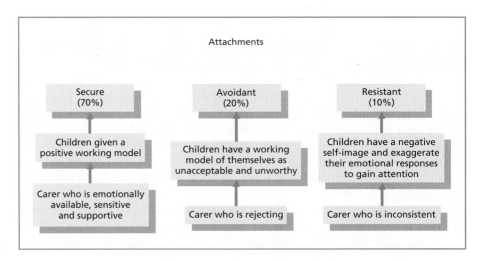

Ainsworth and Bell's (1970) attachment types.

Main et al. (1985) identified a fourth type of attachment behaviour in the Strange Situation: disorganised and disoriented attachment. Infants with this type of attachment lacked any coherent strategy for coping with the Strange Situation; their behaviour was a confusing mixture of approach and avoidance.

Dimensional approach

It is neat and tidy to assign all children to three or four attachment categories. However, reality isn't neat and tidy. For example, two children might both be classified as showing avoidant attachment, but one might display much more avoidant behaviour. We can take account of such individual differences by using *dimensions* (going from very low to very high) instead of *categories*. Fraley and Spieker (2003) identified two dimensions of attachment (see the figure below):

1. *Avoidant/withdrawal vs. proximity-seeking strategies*: This is concerned with the extent to which the child tries to maintain physical closeness with his/her mother.
2. *Angry and resistant strategies vs. emotional confidence*: This is concerned with the child's emotional reactions to the attachment figure's behaviour.

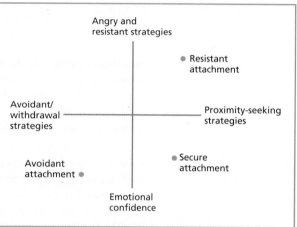

As can be seen in the figure, secure, resistant, and avoidant attachment all fit into this two-dimensional framework. Why is this approach preferable to the categorical one put forward by Ainsworth and Bell (1970)? It provides a more accurate assessment of each child's attachment behaviour because it takes more account of small individual differences in attachment behaviour.

The locations of secure, resistant, and avoidant attachments within a two-dimensional framework (proximity seeking vs. avoidance/withdrawal, angry and resistant vs. emotional confidence).

Cross-cultural differences

So far we have focused on findings obtained mainly from middle-class American culture. Are there important cultural differences in child attachment? This issue was addressed by Sagi et al. (1991) using the Strange Situation test with infants in the United States, Israel, Japan, and Germany.

The findings of Sagi et al. (1991) are shown in the figure overleaf. German infants were the ones least likely to be securely attached but most likely to be anxious and avoidant. Why was this? Grossman et al. (1985) found that Germans parents prefer infants to be independent, non-clinging, and obedient.

None of the Japanese infants was avoidant. This may have happened because Japanese mothers in the 1980s practically never left their infants alone with a stranger. As a result, the infants in the Strange Situation were faced with the totally new experience of being on their own with a stranger. Very few Israeli infants were avoidant. These infants lived on a kibbutz (collective farm) and were looked after by strangers much of the time. However, they had a close relationship with their mothers, and so tended not to be avoidant.

We mustn't exaggerate cultural differences in attachment. Van IJzendoorn and Kroonenberg (1988) analysed numerous studies using the Strange

Which type of attachment to their mothers is exhibited by very few Japanese infants?

Children from different countries vary in their attachment types. The graph summarises research from Sagi et al. (1991).

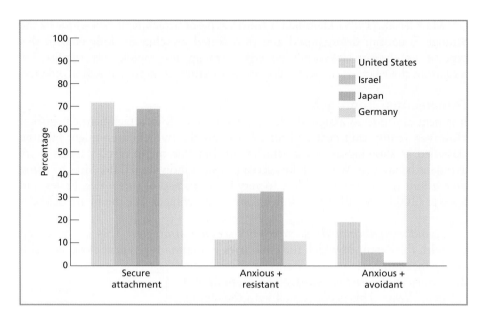

Situation. Variations in findings *within* countries were much greater than the variations *between* countries. Thus, it would be misleading to assume that there is a single culture in the UK, the United States, or most other countries.

Theories of attachment

Why do some infants have a secure attachment with their mothers, whereas others do not? Ainsworth et al. (1978) put forward the maternal sensitivity hypothesis, according to which the sensitivity of the mother (or other caregiver) is of crucial importance. Most mothers of securely attached children are very sensitive to their needs, and are emotionally expressive.

De Wolff and van IJzendoorn (1997) reviewed research on the maternal sensitivity hypothesis. There was a positive (but fairly weak) association between maternal sensitivity and security of infant attachment. Other aspects of mothers' behaviour of only indirect relevance to maternal sensitivity were also important. These included stimulation (any action of the mother directed at her baby) and attitude (mother's expressions of positive emotion to her baby).

The maternal sensitivity hypothesis exaggerates the mother's role. De Wolff and van IJzendoorn (1997) reviewed studies in which the *father's* sensitivity had been assessed. There was a positive association between paternal sensitivity and infant's security of attachment to the father. However, it was smaller than the association between maternal sensitivity and security of infant–mother attachment.

Temperament hypothesis

The maternal sensitivity hypothesis ignores the role played by the infant him/herself. Kagan (1984) put forward the temperament hypothesis, according to which the infant's temperament or personality influences its attachment to its mother. Belsky and Rovine (1987) reported supporting evidence. Newborns showing signs of behavioural instability (e.g., tremors or shaking) were less likely than other newborns to become securely attached to their mother.

We can study the role of children's personal characteristics (e.g., personality) in influencing attachment by studying pairs of identical twins (sharing 100% of their genes) and fraternal twins (sharing 50% of their genes). If the child's genetically-influenced characteristics influence his/her attachment style, identical twins should show more agreement in attachment style than fraternal twins. O'Connor and Croft (2001) found support for this hypothesis, suggesting that genetic factors influence young children's attachment type.

If attachment type depends on infants' personality, we might expect that attachment type would be the same with their father as with their mother. In fact, however, this is only the case to a modest extent (De Wolff & van IJzendoorn, 1997). This suggests that an infant's attachment to its mother/father depends mainly on its parents' behaviour.

Gene–environment interaction

The theories discussed so far are oversimplified. We can see this by considering a study by Spangler et al. (2009) on 12-month-olds. Disorganised attachment was found mostly in infants who had specific genes. However, this genetic influence was found only among infants with unresponsive mothers. Thus, disorganised attachment depends on a complex interaction between genes and maternal responsiveness—this is known as a gene–environment interaction.

EVALUATION

➕ Most researchers have obtained support for the three attachment types described by Ainsworth.

➕ Attachment type in infancy influences later emotional and social development. Elicker et al. (1992) found that social interactions at school could be predicted from behaviour in the Strange Situation several years earlier.

➖ The maternal sensitivity and temperament hypotheses are limited, because maternal sensitivity and the infant's temperament both influence attachment type (Spangler, 1990).

➖ Most theories are oversimplified because they don't consider complex interactions (e.g., gene–environment interactions) between the factors influencing attachment type.

➖ There are important cross-cultural differences in attachment behaviour. However, we don't yet have a clear understanding of the factors producing these differences.

According to Bowlby's maternal deprivation hypothesis, what are the effects of a breaking of the maternal bond, and how serious are they?

Effects of deprivation

So far we have looked at the factors influencing the nature of the attachment that an infant forms with its mother or caregiver. In the real world, unfortunately, there are several events (e.g., divorce, death of a parent) that can *disrupt* an infant's attachments or even prevent them being formed in the first place. In this section, we will consider the effects on infants of being separated from the most important adult(s) in their lives.

Maternal deprivation hypothesis and beyond

A very influential theory dealing with the effects of separation on children was put forward by the child psychoanalyst John Bowlby (1907–1990). Bowlby (1951) argued that "an infant and young child should experience a warm, intimate and continuous relationship with his mother (or permanent mother-figure) in which both find satisfaction and enjoyment".

No one would disagree with the above statement. However, Bowlby (1951) also proposed the more controversial **maternal deprivation hypothesis**. According to this hypothesis, a breaking of the maternal bond with the child early in life often (but not always) has serious effects on its intellectual, social, and emotional development. He also claimed that these negative effects of maternal deprivation were permanent or irreversible in 25% of children.

Bowlby made two other important assumptions. First, he argued in his **monotropy hypothesis** that infants form only *one* strong attachment (typically with the mother). Second, he argued there is a **critical period** during which the infant's attachment to the mother or caregiver must occur. This critical period ends at some point between 1 and 3 years of age. After that, it isn't possible to establish a powerful attachment to the mother or caregiver.

Rutter (1981) argued that Bowlby's ideas were oversimplified in three main ways. First, he claimed it is important to distinguish between deprivation and privation. **Deprivation** occurs when a child has formed a close attachment and is then separated from the major attachment figure. **Privation** occurs when a child has never formed a close attachment with anyone. Rutter argued that privation is more serious than deprivation. He reanalysed some of Bowlby's own data, and showed that many of the effects Bowlby had attributed to deprivation were actually due to privation.

Second, Rutter disagreed with Bowlby's notion that deprivation *necessarily* causes long-term difficulties. Instead, Rutter suggested that the effects of deprivation depend very much on the precise *reasons* for the separation.

Third, Rutter (1981) was sceptical of Bowlby's assumption that the negative effects of long-term maternal deprivation can be very hard to reverse. Rutter argued that these effects can generally be reversed provided that deprived children are placed with a loving family.

Findings

Bowlby's theorising was based in part on the work of Spitz (1945) and Goldfarb (1947). Spitz visited very poor orphanages and other institutions in South America. Most of the children received little attention or warmth from the staff. As a result, they became apathetic and suffered from helplessness and loss of appetite.

KEY TERMS

Maternal deprivation hypothesis: the notion that a breaking of the bond between child and mother during the first few years typically has serious long-term effects.

Monotropy hypothesis: Bowlby's notion that infants have an innate tendency to form special bonds with one person (generally the mother).

Critical period: according to the **maternal deprivation hypothesis**, a period early in life during which infants must form a strong attachment if their later development is to be satisfactory.

Deprivation: the state of a child who has formed a close attachment to someone (e.g., its mother) but is later separated from that person; see **privation**.

Privation: the state of a child who has never formed a close attachment with another person; see **deprivation**.

Goldfarb (1947) compared two groups of infants from a poor and inadequately staffed orphanage. One group consisted of infants who spent only the first few months of their lives in the orphanage before being fostered. The other group consisted of infants who spent 3 years at the orphanage before being fostered. Those children who had spent longest in the orphanage did less well than the others on intelligence tests at all ages up to 12, they were more often loners, and they were more likely to be aggressive.

Does research support Bowlby's maternal deprivation hypothesis?

It is hard to interpret the findings of Spitz and of Goldfarb. It is possible that maternal deprivation was responsible for the negative effects. However, it is equally likely that these effects were due to deficiencies in the orphanages, which provided very little stimulation for the children.

Bowlby argued that separation from the mother is damaging to children whatever the underlying reasons. Contrary evidence was reported by Rutter (1970). He studied boys aged between 9 and 12 years of age deprived of their mothers for a period of time when they were younger. Some of these boys were well-adjusted but others were not. The well-adjusted boys had been separated because of factors such as housing problems or physical illness. In contrast, the maladjusted boys had mostly been separated because of family problems (e.g., psychiatric illness). Thus, family discord rather than simply separation causes problems for children.

Bowlby assumed the negative effects of maternal deprivation are often irreversible. Evidence disproving that assumption was reported by Tizard (1977) and by Hodges and Tizard (1989) in a study of privation. They considered children who had spent the first 2–7 years of their lives in an institution. On average, each child had been looked after by 24 different caregivers by the age of 2. In spite of this, the children had an average IQ of 105 (above the population average) at the age of 4½. These children suffered less than those in the studies by Goldfarb (1947) and Spitz (1945) because the institutions in which they had lived were markedly better.

Tizard also considered the children's progress at the ages of 8 and 16. Some had returned to their own families whereas others had been adopted. Most of the adopted children had formed close relationships with their adoptive parents. This was less true of the children who had returned to their own families. This was because their parents were often not sure they really wanted to have their children back. Both groups of children tended to show attention-seeking behaviour at school and were over-friendly. As a result, they weren't very popular.

Hodges and Tizard (1989) found the family relationships of the adopted children at the age of 16 were as good as those of ordinary families. However, the 16-year-olds who had returned to their families showed little affection for their parents and their parents weren't very affectionate to them. Both groups were less likely than other children to have a special friend or to regard other adolescents as sources of emotional support.

The important research of Tizard and his colleagues showed that the long-term effects of separation depend very much on what happens *following* a period of deprivation or privation. The love and involvement provided by adoptive parents can do much to allow deprived children to develop close relationships and to become well-adjusted. However, if deprived children are returned to their own families when they aren't wanted, the outlook is much less favourable.

In sum, we have considered some research that appears to support Bowlby's maternal deprivation hypothesis and other research that does not. There is a summary of both types of research in the figure below.

We conclude this section by considering Bowlby's monotropy hypothesis, according to which children form a strong attachment with only one person. Schaffer and Emerson (1964) found 59% of infants had formed more than one strong attachment by 10 months, a figure that rose to 87% by 18 months. At the older age, only half the infants were attached mainly to their mother, with 30% being attached mainly to their father. Thus, relatively few children only have a strong attachment to their mother as assumed by Bowlby.

Extreme privation

We have seen that the adverse effects of maternal deprivation are generally reversible. We turn now to privation, in which children have never experienced a close and loving relationship with anyone. Extreme privation occurs when such children spend several years in terrible conditions before being adopted. In line with Bowlby's theoretical approach, it would be predicted that such children would suffer irreversible damage. Surprisingly, that is often *not* the case.

Koluchová (1976) studied twin boys (Andrei and Vanya) who had spent most of their first 7 years locked in a cellar. They had been treated very badly

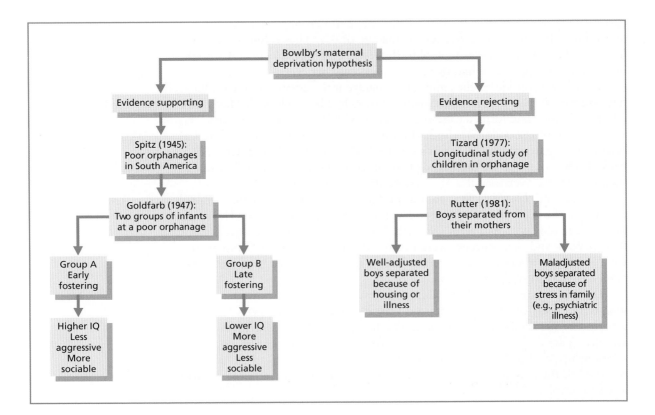

News reports in the 1980s highlighted deprivation in Romanian orphanages, with many children becoming depressed, having received basic sustenance but little human warmth or contact.

and were often beaten. They could barely talk and relied mainly on gestures. The twins were adopted by very dedicated women at about the age of 9.

What happened to the twins after adoption? By the time they were 14, their behaviour was essentially normal. By the age of 20, they were of above-average intelligence and had excellent relationships with their foster family. They took further education and both married and had children.

The findings obtained by Koluchová (1976) are very encouraging, but it would be dangerous to draw general conclusions based on a sample size of two. However, broadly similar findings have been reported by Michael Rutter and his colleagues in very thorough research on much larger samples of children. They studied Romanian children who spent the early months or years of their lives in very poor institutions in Romania receiving very little attention or care. These children were subsequently adopted by caring British families, and were tested several times up to the age of 15.

We will consider four main findings from the above study:

1. Most of these Romanian children showed substantial catch-up in their social and intellectual development in the first few years after adoption (O'Connor et al., 2000).
2. The outcomes varied very much from child to child (Rutter et al., 2010). Most children recovered almost totally from their institutional experiences, but a minority did not.
3. There were surprisingly few long-term negative effects of early institutionalisation on emotional development, behavioural problems, or interactions with children of their own age. These findings are totally inconsistent with Bowlby's maternal deprivation hypothesis.
4. A minority of these children showed various problems (Kumsta et al., 2010). These included cognitive impairment, excessive friendliness with complete strangers, inattention, and overactivity.

> **OVERALL EVALUATION**
>
> ⊕ Children's early experiences often have long-term effects on their social and emotional development.
>
> ⊕ Rutter's assumption that the adverse effects of privation are greater than those of deprivation has received support.
>
> ⊕ Rutter's assumption that most of the negative effects of maternal deprivation can be reversed is strongly supported by research.
>
> ⊕ Rutter's argument that the effects of deprivation depend on the reasons for the separation is correct.
>
> ⊖ Bowlby exaggerated the importance of the attachment between infant and mother. Most young children have formed more than one strong attachment.
>
> ⊖ Bowlby de-emphasised the extent to which a loving environment can reverse the adverse effects of earlier deprivation or privation.

Effects of divorce and day care

Some major sources of disruption in children's attachments in Western societies (and in many other cultures) have become much more common in recent decades. For example, fewer than 5% of marriages in the United Kingdom ended in divorce 50 years ago. Nowadays the figure is 40% and it is even higher in the United States.

There has also been a large increase in the number of young children put into day care for several days a week while their mothers are at work. In the United States, 80% of children under the age of 6 spend an average of 40 hours in non-parent care every week. The effects of divorce and day care on children's well-being are the focus of this section.

Divorce

Divorce involves a series of stages, each of which requires children to adjust. First, there are marital conflicts that are distressing to children. Second, there is the actual separation followed by divorce. Third, children often have to cope with moving house and reacting to new relationships as their parents find new partners and perhaps remarry.

Hetherington et al. (1982) reported the effects of divorce on 4-year-old children over a 2-year period. The first year after the divorce was the **crisis phase**. During that time, mothers became stricter and less affectionate than before. In return, the children (especially boys) behaved in more aggressive and challenging ways. During this first year, the fathers became less strict and often gave treats to their children.

The **adjustment phase** was usually reached about 2 years after divorce. There was more routine and order about the children's everyday lives. In

According to Hetherington et al. (1982), what typically happens in the period following divorce?

KEY TERMS

Crisis phase: this is the first period following divorce; during this phase, the mother is less affectionate than usual.

Adjustment phase: this is the second period after divorce; it follows the crisis phase and is marked by less emotional distress than that phase.

addition, the mothers had returned to treating their children in a more patient and understanding way. Overall, there was less emotional distress than during the crisis phase. However, the boys of divorced parents had worse relations and showed more disobedient behaviour than boys whose parents hadn't divorced.

How negative are the long-term effects of divorce? O'Connor et al. (1999) found women who had experienced divorce in childhood were more likely to be severely depressed than those whose parents hadn't divorced. Hetherington and Kelly (2002) found 25% of children with divorced parents had serious long-term social, emotional, or psychological problems. The comparable figure was 10% for children whose parents hadn't divorced. Wallerstein (1984) found that even 10 years after a divorce, the children involved regarded the divorce as the most stressful event in their lives.

Parents who divorce don't only provide their children with a hard and stressful home environment. They also provide their children's genes. It is thus possible that some negative effects of divorce on children may be due to the genes they have inherited rather than the experience of divorce itself. O'Connor et al. (2003) studied children at genetic risk because their parents had anxious personalities. This genetic risk strongly predicted poor adjustment in children whose parents had separated but not in those that had remained together. Thus, the negative effects of parental separation were much greater on children at genetic risk.

The negative effects of divorce depend in part on how old the child was at the time of the divorce (Lansford, 2009). Children experience more behavioural problems if they are relatively young at the time of divorce. However, they experience more problems with academic achievement and with romantic relationships if they are older when their parents divorce.

In sum, the great majority of children experience the divorce of their parents as extremely stressful. Adults whose parents divorced when they were children are more vulnerable than other adults to various emotional and psychological problems including depression. However, some of this vulnerability is due to the genes these adults inherited from their parents rather than to the divorce itself.

What are the short- and long-term effects of divorce on girls and on boys?

Day care

Most studies discussed so far have been concerned with long and distressing periods of separation. However, 50% of all infants in Western societies experience short periods of separation several days a week because their mother are out at work. Do these infants suffer as a result? Perhaps surprisingly, the answer most of the time is "No".

Much research has focused on the effects of day care on infants' attachment to their mother. In a study of more than 1000 infants, attachment as assessed by the Strange Situation test was not affected by the amount of stimulation infants received in day care (Scarr, 1997). Scarr pointed out that the care received within the home is far more important than day care in determining children's attachment behaviour.

However, it is important to consider the mother's attitudes towards working. Harrison and Ungerer (2002) studied mothers who had returned to paid employment during the first year of their infant's life. Infants were less likely to be securely attached to their mother if she wasn't committed to work and had anxieties about making use of child care.

Erel et al.'s (2000) review of studies on day care found that there were no significant effects on measures of child development such as social interaction with peers and attachment to mother.

Erel et al. (2000) carried out a thorough review of studies on the effects of day care using seven measures of child development:

1. *Secure vs. insecure attachment to the mother.*
2. *Attachment behaviours*: Avoidance and resistance (reflecting insecure attachment), and exploration (reflecting secure attachment).
3. *Mother–child interaction*: Responsiveness to mother, smiling at mother, obeying mother, and so on.
4. *Adjustment*: Self-esteem, lack of behaviour problems, and so on.
5. *Social interaction with peers* (children of the same age).
6. *Social interaction with non-parental adults* (e.g., relatives; teachers).
7. *Cognitive development*: School performance, IQ, and so on.

Erel et al. (2000) found day care had non-significant effects on all seven measures described above. This was the case regardless of the amount of day care per week, the number of months the child had been in day care, and the child's gender.

Subtle effects

In spite of the non-significant findings reported by Erel et al. (2000), day care can have some subtle positive and negative effects. Lucas-Thompson et al. (2010) found day care was most beneficial for infants in families facing challenges due to single parenthood or dependency on welfare. However, day care sometimes had negative effects when the mother returned to work during the child's first year.

The National Institute of Child Health and Development (NICHD) carried out very large studies into the effects of day care. In one of their studies (NICHD, 2003), levels of aggression (e.g., fighting) and assertiveness (e.g., demanding attention) were higher in infants who had received the most day care. However, Love et al. (2003) pointed out that there are many kinds of day care (e.g., being looked after by grandparents; babysitting at home; day-care centres). They reanalysed the data from the NICHD (2003) study, finding that day care provided by relatives did *not* lead to an increase in aggression or assertiveness.

In sum, day care generally has no negative effects on children's social, emotional, or cognitive development. Indeed, it sometimes has positive effects. However, there is some evidence that extensive day care for infants in the first year of life can have adverse effects, especially if the mother is reluctant to go out to work. Adverse effects (e.g., aggression) are less likely if the day care is provided by relatives rather than non-relatives.

At what age do infants generally do better in day care, and do the mother's circumstances matter?

Chapter summary

- Attachment is often assessed by the Strange Situation test. It has been found with this test that American infants' attachment to their mother is secure in 70% of cases, avoidant in a further 20%, and resistant in the remaining 10%.
- Individual differences in children's attachment behaviour in the Strange Situation test can be seen in terms of the two dimensions of avoidant/withdrawal vs. proximity seeking and angry and resistant vs. emotional confidence.
- There are significant cross-cultural differences in the percentages of children displaying the various attachment types. However, the differences are greater within than between cultures.
- Ainsworth argued in her maternal sensitivity hypothesis that an infant's attachment to its mother or caregiver depends mainly on the mother's or caregiver's sensitivity. This de-emphasises the roles played by the infant's father and the infant's personality.
- Any given child's attachment type depends on complex interactions between various factors (e.g., genes; maternal responsiveness).
- Bowlby argued it is very important for children to have a warm and continuous attachment to their mother. According to him, infants experiencing maternal deprivation may suffer severe and irreversible emotional and other problems.
- Bowlby put forward a theory of monotropy according to which babies are born with a tendency to become strongly attached to only one individual. There is little support for this theory.
- Bowlby exaggerated the adverse effects of maternal deprivation. These effects are typically reversible and family discord rather than separation is in most cases the major problem.
- Children generally experience more problems when exposed to privation (never having had a close relationship) than when exposed to deprivation. However, even the adverse effects of extreme privation are mostly reversible.

- There are two stages of reaction to divorce within families. There is an initial crisis phase followed by an adjustment phase.
- Some of the negative effects on children within families experiencing divorce are due to the genes they have inherited.
- Day care typically has few (if any) negative effects on children's social, emotional, or cognitive development. However, increased aggression and assertiveness in children are associated with some forms of day care.

Further reading

- Berk, L.E. (2006). *Child development (7th ed.)*. New York: Pearson. Psychological research on children's attachments is discussed in detail in this textbook.

- Meins, E. (2011). Emotional development and early attachment relationships. In A. Slater & G. Bremner (Eds.), *An introduction to developmental psychology (2nd ed.)*. Chichester: Wiley-Blackwell. Elizabeth Meins reviews research concerned with attachments in early life.

- Rutter, M., Sonuga-Barke, E.J., & Castle, J. (2010). I. Investigating the impact of early institutional deprivation on development: Background and research strategy of the English and Romanian adoptees (ERA) study. *Monographs of the Society for Research in Child Development*, 75, 1–20. Michael Rutter and his colleagues discuss their important research on the effects of severe privation on children's subsequent development.

Essay questions

1. Describe the various types of attachment that an infant may have with his/her mother. Which factors influence the attachment type found in any given mother–infant relationship?

2. What is the maternal deprivation hypothesis? To what extent does the available evidence support it?

3. Provide an account of the effects of divorce on children's attachment behaviour.

4. What are the advantages of day care for young children? What are the disadvantages?

You probably know some people who are prejudiced against one or more minority groups. Indeed, if you are a member of a minority group yourself, you have probably been on the receiving end of prejudice from other people. Why do you think people are prejudiced? Is it because of their personality, the experiences they have had, the influence of other people, or some other factor?

In view of the harm and misery that are caused by prejudice, it is obviously very desirable that society takes steps to reduce and eliminate it. This is likely to prove difficult to achieve. Given that, how do you think the authorities might attempt to make our society less prejudiced?

Prejudice and discrimination

13

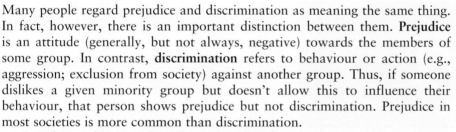

Many people regard prejudice and discrimination as meaning the same thing. In fact, however, there is an important distinction between them. **Prejudice** is an attitude (generally, but not always, negative) towards the members of some group. In contrast, **discrimination** refers to behaviour or action (e.g., aggression; exclusion from society) against another group. Thus, if someone dislikes a given minority group but doesn't allow this to influence their behaviour, that person shows prejudice but not discrimination. Prejudice in most societies is more common than discrimination.

What is the difference between prejudice and discrimination?

In a thorough review, Dovidio et al. (1996) found only a modest association between prejudice and discrimination. One reason is that there are generally greater social pressures to avoid discrimination (which is readily observable by others) than to avoid prejudice (which is less obvious to other people).

Discrimination can take many forms. Allport (1954) argued there are five stages of discrimination. In some situations (e.g., Nazi Germany), the level of discrimination increases rapidly from the early stages to the later ones. Here are Allport's five stages:

1. *Anti-locution*: Verbal attacks are directed against some other group.
2. *Avoidance*: The other group is systematically avoided. Sometimes this involves steps to make it easier to identify members of that group (e.g., the Star of David worn by Jews in Nazi Germany).
3. *Discrimination*: The other group is deliberately treated worse than other groups in civil rights, job opportunities, and so on.
4. *Physical attack*: Members of the other group are attacked, and their property is destroyed.
5. *Extermination*: There are deliberate attempts to kill all members of the other group (e.g., the gas chambers built by the Nazis to murder the Jews).

Is prejudice in decline?

Superficial evidence suggests that prejudice is in decline in countries such as the United Kingdom and the United States. For example, only about 10% of individuals living in Western societies have obvious racial biases, which is

> **KEY TERMS**
>
> **Prejudice:** attitudes and feelings (typically negative) about the members of some group solely on the basis of their membership of that group.
>
> **Discrimination:** negative actions or behaviour directed towards the members of some other group.

much lower than 50 or 60 years ago (S.T. Fiske, 2002). However, as many as 80% of people possess various subtle racial biases leading to "awkward social interactions, embarrassing slips of the tongue, unchecked assumptions, stereotypic judgments, and spontaneous neglect" (S.T. Fiske, 2002, p. 124).

The term "modern racism" refers to subtle prejudicial attitudes towards members of other racial groups. How does modern racism manifest itself? According to Swim et al. (1995), there are three main ways:

1. Modern racists deny there is prejudice and discrimination against minority groups.
2. They show annoyance and impatience because minority groups demand equal treatment with the majority group.
3. They have feelings of resentment at the prospect of minority groups receiving positive action to assist them.

The impact of racism is so subtle that it even influences basic perceptual processes. Payne (2001) presented briefly a photograph of a male face (white or black). The photograph of an object was then presented, and participants decided rapidly whether it was a handgun or a handtool. White participants were more likely to identify a tool mistakenly as a gun when preceded by a black face than by a white face, and this happened automatically.

Discrimination against specific groups is sometimes aided by distinguishing visual characteristics such as skin colour, or style of dress. Sometimes, however, minority group members are not clearly distinguishable from the majority, and are forced to identify themselves. This was the case in Nazi Germany where Jews had to wear a Star of David on their clothing, making them a focus for racial hatred.

Stereotypes

Prejudiced individuals generally regard all members of a disliked minority as being similar to each other. This focus on group membership rather than on an individual's personal qualities is known as stereotyping. A **stereotype** is "a cognitive representation or impression of a social group that people form by associating particular characteristics and emotions with the group" (Smith & Mackie, 2000). For example, many people have a stereotype of the English as intelligent, tolerant, and reserved, even though they know many English people who are totally different!

Brauer and Er-rafiy (2011) studied the role of stereotypes in producing prejudice and discrimination towards other groups (e.g., Moroccans; Chinese) among French students. They reduced stereotypes by emphasising the *variability* among members of the other group (e.g., by portraying them as having diverse opinions). As predicted, perceived variability of the other group decreased prejudice and discrimination because it reduced the relevance of negative stereotypes.

KEY TERM

Stereotype: an oversimplified generalisation (typically negative) concerning some group (e.g., the English; the Welsh).

How accurate are stereotypes? Stereotypes are nearly always oversimplified and often represent distorted views of other groups. Terracciano et al. (2005) compared stereotypical views of national character in 49 cultures with actual average personality. There was no validity to stereotypes about national character. For example, the stereotypical view is that that the Germans are more conscientious than the Chileans. In fact, however, the average level of conscientiousness in those two countries is almost identical.

Even though most stereotypes are distorted, many contain a kernel of truth. For example, many white Americans have a negative stereotype of black Americans. As a result, they believe black Americans are especially likely to have dropped out of high school, to be illegitimate, and so on.

What is the truth? McCauley and Stitt (1978) found in many cases that white Americans' estimates were *less* than the actual figures. Thus, there was some factual basis to their stereotype. Note, however, that the assumption that *all* members of any group share the same negative characteristics is entirely untrue.

Many people have a stereotype of the English as intelligent, tolerant, and reserved.

Assessing stereotypes

Traditionally, stereotypes were assessed mainly by questionnaires. The major limitation with this approach is that individuals having very negative stereotypes of other groups may pretend those stereotypes are less negative than is actually the case. As you can imagine, it is hard to prevent such biased responding from distorting the findings.

Cunningham et al. (2001) addressed the above problem in a study with white participants using a version of the Implicit Association Test. In condition 1, participants pressed one key if a white face or a good word (e.g., love) was presented and another key if a black face or a bad word (e.g., terrible) was presented. In condition 2, white faces and bad words involved one key and black faces and good words the second key

Cunningham et al. (2001) found that reaction times were much faster in condition 1, suggesting the existence of implicit or *unconscious* pro-white and anti-black stereotypes. They also found a modest tendency for those showing much conscious or explicit prejudice on a questionnaire also to show unconscious prejudice. Of importance, participants showed more evidence of prejudice on the implicit measure than the explicit one. This suggests that the implicit measure revealed prejudice *not* observable on the questionnaire.

The stereotypical image of Italian matriarchs being wonderful cooks has given rise to several advertising campaigns for Italian food products.

Why do we have stereotypes?

Nearly everyone possesses numerous stereotypes. This suggests that stereotypes probably fulfil important functions. Two major functions have been identified. First, stereotypes provide a simple way of perceiving the world and so reduce

Not everyone conforms to stereotypes

processing effort. Thus, for example, we can easily categorise a stranger on the basis of their sex, age, clothing, and so on.

Second, stereotypes also fulfil important social and motivational functions. How we think about ourselves is determined in part by the various social groups (e.g., school; clubs) to which we belong. Stereotypes allow us to distinguish ourselves (and our groups) clearly from other groups (Oakes et al., 1994). For example, there is a stereotype of the British as reserved and industrious. This stereotype became stronger when British students compared the British against the Italians. This was because the British students wanted to *emphasise* the differences between the two nationalities (Cinnirella, 1998).

Why are stereotypes hard to change?

It is generally very hard to produce long-lasting changes in someone's negative stereotypes about some minority group. Why is this? Part of the answer lies in the attributions we make about others' behaviour. Other people's behaviour can be attributed to *internal* causes (e.g., personality) or to *situational* causes (see Chapter 16). When someone's behaviour is attributed to internal causes, we expect that behaviour to continue in future. However, we don't expect behaviour attributed to external causes to continue when the situation changes.

Sherman et al. (2005) assessed people's attributions for the behaviour of a gay man from Chicago called Robert. Those prejudiced against homosexuality gave *internal* attributions to Robert's stereotype-consistent behaviour but *external* attributions to his stereotype-inconsistent behaviour. Thus, even prejudiced individuals found some of Robert's behaviour inconsistent with their stereotypical views of gays. However, they still expected that in future he would mainly behave in a stereotype-consistent way.

Explanations of prejudice

There are several causes of prejudice. However, there are *three* main types of causes. First, prejudice may depend on the individual's personality, which in turn is influenced by genetic factors. Second, environmental factors may be important in producing prejudice. For example, a dramatic increase in the level of unemployment within any given country may lead to greater prejudice against minority groups.

Third, simply belonging to a group may cause prejudice. The groups to which an individual belongs (known as ingroups) may be regarded favourably, whereas most or all other groups (known as outgroups) may be regarded unfavourably or with prejudice.

Personality

Adorno et al. (1950) argued that individuals with an authoritarian personality are the ones most likely to be prejudiced. The **authoritarian personality** includes the following characteristics (see the figure overleaf for all the traits):

What attitude do individuals with an authoritarian personality have towards authority figures and values?

- Rigid beliefs in conventional values.
- General hostility towards other groups.
- Intolerance of ambiguity.
- Submissive attitude towards authority figures.

Adorno et al. devised the F (Fascism) Scale to measure the attitudes associated with the authoritarian personality. Here is a sample item: "Most of our social problems would be solved if we could somehow get rid of the immoral, crooked, and feeble-minded people."

How does the authoritarian personality develop? According to Adorno et al. (1950), it has its roots in childhood experiences. Children receiving a harsh upbringing with little affection and much punishment from their parents are most likely to develop an authoritarian personality. The treatment they receive from their parents creates hostility, but they can't express it towards their parents. As a result, they re-direct it towards non-threatening minority groups.

In the early 1960s, during a period of high immigration from the West Indies to the UK, the MP Enoch Powell warned of the dangers of social unrest following the distortion of the labour market. His "rivers of blood" speech was taken by many as a call for repatriation of immigrants, and was quoted by both those for and those against immigration.

Findings

Adorno et al. (1950) found adults with an authoritarian personality tended to have been treated harshly by their parents. There are two possible ways of interpreting these findings. First, a harsh family *environment* may cause children to develop an authoritarian personality. Second, *genetic* factors may mean that authoritarian parents tend to have authoritarian children.

Twin studies are an effective way of deciding between the above two interpretations. Identical twins share 100% of their genes whereas fraternal twins share only 50% of their genes. If individual differences in the authoritarian personality depend in part on genetic factors, we would expect identical twins to be more similar to each other than fraternal twins. That is exactly what has been found (McCourt et al., 1999). These findings leave open the possibility that a harsh family environment may also play a role in causing children to develop the authoritarian personality.

Altemeyer (2004) studied individuals high in right-wing authoritarianism and social dominance. These individuals were very dogmatic and prejudiced because of their authoritarianism. They were also very intimidating and manipulative because of their social dominance. Such individuals were the ones most likely to stir up prejudice among other people.

It is important not to exaggerate the importance of personality in creating prejudice. For example, prejudice can depend more on cultural norms than

> **KEY TERM**
>
> **Authoritarian personality:** a type of personality consisting of intolerance of ambiguity, hostility towards other groups, rigid beliefs, and submissiveness towards authority figures.

The nine personality traits of the authoritarian personality from Adorno et al.'s F-Scale.

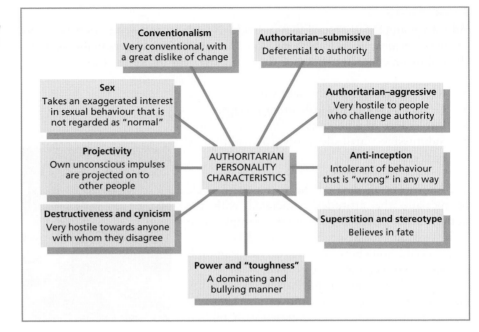

on personality. Pettigrew (1958) studied prejudice in South Africa and the United States. The levels of authoritarianism were similar in the two countries, but there was much more prejudice towards black people in South Africa.

Major historical events can cause a general increase in prejudice. Consider the impact of the attack on the US fleet in Pearl Harbor on Americans' attitudes to the Japanese. There was an immediate large increase in prejudice against Japanese people among those with (and without) authoritarian personalities. Such widespread prejudice can't be explained by Adorno et al.'s theory.

EVALUATION

➕ Individuals differ in prejudice, and these differences can be assessed by the F-Scale.

➕ Genetic factors (and probably certain environmental ones) help to determine whether someone will develop an authoritarian personality.

➖ Prejudice generally depends more on cultural and social factors than on personality. This can be seen when there are rapid increases in prejudice within a society (e.g., Nazi Germany).

➖ Adorno et al. (1950) exaggerated the role of the family environment in producing the authoritarian personality.

Realistic group conflict

Sherif (1966) put forward realistic conflict theory, according to which prejudice often results from conflict between two groups. When two groups compete for the same goal, the members of each group become prejudiced against those of the other group. In contrast, if two groups work together to achieve the same goal, they will cooperate with each other and there will be no prejudice.

According to realistic conflict theory, what does prejudice result from?

Findings

The origins of realistic conflict theory lie in the Robbers Cave study (Sherif et al., 1961). Twenty-two boys spent two weeks at a summer camp in the United States. They were put into two groups (the Eagles and the Rattlers). The boys were told that whichever group did better in various sporting events and other competitions would receive a trophy, knives, and medals. As a result of this competition, a fight broke out between the members of the two groups and the Rattlers' flag was burned.

Prejudice was shown in the Robbers Cave study—each group regarded its own members as friendly and courageous, whereas the members of the other group were regarded as smart alecs and liars. When the boys indicated who their friends were, 93% of the choices were members of the same group. However, prejudice was greatly reduced when the experimenters replaced the competitive situations with a cooperative one in which the success of each group required the cooperation of both groups.

Zárate et al. (2004) studied prejudice against Mexican immigrants at the University of Texas at El Paso, which is on the border between the United States and Mexico. There were concerns about job security among Americans at this university because of the presence of these immigrants. Such concerns could provide the basis for intergroup conflict and prejudice. As predicted, the Americans showed more prejudice against the immigrants when they focused on similarities between the two groups in work-related traits.

Ember (1981) studied 26 small societies. As predicted by realistic conflict theory, intergroup violence was much more frequent when societies competed for resources because of population pressures or severe food shortages.

Tyerman and Spencer (1983) argued that competition and realistic conflict cause prejudice only when those involved don't already have long-term friendships. They observed scouts who knew each other well as they competed in groups against each other at their annual camp. Competition didn't produce the negative effects observed by Sherif et al. (1961). The fact that the boys in the Sherif et al. (1961) study didn't know each other before the summer camp probably explains the difference in the findings.

EVALUATION

✚ Competition between groups can lead to prejudice.

✚ Realistic conflict theory helps to explain the large increases in prejudice found when countries are at war with each other.

➕ Replacing competition with cooperation can be an effective way of reducing prejudice.

➖ According to the theory, conflicts arise when group interests are threatened. However, group interests are defined very vaguely: "A real or imagined threat to the safety of the group, an economic interest, a political advantage, a military consideration, prestige, or a number of others" (Sherif, 1966, p. 15).

➖ Realistic conflict isn't always sufficient to produce prejudice (e.g., Tyerman & Spencer, 1983). It is also not necessary, because millions of people have prejudiced attitudes towards people in other cultures with whom they aren't in competition.

Social identity

What does social identity theory assume about people?

Suppose someone asked you to describe your best friend in detail. Your description would certainly refer to their personal qualities (e.g., personality). In addition, it would probably include some indication of the groups to which they belong (e.g., student at college; hockey team member). According to social identity theory (Tajfel & Turner, 1979), we all have various social identities based on the different groups to which we belong (see Chapter 19). Our sense of ourselves is strongly influenced by our social identities.

Why is it important for us to possess social identities? Having a positive social identity makes us feel good about ourselves and enhances our self-esteem. One way we can achieve a positive social identity is by comparing a group to which we belong (an ingroup) favourably to some other group (an outgroup). This produces **ingroup bias** (the tendency to favour one's ingroup over outgroups), and can lead to prejudice.

There is another way prejudice can occur. When someone belongs to a group, they generally accept the values or norms of that group. If those norms include negative views about a given outgroup, prejudice will result.

Findings

Support for social identity theory was reported by Verkuyten et al. (1999). Dutch participants indicated how strongly they identified themselves with

How many social identities do you have?

the Dutch majority ingroup in the Netherlands. Those identifying themselves most strongly with the Dutch ingroup revealed the greatest negative emotions towards ethnic minorities.

Barlow et al. (2010) studied prejudice in Asian Australians who felt rejected by Aboriginal Australians. Those Asian Australians who identified themselves most strongly with their ingroup had greater prejudice towards Aboriginal Australians than those who identified less strongly.

Social identity theory is more applicable to some cultures than to others. Wetherell (1982) compared the attitudes and behaviour of white and Polynesian children in New Zealand. The white children were biased against the Polynesian children. However, the Polynesian children were cooperative towards the white children and showed very little prejudice against them. This reflected the power structure in New Zealand at the time—the white group was much more powerful than the Polynesian group.

Mullen et al. (1992) reviewed numerous studies. Members of poorly regarded minority groups showed *favouritism* towards more highly regarded outgroups. This is the opposite of what is predicted by social identity theory, and probably occurred in part because of the greater power possessed by the outgroups.

EVALUATION

➕ Group membership and the formation of social identities have strong effects on attitudes towards the ingroup and outgroups.

➕ An individual's social identities can lead to prejudice.

➖ The effects of social identities on attitudes and behaviour vary across cultures. In particular, weak minority groups often fail to show prejudice towards more powerful outgroups.

➖ Individuals can have a strong sense of identity with an ingroup *without* necessarily being prejudiced against outgroups.

Reducing prejudice and discrimination

It is very important to find ways of reducing (and ideally eliminating) prejudice and discrimination. Psychologists have identified various approaches that can be taken, one of which was mentioned earlier in the chapter. Reducing the strength of stereotypes by emphasising the differences among members of another group had beneficial effects on prejudice and discrimination (Brauer & Er-rafiy, 2011). Other approaches are discussed below.

Intergroup contact hypothesis

According to Allport's (1954) intergroup contact hypothesis, prejudice can be reduced by increased social contact between prejudiced individuals and the groups against which they are prejudiced. Why is this the case? Prejudice

How does intergroup contact reduce prejudice?

often involves stereotypes, and stereotypes are based on the assumption that everyone in a given group is very similar. Frequent contact with members of that group can help to disprove that stereotype.

There is another important reason why intergroup contact might reduce prejudice. Interacting with members of another group often makes it clear they are more similar to the prejudiced individual in their attitudes and behaviour than he/she had thought. In other words, prejudice is partly based on *ignorance*, and social contact can remove ignorance and thus reduce prejudice.

Allport (1954) realised that social contact on its own is not enough. If such contact is to prove successful, *four* conditions need to be met:

1. The two groups have equal status within the situation in which the contact takes place.
2. The two groups are working towards common goals.
3. Efforts to achieve these common goals are based on intergroup cooperation rather than intergroup competition.
4. There is formal institutional support for intergroup acceptance.

Findings

The contact hypothesis was tested at Wexler Middle School in Waterford in the United States (Brown, 1986). There were similar numbers of white and black children, and much was done to make all the students feel equal. For example, there was very little streaming by ability. Cooperation was encouraged by having the students work together to buy special equipment they could all use.

There was a steady reduction in discrimination, with the behaviour of the black and white students towards each other being friendly. However, some stereotypical beliefs remained. For example, black and white students agreed that black students were tougher and more assertive than white ones.

Tropp and Pettigrew (2005) reviewed numerous studies on the contact hypothesis. The beneficial effects of intergroup contact on reducing prejudice were greater for majority than minority groups. Why did intergroup contact have only a modest effect within minority groups? Minority groups may be so aware of their lower status that it reduces any positive effects of intergroup contact.

Pettigrew and Tropp (2008) found that reduced prejudice among majority group members following intergroup contact was due to three reasons:

1. Intergroup contact reduced anxiety about interacting with minority group members.
2. It increased empathy (understanding of the feelings of those within the minority group).
3. It increased knowledge about the other group.

Allport (1954) de-emphasised individual differences in the effects of intergroup contact. Dhont et al. (2011) considered the effects of intergroup contact on individuals varying in need for closure (preference for firm answers and an aversion to ambiguity). Intergroup contact reduced prejudice more in those high in need for closure because it reduced their anxiety about the other group.

EVALUATION

➕ Social contact (especially between groups of equal social status) can lead to reduced prejudice.

➕ Key factors (reduced anxiety; empathy; increased knowledge) responsible for the beneficial effects of social contact have been identified.

➖ Intergroup contact typically has little effect on prejudice within minority groups (Tropp & Pettigrew, 2005).

➖ The intergroup contact hypothesis doesn't indicate clearly how positive contact with individual members of an outgroup might *generalise* to include other members of that outgroup.

➖ Individual differences (e.g., in need for closure) are more important in influencing the effects of intergroup contact than assumed by the hypothesis.

Salient categorisation and recategorisation

Suppose someone who is prejudiced against an outgroup has positive social interactions with a member of that outgroup. Such interactions may well lead to liking for that individual. However, it isn't clear this would generalise to reduced prejudice towards the entire outgroup. We will consider two attempts to understand how intergroup contact can lessen prejudice towards all the members of an outgroup.

Salient categorisation

According to Hewstone and Brown (1986), the liked member of an outgroup is generally regarded as "an exception to the rule". They argued that this individual must be perceived as *typical* of his/her group in order to reduce prejudice. This can be done by making his/her group membership as salient or obvious as possible. Thus, **salient categorisation** is the key.

Van Oudenhouven et al. (1996) tested the above hypothesis. Dutch participants spent 2 hours interacting with a Turkish person in the following two conditions:

1. The experimenter never mentioned the person was Turkish (low salience).
2. The fact that the person was Turkish was emphasised throughout (high salience).

Attitudes towards Turks in general were more favourable in the second condition than in the first, indicating the importance of salient categorisation.

Brown et al. (1999) carried out a study in which British participants worked with a German confederate to obtain a substantial reward. The

KEY TERM

Salient categorisation: the notion that someone needs to be regarded as typical or representative of a group if positive encounters with that individual are to lead to reduced prejudice towards the entire group.

German confederate either seemed to correspond closely to the German stereotype or was clearly atypical. In addition, participants were given false information about how similar or dissimilar German people are with respect to several characteristics.

Brown et al. (1999) assumed it would be easier to generalise from the German confederate to all Germans when the confederate was regarded as typical and when the Germans were thought to be similar to each other. As predicted, participants in that condition had the most favourable attitudes towards the Germans.

EVALUATION

➕ Salient categorisation often reduces prejudice to entire outgroups rather than simply to specific individuals.

➕ Much research in education has focused on multiculturalism, which involves the acceptance and promotion of group differences. It resembles salient categorisation, and is effective in improving intergroup relations (see Richeson & Nussbaum, 2004, and next section).

➖ When people already have a definite stereotype of another group, it can be very hard to persuade them that a given member is actually a typical member of that group.

➖ If the interaction with an outgroup member who is allegedly typical of that group goes badly, there is a danger that the entire outgroup will be perceived negatively.

What does reducing prejudice by recategorisation involve?

Recategorisation

There is another method of reducing prejudice towards an entire outgroup. It involves **recategorisation**, in which the ingroup and the outgroup are recategorised to form a single group. The hope is that outgroup members will in a sense become members of the individual's favoured ingroup.

The above hypothesis was tested by Gaertner et al. (1994) in a study within a multi-ethnic high school in the United States. They carried out a survey, part of which consisted of items focusing on the notion that there was a single ingroup within the school. Those students who thought the school consisted of one large ingroup had the most positive attitudes towards other ethnic groups in the school.

Dovidio et al. (2004) also tested the above hypothesis. White participants saw a video showing examples of racial discrimination. Those who had previously been exposed to a recategorisation manipulation (told a terrorist

KEY TERM

Recategorisation: merging the **ingroup** and **outgroup** to form a single large ingroup; it is designed to reduce **prejudice.**

threat was directed at both black and white Americans) showed reduced prejudice following the video.

Recategorisation doesn't *always* have beneficial effects. Turner and Crisp (2010) asked British students to think of themselves as Europeans. This recategorisation reduced prejudice against the French among British students who didn't identify very strongly with being British. However, it *increased* prejudice against the French among students who strongly identified with being British. These students wanted to preserve a strong sense of British identity, and this was threatened when told to think of themselves as European.

Richeson and Nussbaum (2004) compared the effects of multiculturalism (which resembles salient categorisation) and a colour-blind (recategorisation) approach on an American sample. There was more prejudice following recategorisation than following multiculturalism. This happened because participants in the recategorisation condition didn't want to regard all Americans as forming a single group.

EVALUATION

➕ Recategorisation often reduces prejudice even among those whose initial prejudice is high.

➖ Recategorisation can *increase* prejudice among those who identify strongly with their ingroup and so don't want to recategorise.

➖ Some research suggests that recategorisation can be less effective than salient categorisation at reducing prejudice.

Chapter summary

- Prejudice involves negative attitudes toward the members of some group. In contrast, discrimination involves negative actions directed at the members of some other group.
- There has been a decline in overt racism, but this has largely been replaced by more subtle forms of racism.
- Stereotypes are useful because they provide a simple way of perceiving the world. They also serve social and motivational purposes.
- Adorno et al. argued that prejudiced people tend to have an authoritarian personality stemming from a harsh and affectionless childhood.
- Adorno et al. minimised the role of genetic factors in producing individual differences in prejudice. They also minimised the importance of cultural and intergroup factors.

- According to realistic conflict theory, competition between two groups for the same goal can cause intergroup conflict and prejudice.
- Realistic conflict is often neither necessary nor sufficient to produce prejudice.
- Individuals' social identities can produce ingroup bias, which can lead to prejudice against outgroups.
- Intergroup contact can reduce prejudice by reducing anxiety about the other group and by increasing empathy for (and knowledge of) that group. However, the beneficial effect of intergroup contact often fail to generalise to all the members of the other group.
- Prejudice can be reduced by salient categorisation and by recategorisation. However, these techniques are often ineffective when the initial level of prejudice is high.
- There is some evidence that salient categorisation is more effective than recategorisation at reducing prejudice.

Further reading

- Hewstone, M., Rubin, M., & Willis, H. (2002). Intergroup bias. *Annual Review of Psychology, 53*, 575–604. This chapter contains a good account of various theoretical accounts of intergroup bias and conflict.

- Hogg, M.A., & Vaughan, G.M. (2010). *Social psychology (6th ed.)*. Harlow: Pearson Education. Chapter 10 of this leading textbook in social psychology is concerned with prejudice and discrimination.

- Peluck, E.L., & Green, D.P. (2009). Prejudice reduction: What works? A review and assessment of research and practice. *Annual Review of Psychology, 60*, 339–367. The authors provide a comprehensive analysis of the main approaches used in the attempt to reduce prejudice.

Essay questions

1. Define prejudice and discrimination. Why is prejudice more common than discrimination?

2. What are stereotypes and how can they be assessed? What functions do they serve?

3. Discuss the evidence relating to the roles played by personality and intergroup conflict in producing prejudice.

4. Describe (and evaluate) some of the main approaches to reducing prejudice.

In the course of your life, you will have met some people who are very helpful and cooperative, and others who are the exact opposite. What are some of the reasons leading people to behave in a pro-social or cooperative way? It is sometimes argued that people in Western societies are more self-centred and less helpful than those in non-industrialised societies. Do you think that is true or is it just a myth?

Bystanders who see some someone needing help (e.g., someone who has been injured while crossing the road) often fail to go to that person's assistance. Why do you think bystanders are often so reluctant to help? Does it reflect an increase in selfishness in today's society?

Pro-social behaviour

14

The central focus of this chapter is on cooperative and helpful behaviour, and on the factors determining whether someone will behave in that way. **Pro-social behaviour** is defined as any behaviour of benefit to someone else; it includes actions that are cooperative, affectionate, and helpful to others. Such behaviour may or may not be costly to the person who engages in such behaviour; indeed, it is often beneficial to that person as well as to the person who is assisted.

Altruism is an especially important type of pro-social behaviour. It is helping behaviour that is potentially costly to the person who is altruistic. In other words, altruism is based on a desire to help someone else rather than on any possible rewards for the person doing the helping. It has often been assumed that altruism depends on **empathy**—the ability to share the emotions of another person and to understand that person's point of view.

We will initially discuss factors involved in the development of pro-social behaviour in children. For example, when do young children start to show signs of wanting to help others?

After that, we will consider pro-social and altruistic behaviour from the evolutionary perspective. According to that perspective, pro-social behaviour is important because it helps to ensure the survival of the human species.

Most research on pro-social behaviour has been carried out in a small number of relatively affluent Western societies differing markedly from most other human cultures. As a result, it is important to assess the similarities and differences in pro-social behaviour across numerous cultures.

It is often argued that most individuals in Western cultures tend to be selfish and that this state of affairs is undesirable. As a result, it is important to devise ways of encouraging children and adults to engage in more pro-social behaviour. That is the fourth topic discussed in this chapter.

A form of pro-social behaviour that has been studied in detail is **bystander intervention**. Those who study bystander intervention want to understand the factors determining whether or not bystanders give help to a victim. This research is discussed later in the chapter.

> ## KEY TERMS
>
> **Pro-social behaviour:** behaviour that is positive (e.g., cooperative; affectionate) and that is designed to be of benefit to someone else.
>
> **Altruism:** a form of **pro-social behaviour** that is generally costly to the altruistic person, and which is motivated by the desire to help someone else.
>
> **Empathy:** the capacity to enter into another person's feelings and more generally to understand that person's perspective.
>
> **Bystander intervention:** an area of research focusing on the reasons why bystanders to a crime or incident decide whether to help the victim.

Development of pro-social behaviour

Do you think young children often show pro-social behaviour? Many psychologists doubt that they do. For example, Freud and Piaget emphasised children's tendency to engage in antisocial rather than pro-social behaviour. In the words of Schaffer (1996, p. 269), "The child emerged from these accounts as a selfish, self-centered, aggressive, and uncooperative being, with little interest in other people in their own right and little understanding of anyone else's needs."

Even quite small children can show concern when they see others are unhappy.

Findings

The above account provides an exaggerated account of children's selfishness. For example, Zahn-Waxler et al. (1992) studied empathic concern in children between 13 and 20 months of age. Such concern was shown on 10% of occasions on which someone else's distress wasn't caused by the child. This empathic concern took several forms including sad or upset facial expressions and expressing concern (e.g., "I'm sorry"). The level of empathic concern more than doubled among children aged between 23 and 25 months.

Zahn-Waxler et al. (1992) also found that young children engaged in pro-social behaviour in response to another person's distress. The kinds of pro-social behaviour shown by the children included sharing food, hugging, and giving a bottle to a crying baby. There was a marked increase with age in pro-social behaviour in response to distress not caused by the child. More specifically, children aged 13–15 months responded pro-socially on 9% of occasions, and this increased to 49% among children 23–25 months of age (see the figure on the left).

It is important to note that the pro-social behaviour of young children is limited in scope. Svetlova et al. (2010) studied three kinds of pro-social behaviour in 18- and 30-month-olds:

1. *Instrumental helping*: Assisting another person to achieve an action-based goal (e.g., finding a toy).
2. *Empathic helping*: Showing concern about another person.
3. *Altruistic helping*: Giving up an object owned by the child.

The children showed much instrumental helping, rather less empathic helping, and little altruistic helping. Their altruistic helping was rarely costly and was mostly produced in response

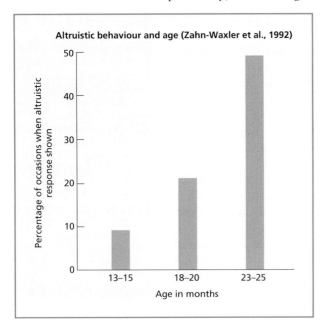

Altruistic behaviour and age (Zahn-Waxler et al., 1992)

y-axis: Percentage of occasions when altruistic response shown

x-axis: Age in months — 13–15, 18–20, 23–25

to an adult's direct request rather than being spontaneous. Thus, young children display pro-social behaviour but it is only occasionally genuinely altruistic.

Individual differences

There are substantial differences in pro-social behaviour among children of any age. Why is this? Environmental factors such as the influence of parents and peers are important. In addition, however, genetic factors are also involved. Knafo et al. (2011) studied environmental and genetic influences on pro-social behaviour in young twins. Their key finding was that 45% of individual differences in pro-social behaviour were due to genetic factors.

Empathy (often associated with pro-social behaviour) also involves genetic factors. Knafo et al. (2008) found in young children of 24 and 36 months that 25% of individual differences in empathy depended on genetic factors. In addition, the amount of pro-social behaviour shown by children depended in part on their empathy level.

In sum, some infants display pro-social behaviour below the age of 2, and the percentage increases rapidly thereafter. However, much of this behaviour is performed to receive reward (e.g., parental attention and praise) and doesn't indicate genuine altruism.

What explains altruism?

It is often argued that it is natural for people to behave selfishly to further their own ends. That makes it hard to explain why people sometimes behave unselfishly or altruistically. An influential attempt to explain altruistic behaviour has come from evolutionary psychology (an approach assuming human behaviour can be explained in evolutionary terms).

Parents invest a lot of time and resources in their children, which may be explained by biological theories of relationships—the parents' chances of passing on their genes are improved if they can help their children to survive and succeed.

According to evolutionary psychologists, individuals are highly motivated to ensure their genes survive. This is so even though most people aren't consciously aware of it. How can we explain altruism in evolutionary terms? As Gross (1996, p. 413) pointed out, "If a mother dies in the course of saving her three offspring from a predator, she will have saved 1½ times her own genes (since each offspring inherits one half of its mother's genes). So, in terms of genes, an act of apparent altruism can turn out to be extremely selfish."

So far, we have seen why people might behave altruistically towards their own *family*. However, most people also behave altruistically towards non-relatives. Evolutionary psychologists (e.g., Trivers, 1971) explain this in terms of **reciprocal altruism**: "I'll scratch your back if you scratch mine."

Trivers (1971) argued that reciprocal altruism is most likely to be found in *two* conditions:

1. The costs of helping are fairly low and the benefits are high.
2. We can identify those who cheat by receiving help but not helping in return.

However, many individuals behave altruistically even when those they help are unlikely to reciprocate (return the favour). *Why* does this happen? According to Fehr and Fischbacher (2003), it allows those individuals to gain a *reputation* for behaving altruistically. That increases the likelihood they will be assisted by others in the future.

Most societies have various norms (socially accepted standards of behaviour) that involve treating others fairly. One example is the distribution norm (goods should be distributed equally). Suppose one person (X) is given some money and decides to give very little of it to another person (Y). You are person Z. If you believe strongly in the distribution norm, you might be willing to punish person X by removing some of his/her money even if it involved a sacrifice (e.g., of money) on your part. This is known as **third-party punishment** (Fehr & Fischbacher, 2004). Such punishment can reduce selfishness and increase cooperation.

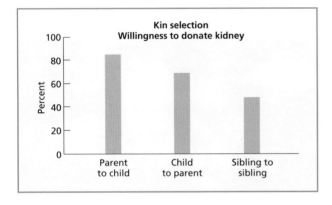

Findings

Much research shows the importance of genetic relatedness or kinship, especially in life-and-death situations. Fellner and Marshall (1981) found that 86% of people were willing to be a kidney donor for their children, 67% would do the same for their parents, and 50% would be a kidney donor for their siblings (see the figure on the left).

Korchmaros and Kenny (2001) argued that we should distinguish between genetic relatedness and emotional closeness. College students chose which family member they would be most likely to provide with life-saving assistance. Altruistic behaviour was determined partly by genetic relatedness (predicted by evolutionary psychology) and partly by emotional closeness (not predicted by evolutionary psychology).

Madsen et al. (2007) wondered whether the effects of kinship on altruistic behaviour are similar in very different cultures (British students and South African Zulu populations). The length of time for which participants were willing to tolerate pain from a physical exercise was affected similarly by kinship in both cultures.

The extent to which people's behaviour is influenced by the desire to have a reputation for altruism was studied by Fehr and Fischbacher (2003). Participants decided whether to help another person who couldn't reciprocate that help. Of those who could nevertheless gain a reputation for altruism, 74% provided help, compared to only 37% of those who couldn't. Thus, many people are willing to behave altruistically to gain a general reputation for altruism that may benefit them in future.

The impact of reputational concerns was also shown in an interesting study by Bateson et al. (2006). Those making themselves tea or coffee in a university coffee room were supposed to put money in an honesty box. As they did so, they saw a photo of flowers or a pair of eyes. The pair of eyes increased participants' concerns about their reputation for making a fair contribution. It

KEY TERM

Third-party punishment: punishing someone else who has treated a third party unfairly even though it involves a personal sacrifice.

was surprisingly effective—on average, people paid almost three times as much for their drinks in the eyes condition as the flowers condition.

Fehr and Fischbacher (2004) studied third-party punishment among students at a Swiss university. Almost two-thirds of third parties decided to punish violations of the distribution norm at a significant cost to themselves. The punishment tended to be more severe with greater violations of the norm.

Henrich et al. (2006) extended the above research by studying 15 diverse cultures in Africa, North America, South America, Asia, and Oceania. There was evidence of third-party punishment in all 15 cultures. However, the percentage of individuals willing to lose some of their own money to punish others who violated the distribution norm varied considerably across cultures. The incidence of third-party punishment was greatest in the most altruistic cultures suggesting third-party punishment is an altruistic way of behaving.

The emphasis of the evolutionary approach is on the *general* principles underlying altruistic behaviour. However, we also need to consider the *individual* level. In your everyday life, you must have noticed that some people are very selfish whereas others are altruistic. These individual differences depend on personality. Krueger et al. (2001) found altruistic individuals tended to be high in positive emotionality, a personality dimension including well-being and social closeness. John et al. (2008) found that individuals high in agreeableness (warmth, generosity, tender-mindedness) were much more altruistic than low scorers.

EVALUATION

➕ Evolutionary psychologists focus more than other psychologists on the key issue of *why* altruism is so important to the human species.

➕ The evolutionary approach explains why altruistic behaviour (especially costly altruistic behaviour) is more likely to be shown to close relatives than to non-relatives.

➕ Evolutionary psychologists have put forward plausible reasons for the existence of altruistic or unselfish behaviour towards non-relatives and even strangers. These reasons include reciprocal altruism, the desire to have a reputation for altruism, and the risk of third-party punishment.

➖ The evolutionary approach largely ignores factors (e.g., emotional closeness; the individual's personality) that help to determine *who* will behave altruistically in a *specific* situation.

➖ Evolutionary psychology provides only a partial account of the substantial cross-cultural differences in third-party punishment (Henrich et al., 2006; see next section).

Is it the case that children in non-industrialised societies are given family responsibilities, and that this increases their altruism?

Cross-cultural differences

Most research on altruism and other forms of pro-social behaviour has been carried out in the United States. However, what is true in that culture is not necessarily true in other cultures. As Darley (1991) pointed out, "In the United States ... , it is generally accepted that the true and basic motive for human action is self-interest."

Evidence that this selfish approach isn't dominant in all cultures was reported by Whiting and Whiting (1975). They studied young children in six cultures: United States, India, Okinawa (a Japanese island), the Philippines, Mexico, and Kenya. At one extreme, 100% of young children in Kenya were high in altruism. At the other extreme, only 8% of young children in the United States were altruistic. The other cultures were in between (see the figure below).

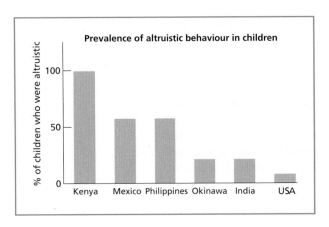

Prevalence of altruistic behaviour in children

What do these findings mean? Three main factors are involved. First, industrialised societies such as those in the United States and Okinawa place much emphasis on competition and personal success. This emphasis reduces cooperation and altruism. Such societies are often termed individualistic cultures (see Chapter 1).

Second, the family structure in non-industrialised cultures such as those of Kenya and Mexico is very different from that in industrialised cultures (or at least it was 40 years ago). Children in non-industrialised societies are often given major family responsibilities (e.g., caring for younger siblings). These responsibilities help to develop altruistic behaviour. Such societies are often termed collectivistic cultures because the emphasis is on the group's needs rather than the individual's.

Third, in spite of the differences, individualistic and collectivistic cultures are more similar than generally recognised. Fijneman et al. (1996) found those living in non-industrialised or collectivistic cultures expect more help from others than those living in industrialised or individualistic cultures. Both kinds of cultures are similar in that individuals anticipate giving only a little more help than they expect to receive. Thus, a norm of reciprocity or mutual exchange applies in both types of cultures and they may differ little in altruism.

Earlier we discussed evidence that third-party punishment (which involves costs to the punisher) can persuade individuals to behave unselfishly. Marlowe and Berbesque (2007) predicted that such punishment would be used more often in larger, more complex societies than in smaller ones. Why is that? It is harder to detect individuals who behave selfishly in larger societies because of greater anonymity. That makes third-party punishment more important in such societies if altruistic behaviour is to be encouraged.

Marlowe and Berbesque (2007) assessed the minimum acceptable offer—the lowest amount of the money available that person A could give to person B without being punished by the third party (person C). As predicted, the minimum acceptable offer was higher in larger societies. It was about 5% of the money available in some of the smallest groups (e.g., in Tanzania or Fiji). However, it was 30% in the largest groups (e.g., in Kenya or Ghana).

EVALUATION

➕ There are substantial cross-cultural differences in pro-social behaviour and altruism.

➕ There is more altruistic behaviour in collectivistic than in individualistic cultures.

➕ Third-party punishment encourages altruism in large societies in which individuals are relatively anonymous and so can easily "cheat" on their obligations to others.

➖ It is an oversimplification to assume that all collectivist cultures display similar levels of pro-social and altruistic behaviour. In similar fashion, there are important differences in such behaviour among individualistic cultures.

➖ What is true at the cultural level is generally not true at the level of all the *individuals* within any given culture (see Chapter 1).

Encouraging pro-social behaviour and altruism

How can children and adults be encouraged to behave in more pro-social ways? There are many answers, and we will consider a few of the most important ones. Most research in this area has focused on children, perhaps because it is easier to change the behaviour of children than of adults.

Parental influence

For the great majority of young children, their parents are easily the most important adults in their lives. How can parents promote pro-social behaviour in their offspring? Schaffer (1996) argued that several types of parental behaviour are of special value in teaching children to be pro-social and altruistic, including the following:

1. *Provision of clear and explicit guidelines* (e.g., "You mustn't hit other people because you will hurt and upset them").
2. *Emotional conviction*: Guidelines to children should be given in a fairly emotional way.
3. *Parental modelling*: Parents should behave altruistically towards their children.
4. *Empathic and warm parenting*: Parents should have a good understanding of their children's needs and emotions.

Findings

There is support for all the parental factors identified by Schaffer (1996) as promoting children's pro-social behaviour. Krevans and Gibbs (1996)

One of the ways in which parents can encourage pro-social behaviour in their children is by behaving altruistically themselves, and by providing warm and empathic parenting.

considered the first factor (clear and explicit guidelines). Children showed more empathy for other people and exhibited more pro-social behaviour when their mothers repeatedly asked them to consider the likely effects of their behaviour on others.

Evidence showing the importance of parental emotional conviction was reported by Zahn-Waxler et al. (1979). They observed the reactions of children between the ages of 18 and 30 months towards the victims of distress. The average percentage of occasions on which children showed altruistic behaviour was twice as high (42% vs. 21%) when the mother made extensive use of emotional explanations than when she did not.

Parental modelling was studied by Burleseon and Kunkel (2002). Mothers' comforting skills predicted their children's emotional support skills. The comforting skills of the children's peers also predicted their emotional support skills.

Finally, we consider empathic and warm parenting. Robinson et al. (1994) found children having a warm and loving relationship with their parents were most likely to show pro-social behaviour. Davidov and Grusec (2006) focused on mothers' responsiveness to distress (e.g., encouraging their child to talk about his/her troubles). Their responsiveness to distress predicted their children's empathic capacity and pro-social behaviour towards distressed others.

Television

How do the effects of pro-social television programmes on pro-social behaviour compare to those of violent television programmes on aggressive behaviour?

Pro-social or helping behaviour shown on television can have beneficial effects on children's behaviour. Hearold (1986) reviewed more than 100 studies on the effects of pro-social television programmes on children's behaviour. She concluded such programmes generally make children's behaviour more helpful. Indeed, the beneficial effects of pro-social television programmes on pro-social behaviour were almost *twice* as great as the adverse effects of television violence on aggressive behaviour. Note that helping behaviour was only assessed shortly after watching a pro-social television programme in most of the studies.

Mares and Woodard (2005) reviewed 34 studies concerned with the effects on children's behaviour of watching pro-social television programmes. The effects were consistently moderately positive. The beneficial effects were especially great when children viewed altruistic behaviour that was easy to imitate.

In spite of the existence of many studies showing that watching pro-social television is associated with pro-social behaviour, there are two major limitations with much of the evidence. First, we can't assume the *only* reason for this association is because watching pro-social television enhances pro-social behaviour. The reason is that children who already display much pro-social behaviour are probably more likely than other children to watch pro-social television. Second, most studies have considered only short-term effects of pro-social television on pro-social behaviour. This is important because the long-term effects are often rather weak or even non-existent (Sagotsky et al., 1981).

Video games

There is much evidence that playing violent video games can lead to increased aggression (Chapter 6). There is much less evidence concerning the effects of playing pro-social video games. However, this is an important area for research given that over 90% of American teenagers play video games and the figures are similar in many other countries.

Greitemeyer and Osswald (2010) carried out four experiments in this area. Students who played a pro-social video game were more likely to provide help after a mishap and were also more willing to take part in future experiments. *Why* did playing pro-social video games have these beneficial effects? Greitemeyer and Osswald found that playing such games made pro-social thoughts more accessible, and these thoughts led to an increase in pro-social behaviour.

Playing pro-social video games clearly enhances pro-social behaviour in the short-term (see Gentile et al., 2009, for a review). However, relatively few studies have considered possible long-term effects. Gentile et al. found the amount of pro-social game playing predicted pro-social behaviour 3 or 4 months later. In addition, individuals displaying much pro-social behaviour spent more time than other people playing pro-social games. Thus, pro-social games promote pro-social behaviour in the long-term. In addition, pro-social behaviour promotes pro-social game playing.

OVERALL EVALUATION

⊕ Several types of parental behaviour that increase pro-social behaviour in their children have been identified.

⊕ Children who devote much time to watching pro-social television programmes and/or playing pro-social video games show more pro-social behaviour than other children.

⊖ Pro-social television programmes and video games are probably associated with pro-social behaviour in part because pro-social children are more likely to watch such programmes and play such games.

⊖ We mustn't exaggerate the impact of environmental factors on children's pro-social behaviour. As we saw earlier, children's empathy and pro-social behaviour depend in part on genetic factors (Knafo et al., 2008, 2011).

Bystander intervention

A haunting image of our time is of someone being attacked violently in the middle of a city with no one coming to their assistance. This reluctance to

Is a bystander more or less likely to help a victim if there are several other bystanders?

help was shown in the case of Kitty Genovese, who was stabbed to death as she returned home at 3 o'clock in the morning on March 13, 1964. According to the *New York Times*, 38 witnesses watched Kitty Genovese being attacked three times over a 30-minute period. No one intervened and only one person called the police. This suggests a truly horrifying reluctance of people to help a victim in desperate need of assistance.

There is just one problem with this account—it is grossly exaggerated. In fact, only *three* people saw either of the stabbings (there were two not three). Even those three eyewitnesses saw Kitty being attacked for only a few seconds.

John Darley and Bibb Latané (1968) were interested in the Kitty Genovese case (but didn't realise how distorted the *New York Times* account was). It led them to initiate research on bystander intervention, which is concerned with the factors influencing whether bystanders help a victim they don't know. Darley and Latané (1968) argued that a victim may be more likely to receive help when there is only one bystander rather than several. In such a situation, responsibility for helping the victim falls firmly on one person, and so he/she has a sense of personal responsibility.

Why is a victim less likely to be helped when there are several observers of a crime or other incident? According to Darley and Latané (1968), the answer is **diffusion of responsibility**—when there are many observers, each person bears only a small portion of the blame for not helping.

Findings

In their research, Darley and Latané (1968) placed participants in separate rooms and told them to put headphones on and to take part in a discussion. The participants were told there were one, two, three, or six people involved in the discussion. In fact, however, all the contributions by other participants were tape recordings.

Each participant heard that one of the other people in the discussion was prone to seizures. Later on, they heard him say, "I—er—I—uh—I've got one of these—er—seizure—er—er—things coming one and—and—I could really—er—use some help so if somebody would—er—er—help—er—er—help—er—uh—uh—uh [choking sounds] ... I'm gonna die—er—er—I'm ... gonna die—er—help—er—er—seizure—er ... [choking sounds, silence]."

Of those who thought they were the only person to know that someone was having an epileptic fit, 100% left the room and reported the emergency. In contrast, only 62% of participants responded if they thought five other bystanders knew about it (see the figure on the left). Furthermore, those participants who thought they were the only bystander responded much more rapidly than did those who thought there were five other bystanders. Fifty per cent of them responded within 45 seconds of the fit starting, whereas none of those who believed there were five other bystanders did so.

> **KEY TERM**
>
> **Diffusion of responsibility:** the larger the number of bystanders who observe what happens to a victim, the less the sense of personal responsibility to help experienced by each one.

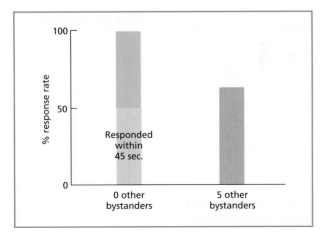

Two other interesting findings emerged from the research of Darley and Latané (1968). First, participants who believed there were five other bystanders denied this had influenced their behaviour. Thus, people aren't fully aware of the factors determining whether they behave pro-socially. Second, those participants who failed to report the emergency weren't apathetic or uncaring. Most had trembling hands and sweating palms. Indeed, they seemed more emotionally aroused than the participants who reported the emergency.

Is it always bad news for victims when there are several bystanders rather than one? The answer is "No". In Darley and Latané's (1968) research, the bystanders didn't know each other. As a result, they didn't share a social relationship. In contrast, victims are more likely to be helped when there are several bystanders rather than one when the bystanders are all friends (Levine & Crowther, 2008). Thus, there is strength in numbers (rather than diffusion of responsibility) when bystanders share social relationships.

Other factors

Many other factors influence the behaviour of bystanders, and we will briefly consider five. First, bystanders are generally more likely to help a victim who is *similar* to themselves. Levine (2002) used a situation in which a victim was exposed to physical violence. Victims were more likely to be helped when described as belonging to the bystanders' ingroup (a group with which they identified) rather than an outgroup (a group with which they didn't identify).

Second, bystanders are more likely to help "deserving" rather than "undeserving victims". A man who staggered and collapsed on the floor of a New York subway was much more likely to be helped if he appeared to be sober rather than drunk (Piliavin et al., 1969).

Third, bystanders are reluctant to become involved in strangers' personal lives. Bystanders witnessing a fight between a man and a woman were *three* times more likely to intervene when they thought the fight involved strangers rather than a married couple (Shotland & Straw, 1976).

Fourth, bystanders' willingness to provide help depends on what they were doing before the incident. Batson et al. (1978) sent participants from one building to another to perform a task. On the way, they passed a male student slumped on the stairs coughing and groaning. Only 10% of those told their task was important stopped to assist the student compared to 80% told the task was trivial.

Fifth, Huston et al. (1981) argued that bystanders with relevant skills or expertise will be especially likely to provide assistance. As predicted, those helping in dangerous emergencies generally had relevant skills (e.g., life-saving; first aid; self-defence).

Arousal: cost–reward model

How can we understand findings on bystander intervention? Piliavin et al. (1981) provided an answer in their arousal: cost–reward model. According to

Bystanders who have some relevant skill to offer are more likely to get involved than those who don't know what to do.

this model, bystanders go through five steps before deciding whether to assist a victim:

1. Becoming aware of someone's need for help; this depends on attention.
2. Experience of arousal.
3. Interpreting cues and labelling their state of arousal.
4. Working out the rewards and costs associated with different actions.
5. Making a decision and acting on it.

Findings

The fourth step is the most important. Some of the major rewards and costs involved in helping and not helping are as follows (relevant studies are in brackets):

- *Costs of helping*: Physical harm; delay in carrying out other activities (Piliavin et al., 1969; Batson et al., 1978).
- *Costs of not helping*: Ignoring personal responsibility; guilt; criticism from friends; ignoring perceived similarity (Darley & Latané, 1968; Levine, 2002; Levine & Crowther, 2008).
- *Rewards of helping*: Praise from victim; satisfaction from having been useful when relevant skills are possessed (Huston et al., 1981).
- *Rewards of not helping*: Able to continue with other activities as normal (Batson et al., 1978).

There is another important prediction from the arousal: cost–reward model. Suppose we compare dangerous and non-dangerous situations. According to the model, dangerous situations should be recognised faster as real emergencies. This should lead to heightened arousal and thus to increased helping. Fischer et al. (2011) reviewed the relevant literature and found good support for this prediction.

According to the arousal/ cost–reward model, when does a bystander give help?

EVALUATION

➕ The model provides a comprehensive account of factors determining bystanders' behaviour.

➕ Potential rewards and costs associated with helping or not helping have a strong influence on bystanders' behaviour.

➕ As predicted by the model, bystanders provide more help in dangerous situations than non-dangerous ones.

➖ The model implies that bystanders *deliberately* consider all the elements in the situation. In fact, bystanders often respond impulsively and without deliberation.

➖ Bystanders don't always need to be aroused before helping a victim. An individual with much relevant experience (e.g., a doctor observing someone having a heart attack) may provide efficient help without becoming very aroused.

Chapter summary

- Children under the age of 3 show considerable pro-social behaviour. Much of this behaviour involves instrumental helping and altruistic helping is rare.
- Differences among children in empathy and pro-social behaviour depend in part on genetic factors.
- According to evolutionary psychologists, the desire to gain a reputation for behaving altruistically and third-party punishment are important reasons for altruistic behaviour.
- Altruistic behaviour is more common in collectivistic than in individualistic cultures. This occurs in part because individuals in collectivistic cultures expect to receive more help.
- Parents can encourage pro-social behaviour in their children by providing clear guidelines in an emotional way, by behaving altruistically themselves, and by providing warm and empathic parenting.
- Watching pro-social behaviour on television and playing pro-social video games can increase children's pro-social behaviour by increasing the accessibility of pro-social thoughts. However, the beneficial effects on behaviour are often short-lived.
- One reason why bystanders don't assist a victim is because of diffusion of responsibility. Bystander intervention is more likely when the bystanders are friends, when the victim is similar to them, or when he/she seems deserving of assistance.

- According to the arousal: cost–reward model, bystanders work out the reward and costs associated with different actions before deciding what to do. The model predicts correctly that bystanders will be more likely to help in dangerous than non-dangerous situations.
- The finding that bystanders often respond rapidly without engaging in a complex assessment of rewards and costs seems somewhat inconsistent with the arousal: cost–reward model.

Further reading

- Bierhoff, H.W. (2008). Pro-social behaviour. In M. Hewstone, W. Stroebe, & K. Jonas (Eds.). *Introduction to social psychology (4th ed.)*. Oxford: Blackwell. This chapter provides a useful overview of research on pro-social behaviour.
- Davidio, J.F., Piliavin, J.A., Schroeder, D.A., & Penner, L.A. (2006). *The social psychology of pro-social behaviour*. Hove, UK: Psychology Press. Most of what is known about pro-social behaviour is discussed thoroughly in this book by four leading experts.
- Fischer, P., Krueger, J.I., Greitemeyer, T., Vogrincic, C., Kastenmuller, A., Frey, D., et al. (2011). The bystander effect: A meta-analytic review on bystander intervention in dangerous and non-dangerous emergences. *Psychological Bulletin*, *137*, 517–537. Peter Fischer and his colleagues provide a thorough and up-to-date review of all the research on bystander intervention.
- Penner, L.A., Dovidio, J.F., Piliavin, J.A., & Schroeder, D.A. (2005). Pro-social behaviour: Multilevel perspectives. *Annual Review of Psychology*, *56*, 365–392. This review chapter provides good coverage of theory and research on pro-social behaviour.

Essay questions

1. How do evolutionary psychologists account for altruistic behaviour? What are the strengths and limitations of this account?

2. Describe cross-cultural differences in altruistic behaviour. Why do these differences exist?

3. What can be done to encourage pro-social behaviour?

4. When are bystanders likely to help a victim? When are bystanders unlikely to help a victim?

Humans are social animals who spend much of their time interacting with other people. To what extent do we behave so as to fit in with the expectations of others? For example, would you go along with the views of the members of a group even though you were confident they were wrong? Would you obey the orders of an authority figure if you thought the orders were wrong? In what circumstances are you most likely to obey authority figures? Why do you think most people in crowds behave differently from the way they behave when they are on their own?

Social influence

What we say and *how* we behave are influenced by other people. We want to be liked and to fit into society. As a result, we often hide what we really think, and try to behave in ways that will meet with the approval of others.

Research by social psychologists has shown that most of us are influenced much more by other people than we think we are. This is true across a very wide range of situations. What we are discussing here is social influence. **Social influence** is "the process whereby attitudes and behaviour are influenced by the real or implied presence of other people" (Hogg & Vaughan, 2005, p. 655).

In this chapter, we consider the main ways in which social influence manifests itself. These include conformity behaviour, obedience to authority, groupthink, group polarisation, social power, and crowd behaviour.

Even the most independent of individuals can feel the need to conform under social pressure from peers.

Conformity

Conformity is defined as yielding to group pressure, something nearly all of us do some of the time. Suppose, for example, you go with friends to see a film. You didn't think the film was much good, but all your friends thought it was brilliant. You might be tempted to conform by pretending to agree with their verdict on the film rather than being the odd one out.

It is argued in most textbooks that conformity is undesirable, and that is certainly often the case. However, there are occasions on which conformity makes sense. Suppose all your friends studying psychology have the same view on a given topic in psychology but it differs from yours. If they know more about the topic, it is probably sensible to conform to their views rather than sticking rigidly to your own!

> **KEY TERMS**
>
> **Social influence:** efforts by individuals or by groups to change the attitudes and/or behaviour of other people.
>
> **Conformity:** changes in attitudes or behaviour that occur in response to group pressure.

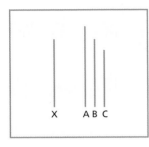

Asch showed lines like the above to his participants. Which line do you think is the closest in height to line X? A, B, or C? Why do you think over 30% of participants answered A?

In what type of culture is Asch's conformity effect stronger?

Solomon Asch: majority influence

Solomon Asch (1951, 1956) carried out some of the best-known research on conformity. He used a situation in which several people (typically seven) sat looking at a display. Their task was to say aloud which one of three lines (A, B, or C) was the same length as a given stimulus line (see the figure left), with the experimenter working his way around the group members in turn.

All but one of the participants were confederates working with the experimenter. These confederates had been told to give the same wrong answer on some trials. The one genuine participant was the last (or last but one) to offer his/her opinion on each trial.

Findings

What do you think the real participants did when faced with the conflict between what the other group members said and what they knew was the right answer? They gave the wrong answer on 37% of these crucial trials. Only 25% of the participants didn't make a single error throughout the experiment. Conformity increased as the number of confederates increased from one to three but didn't increase thereafter (Asch, 1956).

Asch's research is among the most famous in social psychology. Oddly, however, there wasn't anything very social about it because he used groups of strangers! Abrams et al. (1990) studied the role of social factors. They used first-year psychology students as participants. The confederates were said to be first-year psychology students from a nearby university or students of ancient history from the same university.

Abrams et al. (1990) predicted that participants would be more influenced (and so show more conformity) when the confederates appeared similar to them (i.e., fellow psychology students). The findings provided dramatic support. There was conformity on 58% of trials when the confederates were said to be psychology students but only 8% of trials when the confederates were said to study ancient history.

A limitation of Asch's research is that it was carried out in the United States in the late 1940s and early 1950s. That was before it became fashionable for people to "do their own thing". Smith and Bond (1993) reviewed American studies using the Asch task. They found that conformity levels had reduced over time, but even the more recent ones still showed clear conformity effects.

Bond and Smith (1996b) found evidence of important cultural differences. We would expect conformity to be greater in collectivistic cultures (which emphasise group belongingness) than in individualistic ones (which emphasise personal responsibility). As predicted, conformity was greater in collectivistic cultures in Asia, Africa, and elsewhere (37.1% of trials) than in individualistic cultures in North American and Europe (25.3% of trials).

When does conformity break down? The findings were very different when *one* confederate gave the correct answer (Asch, 1956). In those conditions, conformity occurred on only 5% of trials. The comforting feeling of not being entirely isolated made it much easier for the participants to avoid conforming.

Why does conformity occur?

Why do people conform in Asch-type studies? Deutsch and Gerard (1955) identified two reasons (see the figure on the next page). First, there is

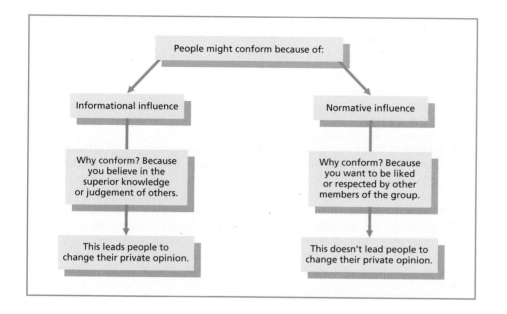

People might conform because of:

Informational influence | Normative influence

Why conform? Because you believe in the superior knowledge or judgement of others. | Why conform? Because you want to be liked or respected by other members of the group.

This leads people to change their private opinion. | This doesn't lead people to change their private opinion.

normative influence: they conform because they want to be liked or respected by group members. Second, there is **informational influence**: they conform because of others' superior knowledge.

Bond (2005) reviewed 125 Asch-type studies. Normative influence was stronger when participants made public responses and were face-to-face with the majority (as in Asch's research). In contrast, informational influence was stronger when participants made private responses and communicated only indirectly with the majority.

Erb et al. (2002) explored factors determining which type of influence was dominant. Normative influence was dominant when an individual's previously formed opinions were strongly opposed to the majority's. However, the influence was mostly informational when an individual's previous opinions differed only moderately from those of the other group members.

Conclusions

What conclusions should we draw from Asch's research? Asch (and many others) argued that his participants had a moral obligation to tell the truth. From that perspective, it is regrettable that 75% produced the wrong answer in response to group pressure at least once, and so exhibited mindless conformity. However, this argument is flawed in various ways.

First, we mustn't overstate the amount of conformity. In fact, 25% of participants did *not* conform to the group's wrong answers at all, and nearly 70% defied the group on a majority of the trials.

Second, Asch and other researchers found many of their participants became aroused and somewhat distressed. Thus, they were aware of a strong conflict between producing the correct answer and their wish not to ignore the group.

Third, the participants were placed in a dilemma to which there was no easy answer. Many of their "errors" can be seen as expressing their respect for group cohesion *and* their desire to avoid ridicule. Most participants

KEY TERMS

Normative influence: one of the factors leading individuals to conform; it is based on people's desire to be liked and/or respected by others.

Informational influence: one of the factors leading individuals to conform; it is based on the perceived superior knowledge or judgement of others.

gave a mixture of correct and incorrect answers because this was the best way to show group solidarity *and* perceptual accuracy (Hodges & Geyer, 2006). Perhaps Asch's participants should be praised rather than criticised!

EVALUATION

➕ There is much more conformity than most people would predict in Asch's unambiguous situation in which the correct answer is obvious.

➕ Several factors affecting conformity (e.g., number of confederates; presence vs. absence of a supporter; type of culture) have been identified.

➕ Many findings can be explained in terms of normative and informational influence.

➖ Asch only studied conformity in a trivial situation in which participants' deeply-held beliefs weren't called into question.

➖ Asch was disappointed in his participants' performance. However, their behaviour can be seen as an effective way of maintaining group cohesion and also showing accurate visual perception.

Serge Moscovici: minority influence

Asch focused on the influence of the majority on a minority (typically of one) within a group. However, minorities can also influence majorities. Serge Moscovici is a central figure in research on minority influence, and so we will focus on his contribution.

What happens when a minority influences a majority? Moscovici (1980) addressed this issue in his dual-process theory. He distinguished between compliance and conversion. **Compliance** is often involved when a majority influences a minority; it is based on the power of the majority. It usually involves public agreement with the majority but not necessarily private agreement. Compliance often occurs rapidly and without much thought.

Conversion is how a minority can influence a majority. It involves convincing the majority that the minority's views are correct. For conversion to occur, the minority must argue *consistently* for its point of view. Conversion often produces private agreement with the minority as well as public agreement. Conversion is generally more time-consuming than compliance and occurs only after cognitive conflict and much thought.

Findings

Wood et al. (1994) identified three conformity effects predicted by Moscovici's dual-process theory:

Is conversion or compliance involved when a majority influences a minority?

KEY TERMS

Compliance: the influence of a majority on a minority based on its power; this influence is generally on public behaviour rather than private beliefs.

Conversion: the influence of a minority on a majority based on convincing the majority that its views are correct; this influence is on private beliefs more than public behaviour.

1. *Public influence*, in which the individual's behaviour in front of the group is influenced by others' views. This should occur mostly when majorities influence majorities.
2. *Direct private influence*, in which there is a change in the individual's private opinions about the issue discussed by the group. This should be found mainly when minorities influence majorities.
3. *Indirect private influence*, in which the individual's private opinions about related issues change. This should also be found mostly when majorities are influenced by minorities.

Wood et al. (1994) reviewed studies relevant to the above three effects. As predicted, majorities in most studies had more public influence than minorities. Also as predicted, minorities had more indirect private influence than majorities, especially when their opinions were consistent. However, majorities had more direct private influence than minorities, which is contrary to Moscovici's theory.

Nemeth et al. (1990) found minorities can make group members engage in more thorough processing than majorities as predicted by Moscovici. Participants listened to word lists. The majority or the minority consistently drew attention to words belonging to certain categories. There was then a recall test for the words. There was much better recall when a minority had drawn attention to them, presumably because they had been processed more thoroughly.

David and Turner (1999) argued that minority influence will be found *only* when the minority is perceived as part of the ingroup. The participants were moderate feminists exposed to the minority views of extreme feminists. These views influenced the participants when the situation was set up as feminists vs. non-feminists—the extreme feminists were part of the ingroup. The views of the extreme feminists had little impact when there was a contrast between a moderate feminist majority and an outgroup of extreme feminists.

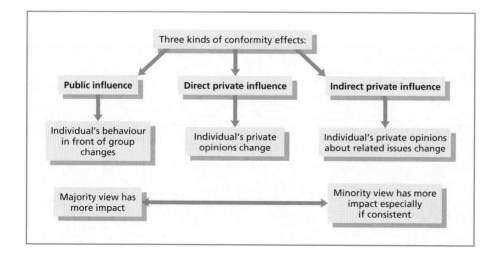

EVALUATION

➕ Minorities often influence majorities.

➕ The influence of minorities on majorities is mainly in the form of private rather than public agreement. The opposite pattern is found when majorities influence minorities.

➖ Majorities generally differ from minorities in several ways (e.g., power; status). Differences in the social influence exerted by majorities and minorities may depend on power or status rather than on their majority or minority position within the group.

➖ Moscovici exaggerated the differences between majority and minority influence. As Smith and Mackie (2000, p. 371) pointed out, "Minorities are influential when their dissent offers a consensus, avoids contamination [i.e., obvious bias], and triggers private acceptance – the same processes by which all groups achieve influence."

Obedience to authority

In nearly all societies, certain people are given power and authority over others. In our society, parents, teachers, and managers are invested with varying degrees of authority. This generally doesn't cause any problems. If a doctor tells us to take some tablets three times a day, we accept that he/she is the expert. As a result, we do as we are told without thinking any more about it.

It is of interest to see how far most people are willing to go in their obedience to authority. What happens if you are asked by a person in authority to do something you think is wrong? The best-known research on this issue was by Stanley Milgram.

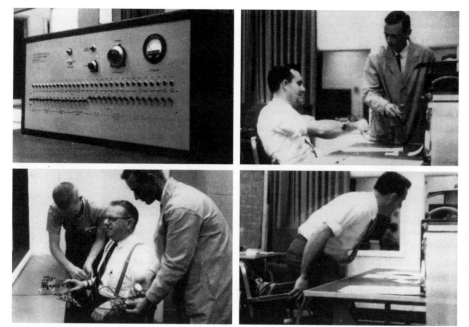

The photographs show the electric shock machine used in Milgram's classic experiment where 65% of the participants gave a potentially lethal shock to the "learner", shown in the bottom left photograph. The learner was actually a confederate of the experimenter, a 47-year-old accountant called "Mr Wallace". The photographs show the experimenter (in the overall) and the true participant, the "teacher".

Stanley Milgram

In Milgram's studies at Yale University in the early 1960s (reported in book form by Milgram, 1974), pairs of participants were used in a simple learning test. The "teacher" gave electric shocks to the "learner" for wrong answers and increased the shock intensity each time. At 180 volts, the learner yelled, "I can't stand the pain!", and by 270 volts the only response was an agonised scream. The maximum shock was 450 volts.

Would you give the maximum (and potentially deadly) 450-volt shock in this situation? Nearly everyone denies they would personally do any such thing. Psychiatrists from a leading medical school predicted only one person in a thousand would go to the 450-volt stage. In fact, about 65% of Milgram's participants gave the maximum shock, 650 times as many people as the expert psychiatrists had predicted!

Did Milgram's research on obedience to authority produce more or less obedience than most people predicted?

A striking case of total obedience was Pasqual Gino, a 43-year-old water inspector. Towards the end of the experiment, he thought, "Good God, he's dead. Well, here we go, we'll finish him. And I just continued all the way through to 450 volts."

Milgram found two main ways obedience to authority could be reduced (see the figure overleaf):

1. Increasing the obviousness of the learner's plight.
2. Reducing the authority or influence of the experimenter.

The first way was studied by comparing obedience in four situations (the percentage of totally obedient participants is in brackets):

- *Remote feedback*: The victim couldn't be seen or his voice heard but his thumping on the wall could be heard (66%).

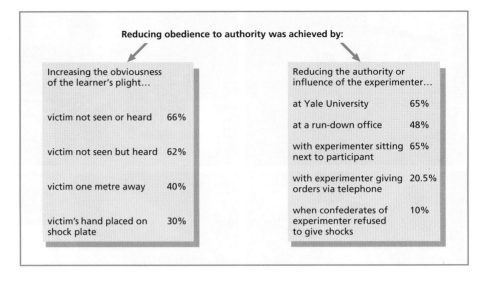

Reducing obedience to authority was achieved by:

Increasing the obviousness of the learner's plight...		Reducing the authority or influence of the experimenter...	
		at Yale University	65%
victim not seen or heard	66%	at a run-down office	48%
victim not seen but heard	62%	with experimenter sitting next to participant	65%
victim one metre away	40%	with experimenter giving orders via telephone	20.5%
victim's hand placed on shock plate	30%	when confederates of experimenter refused to give shocks	10%

- *Voice feedback*: The victim could be heard but not seen (62%).
- *Proximity*: The victim was only 1 metre away from the participant (40%).
- *Touch-proximity*: This was like the proximity condition except the participant had to force the learner's hand onto the shock plate (30%).

In one experiment, Milgram reduced the authority of the experimenter by carrying out the experiment in a run-down office building rather than at Yale University. The percentage of obedient participants went down from 65% at Yale University to 48% in the run-down building. When the experimenter's influence was reduced by having him give orders by phone, obedience fell to only 20%.

Reasons for obedience

Very high levels of obedience have been found in most research using the Milgram paradigm. Bond and Smith (1996a) found the percentage of totally obedient participants was 80% or more in Italy, Spain, Germany, Austria, and Holland.

Why are so many people obedient? Milgram argued that many participants were in an agentic state. In this state, they became the instrument of an authority figure and so ceased to act according to their conscience. Someone in an agentic state thinks, "I am not responsible because I was ordered to do it!"

In fact, Milgram's account is too pessimistic. Most obedient participants experienced a strong conflict between the experimenter's demands and their own conscience. They were very tense, they perspired, and they clenched and unclenched their fists. Such behaviour does *not* suggest they were in an agentic state.

Burger (2011) argued that Milgram only obtained high levels of obedience to authority because of several features of the situation he used. First, the experimenter told concerned participants he took full responsibility for what happened. This is really important, there is much less obedience when participants are told they must accept responsibility (Tilker, 1970).

Second, it was only when participants delivered the *tenth* shock that the learner first protested and demanded to be released. More participants would have refused to obey the experimenter if the learner's anguish had been obvious earlier on.

Third, what was demanded of participants increased slowly in 15-volt increments. This made it hard for them to notice when they began to be asked to behave unreasonably.

Real-life situations

Milgram's studies were carried out in laboratories, and it would be useful to show that what happens in the real world is similar. Hofling et al. (1966) did precisely that. Twenty-two nurses were phoned up by someone claiming to be Dr Smith. He asked the nurse to check that a drug called Astroten was available. When the nurses did this, they saw on the bottle that the maximum dosage of this drug was 10 mg. When they reported back to Dr Smith, he told them to give 20 mg of the drug to a patient.

There were two good reasons why the nurses should have refused to obey. First, the dose was much higher than the maximum safe dose. Second, the nurses didn't know Dr Smith, and were only meant to take instructions from doctors they knew. However, the nurses' training had led them to obey instructions from doctors because they are in a more powerful position than nurses.

What happened? All but one of the nurses did as Dr Smith instructed. Similar findings were obtained in a study on medication errors in American hospitals (Lesar et al., 1997). However, Rank and Jacobsen (1977) found only 11% of nurses obeyed a doctor's instructions to give an overdose of Valium to patients. This low level of obedience occurred because the nurses discussed the issue with other nurses before deciding what to do.

Relevance to Nazi Germany?

Milgram argued that there were links between his findings and the horrors of Nazi Germany. However, he exaggerated the similarities in several ways. First, the values underlying Milgram's studies were the positive ones of understanding more about human learning and memory in contrast to the vile ideas prevalent in Nazi Germany. Second, most participants in Milgram's studies had to be watched closely to ensure their obedience, which wasn't necessary in Nazi Germany. Third, most of Milgram's participants experienced great conflict and agitation. In contrast, those carrying out atrocities in Nazi Germany often seemed unconcerned about moral issues.

EVALUATION

➕ Milgram's important findings are among the most surprising in the history of psychology.

➕ Milgram's findings are of direct relevance to many everyday situations (e.g., doctor and nurse interactions).

- There are limitations with Milgram's notion of an agentic state—most participants found it emotionally distressing to obey the experimenter.

- Milgram exaggerated the extent to which his findings apply to the horrors of Nazi Germany.

- There are serious ethical problems with Milgram's research. Participants didn't give their informed consent and weren't free to leave the experiment if they wanted to.

Group decision making

How do you think decision making differs between individuals and groups? Many people think groups will generally be rather cautious in the decisions they make. This could happen because their decisions reflect the average of the views of all (or most) members of the group.

In fact, what typically happens is **group polarisation**, which is "the exaggeration through group discussion of initial tendencies in the thinking of group members" (Brehm et al., 1999, p. 263). In other words, groups often produce more extreme views and decisions than the individuals within those groups would do on their own.

What factors influence group polarisation? First, there is social comparison. Individuals want to be positively evaluated by other group members. If they see other group members endorsing positions closer to some socially desired goal than their own, they will change their position towards that goal. Isenberg (1986) reviewed numerous studies. Social comparison had a reasonably strong effect on group polarisation, especially when value- or emotion-laden issues were discussed rather than factual ones.

Second, group polarisation is influenced by persuasive arguments. Suppose most members of a group initially favour a given type of decision. During the discussion, individuals are likely to hear new arguments supporting their own position (Larson et al., 1994). As a result, their views are likely to become more extreme. Isenberg (1986) found in a review that persuasive arguments had a powerful overall effect on group polarisation. This was especially the case when groups discussed factual rather than emotional issues.

Third, members of an ingroup often want to distinguish their group from other groups. Suppose an ingroup has a confrontation with a cautious outgroup (not part of the ingroup). They can distinguish themselves from that group by becoming riskier in their decision making (Hogg et al., 1990). In similar fashion, an ingroup that encounters a risky outgroup can distinguish itself by becoming more cautious (Hogg et al., 1990).

Groupthink

The processes within groups leading to group polarisation can have serious consequences. This is especially the case when groups engage in **groupthink**, which is "a mode of thinking in which the desire to reach unanimous agreement

KEY TERMS

Group polarisation: the tendency of groups to produce fairly extreme decisions.

Groupthink: group pressure to achieve general agreement in groups in which dissent is suppressed; it can lead to disastrous decisions.

overrides the motivation to adopt proper rational decision-making procedures" (Hogg & Vaughan, 2005, p. 339). Features of groupthink include suppression of dissent, exaggerating the group consensus, and a sense of group invulnerability.

Groupthink has led to catastrophic decisions in the real world. For example, Sorkin (2009) analysed the factors behind the near collapse of some of the largest American banks in 2008. There was a culture of risk tasking that for a while produced huge profits. Individuals working on risk assessment in those banks who expressed concerns about the excessive risks the banks were taking were ignored or lost their jobs.

Janis (1982) argued that *five* factors increase the chances of groupthink occurring:

1. The group is very cohesive.
2. The group considers only a few options.
3. The group is isolated from information coming from outside the group.
4. There is much stress (e.g., time pressure; threatening circumstances).
5. The group is dominated by a very directive leader.

Is groupthink found more in groups with a strong or a weak leader? Is it useful or dangerous?

Findings

Tetlock et al. (1992) considered eight of the real-world cases used by Janis (1982) to support his groupthink theory. They agreed with Janis that groups showing groupthink typically had a strong leader and a high level of conformity. However, contrary to Janis's theory, groups showing groupthink were generally less (rather than more) cohesive than other groups. In addition, exposure to stressful circumstances didn't contribute to the development of groupthink.

Janis (1982) claimed that high group cohesion can lead to groupthink and poor decision making. However, high group cohesion in the workplace is associated with several positive outcomes including greater loyalty and increased productivity (Haslam et al., 2006).

Baron (2005) argued that groupthink symptoms (e.g., suppression of dissent) are present in most groups and are *not* limited to groups making catastrophic decisions. Support for this view comes from Peterson et al. (1998). They studied top management teams when they made good decisions and bad decisions. Contrary to Janis's theory, the symptoms of groupthink were present almost as much during good as poor decision making.

Baron (2005) reviewed research on the five factors Janis (1982) identified as leading to groupthink. He argued these factors sometimes increase the chances of groupthink occurring. However, they aren't *necessary* for groupthink to occur because most groups naturally strive for consensus even in their absence.

EVALUATION

➕ Groupthink has played a role in many real-world catastrophic decisions.

➕ As Janis predicted, factors such as a strong leader and pressures towards conformity increase the chances of groupthink.

> ⊖ Janis was wrong to focus only on the negative effects of group cohesion. In addition, he exaggerated the role of exposure to threatening circumstances in producing groupthink.

> ⊖ The symptoms of groupthink are present in most groups (successful as as well as unsuccessful) and are found far more often than assumed by Janis.

Social power

According to Franzoi (1996, p. 258), **social power** is "the force available to the influencer to motivate attitude or behaviour change". Philip Zimbardo looked at a situation in which some individuals were given great social power—they had the power to decide whether others should be rewarded or punished. His well-known Stanford prison experiment is discussed below.

Stanford prison experiment

In the 1960s, there were numerous problems in American prisons, many involving brutal attacks by prison guards on prisoners. Why did this brutality occur? Perhaps prison guards have aggressive or sadistic personalities. Alternatively, the social environment of prisons, including a rigid power structure, may be responsible.

In order to decide between these two possibilities, Zimbardo carried out the Stanford prison experiment (Haney et al., 1973). Students who were emotionally stable agreed to act as "guards" and "prisoners" in a mock prison. If hostility was found in spite of not using sadistic warders, this would suggest the social environment of prisons creates hostility.

What happened? The entire experiment was stopped after 6 days instead of the intended 14 days! Violence and rebellion broke out within 2 days of the start. The prisoners ripped off their clothing and shouted and cursed at the guards. In return, the guards violently put down this rebellion using fire extinguishers. One prisoner showed such severe symptoms of emotional disturbance (e.g., disorganised thinking; uncontrollable crying) he had to be released after only one day.

Over time, the prisoners became more subdued and submissive, often slouching and keeping their eyes fixed on the ground. At the same time, force, harassment, and aggression by the guards increased. For example, the prisoners were sleep deprived, put in solitary confinement, and had to clean the toilets with their bare hands.

Zimbardo argued that the mock warders became aggressive because of the role they were playing. However, it emerged many years later that Zimbardo

KEY TERM

Social power: the force that can be used by an individual to change the attitudes and/ or behaviour of other people.

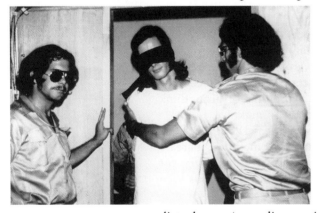

Mock guards and a mock prisoner in Zimbardo's Stanford Prison Experiment. Some of the mock guards became very aggressive during the experiment, and four of the mock prisoners had to be released early.

was much more centrally involved in what happened than he indicated at the time. When he briefed the guards, he told them: "You can create in the prisoners ... a sense of fear to some degree, you can create a notion of arbitrariness that their life is totally controlled by us, by the system, you, me—and they'll have no privacy ... They can do nothing, say nothing that we don't permit" (Zimbardo, 1989).

British study

In December 2001, British researchers carried out a study similar to the Stanford prison experiment for the British Broadcasting Corporation (BBC). Interestingly, the findings of the BBC prison study were very different (Reicher & Haslam, 2006). The guards failed to identify with their role, whereas the prisoners increasingly did identify with their role. As a result, the guards were reluctant to impose their authority on the prisoners and so were overcome by the prisoners. Thus, people don't necessarily assume the role they have been given.

Why were the findings so different from those of the Stanford prison experiment? First, the pressure applied to the guards by Zimbardo to act aggressively was missing from the BBC study. Second, 30 years on from the Stanford prison experiment, people were more aware of the dangers of conforming to stereotyped views. Third, the guards in the BBC prison study knew what they did would be seen by millions on television.

EVALUATION

- Zimbardo apparently showed that situational factors (i.e., the power structure of an organisation) can have large effects on people's behaviour.

- Zimbardo showed that even stable individuals will often abuse the social power they possess.

- The failure of the BBC prison study to repeat the findings of the Stanford prison experiment casts doubt on the importance of situational factors on behaviour.

- It is likely that middle-aged people would have been less affected by the mock prison than were the college students used by Zimbardo.

- There are serious ethical problems in exposing people to degradation and hostility.

Crowd behaviour

Individuals often behave differently when in a crowd than when on their own or with a small group of friends. For example, lynch mobs in the south of the United States murdered about 2000 people (mostly blacks) during the first half of the twentieth century. It is unlikely that those involved in these atrocities would have behaved like that if they hadn't been part of a highly emotional crowd. In similar fashion, groups of people were involved in most of the rioting in London and other English cities in August 2011.

Le Bon (1895) was a French journalist who put forward perhaps the first theory of crowd behaviour. According to him, a man in a crowd "descends several rungs in the ladder of civilization, he is a barbarian ... An individual in a crowd is a grain of sand amid other grains of sand, which the wind stirs up at will."

Le Bon (1895) argued that the anonymity of individuals in a crowd or mob can remove normal social constraints and so lead to violence. In similar fashion, Zimbardo (1970) argued for the importance of **deindividuation**, which is the loss of a sense of personal identity occurring in crowds. It is most likely to occur in conditions of high arousal, anonymity, and diffused responsibility (i.e., responsibility for what happens is spread among the members of the crowd). Deindividuated individuals stop monitoring their own behaviour and so often start behaving aggressively.

The ideas considered so far lead to the pessimistic conclusion that crowds will typically behave in antisocial ways. Reicher et al. (1995) put forward a more positive approach to crowd behaviour in their social identity model. They disagreed with the notion that deindividuated individuals become uninhibited and freed from social constraints. Reicher et al. argued that almost the opposite is the case—the behaviour of deindividuated individuals is strongly influenced by the crowd's **norms** (standards of behaviour). Thus, deindividuation may or may not lead to antisocial behaviour by crowd members depending on the current group or social norms.

When members of a crowd become deindividuated, do they tend to follow or ignore society's norms and group norms?

Findings

There is some support for Zimbardo's (1970) deindividuation theory. Mann (1981) analysed newspaper accounts of crowds watching someone threatening to commit suicide by jumping from a bridge or building. The person was most likely to be encouraged to jump when those in the crowd were fairly anonymous and deindividuated because the crowd was large or the incident took place after dark. Zimbardo (1970) found that the intensity of shocks given in a Milgram-type study was twice as great when participants were deindividuated by wearing lab coats and hoods covering their faces.

Johnson and Downing (1979) pointed out that the clothing worn by the deindividuated individuals in Zimbardo's (1970) study resembled that worn by the Ku Klux Klan (an organisation that favoured violence against American blacks). Johnson and Downing found that deindividuated individuals dressed as nurses actually gave *fewer* electric shocks than those wearing their own clothes. Thus, deindividuation can have desirable effects on behaviour.

Much evidence indicates that Le Bon exaggerated the mindlessness of crowds. Reicher (1984) studied a riot in the St Pauls area of Bristol. There was much violence with many people seriously injured and several police cars destroyed. However, the crowd's behaviour was more controlled than might have been imagined. The crowd displayed violence towards the police but didn't attack or destroy local shops and houses.

KEY TERMS

Deindividuation: loss of a sense of personal identity; it can happen in a large group or crowd.

Norms: standards or rules of behaviour that operate within a group or within society generally.

In addition, the crowd's actions were confined to a small area lying at the heart of the community. If the members of the crowd had simply been intent on behaving violently, the violence would have spread into the surrounding areas.

Postmes and Spears (1998) reviewed 60 studies on group and crowd behaviour. On average, deindividuation (produced by anonymity, large groups, and so on) led to a very small increase in antisocial behaviour. In line with the views of Reicher et al. (1995), deindividuation increased the extent to which individuals adhered to group norms. This often produced positive effects. For example, the death of Princess Diana on 31 August 1997 led very large crowds of people to become deindividuated. However, they behaved in accordance with positive social norms, showing their sadness and sense of loss in a dignified way.

EVALUATION

- Individuals in large crowds often experience deindividuation.

- There is much support for the notion that deindividuation increases adherence to group norms.

- The social identity model accounts for most of the findings, including the varying effects of deindividuation on crowd behaviour.

- Members of a crowd may experience exhilaration or great excitement, but the social identity model has little to say about such emotional states.

- It is sometimes hard to measure "social identity" and "group norms".

Chapter summary

- There is a fairly strong conformity effect in the Asch situation, especially when the participant regards the other group members as similar to himself/herself.
- Conformity in the Asch situation depends on normative and informational influence.
- Majorities often influence minorities through compliance, whereas minorities influence majorities through conversion.
- In Milgram's research, the percentage of fully obedient participants went down when the obviousness of the learner's plight increased and/or the experimenter's authority was reduced.

- Milgram exaggerated the extent to which his participants entered into an agentic state by minimising their obvious distress.
- Group polarisation is influenced by social comparison, persuasive arguments, and group members' desire to distinguish their group from other groups.
- Groupthink involves suppression of dissent, exaggerating the group consensus, and a sense of group invulnerability.
- Groupthink is more likely when a group has a strong leader and there are pressures towards conformity.
- The Stanford prison experiment suggested that brutality in American prisons is due to the power structure within prisons. However, the experiment was poorly designed and the findings haven't been replicated.
- It has often been argued that deindividuation within crowds leads to uninhibited and aggressive behaviour.
- In fact, the main effect of deindividuation within crowds is to increase individuals' adherence to group norms, which can produce positive effects.

Further reading

- Burger, J.M. (2011). Alive and well after all these years. *Psychologist, 24,* 654–657. Jerry Burger shows very clearly how Milgram set up his research so that most participants had no alternative but to show extreme obedience to authority.
- Hewstone, M., Stroebe, W., & Jonas, K. (Eds) (2008). *Introduction to social psychology: A European perspective (4th ed.).* Oxford: Blackwell. The topics discussed in this chapter are considered at greater length in Chapters 11 and 12 of this textbook.
- Hodges, B.H., & Geyer, A.L. (2006). A nonconformist account of the Asch experiments: Values, pragmatics, and moral dilemmas. *Personality and Social Psychology Review, 10,* 2–19. Bert Hodges and Anne Geyer show how Asch's conformity research has been misunderstood and misinterpreted.
- Hogg, M.A., & Vaughan, G.M. (2010). *Social psychology (6th ed.).* Harlow, UK: Prentice Hall. Several chapters in this textbook contain comprehensive coverage of the topics discussed in this chapter.

Essay questions

1. What is conformity? What are some of the main reasons why people conform?

2. Discuss some of the evidence on conformity. How relevant are these findings to real-life situations?

3. What is groupthink? Why does it occur?

4. How can we explain the behaviour of crowds?

We like some of the people we meet and dislike others. We often possess so much information about other people that it is hard to know which information has been crucial in determining our emotional reactions to them. What kinds of information do you think influence your reactions to other people? Are you more affected by their personality or by their personal appearance? Why do you find some people more attractive than others? Do the factors determining romantic attraction to members of the opposite sex differ between men and women?

Social perception and attraction 16

This chapter is concerned with **social perception**—how we perceive and understand other people and form impressions of them. Humans are social beings who spend much of their time interacting with other people within the family, at work, and at various leisure and social activities.

Almost every time we meet someone for the first time, we form an impression of that person. We may find him/her friendly or unfriendly, aggressive or timid, clever or unintelligent. We generally form these impressions very rapidly and often we don't really know *why* our immediate impressions are positive or negative. In view of this lack of conscious awareness, it is necessary to devise ingenious experiments to shed light on the mysteries of social perception and attraction.

Our discussion of social perception is divided into two main sections. First, we will consider the most important mechanisms involved in social perception. For example, how do we interpret or make sense of other people's behaviour? Are some of their personality traits more important than others in forming a global impression of them?

Second, we consider factors determining whether we find another person attractive or unattractive. These factors include physical attractiveness, our familiarity with the other person, and their similarity to us in beliefs, attitudes, personality, and so on. The factors involved in romantic attraction are also discussed.

When deciding why someone has behaved in a certain way, what types of information do we typically use?

Attributions about others' behaviour

In our everyday lives, we spend much of our time in the company of other people. It is often important to work out *why* they behave in certain ways. For example, someone you meet is very friendly towards you. There are various possible interpretations of this behaviour. They may be naturally warm and friendly, they may really like you, or they may want something from you. In order to decide how to interact with them, you need to understand the reasons for their apparent friendliness.

According to Heider (1958), people are naive scientists who relate observable behaviour to unobservable causes. We produce **attributions**, which are beliefs about the reasons why other people behave as they do.

KEY TERMS

Social perception: the processes involved when one person perceives, evaluates, and forms an impression of another person.

Attributions: our inferences concerning the causes of patterns of behaviour in other people.

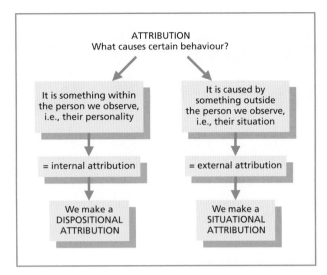

Heider argued there is a key distinction between *internal* attributions (based on something within the individual being observed) and *external* attributions (based on something outside the individual) (see the figure on the left).

Internal attributions are called dispositional attributions, whereas external attributions are called situational attributions. A **dispositional attribution** is made when we decide that someone's behaviour is due to their personality or other characteristic. In contrast, a **situational attribution** is made when someone's behaviour is attributed to the current situation. When we make a dispositional attribution, we generally expect the behaviour in question to be repeated frequently. However, that isn't the case when we make a situational attribution for someone's behaviour unless they are likely to find themselves in similar situations in the future.

The distinction between dispositional and situational attributions can be seen by considering a man at a social gathering who almost ignores everyone else. A dispositional attribution would be that he has an unsociable personality. A possible situational attribution is that he is very concerned about personal matters (e.g., his wife's health).

Fundamental attribution error

Suppose you meet someone for the first time and find them rather aggressive. You might decide they are behaving like that because someone has just been appallingly rude to them. Alternatively, you might decide that their behaviour is a reflection of their hostile personality. In ambiguous situations like that, we tend to exaggerate the extent to which other people's actions are due to their personality and minimise the role of the situation. This is the **fundamental attribution error**.

Why do we possess the fundamental attribution error? Gilbert (1995) suggested two plausible answers. First, "We like to think that life is fair, and using dispositional [personality] attributions can help us to preserve the belief that we get what we deserve" (Gilbert, 1995, p. 108).

Second, the fundamental attribution error makes our lives seem more predictable. If others' behaviour is determined by their personality, this makes their future behaviour more predictable than if it varied greatly across situations.

Do we *always* underestimate the importance of situational factors when explaining someone else's behaviour? The answer is "No", especially when the other person has a hidden motive for suppressing his/her true attitudes. For example, suppose a politician tells you just before an important election that he has no intention of raising taxes if elected. When interpreting this statement, you are likely to take account of the situation (i.e., his motive to win the election).

KEY TERMS

Dispositional attribution: deciding that someone's behaviour is due to their personality rather than to the situation.

Situational attribution: deciding that someone's behaviour is due to the situation in which they find themselves rather than to their personality.

Fundamental attribution error: the tendency to think that the behaviour of other people is due more to their personality and less to the situation than is actually the case.

Findings

Fein et al. (1990) carried out a study in which participants read an essay written by a student called Rob Taylor on a controversial topic. In one condition, they were told Rob had been told to write in favour of (or against) a particular point in view. In this condition, participants made the fundamental attribution error; they decided that Rob's true attitudes were those expressed in the essay even though they knew he had been told which attitudes to convey.

In a second condition, participants were told that Rob had chosen what point of view to express. However, the professor who would be marking the essay had very strong views on the topic. These participants avoided the fundamental attribution error; they decided that Rob's desire to please his professor (a situational factor) led him to hide his real attitudes.

The study by Fein et al. (1990) shows that we focus on a person's motives as well as their behaviour when engaged in person perception. Clear evidence of the importance we attach to motives was reported by Krull et al. (2008). A teenager's mother asked her to help an elderly neighbour by mowing her lawn. The teenager agreed to do this either in a cheerful way or while grumbling. Participants formed a more positive impression of the teenager when she helped willingly.

Krull et al. (2008) found that the impression formed of the teenager depended more on her motives than her actual behaviour. Her willingness to help influenced impression formation more than did the actual amount of help she provided (e.g., mowing the front and back lawns vs. only the back lawn).

Are we more likely to assume this man is sleeping rough because of situational factors (he's been taken ill, forgotten his house keys) or dispositional factors (he can't keep a job, he's drunk and rowdy in accommodation, for example)?

Cultural differences

We might expect the fundamental attribution error to be common in individualistic cultures (e.g., UK; the United States) in which the emphasis is on individual responsibility and independence (see Chapter 1).

However, many cultures (especially in the Far East) are collectivistic and have an emphasis on group cohesiveness. Such cultures focus on situational explanations of people's behaviour because their members are responsive to the wishes of others. Accordingly, we might expect to find little evidence of the fundamental attribution error in collectivistic cultures.

Choi and Nisbett (1998) obtained support for the above predictions in a study involving members of an individualistic culture (United States) and a collectivistic one (Korea). The American participants showed a much stronger fundamental attribution error than the Korean ones.

Knowles et al. (2001) considered attributions for someone else's behaviour among American and Hong Kong participants. Only those from Hong Kong (a collectivistic culture) automatically took account of situational influences in their attributions.

In what type of culture is the fundamental attribution error more common?

EVALUATION

➕ We spend much of our time trying to work out why other people behave as they do; this involves making attributions.

➕ The distinction between dispositional and situational attributions is an important one.

➕ There is some support for the fundamental attribution error.

➖ The distinction between dispositional and situational attributions is oversimplified. For example, neither type of attribution is involved when someone's behaviour is influenced by a headache.

➖ It is important to consider an individual's motives as well as his/her behaviour.

➖ The fundamental attribution error is found much more in individualistic than in collectivistic cultures.

Implicit personality theory

According to implicit personality theory, what do we assume about others? What does the primacy effect mean?

What happens when we form an initial impression of another person? We use an **implicit personality theory**—we assume a person who has one particular personality trait will also have other, related traits. For example, if we know X is friendly, we might assume she is also honest and tolerant.

Asch (1946) argued we should distinguish between key aspects of personality (*central* traits) and less important ones (*peripheral* traits). Central traits have much more influence on our impressions of another person than peripheral ones. Asch assumed that the most important central trait is warmth. Individuals who are warm are thought to possess many other positive traits whereas those who are cold are regarded as possessing mostly negative traits.

Why is the warm–cold dimension of central importance? When we first meet someone, we need to know whether they intend good or ill towards us. Warmth and good intentions go together just as coldness and bad intentions go together.

Asch (1946) also claimed that the initial information we receive about another person affects our perception of him/her more than information presented later. The term **primacy effect** refers to the special importance of first impressions.

There is general agreement with Asch's assumption that the warmth–coldness dimension is of considerable importance in person perception. However, Cuddy et al. (2008) argue that competence is also important. How did they define warmth and competence? "Our warmth scales have included good natured, trustworthy, tolerant, friendly, and sincere. Our competence scales have included capable, skillful, intelligent, and confident" (Cuddy et al., 2008, p. 65).

KEY TERMS

Implicit personality theory: the tendency to believe (sometimes mistakenly) that someone who has a given personality trait will also have other, related traits.

Primacy effect: the finding that first impressions are more important than later ones in determining our opinion of others.

Findings

Asch (1946) gave his participants a list of seven adjectives describing an imaginary person called X. All were given the following six adjectives: intelligent, skilful, industrious, determined, practical, and cautious. The seventh adjective was warm, cold, polite, or blunt.

The findings were clear-cut. The adjectives "warm" and "cold" were central traits because they had marked effects on how *all* the information about X was interpreted. When X was warm, 91% of the participants thought he was generous and 94% thought he was good natured. In contrast, when X was cold, only 8% thought he was generous and 17% thought he was good natured. The adjectives "polite" and "blunt" were peripheral traits because they had little impact on impression formation.

Asch (1946) also studied the primacy effect. Some participants were told another person was "intelligent, industrious, impulsive, critical, stubborn, and envious". Thus, they were given positive information followed by negative information. Other participants were given the same adjectives in reverse order. What did Asch (1946) find? There was a clear primacy effect—those hearing the positive traits first formed a much more favourable impression than those hearing the negative traits first. For example, 90% of those in the first group predicted the person was generous compared to only 10% in the second group.

What causes this primacy effect? When someone feels they have formed an accurate impression of someone else based on the initial information, they pay less attention to subsequent information. Participants reading statements about a person spent less and less time on each successive statement (Belmore, 1987).

The primacy effect isn't always obtained, especially when the information about another person focuses on their behaviour rather than their personality traits. Ybarra (2001) found there was no primacy effect when positive information about someone's behaviour was followed by negative information. However, there was a primacy effect when negative information was followed by positive information.

How can we explain the above findings? According to Ybarra, positive behaviour (e.g., "completed his time sheet accurately at work") is often attributed to the social demands of the situation rather than to the individual's personality. In contrast, negative behaviour is generally attributed to the individual's personality.

What causes the primacy effect?

Warmth vs. competence

There is considerable evidence that our overall impression of another person is much influenced by their perceived competence or incompetence as well as by their warmth or coldness (see Cuddy et al., 2008, for a review). However, Wojciszke et al. (1998) found that warmth judgements were more than twice as important as competence judgements in determining participants' global impressions of familiar others.

Positive warmth judgements were always associated with positive global evaluations and negative warmth judgements always led to negative global evaluations. Competence judgements influenced *how* positive or negative those global evaluations were.

Cultural differences

There are important differences in the implicit personality theories of individuals living in different cultures. Hoffman et al. (1986) asked bilingual English–Chinese speakers to read descriptions of individuals. They then provided free interpretations of the individuals described using the English or Chinese language.

Participants' initial descriptions conformed to Chinese or English stereotypes of personality. For example, there is a stereotype of the artistic type in English (i.e., artistic skills; moody and intense temperament; a bohemian lifestyle), but this stereotype doesn't exist in Chinese.

Bilinguals thinking in Chinese used Chinese stereotypes in their free impressions, whereas those thinking in English used English stereotypes. Thus, the inferences we draw about other people are influenced by our implicit personality theories.

EVALUATION

⊕ There is much support for implicit personality theory, and for the notion that some traits are of more central importance than others.

⊕ There is generally a primacy effect in impression formation.

⊖ Asch de-emphasised the importance of competence as a personality trait that influences our global impressions of others.

⊖ Much of the research has involved asking participants to form impressions of imaginary others on the basis of lists of adjectives. This is very artificial, and may involve different processes from those used in everyday life.

Physical attractiveness

The first thing we generally notice when meeting a stranger is their physical appearance. This includes how they are dressed and whether they are clean or dirty. It often includes an assessment of their physical attractiveness.

People tend to agree with each other whether someone is physically attractive. Women whose faces resemble those of young children are often perceived as attractive. Thus, photographs of females with fairly large and widely separated eyes, a small nose, and a small chin are regarded as more attractive. However, wide cheekbones and narrow cheeks are also seen as attractive (Cunningham, 1986), and these features aren't usually found in young children.

Cunningham (1986) also studied physical attractiveness in males. Men having features such as a square jaw, small eyes, and thin lips were found attractive by women. These features can be regarded as indicating maturity, since they are rarely found in children.

How important is physical attractiveness in everyday life? Dion et al. (1972) found physically attractive people were thought to have more positive traits and characteristics than less attractive ones. They interpreted their findings

Cheryl Cole (top left) fits Cunningham's "attractive female" characteristics— note how her features are similar to the little girl's (top right). Colin Firth (bottom left), however, looks very different from the little boy (bottom right).

as supporting the "beauty-is-good" stereotype. However, their findings were actually equally consistent with the "unattractiveness-is-bad" stereotype. Griffin and Langlois (2006) found that being unattractive is a disadvantage rather than that being attractive is a positive advantage.

So far we have considered only people's *beliefs* about physically attractive and unattractive people. A saying such as "You can't judge a book by the cover" suggests physical attractiveness is relatively unimportant in real life. However, the evidence indicates otherwise.

Langlois et al. (2000) reported several significant differences between physically attractive and unattractive adults. Below in brackets are the percentages having each characteristic (attractive people first). Attractive individuals had more self-confidence (56% vs. 44%), better social skills (55% vs. 45%), better physical health (59% vs. 41%), more extraversion (56% vs. 44%), and more sexual experience (58% vs. 42%). Thus, beauty is more than skin deep!

Are heavy women regarded as more attractive than slender women in most, some, or no cultures? How does the reliability of the food supply affect this perception?

Cultural variations

It has sometimes been assumed that perceptions of physical attractiveness are similar in other cultures. In fact, this is often *not* the case. For example, consider body mass index (BMI). This is based on the relationship between height and weight and is between 20 and 30 in the most fertile women.

Rubinstein and Caballero (2000) found there was a steady decrease in BMI for the winners of the Miss America Pageant between 1922 and 1999. Towards the end of that time period, several winners had a BMI of under 20, indicating they were suffering from undernourishment. As we will see, matters are very different in some other cultures.

Anderson et al. (1992) studied body size preferences for females in 54 cultures. As you can see in the table below, heavy women were preferred to slender ones in most cultures, especially those in which the food supply was moderately or very unreliable. This can be explained on the basis that heavy women in cultures with unreliable food supplies are better equipped than slender women to survive food shortages and to provide nourishment for their children.

	FOOD SUPPLY			
Preference	Very unreliable	Moderately unreliable	Moderately reliable	Very reliable
Heavy body	71%	50%	39%	40%
Moderate body	29%	33%	39%	20%
Slender body	0%	17%	22%	40%

Similarity

There are several ways two people can be similar or dissimilar. These include similarity in personality, attitudes, and demographic similarity (e.g. age, race, gender). We will start by considering similarity in personality. The saying "Opposites attract" implies we are most likely to be attracted to those very *different* from us. However, there is another saying, "Birds of a feather flock together". This implies we are attracted to *similar* people.

Actual vs. perceived similarity

It is important at the outset to distinguish between *actual* similarity and *perceived* similarity. It is entirely possible for someone to believe another person's attitudes and/or personality are similar to their own even when that isn't the case.

Indeed, there is much evidence for the **false consensus effect**—the tendency to overestimate how similar other people are to us in their opinions, behaviour, and personality.

Krueger and Clement (1994) obtained evidence of the false consensus effect. Participants completed a personality test in which they agreed

KEY TERM

False consensus effect: the mistaken belief that most other people are similar to us in their opinions, behaviour, and personality.

or disagreed with various statements. They were then asked to estimate the percentage of the population who would agree with each statement. The estimates produced by the participants were influenced by their own answers. For example, those who agreed they would like to be a singer predicted that 56% of the population would also like to be singers. The corresponding figure was only 40% for those who didn't want to be singers.

When is the false consensus effect weak or non-existent? Robbins and Krueger (2005) provided an answer in their review of the literature. The false consensus effect was stronger when individuals were making judgements about ingroups (groups to which they belonged) than about outgroups (groups to which they didn't belong). It matters more that ingroup members are similar to us than is the case with outgroup members.

Findings: Actual vs perceived similarity

Does attraction depend more on *actual* similarity or on *perceived* similarity? Montoya et al. (2008) addressed this question in a review of hundreds of studies on attitudes and personality. Actual and perceived similarity were both important when individuals interacted for only a short time with each other.

Within existing relationships, attraction continued to be well predicted by perceived similarity. However, attraction within such relationships wasn't predicted at all by actual similarity. What is going on here? Attraction within relationships leads to perceived similarity even in the absence of actual similarity.

Findings: Overall similarity

Most evidence supports the notion that we are attracted to individuals similar to us in personality. Burgess and Wallin (1953) obtained information on 42 personality characteristics from 1000 engaged couples. There was no evidence that opposites attract. The couples showed a significant amount of similarity for 14 personality characteristics (e.g., feelings easily hurt; leader at social events).

Byrne (1971) found that strangers holding similar attitudes to participants were rated as more attractive than those holding dissimilar attitudes. Is this difference more a result of our liking of those with similar attitudes or of our dislike of those having dissimilar attitudes? Rosenbaum (1986) found that dissimilarity of attitudes increased disliking more than attitude similarity increased liking. This may happen because we feel threatened and fear disagreements when we discover the other person has very different attitudes.

Sprecher (1998) studied the importance of similarity in romantic relationships, opposite-sex friendships, and same-sex friendships. Similarity of interests and leisure activities was more important than similarity of attitudes and values in same- and opposite-sex friendships. However, the opposite was the case for romantic relationships.

Are there exceptions to the general rule that we are more attracted to those who are (or appear to be) similar to us? The answer is, "Yes". Heine et al.

Similarity of leisure activities, such as a shared interest in football, is more important than similarity of attitudes and values in friendships. However, the opposite is the case for romantic relationships.

(2009) studied the relationship between similarity and attraction in American and Japanese samples. With respect to several kinds of similarity (personality; activities; attitudes; demographics), the American participants showed a stronger impact of similarity on attraction.

Why did Heine et al. (2009) obtain the above cultural difference? As is discussed in Chapter 19, Americans attach much more importance than the Japanese to having a high level of self-esteem. The Americans are more attracted to those who are like them because such individuals serve to confirm their own level of self-esteem.

Conclusions

There is convincing evidence that we are more attracted to those similar to us in attitudes and personality. Of interest, in established relationships, what really matters is perceived rather than actual similarity—attraction makes us perceive the other person as more similar to us than is actually the case.

However, there are cultural differences. Similarity plays a more important role in attraction within American than Japanese society. The self-esteem of Americans is confirmed by forming relationships with those who are very similar to them, whereas the Japanese attach little value to high self-esteem.

Familiarity

We can assess another person's physical attractiveness very rapidly. However, many factors that influence how generally attractive we find another person have an increasing impact over time. Some people seem increasingly attractive as we discover more about them, whereas the opposite is the case for others. In this section, we will briefly consider ways in which increasing familiarity with another person affects our assessment of their attractiveness.

Do you think increased familiarity with another person generally makes them appear more or less attractive? As we will see, psychologists differ in their answers. Some agree with the saying, "Familiarity breeds contempt", whereas others believe the opposite. In fact, as we will see, familiarity sometimes increases liking and sometimes decreases it. Thus, the real question is the following: what factors determine whether familiarity has positive or negative effects on liking?

Positive factors

Reis et al. (2011) carried out two studies in which two same-sex strangers chatted with each other face-to-face or online. In both studies, the participants were increasingly attracted to each other the more they interacted. Why did this happen? Reis et al. identified three factors:

1. increased knowledge about the other person;
2. increased comfort and satisfaction over time;
3. increased responsiveness of the other person.

What often happens with increased familiarity is that there is an increase in **self-disclosure,** in which revealing information of a personal nature is communicated to someone else. Self-disclosure is often associated with increased attraction.

Collins and Miller (1994) reported several findings based on a review of numerous studies of self-disclosure. First, individuals disclosing much intimate information about themselves are liked more than those who disclose little. Second, individuals disclose more personal information to those whom they already like than to those about whom they are more neutral. Third, individuals who disclose personal information to someone else tend to like that person more as a result.

Negative factors

Increased familiarity sometimes has negative effects on liking and attraction for another person. West et al. (2009) found that college roommates on average liked each other less over time. Of the 11 American presidents from Harry Truman to George W. Bush, 10 had higher disapproval ratings when they left office than when they became president.

Norton et al. (2011) discussed a study in which participants were presented with information about a potential interaction partner. This information consisted of random positive and negative personality traits. The key finding was that liking for the other person decreased as the amount of information provided increased.

Why did familiarity have a negative effect on liking in the study discussed by Norton et al. (2011)? Participants were presented with much negative information about the potential interaction partner, which led them to doubt whether they were similar to the other person. In everyday life, people meeting for the first time typically focus on positive information about themselves and look for common beliefs and interests. The artificiality of Norton et al.'s study means it probably has little relevance to the real world.

Conclusions

Increasing familiarity generally provides the opportunity for important similarities between two people to become apparent. It also allows for increasing self-disclosure and an increased understanding of the other person. These factors jointly mostly lead to increased liking and attraction. However, increased familiarity can produce decreased liking and attraction when it becomes apparent the two people are dissimilar in important ways or that the other person possesses undesirable qualities.

Romantic attraction

So far we have discussed the factors that make another person attractive (or unattractive) to us. Unsurprisingly, most of these factors are also relevant with regard to explaining romantic attraction, as we will see in this section.

Sex differences

A key issue is whether men and women differ with respect to the factors influencing their romantic attraction to members of the opposite sex.

KEY TERM

Self-disclosure: revealing personal or private information about oneself to another person.

An influential approach to this issue has been provided by evolutionary psychologists, who argue we can understand sexual attraction and behaviour in terms of natural selection.

According to evolutionary psychologists, what men and women find attractive in the opposite sex are features maximising the chances of producing offspring who will survive and prosper. The reason is that we want our genes to carry over into the next generation. It follows that men will prefer younger women to older ones because older women are less likely to be able to have children. In contrast, women should prefer older men because they are more likely to provide for their offspring's needs.

Findings

Some support for the evolutionary approach was reported by Buss (1989). In 37 cultures around the world, men preferred younger women as mates and women preferred men older than themselves in all cultures except Spain.

If men prefer younger women because they are more likely to be fertile, this preference should increase as men become older. This prediction was supported by Kenrick and Keefe (1992) using marriage statistics from the United States and the Philippines.

It is often assumed that men attach more importance than women to physical attractiveness, whereas women are more concerned about a man's social status and resources. In other words, men are looking for "sex objects" whereas women seek "success objects".

Shackleford et al. (2005) obtained support for the above assumptions in a re-analysis of Buss's (1989) cross-cultural data. Men attached more importance than women to physical attractiveness and health in a potential long-term mate. In contrast, women focused more than men on social status, financial resources, intelligence and dependability.

Townsend et al. (1995) found that both sexes agreed that males' sexual attractiveness depended more than females' on their status. Males who achieved high status (e.g., via athletic stardom) became much more sexually attractive to females and had a greatly increased number of sex partners. This phenomenon can be seen with numerous male celebrities whose attractiveness to women was transformed by success.

We mustn't exaggerate sex differences in what is found attractive in the other sex. Consider a review by Feingold (1990). Physical attractiveness was rated as more important for romantic attraction by men. However, this sex difference was greater when based on self-reports rather than behavioural data. Thus, women may not be fully aware of the importance they actually attach to male physical attractiveness.

Luo and Zhang (2009) considered the factors associated with romantic attraction in a study on speed dating. Both sexes attached considerable importance to physical attractiveness and there was no difference between men and women. Asendorpf et al. (2011) also found that physical attractiveness was the most important factor for both men and women in a speed-dating situation. In addition, however, women attached some importance to men's shyness, education, and income.

There are major similarities between men and women in the factors they focus on in romantic attraction. For example, let us return to the cross-cultural study by Buss (1989). The personal qualities of kindness and intelligence were regarded as important by both sexes in virtually every culture.

Related findings were reported by Bryan et al. (2011). They found that men and women both attached much importance to agreeableness when looking for a serious relationship. In addition, agreeableness was the strongest predictor of current and future relationship satisfaction.

Similarity

We saw earlier in the chapter that we are more attracted to those who are similar to us than those who are dissimilar. Similarity with respect to several factors is important in determining the person we choose to marry.

The evidence was reviewed by Lykken and Tellegen (1993). Married couples are generally moderately similar with respect to physical attractiveness and educational attainment. Slightly weaker effects were found with respect to intelligence and personal values. Finally, there is a modest tendency for married couples to have similar personalities.

Chapter summary

- According to attribution theory, we try to understand people's behaviour by making dispositional or situational attributions.
- The fundamental attribution error involves an exaggerated tendency to infer that people's behaviour is due to their personality rather than the situation in which they find themselves. This error is less common in collectivistic cultures than in individualistic ones.
- The attributions we make about other people's behaviour depend very much on their perceived motives as well as on their behaviour.
- According to implicit personality theory, we assume an individual who has one particular personality trait will have other, related traits. It is of central importance whether another person is warm or cold, and their competence vs. incompetence is also important.
- Studies of how we form impressions of others indicate we are often strongly influenced by first impressions.
- Physically attractive individuals are perceived to possess more positive qualities than unattractive ones. The evidence indicates there is some validity to these perceptions.
- There is a preference for slim women over heavy ones in most Western cultures. However, heavy women are preferred to slender ones in many cultures, especially those in which the food supply is unreliable.

- We tend to overestimate how similar the opinions, behaviour, and personality of other people are to our own (the false consensus effect).
- Attraction within existing relationships is associated with perceived rather than with actual similarity.
- Attraction depends more on several kinds of similarity in the United States than in Japan.
- There is support for the view that men are looking for "sex objects" whereas women are looking for "success objects". However, physical attractiveness in men is also of importance to women seeking a romantic partner.
- Men and women both attach considerable importance to kindness, agreeableness, and intelligence in a romantic partner.

Further reading

- Eysenck, M.W. (2009). *Fundamentals of psychology*. Hove, UK: Psychology Press. Chapter 18 of this textbook is devoted to a discussion of theory and research on social behaviour and relationships.

- Gilovich, T., Keltner, D., & Nisbett, R. (2010). *Social psychology (2nd ed.)*. New York: W.W. Norton. Most of the topics discussed in this chapter receive detailed coverage in this textbook on social psychology.

- Hogg, M.A., & Vaughan, G.M. (2011). *Social psychology (6th ed.)*. New York: Prentice Hall. Attribution theory is discussed in Chapter 3 of this textbook and research on attraction is considered in Chapter 14.

Essay questions

1. What is attribution theory? What kinds of information are used when making attributions?

2. Describe implicit personality theory. To what extent does the evidence support this theory?

3. Discuss similarities and differences in the factors that men and women find sexually attractive in members of the opposite sex.

Part 5

Individual differences

The extraordinary diversity of human behaviour is obvious to us nearly all the time in the course of our everyday lives. As a result, psychologists have devoted considerable research to trying to identify (and understand) some of the most important aspects of individual differences.

Individual differences have a great influence on our behaviour. For example, if you have a problem, you would probably discuss it with a friend who is warm and approachable rather than one lacking those qualities.

Chapter 17 • Intelligence

Issues such as what we mean by intelligence and why some individuals are more intelligent than others will be discussed.

Chapter 18 • Personality

We will address issues such as the number and nature of personality dimensions and why individuals differ in terms of those dimensions.

Chapter 19 • The self-concept

We will consider major aspects of our self-concept and the ways in which the self-concept differs as a function of gender and culture.

Some of the people you meet from day to day seem very intelligent whereas others are much less so. How do you think we could best measure intelligence: are intelligence or IQ tests adequate? Do you think that people can be intelligent in several different ways? If so, what are the major dimensions of intelligence?

Finally, we come to an especially difficult and controversial issue: where do you think intelligence comes from? Is it something we are born with, or is it largely determined by education and other environmental factors? Alternatively, does an individual's level of intelligence depend on a combination of genes and environment?

Intelligence

17

There has been much controversy about the meaning of the term "intelligence". However, most people accept that intelligence is important in everyday life. For example, those who are very successful in their careers tend to be more intelligent (and also more motivated) than those who are less successful. It is also generally the case (but with many exceptions) that students who perform best on examinations are more intelligent than those who do less well.

What does "intelligence" mean to psychologists? There is general agreement among them that individuals good at abstract reasoning, problem solving, and decision making are more intelligent than those who are poor at these mental activities. It is also generally agreed that an individual's level of intelligence remains fairly constant over time (or at least until old age).

There is more to intelligence than indicated so far. According to Sternberg (2004, p. 472), intelligence involves "the capacity to learn from experience and adaptation to one's environment." An important implication is that we should pay attention to cultural differences; what is needed to adapt successfully in one culture may be very different from what is required in a different culture.

Many psychologists distinguish between individualistic cultures (e.g., the United States; the United Kingdom) and collectivistic cultures (e.g., many Asian and African cultures) (see Chapter 1). There is an emphasis on individuals accepting responsibility for their own behaviour in individualistic cultures but more of a focus on the group within collectivistic cultures.

Social considerations loom larger in definitions of "intelligence" in collectivistic cultures than in individualistic ones (Sternberg & Kaufman, 1998). For example, the word for intelligence in Zimbabwe is *ngware*, meaning to be careful and prudent in social relationships. In similar fashion, the Taiwanese Chinese people emphasise interpersonal intelligence (the ability to understand and to get on well with other people).

Street-wise skills such as the commercial, bargaining, and economic abilities that children such as this young street vendor possess are not measured by conventional intelligence tests.

The trickiest issue about the definition of intelligence concerns the range of abilities to be included. Are "street-wise" individuals (who are skilful at finding ways of furthering their own ends) very intelligent? Then there is emotional intelligence, which involves being sensitive to the needs of others. Should the notion of intelligence be extended to include emotional intelligence?

There are no definite answers to the above questions. However, most psychologists accept that the definition of intelligence should include skills (e.g., being street-wise) valued by the culture or society in which one lives. In contrast, emotional intelligence is very related to personality and probably less so to intelligence.

Intelligence testing

How is the intelligence quotient usually assessed? What is the average IQ and standard deviation?

Numerous intelligence tests have been produced over the years. In 1905, the French psychologist Alfred Binet and his associate Théophile Simon produced the first proper intelligence test. It measured comprehension, memory, and other psychological processes. Among the well-known tests that followed were the Stanford–Binet test produced at Stanford University in the United States, the Wechsler Intelligence Scale for Children, and the British Ability Scales.

These, and other, tests measure several aspects of intelligence. They typically contain mathematical items and many contain vocabulary tests in which individuals define the meanings of various words. They often include problems based on analogies (e.g., "Hat is to head as shoe is to ___") and tests of spatial ability. A sample item might be as follows: "If I start walking northwards, then turn left, and turn left again, what direction will I be facing?"

Calculating IQ

All the major intelligence tests are **standardised tests**. This means the test has been given to large, representative samples of the age groups covered by the test. As a result, the meaning or significance of an individual's score on the test can be assessed by comparing it against the scores of those on whom the test was standardised. Standardisation is important—we can only interpret an individual's score of, say, 47 out of 100 on an intelligence test by comparing that score against those obtained by numerous other people.

The best-known measure obtained from intelligence tests is IQ or **intelligence quotient**. This is based on performance across all of the sub-tests contained in an intelligence test. As a result, it provides an overall measure of intellectual ability.

Another feature of all the major intelligence tests is that they have manuals indicating how the test should be administered. This is important because the precise instructions can influence the tested person's score.

The most common way of assessing an individual's IQ is to compare his/her performance against those of others of the same age. Most intelligence tests are devised so IQs from the general population are normally distributed. The normal distribution is a bell-shaped curve in which there are as many scores above the mean as below it (see the figure on the next page). Most scores are close to the mean, and there are fewer and fewer scores as we move away from the mean in either direction.

KEY TERMS

Standardised tests: tests that have been given to large representative samples, and on which an individual's ability (or personality) can be compared to that of other people.

Intelligence quotient (IQ): a measure of general intelligence; the average IQ is 100 and most people have IQs lying between 85 and 115.

The spread of scores in a normal distribution is usually indicated by a statistical measure known as the standard deviation (sd). In a normal distribution, 68% of the scores fall within one standard deviation of the mean or average, 95% fall within two standard deviations, and 99.73% are within three standard deviations.

Intelligence tests are designed to produce a mean IQ of 100 and a standard deviation of about 16. Thus, an individual with an IQ of 116 is more intelligent than 84% of the population. That is so because 50% of people are below the mean and a further 34% are between the mean and one standard deviation above it.

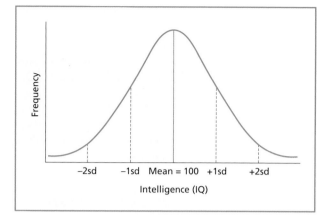

Reliability and validity

Good intelligence tests have high reliability and validity. **Reliability** refers to the extent to which a test provides *consistent* findings. **Validity** refers to the extent to which a test measures what it is supposed to be measuring. We will consider these two requirements in turn.

Should intelligence tests possess high/low reliability and/or validity?

Reliability

Suppose someone obtained an IQ of 135 when taking an intelligence test on one occasion but an IQ of 80 when retaking the same test a short time later. If that happened, the test would clearly be unreliable. As a result, it couldn't possibly be an adequate measure of something as relatively unchanging as intelligence.

Reliability is usually worked out by means of the test–retest method. A group of people take exactly the same test on two occasions. Their scores on the two occasions are compared. The higher the correlation (a measure of the relationship between the two scores), the greater is the reliability of the test. The highest possible correlation is +1.00, which would indicate perfect agreement or reliability. In contrast, a correlation of 0.00 would indicate no reliability at all.

In practice, reliability correlations are about +.85, which is not far short of perfect reliability. This is especially impressive in view of the fact that some individuals show a practice effect—they perform better on the second testing occasion.

Validity

Validity is harder to assess than reliability. The most direct approach to validity involves relating IQ to some external criterion or standard. For example, we would expect highly intelligent individuals to do well at school, to succeed in their careers, and so on. This approach has its limitations, because academic and career success obviously depend on motivation, quality of teaching, and so on as well as on the individual's level of intelligence.

What do studies on validity indicate? IQ generally correlates about +.5 with school or college academic performance (Mackintosh, 1998). This means there is a moderate tendency for more intelligent students to perform better academically than less intelligent ones. However, it is indisputable that other factors (e.g., motivation; study skills) also determine the academic performance of students.

Another way to assess the validity of intelligence tests is to consider the relationship between IQ and occupational performance for those working in intellectually demanding jobs. Hunter (1986) found IQ correlated moderately highly (+.58) with work performance among individuals with high-complexity jobs (e.g., biologist; city circulation manager). The fact that IQ predicted job performance reasonably well strongly suggests that intelligence tests possess high validity.

EVALUATION

➕ Intelligence tests generally have good reliability.

➕ Intelligence tests have proved useful for predicting academic performance and career success. Thus, they possess reasonable validity.

➖ Most intelligence tests are rather narrow in scope. They focus on the individual's thinking ability at the expense of his/her ability to interact successfully with other people (emotional intelligence).

➖ IQ is a very *general* measure of intelligence. It can obscure the fact that intelligence also involves more *specific* abilities (e.g., spatial, numerical, verbal).

➖ Most intelligence tests are devised by white, middle-class psychologists from Western societies. Such tests may be biased against those from other cultures.

Heredity and environment

Where do individual differences in intelligence come from? One possibility is that they depend on heredity. In other words, it could be that our level of intelligence depends mainly on the genes we inherit from our parents.

Another possibility is that individual differences in intelligence depend on the environment. According to this view, some individuals are more intelligent than others because of more favourable environmental conditions (e.g., good teaching; supportive family and friends). Finally, and most plausibly, individual differences in intelligence may depend partly on genetic factors and partly on environmental ones.

It is perhaps natural to think of heredity and environment as having entirely separate or *independent* effects on intelligence. However, the reality is very different. This is because our genetic make-up influences the kinds of environmental experiences we have. Individuals with high genetic ability are much more likely than those with less ability to read many books and go to university. As Dickens and Flynn (2001, p. 347), pointed out, "Higher IQ leads one into better environments causing still higher IQ, and so on." In other words, to him that hath shall be given.

Twin studies

Some of the most important work on individual differences in intelligence has made use of twins. Identical twins (technically known as monozygotic twins) have the same heredity, meaning they inherit the same genes. Fraternal twins (known as dizygotic twins) share 50% of their genes. They are thus no more similar in their heredity than ordinary brothers and sisters.

What is generally found in studies of intelligence on identical and fraternal twins?

What predictions can we make about identical and fraternal twins? Suppose heredity is important in producing individual differences in intelligence. We would then expect identical twins to be more similar in intelligence than fraternal twins. Suppose the environment is the *only* important factor in determining individual differences in intelligence. It might then be reasonable to predict that identical twins would be no more similar in intelligence than fraternal twins.

The degree of similarity in intelligence shown by pairs of twins is usually reported in the form of a correlation. A correlation of +1.0 would mean that both twins in a pair have exactly the same IQ, whereas a correlation of 0.0 would mean there was no relationship at all.

McCartney et al. (1990) considered the findings from numerous studies. The average correlation for identical twins was +.81 compared to +.59 for fraternal twins (see the figure below). Thus, identical twins are more alike in intelligence than fraternal twins. This suggests that heredity influences individual differences in intelligence.

A problem in interpreting these findings is the possibility that identical twins tend to have more similar environments than fraternal twins. In that case, the higher correlation for identical twins might be due to environmental factors rather than heredity. Identical twins spend more time together than fraternal twins, and their parents are more likely to try to treat them exactly alike (Loehlin & Nichols, 1976). In fact, however, the more similar environments of identical than fraternal twins play only a small part in accounting for their greater similarity in intelligence.

We also need to consider the prenatal (before birth) environment. All fraternal twins have separate placentas in the womb, whereas two-thirds of identical twins share a placenta. As a result, the prenatal environment of most identical twins is more similar than that of fraternal twins.

Identical twins sharing a single placenta are more similar in intelligence than those having separate placentas (Phelps et al., 1997). Thus, the greater similarity in IQ between identical twins than fraternal twins may depend in part on the greater similarity of the prenatal environment for most identical twins.

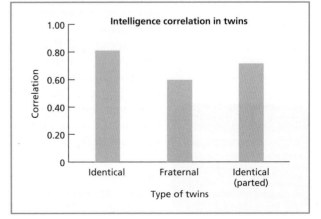

Identical twins brought up apart

Important evidence on the role of heredity in intelligence comes from the small number of identical twins separated in early life and then

Do adoption studies indicate that the IQ of adopted children is more similar to that of their biological mother or their adoptive mother?

reared apart. Such twins are of special interest because they have the same heredity but grow up in a different environment. If heredity is of major importance, such twins should have very similar measured intelligence. If environment is of more importance, there should be little similarity in intelligence.

Bouchard et al. (1990) studied adult identical twin pairs separated at a mean age of 5 months. Even though these twin pairs had been separated in infancy, their IQs correlated +.75 (see the figure on the previous page). This high similarity in the IQs of the twin pairs depended very little on their age at separation or on the total amount of contact with each other.

There is one significant limitation with Bouchard et al.'s (1990) study. More than half the twin pairs were brought up in separate branches of the same family. As a result, their environments may well have been rather similar. This could explain at least some of the similarity in their IQs.

Adoption studies

Adoption studies provide another way of assessing the relative importance of heredity and environment in determining individual differences in

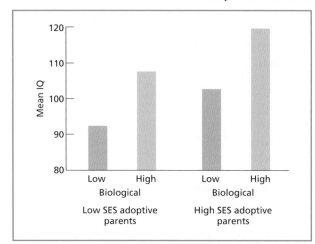

Mean IQs of adopted children as a function of socioeconomic status (SES) of their biological parents (low vs. high) and their adoptive parents (low vs. high). Data from Capron and Duyme (1989).

intelligence. If heredity is more important than environment, then adopted children's IQs will be more similar to those of their biological parents than their adoptive parents. However, the opposite pattern will be found if environment is more important.

The evidence indicates that the IQs of adopted children are generally more similar to those of their biological parents than their adoptive parents. This suggests heredity may be more important than environment in determining individual differences in intelligence.

However, it is often hard to interpret the findings of adoption studies. A key problem is **selective placement**—adoption agencies often try to place infants in homes with similar educational and social backgrounds to those of their biological parents. As a result, some of the similarity in IQ between adopted children and their biological mothers may occur because they are living in an environment resembling the home environment.

Capron and Duyme (1989) carried out an important study on adopted children. It had the great advantage that there was little or no evidence of selective placement. The socioeconomic status of the biological parents had a major impact on the adopted children's IQ, and the same was true of the socio-economic status of the adoptive parents (see the figure above). Favourable heredity or favourable environment both led to significant (and similar) increases in the children's level of intelligence.

Environmental factors

Environmental factors can have large effects on intelligence if the environment is sufficiently extreme. For example, Wheeler (1942) studied

KEY TERM

Selective placement: placing adopted children in homes resembling those of their biological parents in social and educational terms.

an isolated community in East Tennessee in the United States. This community gradually became more integrated into society as schools and roads were built and communications with the outside world developed. The children's IQs increased by 10 points on average during the time these environmental changes were occurring.

Hall et al. (2010) identified several environmental factors associated with the intelligence of British children. Some factors were at the *child* level (e.g., whether he/she was part of a large family; whether the first language was English). Other factors were at the *family* level (e.g., whether the father was employed; father's social class; the mother's qualifications). A final factor was at the *home* level (home learning environment).

Evidence that environmental factors typically have a great influence on intelligence was reported by Flynn (1987). He identified the **Flynn effect,** a surprisingly rapid rise in average IQ in numerous Western countries over the past half-century. Non-verbal IQ (intelligence not dependent on language ability) had increased 5.9 points per decade and verbal IQ (intelligence dependent on language ability) by 3.7 points. The increase has been so rapid it can't be due to genetic factors.

Why does the Flynn effect occur? Ang et al. (2010) found the effect occurred in *all* American groups regardless of gender, race, or rural vs. urban living. This suggests that *general* factors are important. Such factors might include increased years of education, greater access to information (e.g., internet), and increased job complexity. Education may be of special importance, because children whose mothers had higher levels of education had the largest Flynn effect.

Conclusions

We have seen that heredity and environment both play a major role in determining individual differences in intelligence. Can we be more specific? As discussed in Chapter 3, all we can do is to consider the impact of genetic and environmental factors *within a given population*. As a result, it would make no sense to assume that the role of, say, genetic factors in determining individual differences in intelligence can be expressed by a *single* percentage figure.

Striking evidence that the roles of genetic and environmental factors vary across populations comes from twin studies in which the populations are defined by age. According to Plomin (1988, p. 420), the genetic influence on individual differences in IQ "increases from infancy (20%) to childhood (40%) to adulthood (60%)". This happens because adolescents and adults select and control their own environment more than children; this reduces the impact of the environment on intelligence.

Even more dramatic evidence was reported by Turkheimer et al. (2003) in a study on American children. Within affluent families high in

KEY TERM

Flynn effect: the progressive increase in **intelligence quotient (IQ)** in numerous countries over the past 40 or 50 years.

socioeconomic status, genetic factors accounted for 72% of individual differences in intelligence. In contrast, genetic factors accounted for only 10% of individual differences in intelligence in impoverished families low in socio-economic status.

Why was there this very large difference? If the great majority of children within a population have a *similarly* supportive environment, individual differences in intelligence would depend heavily on genetic factors. That was the case for the high socioeconomic status children in Turkheimer et al.'s (2003) study. In contrast, the environmental conditions of the low socioeconomic status children varied much more. This increased considerably the impact of environmental factors on individual differences in intelligence.

Types of intelligence

So far we have focused mainly on IQ, which is a very general measure of intelligence. However, as mentioned earlier, we also need to take into account more specific abilities. For example, some individuals with average IQ have highly developed abilities in language, mathematics, or some other aspect of intelligence. In this section, we will consider the search for the main types or varieties of intelligence.

Factor theories

What is the range of factor types in the hierarchical model of intelligence?

During the first half of the twentieth century, theorists such as Spearman, Thurstone, and Burt tried to identify the main specific forms of intelligence. They used a statistical technique known as **factor analysis**. The first step in factor analysis is to give a series of tests to a large number of individuals and to obtain scores for each individual on each test.

What happens next? The extent to which individuals who perform well on one test perform well on other tests is assessed. If individuals who perform well on test A also tend to perform well on test B (i.e., performance on the two tests is highly correlated), it is assumed both tests assess the same aspect (or factor) of intelligence. If you can't predict an individual's performance on test B from his/her performance on test A, it is assumed the two tests assess different aspects of intelligence.

Hierarchical theory

Carroll (1993) reviewed the evidence based on factor analysis of over 460 data sets obtained over a 60-year period from more than 130,000 people. The findings were consistent with a hierarchical theory having three levels (see the figure on the next page):

- At the top level, there is the general factor of intelligence; this is basically what is measured by IQ.
- At the middle level, there are various fairly general group factors. They include crystallised intelligence (acquired knowledge and ways of thinking) and fluid ability (used when dealing with novel problems).
- At the bottom level, there are very specific factors associated with only one test or a small number of tests.

KEY TERM

Factor analysis: a statistical technique used to find out the number and nature of the aspects of intelligence (or personality) measured by a test.

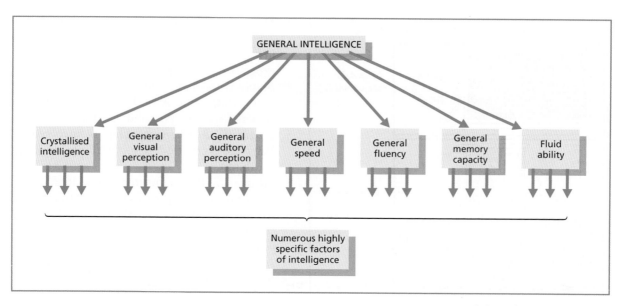

A three-level hierarchical model of intelligence.

EVALUATION

➕ The factorial approach has produced reasonable agreement on the notion that intelligence has a hierarchical structure.

➕ Evidence for the existence of a general factor of intelligence justifies the widespread use of IQ as a general measure of intelligence.

➖ Factor theories *describe* the structure of intelligence. However, they don't *explain* the processes and mechanisms underlying intelligent behaviour.

➖ Factor analysis is like a sausage machine: what you get out depends on what was put into it in the first place. If, for example, no mathematical tests are given to participants, then no factor of mathematical ability will emerge from the factor analysis.

Multiple intelligences

Howard Gardner (1983) argued strongly that most intelligence tests (and most theories of intelligence) are based on an excessively narrow view of intelligence. Traditionally, intelligence tests have assessed language ability, spatial ability, and mathematical ability. However, they haven't considered other abilities of great value in coping successfully with the environment.

Gardner (1983) identified the following seven intelligences, which he claimed were all reasonably separate or independent of each other:

1. *Logical-mathematical intelligence*: This is of special value in handling abstract problems of a logical or mathematical nature.
2. *Spatial intelligence*: This is used when deciding how to go from one place to another, how to arrange suitcases in the boot of a car, and so on.

Gardner's seven intelligences

Logical-mathematical

Spatial

Musical

Bodily-kindesthetic

Linguistic

Intrapersonal

Interpersonal

3. *Musical intelligence*: This is used both for active musical processes (e.g., playing an instrument; singing) and for more passive processes (e.g., appreciating music).
4. *Bodily/kinaesthetic intelligence*: This is involved in the fine control of bodily movements in activities such as sport and dancing.
5. *Linguistic intelligence*: This is involved in language activities (e.g., reading; writing; speaking).
6. *Intrapersonal intelligence*: This intelligence "depends on core processes that enable people to distinguish among their own feelings" (Gardner et al., 1996, p. 211); it closely resembles self-awareness.
7. *Interpersonal intelligence*: This intelligence involves understanding other people; high scorers are regarded as warm and sympathetic.

Findings

It is hard to test Gardner's theory of multiple intelligences. Why is this? A major reason is because good ways of measuring some of the intelligences (e.g., intrapersonal intelligence; interpersonal intelligence) are not available.

Gardner (1993) provided an indirect test of the theory by selecting seven individuals who displayed outstanding creativity with respect to one of the seven intelligences. The representative of logical-mathematical intelligence was Albert Einstein. The other outstanding figures were Pablo Picasso (spatial intelligence), the composer Igor Stravinsky (musical intelligence), the poet T. S. Eliot (linguistic intelligence), the dancer and choreographer Martha Graham (bodily/kinaesthetic intelligence), the psychologist Sigmund Freud (intrapersonal intelligence), and the political leader and freedom fighter Mahatma Gandhi (interpersonal intelligence).

Gardner (1993) reported there were great similarities in the upbringing of these creative geniuses. With the exception of Martha Graham, they were brought up in families that imposed high moral requirements on them and forced them to meet standards of excellence. Gardner was also impressed by their child-like qualities, with each of them showing signs of behaving like a "wonder-filled child" (p. 32).

The lives of these seven outstanding individuals suggested that environmental factors played a major role in allowing them to develop one intelligence to an outstanding extent. Picasso was the only one who displayed obvious talent at an early age. The other six showed no clear signs of their outstanding creativity and future career success even at the age of 20.

This genius-based approach to identifying intelligences is open to criticism. As Jensen (in Miele, 2002, p. 58) pointed out sarcastically, the logic of this approach is that we could claim that, "Al Capone displayed the highest level of 'Criminal Intelligence', or that Casanova was 'blessed' with exceptional 'Sexual Intelligence'."

Real-world applications

Gardner's theory has had a considerable impact within education. The theory implies that teachers need to be responsive to the different patterns of abilities and personal preferences of the students. Lisle (2007) studied adults with intellectual difficulties. Among these adults, 34% expressed a preference for learning through visual presentation of material, 34% through auditory presentation, 23% through kinaesthetic presentation, and 9% through multi-modal presentation.

Emotional intelligence (see below) is basically a combination of intrapersonal and interpersonal intelligence. There is evidence that high emotional intelligence is valuable in the real world. For example, Rode et al. (2007) found that business students high in emotional intelligence showed greater group behaviour effectiveness and higher levels of academic performance.

EVALUATION

➕ Gardner was correct in arguing that traditional intelligence tests fail to consider all aspects of intelligence.

➕ There is reasonable evidence for each of the seven intelligences suggested by Gardner.

➕ Gardner's notion that students differ in their preferred ways of being taught has been influential in the field of education.

➖ Individuals scoring highly on a given intelligence tend to score highly on the other intelligences as well. Thus, the seven intelligences are much less independent or separate than Gardner claimed.

➖ The musical and bodily-kinaesthetic intelligences are less important in everyday life than the other intelligences, which serve more of a practical purpose. You can be tone-deaf and poorly coordinated and still lead a very successful life.

➖ The theory is descriptive rather than explanatory. It fails to explain *how* each intelligence works or *why* some individuals are more intelligent than others.

Emotional intelligence

Over the past 30 years, there have been various attempts to assess the more social and interpersonal aspects of intelligence emphasised in many non-Western cultures. Most of these attempts have focused on emotional intelligence. **Emotional intelligence** has been defined as "the ability to monitor one's own and others' emotions, to discriminate among them, and to use the information to guide one's thinking and actions" (Salovey & Mayer, 1990, p. 189).

Most early research on emotional intelligence used self-report questionnaires. One such test is the Emotional Quotient Inventory (EQ-i) (Bar-On, 1997). High scorers on the EQ-i tend to be high on extraversion and low on neuroticism (Geher, 2004; see Chapter 18). However, EQ-i scores are generally not associated or correlated with IQ (Geher, 2004).

The above findings suggest that emotional intelligence assessed by the EQ-i mainly involves re-packaging well-established personality dimensions. They also suggest it has little resemblance to intelligence as conventionally defined. The same limitations apply to most other self-report measures of emotional intelligence (Zeidner et al., 2009).

In recent years, various ability-based measures of emotional intelligence have been developed. One of the most-used of such measures is the Mayer-Salovey-Caruso Emotional Intelligence Test (MSCEIT) (Mayer et al., 2003). It is based on the notion that *four* main abilities underlie emotional intelligence:

1. *Perceiving emotions*: Identification of emotions in oneself and others. This is assessed by asking participants to identify the emotions shown in faces.
2. *Using emotions*: Facilitating thought and action through experiencing the most suitable emotion.
3. *Understanding emotions*: Comprehending the language of emotion.
4. *Managing emotions*: Regulation of emotions in oneself and others.

Findings

The MSCEIT has proved reasonably effective at predicting several kinds of behaviour. For example, it predicted deviant behaviour in male adolescents (Brackett et al., 2004) over and above the effects of major personality dimensions. Brackett et al. also found that heterosexual couples in which both individuals had high MSCEIT scores were much happier than those in which both had low scores.

Lopes et al. (2004) compared workers having low and high scores on the MSCEIT. Those with high scores were rated by colleagues as easier to deal with, more interpersonally sensitive, more tolerant of stress, and more sociable.

Some findings showing the MSCEIT can predict job performance are less impressive than they appear. This is because the MSCEIT in part assesses aspects of ability and personality duplicating those assessed by previous tests. This was shown by Rossen and Kranzler (2009). The MSCEIT predicted academic achievement, psychological well-being, peer attachment, positive relations with others, and alcohol use.

KEY TERM

Emotional intelligence: an individual's level of sensitivity to his/her own emotional needs and those of others; more related to personality than to intelligence.

However, most of the above effects occurred because high scorers on the MSCEIT differed from low scorers in traditional measures of personality (e.g., extraversion; neuroticism) and intelligence. Thus, the individual differences identified by the MSCEIT resemble those identified by well-established measures of personality and intelligence.

EVALUATION

➕ Emotional intelligence is of importance and was neglected by intelligence theorists for several decades.

➕ Ability-based measures of emotional intelligence have successfully predicted various aspects of job performance and relationship satisfaction.

➖ Self-report measures of emotional intelligence are limited because they are essentially assessing personality but not intelligence.

➖ It has proved hard to show that most ability-based measures of emotional intelligence assess anything more than extraversion, neuroticism, and intelligence as traditionally defined.

Chapter summary

- Intelligence involves abilities such as problem solving and reasoning. Of crucial importance, it involves successful adaptation to one's cultural environment.
- Intelligence tests assess IQ. It is a general measure of intelligence having a population average of 100 and with two-thirds of people having IQs between 85 and 115.
- All good intelligence tests have high reliability (consistency of measurement) and validity (e.g., predicting career success).
- Identical twins (even those reared apart) tend to be more similar in IQ than fraternal twins. Such findings indicate that genetic factors partly determine individual differences in IQ.
- The rapid rise in IQ in recent decades (the Flynn effect) is due to various environmental factors (e.g., increased years of education).
- The impact of genetic factors on individual differences in intelligence is greater in populations (e.g., children with high socioeconomic status parents) in which most individuals have a supportive environment.
- Factor theories suggest that intelligence possesses a hierarchical structure with a general factor at the top. Such theories are descriptive rather than explanatory.

- Gardner proposed an approach based on multiple intelligences. His approach has been influential in education. However, he exaggerated the extent to which each intelligence is independent of all the others.
- There has been considerable interest in the notion that individuals differ in terms of emotional intelligence.
- Some research on emotional intelligence has produced promising findings. However, high emotional intelligence often means little more than a combination of high extraversion and low neuroticism.

Further reading

- Eysenck, M.W. (2009). *Fundamentals of psychology*. Hove, UK: Psychology Press. Chapter 11 of this textbook focuses on the topic of intelligence.

- Mackintosh, N.J. (1998). *IQ and human intelligence*. Oxford: Oxford University Press. This is an excellent book by a leading British psychologist. It stands out for providing a balanced and insightful account of human intelligence.

- Zeidner, M., Matthews, G., & Roberts, R.D. (2009). *What we know about emotional intelligence: How it affects learning, work, relationships, and our mental health*. Cambridge, MA: MIT Press. Moshe Zeidner and his co-authors present a thorough evaluation of research on emotional intelligence.

Essay questions

1. What is intelligence? What are the features of a good intelligence test?

2. Discuss ways of trying to study the relative roles of heredity and environment in influencing individual differences in intelligence.

3. Describe Gardner's theory of multiple intelligences. To what extent is this theory supported by the evidence?

4. What is emotional intelligence? How can it be measured?

One of the most fascinating things in our lives is the rich diversity of people we meet. Of course, they differ in numerous ways. However, one of the most important ways in which they differ is in terms of their personality. In view of the richness of human personality, is it really possible to measure it? How can we be sure we have measured it accurately?

What do you think are the most important ways in which people's personalities differ? Is personality determined largely by heredity or does it depend more on the experiences we have had during our lives?

Personality

18

Some of the people we know are nearly always cheerful and friendly. In contrast, others tend to be unfriendly and depressed, and still others are aggressive and hostile. This chapter is concerned with attempts to understand these individual differences in personality.

What is meant by the word "personality"? According to Child (1968, p. 83), personality consists of "the more or less stable, internal factors that make one person's behaviour consistent from one time to another, and different from the behaviour other people would manifest in comparable situations."

There are four key words in the above definition:

- *Stable*: Personality remains relatively constant or unchanging over time.
- *Internal*: Personality lies within us, but how we behave is determined in part by our personality.
- *Consistent*: If personality remains constant over time, and if personality determines behaviour, then we would expect people to behave in fairly consistent ways.
- *Different*: When we talk of personality, we assume there are large individual differences leading different people to behave differently in similar situations.

Cross-cultural differences

Do people's personalities remain stable over time in *all* cultures? The answer is, "No" (Heine & Buchtel, 2009). Consider the important distinction between individualistic and collectivistic cultures (Oyserman et al., 2002; see Chapters 1 and 19). Individualistic cultures (e.g., the UK; the United States) emphasise independence and personal responsibility. In contrast, collectivistic cultures (e.g., China; Japan) emphasise interdependence and group membership. The notion of stable personality characteristics determining behaviour is less applicable to collectivistic cultures because individuals in those cultures are supposed to fit in flexibly with group expectations.

There is much evidence indicating the importance of cross-cultural differences. Some of this research involved the Twenty Statements Test, in which individuals provide descriptions of their self-concept. Those from collectivistic cultures use fewer personality characteristics to describe themselves than those from individualistic cultures (see Heine & Buchtel, 2009, for a review). Instead, people living in collectivistic cultures emphasise their various social roles (i.e., parent; teacher; club member) more than those in individualistic cultures.

What would we expect if members of collectivistic cultures have less stable personality characteristics than members of individualistic cultures? They should show less *consistency* across situations. Precisely that was found by Oishi et al. (2004). Participants reported their positive and negative moods in various situations (e.g., alone; with a stranger; with a romantic partner). Participants from collectivistic cultures (e.g., India; Japan) showed less consistency of mood state across situations than those from an individualistic culture (i.e., United States).

Determinants of personality

What factors determine adult personality? According to Freud, adult personality is influenced mainly by childhood experiences, although he accepted that biological factors are also important. In contrast, trait theorists such as Raymond Cattell and H.J. Eysenck emphasised the importance of genetic factors in determining personality. Bandura argued that individual differences in personality depend to a large extent on the particular learning experiences we have had.

Which of the above views is correct? There is no simple answer to that question. In fact, there is some truth in all the views—a complete account of the determinants of personality would combine the factors emphasised by each theorist.

Freud's psychoanalytic approach

According to Sigmund Freud (1856–1939), the experiences children have during the first 5 years of life are very important. Their personalities develop during that period and adult personality depends very much on the experiences of early childhood. Most of Freud's approach to personality development was

There are great differences in personality, sometimes within the same family.

contained in his theory of psychosexual development, according to which children pass through five stages:

1. *Oral stage*: This lasts up to the age of 18 months. Infants in this stage enjoy various activities involving their mouths, lips, and tongues. Children may experience problems at this stage (e.g., due to rapid weaning). These problems can produce adults with an oral receptive character (very dependent on other people) or an oral aggressive character (hostile and domineering).
2. *Anal stage*: This lasts between the ages of 18 and 36 months and involves the anal area as the main source of satisfaction. This is the stage at which toilet training occurs. Children experiencing problems at this stage may develop an anal retentive character (mean, stubborn, and orderly) or may become very generous and giving (anal receptive character).
3. *Phallic stage*: This stage lasts between the ages of 3 and 6. During this stage, the penis or clitoris becomes the major source of satisfaction. Problems at this stage lead to the development of a phallic character. Men with a phallic character are vain and self-assured, whereas women with a phallic character fight hard for superiority over men.
4. *Latency stage*: This lasts from the age of 6 until puberty. During this stage, boys and girls ignore each other and experience few sexual feelings.
5. *Genital stage*: This lasts from puberty onwards. In this stage, the main source of sexual pleasure is the genitals as was the case in the phallic stage. However, the key difference is that in the genital stage the focus is on sexual pleasure with another person. Children who develop a genital character are mature, and are able to love and be loved.

What happens when children have problems at a given psychosexual stage? According to Freud, this leads to **fixation**, in which basic sexual energy

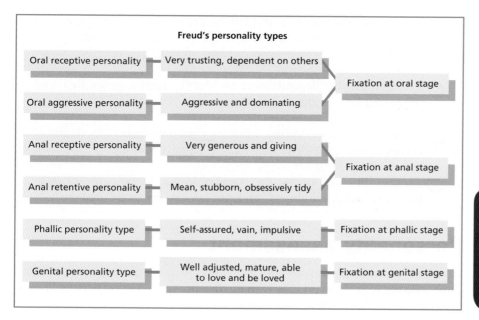

Freud's personality types

Oral receptive personality — Very trusting, dependent on others

Oral aggressive personality — Aggressive and dominating

Fixation at oral stage

Anal receptive personality — Very generous and giving

Anal retentive personality — Mean, stubborn, obsessively tidy

Fixation at anal stage

Phallic personality type — Self-assured, vain, impulsive — Fixation at phallic stage

Genital personality type — Well adjusted, mature, able to love and be loved — Fixation at genital stage

KEY TERM

Fixation: the long-term attachment of basic energy to a stage of psychosexual development at which problems were experienced.

remains attached to that stage during adulthood. When adults experience great problems, they show **regression**. This involves displaying behaviour similar to that exhibited during the stage at which they fixated as children. Such behaviour (which is inappropriate in adults) is often a sign of mental disorder.

Findings

There is reasonable support for the *general* approach taken by Freud, in that childhood experiences clearly influence the development of adult personality (see Westen, 1998, for a review). For example, Mickelson et al. (1997) found that parental loss or separation in childhood was associated with insecure attachment in adults. In addition, adults who experienced serious traumas in childhood (e.g., sexual abuse; severe neglect) were more likely than other adults to have anxious attachments to other people.

Franz et al. (1996) also reported evidence suggesting that childhood experiences have a long-term impact. Adult levels of depression at the age of 41 were predicted well by parental coldness when they were only 5 years old. In addition, an overall measure of difficult childhood experiences (e.g., parental divorce; frequent moves; loss) predicted depression in middle age.

Knappe et al. (2009) studied social phobia (severe anxiety for social situations) in adolescents. Social phobia was more common (and lasted longer) in adolescents whose parents lacked emotional warmth. However, this finding doesn't provide direct support for Freud's *specific* theoretical assumptions.

EVALUATION

➕ Freud put forward the first systematic theory of personality.

➕ Adult personality depends in part on the experiences of early childhood.

➕ The notion that individuals with certain types of personality are more vulnerable than others to developing mental disorders is a powerful one.

➖ Adult personality depends more on heredity than assumed by Freud (discussed later in the chapter).

➖ Freud's stage-based theory assumes that personality development occurs in a more orderly way than is actually the case.

➖ There is little support for the assumption that Freud's five stages of psychosexual development influence personality as he predicted.

KEY TERM

Regression: returning to a less mature way of behaving within Freud's psychosexual theory.

Personality assessment

How can we assess personality? As we will see shortly, there are several kinds of personality tests. However, as with intelligence tests, a good personality test needs to possess three important characteristics:

1. *Reliability*: The test produces similar results on different occasions. A test indicating that a given individual was very extraverted on the first testing occasion but very introverted on the second occasion would be useless.
2. *Validity*: The test measures what it is supposed to be measuring. A personality test might be reliable and yet fail to assess the relevant aspects of personality.
3. *Standardisation*: This involves giving the test to large, representative samples of people so the meaning of any given individual's scores can be evaluated. For example, a score of 19 on a test of extraversion has no meaning on its own. However, it becomes meaningful if we know that only 10% of the population have such a high score.

What is the greatest problem with personality questionnaires?

Questionnaires

You have probably filled in several personality questionnaires. What happens is that you have to decide on the truth of various statements about your thoughts, feelings, and behaviour. Here are some sample items: Do you tend to be moody? Do you have many friends? Do you like to be involved in numerous social activities?

One advantage of the questionnaire-based approach is that it is easy to use. Another advantage is that an individual knows more about himself/herself than do other people. The greatest disadvantage is that individuals may fake their responses. Most faking involves **social desirability bias**, which is the tendency to respond to questionnaire items in the socially desirable (but inaccurate) way. This bias is especially likely to be present in job applicants. As Cook (1993, p. 144) pointed out, "No one applying for a sales job is likely to say true to 'I don't much like talking to strangers', not is someone trying to join the police force likely to agree that he/she has pretty undesirable acquaintances."

How can we detect social desirability bias? The most common method is to use a Lie scale consisting of items where the socially desirable answer is very unlikely to be the honest answer (e.g., "Do you ever gossip?"; "Do you always keep your promises?"). If someone answers most questions on the Lie scale in the socially desirable direction, it is assumed they are faking their responses. Of course, this is unfair on the small minority of genuinely saintly individuals!

Social desirability bias is the desire to give false answers in order to be deemed socially desirable. This could have ramifications in terms of the accuracy of a job application, for example!

Reliability

How can we assess reliability? The most common approach involves giving a personality questionnaire to a group of people on two occasions. This is known as the test–retest method. The test has high reliability if most individuals have similar scores on both occasions, as is the case with the great majority of personality questionnaires.

Validity

How can we assess validity? One approach is to consider differences in behaviour between high and low scorers on some personality dimension. For example, consider sociability. We might assume that those high in sociability should have more friends than those low in sociability. The evidence supports that assumption (Eysenck, 2009b). However, this approach is limited. No one believes an individual's level of sociability is the *only* factor determining how many friends he/she has.

There is another approach to validity. Suppose you fill in a personality questionnaire (self-report measure). Your best friend also completes the same questionnaire, but does so by providing an assessment of *your* personality (rating measure). A questionnaire has good validity if there is much similarity between self-report and rating scores. McCrae and Costa (1990) did precisely this for five major personality factors. Ratings were obtained from spouses. There was good agreement between self-reports and spouse ratings for all five personality factors.

In sum, the questionnaire-based approach to personality assessment has proved valuable. Most of the leading tests possess high reliability as assessed by the test–retest method. In addition, they possess reasonable validity.

Trait theories

In our everyday lives, we may refer to Susan as "sociable", to Fred as "neurotic", and to Catherine as "aggressive". What we are doing is focusing on their **traits** (stable aspects of a person that influence his/her behaviour). For example, we think Susan is sociable because she is talkative, smiles a lot, is much involved in social events, and has many friends.

Personality traits have mostly been assessed by questionnaires. As we have just seen, such questionnaires provide a reliable and valid assessment of human personality. In what follows, we will be discussing some of the major trait theories.

Cattell's trait theory

How can trait theorists ensure they include *all* the important personality traits in their questionnaires? Raymond Cattell adopted an ingenious approach. He used the **fundamental lexical hypothesis**, according to which each language contains words describing all the main personality traits. This makes sense—it would seem odd if there were no words in the English language referring to an important personality trait!

Cattell's use of this hypothesis led him to the work of Allport and Odbert (1936), who tracked down 4500 words used to describe personality. These 4500 words were reduced to 160 trait words by eliminating unfamiliar words and words having the same meaning. Cattell (1946) then added 11 traits from the personality literature, producing a total of 171 trait names claimed to cover almost everything of importance in personality. Cattell used these trait names to construct the Sixteen Personality Factor (16PF) test, which was designed to measure 16 personality traits.

Cattell (e.g., 1946) identified three main methods for assessing personality:

1. *Life (L) data*: observers' ratings of other people's behaviour.
2. *Questionnaire (Q) data*: self-report questionnaires.

The factors of Cattell's 16PF

Reserved ... ... Outgoing
Less intelligent ... ... More intelligent
Affected by feelings ... ... More emotionally stable
Humble ... ... Assertive
Sober ... ... Happy-go-lucky
Expedient ... ... Conscientious
Shy ... ... Venturesome
Tough-minded ... ... Tender-minded
Trusting ... ...Suspicious
Practical ... ... Imaginative
Forthright ... ...Shrewd
Placid ... ... Apprehensive
Conservative ... ... Experimenting
Group-dependent ... ...Self-sufficient
Casual ... ... Controlled
Relaxed ... ... Tense

3. *Objective test (T) data)*: careful assessment of some aspect of personality under controlled conditions (e.g., measuring anxiety by seeing how much people sway when standing on tiptoe).

Findings

The 16PF, one of the world's most popular personality tests, has been examined carefully in numerous studies. Systematic factor analyses of the test have shown it doesn't actually measure anything like 16 different personality traits. For example, Barrett and Kline (1982) gave the 16PF to almost 500 participants. There was evidence for only seven to nine factors and these factors generally didn't relate closely to those proposed by Cattell.

> What did Cattell find in relation to personality traits using life, questionnaire, and objective test data?

Why have findings with the 16PF been so disappointing? The main problem is that many of the 16 traits resemble each other so closely it is hard to discriminate between them. For example, the tense and apprehensive traits are very similar and both are almost the opposite of emotionally stable.

Cattell (1946, 1957) carried out much research to see whether the same personality traits would be found in L, Q, and T data. This was largely true of life and questionnaire data. However, objective tests produced rather different traits. One of the main reasons is that objective tests tend to be rather unreliable and inconsistent.

EVALUATION

➕ Cattell's use of the fundamental lexical hypothesis is potentially a suitable way of identifying the main personality traits.

➕ Cattell's attempt to combine information from several different methods (questionnaire, rating, objective tests) was thorough and systematic.

○ Cattell's approach wasn't very theoretical or explanatory. As Cattell (1957, p. 50) admitted, "I have always felt justifiably suspicious of theory built much ahead of data."

○ There are only about eight different personality traits in the 16PF. Thus, Cattell's main questionnaire is flawed.

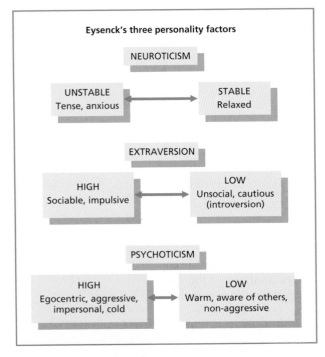

Eysenck's three personality factors

NEUROTICISM

UNSTABLE
Tense, anxious → STABLE
Relaxed

EXTRAVERSION

HIGH
Sociable, impulsive → LOW
Unsocial, cautious
(introversion)

PSYCHOTICISM

HIGH
Egocentric, aggressive,
impersonal, cold → LOW
Warm, aware of others,
non-aggressive

H.J. Eysenck's trait theory

Cattell identified numerous correlated personality traits, many of which resemble each other. In contrast, H.J. Eysenck argued it is preferable to focus on a small number of uncorrelated or *independent* factors that are quite separate from each other.

H.J. Eysenck identified three major personality traits or "superfactors" (see the figure on the left). All of these superfactors are measured by the Eysenck Personality Questionnaire (EPQ; Eysenck & Eysenck, 1975):

- **Extraversion:** Those scoring high on extraversion (extraverts) are more sociable and impulsive than those scoring low (introverts).
- **Neuroticism:** Those scoring high on neuroticism are more anxious and depressed than those scoring low.
- **Psychoticism:** Those scoring high are aggressive, hostile, and uncaring.

KEY TERMS

Extraversion: a personality **trait** reflecting individual differences in sociability and impulsiveness.

Neuroticism: a personality **trait** reflecting individual differences in negative emotional experiences (e.g., anxiety; sadness).

Psychoticism: a personality **trait** that reflects individual differences in hostility, coldness, and aggression.

You probably feel there must be more to personality than just these three factors (and you're right!). However, many aspects of personality can be understood as consisting of *combinations* of two (or even all three) of these factors. For example, there is no trait of "optimism" in the theory. However, people high in extraversion and low in neuroticism are typically optimistic.

Where do individual differences in extraversion, neuroticism, and psychoticism come from? According to H.J. Eysenck (1982), genetic factors account for two-thirds of these differences. These genetic factors influence the responsiveness of the physiological system. Introverts were assumed to have a high level of cortical arousal (brain activity). As a result, they can become over-aroused, and so tend to prefer reading books to going to exciting parties.

Those high in neuroticism were assumed to have high activation of the visceral brain. This consists of several parts of the brain including some (e.g., amygdala) involved in fear processing, and helps to explain why individuals high in neuroticism have strong negative emotions. Differences in brain functioning between those high and low in psychoticism are unclear.

Findings

Extraversion and neuroticism are major personality traits, but psychoticism is less important (Eysenck & Eysenck, 1985). Convincing evidence for the importance of extraversion and neuroticism comes from considering personality questionnaires *not* explicitly designed to measure those traits. For example, Saville and Blinkhorn (1976) studied Cattell's 16PF questionnaire to find out which independent or separate factors it contained. They found it largely measured extraversion and neuroticism (but not psychoticism).

Pedersen et al. (1988) studied large numbers of identical and fraternal twins brought up together or apart. When they analysed the data in complex ways they found 31% of individual differences in neuroticism were due to genetic factors, and the figure was 41% for extraversion. With psychoticism, about 40% of individual differences stem from heredity.

There is evidence that introverts are generally more cortically aroused than extraverts (Gale, 1983). This could help to explain why introverts enjoy stimulating situations (e.g., loud parties) less than extraverts. However, there is very little support for the notion that individual differences in neuroticism depend on the amount of activation within the visceral brain (Fahrenberg, 1992).

Jack Nicholson in The Shining—*perhaps this character would score highly on Eysenck's psychoticism personality factor—he is aggressive, impulsive, impersonal, cold, and lacking in empathy and concern for others.*

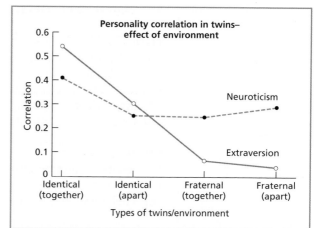

EVALUATION

➕ It has proved more useful to identify a small number of unrelated or independent personality traits (as in H.J. Eysenck's approach) than a larger number of related ones (as in Cattell's approach).

➕ Extraversion and neuroticism are major personality traits or factors.

➕ H.J. Eysenck made a thorough attempt to find the mechanisms underlying individual differences in personality.

➖ The role of genetic factors in determining individual differences in personality is much smaller than claimed by H.J. Eysenck.

What do studies based on H.J. Eysenck's theory indicate about major personality traits?

⊖ There is little support for the physiological bases of personality proposed by H.J. Eysenck.

⊖ Psychoticism is not a major personality trait. It is also poorly named, being more closely related to antisocial personality disorder than to psychotic disorders such as schizophrenia (Corr, 2010).

Big Five model

There is now general agreement among trait theorists that there are *five* personality traits (known as the Big Five). The most influential Big Five theorists are McCrae and Costa (1985). They identified the following five traits (the characteristics of high scorers on each trait are shown in brackets):

1. *Openness* (curious, imaginative, creative)
2. *Conscientiousness* (hard-working, ambitious, persistent)
3. *Extraversion* (sociable, optimistic, talkative)
4. *Agreeableness* (good-natured, cooperative, helpful)
5. *Neuroticism* (anxious, insecure, emotional)

Have a look at the first letters of the five traits or factors. They form the word OCEAN; this may help you to remember the names of the traits.

Costa and McCrae (1992) produced the NEO-PI Five-Factor Inventory to measure the above five factors. They assumed these five traits or factors were all independent or *unrelated* to each other. They also assumed that individual differences in each trait depend importantly on genetic factors.

Findings

Five traits or factors closely resembling those put forward by McCrae and Costa (1985) have been reported many times. For example, Goldberg (1990) collected hundreds of words describing personality. He then obtained self-report and rating data based on these words, finding clear evidence for the Big Five personality factors.

Several twin studies have considered the role of genetic factors in accounting for individual differences in the Big Five factors. Loehlin et al. (1998) found genetic factors accounted for between 51% and 58% of individual differences in the various factors. Similar findings (but with slightly lower percentages) were reported by Distel et al. (2009). In their study, the contribution of genetic factors ranged between 36% (agreeableness) and 54% (openness).

Are the Big Five factors important in everyday life? There is much evidence that they are. Paunonen (2003) compared introverts and extraverts. Extraverts consumed more alcohol,

The results of twin studies suggest that genetic factors account for 45% to 50% of individual differences in each of the Big five factors.

were more popular, attended more parties, and had more dating variety. Those high in conscientiousness had higher academic achievement, were more intelligent, and more honest than those low in conscientiousness. The other factors (neuroticism, agreeableness, and openness) also predicted aspects of behaviour.

Kotov et al. (2010) wondered whether patients suffering from various mental disorders (e.g., anxiety disorders; depressive disorders) differed in personality from healthy individuals. In every case, the patients on average had a high level of neuroticism and a low level of conscientiousness. In addition, patients tended to have a low level of extraversion. These findings suggest that individuals with certain types of personality may be vulnerable to the development of mental disorders. However, it is also possible that having a mental disorder leads to high neuroticism and low extraversion.

The assumption that the Big Five factors are all independent of each other has been disproved. For example, Van der Linden et al. (2010) found high neuroticism was associated with low conscientiousness, low extraversion, and low agreeableness. High extraversion was associated with high openness and high conscientiousness. The take-home message is that the factors are *not* totally separate from each other in the neat and tidy way assumed by McCrae and Costa (1985).

It is assumed by Big Five theorists that individuals behave in ways reasonably consistent with their personality. The validity of this assumption was tested by Fleeson and Gallagher (2009). They asked numerous individuals to report on their behaviour several times a day for one or two weeks. Their key finding was that most people's behaviour was reasonably consistent over time. Extraverted individuals behaved in an extraverted way much more often than introverted ones, those high in conscientiousness behaved more often in a conscientious way than low scorers, and so on.

EVALUATION

➕ The Big Five personality traits or factors have been obtained repeatedly in self-report and rating studies and predict everyday behaviour.

➕ The Big Five approach builds on and extends the earlier theory of H.J. Eysenck.

➕ Genetic factors account for 45% to 50% of individual differences in each of the Big Five factors.

➖ The Big Five factors are more related to each other than assumed theoretically.

➖ Some of the richness of personality is lost by reducing an individual to five scores, one for which each factor.

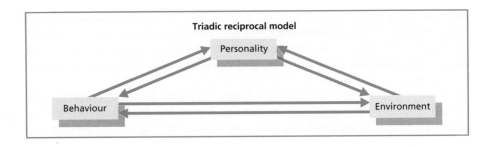

Social cognitive theory

What are the main differences between Bandura's social cognitive theory of personality and the trait theories?

Albert Bandura, an American psychologist born in 1925, has spent many years developing his social cognitive approach. Bandura (1999) argued that the trait approach to personality is *oversimplified*. According to him, we need to consider personal factors (personality), environmental factors, and the individual's own behaviour to obtain a full picture of what is happening.

The essence of Bandura's approach is shown in the figure above. It is assumed that personality, behaviour, and the environment influence each other in complex ways. Thus, the environment influences our behaviour, but our personality and behaviour also help to determine the environment. For example, extraverts actively seek out social situations more often than introverts (Furnham, 1981).

Bandura's approach is more complex than that of traditional trait theorists. Trait theorists emphasise the notion that personality influences behaviour, which corresponds to only *one* of the six arrows in Bandura's model. Trait theorists also argue that the environment influences behaviour (a second arrow in Bandura's model). However, few trait theorists focus on the other four arrows in the model. This is a real limitation. People's personalities influence the situations in which they find themselves as well as how they behave in those situations.

There are two other important differences between Bandura's social cognitive approach and trait theories. Bandura argued we must take full account of the *specific* situation in which individuals find themselves to predict their behaviour. In contrast, most trait theorists claim an individual's personality will influence their behaviour in similar ways in most situations.

Second, Bandura argued that individual differences in *cognitive* processes and strategies play an important role in determining differences in behaviour. In contrast, trait theorists have generally had little or nothing to say about such processes. Indeed, the neglect of the cognitive system is one of the greatest limitations of most trait theories.

Self-efficacy

The notion of self-efficacy is of central importance within Bandura's social cognitive approach. **Self-efficacy** refers to the beliefs individuals have concerning their ability to cope with a particular task or situation and achieve the desired outcome. In the words of Bandura (1977, p. 391), self-efficacy judgements are concerned, "not with the skills one has but with judgements of what one can do with the skills one possesses". It is assumed that high self-efficacy has beneficial effects on performance because it leads to increased task motivation.

What determines an individual's level of self-efficacy in any given situation? First, there are the individual's experiences of success and/or failure in that situation. Second, there are relevant second-hand experiences—if you see someone else cope successfully with that situation, it will increase your self-efficacy beliefs. Third, there is social persuasion—your level of self-efficacy will increase if someone argues persuasively you have the necessary skills to succeed in that situation. Fourth, self-efficacy will be reduced if you experience the high level of arousal associated with anxiety and failure.

Self-regulation

Bandura (1986) argued that our behaviour is also influenced by self-regulation. **Self-regulation** involves using your cognitive processes to regulate and control your own behaviour. For example, you may reward yourself if you achieve a given standard of performance by thinking positively about your achievement or by having a celebratory drink. In general terms, our behaviour is often controlled by *internal* factors. It is assumed that self-regulation leads to enhanced performance.

Bandura (1986) identified three processes of central importance to self-regulation:

According to Bandura's social cognitive theory, our behaviour is influenced by self-efficacy and self-regulation. Individuals high in self-efficacy and self-regulation tend to have healthier lifestyles than other people.

1. *Self-observation*: Individuals observe their own behaviour (e.g., the quality of their work; their productivity).
2. *Judgemental processes*: Individuals take account of their personal standards and the role of personal and external factors in influencing their performance.
3. *Self-reaction*: Individuals experience pride or self-satisfaction when their behaviour reaches or exceeds their personal standards; they experience self-criticism when it falls short of those standards.

Findings

Self-efficacy beliefs typically predict behaviour. For example, Dzewaltowski (1989) assessed the ability of various factors to predict the amount of exercise students would take over a 7-week period. Self-efficacy beliefs concerning

> **KEY TERM**
>
> **Self-regulation:** according to Bandura, the notion that individuals learn to reward and punish themselves internally to regulate their own behaviour and achieve desired outcomes.

their ability to take part in an exercise programme when faced with competing demands emerged as the best single predictor.

Stajkovic and Luthans (1998) found there was a moderately strong association between self-efficacy and work performance across 114 studies. High self-efficacy was associated with a 28% increase in performance. This was much greater than the beneficial effects of other factors such as goal setting (10% increase) or being provided with feedback concerning performance (13.6% increase).

Stajkovic and Luthans (1998) found self-efficacy was more strongly associated with high task performance on easy than complex tasks. In addition, the strength of the association was higher in laboratory settings than in more naturalistic ones.

Why did the above differences occur? We would expect the relationship between self-efficacy and performance to be greater when participants possess detailed information about task demands, the best strategy to adopt, and so on. People performing difficult tasks in real-world settings often lack sufficient information to make accurate self-efficacy judgements.

How does self-efficacy compare to standard personality factors in its ability to predict behaviour? Judge et al. (2007) considered this issue by reviewing studies on work-related performance. Self-efficacy predicted performance to a modest extent, but this didn't seem to be due to self-efficacy itself. Instead, it occurred mainly because individuals high in self-efficacy tended to be high in intelligence, conscientiousness, and extraversion, and low in neuroticism. Performance was much better predicted by intelligence and conscientiousness than by self-efficacy.

Self-regulation: Eating behaviour

The prediction that individuals using self-regulation strategies will outperform those not using such strategies has received much support in studies on eating behaviour. For example, Kitsantas (2000) carried out a study on three groups of college students: overweight students who had failed to lose weight; previously overweight students who had successfully lost weight; and students with no weight problems.

All the participants in the study by Kitsantas (2000) completed a questionnaire indicating the self-regulation strategies they used. They also recorded their self-efficacy beliefs concerning their ability to use these strategies successfully. The self-regulation strategies used included the following: goal setting and/or planning (e.g., setting a desired weight); self-evaluation of progress in losing weight; and attempts to seek help in efforts to lose weight.

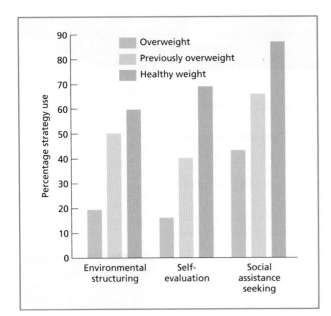

Use of various self-regulation strategies by overweight, previously overweight, and healthy weight participants. Data from Kitsantas (2000).

What did Kitsantas (2000) find? First, overweight students who didn't lose weight used fewer self-regulation strategies than did the other two groups (see the figure on the left). This was especially the case for self-evaluation of progress, a strategy used far less by overweight students than by those in the other groups.

Second, overweight students who didn't lose weight had lower levels of self-efficacy than students in the other two groups. Third, the use of several self-regulation strategies was only effective when combined with high self-efficacy. Thus, there is little point in using self-regulation strategies if you use them half-heartedly—you have to believe they are going to be effective.

Similar findings have been obtained in research on eating behaviour in adolescents. Kalavana et al. (2010) found that self-regulation strategies were positively related to healthy eating. In addition, self-regulation strategies were negatively related to unhealthy eating (e.g., junk food).

EVALUATION

⊕ Self-efficacy and self-regulation both influence how an individual will behave in a given situation.

⊕ Bandura's approach has been very influential within health psychology.

⊕ The extent to which people adopt healthy forms of behaviour (e.g., giving up smoking; losing weight; taking exercise) depends to an important extent on self-efficacy and self-regulation.

⊖ The social cognitive approach focuses on cognitive factors and de-emphasises emotional ones. In fact, our motivation and behaviour are often influenced by our emotions rather than by cool calculation.

⊖ It is hard to interpret associations between self-efficacy and performance. Bandura assumed that self-efficacy influences performance. However, past performance influences self-efficacy judgements. It is often unclear whether self-efficacy influences performance more than performance influences self-efficacy.

⊖ Bandura has focused on predicting and understanding people's behaviour in *specific* situations. It is unclear whether his approach can account for individual differences in *broad* areas of life.

Chapter summary

- The notion that our behaviour is strongly influenced by our stable personality characteristics is more relevant in individualistic than in collectivistic cultures.
- Freud identified five stages of psychosexual development: oral; anal; phallic; latency; and genital.

- Freud argued that many adult mental disorders depend in large part on childhood experiences. There is some truth in this argument, but Freud didn't fully appreciate the importance of *current* adult concerns in producing mental disorder.
- Personality tests need to be standardised and to have high levels of reliability and validity.
- Cattell argued there are 16 personality traits, many of which are fairly closely related. However, there are no more than 8 personality traits in his questionnaire designed to assess 16.
- H.J. Eysenck identified three unrelated superfactors (extraversion; neuroticism; psychoticism). Genetic factors account for about 40% of individual differences in all three superfactors.
- Costa and McCrae argued that there are five major personality factors (the Big Five: openness; conscientiousness; extraversion; agreeableness; and neuroticism). Individual differences in all five factors depend in part on genetic factors.
- Costa and McCrae argued incorrectly that the Big Five factors are all unrelated to each other.
- According to Bandura's social cognitive theory, our behaviour is influenced by self-efficacy and self-regulation. Individuals high in self-efficacy and self-regulation tend to have healthier lifestyles than other people.
- Bandura's approach involves a strong emphasis on cognitive factors and a relative neglect of emotional factors.

Further reading

- Carver, C.S., & Scheier, M.F. (2011). *Perspectives on personality (7th ed.).* Pearson: New York. This textbook provides good basic coverage of major approaches to personality.

- Cervone, D., & Pervin, L.A. (2008). *Personality: Theory and research (10th ed.).* Hoboken, NJ: Wiley. This well-established textbook has full discussions of all the theoretical approaches included in this chapter.

- Eysenck, M.W. (2009). *Fundamentals of psychology.* Hove, UK: Psychology Press. Chapter 12 of this introductory textbook is devoted to a discussion of various personality theories.

- Heine, S.J., & Buchtel, E.E. (2009). Personality: The universal and the culturally specific. *Annual Review of Psychology, 60,* 369–394. This chapter contains much discussion of cross-cultural differences in personality.

Essay questions

1. What is Freud's psychosexual theory? How adequate is it as an account of personality development?

2. Describe Cattell's and H.J. Eysenck's trait theories of personality. What do they have in common? How do they differ?

3. What is the Big Five approach to personality? How successful has that approach been?

4. Describe Bandura's social cognitive theory. What are its main strengths and limitations?

The way we see ourselves is our self-concept. Like everyone else, you have many thoughts and feelings about yourself, about the kind of person you are, and about your relationships with other people. What do you think are some of the most important influences that have shaped your self-concept? Do you agree that your self-concept has been influenced by other people (especially those who play or have played a major role in your life)?

In Western cultures, most people have a sense of themselves as individuals whose behaviour is determined by their personality, personal goals, and so on. Do you think this Western view of the self is universal? More specifically, do you think that people living in very different cultures (e.g., in the Far East) have a sense of self revolving around their social roles and obligations?

The self-concept

19

What is the self-concept? According to Baumeister (1995, p. 58), the **self-concept** is, "the total organized body of information that any given person has about himself or herself". Baumeister and Bushman (2009) argued that the self has three basic aspects:

1. Self-knowledge (our awareness of having a self).
2. The self exists almost entirely within a social context and is used when relating to others.
3. The self seems to make decisions and to cause us to behave in certain ways.

The self-concept is influenced by numerous factors. However, as mentioned already, our relationships with other people are of crucial importance. Charles Cooley (1902) used the term "looking-glass self" to convey the notion that our self-concept reflects other people's evaluations. In other words, we tend to see ourselves as others see us. Unsurprisingly, those of greatest importance in our lives (e.g., partners, parents, close friends) have the most influence on our self-concept.

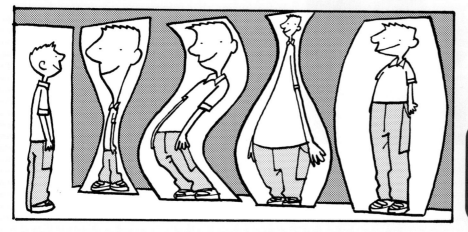

William James (1890) distinguished between two aspects of the self-concept: the "I" or self as the *subject* of experience and the "me" or self as the *object* of experience. Young children start to develop a sense of being separate from other people. This is the "I". After that, the "me" develops. This involves an awareness of the self as an object that can be perceived by others, which in turn leads to the development of the self-concept.

It seems natural for people living in Europe or the United States to think in terms of a self-concept. As is discussed in Chapter 1, these cultures are individualistic ones in which the emphasis is on personal responsibility and achievement. However, the views we have of ourselves as separate individuals differ considerably from those held in most societies throughout human history. As Westen (1996, p. 696) pointed out:

> The contemporary Western view of the person is of a bounded individual, distinct from significant others, who is defined by idiosyncratic attributes. In contrast, most cultures, particularly the non-literate tribal and band societies in which people lived throughout the vast expanse of human history, have understood the person in social and familial context.

Westen's point is illustrated by contemporary Asian cultures. They are collectivistic cultures, meaning the emphasis is on the group rather than the individual. For example, the Chinese word *ren* (meaning person) refers to the ways in which an individual's behaviour fits (or doesn't fit) group standards. More will be said about cultural differences later in the chapter.

Development of the self-concept

The self-concept develops during the early years of life. It is hard to study its development because young children have a very limited command of language. In spite of this, progress has been made in studying how the self-concept develops in infants.

Self-recognition

An early sign that infants are starting to develop a sense of self is when they recognise themselves in a mirror. Lewis and Brooks-Gunn (1979) carried out a study in which infants who had had a red spot applied to their nose were held up to a mirror.

Those infants who reached for their own nose (and so recognised their own reflection) were claimed to show evidence of self-awareness. Practically no infants in the first year of life showed self-awareness. However, 70% of infants between 21 and 24 months did so.

Evidence that visual self-recognition is a sign of self-awareness was reported by Courage et al. (2004). In most infants, visual self-recognition was

When infants start to recognise themselves in a mirror it is a sign that they are starting to develop a sense of self.

followed closely by the use of personal pronouns (e.g., "I", "me") and an ability to identify themselves in photographs.

What are the changes in the self-concept during childhood?

Howe and Courage (1997) claimed the initial development of a sense of self (revealed by visual self-recognition) is crucial in the emergence of autobiographical memory. Autobiographical memory is memory for the events of one's life and is important to our sense of self.

The finding that visual self-recognition appears shortly before the onset of autobiographical memory around a child's second birthday is consistent with the above claim. However, it doesn't show that the former plays a role in *causing* the latter. Howe et al. (2003) obtained stronger evidence. Among infants aged between 15 and 23 months, self-recognisers had better memory for personal events than infants who weren't self-recognisers. More strikingly, not a single child showed good performance on a memory test for personal events *before* achieving self-recognition.

Self-descriptions

We can study the development of the self-concept in older children by asking them to describe themselves and seeing the kinds of information they regard as important. However, there are real limitations with this approach. Children may *distort* their self-descriptions to impress the investigator. Alternatively, children may ignore important aspects of their self-concept when providing self-descriptions. Nevertheless, the use of self-descriptions is a valuable approach.

Damon and Hart (1988) argued that children's self-descriptions fall into four categories:

1. *Physical features*: external characteristics (e.g., being tall or overweight).
2. *Activities*: the things the child spends time doing (e.g., "I like playing netball").
3. *Social characteristics*: self-descriptions relating the self to other people (e.g., "I have a brother and a sister").
4. *Psychological characteristics*: internal characteristics (e.g., "I am very friendly").

According to Damon and Hart (1988), there are some common themes in the self-concept throughout childhood, with all four categories being included in most self-descriptions. However, the relative importance to the self-concept of each category changes considerably during the course of development. For example, physical characteristics become less important and psychological ones become more important.

Findings

Hart et al. (1993) provided detailed evidence on the salience or centrality of the four categories of self-descriptions among 6- to 16-year-olds. The relative importance to the self-concept of social characteristics didn't change during childhood, but there was a reduction in the importance of physical characteristics. Children of 9 or 10 defined themselves less in terms of their activities than did children of 6 to 8. In addition, adolescents attached much more significance than 11- to 13-year-olds to psychological characteristics.

Wellman and Gelman (1988) pointed out there are *two* kinds of psychological or internal characteristics contained in self-descriptions:

1. Dispositions (e.g., personality traits), which are relatively permanent.
2. Internal states (e.g., feeling sad), which are short-lived.

According to Damon and Hart's (1988) theory, psychological characteristics only become important towards the end of childhood. That is much more the case for dispositions than internal states. Children typically don't include dispositions in their self-descriptions before the age of 7. However, they apply psychological characteristics in the form of internal states to themselves from the age of 3 onwards.

Autobiographical memory

As mentioned earlier, there are close connections between the self-concept and autobiographical memory. **Autobiographical memory** is concerned with our memories of the events of our own life. For example, consider patients suffering from Alzheimer's disease, in which there is a severe impairment in autobiographical memory. Those patients whose autobiographical memory for childhood and early adulthood was most impaired also had the weakest self-concept or sense of identity (Addis & Tippett, 2004).

How does autobiographical memory change during development? Pasupathi and Wainryb (2010) asked children and adolescents to construct autobiographical memory narratives. Adolescents were much more likely than children to focus on their desires, emotions, and beliefs in their narratives. Thus, the notion of a self that can succeed or fail only fully develops during adolescence.

Why do we spend time recalling autobiographical memories from the past? Three key reasons are as follows (Bluck & Alea, 2009):

1. maintenance of social bonds;
2. directing future behaviour;
3. creating a sense of self-continuity over time.

Bluck and Alea (2009) asked young and older adults why they thought and talked about their past. The younger group used autobiographical memory more often to direct future plans and to produce a sense of self-continuity. Thus, the self-concept is still developing in early adulthood.

Suppose we asked people to describe a positive or negative personal experience. Since autobiographical memory and the self are closely related, the content of such memories might reveal much about each individual's self-concept. Precisely this was done by Woike et al. (1999). The memories that were recalled were categorised as *agentic* (e.g., involving success or failure; power or powerlessness) or *communal* (e.g., involving love or friendship).

What did Woike et al. (1999) find? Most individuals whose self-concept was agentic (with an emphasis on independence, achievement, and personal power) recalled agentic personal memories. In contrast, individuals whose self-concept was communal (with an emphasis on interdependence and similarity to others) recalled communal memories. Thus, our self-concept partly determines which autobiographical memories are important to us.

> **KEY TERM**
>
> **Autobiographical memory:** memory across the lifespan for specific events involving the individual (especially those of personal significance).

You might find it interesting to think of two very positive autobiographical memories and two very negative ones. Are most of these memories agentic or communal? Do they seem of relevance to your self-concept?

Cross-cultural and gender differences

Markus and Kitayama (1991) argued there are major cultural differences in the conception of the self. Those living in individualistic cultures such as the United States and the United Kingdom have an **independent self**: the individual is seen as "an independent, self-contained autonomous entity who (1) encompasses unique configurations of internal attributes (e.g., traits, abilities, morals, and values), and (2) behaves primarily as a consequence of these internal attributes" (p. 224).

In contrast, people living in collectivistic cultures (especially those in East Asia) have an **interdependent self**. They define themselves mainly with respect to their relationships and group memberships. There is more on the differences between individualistic and collectivistic cultures in Chapter 1.

Cross and Madsen (1997) argued that the distinction between an independent self and an interdependent self also applies to gender differences. More specifically, they argued that, "Men in the United States are thought to construct and maintain an independent self-construal, whereas women are thought to construct and maintain an interdependent self-construal" (p. 5).

What Cross and Madsen (1997) had in mind was that men and women *on average* differ in the nature of the self-concept. In spite of that, some men have an interdependent self and some women have an independent self.

Findings

We can study cultural differences in the self-concept by using the Twenty Statements Test. This test requires people to provide 20 answers to the question, "Who am I?" The predicted cultural differences have generally been reported. For example, Triandis et al. (1990) compared the test responses of students from mainland United States, Hawaii, Hong Kong, Greece, and China. There were far more references to oneself as a member of a social category or group in the responses of the Chinese students than in any other group.

Interesting evidence that cultural differences in the conception of the self influence social processes was obtained by Gudykunst et al. (1996). American and British participants reported greater monitoring of their *own behaviour* in social situations than did Japanese and Chinese participants. This suggests their self-concept is mostly concerned with themselves as individuals. In contrast, the Japanese and Chinese participants monitored *others' behaviour* more in social situations. That is as expected given that their self-concept is concerned with their relationships with others.

Cross and Madsen (1997) reviewed many studies supporting the notion of gender differences in self-concept. Men typically evaluate themselves more positively on independence (e.g., power, self-sufficiency) than interdependence (e.g., sociability, likeability). In contrast, women exhibit the opposite pattern.

Stein et al. (1992) found a measure of interdependence predicted self-esteem 2 years later for women but not men, suggesting that interdependence is

Is the interdependent self found mainly in men and/or women, and in members of collectivistic and/or individualistic societies?

more important for women. In addition, a measure of independence predicted self-esteem 2 years later for men but not women. Thus, men's self-concept depends more than women's on independence.

EVALUATION

➕ The distinction between independent and interdependent selves captures important cultural differences in the self-concept.

➕ The distinction between independent and interdependent selves sheds light on gender differences in the self-concept.

➖ It is an oversimplification to use only two categories (i.e., independent; interdependent) to describe the self. In addition, some people living in individualistic cultures have an interdependent self and some in collectivistic cultures have an independent self.

➖ Cross and Madsen's (1997) assumption that men are less concerned about other people than are women may be only partially correct. Women may attach more importance than men to close relationships. However, men tend to have a greater number of social relationships (Baumeister & Sommer, 1997).

➖ Research has been based on the assumption that the self is relatively *unchanging* over time. In fact, however, our views of the self vary with changing social contexts (see discussion below).

Changing the self-concept

Adults' self-concepts are generally reasonably stable and resistant to change. However, some people's self-concepts evolve and change over time. There are various reasons why such changes occur, two of which are discussed below.

Public self-presentation

Suppose you were asked to present yourself as an extraverted person (outgoing, socially skilled, eager to meet new people) while being videotaped. In order to do this effectively, you are told to describe yourself as you are on your most extremely extraverted day. Would this cause your self-concept to change in the direction of perceiving yourself as more extraverted? Would describing yourself as introverted (shy, thoughtful, quiet) make your self-concept more introverted?

Kelly and Rodriguez (2006) carried out a study resembling the above account. They found it was crucially important whether participants believed the videotape would be seen by a graduate student rather than simply being erased. More specifically, it was only when participants *publicly* committed themselves to a given identity that their self-concept changed. This is consistent

with the notion that the self-concept has a strong social emphasis and depends heavily on our interactions with others.

Social identity

The approaches discussed in the previous section focus on the notion of a *single* self-concept. Other theorists (e.g., Tajfel, 1981) have argued that we actually possess several social identities. These social identities depend on the various groups to which we belong (e.g., student; woman; European; tennis player).

Your social identity as a student may be especially important when you are at school or university chatting with other students. In contrast, your social identity as a tennis player may be dominant when you are playing tennis with a friend.

What is the relationship between our self-concept and social identities? Rogers et al. (2007) argued that we look for the *similarities* among our various social identities and try to resolve conflicts among them. After that, our social identities are *integrated* so that they jointly become important to our self-concept. Such integration is important because in its absence our self-concept would be fragmented and somewhat chaotic.

Why is it important for people to possess social identities? According to social identity theory, having a positive social identity increases the individual's self-esteem (Hogg & Vaughan, 2005). A major way we can achieve a positive social identity is by comparing a group to which we belong (the ingroup) with some relevant outgroup. Social identity theory predicts ingroup bias, in which one's own ingroup is perceived as superior to some outgroup. There is much evidence for ingroup bias, and it helps to explain the existence of prejudice against minority outgroups (see Chapter 13).

Why are most social identities positive?

What determines which social identity is dominant at any given time? Several factors are involved. First, the current situation is important. For example, if I attend a psychology conference, my identity as a psychologist is likely to be dominant. Second, there are our past experiences. If it has made me happy to identify myself as a psychologist in the past, that increases the likelihood I will do so across a range of situations. Third, there are present expectations. If I expect the people I am with to be more positively disposed towards a writer than a psychologist, I may be tempted to adopt the identity of a writer rather than a psychologist!

Situation can affect social identity. For example, a person's identity as a football fan is more dominant when watching a match than it would be in a work situation.

Self-knowledge

Do we know ourselves better than anyone else? Most people believe the answer to that question is, "Yes". That makes sense because we all have detailed knowledge about our own lives, our thoughts and feelings, and so on that isn't available to other people. However, many people have "blind spots", especially with respect to their faults.

Vazire and Carlson (2011) addressed the above issues. They obtained personality ratings from the participants themselves and also from their friends. They then compared these self-ratings and friend-ratings with the participants' actual behaviour in various situations.

What did Vazire and Carlson (2011) find? First, they considered traits low in evaluativeness (e.g., anxiety). With such traits, self-ratings were more accurate than friend-ratings. Second, with traits high in evaluativeness (e.g., intelligence; creativity), self-ratings were *less* accurate than friend-ratings. Thus, we are motivated to distort our self-perceptions for important, high-evaluative traits such as intelligence.

More evidence that we can be better at judging other people than ourselves was reported by Balcetis and Dunning (2011). The situation they used involved the experimenter bumping into a cart loaded with boxes of puzzle pieces, spilling about 300 of the pieces. Some participants simply predicted whether they would help to clear up the mess when they were on their own in that situation or when other participants were present. Additional participants predicted whether other people would help. Note that this study relates to research on bystander intervention (see Chapter 14).

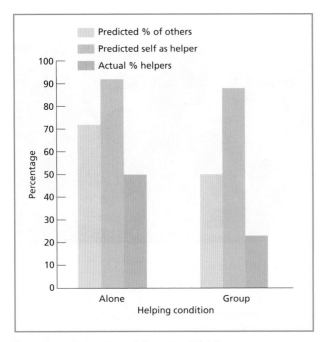

Data from Balcetis and Dunning (2011).

As you can see in the figure left, help was much more likely to be given when participants were on their own than when with other participants. The participants predicted this pattern accurately when judging whether others would help. However, and more importantly, the participants predicted incorrectly they would be equally likely to help regardless of whether or not they were alone.

Finally, the participants exaggerated their own helpfulness more than that of other people. Overall, help was offered 36.5% of the time. The participants predicted they would help 90% of the time and that other participants would help 61% of the time.

What are the take-home messages from this study? First, most people have a much more flattering view of themselves than of others. This is consistent with much other evidence. For example, 31% of adult Americans are obese. However, only 5% of adult Americans consider they themselves are obese, but estimate that 37% of other Americans are.

Second, participants focused almost exclusively on their own caring nature when predicting whether they would help. In so doing, they showed poor understanding of the impact of the situation (i.e., on their own vs. with others) on their behaviour. The poor self-knowledge often shown by people depends on focusing too much on their own personality traits and not enough on the situation.

Self-esteem

Self-esteem is an important part of the self-concept. It is the evaluative part of the self-concept; it concerns how worthwhile and confident an individual feels about himself/herself.

Several theorists (e.g., Baumeister, 1998) have argued that most people are highly motivated to maintain or enhance their self-esteem. As a result, much social behaviour has the goal of maximising self-esteem (e.g., by achieving career success; by being positively evaluated by others). The motivation to maximise self-esteem helps to explain the excessively positive views of the self held by many people.

A person's show of confidence can reflect how high their self-esteem is.

Why are most people keen to have high self-esteem? Leary and Downs (1995) provided an answer in their sociometer theory. According to this theory, self-esteem is an internal assessment of the extent to which we are accepted and liked by other people. Sociometer theory was supported by Leary et al. (1998). Participants who were evaluated positively showed increased self-esteem whereas those evaluated negatively had decreased self-esteem.

Findings

Pass et al. (2010) argued that men and women differ in the effects of different types of negative evaluation on their self-esteem. Women's self-esteem was reduced when rejected as a potential mate because of their low physical attractiveness. However, their self-esteem wasn't reduced when they were rejected because of their poor competence and status.

The opposite was the case for men—their self-esteem was only lowered by rejection on the grounds of inadequate competence and status. These findings support much other research in showing that women regard their own physical attractiveness as especially important whereas men attach most weight to competence and status.

If people are motivated to maintain or enhance their self-esteem, we might expect them to take credit for success by attributing it to internal or dispositional factors (e.g., "I worked very hard"; "I have a lot of ability") (see Chapter 16). In contrast, they should deny responsibility for failure by attributing it to external or situational factors (e.g., "The task was very hard"; "I didn't have enough time to prepare myself"). Taking credit for success but refusing to accept responsibility for failure defines the **self-serving bias**.

To what does the self-serving bias attribute success and failure?

There is considerable evidence for self-serving bias. Mezulis et al. (2004) reviewed 266 studies, and found there was a large overall bias. This bias was especially large in individualistic cultures (e.g., UK; USA) in which there is an emphasis on personal achievement.

The response to failure varies as a function of the individual's self-esteem. Van Dellen et al. (2011) found those high in self-esteem attributed failure to external factors. In some cases, failure even led to increased self-esteem. In contrast, individuals low in self-esteem were more likely to attribute failure to internal factors and this led to reduced self-esteem.

Does the self-serving bias cause high self-esteem or does high self-esteem lead to the self-serving bias? The causality probably operates in both directions. Blaine and Crocker (1993) argued that those high in self-esteem have higher (and clearer) expectations of what will happen in their lives. As a result, high self-esteem creates a self-serving bias.

Several other biases reflect people's desire to enhance their self-esteem. Examples include the **false uniqueness bias** (the tendency to regard oneself as better than most other people) and various optimism biases (e.g., the expectation that one's future health will be better than that of others). Heine and Hamamura (2007) reviewed research on these and other biases. Those living in Western societies possessed all the biases studied.

In sum, there is much evidence that those living in individualistic cultures strive for high self-esteem. Self-esteem is more associated with status or competence in men than in women, whereas the opposite is the case with physical attractiveness. Men and women both possess numerous biases that serve to enhance their self-esteem.

Is high self-esteem desirable?

I imagine your answer to the above question is "Yes". In Western cultures, it is generally accepted that high self-esteem confers various benefits. For example, individuals high in self-esteem are less likely to be depressed or anxious than those low in self-esteem (Baumeister, 1998).

Does low self-esteem help to cause anxiety and depression or do anxiety and depression lead to low self-esteem? Evidence that low self-esteem can lead to subsequent mental disorders was reported by Trzesniewski et al. (2006). They assessed self-esteem in adolescents and then followed them up for 11 years into adulthood.

Of adults having five or more problems (e.g., major depressive disorder; anxiety disorder; criminal convictions), 65% had had low self-esteem in adolescence and only 15% had had high self-esteem. Of adults with no problems, 16% had had low adolescent self-esteem but 50% had had high self-esteem. Thus, the level of self-esteem in adolescence was highly predictive of whether an individual would experience major problems in adulthood.

Other researchers argue that high self-esteem can be undesirable. For example, those who behave aggressively (e.g., bullying) have relatively high self-esteem (Baumeister et al., 2005). Colvin et al. (1995) studied individuals with inflated self-esteem (their self-descriptions were more favourable than descriptions of them provided by acquaintances). These individuals had poor social skills and signs of psychological maladjustment (e.g., hostility towards others; distrustful of people; self-defensive).

KEY TERM

False uniqueness bias: the mistaken belief that one is better than most other people.

There is no straightforward answer to the question of whether high self-esteem is desirable. Kernis (2003) distinguished between secure and fragile high self-esteem. Secure high self-esteem is genuine and is stable over time. In contrast, fragile high self-esteem is defensive and changeable over time.

Those with fragile high self-esteem have an excessively positive view of themselves, and are often at least partly aware of this. Unsurprisingly, the evidence suggests that secure high self-esteem is much more desirable than fragile high self-esteem (Kernis, 2003).

Cross-cultural differences

So far I have focused on the role of high self-esteem within individualistic cultures (especially the United States) in which the emphasis is on individual achievement. In fact, the desirability of having high self-esteem or self-confidence varies across cultures. It is regarded as least desirable in collectivistic cultures in which the emphasis is on the group and social cohesion rather than the individual.

Why don't collectivistic cultures regard high self-esteem as desirable? According to Heine et al. (1999, p. 785), "In Japanese culture, ... to say that an individual is self-confident has negative connotations because it reflects how self-confidence gets in the way of interdependence, or it reveals one's failure to recognise higher standards of excellence, and thus to continue to self-improve, or both."

Are members of collectivistic societies highly motivated to have high self-esteem, and do they show self-serving bias?

Findings

From what has been said so far, we wouldn't expect those living in collectivistic cultures to show biases designed to enhance self-esteem. In a study discussed earlier, Mezulis et al. (2004) reviewed studies on self-serving bias. This bias was much stronger in individualistic cultures than the collectivistic cultures of Asia. One reason why the self-serving bias is weak (or even non-existent) in collectivistic cultures is because they attach much importance to being self-critical.

Earlier I also discussed Heine and Hamamura's (2007) review of numerous biases (e.g., false uniqueness bias) used by those in individualistic cultures to enhance their self-esteem. Those living in individualistic societies possessed all the biases, whereas those living in East Asia had practically none of them. East Asians don't show these biases because they are concerned that what they claim about themselves matches other people's judgements about them.

Lee et al. (2010) argued that what is important is the individual's **cultural mindset** (way of thinking about things). They asked Chinese students in Hong Kong to decide whether various desirable and undesirable personality traits applied more or less to them than to the average student. When the students responded in English, they showed more evidence of false uniqueness bias than when they responded in Chinese. Thus, use of English evoked an individualistic mindset that led them to regard desirable traits as self-descriptive and undesirable ones as more defining of the average student.

> **KEY TERM**
>
> **Cultural mindset:** the beliefs and values that are active at any given time; individuals who have extensive experience of two cultures have two cultural mindsets, with the one that influences thinking and behaviour being determined by the immediate social context.

Lo et al. (2011) argued we shouldn't exaggerate the self-enhancing tendencies of people in individualistic cultures or the self-critical tendencies of people in individualistic cultures. In their study, Lo et al. asked participants to write down five important positive qualities and five important negative qualities they possessed. Participants from individualistic and collectivistic cultures had both self-enhancing and self-critical tendencies. However, those from collectivistic cultures were less self-enhancing and more self-critical than those from individualistic cultures.

Conclusions

Most of the biases used to enhance self-esteem among people living in individualistic cultures are not found among those living in collectivistic cultures. There are various reasons for this, including the greater emphasis on social cohesion and the need for self-improvement rather than self-congratulation in collectivistic cultures. There is some truth in the notion that members of collectivistic cultures are self-critical whereas those in individualistic cultures are self-enhancing. However, most people in both cultures show evidence of self-critical and self-enhancing tendencies.

Chapter summary

- The self-concept corresponds to the set of ideas individuals have about themselves. It depends crucially on social interaction and social relationships.
- Infants develop basic self-awareness (indexed by self-recognition) during the second year of life.
- Self-recognition is followed by the development of autobiographical memory. This is of much relevance to the self-concept because it provides us with a sense of personal continuity over time.
- During childhood, psychological characteristics form an increasingly important part of the self-concept. In contrast, physical characteristics become less important.
- Those living in individualistic cultures have an independent self, whereas those living in collectivistic cultures have an interdependent self.
- Men in the United States have a more independent self than women, whereas women have a more interdependent self than men.
- Part of the self-concept is formed out of social identities, which are based on membership of various groups.
- Most social identities are positive. This is because of ingroup bias, in which one's own group is compared favourably to other groups. This ingroup bias can increase an individual's self-esteem.
- People's knowledge of themselves is greater than that of their friends with respect to low-evaluativeness personality traits. However, the opposite is the case with high-evaluativeness traits. This occurs in part because those in Western cultures tend to have excessively positive views of themselves.

- High self-esteem in Western cultures is maintained by various biases including the self-serving bias, the false uniqueness bias, and various optimism biases.
- In Western cultures, individuals with high self-esteem tend to suffer less than those with low self-esteem from anxiety, depression, and criminality. However, individuals whose self-descriptions are inflated or exaggerated are more susceptible to psychological maladjustment.
- Secure high self-esteem confers benefits on individuals whereas fragile high self-esteem has negative effects.
- High self-esteem is much less highly valued in collectivistic cultures than in individualistic (predominantly Western) ones. Those living in collectivistic cultures typically do not show the biases (e.g., self-serving bias) found in individualistic cultures.

Further reading

- Baumeister, R.F., & Bushman, B.J. (2011). *Social psychology and human nature (2nd ed.).* Belmont, CA: Wadsworth. Chapter 3 in this introductory textbook is devoted to the self.

- Gilovich, T., Keltner, D., & Nisbett, R. (2010). *Social psychology (2nd ed.).* New York: W.W. Norton. This textbook on social psychology contains interesting material of relevance to the self-concept.

- Hogg, M.A., & Vaughan, G.M. (2011). *Social psychology (6th ed.).* New York: Prentice Hall. Chapter 4 of this excellent textbook is devoted to self and identity.

Essay questions

1. What is the self-concept? Describe some of the factors involved in its development during childhood.

2. How is the conception of the self influenced by cross-cultural and gender differences?

3. Are most people motivated to enhance their self-esteem? How desirable is high self-esteem?

Part 6

Cognitive approach

Cognitive psychology is concerned with our internal mental processes (e.g., perception; attention; memory) and with the ways these mental processes influence our behaviour. We differ from other species in many ways, but perhaps the most important are in terms of cognitive abilities such as thinking, reasoning, and problem solving.

Cognitive psychology is of major relevance to most of the other approaches discussed in this book. For example, our behaviour in social situations depends in part on our perceptions of others and on our beliefs and attitudes.

Chapter 20 • Visual perception

We will examine how it is that we generally manage to make sense of visual information in order to perceive the world accurately.

Chapter 21 • Memory

We will look at the ways in which we remember information and also why it is that we often forget things we wanted to remember.

Chapter 22 • Problem solving and creativity

We will consider some of the factors that allow us to succeed at solving complex problems and showing creativity when it is required.

Visual perception is normally very rapid and accurate in spite of the problems we face in making sense of visual information. When looking at the world, we somehow manage to turn a two-dimensional retinal image into complete three-dimensional perception of the objects in the environment. What kinds of cues do you think we use to see the world as it is rather than as it appears on the retina?

In spite of our perceptual abilities, we are nevertheless taken in by many so-called visual illusions. We think we have a clear picture of the visual scene in front of us. However, we often fail to notice even fairly large changes in that scene. Why is visual perception so prone to these errors?

Visual perception 20

This chapter is concerned with the area of psychology known as perception. **Perception** is "the acquisition and processing of sensory information in order to see, hear, taste, or feel objects in the world; it also guides an organism's actions with respect to those objects" (Sekuler & Blake, 2002, p. 621). In this chapter, we will be considering our most important sense: vision. Unsurprisingly, more of the cortex in the brain is devoted to visual processing than to processing in any other sense modality.

Visual perception is much more of an achievement than you might imagine. It generally seems very easy to us. Most of the time, we simply look around and immediately make coherent sense of the objects in front of us. In fact, however, the information arriving at the retina is generally confusing and disorganised. There is a mosaic of colours, and the retinal shapes and sizes of objects are often very different from their actual shapes and sizes.

Another complication is that the retinal image is two-dimensional. In spite of that, we perceive the world as well-organised and three-dimensional. In what follows, we consider how we manage to do this. We will also consider some of the deficiencies in visual perception. For example, we sometimes misperceive visual stimuli. We also find it surprisingly hard to detect changes in the visual world around us.

Perceptual organisation

It would be fairly easy to work out accurately which parts of the visual information presented to us belong together (and thus form objects) if those objects were spread out in space. Instead, the visual environment is often complex and confusing, with many objects overlapping others and so hiding parts of them from view. As a result, it can be difficult to achieve perceptual segregation of visual objects.

The first systematic attempt to study perceptual segregation (and the perceptual organisation to which it gives rise) was made by the Gestaltists. They were German psychologists (including Koffka, Köhler, and Wertheimer), most of whom emigrated to the United States before the Second World War. Their fundamental principle was the **law of Prägnanz**, according to which we typically perceive the simplest possible organisation.

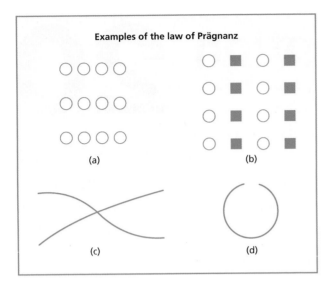

Examples of the law of Prägnanz

(a)

(b)

(c)

(d)

What the Gestaltists had in mind with their law of Prägnanz can be seen by considering some concrete examples (set out in the figure on the left). Pattern (a) is more easily seen as three horizontal lines of dots than four vertical lines. It shows the Gestalt law of proximity, according to which visual elements close to each other tend to be grouped together.

In pattern (b), vertical columns rather than horizontal rows are seen. This fits the law of similarity, according to which similar visual elements are grouped together. In pattern (c), we tend to see two crossing lines rather than a V-shaped line and an inverted-V shaped line. This fits the law of good continuation, which states that those visual elements producing the fewest interruptions to smoothly curving lines are grouped together.

Finally, pattern (d) shows the law of closure. The missing parts of a figure are filled in to complete it (in this case, a circle). All four laws discussed here are more specific statements of the basic law of Prägnanz.

Where do these organisational processes come from? The Gestaltists argued that most perceptual organisation depends on innate factors. In other words, we naturally organise our perceptual experience in line with the law of Prägnanz. An alternative view is that we *learn* that visual elements close (or similar) to each other generally belong to the same object. As we will see, the evidence favours the learning account.

When does perceptual organisation occur? The Gestaltists argued that the grouping of visual elements occurs *early* in processing, and before most other visual processes.

The Gestaltists emphasised **figure–ground organisation**. One part of the visual field is identified as the figure (central object). The rest of the visual field is less important and forms the ground. The Gestaltists claimed the figure is perceived as having distinct form or shape, whereas the ground lacks form. In addition, the figure is perceived in *front* of the ground, and the contour separating the figure from the ground belongs to the figure.

Check the validity of the above claims by looking at the faces–goblet illusion (see the figure on the left). When the goblet is the figure, it seems to be in front of a dark background. In contrast, the faces are seen in front of a light background when they form the figure.

When does figure–ground segregation occur? According to the Gestaltists, it occurs very *early* in visual processing and so always precedes object recognition.

The faces–goblet ambiguous figure is an example of figure and ground—which is figure and which is ground?

Findings

The Gestaltists used artificial figures, and it is important to see whether their findings also apply to more realistic stimuli. Elder and Goldberg (2002) presented observers with pictures of natural objects. Proximity or closeness was a very powerful cue when deciding which contours belonged to which objects. In addition, the cue of good continuation also made a positive contribution.

Weisstein and Wong (1986) obtained evidence showing the importance of the distinction between figure and ground. They flashed vertical lines and slightly tilted lines onto the faces–goblet illusion, and observers decided whether the line was vertical. Performance was much better when the line was presented to what the observers perceived as the figure rather than to the ground. Thus, there was more attention to (and processing of) the figure than of the ground.

Does the grouping of visual elements *always* occur early in processing? Evidence that the answer is "No" was reported by Rock and Palmer (1990). They presented luminous beads on parallel strings in the dark. The beads were closer to each other in the vertical direction than the horizontal one. However, the situation was more complex when the display was tilted backwards. The beads remained closer to each other vertically in three-dimensional space but were closer to each other horizontally in the two-dimensional retinal image.

What did the observers report? If the grouping of the beads occurred *before* depth perception (as predicted by the Gestaltists), they should have seen the beads organised in horizontal rows. On the other hand, if grouping occurred *after* depth perception, the observers should have seen the beads organised in vertical columns. That is what happened.

The assumption that figure–ground segregation always precedes object recognition (and so happens faster) was tested by Grill-Spector and Kanwisher (2005). Photographs were presented briefly. On some trials, participants decided whether the photograph contained an object to assess figure–ground segregation. On other trials, they decided whether the photograph showed an object from a given category (e.g., "car"). Performance speed was very similar on both tasks, whereas the Gestaltists would predict it should have been faster on the figure–ground task.

According to the Gestaltists, figure–ground segregation depends very little on past knowledge and experience. That led them to de-emphasise the role of experience. In a study by Schwarzkopf et al. (2009), observers were presented with atypical-shape contours that were hard to interpret. However, the observers showed rapid and flexible learning leading to a rapid improvement in performance.

EVALUATION

➕ The Gestaltists correctly emphasised the importance of perceptual organisation and figure–ground segregation.

➕ The Gestaltists discovered several major laws of perceptual organisation.

➖ The Gestaltists de-emphasised the importance of experience in determining perceptual organisation.

➖ Grouping and figure–ground organisation don't always precede other aspects of visual processing as assumed by the Gestaltists.

➖ The Gestalt laws are descriptive rather than explanatory. They don't tell us *why* similar elements (or those close together) are grouped.

Texture gradients communicate texture and depth. The flowers appear to become closer together as they recede into the distance.

Depth perception

A central achievement of visual perception is the way the *two-dimensional* image on our retina changes into our perception of a *three-dimensional* world. This is the issue of depth perception.

It is very important for us to have good depth or distance perception. For example, consider what happens when we cross the road. We need to be confident that a car coming in our direction is far enough away that we can get safely to the other side of the road. As we will discover, people use many different cues to achieve accurate depth or distance perception.

Monocular cues

Many cues to distance are **monocular cues**. These cues require the use of only one eye, but can still be used when someone has both eyes open. We know monocular cues exist because the world still retains a sense of depth when we close one eye.

Monocular cues are sometimes called pictorial cues because artists use them to create the impression of three-dimensional scenes when painting. One such cue is **linear perspective**. Parallel lines pointing away from us (e.g., railway tracks) seem to get closer as they recede into the distance.

Another cue to perspective is texture. Most objects (e.g., cobbled roads; carpets) possess texture, and textured objects slanting away from us have a **texture gradient**. This means the texture becomes more dense as you look from the front to the back of a slanting object.

A further cue is **interposition**, in which a nearer object hides part of a more distant one from view. The power of this cue can be seen if you look at Kanizsa's (1976) illusory square (see the figure on the next page). It looks as if there is a square in front of four circles in spite of the fact that most of the contours of the square are missing.

Another cue to depth is given by shading. Flat, two-dimensional surfaces don't cast shadows. As a result, the presence of shading indicates the presence of a three-dimensional object. Ramachandran (1988) presented observers with a visual display consisting of numerous shaded circular patches. Some were illuminated by one light source and the rest were illuminated by a different light source. The observers incorrectly assumed the visual display was lit by a *single* light source above the display. This led them to use shading information to misperceive some "dents" as bumps.

Finally, there is **motion parallax**. This refers to the movement of an object's image over the retina due to movement of the observer's head. If you look into the far distance through the windows of a moving train, the apparent speed of objects passing by seems faster the nearer they are to you. In addition, distant objects seem to move in the same direction as the train whereas nearby ones apparently move in the opposite direction.

Binocular and oculomotor cues

Binocular cues are ones that can be used only when someone has both eyes open. The most important of such cues is **stereopsis**. It depends for its effectiveness on the fact that there are slight differences between the two retinal images of objects. Stereopsis plays an important role in three-dimensional films such as *Avatar*. What happens is that each scene is recorded with two cameras to simulate what can be seen with the left and right eyes. When people watch the film, they wear special glasses. This is done so that the visual input to the spectator's two eyes corresponds to what each eye would have seen in the original scene.

The effectiveness of stereopsis depends on the disparity or discrepancy in the retinal images of the visual scene. The disparity in the retinal images of an object decreases by a factor of 100 as its distance increases from 6 to 65 feet (Bruce et al., 2003). Thus, stereopsis rapidly becomes less effective at greater distances.

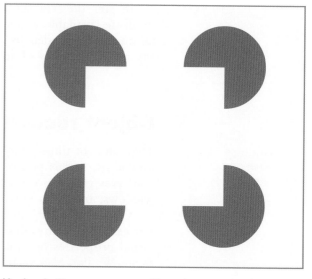

Kanizsa's illusory square—although no square is present, people see the diagram as if it were four circles with a square lying on them.

Oculomotor cues are kinaesthetic, depending on the sensations from muscles around the eye. One such cue is **convergence**—the eyes turn inwards to focus on an object to a greater extent with a very close object than one that is further away. **Accommodation** refers to the variation in optical power produced by a thickening of the lens of the eye when focusing on a close object. Convergence and accommodation are only of use with objects very close to the observer.

Integrating cue information

So far we have considered cues to distance one at a time. In the real world, of course, we typically have access to several cues at the same time. How do we combine or integrate information from different cues? Jacobs (2002) argued that observers assign more weight or importance to *reliable* cues than to unreliable ones.

There are two ways a cue can be reliable. First, it may provide unambiguous information. Triesch et al. (2002) used a virtual reality situation in which observers tracked an object defined by the attributes of colour, shape, and size. On each trial, two attributes were ambiguous and one was unambiguous. Observers attached increased weight to the reliable cue and less to the ambiguous ones.

Second, it may provide information consistent with that provided by other cues. Atkins et al. (2001) used a virtual reality environment in which observers viewed and grasped elliptical cylinders. There were three cues to cylinder depth: texture, motion, and touch. When only one of the visual cues (i.e., texture or motion) indicated the same distance as the touch cue, that cue was preferred.

In sum, the evidence shows that observers don't attach equal importance to all the available visual cues. Instead, they attach most importance to the information provided by reliable cues. This is sensible because it generally ensures the accuracy of depth or distance perception.

Object recognition

What processes are involved in object recognition?

Thousands of times every day we identify or recognise objects in the world around us. At this precise moment, you are looking at a book (possibly with your eyes glazed over). If you raise your eyes, perhaps you can see a wall, windows, and so on in front of you.

Object recognition is much more complex than you might imagine. For example, many objects (e.g., chairs; houses) vary enormously in their visual properties (e.g., colour, size, shape) and yet we can still recognise them. We can also recognise many objects over a wide range of viewing distances and orientations. For example, most plates are round but we can identify plates seen from an angle so they appear elliptical. Thus, there is much more to object recognition than might initially be supposed (than meets the eye?).

Recognition-by-components theory

What processes are involved in object recognition? An influential answer was provided by Irving Biederman (1987) in his recognition-by-components theory. He argued that objects consist of basic shapes or components known as **geons** (geometric ions). Examples of geons are blocks, cylinders, spheres, arcs, and wedges.

How many geons are there? According to Biederman (1987), there are about 36 different geons. That may sound suspiciously few to provide descriptions of all the objects we can recognise and identify. However, we can identity enormous numbers of spoken English words even though there are only about 44 phonemes (basic sounds) in the English language. This is because they can be arranged in almost limitless combinations.

The same is true of geons—the reason for the richness of the object descriptions provided by geons stems from the different possible spatial relationships among them. For example, a cup can be described by an arc connected to the side of a cylinder. A pail can be described by the same two geons but with the arc connected to the top of the cylinder.

Geon-based information about common objects is stored in long-term memory. As a result, object recognition depends crucially on the identification of geons. Of major importance, an object's geons can be identified from numerous viewpoints. Thus, object recognition should generally be easy unless one or more geons are hidden from view. In technical terms, we have **viewpoint-invariant perception**.

How do we recognise objects when only some of the relevant visual information is available? According to Biederman (1987), the concavities (hollows) in an object's contour provide especially useful information.

KEY TERMS

Geons: basic shapes or components that are combined in object recognition; an abbreviation for "geometric ions" proposed by Biederman.

Viewpoint-invariant perception: the notion that it is equally easy to recognise objects from numerous different viewpoints.

Findings

Biederman (1987) studied the role of concavities in object recognition by presenting observers with degraded line drawings of objects (see the figure on the right). As predicted, object recognition was much harder to achieve when parts of the contour providing information about concavities were omitted than when other parts of the contour were deleted.

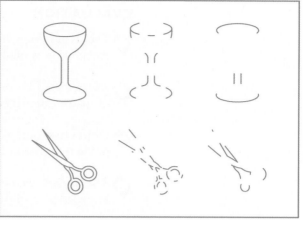

Intact figures (left-hand side), with degraded line drawings either preserving (middle column) or not preserving (far-right column) parts of the contour providing information about concavities.

Form a visual image of a bicycle. Your image probably involves a side view in which the bicycle's two wheels can be seen clearly. Suppose some people were presented with a picture of a bicycle shown in the typical view as in your visual image. In contrast, other people were presented with a picture of the same bicycle viewed end on or from above. Both groups are instructed to identify the object as rapidly as possible. Would the group given the typical view of a bicycle perform this task faster than the other group?

Biederman (1987) claimed object recognition is equally rapid and easy regardless of the angle from which an object is viewed. In other words, he assumed it is viewpoint-invariant. However, it is possible that object recognition is generally faster and easier when objects are seen from certain angles (**viewpoint-dependent perception**).

As you may have guessed, object recognition is sometimes viewpoint-dependent and sometimes viewpoint-invariant. According to Tarr et al. (1998), viewpoint-invariant mechanisms are typically used when object recognition involves making easy discriminations (e.g., between cars and bicycles). In contrast, viewpoint-dependent mechanisms are more important when the task requires difficult within-category discriminations (e.g., between different makes of car; between faces). Tarr et al. obtained support for these hypotheses when observers recognised 3-D objects under various conditions.

One factor influencing the extent to which object recognition is viewpoint-dependent is the amount of information available to the observer. For example, consider face recognition. Face recognition is typically strongly viewpoint-dependent when faces are presented two-dimensionally on computer monitors (Burke et al., 2007). However, we typically perceive faces in three dimensions. Burke et al. found face recognition was much less strongly viewpoint-dependent with three-dimensional faces than with two-dimensional ones. This occurred because three-dimensional faces provided the observers with much more information than two-dimensional ones.

Recognition-by-components theory strongly emphasises the processing of object features or geons in object recognition. However, other factors such as expectation and knowledge are often important, especially when object recognition is difficult.

Viggiano et al. (2008) studied object recognition with animal photographs that were clear or blurred to make them harder to recognise. Observers relied more on their expectations and knowledge with the blurred photographs because information about object features or geons was less accessible.

KEY TERM

Viewpoint-dependent perception: the notion that objects can be recognised more easily from some viewpoints or angles than from others.

EVALUATION

➕ The assumption that geon-like components are involved in object recognition is plausible and in line with much of the evidence.

➕ As predicted by recognition-by-components theory, concavities are of major importance in object recognition.

➖ Object recognition is often viewpoint-dependent, whereas the theory predicts it should be viewpoint-invariant.

➖ The theory de-emphasises the importance of expectations and knowledge in object recognition.

Visual illusions

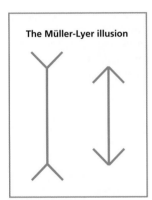

The Müller-Lyer illusion

The Müller-Lyer illusion.

Visual perception is usually very accurate. If it weren't, we would be in danger of falling over the edges of cliffs or stumbling over obstacles in our path. However, the situation is very different with **visual illusions**. These are generally two-dimensional drawings that most people see inaccurately. In the Müller-Lyer illusion (see the figure on the left), for example, the vertical line in the figure on the left seems longer than the vertical line in the figure on the right. In fact, they are the same size as can be shown with a ruler.

Expectations

How can we explain illusions such as the Müller-Lyer? Even though the Müller-Lyer figures look flat and two-dimensional, Richard Gregory (1970) argued that we treat them as if they were three-dimensional. The figure on the left looks like the inside of a room whereas the figure on the right is like the outside corner of a building. Thus, the outgoing fins represent lines approaching us whereas the ingoing fins stand for receding lines. Our *expectations* concerning what the figures would look like in three-dimensional space create the illusion effect (Redding & Vinson, 2010).

The importance of our expectations can be seen clearly with the **Ames room**. This is a specially constructed room with a most peculiar shape (see the figure on the next page). The floor slopes and the rear wall isn't at right angles to the adjoining walls. The fact that one end of the rear wall is much further from the viewer is disguised by making it much higher.

In spite of the oddities of the Ames room, it creates the same retinal image as a normal rectangular room. Our *expectation* that rooms are rectangular and have level floors causes us to see the room as normal. This effect is so strong that a person walking backwards and forwards in front of the rear wall seems to grow and shrink! This is somewhat puzzling since we certainly don't expect people to change size as they move around.

In one study (Glennerster et al., 2006), participants walked through a virtual-reality room as it expanded or contracted considerably. Even though there was much information available indicating the room's size was changing,

KEY TERM

Visual illusions: two-dimensional drawings that are seen inaccurately by nearly everyone; the best-known is the Müller-Lyer illusion.

Ames room: a special room with a very unusual shape, which looks like an ordinary room under some viewing conditions.

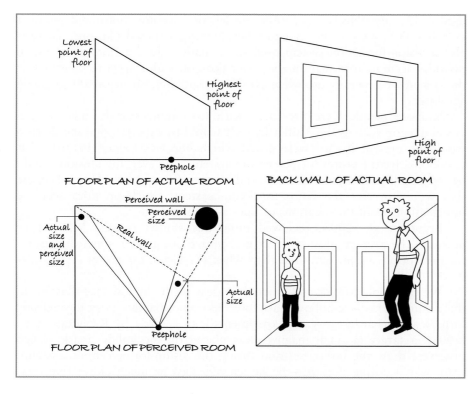

no participants noticed the changes. Their expectation that the size of the room wouldn't alter led participants to be very inaccurate in their judgements of the sizes of objects in the room.

Illusions due to artificiality?

The existence of numerous visual illusions leaves us with an intriguing paradox. *How* has the human species survived if our visual perceptual processes are so error-prone? A plausible answer is that most visual illusions involve artificial figures. As a result, they can be dismissed as tricks played by psychologists with nothing better to do.

What can the study of visual illusions tell us about how our visual system operates?

The above argument doesn't account for all illusions. For example, you can show the Müller-Lyer illusion with real three-dimensional objects (DeLucia & Hochberg, 1991). Place three open books in a line with the ones on the left and the right open to the right and the middle one open to the left (see the figure on the right). The spine of the book in the middle should be the same distance from the spines of each of the other two books. In spite of this, the distance between the spines of the middle book and the book on the right appears longer.

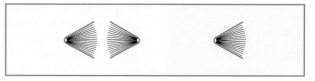

The spine of the middle book is closer to the spine of which other book? Now check your answer with a ruler.

Two perception systems

An alternative viewpoint was offered by Milner and Goodale (e.g., 2008), who argued we have *two* visual systems. There is a vision-for-perception system used to identify objects (e.g., to decide whether we are confronted by a cat or a buffalo). We use this system when looking at visual illusions. There is also a vision-for-action system used for visually guided action. This system provides accurate information about our position with respect to objects. It is the system we generally use when avoiding a speeding car or rapidly grasping an object.

Suppose people were presented with three-dimensional versions of a visual illusion such as the Müller-Lyer. It would be expected that the illusion would be present if they were asked which line was longer, because that would involve the vision-for-perception system. However, the illusion should be reduced if people pointed at the end of one of the figures. This is because that would involve the vision-for-action system, which provides accurate information about the locations of lines and objects.

Bruno et al. (2008) reviewed numerous studies on the Müller-Lyer illusion. The average illusion effect was *four* times greater when the vision-for-perception system was used than when the vision-for-action system was used.

We can apply Milner and Goodale's ideas to the hollow-face illusion. In this illusion, a realistic hollow mask looks like a normal face (visit the website: http://www.richardgregory.org/experiments/). In a study by Króliczak et al. (2006), a target (a small magnet) was placed on the hollow mask. When observers drew the target position (using the vision-for-perception system), there was a strong illusion—the target was seen as much closer than was actually the case. In contrast, when observers made a fast flicking finger movement to the target (using the vision-for-action system) there was no illusion effect.

In sum, visual illusions are strongly influenced by our expectations concerning the world around us. However, this is *only* the case when we make judgements about visual figures using the vision-for-perception system. When we point at visual figures using the vision-for-action system, there is little or no illusion effect and our expectations are unimportant. The vision-for-action system allows us to avoid falling over cliffs even though the vision-for-perception system is fooled by visual illusions.

KEY TERMS

Inattentional blindness: the failure to perceive the appearance of an unexpected object in the visual environment; see **change blindness**.

Change blindness: the failure to detect that a visual stimulus has moved, changed, or been replaced by another stimulus; see **inattentional blindness**.

Change blindness

Have a look around you (go on!). I imagine you have the strong impression of seeing a vivid and detailed picture of the visual scene in front of your eyes. In fact, however, you may be deluding yourself. Suppose you walked across a large square close to a unicycling clown wearing a vivid purple and yellow outfit, large shoes, and a bright red nose. Do you think you would spot him? I imagine your answer is "Yes". However, Hyman et al. (2009) found only 51% of people walking on their own spotted the clown and this figure dropped to 25% of people chatting on a cell or mobile phone.

The study by Hyman et al. (2009) focused on **inattentional blindness**, which is the failure to notice an unexpected object appearing in a visual display. A closely related phenomenon is known as **change blindness**. This is the failure to detect that an object has moved, changed, or disappeared.

We will focus on change blindness because more is known about it than inattentional blindness.

We greatly overestimate our ability to detect visual changes. Consider a study by Levin et al. (2002). Observers saw various videos involving two people having a conversation in a restaurant. In one video, the plates on their table changed from red to white, and in another a scarf worn by one of them disappeared.

It had been found in previous research that no observers detected any of the changes. Levin et al. (2002) asked their participants whether they thought they would have noticed the changes. Forty-six per cent claimed they would have noticed the change in the colour of the plates, and 78% the disappearing scarf. Levin et al. used the term **change blindness blindness** to describe our wildly optimistic beliefs about our ability to detect visual changes.

What is the difference between inattentional blindness and change blindness? Can you think of examples of both from your own life?

When is change blindness found?

The extent to which we show change blindness or inattentional blindness depends on several factors. You can (hopefully!) see the effects of one of these factors if you look at the figure overleaf and try to spot the difference between the pictures. Rensink et al. (1997) found observers took an average of 10.4 seconds to spot the difference between the first pair of pictures but only 2.6 with the second pair of pictures. This difference occurred because the height of the railing is of *marginal* interest whereas the position of the helicopter is of *central* interest.

What factors could lead you to fail to notice a change in your visual environment?

Another important factor is the *similarity* between an unexpected object and other objects in the visual environment. In a famous study by Simons and Chabris (1999), a woman dressed in black as a gorilla strolled across a scene in which there were two teams, one dressed in white and the other in black. When observers counted the number of passes made by the team in white, 58% of them failed to detect the gorilla!

Simons and Chabris (1999) obtained different findings when the attended team was dressed in black. In this condition, the gorilla's presence was detected by 83% of observers. What do these findings mean? An unexpected object (i.e., the gorilla) attracts more attention and so is more likely to be detected when *similar* to task-relevant stimuli.

In studies such as those of Simons and Chabris (1999) and Hyman et al. (2009), observers weren't told beforehand to expect a change in the visual display (incidental approach). Observers are much more likely to detect a change when told in advance to expect one (intentional approach). Beck et al. (2007) found that observers detected visual changes 90% of the time using the intentional approach but only 40% using the incidental approach.

What causes change blindness?

It is generally agreed that attentional processes play an important role in change blindness. More specifically, we would expect observers to be more likely to detect changes in objects that had previously received attention than ones that hadn't.

Hollingworth and Henderson (2002) studied the role of attention in change blindness. Observers looked at a visual scene (e.g., kitchen; living

> **KEY TERM**
>
> **Change blindness blindness:** the tendency of individuals to exaggerate greatly their ability to detect visual changes and so avoid **change blindness**.

(a) The object that is changed (the railing) undergoes a shift in location comparable to that of the object that is changed (the helicopter) in (b). However, the change is much easier to see in (b) because the changed object is more important.

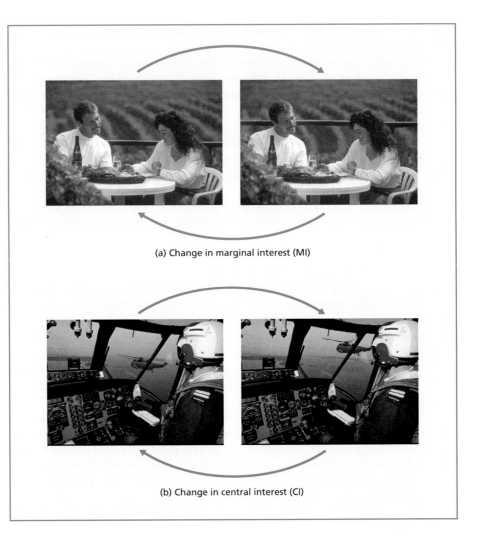

(a) Change in marginal interest (MI)

(b) Change in central interest (CI)

room) for several seconds, and it was assumed the object fixated at any given moment was being attended. Two kinds of changes could occur:

- *Type change*, in which an object was replaced by one from a different category (e.g., a plate replaced by a bowl).
- *Token change*, in which an object was replaced by one from the same category (e.g., a plate replaced by a different plate).

There were two main findings (see the figure on the next page). First, changes were much more likely to be detected when the changed object had received attention (been fixated) before the change occurred. That supports the view that lack of attention plays an important role in producing change blindness.

Second, change detection was much better when there was a change in the type of object rather than merely swapping one member of a category for another (token change). That finding occurred because there is a much larger change in the visual information available when the type of object changes.

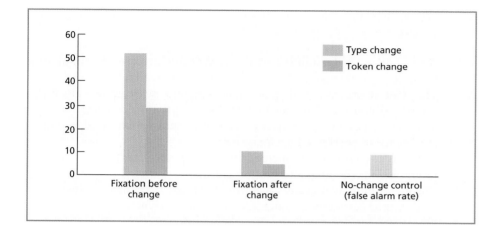

Percentage of correct change detection as a function of form of change (type vs. token) and time of fixation (before vs. after change); also false alarm rate when there was no change.

More recent evidence indicates that detection of change blindness doesn't merely involve fixating the object that changes. Caplovitz et al. (2008) presented observers with photos of natural scenes and told them to look out for possible changes. When observers were fixating the target object as it changed, they failed to detect the change on 18% of trials. Caplovitz et al. described these failures as "attentive blank stares".

How can we account for attentive blank stares? Perhaps observers sometimes attend to aspects of the object or part of the scene that don't change rather than the aspect that does change. For example, one change involved a scene in which the horizon between the sea and the sky moved up and down. Even though the horizon changed position, everything else (e.g., the colours of the sky and sea) remained the same. Thus, change detection may require fixating the object that changes *and* attending to the *specific* aspect of it that changes.

EVALUATION

➕ Change blindness and inattentional blindness are important phenomena that reveal surprising fallibilities with visual perception.

➕ Several factors increasing or decreasing the likelihood of change blindness have been identified.

➕ Attentional processes play a major role in producing change blindness and inattentional blindness.

➖ More remains to be discovered about precisely *how* attentional processes determine change blindness and change detection.

➖ It is too often assumed that failure to report detecting a change in a scene means that there has been little or no processing of the changed object. Undetected changes often trigger brain activity indicating that some processing of those changes has occurred (Fernandez-Duque et al., 2003).

Chapter summary

- According to the Gestaltists, observers typically perceive the simplest possible organisation of the visual information available to them.
- The Gestaltists assumed that figure–ground segregation always occurs early in visual processing. This assumption is incorrect.
- The Gestaltists underestimated the importance of knowledge and experience in perceptual organisation.
- Monocular cues to depth include linear perspective, texture gradient, interposition, shading, and motion parallax.
- The major binocular cue is stereopsis. There are two rather ineffective oculomotor cues: convergence and accommodation.
- Observers integrate information from different cues by assigning more weight to reliable cues. Such cues provide unambiguous information and/or information consistent with that provided by other cues.
- According to Biederman's recognition-by-components theory, object recognition involves identifying an object's basic shapes (known as geons).
- Biederman assumed that object recognition was viewpoint-invariant. However, it is actually viewpoint-dependent when object recognition is difficult.
- Biederman emphasised bottom-up processes and de-emphasised the roles of expectation and knowledge in object recognition.
- Many visual illusions occur when observers' expectations are mistaken.
- Some illusions reflect the artificiality of the visual displays presented to observers.
- Illusion effects are typically much greater when observers use the vision-for-perception system rather than the vision-for-action system.
- Most people greatly exaggerate their ability to detect visual changes in objects. In fact, most of us exhibit much change blindness.
- Change blindness is most commonly found when observers aren't expecting a change and when the object changed is of marginal interest.
- Change in an object is more likely to be detected when observers are attending to that object, especially when they are attending to the specific aspect of it that changes.

Further reading

- Eysenck, M.W. (2012). *Fundamentals of cognition*. Hove, UK: Psychology Press. Most of Chapter 2 of this textbook is devoted to topics in visual perception.

- Goldstein, E.B. (2009). *Sensation and perception (8th ed.)*. Belmont, CA: Thomson. There is much information on major issues in visual perception in this textbook.

- Mather, G. (2009). *Foundations of sensation and perception (2nd ed.)*. Hove, UK: Psychology Press. George Mather provides good introductory coverage of most of the topics discussed in this chapter. For example, Chapter 10 is devoted to depth perception.

- Peissig, J.J., & Tarr, M.J. (2007). Visual object recognition: Do we know more now than we did 20 years ago? *Annual Review of Psychology, 58*, 75–96. Thankfully, the answer to the question posed by the authors is positive! They provide a good overview of developments in our understanding of object recognition in recent decades.

Essay questions

1. What processes are involved in perceptual organisation?
2. What cues determine depth perception?
3. Discuss factors involved in object recognition.
4. Why are we susceptible to visual illusions?
5. In what circumstances does change blindness occur?

In your everyday life, you probably find your memory for some things is very good, whereas you find it very hard to remember other things. Why do you think this is? How many different types of memory do you think we have? As we have all discovered to our cost, it is very common to forget information (even important information). What are some of the main reasons that forgetting occurs?

It is very important for eyewitnesses to a crime to remember in detail what happened. However, their memories of the crime are often limited and inaccurate. Why do you think eyewitness testimony tends to be so poor?

Memory

21

How important is memory to us? Imagine what our lives would be like without it. For a start, we wouldn't recognise anyone or anything as familiar. In addition, we wouldn't be able to talk, read, or write, because we would remember nothing about language. Furthermore, we would have no sense of self, because we wouldn't be able to access any information about our own personal history. In sum, experience would have taught us absolutely nothing, and we would have the same lack of knowledge as a newborn infant.

There are very close links between memory and learning. Every time we remember something, it involves recall of previous learning (see Chapter 23). Thus, memory depends on learning. It is also true that learning depends on memory—we could never learn anything properly if we forgot everything we had just learned. Such considerations lead memory theorists to argue that learning and memory involve three stages:

- *Encoding*: This is the process occurring during learning; it typically includes extracting the meaning of the to-be-learned material.
- *Storage*: At this stage, some of the information encoded during the first stage is stored within long-term memory.
- *Retrieval*: The final stage includes gaining access to some of the information stored in long-term memory.

The above three stages are closely linked together. For example, in order for information to be retrieved it must previously have been stored.

Your ability to retrieve or remember stored information can be tested in several ways. You could show you remember someone you have met before by *recognising* their face as familiar, or you might *recall* their name. As you have probably found, it is perfectly possible (and somewhat embarrassing!) to recognise someone's face without being able to put a name to it.

Suppose you were asked to learn the following list of words: CHAIR, TABLE, LEOPARD, WATCH, FOREST, MOUTH, GARDEN, WATER. Some of the ways your memory could be tested are as follows:

- **Free recall**: This involves writing down all the words you remember in any order.

Are learning and memory different? If so, what are the differences?

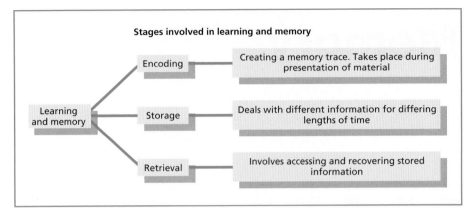

Stages involved in learning and memory

Learning and memory

Encoding — Creating a memory trace. Takes place during presentation of material

Storage — Deals with different information for differing lengths of time

Retrieval — Involves accessing and recovering stored information

- **Cued recall**: This might involve being given the first few letters of each word (e.g., CHA___ ; TAB___) and trying to think of the appropriate list words.
- **Recognition**: This might involve being given the list words as well as other non-list words (e.g., CHAIR SHELF ELBOW MOUTH FRAME TABLE WATER PHOTO TIGER GARDEN FOREST WATCH STATUE LEOPARD ROBIN TICKET) and selecting the list words.

Short-term vs. Long-term memory

There are several different forms of memory. A crucial distinction is between short-term and long-term memory. Short-term memory is rather fragile and short-lived, lasting only for a few seconds. It is used when we remember a telephone number for a few seconds or when listening to a conversation. Long-term memory is less fragile. It is used when we recall what happened today or the happiest time of our lives, or when we play a sport or ride a bicycle.

Multistore model

According to Atkinson and Shiffrin's (1968) multistore model, information we attend to is processed in a short-term memory store having very limited capacity. Some of that information then proceeds to the long-term store if there is **rehearsal** (saying the items over to ourselves silently) (see the figure on the next page). Suppose you were asked to learn a list of words. The more you rehearsed the list words to yourself, the better your long-term memory would be.

Findings

Convincing evidence that there are separate short-term and long-term memory systems comes from work on brain-damaged patients. Suppose there is only *one* memory system covering both short-term and long-term memory. Patients with brain damage to this system would show poor short-term and long-term memory.

In contrast, suppose there are *two* memory systems, one for short-term memory and one for long-term memory. If these two systems are in different

KEY TERMS

Cued recall: a form of memory test in which cues or clues are given to assist remembering; the first few letters of words can be used as cues.

Recognition: a form of memory test in which decisions have to be made as to whether the items on the test were presented before.

Rehearsal: the verbal repetition of information (often words), which typically has the effect of increasing our long-term memory for the rehearsed information.

parts of the brain, some patients would have poor short-term memory but intact long-term memory. Other patients would have intact short-term memory but poor long-term memory.

What has been found? Most brain-damaged patients with memory problems suffer from **amnesia**. These patients have intact short-term memory but their long-term memory is severely disrupted. They will re-read a newspaper without realising they read it a short time ago, and often fail to recognise someone they met only recently.

A few patients show the opposite pattern. Shallice and Warrington (1974) studied a patient, KF, who had suffered brain damage as a result of a motorcycle accident. He had very poor short-term memory but essentially intact long-term memory.

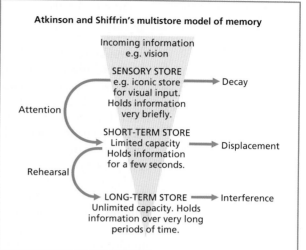

Atkinson and Shiffrin's multistore model of memory

EVALUATION

⊕ Atkinson and Shiffrin's (1968) multistore model has been very influential.

⊕ There is good evidence for separate short-term and long-term memory systems.

⊖ The role played by rehearsal in producing long-term memory was exaggerated in the model. Most of the information stored in long-term memory wasn't rehearsed during learning.

⊖ As is discussed below, the assumptions that we have a *single* short-term memory system and a *single* long-term memory system are gross oversimplifications.

Short-term memory

In approximate terms, short-term memory consists of the information we are consciously aware of at any given time. What is its capacity? John Jacobs (1887) presented participants with a random sequence of digits or letters, after which they repeated the items back in the same order. **Memory span** was the longest sequence of items recalled accurately at least 50% of the time. Digit span was greater than letter span (9.3 vs. 7.3 items, respectively).

George Miller (1956) argued that the capacity of short-term memory is "seven, plus or minus two". This is the case whether the units are numbers, letters, or words. He claimed we should focus on **chunks** (integrated pieces of information). What forms a chunk depends on your personal experience. For example, "IBM" is *one* chunk for those familiar with the company name International Business Machines but *three* chunks for everyone else.

KEY TERMS

Amnesia: a condition produced by brain damage in which patients have normal short-term but poor long-term memory.

Memory span: an assessment of how much can be stored in short-term memory based on the individual's ability to repeat back digits or other items in the correct order immediately after they have been presented.

Chunks: familiar units of information.

What is the approximate capacity of short-term memory?

Simon (1974) found memory span in chunks was less with larger chunks than with smaller ones. He studied memory span for words, two-word phrases, and eight-word phrases arguing that each phrase formed a chunk. The number of chunks recalled fell from six or seven with unrelated words to four with two-word phrases and three with eight-word phrases.

Cowan (2000) argued that the capacity of short-term memory is often exaggerated for two reasons. First, people may recall some of the information from long-term memory rather than short-term memory. Second, they may engage in rehearsal to increase recall. When these factors are largely eliminated, the capacity of short-term memory is about four chunks (Cowan et al., 2005).

Is short-term memory useful in everyday life? Textbook writers (including me earlier!) sometimes point out that it allows us to remember a telephone number for the few seconds required to dial it. However, that is no longer of much relevance—nearly everyone has a mobile phone storing the phone numbers needed regularly.

Working memory

In 1974, two British psychologists (Alan Baddeley and Graham Hitch) came up with a convincing answer to the question of whether short-term memory is useful in everyday life. They argued we generally use short-term memory when engaged in the performance of complex tasks. With such tasks, you have to carry out various processes to complete the task. However, you also have to store briefly information about the outcome of early processes in short-term memory as you move on to later processes.

Suppose you were given the addition problem 13 + 18 + 24. You would probably add 13 and 18 and keep the answer (31) in short-term memory. You would then add 24 to 31 and produce the correct answer of 55.

Baddeley and Hitch (1974) argued we should replace the notion of short-term memory with that of working memory. **Working memory** refers to a system combining processing and short-term memory functions. Baddeley and Hitch's crucial insight was that short-term memory is essential in the performance of numerous tasks that aren't explicitly memory tasks.

Baddeley and Hitch (1974) proposed the original version of the working memory model. We will focus on the most recent version (e.g., Baddeley, 2007) consisting of four components:

- **Central executive:** This is a limited capacity processing system acting as an attentional controller. It is the "boss" of the working memory system and controls what happens within the other components. It can process information from any sensory modality (e.g., visual, auditory) but has no storage capacity.
- **Phonological loop:** This is involved in the processing and brief storage of phonological (speech-based) information. For example, it is used to rehearse words on a short-term memory task.
- **Visuo-spatial sketchpad:** This is involved in the processing and brief storage of visual and spatial information. It is used when finding the route from one place to another or when watching TV. There is an important distinction between visual and spatial processing. For example, blind

KEY TERMS

Working memory: a system that has separate components for rehearsal and for other processing activities; it has been proposed as a replacement for the short-term memory store.

Central executive: the most important component of working memory; it is involved in planning and the control of attention and has limited capacity.

Phonological loop: a component of working memory in which speech-based information is processed and stored and subvocal articulation occurs.

Visuo-spatial sketchpad: a component of working memory that is used to process visual and spatial information and to store this information briefly.

people often have good spatial processing in the absence of visual processing: Fortin et al. (2008) found blind people were better than sighted ones at finding their way through a human-size maze.

- **Episodic buffer**: This is a storage system holding information from the phonological loop, the visuo-spatial sketchpad, and long-term memory.

It is assumed that all four components of working memory have limited capacity. It is also assumed each component can function fairly independently of the others.

You are probably thinking the working memory model seems rather complicated. However, the basic ideas are straightforward. When we carry out a task, we can use verbal processing (phonological loop), visual processing, or spatial processing (visuo-spatial sketchpad).

Performing the task successfully requires that we attend to relevant information and use verbal, visual, and spatial processes effectively (central executive). During the performance of a task, we often need a general storage system combining and integrating information from the other components and from long-term memory (episodic buffer).

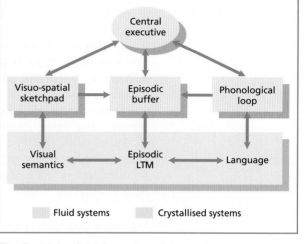

The Baddeley (2000) version of the multi-component working memory. Links to long-term memory have been specified and a new component, the episodic buffer, added. Fluid systems involve active processing whereas crystallised systems involve stored knowledge.

Long-term memory

Atkinson and Shiffrin (1968) argued there is only one long-term memory system. However, that seems unlikely when you consider the huge range of information stored in long-term memory: personal experiences, general knowledge, motor skills, language, and so on.

The most important distinction between different types of long-term memory is between declarative memory and non-declarative memory. **Declarative memory** involves conscious recollection of events and facts; it refers to memories that can be "declared" or described. Declarative memory is sometimes referred to as explicit memory, defined as memory that "requires conscious recollection of previous experiences" (Graf & Schacter, 1985, p. 501). It involves "knowing that" something is the case. Declarative memory is what you use when you remember someone's name when you see them, when you remember some fact in psychology, or when you remember how to get to your friend's house.

In contrast to declarative memory, **non-declarative memory** does *not* involve conscious recollection, and is sometimes referred to as implicit memory. Typically, we obtain evidence of non-declarative memory by observing changes in behaviour.

The differences between the two types of memory can be seen in the following anecdote from Edouard Claparède (1873–1940) reported by him in 1911. He studied a female patient suffering from amnesia due to chronic alcoholism. She couldn't recognise doctors and nurses she had seen virtually

How does amnesia affect procedural and declarative memory?

every day over a period of several years, indicating her declarative memory was extremely poor. One day Claparède hid a pin in his hand before shaking hands with the patient. The following day she was very sensibly reluctant to shake hands with him. However, she felt embarrassed because she couldn't explain her reluctance. Her behaviour indicated the presence of non-declarative memory of what had happened the previous day even though she had no conscious recollection of it.

Evidence for the distinction between declarative and non-declarative memory has been obtained from numerous amnesic patients (see Chapter 2). Spiers et al. (2001) reviewed findings from 147 amnesic patients. All the patients had severely impaired declarative memory but *none* had impaired non-declarative memory. Thus, declarative and non-declarative memory involve different memory systems.

Declarative memory

How many types of declarative or explicit memory are there? As we will see, there are three main types: episodic memory; semantic memory; and autobiographical memory.

Episodic memory

Episodic memory is the memory system we use when we remember the word *chair* appeared in the last list we learned, that we had cereal for breakfast, or that we went to the cinema yesterday.

More generally, we use **episodic memory** to remember past events we have experienced. Episodic memories fulfil the www criteria: they contain information about *what* happened, *where* it happened, and *when* it happened. You might expect the episodic memory system would work like a video recorder, providing us with accurate and detailed information about past events. That is *not* the case. As Schacter and Addis (2007, p. 773) pointed out, "Episodic memory is . . . a fundamentally constructive, rather than reproductive process that is prone to various kinds of errors and illusions."

Why is episodic memory prone to error? It would require an incredible amount of processing to produce a semi-permanent record of all our experiences. In addition, we typically only want to remember the essence of an experience rather than the details.

Semantic memory

Semantic memory is the memory system we use when remembering facts and information (e.g., the name of the current American President, the number of planets in the solar system, or the meaning of the word *psychology*). More generally, semantic memory consists of our knowledge of language and the world. Much of that knowledge is in the form of schemas (discussed later).

Semantic memory is less *vulnerable* to brain damage than episodic memory. I mentioned earlier that Spiers et al. (2001) reviewed 147 cases of patients with amnesia. Episodic memory was severely impaired in all cases, but semantic memory was often only slightly impaired.

In some cases of amnesia, semantic memory is intact. Vargha-Khadem et al. (1997) studied two patients (Beth and Jon) who had very poor episodic memory for the day's activities, television programmes, and telephone conversations.

KEY TERMS

Episodic memory: long-term memory for personal events.

Semantic memory: a form of **declarative memory** consisting of general knowledge about the world, concepts, language, and so on; see **episodic memory**.

However, Beth and Jon both attended ordinary schools, and their levels of speech and language development, literacy, and factual knowledge were normal.

Autobiographical memory

We use **autobiographical memory** when we remember personal experiences of importance in our lives. For example, we might think about our first boyfriend/girlfriend or the best holiday of our lives. It resembles episodic memory, but differs in that episodic memory tends to be concerned with relatively trivial experiences.

According to Conway and Pleydell-Pearce (2000, p. 266), "Autobiographical memories are primarily records of success or failure in goal attainment." An individual's goals depend in part on his/her personality. As a result, the autobiographical memories an individual regards as important should reflect his/her personality.

Woike et al. (1999) tested the above hypothesis. They distinguished between two types of personality. First, there is the agentic personality type with an emphasis on independence and achievement. Second, there is the communal personality type with an emphasis on interdependence and similarity to others.

Woike et al. (1999) asked participants to write about positive or negative personal experiences. Those with an agentic personality mostly recalled agentic autobiographical memories (e.g., involving success or failure). In contrast, those with a communal personality recalled communal memories (e.g., involving love, friendship, or betrayal of trust).

Non-declarative memory

The essence of non-declarative memory is that it doesn't involve conscious recollection but instead reveals itself through behaviour. There are two main forms of non-declarative memory: priming and skill learning. **Priming** is what happens when processing of a stimulus is easier because the same (or a similar) stimulus was presented previously. When children learn to read they show priming as they recognise familiar words more and more easily.

Tulving and Schacter (1990) found that people found it easier to identify briefly presented words if they had been presented previously. This occurred even though the participants were unaware that their ability to perceive the flashed words had been influenced by the study list. This is an example of a priming effect.

What is involved in priming? Repeated presentation of a stimulus means it can be processed more *efficiently* using fewer resources. As a result, priming is associated with reduced levels of brain activity (Poldrack & Gabrieli, 2001).

Skill learning is involved when we learn how to ride a bicycle or play a sport. There are several differences between priming and skill learning:

1. Priming often occurs rapidly whereas skill learning is typically slow and gradual (Knowlton & Foerde, 2008).

KEY TERMS

Autobiographical memory: memory across the lifespan for specific events involving the individual (especially those of personal significance).

Priming: this is a form of **non-declarative memory** involving facilitated processing of (and response to) a target stimulus because the same or a related stimulus was presented previously.

Skill learning: this is a form of learning in which there is little or no conscious awareness of what has been learned.

2. Priming involves learning tied to *specific* stimuli, whereas skill learning *generalises* to other stimuli. For example, it wouldn't be much use if you learned how to hit backhands at tennis very well, but could only do so provided the ball came towards you from a given direction at a given speed!

Hamann and Squire (1997) studied an amnesic patient, EP, who seemed to have no declarative memory at all. On a test of recognition memory he was correct on only 52% of trials (chance = 50%) compared to 81% for healthy controls. However, his performance on priming tasks was as good as that of healthy controls.

Cavaco et al. (2004) used five tasks requiring skills similar to those needed in the real world. For example, there was a weaving task and a control stick task requiring movements similar to those involved in operating machinery. Amnesic patients showed comparable rates of learning to those of healthy individuals on all five skill-learning tasks in spite of having impaired declarative memory for the tasks assessed by recall and recognition tests. Such findings strengthen the notion that non-declarative memory is very different from declarative memory.

Categorical clustering is a useful tool for sorting and storing a mass of information. Imagine how difficult it would be to find anything in a library if books were organised by colour or size.

Organisation in memory

Human memory is generally highly organised, with well-organised information being better remembered than poorly organised information. The existence of organisation in memory can be shown very simply. A categorised word list is prepared, with words belonging to different categories (e.g., four-footed animals; sports; flowers). The list is then presented in random order (e.g., tennis, cat, golf, tulip, horse, and so on) followed by a test of free recall (words are recalled in any order).

The words are *not* recalled in a random order. Instead, they are mostly recalled category by category (Shuell, 1969). This is known as **categorical clustering**. It shows that to-be-remembered information is organised on the basis of knowledge stored in long-term memory.

Schema theory

We have seen that people use their previous relevant knowledge to assist learning and memory. Much of this relevant knowledge is in the form of **schemas** (organised packets of knowledge stored in long-term memory). In a study on schemas, Bower et al. (1979) asked people to list 20 actions or events that usually occur in a restaurant. There was much agreement with respect to the restaurant schema. Most people mentioned sitting down, looking at the menu, ordering, eating, paying the bill, and leaving.

Schemas often enhance long-term memory. Read the following passage from Bransford and Johnson (1972, p. 722) and try to make sense of it:

The procedure is quite simple. First, you arrange items into different groups. Of course one pile may be sufficient depending on how much there is to do. If you have to go somewhere else due to lack of facilities, that is the next step; otherwise, you are pretty well set. It is important not to overdo things. That is, it is better to do too few things at once than too many. In the short run this may not seem important, but complications from doing too much can easily arise ...

I imagine you found it very difficult to understand the passage. The reason is that you lacked the relevant schema. In fact, the title of the passage is "Washing clothes". Now re-read the passage, which should be much easier to understand armed with that schematic information.

Bransford and Johnson (1972) found that participants hearing the passage in the absence of a title recalled an average of only 2.8 idea units. In contrast, those supplied beforehand with the title "Washing clothes" found it easy to understand and recalled 5.8 idea units on average. Thus, making it easier for the participants to use the relevant schema *doubled* long-term memory.

Bartlett (1932) argued that our schematic knowledge can disrupt our long-term memory. He presented English students with stories from a different culture (North American Indian) to produce a *conflict* between the story and their prior knowledge. Bartlett (1932) found that people's schematic knowledge caused systematic distortions in their story memory. These distortions involved making the story conform to the readers' cultural expectations, a type of error Bartlett termed **rationalisation**. Such distortions are also found when eyewitnesses recall a crime they have witnessed (discussed later in this chapter).

Bartlett (1932) argued that memory for the precise information presented is forgotten over time, whereas memory for the underlying schemas is not. Thus, there should be more rationalisation errors (which depend on schematic knowledge) at longer retention intervals.

Support for Bartlett's schema theory was reported by Sulin and Dooling (1974). Some participants read a story about Gerald Martin, who was described as a ruthless dictator who caused the downfall of his country. Other participants read the same story, but the main actor's name was given as Adolf Hitler. It was expected that these participants would make use of their schematic knowledge of Hitler when remembering the story.

The participants told the story was about Adolf Hitler were much more likely than the other participants to believe incorrectly they had read the sentence, "He hated the Jews particularly and so persecuted them." This type of distortion was more common at a long than a short retention interval, because schematic information was more long-lasting than the information in the text.

KEY TERM

Rationalisation: in Bartlett's theory, the tendency in story recall to produce errors conforming to the cultural expectations of the rememberer; it is attributed to the influence of schemas.

EVALUATION

➕ Schematic knowledge of the world is used when we learn and remember.

➕ Schemas provide an organisational framework that often enhances long-term memory.

➕ Many errors and distortions in long-term memory are due to the influence of schematic information.

➖ It is hard to assess how much information is contained in schemas.

➖ The conditions determining *when* a given schema will be activated are unclear.

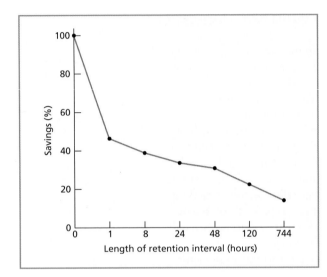

Forgetting over time as indexed by reduced savings during relearning. (0% savings would indicate total forgetting.) Data from Ebbinghaus (1885/1913).

Forgetting

So far we have focused mostly on what we remember. However, most of us feel that we have a really poor memory. Evidence that our memories can be poor for important information comes from the study of passwords. In one study (Brown et al., 2004), 31% of American students admitted to having forgotten passwords.

How can we minimise the risk of forgetting passwords? As we would expect, meaningful and familiar passwords are best remembered (Ostojic & Phillips, 2009).

The rate of forgetting is generally fastest shortly after learning and decreases progressively after that. The German psychologist Hermann Ebbinghaus (1885/1913) found that forgetting of lists was most rapid over the first hour or so after learning.

It is generally assumed that forgetting should be avoided. However, that is often *not* the case (Schacter, 1999; Schacter et al., 2011). For example, it isn't useful to remember where you parked your car yesterday, what your schedule of lectures was last term, or where your friends used to live. What you need to do is *update* your memory of such information and forget what was previously the case. Fortunately, our memory system is reasonably efficient at doing precisely that.

There are many reasons why forgetting occurs. Below we will consider some of the main theories of forgetting.

Interference

One of the main reasons for forgetting is interference. Our ability to remember what we are currently learning can be disrupted (or interfered with) by what we have previously learned (**proactive interference**). What we are currently learning can also be interfered with by future learning (**retroactive interference**) (see the figure on the next page).

Proactive and retroactive interference are both greatest when two different responses have been associated with the same stimulus. An example concerns the German psychologist Hugo Münsterberg (1863–1916), who put forward interference theory in the nineteenth century. Men had pocket-watches in those days, and Münsterberg kept his watch in one particular pocket. When he started to keep it in a different pocket, he often fumbled around in confusion when asked the time.

The above story shows the key features of interference theory. Münsterberg had learned an association between the stimulus, "What's the time, Hugo?", and the response of removing the watch from his pocket. Subsequently the stimulus remained the same but a different response was now associated with it. This produced proactive interference, in which previous learning disrupts later learning.

What causes proactive interference? There is *competition* between the correct and incorrect responses. Jacoby et al. (2001) found that proactive interference was due much more to the strength of the incorrect response than the weakness of the correct response.

Retroactive interference

There is also retroactive interference, in which later learning disrupts memory for previous learning. Suppose you became skilful in carrying out tasks on one computer. After that, you become expert at performing the same tasks on a different computer with different software. If you went back to your first computer, you might keep doing things that were correct with the second computer even though they were wrong with this computer.

Isurin and McDonald (2001) argued that retroactive interference explains why people forget

some of their first language when acquiring a second one. Bilingual participants fluent in two languages were first presented with various pictures and the corresponding words in Russian or Hebrew. Some were then presented with the same pictures and the corresponding words in the other language. Finally, they were tested for recall of the words in the first language. There was substantial retroactive interference—recall of the first-language words became progressively worse the more learning trials there were with the second-language words.

Lustig et al. (2004) argued that retroactive interference could occur because (1) the correct response is hard to retrieve; or (2) the incorrect response is very strong. They discovered that the second reason was more important.

Retroactive interference is generally greatest when the new learning resembles previous learning. However, there is some retroactive interference when people expend mental effort during the retention interval by performing a simple task (e.g., detecting tones) (Dewar et al., 2007). Dewar et al. concluded that retroactive interference can occur in two ways:

1. Expenditure of mental effort during the retention interval.
2. Learning of material similar to the original learning material.

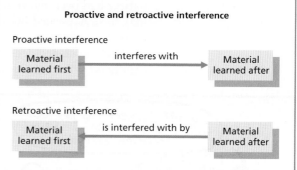

Proactive and retroactive interference

Proactive interference

| Material learned first | interferes with | Material learned after |

Retroactive interference

| Material learned first | is interfered with by | Material learned after |

Repression

One of the best-known theories of forgetting was put forward by the bearded Austrian psychologist Sigmund Freud. He claimed that much forgetting occurs as a result of **repression** (motivated forgetting of traumatic memories). For example, children who suffered sexual abuse when young may be highly motivated to forget or repress their terrible experiences.

Much evidence on repression comes from adults who have apparently recovered repressed memories of childhood physical and/or sexual abuse. There has been a fierce controversy about the genuineness of these recovered memories. Some theorists (e.g., Loftus & Davis, 2006) argue that many of these so-called recovered memories are false memories—they refer to events and experiences that never actually happened.

It is hard to obtain clear-cut evidence for two main reasons. First, there are generally no independent witnesses of the alleged sexual abuse. Second, we can't be sure that adults claiming to have recovered memories had *no* conscious recollection of childhood sexual abuse during adolescence.

Findings

Some patients have admitted that their "memories" of childhood abuse are false. In most such cases, the therapist had made direct suggestions that the patient had been the victim of childhood abuse (Lief & Fetkewicz, 1995). This may have happened because many therapists believe strongly in the reality of repressed memories.

Such evidence led Geraerts et al. (2007) to divide adults reporting childhood sexual abuse into three groups:

What bothers me is, how will I know when I have forgotten everything?

1. Those whose recovered memories had been recalled *inside* therapy.
2. Those whose recovered memories had been recalled *outside*.
3. Those who had continuous memories of abuse.

Geraerts et al. (2007) assessed how many of these memories had supporting evidence (e.g., the culprit had confessed). There was supporting evidence for 45% of the individuals with continuous memories, for 37% of those who had recalled memories outside therapy, and for 0% of those who had recalled memories inside therapy.

The above findings suggest that recovered memories fall into two categories. First, many recalled inside therapy are false memories produced by patients under the therapist's influence. Second, many of those recalled spontaneously outside therapy are genuine.

EVALUATION

➕ There is good evidence that repressed memories of childhood abuse exist.

- Genuine recovered memories are generally recalled spontaneously without prompting from a therapist.

- Recovered memories produced inside therapy are often false.

- Repression theory is limited because most forgetting doesn't relate to traumatic events.

Everyday memory

The study of everyday memory is concerned with how we use memory in our daily lives. A key issue is that of ecological validity (the extent to which laboratory findings apply to the real world).

The greatest difference between memory as traditionally studied and memory in everyday life relates to *motivation*. Laboratory participants are generally motivated to be as *accurate* as possible in their memory performance. This is less true of everyday life. For example, Marsh and Tversky (2004) found students admitted that 42% of their retellings of personal memories were inaccurate.

Laboratory studies are generally more carefully controlled than studies in the real world, and so the findings are more reliable. We will be considering laboratory research on **eyewitness testimony** (the evidence provided by the observer of a crime), which possesses a high level of ecological validity.

Eyewitness testimony

Suppose you are the only eyewitness to a serious crime in which someone is killed. Subsequently the person you identify as the murderer on a line-up is found guilty solely based on your evidence. Such cases raise the following question: is it safe to rely on eyewitness testimony?

The introduction of DNA tests has made it easier to answer the above question. In the United States, over 200 falsely convicted individuals have been shown to be innocent by DNA tests. More than 75% were found guilty on the basis of mistaken eyewitness identification.

Why is eyewitness testimony often inaccurate? There are two major reasons:

1. The eyewitness failed to attend closely to the crime and/or the criminal.
2. The eyewitness' memory became distorted *after* the crime was committed.

It may seem likely that failures of attention cause most cases of inaccurate eyewitness memory. However, as we will see, eyewitness memories are fragile and can easily be influenced by later information.

Fragility of memory

Elizabeth Loftus and John Palmer (1974) showed people a film of a multiple car accident. Afterwards, they answered various questions. Some were asked, "About how fast were the cars going when they smashed into each other?", whereas for other eyewitnesses the verb "hit" replaced "smashed into".

> **KEY TERM**
>
> **Eyewitness testimony:** the evidence relating to a crime that is provided by someone who observed the crime being committed.

Loftus and Palmer (1974) found that assessment of speed of a videotaped car crash and recollection of whether there was broken glass present were affected by the verb used to ask the question. Use of the verbs "hit" and "smash" have different implications as shown in (a) and (b).

One week later, the eyewitnesses were asked whether they had seen any broken glass. Even though there was actually no broken glass, 32% of those who had been asked before about speed using the verb "smashed" said they saw broken glass. In contrast, only 14% of those asked using the verb "hit" said they saw broken glass (see the figure left). Thus, our memory is so fragile it can be distorted by changing *one* word in *one* question!

The study by Loftus and Palmer (1974) focused on distortions for *minor* details (e.g., presence of broken glass) rather than central features. That may be important. Dalton and Daneman (2006) found that memory distortions were more common following misinformation about *peripheral* features than following misinformation about *central* features.

Leading questions

Lawyers in most countries aren't allowed to ask leading questions implying the desired answer (e.g., "When did you stop beating your wife?"). There are good reasons for this, as was shown by Loftus and Zanni (1975). Eyewitnesses watched a short film of a car accident. Some were asked the leading question, "Did you see *the* broken headlight?" The other eyewitnesses were asked the neutral question, "Did you see *a* broken headlight?" Even though there was no broken headlight, 17% asked the leading question said they had seen it compared to only 7% asked the neutral question.

Remembering faces

Are the findings of laboratory studies on eyewitness testimony applicable to real-life crime scenarios?

Information about the culprit's face is often the most important information eyewitnesses may or may not remember. In several countries, there has been a dramatic increase in the number of closed-circuit television (CCTV) cameras. How easy is it to identify someone on the basis of CCTV images? Burton et al. (1999) considered this question. They presented people with a target face taken from a CCTV video together with an array of 10 high-quality photographs (see the figure on the next page).

The participants selected the matching face or indicated the target face wasn't present in the array. When the target face was present, it was selected only 65% of the time. When it wasn't present, 35% of the participants nevertheless claimed a face in the array matched the target face!

Same-race faces are recognised better than cross-race faces—the **cross-race effect**. In actual criminal cases, the suspect was much more likely to be identified when he/she was of the same race as the eyewitness (Behrman & Davey, 2001).

How can we explain the cross-race effect? Expertise is a factor. Eyewitnesses having the most experience with members of another race show a smaller cross-race effect than others (Shriver et al., 2008). It is also possible that we process the faces of individuals with whom we identify (our ingroup) more thoroughly than those of outgroup members.

Shriver et al. (2008) carried out a study on white, middle-class students. The cross-race effect disappeared when white and black faces were seen in an

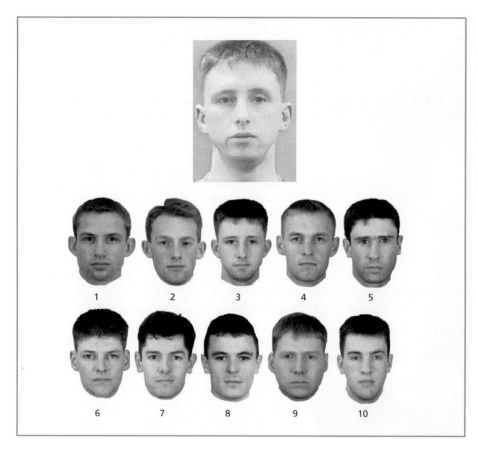

Example of full-face neutral target with an array used by Burton et al. (1999). You may wish to attempt the task of establishing whether or not the target is present in this array and which one it is. The studio and video images used are from the Home Office Police Information Technology Organisation. Target is number 3.

impoverished context. This was because the white faces weren't regarded as belonging to the students' ingroup and so weren't processed in detail.

Memory bias

Eyewitness testimony can be distorted via **confirmation bias,** i.e., event memory is influenced by what the observer expects to see. This can happen because of the schemas (packets of knowledge) we possess. Most people's bank-robbery schema includes information that robbers are typically male, wear dark clothes, and are in disguise (Tuckey & Brewer, 2003a). This schema leads us to form certain expectations. It can distort memory by causing eyewitnesses to reconstruct an event's details by including information from the bank-robbery schema even when it doesn't correspond to what they have observed (Tuckey & Brewer, 2003b).

Violence and anxiety

What are the effects of anxiety and violence on eyewitness memory? There is evidence for **weapon focus**—eyewitnesses attend to the criminal's weapon, which reduces their memory for other information. In one study, Loftus et al. (1987) asked participants to watch one of two sequences: (1) a person pointing a gun at a cashier and receiving some cash; (2) a person handing a cheque to the cashier and receiving some cash. The participants looked more at the gun

Eyewitnesses pay so much attention to the criminal's weapon that their memory for other details is reduced.

than at the cheque. As predicted, memory for details unrelated to the gun/cheque was poorer in the weapon condition.

Pickel (2009) pointed out that people often attend to stimuli that are *unexpected* in a current situation (inconsistent with their schema of that situation). This impairs their memory for other stimuli. As predicted, the weapon focus effect was greater when the presence of a weapon was very unexpected (e.g., a female criminal carrying a folding knife).

Deffenbacher et al. (2004) combined the findings from several studies. Culprits' faces were identified 54% of the time in low anxiety or stress conditions compared to 42% for high anxiety or stress conditions. Thus, stress and anxiety generally impair eyewitness memory.

From laboratory to courtroom

Can we apply findings from laboratory studies to real-life crimes? There are certainly some important differences. For example, eyewitnesses to real crimes are often the victims of an attack and are exposed to a highly stressful experience. In addition, the evidence they provide may be literally a matter of life or death in an American courtroom.

However, there are important similarities. Ihlebaek et al. (2003) used a staged robbery involving two robbers armed with handguns. In the live condition, eyewitnesses were ordered repeatedly to "Stay down". A video taken during the live condition was presented to eyewitnesses in the video condition. Participants in both conditions exaggerated the duration of the event, and showed similar patterns in what was well and poorly remembered. However, eyewitnesses in the video condition recalled more information.

Tollestrup et al. (1994) analysed police records concerning the identifications by eyewitnesses to crimes involving fraud and robbery. Factors important in laboratory studies (e.g., weapon focus; retention interval) were also important in real-life crimes.

In sum, artificial laboratory conditions typically don't distort the findings. If anything, the errors in eyewitness memory obtained under laboratory conditions *underestimate* memory deficiencies for real-life events. Overall, laboratory research provides evidence of genuine relevance to the legal system.

Chapter summary

- Learning and memory involve three successive stages: encoding, storage, and retrieval.
- There are several ways an individual's memory can be tested. Memory tests include free recall, cued recall, and recognition.
- There is a major distinction between short-term and long-term memory systems. According to the multistore model, rehearsal causes information to proceed from short-term to long-term memory.
- Amnesic patients have impaired long-term memory but intact short-term memory, whereas some other brain patients show the opposite pattern.
- It has been claimed that the capacity of short-term memory is seven chunks. However, when the contributions of long-term memory and rehearsal are removed, its capacity is only four chunks.
- The notion of a short-term store has been replaced with that of working memory, a system combining brief storage and processing.
- According to Baddeley's working memory model, working memory consists of four components: central executive; phonological loop; visuo-spatial sketchpad; and episodic buffer.
- Declarative memory involves conscious recollection of events and facts. Non-declarative memory doesn't involve conscious recollection and is often assessed by observing behaviour changes.
- Amnesic patients have severely impaired declarative memory but intact non-declarative memory.
- The major types of declarative memory are episodic memory (for personal events), semantic memory (for remembering facts and information), and autobiographical memory (for important personal experiences).
- The major types of non-declarative memory are priming (enhanced stimulus processing with repetition) and skill learning (e.g., riding a bicycle).
- Human memory is generally highly organised as is shown by categorical clustering.
- Schematic knowledge often enhances long-term memory. However, it can cause memory distortions (especially at long retention intervals).
- Forgetting can be due to interference from what we have previously learned (proactive interference) or to interference from what we learn between learning and retrieval (retroactive interference). Both kinds of interference are greatest when two different responses are associated with the same stimulus.
- Motivated forgetting of traumatic memories is known as repression. The recovered memories of adults abused as children often involve repression. However, some are false memories produced under the therapist's influence.

- In laboratory research, people are motivated to recall information as accurately as possible. In everyday life, in contrast, the emphasis is often on sounding impressive or being entertaining.
- Eyewitness memory is often distorted by information presented after the crime. It can also be inaccurate because it is hard to remember detailed information about faces.
- Eyewitnesses may be over-influenced by their expectations (confirmation bias) based on crime schemas. In addition, stress and anxiety can impair their memory.

Further reading

- Baddeley, A., Eysenck, M.W., & Anderson, M.C. (2009). *Memory*. Hove, UK: Psychology Press. This textbook provides more detailed coverage of the topics discussed in this chapter.

- Della Sala, S. (Ed.). (2010). *Forgetting*. Hove, UK: Psychology Press. The major contemporary approaches to understanding forgetting are discussed in this edited book.

- Eysenck, M.W. (2012). *Fundamentals of cognition (2nd Ed.)*. Hove, UK: Psychology Press. Chapters 4–6 of this textbook cover the topics discussed in this chapter in more detail.

- Lindsay, R.C.L., Ross, D.F., Read, J.D., & Toglia, M.P. (Eds.) (2007). *The handbook of eyewitness psychology: Volume II: Memory for people*. Mahwah, NJ: Lawrence Erlbaum Associates, Inc. This edited book contains contributions from the world's leading experts on eyewitness memory for people.

Essay questions

1. Compare and contrast the concepts of "short-term memory" and "working memory".

2. Describe the various types of long-term memory.

3. Discuss factors responsible for forgetting.

4. Why is eyewitness memory often inaccurate?

You probably spend much of your time trying to solve problems. Some are related to your studies, whereas others are to do with your personal life. How useful is past experience when it comes to problem solving?

Creativity is regarded as a very useful ability. Some people argue that scientific creativity involves special processes whereas others argue that it mostly depends on cognitive processes that we use much of the time. What do you think?

Problem solving and creativity

Life provides us with many problems. These problems come in many shapes and sizes. Most problems are fairly trivial and short-term (e.g., "How am I going to travel from A to B?"). However, a few are important and long-term (e.g., "How am I going to pass my psychology exam?"). What, if anything, do all attempts at problem solving have in common?

According to Mayer (1990, p. 284), problem solving is "cognitive processing directed at transforming a given situation into a goal situation when no obvious method of solution is available to the problem solver." Thus, there are three major aspects to problem solving:

- It is purposeful or goal-directed.
- It requires the use of cognitive processes rather than automatic ones.
- A problem only exists when someone lacks the relevant knowledge to produce an immediate solution.

There are many different kinds of problems. There are well-defined problems in which everything is clearly specified including the range of possible moves and the goal or solution. Mazes are well-defined problems in which reaching the centre is the goal.

In contrast, ill-defined problems are underspecified. Suppose you set yourself the goal of obtaining a well-paid and interesting job. There are numerous strategies you could adopt, and it is very hard to know in advance which ones would be most effective. The goal is also not very specific—*how* well-paid and interesting does a job need to be to achieve it?

Most everyday problems are ill-defined but psychologists focus mainly on well-defined problems. Why is this? Well-defined problems have a best strategy for their solution. Thus, it is easy for psychologists to identify clearly the errors and deficiencies in the strategies used by problem solvers.

Insight vs. non-insight problems

We have all found ourselves working slowly but surely through problems until we reach the solution: "grind-out-the-answer" problems. For example, solving a hard problem in multiplication involves several processing operations that must be performed in the correct sequence.

Do you believe that most problems involve moving slowly towards the solution? If you do, you are in for a rude shock! There are many problems in which the solution depends on **insight** or an "aha" experience involving a sudden transformation of the problem.

Findings

Gilhooly and Murphy (2005) considered performance on insight and non-insight problems. Here are two of the insight problems they used:

1. You have six matches and have to put them together to form four triangles with all sides equal in length.
2. You have black and brown socks in your drawer in a ratio of 4 to 5. How many socks do you need to take out to ensure you have a pair the same colour?

The answer to problem (1) is shown in the figure below. The answer to problem (2) is three, the ratio of the two sock colours is irrelevant.

Why do many people find it hard to solve such insight problems? How we think about a problem (the problem representation) is often of great importance. Our initial problem representation is often misleading with insight problems—we think of forming a two-dimensional structure with the matches rather than a three-dimensional pyramid, and we think the total number of socks of each colour matters. Insight occurs when there is a sudden restructuring of the problem to form the correct problem representation (Ohlsson, 1992).

Gilhooly and Murphy (2005) also used various non-insight problems. Examples include anagram problems (rearranging letters to form words) and reasoning problems (deciding whether a conclusion follows validly from previous statements). Some individuals were better at insight problems than at non-insight problems whereas others showed the opposite pattern. These findings suggest the two types of problems involve different processes.

Evidence supporting the notion there are important differences between insight and non-insight problems was provided by Metcalfe and Wiebe (1987). There was a *gradual* increase in "warmth" (closeness to solution) during non-insight problems. This is as expected since they involve a sequence of processes. In contrast, the warmth ratings during insight problems remained at the same low level until *suddenly* increasing just before the solution was reached.

Brain-imaging findings have also revealed important differences in the processing of insight and non-insight problems. Bowden et al. (2005) used Remote Associate problems. Three words were presented (e.g., "fence"; "card"; "master"), and participants had to think of a word (e.g., "post")

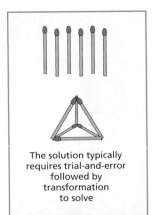

The solution typically requires trial-and-error followed by transformation to solve

KEY TERM

Insight: a sudden understanding or "a-ha" experience, in which an entire problem is looked at in a different way.

that would go with each of them to form compound words. The participants indicated whether their answers involved insight (i.e., sudden awareness).

Bowden et al. (2005) found using fMRI (functional magnetic resonance imaging) to assess brain activity that the right anterior superior temporal gyrus (ridge) was activated *only* when solutions involved insight. In their second experiment, event-related potentials (ERPs) were recorded. There was a burst of high-frequency brain activity one-third of a second before the participants indicated they had achieved an insightful solution. This brain activity was centred in the same brain area. According to Bowden et al., this area is vital to insight because it is involved in processing general semantic (meaning) relationships.

Insightful solutions to problems seem to "pop into the mind" in a relatively automatic and effortless way. In contrast, deliberate processes involving working memory are required to solve non-insight problems. Lavric et al. (2000) considered the effects of counting auditory stimuli (requiring the involvement of working memory) on the performance of various problems. The counting task impaired performance on non-insight problems but not on insight ones. Thus, working memory is more important for non-insight problems than for insight ones.

How can we increase insightful problem solving? Slepian et al. (2010) pointed out that a lightbulb is often used to represent insight. That led them to wonder whether an illuminating lightbulb would activate concepts associated with insight and thereby enhance insightful problem solving. Many more of the participants exposed to the illuminating lightbulb solved a complex insight problem than those not exposed to it (44% vs. 22%, respectively).

EVALUATION

⊕ Insight problems differ from non-insight ones in suddenness of solution, the involvement of specific brain areas, and the involvement of working memory.

⊕ Solving insight problems typically involves a sudden replacing of an incorrect problem representation with the correct one.

⊖ The factors leading to changes in the problem representation aren't well understood.

⊖ Many problems can be solved in an insightful or non-insightful way. This blurs the distinction between problem types.

Past experience

Common sense tells us that our ability to solve a problem is improved if we have past experience with similar problems. Indeed, a crucial reason why adults solve most problems much faster than children is because of their much greater relevant past experience.

What is the name of the tendency to think that objects can only be used for functions for which they have been used in the past?

Research showing how past experience can benefit present problem solving is discussed later. Before that, however, we will focus on the notion that past experience sometimes has *negative* effects on problem solving.

Is past experience useful? No

Evidence that past experience can impair problem solving was reported by Duncker (1945). He studied **functional fixedness**, which is the tendency to think that objects can only be used for a narrow range of functions for which they have been used in the past. Duncker asked participants to mount a candle on a vertical screen. Various objects were spread around including a box full of nails and a book of matches (see the figure on the left).

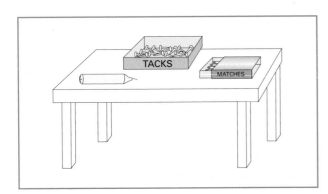

Some of the materials provided for participants instructed to mount a candle on a vertical wall in the study by Duncker (1945).

The solution involves using the box as a platform for the candle. Only a few participants solved this problem because their past experience led them to regard the box as a container rather than a platform. Their performance was better when the box was empty rather than full of nails—the latter set-up emphasised the container-like quality of the box.

More evidence that functional fixedness is hard to avoid was reported by Chrysikou and Weisberg (2005). Participants designed various objects (e.g., a disposable, spill-proof coffee cup). In one condition, they were shown a picture of an inadequate coffee cup with the accompanying description explicitly stating problems with it. Nevertheless, the participants' designs consistently included elements of the deficient coffee cup. The take-home message is that the ideas we encounter often *limit* our subsequent thinking.

Mental set

Suppose you were given the following problem (Luchins, 1942):

> Jar A can hold 28 quarts of water, Jar B 76 quarts, and Jar C 3 quarts (a quart is 2 pints or 1.14 litres). The task is to end up with exactly 25 quarts in one of the jars.

The solution is easy: Jar A is filled, and then Jar C is filled from it, leaving 25 quarts in Jar A.

Luchins (1942) found that 95% of participants who had previously been given similar problems solved it. More interestingly, the success rate on this problem was only 36% for participants who had been trained on problems with complex three-jar solutions.

What is going on here? According to Luchins (1942), the participants in the latter condition developed a **mental set** or way of approaching the problems that led them to think rigidly. In the words of Luchins (1942, p. 1), "The successive, repetitive use of the same method mechanised many of the subjects – blinded them to the possibility of a more direct and simple procedure."

We might expect experts given a problem in their area of expertise would be relatively immune from the damaging effects of mental set. In fact, this is *not* the case. Bilalić et al. (2008a) presented expert chess players with a chess problem and told them to find the shortest way to win. The problem could be solved in five moves using a familiar strategy but in only three moves using a less familiar solution. Only 50% of the International Masters found the shorter solution and 0% of the Candidate Masters.

Bilalić et al. (2008b) carried out a similar study. After expert players had found the familiar solution, they reported they were looking hard for a better one. However, their eye movements showed they were still looking at features of the chessboard position related to the familiar solution. Thus, their attentional processes were still partly under the control of mental set.

How can past experience both impair and promote problem solving?

Is past experience useful? Yes

We have seen that past experience can have negative effects on problem solving. In everyday life, however, the effects of past experience are mostly positive. When we try to solve a problem, we often make use of analogies or similarities between that problem and those we have solved in the past. We turn now to research on analogical problem solving.

The history of science provides numerous examples of successful analogical problem solving. For example, the New Zealand physicist Ernest Rutherford used a solar system analogy to understand the structure of the atom. He argued that electrons revolve around the nucleus in the same way that planets revolve around the sun.

In order for someone to make successful use of a previous problem to solve a current one, they must detect *similarities* between the two problems. There are two main types of similarity:

1. *Superficial similarity*: Solution-irrelevant details (e.g., specific objects) are common to both problems.
2. *Structural similarity*: Causal relations among some of the main components are shared by both problems.

Findings

Suppose you are given a problem to solve. How likely is it that you will use a relevant analogy to solve it? The findings are mixed. In one study, Gick and Holyoak (1980) used a problem on which a patient with a malignant tumour can only be saved by a special kind of ray. A ray strong enough to destroy the tumour will also destroy the healthy tissue. However, a ray that won't harm healthy tissue will be too weak to destroy the tumour.

What is the answer to the above problem? Before providing the answer, here is an analogy to help you. A general wants to capture a fortress but the roads leading to it are mined, making it too dangerous for the entire army to march along any one of them. The general solved the problem by dividing his army into groups that marched along several different roads. Hopefully, this analogy helped you to solve the radiation problem—this involves having several weak rays all directed at the tumour.

Gick and Holyoak (1980) found that 80% of participants solved the radiation problem when told that the fortress story (which they encountered previously) was relevant. This dropped to 40% for participants who had encountered the fortress story earlier but were *not* informed of its relevance. Finally, only 10%

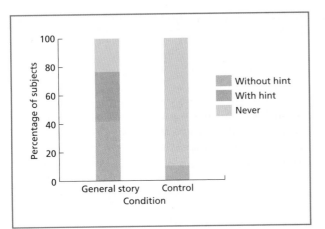

Some of the results from Gick and Holyoak (1980, Experiment 4) showing the percentage of subjects who solved the radiation problem when they were given an analogy (general-story condition) or were just asked to solve the problem (control condition). Note that just under half of the subjects in the general-story condition had to be given a hint to use the story analogue before they solved the problem.

Define heuristic methods.

of participants solved the radiation problem in the absence of the fortress story (see the figure on the left).

What do these findings mean? They indicate that having a relevant analogy stored in long-term memory is no guarantee it will be used. The main reason was that there were few superficial similarities between the two problems. People are much more likely to recall spontaneously a previous story superficially similar to the radiation problem (story about a surgeon using rays on a cancer) than one lacking superficial similarities (fortress story) (Keane, 1987).

We have seen that people focus on superficial rather than structural similarities between problems when *given* a relevant analogy beforehand. In everyday life, people generally *produce* their own analogies rather than being given them. Dunbar and Blanchette (2001) found with scientists generating hypotheses that the analogies they used involved structural rather than superficial similarities. Thus, we can focus on structural similarities between problems in certain circumstances.

How can we improve analogical problem solving? Kurtz and Loewenstein (2007) argued that it is easier to understand the underlying structure of a problem if we compare it *directly* with another problem sharing the same structure. As predicted, performance on the radiation problem was much better among participants who considered similarities between the radiation problem and an analogous problem than among those who didn't.

Problem-solving strategies

A major landmark in research on problem solving was the publication in 1972 of a book entitled *Human Problem Solving* by Allen Newell and Herb Simon. Their key notion was that the strategies we use when tackling complex problems reflect our limited ability to process and store information. Newell and Simon assumed we have very limited short-term memory capacity (see Chapter 21) and that complex information processing is typically serial (one process at a time). These assumptions were included in their General Problem Solver, a computer program designed to solve well-defined problems.

How do we cope with our limited processing capacity? According to Newell and Simon (1972), we rely heavily on **heuristics** or rules of thumb. Heuristics have the advantage that they don't require extensive information processing and so are very easy to use. However, they have the disadvantage that they may not lead to problem solution.

Means–ends analysis

The most important heuristic identified by Newell and Simon (1972) was **means–ends analysis:**

- Note the difference between the current state of the problem and the goal state.

- Form a sub-goal to reduce the difference between the current and goal states.
- Select a mental operator that permits attainment of the sub-goal.

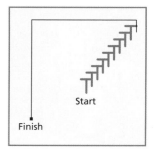

The maze used in the study by Sweller and Levine (1982).

Means–ends analysis is generally very useful. However, Sweller and Levine (1982) found that people used that heuristic even when it wasn't useful. Participants were given the maze shown in the figure on the right, but most of it wasn't visible to them. All participants could see where they were in the problem. Some could also see the goal state (goal-information group), whereas others could not (no-goal-information group).

Use of means–ends analysis requires knowledge of the location of the goal, so only the goal-information group could have used that heuristic. However, means–ends analysis wasn't useful, because every move involved turning *away* from the goal. Participants in this group performed very poorly—only 10% solved the problem in 298 moves! In contrast, participants in the no-goal-information group solved the problem in an average of only 38 moves. Thus, people are so attached to means–ends analysis they use it even when it prevents them from discovering the problem structure.

Hill climbing

One of the simplest heuristics is **hill climbing**, which involves changing the present state within the problem into one closer to the goal. It is called hill climbing because it resembles a climber whose strategy for reaching the highest mountain peak in the area is always to move upwards. It is a simpler strategy than means–ends analysis, and is mostly used when the problem solver has no clear understanding of a problem's structure.

The hill-climbing heuristic involves a focus on *short-term* goals. As a result, it often fails to lead to problem solution (Robertson, 2001). A climber using the hill-climbing heuristic may achieve his/her goal of ascending the highest mountain in the area. However, it is more likely he/she will be trapped on top of a hill separated by several valleys from the highest peak.

Planning

Newell and Simon (1972) assumed that most problem solvers engage in only a modest amount of planning because of limited short-term memory capacity. Another possible reason for limited planning is because simple heuristics are often sufficient. Evidence favouring the latter possibility was reported by Delaney et al. (2004). They used water-jar problems in which the task was to finish up with a specified amount of water in one of the jars. Some participants were told to generate the complete solution before making any moves. Others (control group) were free to adopt their preferred strategy.

The control participants showed little evidence of planning. However, those in the planning group engaged in much planning, and solved the problem in far fewer moves than did control participants. Thus, we have a greater ability to plan than is usually assumed. However, we often choose not to plan unless required to do so.

As would be expected, the amount of forward planning is strongly influenced by the level of expertise. Charness (1981) presented chess players with various chess positions and asked them to think aloud as they planned

KEY TERM

Hill climbing: a simple heuristic used by problem solvers in which they focus on making moves that will apparently put them closer to the goal or problem solution.

Expert chess players plan their moves further ahead than non-expert players.

their next move. A move in chess is defined as a turn by each player, and a ply is a half-move (i.e., one player has a turn). Expert chess players worked out the implications of possible moves about three plies further ahead in the game than did non-expert ones.

Summary

The strategies we use when solving problems take account of our limited processing and short-term memory capacities. Many of these strategies consist of heuristics or rules of thumb such as means–ends analysis and hill climbing. In spite of our limited processing capacity, most people (especially experts) can engage in a reasonable amount of planning. However, we often choose not to plan because it is effortful and cognitively demanding.

Creativity

What is **creativity**? It involves "the generation of ideas, insights, or problem solutions that are both novel and potentially useful" (Baas et al., 2008, p. 780). The distinction between ordinary problem solving and creativity resembles that between convergent thinking and divergent thinking (Guilford, 1967). **Convergent thinking** is rational thinking in which there is only one right answer. Arithmetic problems such as 4 × 8 = ? are clear examples of problems that require convergent thinking. **Divergent thinking** involves the ability to produce many useful ideas in novel situations or problems where several answers are possible.

Are originality and creativity easy or hard to measure?

Numerous tasks have been used to assess divergent thinking or creativity. For example, there is the Uses of a Brick test, on which individuals list as many uses of a brick as possible. Test performance can be assessed in various ways (e.g., Lamm & Trommsdorff, 1973):

- First, there is *fluency*—the number of different uses produced.
- Second, there is *flexibility*—the breadth and number of distinct categories produced.
- Third, there is *originality*—the uncommonness of the uses produced.

Note that the Uses of a Brick test doesn't necessarily provide a good assessment of creativity. For example, someone could obtain a high score for originality even though their responses lacked the quality and usefulness associated with creativity. There is also evidence that different tests of divergent thinking involve rather different processes (Dietrich & Kanso, 2010). This makes it hard to draw any general conclusions about divergent thinking.

Factors relevant to creativity

It seems reasonable to assume that individuals of high intelligence tend to be more creative than those of lower intelligence. There is support for that assumption. For example, Silvia (2008) considered the findings from several studies, and found that overall there was a significant (but fairly small) positive relationship between intelligence and creativity.

It seems that reasonably high intelligence is a necessary (but not a sufficient) condition for high creativity. Creative individuals need to have the good knowledge base found in those of high intelligence for their divergent thinking skills to be put to best use.

Why is the relationship between intelligence and creativity so modest? The main reason is that rather different kinds of thinking are involved. In general terms, the items on intelligence tests require convergent thinking, whereas most creativity tests focus more on divergent thinking.

It has often been claimed that people are more creative in certain mood states. This issue was addressed by Baas et al. (2008) in a review. Positive moods were associated with a slight increase in creativity, but negative moods had no effect on creativity. On tests such as the Uses of a Brick, positive moods were associated with increased fluency, flexibility, and originality, with the largest effect being on originality.

One of the most important factors of personality is openness to experience, with high scorers having more curiosity and being more imaginative than low scorers (see Chapter 18). Unsurprisingly, high openness is associated with high creativity. Indeed, Batey et al. (2010) found that openness predicted creativity better than did intelligence.

Incubation

Graham Wallas (1926) argued that there are five stages in the creative process:

1. *Preparation*: The problem is identified and initial attempts are made to solve it.
2. *Incubation*: The problem is set aside while other tasks are worked on, thus allowing unconscious problem solving activities to occur.
3. *Intimation*: The problem solver has a feeling that a solution is on the way.
4. *Illumination*: The solution emerges as a sudden insight.
5. *Verification*: The problem solver checks that the proposed solution works.

Wallas's (1926) most interesting idea was the notion that **incubation** is important. There is support for this in the lives of famous creative individuals. For example, the French mathematician Poincaré suddenly solved a complex problem in mathematics he hadn't been thinking about as he stepped onto a bus (Ghiselin, 1952).

Sio and Ormerod (2009) reviewed 117 studies on incubation, and reported three main findings:

1. An incubation effect was obtained in over 70% of the studies, although it was often fairly small.
2. There was a stronger incubation effect with creative problems having multiple solutions than with verbal problems having a single solution. Incubation often leads to a widening of the search for knowledge, and this may well be more useful with multiple-solution problems than with single-solution ones.
3. The effects were greater when there was a relatively long preparation time prior to incubation. This may have occurred because a block in thinking is more likely to develop when the preparation time is long.

KEY TERM

Incubation: the notion that complex problems can sometimes be solved by setting the problem aside for a while before returning to it.

Simon (1966) argued that incubation involves a special type of forgetting. What is forgotten over time is control information relating to the strategies tried by the problem solver. This forgetting makes it easier for problem solvers to adopt a new approach following incubation. This approach was supported by Vul and Pashler (2007). Misleading information was presented (or not presented) at the start of each problem. There was an incubation effect *only* when the break allowed misleading information to be forgotten.

It is often claimed that "sleeping on a problem" can be a very effective form of incubation. For example, the dreams of August Kekulé led to the discovery of a simple structure for benzene. Wagner et al. (2004) tested the value of sleep. Participants performed a complex mathematical task and were then retested several hours later. The mathematical problems were designed so they could be solved in a much simpler way than the one initially used by nearly all the participants. Of those who slept between training and testing, 59% found the short cut, compared to only 25% of those who did not.

In sum, there is much evidence for the existence of an incubation effect. This effect occurs because it gives time for information about inappropriate strategies to be forgotten rather than because of the presence of unconscious processes.

Scientific creativity

We can distinguish between "Little c" or everyday creativity and "Big C" or eminent creativity (Hennessey & Amabile, 2010). Our focus so far has been on Little c creativity. However, Big C creativity that has a major impact is also important. In this section, we will consider Big C creativity in the context of scientific discoveries.

Sternberg (1985) pointed out that scientific discoveries can involve various processes:

- *Selective encoding*: Identifying what is of crucial importance from all the available information. For example, Alexander Fleming noticed that bacteria close to a culture that had become mouldy were destroyed, and this led to the discovery of penicillin.
- *Selective combination*: Realising how the relevant pieces of information fit together. This was used by Charles Darwin. He had known the relevant facts about natural selection for many years before he combined them in his theory of evolution.
- *Selective comparison*: Relating information in the current problem to relevant information from another problem (problem solving by analogy). This was used by Kekulé. He dreamed of a snake curling back on itself and catching its own tail. When he awoke, he realised this was an analogy for the molecular structure of benzene.

Strong vs. weak methods

A popular view of scientific creativity is that a few "great" individuals (e.g., Newton; Einstein) are responsible for nearly all the major scientific achievements. The creative and intellectual abilities of these individuals stretch far beyond those of the mass of humanity (otherwise known as *us*). The essence of this view is, "the belief that scientific discovery is the result of genius, inspiration, and sudden insight" (Trickett & Trafton, 2007, p. 868). As we will see, this view is largely incorrect.

Klahr and Simon (2001) distinguished between two kinds of methods that might be used by creative scientists:

1. *Strong methods*: These methods are acquired through a lengthy process of acquiring huge amounts of detailed domain-specific knowledge (knowledge in a specific area) about scientific phenomena, theories, procedures, experimental paradigms, and so on. Such methods are often sufficient to solve relatively simple scientific problems. However, they are insufficient to permit creative scientific discoveries.
2. *Weak methods*: These methods are very general and can be applied to almost any scientific problem. Indeed, they are so general they are also used in most everyday problem solving. Weak methods include means–ends analysis, hill climbing, and use of analogies (all discussed earlier).

Numerous studies have considered the weak methods used by scientists. Kulkarni and Simon (1988) found scientists made extensive use of the unusualness heuristic or rule of thumb. This involves focusing on unusual or unexpected findings, which are then used to generate new hypotheses and experiments.

Zelko et al. (2010) asked leading biomedical scientists in several countries to identify their research strategies. Every researcher had a main heuristic or rule of thumb that he/she used much of the time. The heuristics included the following: challenge conventional wisdom; adopt a planned, step-by-step approach; carry out numerous experiments on an unplanned or trial-and-error basis.

Another method used by scientists is "what if" reasoning, in which they work out what would happen in certain imaginary circumstances (Trickett & Trafton, 2007). A famous example of such reasoning involves Albert Einstein. At the age of 16, he imagined himself riding a beam of light, which led to his theory of relativity.

Simonton (e.g., 2010) endorsed the notion that creative scientists use weak methods when making important discoveries. Indeed, he went further and argued that such discoveries often result from an almost random process ("blind variation"). This viewpoint received some support in the study by Zelko et al. (2010) discussed above in which scientists often admitted a random element was involved in their major discoveries.

Simonton (2010) argued that creative scientists possess a high ability to *discriminate* between valuable ideas and findings and relatively useless ones. He called this process "selective retention". Zelko et al. (2010) found his elite scientists typically realised rapidly when they had made an important discovery.

EVALUATION

➕ The processes involved in scientific discovery are less mysterious than is often assumed.

➕ Scientists entering the unknown often rely on the same weak methods most of us use in our everyday lives.

➖ The role of scientists' huge relevant knowledge in leading to major scientific discoveries has been de-emphasised.

➖ The scientific creative process is rather more systematic and less random than Simonton suggested. The ideas considered by scientists are generally pre-selected to some extent rather than being random (Runco, 2010).

Chapter summary

- Psychologists generally study well-defined problems, but most everyday problems are ill-defined.
- Solutions to insight problems often occur suddenly and relatively effortlessly. In contrast, solutions to non-insight or analytic problems emerge slowly and effortfully.
- Past experience can impair present problem solving through functional fixedness (focusing on only a few functions of objects) or mental set (rigid strategy).
- Past experience can enhance present problem solving when analogies are used. However, individuals often fail to detect the relevance of previous problems to the current one.
- The strategies we use to solve problems reflect our limited ability to process and store information.
- Means–ends analysis is a very common problem-solving strategy. It is designed to reduce the difference between the current and goal states.
- Problem solvers often engage in limited planning when less effortful heuristics are available. However, experts exhibit more planning than do non-experts.
- Creativity involves the generation of ideas that are original and of potential value.
- Creativity is greater in individuals who are intelligent, high in openness, and in a positive mood.
- Creative performance improves following incubation (setting the problem aside).
- Creative scientists make extensive use of various heuristics or rules of thumb. These include the unusualness heuristic, "what if" reasoning, challenging conventional wisdom, and the step-by-step approach.

Further reading

- Eysenck, M.W. (2012). *Fundamentals of cognition*. Hove, UK: Psychology Press. Chapter 11 of this textbook covers problem solving in more detail than has been done here.

- Hennessey, B.A., & Amabile, T.M. (2010). Creativity. *Annual Review of Psychology, 61*, 569–598. Beth Hennessey and Teresa Amabile discuss major approaches to creativity and emphasise the importance of interdisciplinary research.

- Robertson, S.I. (2001). *Problem solving*. Hove, UK: Psychology Press. This book contains comprehensive coverage of theory and research on problem solving.

- Zelko, H., Zammar, G.R., Ferreira, A.P.B., Phadtare, A., Shah, J., & Pietrobon, R. (2010). Selection mechanisms underlying high impact biomedical research – A qualitative analysis and causal model. *Public Library of Science One, 5*, e10535. This article provides insights into individual differences in the problem-solving strategies used by leading scientists.

Essay questions

1. Discuss the main differences between insight and non-insight problems.

2. How does past experience affect problem solving?

3. Discuss some of the strategies used in problem solving.

4. What are the main methods used by creative scientists?

Part 7

Effective learning

Psychologists have discovered a considerable amount about the factors promoting effective learning. This knowledge is of great potential value to students who frequently find themselves needing to learn (and remember!) lots of information about any given topic. For example, it has been found that students who devote much of their revision time to trying to recall relevant course material typically perform better than other students on examinations.

Chapter 23 • Effective studying and learning

Ways in which research on learning and motivation can be used to enhance student examination performance are considered in detail.

You will almost certainly have had to write essays and prepare for tests. You may have wondered why some people seem to find it much easier and less effortful than others to cope with these tests. An important part of the answer lies in good learning and study skills. What do you think are the key study skills required for successful academic performance? How do you think that most people could learn to improve their study skills?

Effective studying and learning

23

Students of psychology should find it easier than other students to develop good study skills and effective learning (at least in theory!). Psychological principles are of central importance to effective learning and remembering, and learning and memory are key areas within psychology (see Chapters 7 and 21). Study skills are also concerned with motivation and developing good work habits, and these fall very much within the scope of psychology.

In this chapter, I will discuss several topics in this area. First, I focus on factors determining the effectiveness of learning. My coverage is based on the levels-of-processing approach developed in the early 1970s. Second, we will consider techniques that have been devised to enhance people's ability to remember information over long periods of time.

Third, we will discuss an issue of central importance to students busy revising for a forthcoming exam. Should they devote their revision time to studying and restudying the material they need to remember or should they concentrate on trying to recall that material? Fourth, what can students do to motivate themselves?

Learning: levels of processing

What determines how well we remember information? A very influential answer was proposed by Fergus Craik and Robert Lockhart (1972). They argued in their levels-of-processing approach that what is crucial is how we *process* that information during learning. In essence, the greater the extent to which *meaning* is processed, the deeper the level of processing.

Craik and Lockhart's (1972) main theoretical assumptions were as follows:

* The level or depth of processing of a stimulus has a large effect on its memorability.
* Deeper levels of analysis produce more elaborate, longer lasting and stronger memory traces than shallow levels of analysis (e.g., processing the sound of a word).

Numerous studies support the main assumptions of the levels-of-processing approach. Craik and Tulving (1975) compared recognition performance as a function of the task performed at learning:

* *Shallow grapheme task*: Decide whether each word is in uppercase or lowercase letters.
* *Intermediate phoneme task*: Decide whether each word rhymes with a target word.
* *Deep semantic*: Decide whether each word fits a sentence containing a blank.

Depth of processing had impressive effects on memory performance—it was *three* times higher with deep than with shallow processing.

Elaboration

Craik and Tulving (1975) argued that *elaboration* of processing (i.e., the amount of processing of a given kind) is important as well as processing depth. They used the deep semantic task discussed above and varied elaboration by using simple sentence frames (e.g., "She cooked the ___" and complex ones (e.g., "The great bird swooped down and carried off the struggling ____". Cued recall was twice as high for words accompanying complex sentences, showing that memory is better following more elaborate processing.

Distinctiveness

Another important factor in determining long-term memory is distinctiveness (Hunt, 2006). **Distinctiveness** means that a memory trace differs from other memory traces because it was processed differently at the time of learning. There is much evidence that distinctive memories are generally better remembered than non-distinctive ones (see Demonstration).

Why are distinctive memories so well remembered? Much forgetting is due to interference (see Chapter 21)—our long-term memory for information can be distorted (or interfered with) by information learned beforehand or afterwards. That is especially so when the other information is very *similar* to what we are trying to remember. Distinctive memories are easy to remember because they are *dissimilar* to other memories and so less liable to interference (Eysenck, 1979).

KEY TERM

Distinctiveness: this characterises memory traces that are distinct or different from other memory traces stored in long-term memory; it leads to enhanced memory.

DEMONSTRATION: Distinctiveness and long-term memory

Below is a list of 45 words (5 in each of 9 categories):

CHAIR	CAT	TANK
PIANO	ELEPHANT	KNIFE
CLOCK	GIRAFFE	POISON
TELEPHONE	MOUSE	WHIP
CUSHION	TIGER	SCREWDRIVER
APPLE	BICYCLE	DRESS
GRAPEFRUIT	TRACTOR	MITTENS
COCONUT	TRAIN	SWEATER
PEACH	CART	SHOES
BLUEBERRY	SLED	PYJAMAS
CARROTS	MICHAEL	DONNA
LETTUCE	DANIEL	PAULA
ASPARAGUS	JOHN	BETH
ONION	RICHARD	SUSAN
POTATO	GEORGE	ANNE

Ask a friend of yours to consider the list words category by category. Their task is to write down one thing common to all 5 words within a category (Condition 1). After your friend has finished, present them with everything they have written down and ask them to recall as many list words as possible.

Ask another friend to consider the list words category by category. Within each category, they should write beside each word one thing they know about that word that isn't true of any other word in that category (Condition 2). After that, present them with what they have written down, and ask them to recall as many words as possible.

This task is based on an experiment reported by Hunt and Smith (1996). They found recall was far higher in Condition 2 than Condition 1 (97% correct vs. 59%). The reason is that the instructions in Condition 2 led to much more distinctive or unique memory traces than those in Condition 1 because each word was processed differently from the others.

Limitations

So far we have emphasised the importance of what happens during *learning*. However, memory depends very much on the *relevance* of our stored information to the requirements of the memory test. Consider a study by Morris et al. (1977). Participants answered semantic or shallow (rhyme) questions for lists of words. Memory was tested one of two ways:

1. Standard recognition test on which participants selected list words and avoided non-list words.
2. Rhyming recognition test on which participants selected words that rhymed with list words; the words themselves had *not* been presented on the list.

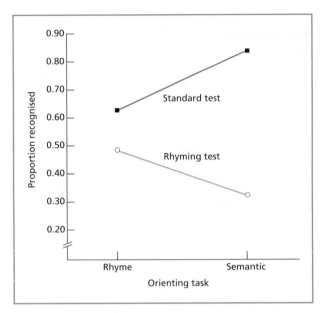

Mean proportion of words recognised as a function of orienting task (semantic or rhyme) and of the type of recognition task (standard or rhyming). Data are from Morris et al. (1977), and are from positive trials only.

For example, if the word FABLE appeared on the test and TABLE was a list word, participants should have selected it.

With the standard recognition test, there was the typical superiority of deep over shallow processing (see the figure on the left). More interestingly, the *opposite* result was reported with the rhyme test. This disproves the notion that deep processing always enhances long-term memory.

Morris et al. (1977) explained these findings in terms of **transfer-appropriate processing**. Whether what we have learned leads to good performance on a subsequent memory test depends on the *relevance* of that information (and its associated processing) to the memory test. For example, storing semantic information is irrelevant when the memory test requires the identification of words rhyming with list words. What is required for this kind of test is shallow rhyme information.

We turn now to another limitation of the levels-of-processing approach. The research discussed so far mainly involved explicit memory (conscious recollection). The effects of depth of processing are typically much less with implicit memory (memory not involving conscious recollection).

Challis et al. (1996) used various tests of explicit and implicit memory. One test of implicit memory was the word-fragment task. Participants were originally presented with a list of words. Later they completed word fragments (e.g., c _ pp _ _) with the first word coming to mind. Implicit memory was assessed by the tendency to complete these word fragments with list words.

Challis et al.'s (1996) findings were clear-cut. There was a strong effect of processing depth on performance of all the explicit memory tests (e.g., recognition memory; free recall). In contrast, there was no effect of processing depth on the word-fragment task.

KEY TERM

Transfer-appropriate processing: this is the notion that long-term memory will be greatest when the processing at the time of retrieval is very similar to the processing at the time of learning.

EVALUATION

➕ The notion that long-term memory depends heavily on the extent to which meaning is processed at learning has been very influential.

➕ The levels-of-processing approach has led to the identification of elaboration and distinctiveness of processing as important factors in learning and memory.

➖ Craik and Lockhart (1972) underestimated the importance of the relationship between what has been learned and the nature of the retrieval environment.

- The relative importance of depth, elaboration, and distinctiveness in enhancing long-term memory hasn't been established.

- Processing depth is much less important for implicit than for explicit memory. As yet, the reasons for this difference remain unclear.

Mnemonics

Every self-help book designed to improve your memory provides many examples of effective techniques (e.g., McPherson, 2004). Indeed, there are more such techniques than you can shake a stick at. Here we will focus on a few of the most important ones including an assessment of their strengths and limitations.

Visual imagery techniques

Mnemonics are techniques used to improve memory. Some of the most effective mnemonics involve visual imagery. For example, there is the **method of loci**. What happens is that the to-be-remembered items of information are associated with well-known locations (e.g., places along a walk) (see Demonstration).

The method of loci is remarkably effective. Bower (1973) compared recall of 5 lists of 20 nouns each for groups using (or not using) the method of loci.

DEMONSTRATION: Method of loci

Think of 10 locations in your home, choosing them so the sequence of moving from one to the next is obvious; for example, from front door to entrance hall to kitchen to bedroom. Check you can imagine moving through your 10 locations in a consistent order without difficulty.

Now think of 10 items and imagine them in those locations. If your first item is a *pipe*, you might imagine it poking out of the letterbox in your front door with great clouds of smoke billowing into the street. If the second item is a *cabbage*, you might imagine your hall obstructed by an enormous cabbage, and so on. When it comes to recall, walk mentally the route around your house.

Now try to create similarly striking images associating your 10 chosen locations with the words below:

shirt	eagle	paperclip	rose	camera
mushroom	crocodile	handkerchief	sausage	mayor

The same set of locations can be used repeatedly as long as only the most recent item in a given location is remembered.

Try to recall the 10 items listed two paragraphs ago. No, don't look! Rely on the images you created.

KEY TERMS

Mnemonics: these consist of numerous methods or systems that learners can use to enhance their long-term memory for information.

Method of loci: a memory technique in which the items that are to be remembered are associated with various locations that are well known to the learner.

The former group recalled 72% of the nouns against only 28% for the latter group.

The effectiveness of the method of loci depends on which locations are used. It leads to better recall when based on a route to work rather than a route in the participant's house (Massen et al., 2009). An individual's route to work is generally more constant than the ways they move around their own house, and is thus easier to use.

The method of loci is limited in that it is hard to recall any given item without working your way through the list until you come to it. Another apparent limitation occurs when the method of loci is used with several lists of items. If the same locations are used with each list, there is a danger of proactive interference (previous learning disrupting the learning and memory of subsequent lists; see Chapter 21). In fact, however, there is little or no proactive interference provided the words on successive lists are dissimilar (Massen & Vaterrodt-Plünnecke, 2006).

It is often argued that the method of loci isn't useful when people learn material in the real world. De Beni et al. (1997) addressed this issue. They presented a 2000-word text orally or in written form to students who used the method of loci or rehearsed parts of the text. Memory was tested shortly after presentation and 1 week later.

The method of loci led to much better recall than rehearsal at both retention intervals with oral presentation of the material. Thus, it was very effective when there was a lecture-style presentation. In contrast, there was *no* effect of learning method when the text was presented in written form. Similar findings were reported by De Beni and Moè (2003). The method of loci was ineffective with written presentation because the visual nature of the presentation *interfered* with the use of visual imagery associated with the method of loci.

Pegword system

The pegword system resembles the method of loci in that it relies on visual imagery and allows you to remember sequences of 10 unrelated items. First of all you memorise 10 pegwords. As each pegword rhymes with a number from one to ten, this is relatively easy. Try it for yourself:

One = *bun* Two = *shoe* Three = *tree* Four = *door* Five = *hive* Six = *sticks* Seven = *heaven* Eight = *gate* Nine = *wine* Ten = *hen*

Having mastered this, you are ready to memorise 10 unrelated words. Suppose these are as follows: battleship, pig, chair, sheep, castle, rug, grass, beach, milkmaid, binoculars. Take the first pegword (bun) and form an image of a bun interacting with battleship (e.g., a battleship sailing into an enormous floating bun). Now take the second pegword (shoe) and imagine it interacting with pig (e.g., a large shoe with a pig sitting in it). Work through the rest of the items forming a suitable interactive image in each case.

The pegword technique is very effective. Morris and Reid (1970) found it *doubled* the number of words recalled. Other research indicates it is as effective as the method of loci (Wang & Thomas, 2000). However, the technique has some limitations:

1. It requires extensive training.
2. It is easier to use with concrete than with abstract material. For example, it isn't easy to form interactive images involving abstract concepts (e.g., *morality*; *insincerity*).
3. There are doubts about its applicability to real life, since we rarely need to remember a sequence of several unrelated items.

Remembering names

Most people have problems remembering names. When being introduced to someone new, we tend to look at them and make whatever initial remarks are appropriate. As a result, their name "goes in one ear and out the other". As you have probably discovered, it can be socially embarrassing to admit you have completely forgotten someone's name.

The pegword method is a very effective way of memorising a list of items, for example a shopping list but not so good for memorising abstract concepts.

One way of remembering people's names is based on a visual imagery mnemonic. You start by searching for an imageable substitute for the person's name (e.g., Eysenck becomes "ice sink"). Then some prominent feature of the person's face is selected, and the image is linked with that feature. For example, the nose might be regarded as a tap over the sink. Brief training in this method improved recall of names to faces by almost 80% under laboratory conditions (Morris et al., 1978). This finding is consistent with much evidence that long-term memory is better for information previously processed in a distinctive fashion (Eysenck, 1979).

The imagery mnemonic for learning names works well in the peace and quiet of the laboratory. In real-life social situations, however, it may be hard to form good imagery mnemonics. Morris et al. (2005) invited university students to attend a party having received instructions about learning the other students' names. One group was trained to use the imagery mnemonic. A second group tried to retrieve the name at increasing intervals after first hearing them (expanded retrieval practice). There was also a control group simply told to learn people's names.

Between 24 and 72 hours after the party, the students were shown photographs of the students who had been at the party and wrote their names underneath. Students in the expanded retrieval practice condition recalled 50% more names than those in the control group. The imagery mnemonic was even less effective than no specific memorising strategy. Thus, it is important to combine use of the visual imagery mnemonic with repeated attempts to recall the name.

The imagery mnemonic for learning names works well in the laboratory but how well do you think it works in real-life social situations?

Verbal techniques

There are several verbal mnemonics (see Baddeley et al., 2009). One of the most effective is the story method. It is used to remember a series of unrelated words in the correct order by linking them together within the context of a story. Note that the story method often involves the use of visual imagery as well as producing sentences. Suppose we apply the story method to the 10 words used to illustrate use of the pegword technique:

> In the kitchen of the *battleship*, there was a *pig* that sat in a *chair*. There was also a *sheep* that had previously lived in a *castle*. In port, the sailors took a *rug* and sat on the *grass* close to the *beach*. While there, they saw a *milkmaid* watching them through her *binoculars*.

The story method is very effective. Bower and Clark (1969) gave participants the task of recalling 12 lists of 10 words each in the correct order when given the first words of each list as cues. Those who had formed narrative stories recalled 93% of the words compared to only 13% for those who didn't do so. Thus, there was a massive *sevenfold* advantage for the story method.

The story method is limited in that it requires fairly extensive training—it took me a few minutes to form the story given above! Another limitation is that you generally have to work your way through the list if you want to find a given item (e.g., the seventh one).

Why do mnemonic techniques work?

The success of mnemonic techniques owes much to the fact that they allow us to use our knowledge (e.g., about familiar walks). However, detailed knowledge isn't always enough. Suppose we asked taxi drivers and students to recall lists of streets in the city in which they lived. You might imagine that the taxi drivers (with their superb knowledge of the spatial layout of the city's streets) would always outperform the students. As we are about to see, that is *not* the case.

Kalakoski and Saariluoma (2001) asked Helsinki taxi drivers and students to recall lists of 15 Helsinki street names in the order presented. The taxi drivers did much better than the students when the streets formed a continuous route through the city. However, their advantage disappeared when non-adjacent street names taken from all over Helsinki were presented in a random order.

What can we conclude from the study by Kalakoski and Saariluoma (2001)? In essence, the findings show the importance of *organisation*—the taxi drivers couldn't use their special knowledge effectively to organise the to-be-remembered information when the street names were random.

Why are techniques such as the method of loci, the pegword method, and the story method so effective? According to Ericsson (1988), there are three requirements to achieve very high memory skills:

1. *Meaningful encoding*: The information should be processed meaningfully, relating it to pre-existing knowledge. This is clearly the case when you use known locations (method of loci) or the number sequence (pegword method), or when taxi drivers use their knowledge of their own town or city. This is the encoding principle.
2. *Retrieval structure*: Cues should be stored with the information to aid subsequent retrieval. A connected series of locations or the number

sequence provides an immediately accessible retrieval structure, as does the knowledge of spatial layout possessed by taxi drivers. This is the retrieval structure principle.

3. *Speed-up*: Extensive practice allows the processes involved in encoding and retrieval to function faster and faster. The importance of extensive practice can be seen in the generally superior memory for street names shown by taxi drivers compared to students in Kalakoski and Saariluoma's (2001) study. This is the speed-up principle.

Extensive practice, such as that used by taxi drivers to learn street names, is important in achieving high memory skills.

We can see the above principles at work in a study by Ericsson and Chase (1982) on SF. He was paid to practise the digit-span task for 1 hour a day for 2 years. The digit span (the number of random digits that can be repeated back immediately in the correct order) is typically about 6 or 7 items. SF eventually attained a span of 80 items!

How did SF do it? He reached a digit span of 18 items by using his extensive knowledge of running times (encoding and retrieval principles). For example, if the first few digits were "3594" he would note this was Bannister's time for the first sub-four-minute mile, and so he would store these digits away as a single chunk or unit. He then increased his digit span to 80 items by organising those chunks into a hierarchical structure and by extensive practice (the speed-up principle). Sadly, his outstanding digit span didn't generalise to other memory tasks—SF had only average letter and word spans.

Learning by remembering

Answer this question taken from research by Karpicke et al. (2009):

> Imagine you are reading a textbook for an upcoming exam. After you have read the chapter one time, would you rather:
> A: Go back and restudy either the entire chapter or certain parts of the chapter.
> B: Try to recall material from the chapter (without the possibility of restudying the material)
> C: Use some other study technique.

Karpicke et al. (2009) found that 57% of their students gave answer A, 21% gave answer C, and only 18% gave answer B. What is interesting about this pattern of responses is that the least frequent answer (B) is actually the correct one in terms of its effectiveness in promoting good long-term memory!

Findings

There is convincing evidence that long-term retention for material is better when memory is tested during the time of learning. This is the **testing effect**. Bangert-Drowns et al. (1991) reviewed the findings from 35 classroom studies. A significant testing effect was found in 83% of these studies, and the magnitude of the effect increased as the number of testing occasions went up.

KEY TERM

Testing effect: the finding that long-term memory is enhanced when some of the learning period is devoted to retrieving the to-be-remembered information.

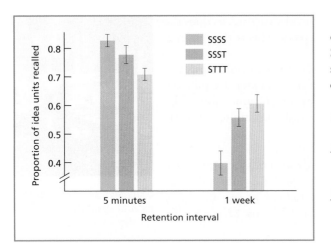

Memory performance as a function of learning conditions (S, study; T, test) and retention interval (5 min vs. 1 week).

Roediger and Karpicke (2006) carried out a thorough study on the testing effect. Students read a prose passage covering a general scientific topic and memorised it in one of three conditions:

1. *Repeated study*: The passage was read four times and there was no test.
2. *Single test*: The passage was read three times and then students recalled as much as possible from it.
3. *Repeated test*: The passage was read once and then students recalled as much as possible on three occasions.

Finally, memory for the passage was tested after 5 minutes or 1 week.

The findings are shown in the figure above. Repeated study was the most effective strategy when the final test was given 5 minutes after learning. However, there was a dramatic reversal in the findings when the final test occurred after 1 week. There was a very strong testing effect—average recall was 50% higher in the repeated test condition than the repeated study condition! That could easily make the difference between doing very well on an examination and failing it.

Students in the repeated study condition predicted they would recall more of the prose passage than did those in the repeated test condition. This helps to explain why many students mistakenly devote little or no time to testing themselves when preparing themselves for an examination.

Explanations

How can we explain the above findings? Many people feel reassured if they find it easy to retrieve material they have been learning. However, only *effortful* or demanding retrieval improves long-term memory (Bjork & Bjork, 1992). One reason is because it provides *practice* in the effortful retrieval generally required during examinations.

Evidence that effortful retrieval is useful was reported by Metcalfe and Kornell (2007) in a study on the learning of foreign vocabulary (e.g., house–maison). During learning, the French word was presented at the same time as the English word or there was a short delay. Subsequent long-term memory was much better when there was a short delay, because it allowed the participants to engage in effortful retrieval.

Motivation

Motivation is often a problem for students who have to learn and remember large amounts of information for an examination. There are many theories of motivation. However, some of the most useful ones focus on cognitive processes. Examples include goal-setting theory and the theory of implementation intentions, both of which are discussed below.

Goal-setting theory

Useful ideas about how to motivate yourself are contained in goal-setting theory. This theory was originally put forward by Edwin Locke (1968) and later developed by Latham and Locke (2007).

The key assumption of goal-setting theory is that *conscious goals* have a major impact on people's motivation and behaviour. More specifically, the harder the goals we set ourselves, the better our performance is likely to be. Wood et al. (1987) reviewed 192 studies testing that hypothesis and found support in 175 of them.

Why do hard goals lead to better performance than easy ones? According to goal-setting theory, the reason is that individuals are more motivated and try harder when difficult goals are set.

Motivation doesn't consist only in setting difficult goals. It is also important that the goals you set yourself should be specific and clear—make sure to avoid very vague goals such as simply "doing well". Latham (2003, p. 309) summarised some of the key points of goal-setting theory: the goal should be "specific, measurable, attainable, relevant, and have a time-frame (SMART)".

There is little point in setting yourself the goal of obtaining an excellent examination result if you don't *commit* yourself fully to the achievement of that goal. According to goal-setting theory, high performance occurs only when goal difficulty and goal commitment are both high. Goal commitment is especially important when goals are difficult because such goals require high levels of effort and are associated with smaller chances of success than easy goals.

Findings

Latham and Brown (2006) studied the academic performance of students doing an MBA (Master's in Business Administration). Some of the students set themselves vague general goals (e.g., performing well at the end of the programme). In contrast, other students set themselves hard, specific goals (e.g., learning to network; master key course subject matter). Those who set themselves hard, specific goals performed better and had greater satisfaction with their course than did those setting themselves general goals.

Set a realistic goal.   Commit to achieving the goal.   Enjoy your achievement!

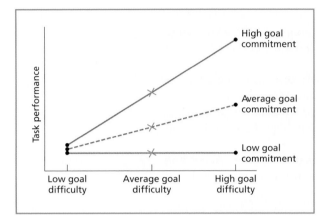

The effects of goal difficulty and goal commitment on task performance according to Locke's goal-setting theory.

Klein et al. (1999) reviewed numerous studies on the effects of goal setting and goal commitment on task performance. The pattern of the findings was as predicted from goal-setting theory (see the figure on the left). Higher levels of goal commitment were associated with higher levels of performance, especially when goal difficulty was high.

Various factors influenced the level of goal commitment. Two of the key ones were attractiveness of goal attainment and expectancy of goal attainment provided the individual applied reasonable effort. Other factors producing high goal commitment were having high ability, being personally involved in goal setting, and receiving performance feedback.

Most research on goal-setting theory has involved situations in which a single, specific task is performed over a short period of time in the absence of distractions. Such situations are very different from those found in many companies in which employees are set performance targets over a period of several months and are exposed to numerous distractions (e.g., knocks on the door; phone calls).

Do the above differences matter? They probably do. Yearta et al. (1995) studied scientists and professional staff working at the research centre of a large multi-national company. Within that organisation, work performance was *negatively* related to goal difficulty—this is diametrically opposite to the prediction from goal-setting theory.

EVALUATION

➕ Performance is generally best when individuals set themselves hard goals accompanied by high goal commitment.

➕ The most effective goals are specific, measurable, attainable, relevant, and with a time-frame.

➖ Most laboratory studies are artificial in that participants perform a single task for a relatively short period of time.

➖ Goal setting can have unpredictable effects on performance when complex tasks are performed over long periods of time in the presence of distraction.

Implementation intentions

Yearta et al.'s (1995) research suggests that the issue of how people move from goal setting to goal attainment in a world of complications and distractions is de-emphasised within goal-setting theory. Gollwitzer has focused on precisely this issue. His key concept is that of **implementation intentions**, which "specify the when, where, and how of responses leading to goal attainment" (Gollwitzer, 1999, p. 494).

We can see the importance of implementation intentions by considering a student called Natalie who has set herself the goal of spending 4 hours every Saturday revising for an exam. However, Natalie normally chats for several hours a day with her friends and also likes to watch television.

How can Natalie ensure her revision gets done? According to Gollwitzer's (1999) theory, this is where implementation intentions come in. Here are two possible ones: "When one of my friends knocks on the door, I will tell her that I'll see her at McDonald's at 8 o'clock"; "If I discover there's something interesting on television, I'll record it so I can watch it later".

Evidence supporting the importance of implementation intentions was reported by Gollwitzer and Brandstätter (1997). Participants were given the goal of writing a report on how they spent Christmas Eve within the following two days. Half of them formed implementation intentions by indicating *when* and *where* they intended to write the report. The goal of writing the report very shortly after Christmas was achieved by 75% of those who formed implementation intentions but by only 33% of those who didn't.

There is much additional evidence that implementation intentions have beneficial effects on behaviour. For example, people can be persuaded to adopt a healthier diet by making use of implementation intentions (Adriaanse, Gollwitzer et al., 2011; see Chapter 1).

Why are implementation intentions so effective? According to Gollwitzer (1999), forming an implementation intention is like creating an "instant habit". Our habits are reliably triggered by relevant cues providing information about *when* and/or *where* certain actions occur. In a similar way, implementation intentions specify when and where we are going to initiate behaviour to attain our goal.

Much evidence is consistent with this view. Our ordinary everyday intentions typically have only a small effect on behaviour in situations in which individuals have alternative habitual ways of responding (Webb & Sheeran, 2006). This occurs in part because habitual responses are accessed more rapidly than intended responses and so have a strong influence on behaviour. However, the situation is very different with implementation intentions, which are as readily accessible as habitual ones (Adriaanse, Gollwitzer et al., 2011). As a result, they can compete successfully with habitual responses.

Chapter summary

- Long-term memory depends on the depth of processing at the time of learning. It also depends on elaboration of processing and distinctiveness.
- Long-term memory also depends on the relevance of stored information to the requirements of the memory test.
- The method of loci is effective with lists of words and also with lecture-style presentations. However, it is ineffective with written texts because visual material interferes with visual imagery.

- The pegword technique is a useful way of learning lists of unrelated words. However, there are doubts about its applicability to real life.
- One of the best ways of remembering a stranger's name is to use an imagery mnemonic combined with repeated attempts to recall the name.
- The story method is a very effective way of learning a list of unrelated words.
- Successful mnemonic techniques involve meaningful encoding, an effective retrieval structure, and extensive practice.
- Long-term memory is generally much better when revision time is mostly devoted to recalling the material rather than to further study. This is known as the testing effect.
- According to goal-setting theory, the harder the goals we set ourselves, the higher the level of performance. This is especially the case when goal commitment is high.
- Implementation intentions (which have been described as instant habits) increase the probability of carrying out the actions required to attain a goal.

Further reading

- Baddeley, A., Eysenck, M.W., & Anderson, M. C. (2009). *Memory*. Hove, UK: Psychology Press. Chapter 16 in this introductory textbook contains full coverage of the main techniques that can be used to improve your memory.

- Gollwitzer, P.M., & Sheeran, P. (2006). Implementation intentions and goal achievement: A meta-analysis of effects and processes. *Advances in Experimental Social Psychology, 38*, 69–119. This chapter by Peter Gollwitzer and Paschal Sheeran provides a thorough discussion of theory and research on implementation intentions.

- Hunt, R.R., & Worthen, J.B. (2010). *Mnemonology: Mnemonics for the 21st century*. New York: Psychology Press. Reed Hunt and James Worthen identify the underlying cognitive processes responsible for numerous successful mnemonic techniques.

- Morris, P.E., & Fritz, C.O. (2006). How to … improve your memory. *The Psychologist, 19*, 608–611. Peter Morris and Catherine Fritz discuss several ways of improving your memory based on solid experimental evidence.

Essay questions

1. What is the levels-of-processing approach to memory? What are its strengths and weaknesses?

2. Describe some of the main mnemonic techniques. How effective are they likely to be in real-life situations?

3. How should students allocate their time when revising for an examination?

4. What are the main assumptions of goal-setting theory? To what extent have these assumptions been supported by research?

Glossary

accommodation: (1) in Piaget's theory, changes in an individual's cognitive organisation that are designed to deal more effectively with the environment; (2) a cue to depth involving a thickening of the eye's lens when focusing on close objects.

adjustment phase: this is the second period after divorce; it follows the **crisis phase** and is marked by less emotional distress than that phase.

adrenaline: this hormone produces increased arousal within the **sympathetic nervous system**.

adrenocorticotrophic hormone (ACTH): a hormone that leads to the release of the stress hormone cortisol.

affective blindsight: the ability found in some brain-damaged patients to identify emotional stimuli that aren't perceived consciously.

aggression: forms of behaviour that are deliberately intended to harm or injure someone else.

altruism: a form of **pro-social behaviour** that is generally costly to the altruistic person, and which is motivated by the desire to help someone else.

Ames room: a special room with a very unusual shape, which looks like an ordinary room under some viewing conditions.

amnesia: a condition produced by brain damage in which patients have normal short-term but poor long-term memory.

amygydala: a small, almond-shaped part of the brain buried deep within the temporal lobe; it is associated with several emotional states (e.g., fear).

androgyny: used to describe an individual who possesses a mixture or combination of masculine and feminine characteristics.

assimilation: in Piaget's theory, dealing with new environmental situations by using existing cognitive organisation.

attributions: our inferences concerning the causes of patterns of behaviour in other people.

authoritarian personality: a type of personality consisting of intolerance of ambiguity, hostility towards other groups, rigid beliefs, and submissiveness towards authority figures.

autism: a severe disorder involving very poor communication skills, deficient social and language development, and repetitive behaviour.

autobiographical memory: memory across the lifespan for specific events involving the individual (especially those of personal significance).

autonomic nervous system: the part of the **peripheral nervous system** that controls the involuntary movement of non-skeletal muscles; it is divided into the **sympathetic nervous system** and the **parasympathetic nervous system**.

avoidance learning: a form of operant conditioning in which an appropriate avoidance response prevents presentation of an unpleasant or aversive stimulus.

avoidant attachment: an insecure attachment of an infant to its mother, combined with an avoidance of contact with her when she returns after an absence.

behaviourism: an approach to psychology started in the United States by John Watson, according to which psychologists should focus on observable stimuli and responses and learning can be accounted for in terms of conditioning principles.

binocular cues: cues to depth that involve the use of both eyes.

blocking effect: the lack of a **conditioned response** to a **conditioned stimulus** if another **conditioned stimulus** already predicts the onset of the **unconditioned stimulus**.

bystander intervention: an area of research focusing on the reasons why bystanders to a crime or incident decide whether to help the victim.

case study: the intensive study of one or two individuals.

categorical clustering: the tendency in free recall to produce words on a category-by-category basis.

catharsis: the notion that behaving aggressively can cause a release of negative emotions such as anger and frustration and thus reduce subsequent aggression.

central coherence: the ability to interpret information taking account of the context; being able to "see the big picture".

central nervous system: the brain and spinal cord; it is protected by bone and cerebrospinal fluid.

central executive: the most important component of working memory; it is involved in planning and the control of attention and has limited capacity.

centration: in Piaget's theory, the tendency of young children to attend to only part of the information available in a given situation.

cerebral cortex: the outer layer of the **cerebrum**; it is involved in perception, thinking, and language.

cerebrum: a part of the forebrain crucially involved in thinking and language.

change blindness: the failure to detect that a visual stimulus has moved, changed, or been replaced by another stimulus; see **inattentional blindness**.

change blindness blindness: the tendency of individuals to exaggerate greatly their ability to detect visual changes and so avoid **change blindness**.

child-directed speech: the short, simple, slowly-spoken sentences used by mothers, fathers, or caregivers when talking to their young children; designed to be easy for children to understand.

chunks: familiar units of information.

classical conditioning: a basic form of learning in which simple responses (e.g., salivation) are associated with a new or **conditioned stimulus**.

coercive cycle: a pattern of behaviour within families in which aggression by one family member produces an aggressive response that leads to an escalation in aggression.

cognitive appraisal: the individual's interpretation of the current situation; it helps to determine the nature and intensity of his/her emotional experience. It also helps the individual to decide whether he/she has the resources to cope with the situation.

collectivistic cultures: **cultures** (such as many in the Far East) in which the emphasis is on group solidarity rather than on individual responsibility.

compliance: the influence of a majority on a minority based

on its power; this influence is generally on public behaviour rather than private beliefs.

conditioned reflex: the new association between a **conditioned stimulus** and an **unconditioned stimulus** that produces a **conditioned response**.

conditioned response: the new response that is produced as a result of **classical conditioning**.

conditioned stimulus: a neutral stimulus that is paired with an **unconditioned stimulus** to produce **classical conditioning**.

confirmation bias: (1) distortions of memory caused by the influence of expectations concerning what is likely to have happened; (2) in hypothesis testing, a tendency to emphasise evidence that seems to confirm one's hypothesis and to ignore or reject evidence inconsistent with the hypothesis.

conformity: changes in attitudes or behaviour that occur in response to group pressure.

confounding variables: variables not of interest to the experimenter that are mistakenly manipulated along with the **independent variable**.

congenital adrenal hyperplasia: an inherited disorder of the adrenal gland causing the levels of male sex hormones in foetuses of both sexes to be unusually high.

conservation: in Piaget's theorising, the child's understanding that various aspects of an object may remain constant even though other aspects are transformed or changed considerably.

conventional morality: the second level of moral development in Kohlberg's theory; at this level, moral reasoning focuses on having the approval of others.

convergence: a cue to depth provided by the eyes turning inwards more when looking at a close object than at one further away.

convergent thinking: logical thinking in which there is only one correct answer.

conversion: the influence of a minority on a majority based on convincing the majority that its views are correct; this influence is on private beliefs more than public behaviour.

correlation: an association between two dependent variables or responses produced by participants.

cortisol: this is often called the "stress hormone" because elevated amounts are typically found in the bodies of highly stressed individuals.

counterbalancing: this is used with the repeated measures design; each condition is equally likely to be used first or second with the participants.

creativity: the ability to produce original, useful, and ingenious solutions to problems.

crisis phase: this is the first period following divorce; during this phase, the mother is less affectionate than usual.

critical period: according to the **maternal deprivation hypothesis**, a period early in life during which infants must form a strong attachment if their later development is to be satisfactory.

cross-cultural psychology: the systematic study of similarities in and differences between cultures around the world.

cross-race effect: the finding that recognition memory for same-race faces is more accurate than for other-race faces.

cross-sectional method: this method uses different groups (e.g., of different ages) which are all studied at the same time.

cued recall: a form of memory test in which cues or clues are given to assist remembering; the first few letters of words can be used as cues.

cultural mindset: the beliefs and values that are active at any given time; individuals who have extensive experience of two cultures have two cultural mindsets, with the one that influences thinking and behaviour being determined by the immediate social context.

culture: the values, beliefs, and practices shared by members of a given society.

decentration: in Piaget's theorising, the ability to focus on several aspects of a problem at once and make coherent sense of them.

declarative memory: a long-term memory system concerned with personal experiences and general knowledge; it usually involves conscious recollection of information.

deindividuation: loss of a sense of personal identity; it can happen in a large group or crowd.

demand characteristics: cues that are used by participants to try to guess the nature of the study or to work out what the experiment is about.

dependent variable: some aspect of the participants' behaviour that is measured in an experiment.

deprivation: the state of a child who has formed a close attachment to someone (e.g., its mother) but is later separated from that person; see **privation**.

diffusion of responsibility: the larger the number of bystanders who observe what happens to a victim, the less the sense of personal responsibility to help experienced by each one.

direct tuition: one way of increasing a child's **gender identity** and **sex-typed behaviour** by being instructed by other people.

discrimination: negative actions or behaviour directed towards the members of some other group.

dispositional attribution: deciding that someone's behaviour is due

to their personality rather than to the situation.

distinctiveness: this characterises memory traces that are distinct or different from other memory traces stored in long-term memory; it leads to enhanced memory.

divergent thinking: thinking involving the ability to think of many useful ideas in novel situations or problems where several answers are possible.

dizygotic twins: twins derived from the fertilisation of two ova or eggs by two spermatozoa at approximately the same time; they share 50% of their genes and are also known as fraternal twins.

ecological validity: the extent to which research findings are applicable to everyday settings and generalise to other locations, times, and measures.

egocentrism: an assumption made by young children that the ways other people see or think are the same as theirs; it is similar to being self-centred.

emotion-focused coping: a general strategy for dealing with stressful situations in which the individual concerned attempts to reduce his/her negative emotional state.

emotion regulation: the management and control of emotional states by various processes (e.g., cognitive reappraisal; distraction).

emotional intelligence: an individual's level of sensitivity to one's own emotional needs and those of others; more related to personality than to intelligence.

empathy: the capacity to enter into another person's feelings and more generally to understand that person's perspective.

enactive experience: this involves the child learning which behaviours are expected of his/

her gender within any given culture as a result of being rewarded or punished for behaving in different ways.

episodic buffer: a component of working memory that is used to integrate and to store briefly information from the **phonological loop**, the **visuo-spatial sketchpad**, and long-term memory.

episodic memory: long-term memory for personal events.

equilibration: in Piaget's theory, responding to cognitive conflicts by using the processes of **accommodation** and **assimilation** to return to a state of equilibrium.

equipotentiality: the notion that any response can be conditioned in any stimulus situation.

evolutionary psychology: an approach to psychology based on the assumption that much human behaviour can be understood on the basis of Darwin's theory of evolution.

executive processes: processes that are involved in coordinating an individual's cognitive functioning when performing tasks.

expansions: utterances of adults that consist of fuller and more accurate versions of what a child has just said.

experimental hypothesis: prediction as to what will happen in a given experiment; it typically involves predicting the effects of a given **independent variable** on a **dependent variable** and is often theory-based.

experimental method: a method involving a generally high level of control over the experimental situation (especially the **independent variable**).

experimenter effect: unintended influences of the experimenter's behaviour on the behaviour of the participants in an experiment.

exposure therapy: a form of treatment in which clients are repeatedly exposed to stimuli or situations they fear greatly.

extinction: the elimination of a response when it is not followed by reward (**operant conditioning**) or by the **unconditioned stimulus** (classical conditioning).

extraversion: a personality **trait** reflecting individual differences in sociability and impulsiveness.

eyewitness testimony: the evidence relating to a crime that is provided by someone who observed the crime being committed.

factor analysis: a statistical technique used to find out the number and nature of the aspects of intelligence (or personality) measured by a test.

false consensus effect: the mistaken belief that most other people are similar to us in their opinions, behaviour, and personality.

false uniqueness bias: the mistaken belief that one is better than most other people.

field experiments: experiments carried out in real-world situations using the **experimental method.**

figure–ground organisation: the perception of a scene as consisting of an object or figure standing out from a less distinct background.

fixation: the long-term attachment of basic energy to a stage of psychosexual development at which problems were experienced.

Flynn effect: the progressive increase in **intelligence quotient** (**IQ**) in numerous countries over the past 40 or 50 years.

free recall: a form of memory test in which words from a list are to be produced in any order.

functional fixedness: a form of negative effect in which it is assumed that objects can only be used for purposes or functions for which they have been used in the past.

fundamental attribution error: the tendency to think that the behaviour of other people is due more to their personality and less to the situation than is actually the case.

fundamental lexical hypothesis: the assumption that dictionaries contain words that refer to all of the most important personality **traits.**

gender identity: our awareness of being male or female; it depends to an important extent on social rather than biological factors.

gender schemas: organised knowledge stored in long-term memory in the form of numerous beliefs about the forms of behaviour that are appropriate for each sex.

gender similarities hypothesis: the notion that there are only small differences between males and females with respect to the great majority of psychological variables (e.g., abilities; personality).

geons: basic shapes or components that are combined in object recognition; an abbreviation for "geometric ions" proposed by Biederman.

grammatical morphemes: prepositions, prefixes, suffixes, and so on that help to indicate the grammatical structure of sentences.

group: in Piaget's theorising, the structure that is formed from the organisation of various related cognitive processes or operations.

group polarisation: the tendency of groups to produce fairly extreme decisions.

groupthink: group pressure to achieve general agreement in groups in which dissent is suppressed; it can lead to disastrous decisions.

hemispheric specialisation: each hemisphere or half of the brain carries out its own specific functions to some extent; however, the two hemispheres coordinate their activities most of the time.

heuristics: rules of thumb used to solve problems.

hill climbing: a simple heuristic used by problem solvers in which they focus on making moves that will apparently put them closer to the goal or problem solution.

hindbrain: the "reptilian brain", concerned with breathing, digestion, swallowing, the fine control of balance, and the control of consciousness.

hindsight bias: the tendency to be wise after the event using the benefit of hindsight.

hypothalamus: a part of the forebrain that is involved in controlling body temperature, hunger, thirst, and sexual behaviour.

hypotheses: predictions concerning the effects of some factor(s) on behaviour based on a theory.

immune system: a system of cells in the body that is involved in fighting disease.

implacable experimenter: the typical laboratory situation in which the experimenter's behaviour is uninfluenced by the participant's behaviour.

implementation intentions: action plans designed to achieve some goal (e.g., healthier eating) based on specific information concerning where, when, and how the goal will be achieved.

implicit personality theory: the tendency to believe (sometimes mistakenly) that someone who has a given personality trait will also have other, related traits.

inattentional blindness: the failure to perceive the appearance of an unexpected object in the visual environment; see **change blindness.**

incubation: the notion that complex problems can sometimes be solved by setting the problem aside for a while before returning to it.

independent design: an experimental design in which each participant is included in only one group.

independent self: a type of **self-concept** in which the self is defined with respect to personal responsibility and achievement.

independent variable: some aspect of the experimental situation that the experimenter manipulates in order to test a given **experimental hypothesis**.

individualistic cultures: cultures (mainly in Western societies) in which the emphasis is on personal responsibility rather than on group needs; see **collectivistic cultures**.

informational influence: one of the factors leading individuals to conform; it is based on the perceived superior knowledge or judgement of others.

ingroup bias: the tendency to view one's own group more favourably than other groups.

insight: a sudden understanding or "a-ha" experience, in which an entire problem is looked at in a different way.

intelligence quotient (IQ): a measure of general intelligence; the average IQ is 100 and most people have IQs lying between 85 and 115.

interdependent self: a type of **self-concept** in which the self is defined with respect to one's relationships with others.

inter-observer reliability: the degree of agreement between two observers rating the behaviour of participants.

interposition: a cue to depth in which a closer object hides part of an object that is further away.

interpretive bias: negative biased or distorted interpretations of ambiguous stimuli and/or situations.

law of Prägnanz: the notion that perception will tend to be organised in as simple a way as possible.

law of reinforcement: the probability of a response being produced is increased if it is followed by reward but is decreased if it is followed by punishment.

life events: these are major events (mostly having negative consequences) that create high levels of stress, often over a long period of time.

limbic system: a brain system consisting of the amygdala, the hippocampus, and septal areas, all of which are involved in emotional processing.

linear perspective: a strong impression of depth in a two-dimensional drawing created by lines converging on the horizon.

linguistic universals: features (e.g., preferred word orders; the distinction between nouns and verbs) that are found in the great majority of the world's languages.

longitudinal method: this is a method in which one group of participants is studied repeatedly over a relatively long period of time.

matched participants design: an experimental design in which the participants in each of two groups are matched in terms of some relevant factor or factors (e.g., intelligence; sex).

maternal deprivation hypothesis: the notion that a breaking of the bond between child and mother during the first few years typically has serious long-term effects.

means–ends relationship: the knowledge that behaving in a given way in a given situation will produce a certain outcome.

means–ends analysis: an approach to problem solving based on reducing the differences between the current state of a problem and the solution.

memory span: an assessment of how much can be stored in short-term memory based on the individual's ability to repeat back digits or other items in the correct order immediately after they have been presented.

mental rotation: a task used to assess spatial ability which involves imagining what would happen if the orientation of an object in space were altered.

mental set: a fixed or blinkered approach to problems that prevents people from thinking in a flexible way.

method of loci: a memory technique in which the items that are to be remembered are associated with various locations that are well known to the learner.

microgenetic method: an approach to studying children's changes in cognitive strategies by means of short-term longitudinal studies.

midbrain: the middle part of the brain; it is involved in vision, hearing, and the control of movement.

mnemonics: these consist of numerous methods or systems that learners can use to enhance their long-term memory for information.

monocular cues: cues to depth that only require the use of one eye.

monotropy hypothesis: Bowlby's notion that infants have an innate tendency to form special bonds with one person (generally the mother).

monozygotic twins: twins that are formed from the same fertilised ovum or egg that splits and leads to the development of two individuals sharing 100% of their genes; also known as identical twins.

moods: states resembling emotions, but generally longer lasting, less intense, and of unknown cause.

morality of care: this is a form of morality in which the individual emphasises the importance of compassion and human well-being when deciding what is morally acceptable.

morality of justice: this is a form of morality in which the individual emphasises the importance of laws and of moral principles when deciding what is morally acceptable.

motion parallax: a cue to depth provided by the movement of an object's image across the retina.

negative punishment: a form of operant conditioning in which the probability of a response being produced is reduced by following it with the removal of a positive reinforcer or reward.

negative reinforcers: unpleasant or aversive stimuli that serve to strengthen any responses that prevent these stimuli from being presented.

neuroticism: a personality **trait** reflecting individual differences in negative emotional experiences (e.g., anxiety; sadness).

non-declarative memory: this is memory that does not involve conscious recollection of information; see **declarative memory.**

noradrenaline: a hormone that produces increased arousal within the **sympathetic nervous system.**

normative influence: one of the factors leading individuals to conform; it is based on people's desire to be liked and/or respected by others.

norms: standards or rules of behaviour that operate within a group or within society generally.

null hypothesis: prediction that the independent variable will have no effect on the dependent variable.

object permanence: the belief that objects continue to exist even when they can't be seen.

observational learning: learning based on watching the behaviour of others and copying behaviour that is rewarded and not copying punished behaviour.

oculomotor cues: cues to depth based on sensations produced by muscular contraction of the muscles around the eye.

operant conditioning: a form of learning in which an individual's responses are controlled by their consequences (reward or punishment).

opportunity sampling: selecting a sample of participants simply because they happen to be available.

outgroup: a group to which the individual does not belong; such groups are often regarded negatively and with prejudice.

over-regularisation: this is a language error in which a grammatical rule is applied to situations in which it isn't relevant.

parasympathetic nervous system: the part of the **autonomic nervous system** that is involved in reducing arousal and conserving energy (e.g., by reducing heart rate).

peers: children of approximately the same age as a given child.

perception: making sense of the information presented to the sense organs.

peripheral nervous system: it consists of all the nerve cells in the body not located within the **central nervous system;** it is divided into the **somatic nervous system** and the **autonomic nervous system.**

phobias: extreme fears of certain objects (e.g., snakes) or places (e.g., social situations) that cause avoidance of those objects or places.

phonological loop: a component of working memory in which speech-based information is processed and stored and subvocal articulation occurs.

phonology: the system of sounds within any given language.

population: a large collection of individuals from whom the **sample** used in a study is drawn.

positive punishment: a form of operant conditioning in which the probability of a response is reduced by following it with an unpleasant or aversive stimulus; sometimes known simply as punishment.

post-conventional morality: the third level of moral development in Kohlberg's theory; at this level, moral reasoning focuses on justice and the need for others to be treated in a respectful way.

pragmatics: the rules involved in deciding how to make sure that what is said fits the situation.

pre-conventional morality: the first level of moral development in Kohlberg's theory; at this level, moral reasoning focuses on rewards and punishments for good and bad actions.

prejudice: attitudes and feelings (typically negative) about the members of some group solely on the basis of their membership of that group.

primacy effect: the finding that first impressions are more important than later ones in determining our opinion of others.

primary reinforcers: rewarding stimuli that are essential for survival (e.g., food; water).

priming: this is a form of **non-declarative memory** involving facilitated processing of (and response to) a target stimulus because the same or a related stimulus was presented previously.

privation: the state of a child who has never formed a close attachment with another person; see **deprivation**.

proactive aggression: forms of aggressive behaviour that are planned in advance to achieve some goal; this is cold-tempered aggression.

proactive interference: disruption occurring when previous learning interferes with later learning and memory.

problem-focused coping: a general strategy for dealing with stressful situations in which attempts are made to act directly on the source of the stress.

productive language: this is language production that involves speaking or writing.

pro-social behaviour: behaviour that is positive (e.g., cooperative; affectionate) and that is designed to be of benefit to someone else.

psychoticism: a personality trait that reflects individual differences in hostility, coldness, and aggression.

quota sampling: selecting a **sample** from a **population** in such a way that those selected are similar to it in certain respects (e.g., proportion of females).

random sampling: selecting the individuals for a sample from a population in a random way.

randomisation: placing participants into groups on some random basis (e.g., coin tossing).

rationalisation: in Bartlett's theory, the tendency in story recall to produce errors conforming to the cultural expectations of the rememberer; it is attributed to the influence of schemas.

reactive aggression: this is aggressive behaviour that is triggered by the anger created by a perceived provocation; this is hot-tempered aggression.

recategorisation: merging the **ingroup** and **outgroup** to form a single large ingroup; it is designed to reduce **prejudice**.

receptive language: this is the comprehension or understanding of language (e.g., the speech of others).

reciprocal altruism: the notion that someone will show **altruism** in their behaviour toward someone else if they anticipate that person will respond altruistically.

recognition: a form of memory test in which decisions have to be made as to whether the items on the test were presented before.

regression: returning to a less mature way of behaving within Freud's psychosexual theory.

rehearsal: the verbal repetition of information (often words), which typically has the effect of increasing our long-term memory for the rehearsed information.

reliability: the extent to which an intelligence (or other) test gives consistent findings on different occasions.

repeated measures design: an experimental design in which each participant appears in both groups.

replication: repeating the findings of a study using the same design and procedures.

representative sample: a **sample** of participants that is chosen to be typical or representative of the **population** from which it is drawn.

repression: a term used by Freud to refer to motivated forgetting; it often involves very stressful experiences.

resistant attachment: an insecure attachment of an infant to its mother combined with resistance of contact with her when she returns after an absence.

retroactive interference: forgetting occurring when later learning disrupts memory for earlier learning.

reversibility: in Piaget's theory, the ability to undo mentally (reverse) some operation that has been carried out (e.g., changing an object's shape).

salient categorisation: the notion that someone needs to be regarded as typical or representative of a group if positive encounters with that individual are to lead to reduced prejudice towards the entire group.

sample: the participants actually used in a study drawn from some larger **population**.

schemas: organised packets of information about the world, events, or people, stored in long-term memory and used to guide action.

secondary reinforcers: stimuli that are rewarding because they have repeatedly been associated with **primary reinforcers**; examples are money and praise.

secure attachment: a strong and contented attachment of an infant to its mother including when she returns after an absence.

selective placement: placing adopted children in homes resembling those of their biological parents in social and educational terms.

self-concept: the organised information about ourselves that we have stored away in long-term memory.

self-disclosure: revealing personal or private information about oneself to another person.

self-efficacy: according to Bandura, the beliefs about being able to perform some task so as to achieve certain goals.

self-esteem: the part of the **self-concept** concerned with the feelings (positive and negative) that an individual has about himself/herself.

self-regulation: according to Bandura, the notion that individuals learn to reward and punish themselves internally to regulate their own behaviour and achieve desired outcomes.

self-serving bias: the tendency to attribute your successes to your own efforts and ability, but to attribute your failures to task difficulty and bad luck; it is used to maintain self-esteem.

semantic dementia: a condition caused by brain damage in which the patient experiences considerable problems in accessing word meanings.

semantic memory: a form of **declarative memory** consisting of general knowledge about the world, concepts, language, and so on; see **episodic memory**.

semantics: the meanings that are expressed by words and by sentences.

sex-role stereotypes: culturally-determined expectations concerning the jobs and activities thought suitable for males and for females.

sex-typed behaviour: this is behaviour that conforms to that expected on the basis of any given culture's **sex-role stereotypes**.

shaping: a form of operant conditioning in which behaviour is changed slowly in the desired direction by requiring responses to become more and more like the wanted response in order for reward to be given.

situational attribution: deciding that someone's behaviour is due to the situation in which they find themselves rather than to their personality.

skill learning: this is a form of learning in which there is little or no conscious awareness of what has been learned.

social desirability bias: the tendency to provide socially desirable responses on personality questionnaires even when those responses are incorrect.

social identities: each of the groups with which we identify produces a social identity; our feelings about ourselves depend on how we feel about the groups with which we identify.

social influence: efforts by individuals or by groups to change the attitudes and/or behaviour of other people.

social norms: agreed standards of behaviour within a group (e.g., family; organisations).

social perception: the processes involved when one person perceives, evaluates, and forms an impression of another person.

social phobia: a mental disorder in which the patient experiences very high levels of anxiety in social situations which often cause him/her to avoid such situations.

social power: the force that can be used by an individual to change the attitudes and/or behaviour of other people.

somatic nervous system: the part of the **peripheral nervous system** that controls the voluntary movements of skeletal muscles and hence the limbs.

split-brain patients: individuals in whom the corpus callosum connecting the two halves of the brain has been severed; direct communication between the two hemispheres is not possible.

spontaneous recovery: the re-emergence of responses over time in **classical conditioning** after **extinction**.

standardised tests: tests that have been given to large representative samples, and on which an individual's ability (or personality) can be compared to that of other people.

stereopsis: a cue to depth based on the fact that objects produce slightly different images on the retinas of the two eyes.

stereotype: an oversimplified generalisation (typically negative) concerning some group (e.g., the English; the Welsh).

sympathetic nervous system: the part of the **autonomic nervous system** that produces arousal and energy (e.g., via increased heart rate).

syntax: the grammatical rules that indicate the appropriate order of words within sentences.

technostress: the anxiety and stress caused by difficulties in coping with technological advances (especially in computing).

telegraphic period: the second stage of language development, during which children's speech is like a telegram in that much information is contained in two (or less often) three words.

testosterone: a hormone that is present in much greater quantities in males than in females; it has been linked to aggressive and sexual behaviour.

testing effect: the finding that long-term memory is enhanced when some of the learning period is devoted to retrieving the to-be-remembered information.

texture gradient: a cue to depth given by the increased rate of change in texture density as you look from the front to the back of a slanting stimulus.

thalamus: a part of the forebrain that is involved in wakefulness and sleep.

theory of mind: the understanding by children and adults that other people may have different beliefs, emotions, and intentions than their own.

third-party punishment: punishing someone else who has treated a third party unfairly even though it involves a personal sacrifice.

time-out technique: a form of negative punishment in which undesirable behaviour (e.g., aggression) is reduced by removing the individual from the situation in which he/she has been aggressive.

token economy: a form of therapy based on operant conditioning in which tokens are given to patients when they produce desirable behaviour; these tokens can then be exchanged for rewards.

traits: aspects or dimensions of personality that exhibit individual differences and are moderately stable over time; they have direct and indirect influences on behaviour.

transfer-appropriate processing: this is the notion that long-term memory will be greatest when the processing at the time of retrieval is very similar to the processing at the time of learning.

Type A personality: a personality type characterised by impatience, competitiveness, time pressure, and hostility.

Type D personality: a type of personality that is characterised by high negative affectivity and social inhibition.

unconditioned reflex: a well-established association between an **unconditioned stimulus** and an **unconditioned response**.

unconditioned response: the well-established reaction (e.g., salivation) to a given **unconditioned stimulus** (e.g., food) in an **unconditioned reflex**.

unconditioned stimulus: the stimulus that produces a well-established **unconditioned response** in an **unconditioned reflex**.

validity: the extent to which an intelligence (or other) test measures what it is claimed to be measuring.

viewpoint-dependent perception: the notion that objects can be recognised more easily from some viewpoints or angles than from others.

viewpoint-invariant perception: the notion that it is equally easy to recognise objects from numerous different viewpoints.

visual illusions: two-dimensional drawings that are seen inaccurately by nearly everyone; the best-known is the Müller-Lyer illusion.

visuo-spatial sketchpad: a component of working memory that is used to process visual and spatial information and to store this information briefly.

weapon focus: the finding that eyewitnesses pay so much attention to the culprit's weapon that they ignore other details.

weapons effect: an increase in aggression produced by the sight of a weapon (e.g., gun).

working memory: a system that has separate components for rehearsal and for other processing activities; it has been proposed as a replacement for the short-term memory store.

zone of proximal development: in Vygotsky's theory, the gap between the child's current problem-solving ability and his/her potential ability.

References

Abrams, D., Wetherall, M., Cochrane, S., Hogg, M.A., & Turner, J.C. (1990). Knowing what to think by knowing who you are: Self-categorization and the nature of norm formation, conformity and group polarization. *British Journal of Social Psychology*, 29, 97–119.

Adams, C.H., & Sherer, M. (1985). Sex-role orientation and psychological adjustment: Implications for the masculinity model. *Sex Roles*, 12, 1211–1218.

Addis, D.R., & Tippett, L.J. (2004). Memory of myself: Autobiographical memory and identity in Alzheimer's disease. *Memory*, 12, 56–74.

Adorno, T.W., Frenkel-Brunswik, E., Levinson, D., & Sanford, R. (1950). *The authoritarian personality*. New York: Harper.

Adriaanse, M.A., Gollwitzer, P.M., De Ridder, D.T.D., de Wit, J.B.F., & Kroese, F.M. (2011). Breaking habits with implementation intentions: A test of underlying processes. *Personality and Social Psychology Bulletin*, 37, 502–513.

Adriaanse, M.A., Vinkers, C.D.W., De Ridder, D.T.D., Hox, J.J., & De Wit, J.B.F. (2011). Do implementation intentions help to eat a healthy diet? A systematic review and meta-analysis of the empirical evidence. *Appetite*, 56, 183–193.

Ainsworth, M.D.S., & Bell, S.M. (1970). Attachment, exploration and separation: Illustrated by the behavior of one-year-olds in a strange situation. *Child Development*, 41, 49–67.

Ainsworth, M.D.S., Blehat, M.C., Waters, E., & Wall, S. (1978). *Patterns of attachment: A psychological study of the strange situation*. Hillsdale, NJ: Lawrence Erlbaum Associates, Inc.

Alford, J.R., Funk, C.L., & Hibbing, J.R. (2005). Are political orientations genetically transmitted? *American Political Science Review*, 99, 153–167.

Allport, G.W. (1954). *The nature of prejudice*. Reading, MA: Addison-Wesley.

Allport, G.W., & Odbert, H.S. (1936). Trait-names: A psycho-lexical study. *Psychological Monographs*, 47, No. 211.

Almeida, D.M. (2005). Resilience and vulnerability to daily stressors assessed via diary methods. *Current Directions in Psychological Science*, 14, 64–68.

Altemeyer, B. (2004). Highly dominating, highly authoritarian personalities. *Journal of Social Psychology*, 144, 421–448.

Ambady, N., & Rosenthal, R. (1996). Experimenter effects. In A.S.R. Manstead & M. Hewstone (Eds.), *Blackwell encyclopedia of social psychology*. Oxford: Blackwell.

Anderson, C.A., Anderson, K.B., & Deuser, W.E. (1996). A general framework for the study of affective aggression: Effects of weapons and extreme temperatures on accessibility of aggressive thoughts, affect, and attitudes. *Personality and Social Psychology Bulletin*, 22, 366–376.

Anderson, C.A., Benjamin, A.J., & Bartholow, B.D. (1998). Does the gun pull the trigger? Automatic priming effects of weapon pictures and weapon names. *Psychological Science*, 9, 308–314.

Anderson, C.A., & Bushman, B.J. (2002). Human aggression. *Annual Review of Psychology*, 53, 27–51.

Anderson, C.A., Ihori, N., Bushman, B.J., Rothstein, H.R., Shibuya, A., Swing, E.L. et al. (2010). Violent video game effects on aggression, empathy, and prosocial behavior in Eastern and Western countries: A meta-analytic review. *Psychological Bulletin*, 136, 151–173.

Anderson, J.L., Crawford, C.B., Nadeau, J., & Lindberg, T. (1992). Was the Duchess of Windsor right? A cross-cultural review of the socioecology of ideals of female body shape. *Ethology and Sociobiology*, 13, 197–227.

Andlin-Sobocki, P., Olesen, J., Wittchen, H.-U., & Jonsson, B. (2005). Cost of disorders of the brain in Europe. *European Journal of Neurology*, 12, 1–27.

Andlin-Sobocki, P., & Wittchen, H.-U. (2005). Cost of affective disorders in Europe. *European Journal of Neurology*, 12, 34–38.

Andrews, P.W., & Thomson, J.A. (2009). The bright side of being blue: Depression as an adaptation for analyzing complex problems. *Psychological Review*, 116, 620–654.

Ang, S.C., Rodgers, J.L., & Wänström, L. (2010). The Flynn effect within subgroups in the US: Gender, race, income, education, and urbanization differences in the NLSY-Children data. *Intelligence*, 38, 367–384.

Arnett, J. (2008). The neglected 95%: Why American psychology needs to become less American. *American Psychologist*, 63, 602–614.

Asch, S.E. (1946). Forming impressions of personality. *Journal of Abnormal and Social Psychology*, 41, 258–290.

Asch, S.E. (1951). Effects of group pressure on the modification and distortion of judgments. In H. Guetzkow (Ed.), *Groups, leadership and men*. Pittsburgh, PA: Carnegie.

Asch, S.E. (1956). Studies of independence and conformity: A minority of one against a unanimous majority. *Psychological Monographs, 70* (Whole No. 416).

Asendorpf, J.B., Penke, L., & Back, M.D. (2011). From dating to mating and relating: Predictors of initial and long-term outcomes of speed-dating in a community sample. *European Journal of Personality, 25,* 16–30.

Astington, J.W., & Jenkins, J.M. (1999). A longitudinal study of the relation between language and theory-of-mind development. *Developmental Psychology, 35,* 1311–1320.

Atkins, J.E., Fiser, J., & Jacobs, R.A. (2001). Experience-dependent visual cue integration based on consistencies between visual and haptic percepts. *Vision Research, 41,* 449–461.

Atkinson, R.C., & Shiffrin, R.M. (1968). Human memory: A proposed system and its control processes. In K.W. Spence & J.T. Spence (Eds.), *The psychology of learning and motivation (vol. 2).* London: Academic Press.

Atkinson, R.L., Atkinson, R.C., Smith, E.E., & Bem, D.J. (1993). *Introduction to psychology (11th ed.).* New York: Harcourt Brace College Publishers.

Augustine, A.A., & Hemenover, S.H. (2009). On the relative merits of affect regulation strategies: A meta-analysis. *Cognition & Emotion, 23,* 1181–1220.

Ayllon, T., & Azrin, N.H. (1968). *The token economy: A motivational system for therapy and rehabilitation.* New York: Appleton-Century-Crofts.

Baas, M., De Dreu, C.K.W., Carsten, K.W., & Nijstad, B.A. (2008). A meta-analysis of 25 years of mood-creativity research: Hedonic tone, activation, or regulatory focus? *Psychological Bulletin, 134,* 779–806.

Bachen, E., Cohen, S., & Marsland, A.L. (1997). Psychoimmunology. In A. Baum, S. Newman, J. Weinman, R. West, & C. McManus (Eds.), *Cambridge handbook of psychology, health, and medicine.* Cambridge, UK: Cambridge University Press.

Baddeley, A.D. (2000). The episodic buffer: A new component of working memory? *Trends in Cognitive Science, 4,* 417–423.

Baddeley, A.D. (2007). *Working memory, thought and action.* Oxford: Oxford University Press.

Baddeley, A., Eysenck, M.W., & Anderson, M.C. (2009). *Memory.* New York: Psychology Press.

Baddeley, A.D., & Hitch, G.J. (1974). Working memory. In G.H. Bower (Ed.), *Recent advances in learning and motivation, Vol. 8* (pp. 47–89). New York: Academic Press.

Balcetis, E., & Dunning, D. (2011). Considering the situation: Why people are better social psychologists than self-psychologists. *Self and Identity,* 1–15.

Bandura, A. (1965). Influences of models' reinforcement contingencies on the acquisition of initiative responses. *Journal of Personality and Social Psychology, 1,* 589–593.

Bandura, A. (1973). *Aggression: A social learning analysis.* Englewood Cliffs, NJ: Prentice-Hall.

Bandura, A. (1977). *Social learning theory.* Englewood Cliffs, NJ: Prentice Hall.

Bandura, A. (1986). *Social foundations of thought and action: A social cognitive theory.* Englewood Cliffs, NJ: Prentice Hall.

Bandura, A. (1999). Social cognitive theory of personality. In L.A. Pervin & O.P. John (Eds.), *Handbook of personality: Theory and research (2nd ed.).* New York: Guilford Press.

Bandura, A., Ross, D., & Ross, S.A. (1963). Transmission of aggression through imitation of aggressive models. *Journal of Abnormal and Social Psychology, 66,* 3–11.

Bangert-Drowns, R.L., Kulik, J.A., & Kulik, C.-L.C. (1991). Effects of frequent classroom testing. *Journal of Educational Psychology, 85,* 89–99.

Bannard, C., Lieven, E., & Tomasello, M. (2009). Modeling children's early grammatical knowledge. *Proceedings of the National Academy of Sciences of the United States of America, 106,* 17284–17289.

Barkley, R.A., Ullman, D.G., Otto, L., & Brecht, J.M. (1977). The effects of sex typing and sex appropriateness of modeled behavior on children's imitation. *Child Development, 48,* 721–725.

Barlett, C.P., Harris, R.J., & Baldassaro, R. (2007). Longer you play, the more hostile you feel: Examination of first person shooter video games and aggression during video game play. *Aggressive Behavior, 33,* 486–497.

Barlow, F.K., Louis, W.R., & Terry, D.J. (2010). Minority report: Social identity, cognitions of rejection and intergroup anxiety predicting prejudice from one racially marginalized group towards another. *European Journal of Social Psychology, 40,* 805–818.

Bar-On, R. (1997). *The Emotional Intelligence Inventory (EQ-i): Technical Manual.* Toronto: Multi-Health Systems.

Baron, R. (2005). So right it's wrong: Groupthink and the ubiquitous nature of polarized group decision making. *Advances in Experimental Social Psychology, 37,* 219–253.

Baron-Cohen, S. (1995). *Mindblindness: An essay on autism and theory of mind.* Cambridge, MA: MIT Press.

Baron-Cohen, S., Campbell, R., Karmiloff-Smith, A., Grant, J., & Walker, J. (1995). Are children with autism blind to the mentalistic significance of the eyes? *British Journal of Developmental Psychology, 13,* 379–398.

Baron-Cohen, S., Leslie, A.M., & Frith, U. (1985). Does the autistic child have a "theory of mind"? *Cognition, 21,* 37–46.

Barrett, P.T., & Kline, P. (1982). An item and radial parcel analysis of the 16PF Questionnaire. *Personality and Individual Differences, 3,* 259–270.

Bartlett, F.C. (1932). *Remembering.* Cambridge, UK: Cambridge University Press.

Bassoff, E.S., & Glass, G.V. (1982). The relationship between sex roles and mental health: A meta-analysis of twenty-six studies. *Counseling Psychologist, 10,* 105–112.

Bateson, M., Nettle, D., & Roberts, G. (2006). Cues of being watched enhance cooperation in a real-world setting. *Biological Letters, 2,* 412–414.

Batey, M., Chamorro-Premuzic, T., & Furnham, A. (2010). Individual differences in ideational behavior: Can the Big Five and psychometric intelligence predict creativity scores? *Creativity Research Journal, 22,* 90–97.

Batson, C.D., Cochrane, P.J., Biederman, M.F., Blosser, J.L., Ryan, M.J., & Vogt, B. (1978). Failure to help when in a hurry: Callousness or conflict? *Personality and Social Psychology Bulletin, 4,* 97–101.

Baumeister, R.F. (1995). Self and identity: An introduction. In A. Tesser (Ed.), *Advanced social psychology.* New York: McGraw-Hill.

Baumeister, R.F. (1998). The self. In D.T. Gilbert, S.T. Fiske, & G. Lindzey (Eds.), *The handbook of social psychology (Vol. 1, 4th ed.).* New York: McGraw-Hill.

Baumeister, R.F, & Bushman, B.J. (2009). *Social psychology and human nature.* Belmont, CA: Wadsworth.

Baumeister, R.F., Campbell, J.D., Krueger, J.I., & Vohs, K.D. (2005). Exploding the self-esteem myth. *Scientific American, 292,* 70–77.

Baumeister, R.F., & Sommer, K.L. (1997). What do men want? Gender differences and two spheres of belongingness: Comment on Cross and Madsen (1997). *Psychological Bulletin, 122,* 38–44.

Baynes, K., & Gazzaniga, M. (2000). Consciousness, introspection, and the split-brain: The two minds/ one body problem. In M.S. Gazzaniga (Ed.), *The new cognitive neurosciences.* Cambridge, MA: MIT Press.

Beck, M.R., Levin, D.T., & Angelone, B. (2007). Change blindness blindness: Beliefs about the roles of intention and scene complexity in change blindness. *Consciousness and Cognition, 16,* 31–51.

Bègue, L., Bushman, B.J., Giancola, P.R., Subra, B., & Rosset, E. (2010). "There is no such thing as an accident", especially when people are drunk. *Personality and Social Psychology Bulletin, 36,* 1301–1304.

Behrman, B.W., & Davey, S.L. (2001). Eyewitness identification in actual criminal cases: An archival analysis. *Law and Human Behavior, 25,* 475–491.

Bejjani, B.P., Damier, P., Arnulf, I., Thivard, L., Bonnet, A.M., Dormont, D., et al. (1999). Transient acute depression induced by high-frequency deep-brain stimulation. *New England Journal of Medicine, 340,* 1476–1480.

Belmore, S.M. (1987). Determinants of attention during impression formation. *Journal of Experimental Psychology: Learning, Memory, and Cognition, 13,* 480–489.

Belsky, J., & Rovine, M. (1987). Temperament and attachment security in the Strange Situation: A rapprochement. *Child Development, 58,* 787–795.

Bem, S.L. (1974). Measurement of psychological androgeny. *Journal of Consulting and Clinical Psychology, 42,* 155–162.

Bem, S.L. (1985). Androgyny and gender schema theory: A conceptual and empirical integration. In T.B. Snodegegger (Ed.), *Nebraska symposium on motivation: Psychology and gender.* Lincoln, NE: University of Nebraska Press.

Benenson, J.F., Morash, D., & Petrakos, H. (1998). Gender differences in emotional closeness between preschool children and their mothers. *Sex Roles, 38,* 975–985.

Benigno, J.P., Byrd, D.L., McNamara, P.H., Berg, W.G., & Farrar, M.J. (2011). Talking through transitions: Microgenetic changes in preschoolers' private speech and executive functioning. *Child Language Teaching and Therapy, 27,* 269–285.

Bennett, P. (1994). Should we intervene to modify Type A behavior in patients with manifest heart disease? *Behavioural and Cognitive Psychotherapy, 22,* 125–145.

Berenbaum, S.A., & Beltry, A.M. (2011). Sexual differentiation of human behavior: Effects of prenatal and pubertal organizational hormones. *Frontiers in Neuroendocrinology, 32,* 183–200.

Berk, L. (1994). Why children talk to themselves. *Scientific American* (November), 60–65.

Berk, L. (2006). *Child development (7th ed.)*. New York: Pearson.

Berko, J. (1958). The child's learning of English morphology. *Word, 14*, 150–177.

Berkowitz, L. (1968). Impulse, aggression and the gun. *Psychology Today*, September, 18–22.

Berkowitz, L., & LePage, A. (1967). Weapons as aggression-eliciting stimuli. *Journal of Personality and Social Psychology, 7*, 202–207.

Berndsen, M., & Manstead, A.S.R. (2007). On the relationship between responsibility and guilt: Antecedent appraisal or elaborated appraisal? *European Journal of Social Psychology, 37*, 774–792.

Berndt, T.J. (1979). Developmental changes in conformity to peers and parents. *Developmental Psychology, 53*, 1447–1460.

Bettencourt, B.A., & Miller, N. (1996). Gender differences in aggression as a function of provocation: A meta-analysis. *Psychological Bulletin, 119*, 422–447.

Bickerton, D. (1984). The language bioprogram hypothesis. *Behavioral and Brain Sciences, 7*, 173–221.

Biederman, I. (1987). Recognition-by-components: A theory of human image understanding. *Psychological Review, 94*, 115–147.

Bilalić, M., McLeod, P., & Gobet, F. (2008a). Inflexibility of experts: Reality or myth? Quantifying the Einstellung effect in chess masters. *Cognitive Psychology, 56*, 73–102.

Bilalić, M., McLeod, P., & Gobet, F. (2008b). Why good thoughts block better ones: The mechanism of the pernicious Einstellung (set) effect. *Cognition, 108*, 652–661.

Bjork, R.A., & Bjork, E.L. (1992). A new theory of disuse and an old theory of stimulus fluctuation. In A. Healey, S. Kosslyn, & R. Shiffrin (Eds.), *From learning processes to cognitive processes: Essays in honor of William K. Estes* (Vol. 2). Hillsdale, NJ: Erlbaum.

Bjorkqvist, K., Lagerspetz, K.M.J., & Kaukiainen, A. (1992). Do girls manipulate and boys fight? Developmental trends in regard to direct and indirect aggression. *Aggressive Behavior, 18*, 117–127.

Blaine, B., & Crocker, J. (1993). Self-esteem and self-serving bias in reaction to positive and negative events: An integrative review. In R. Baumeister (Ed.), *Self-esteem: The puzzle of low self-regard*. New York: Plenum Press.

Blandin, Y., & Proteau, L. (2000). On the cognitive basis of observational learning: Development of mechanisms for the detection and correction of errors. *Quarterly Journal of Experimental Psychology, 53A*, 846–867.

Bluck, S., & Alea, N. (2009). Thinking and talking about the past: Why remember? *Applied Cognitive Psychology, 23*, 1089–1104.

Bohannon, J.N., & Warren-Leubecker, A. (1989). Theoretical approaches to language acquisition. In J. Berko-Gleason (Ed.), *The development of language (2nd ed.)*. Columbus, OH: Merrill.

Bolger, N., & Amarel, D. (2007). Effects of social support visibility on adjustment to stress: Experimental evidence. *Journal of Personality and Social Psychology, 92*, 458–475.

Bond, M.H., & Smith, P.B. (1996a). Cross-cultural social and organizational psychology. *Annual Review of Psychology, 47*, 205–235.

Bond, R. (2005). Group size and conformity. *Group Processes and Intergroup Roles, 6*, 331–354.

Bond, R., & Smith, P.B. (1996b). Culture and conformity: A meta-analysis of studies using Asch's (1952b, 1956) line judgment task. *Psychological Bulletin, 119*, 111–137.

Bonta, B.D. (1997). Cooperation and competition in peaceful societies. *Psychological Bulletin, 121*, 299–320.

Bosma, H., Peter, R., Siegrist, J., & Marmot, M. (1998). Two alternative job stress models and the risk of coronary heart disease. *American Journal of Public Health, 88*, 68–74.

Bouchard, T.J., Lykken, D.T., McGue, M., Segal, N.L., & Tellegen, A. (1990). Sources of human psychological differences: The Minnesota study of twins reared apart. *Science, 250*, 223–228.

Bouvier, S.E., & Engel, S.A. (2006). Behavioral deficits and cortical damage loci in cerebral achromatopsia. *Cerebral Cortex, 16*, 183–191.

Bowden, E.M., Jung-Beeman, M., Fleck, J., & Kounios, J. (2005). New approaches to demystifying insight. *Trends in Cognitive Sciences, 9*, 322–328.

Bower, G.H. (1973). How to … uh … remember! *Psychology Today, 7*, 63–70.

Bower, G.H., Black, J.B., & Turner, T.J. (1979). Scripts in memory for text. *Cognitive Psychology, 11*, 177–220.

Bower, G.H., & Clark, M.C. (1969). Narrative stories as mediators for serial learning. *Psychonomic Science, 14*, 181–182.

Bowlby, J. (1951). *Maternal care and mental health*. Geneva: World Health Organization.

Bowlby, J. (1969). *Attachment and love: Vol. 1: Attachment*. London: Hogarth.

Bowlby, J. (1988). *A secure base: Clinical applications of attachment theory*. London: Routledge.

Brace, C.L. (1996). Review of The Bell Curve. *Current Anthropology, 37*, 5157–5161.

Brackett, M.A., Mayer, J.D., & Warner, R.M. (2004). Emotional intelligence and its relationship to everyday behavior. *Personality and Individual Differences, 36*, 1387–1402.

Bradbard, M.R., Martin, C.L., Endsley, R.C., & Halverson, C.F. (1986). Influence of sex stereotypes on children's exploration and memory: A competence versus performance distinction. *Developmental Psychology, 22*, 481–486.

Bradley, B., DeFife, J.A., Guaraccia, C., Phifer, J., Fani, N., Ressler, K.J., et al. (2011). Emotion dysregulation and negative affect: Association with psychiatric symptoms. *Journal of Clinical Psychiatry, 72*, 685–691.

Bradmetz, J. (1999). Precursors of formal thought: A longitudinal study. *British Journal of Developmental Psychology, 17*, 61–81.

Brakke, K.E., & Savage-Rumbaugh, E.S. (1995). The development of language skills in bonobo and chimpanzee. 1. Comprehension. *Language & Communication, 15*, 121–148.

Brakke, K.E., & Savage-Rumbaugh, E.S. (1996). The development of language skills in Pan. 2. Production. *Language & Communication, 16*, 361–380.

Bransford, J.D., & Johnson, M.K. (1972). Contextual prerequisites for understanding. *Journal of Verbal Learning and Verbal Behavior, 11*, 717–726.

Brauer, M., & Er-rafiy, A. (2011). Increasing perceived variability reduces prejudice and discrimination. *Journal of Experimental Social Psychology, 47*, 871–881.

Brehm, S.S., Kassin, S.M., & Fein, S. (1999). *Social psychology (4th ed.)*. New York: Houghton Mifflin.

Breland, K., & Breland, M. (1961). The misbehavior of organisms. *American Psychologist, 16*, 681–684.

Breslow, L., & Enstrom, J.E. (1980). Persistence of health habits and their relationship to mortality. *Preventive Medicine, 9*, 469–483.

British Psychological Society (1990). *Ethical principles for conducting research with human participants*. Leicester, UK: British Psychological Society.

Brody, G.H., & Shaffer, D.R. (1982). Contributions of parents and peers to children's moral socialization. *Developmental Review, 2*, 31–75.

Brody, L.R., & Hall, J.A. (2008). Gender and emotion in context. In M. Lewis, J.M. Haviland-Jones, & L. Feldman Barrett (Eds.), *Handbook of emotion (3rd ed.)* (pp. 395–408). New York: Guilford Press.

Brown, A.S., Bracken, E., Zoccoli, S., & Douglas, K. (2004). Generating and remembering passwords. *Applied Cognitive Psychology, 18*, 641–651.

Brown, G.W., & Harris, T. (1978). *Social origins of depression*. London: Tavistock.

Brown, R. (1986). *Social psychology (2nd ed.)*. New York: Free Press.

Brown, R.J., Vivian, J., & Hewstone, M. (1999). Changing attitudes through intergroup contact: The effects of group membership salience. *European Journal of Social Psychology, 29*, 741–764.

Bruce, V., Green, P.R., & Georgeson, M.A. (2003). *Visual perception: Physiology, psychology and ecology (4th ed.)*. Hove, UK: Psychology Press.

Bruno, N., Bernadis, P., & Gentilucci, M. (2008). Visually guided pointing, the Müller-Lyer illusion, and the functional interpretation of the dorsal-ventral split: Conclusions from 33 independent studies. *Neuroscience and Biobehavioral Reviews, 32*, 423–437.

Bryan, A.D., Webster, G.D., & Mahaffey, A.L. (2011). The big, the rich, and the powerful: Physical, financial, and social dimensions of dominance in mating and attraction. *Personality and Social Psychology Bulletin, 37*, 365–382.

Burger, J.M. (2011). Alive and well after all these years. *Psychologist, 24*, 654–657.

Burgess, R.L., & Wallin, P. (1953). Marital happiness of parents and their children's attitudes to them. *American Sociological Review, 18*, 424–431.

Burke, D., Taubert, J., & Higman, T. (2007). Are face representations viewpoint dependent? A stereo advantage for generalizing across different views of faces. *Vision Research, 47*, 2164–2169.

Burleson, B.R., & Kunkel, A. (2002). Parental and peer contributions to the emotional support skills of the child: From whom do children learn to express support? *Journal of Family Communication, 2*, 81–97.

Burton, A.M., Bruce, V., & Hancock, P.J.B. (1999). From pixels to people: A model of familiar face recognition. *Cognitive Science, 23*, 1–31.

Bushman, B.J., & Anderson, C.A. (2001). Is it time to pull the plug on the hostile versus instrumental aggression dichotomy? *Psychological Review, 108*, 273–279.

Bushman, B.J., & Anderson, C.A. (2002). Violent video games and hostile expectations: A test of the general aggression model. *Personality and Social Psychology Bulletin, 28*, 1679–1686.

Bushman, B.J., Baumeister, R.F., & Stack, A.D. (1999). Catharsis, aggression, and persuasive influence: Self-fulfilling or self-defeating prophecies? *Journal of Personality and Social Psychology, 76*, 367–376.

Buss, D.M. (1989). Sex differences in human mate preferences: Evolutionary hypotheses tested in 37 cultures. *Behavioral & Brain Sciences, 12*, 1–49.

Bussey, K., & Bandura, A. (1999). Social cognitive theory of gender development and differentiation. *Psychological Review, 106*, 676–713.

Byrne, D. (1971). *The attraction paradigm*. New York: Academic Press.

Caplovitz, G.P., Fendrich, R., & Hughes, H.C. (2008). Failures to see: Attentive blank stares revealed by change blindness. *Consciousness and Cognition, 17*, 877–886.

Capron, C., & Duyme, M. (1989). Assessment of effects of socio-economic status on IQ in a full cross-fostering study. *Nature, 340*, 552–554.

Carnagey, N.L., & Anderson, C.A. (2005). The effects of reward and punishment in violent video games on aggressive affect, cognition, and behavior. *Psychological Science, 16*, 882–889.

Carroll, J.B. (1993). *Human cognitive abilities: A survey of factor analytic studies*. New York: Cambridge University Press.

Carver, C.S., & Connor-Smith, J. (2010). Personality and coping. *Annual Review of Psychology, 61*, 679–704.

Cattell, R.B. (1946). *Description and measurement of personality*. Dubuque, IA: Brown Company Publishers.

Cattell, R.B. (1957). *Personality and motivation structure and measurement*. New York: World Book Company.

Cavaco, S., Anderson, S.W., Allen, J.S., Castro-Caldas, A., & Damasio, H. (2004). The scope of preserved procedural memory in amnesia. *Brain, 127*, 1853–1867.

Challis, B.H., Velichkovsky, B.M., & Craik, F.I.M. (1996). Levels-of-processing effects on a variety of memory tasks: New findings and theoretical implications. *Consciousness and Cognition, 5*, 142–164.

Charlton, T., Gunter, B., & Coles, D. (1998). Broadcast television as a cause of aggression? Recent findings from a naturalistic study. *British Journal of Emotional and Behaviour Difficulties, 3*, 5–13.

Charness, N. (1981). Search in chess: Age and skill differences. *Journal of Experimental Psychology: Human Perception and Performance, 7*, 467–476.

Chartrand, T.L., van Baaren, R.B., & Bargh, J.A. (2006). Linking automatic evaluation to mood and information-processing style: Consequences for experienced affect, impression formation, and stereotyping. *Journal of Experimental Psychology: General, 135*, 67–77.

Cheng, C. (2005). Processes underlying gender-role flexibility: Do androgynous individuals know more or know how to cope? *Journal of Personality, 73*, 645–674.

Cherney, I.D. (2008). Mom, let me play more computer games: They improve my mental rotation skills. *Sex Roles, 59*, 776–786.

Chida, Y., & Steptoe, A. (2009). The association of anger and hostility with future coronary heart disease: A meta-analytic review of prospective evidence. *Journal of the American College of Cardiology, 53*, 936–946.

Child, I.L. (1968). Personality in culture. In E.F. Borgatta & W.W. Lambert (Eds.), *Handbook of personality theory and research*. Chicago: Rand McNally.

Choi, I., & Nisbett, R.E. (1998). Situational salience and cultural differences in the correspondence bias and actor-observer bias. *Personality and Social Psychology Bulletin, 24*, 949–960.

Chomsky, N. (1965). *Aspects of the theory of syntax*. Cambridge, MA: MIT Press.

Chomsky, N. (1986). *Knowledge of language: Its nature, origin, and use*. New York: Praeger.

Choy, Y., Fyer, A.J., & Lipsitz, J.D. (2007). Treatment of specific phobia in adults. *Clinical Psychology Review, 27*, 266–286.

Christiansen, M.H., & Chater, N. (2008). Language as shaped by the brain. *Behavioral and Brain Sciences, 31*, 489–512.

Christiansen, M.H., & Chater, N. (2009). The myth of language universals and the myth of universal grammar. *Behavioral and Brain Sciences, 32*, 452–453.

Chrysikou, E.G., & Weisberg, R.W. (2005). Following the wrong footsteps: Fixation effects of pictorial examples in a design problem-solving task. *Journal of Experimental Psychology: Learning, Memory, and Cognition, 31*, 1134–1148.

Cinnirella, M. (1998). Manipulating stereotype ratings tasks: Understanding questionnaire context effects on measures of attitudes, social identity and stereotypes. *Journal of Community and Applied Social Psychology, 8*, 345–362.

Clark, D.M., Ehlers, A., Hackmann, A., McManus, F., Fennell, M., Grey, N., Waddington, L., & Wild, J. (2006). Cognitive therapy versus exposure and applied relaxation in social phobia: A randomised controlled trial. *Journal of Consulting and Clinical Psychology, 74*, 568–578.

Clark, D.M., & Wells, A. (1995). A cognitive model of social phobia. In R.R.G. Heimberg, M. Liebowitz, D.A. Hope, & S. Scheier (Eds.), *Social phobia: Diagnosis, assessment and treatment*. New York: Guilford.

Cobos, P., Sanchez, M., Perez, N., & Vila, J. (2004). Effects of spinal cord injuries on the subjective components of emotions. *Cognition & Emotion, 18*, 281–287.

Coch, D., Sanders, L.D., & Neville, H.J. (2005). An event-related potential study of selective auditory attention in children and adults. *Journal of Cognitive Neuroscience, 17,* 606–622.

Cohen, S., & Williamson, G.M. (1991). Stress and infectious disease in humans. *Psychological Bulletin, 109,* 5–24.

Cohen-Kettenis, P.T., & van Goozen, S.H.M. (1997). Sex reassignment of adolescent transsexuals: A follow-up study. *Journal of American Child Adolescent Psychiatry, 36,* 263–271.

Colby, A., Kohlberg, L., Gibbs, J., & Lieberman, M. (1983). A longitudinal study of moral judgment. *Monographs of the Society for Research in Child Development, 48* (Nos. 1–2, Serial No. 200).

Collins, N.L., & Miller, L.C. (1994). Self-disclosure and liking: A meta-analytic review. *Psychological Bulletin, 116,* 457–475.

Colman, A. (1999). *What is psychology? (3rd ed.).* London: Routledge.

Colman, A.M. (2001). *Oxford dictionary of psychology.* Oxford, UK: Oxford University Press.

Colvin, C.R., Block, J., & Funder, D.C. (1995). Overly positive self-evaluations and personality: Negative implications for mental health. *Journal of Personality and Social Psychology, 68,* 1152–1162.

Colvin, M.K., & Gazzaniga, M.S. (2007). Split-brain cases. In M. Velmans & S. Schneider (Eds.), *The Blackwell companion to consciousness.* Oxford: Blackwell.

Comstock, G., & Paik, H. (1991). *Television and the American child.* San Diego: Academic Press.

Confer, J.C., Easton, J.A., Fleischman, D.S., Goetz, C.D., Lewis, D.M.G., Perilloux, C., & Buss, D.M. (2010). Evolutionary psychology: Controversies, questions, prospects, and limitations. *American Psychologist, 65,* 110–126.

Conner, D.B., Knight, D.K., & Cross, D.R. (1997). Mothers' and fathers' scaffolding of their 2-year-olds during problem-solving and literary interactions. *British Journal of Developmental Psychology, 15,* 323–338.

Conway, M.A., & Pleydell-Pearce, C.W. (2000). The construction of autobiographical memories in the self-memory system. *Psychological Review, 107,* 261–288.

Cook, M. (1993). *Personnel selection and productivity (Rev. ed.).* New York: Wiley.

Cooley, C.H. (1902). *Human nature and the social order.* New York: Scribner.

Corkin, S. (1984). Lasting consequences of bilateral medial temporal lobectomy: Clinical course and experimental findings in HM. *Seminars in Neurology, 4,* 249–259.

Corr, P.J. (2010). The psychoticism-psychopathy continuum: A neuropsychological model of core

deficits. *Personality and Individual Differences, 48,* 695–703.

Costa, P.T., & McCrae, R.R. (1992). *NEO-PI-R, Professional manual.* Odessa, FL: Psychological Assessment Resources.

Courage, M.L., Edison, S.C., & Howe, M.L. (2004). Variability in the early development of visual self-recognition. *Infant Behavior and Development, 27,* 509–532.

Cowan, N. (2000). The magical number 4 in short-term memory: A reconsideration of mental storage capacity. *Behavioral and Brain Sciences, 24,* 87–185.

Cowan, N., Elliott, E.M., Saults, J.S., Morey, C.C., Mattox, S., Hismjatullina, A., & Conway, A.R.A. (2005). On the capacity of attention: Its estimation and its role in working memory and cognitive aptitudes. *Cognitive Psychology, 51,* 42–100.

Coyne, S.M., Archer, J., & Eslen, M. (2004). Cruel intentions on television and in real life: Can viewing indirect aggression increase viewers' subsequent indirect aggression? *Journal of Experimental Child Psychology, 88,* 234–253.

Craik, F.I.M., & Lockhart, R.S. (1972). Levels of processing: A framework for memory research. *Journal of Verbal Learning and Verbal Behavior, 11,* 671–684.

Craik, F.I.M., & Tulving, E. (1975). Depth of processing and the retention of words in episodic memory. *Journal of Experimental Psychology: General, 104,* 268–294.

Cross, S.E., & Madsen, L. (1997). Models of the self: Self-construals and gender. *Psychological Bulletin, 122,* 5–37.

Cuddy, A.J.C., Fiske, S.T., & Glick, P. (2008). Warmth and competence as universal dimensions of social perception: The stereotype content model and the BIAS map. *Advances in Experimental Social Psychology, 40,* 61–149.

Cumberbatch, G. (1990). *Television advertising and sex role stereotyping: A content analysis* (Working paper IV for the Broadcasting Standards Council). Communications Research Group, Aston University, Birmingham, UK.

Cunningham, M.R. (1986). Measuring the physical in physical attractiveness: Quasi experiments on the sociobiology of female facial beauty. *Journal of Personality and Social Psychology, 50,* 925–935.

Cunningham, W.A., Preacher, K.J., & Banaji, M.R. (2001). Implicit attitudes measures: Consistency, stability, and convergent validity. *Psychological Science, 12,* 163–170.

Dalgleish, T. (2009). James–Lange theory. In D. Sander & K.R. Scherer (Eds.), *The Oxford companion to emotion and the affective sciences*. Oxford: Oxford University Press.

Dalton, A.L., & Daneman, M. (2006). Social suggestibility to central and peripheral misinformation. *Memory, 14*, 486–501.

Damon, W., & Hart, D. (1988). *Self-understanding in childhood and adolescence*. Cambridge, UK: Cambridge University Press.

Darley, J.M. (1991). Altruism and prosocial behavior research: Reflections and prospects. In M.S. Clark (Ed.), *Prosocial behavior: Review of personality and social psychology, Vol. 12*. Newbury Park, CA: Sage.

Darley, J.M., & Latané, B. (1968). Bystander intervention in emergencies: Diffusion of responsibility. *Journal of Personality and Social Psychology, 8*, 377–383.

Darwin, C. (1859). *The origin of species*. London: Macmillan.

Davey, G.C.L. (1983). An associative view of human classical conditioning. In G.C.L. Davey (Ed.), *Animal models of human behavior: Conceptual, evolutionary, and neurobiological perspectives*. Chichester, UK: Wiley.

David, B., & Turner, J.C. (1999). Studies in self-categorization and minority conversion: The in-group minority in intragroup and intergroup contexts. *British Journal of Social Psychology, 38*, 115–134.

Davidov, M., & Grusec, J.E. (2006). Untangling the links of parental responsiveness to stress and warmth to child outcomes. *Child Development, 77*, 44–58.

Deady, D.K., North, N.T., Allan, D., Smith, M.J.L., & O'Carroll, R.E. (2010). Examining the effect of spinal cord injury on emotional awareness, expressivity and memory for emotional material. *Psychology, Health & Medicine, 15*, 406–419.

De Beni, R., & Moè, A. (2003). Imagery and rehearsal as study strategies for written or orally presented passages. *Psychonomic Bulletin & Review, 10*, 975–980.

De Beni, R., Moè, A., & Cornoldi, C. (1997). Learning from texts or lectures: Loci mnemonics can interfere with reading but not with listening. *European Journal of Cognitive Psychology, 9*, 401–415.

De Boysson-Bardies, B., Sagart, L., & Durand, C. (1984). Discernible differences in the babbling of infants according to target language. *Journal of Child Language, 16*, 1–17.

De Castro, B.O., Veerman, J.W., Koops, W., Bosch, J.D., & Monshouwer, H.J. (2002). Hostile attribution of intent and aggressive behavior: A meta-analysis. *Child Development, 73*, 916–934.

Declercq, M., & de Houwer, J. (2011). Evidence against an occasion-setting account of avoidance learning. *Learning and Motivation, 42*, 46–52.

Deffenbacher, K.A., Bornstein, B.H., Penrod, S.D., & McGorty, E.K. (2004). A meta-analytic review of the effects of high stress on eyewitness memory. *Law and Human Behavior, 28*, 687–706.

De Fulio, A., Donlin, W.D., Wong, C.J., & Silverman, K. (2009). Employment-based abstinence reinforcement as a maintenance intervention for the treatment of cocaine dependence: A randomized controlled trial. *Addiction, 104*, 1530–1538.

Delaney, P.F., Ericsson, K.A., & Knowles, M.E. (2004). Immediate and sustained effects of planning in a problem-solving task. *Journal of Experimental Psychology: Learning, Memory, and Cognition, 30*, 1219–1234.

Della Sala, S. (Ed.). (2010). *Forgetting*. New York: Psychology Press.

DeLongis, A., Folkman, S., & Lazarus, R.S. (1988). The impact of daily hassles, uplifts and major life events on health status. *Health Psychology, 1*, 119–136.

DeLucia, P.R., & Hochberg, J. (1991). Geometrical illusions in solid objects under ordinary viewing conditions. *Perception & Psychophysics, 50*, 547–554.

Denollet, J. (2005). DS14: Standard assessment of negative affectivity, social inhibition, and Type D personality. *Psychosomatic Medicine, 67*, 89–97.

Deutsch, M., & Gerard, H.B. (1955). A study of normative and informational influence upon individual judgement. *Journal of Abnormal and Social Psychology, 51*, 629–636.

Dewar, M.T., Cowan, N., & Della Sala, S. (2007). Forgetting due to retroactive interference: A fusion of Müller and Pilzecker's (1900) early insights into everyday forgetting and recent research on retrograde amnesia. *Cortex, 43*, 616–634.

de Wied, M., Gispen-de-Wied, C., & van Boxtel, A. (2010). Empathy dysfunction in children and adolescents with disruptive behavior disorders. *European Journal of Pharmacology, 626*, 97–103.

De Wolff, M.S., & van IJzendoorn, M.H. (1997). Sensitivity and attachment: A meta-analysis on parental antecedents of infant attachment. *Child Development, 68*, 571–591.

Dhont, K., Roets, A., & Van Hiel, A. (2011). Opening closed minds: The combined effects of intergroup contact and need for closure on prejudice. *Personality and Social Psychology Bulletin, 37*, 514–528.

Dickens, W.T., & Flynn, J.R. (2001). Heritability estimates versus large environmental effects: The

IQ paradox resolved. *Psychological Review, 108,* 346–369.

Dickerson, S.S., & Kemeny, M.E. (2004). Acute stressors and cortisol responses: A theoretical integration and synthesis of laboratory research. *Psychological Bulletin, 130,* 355–391.

Dickinson, A., & Dawson, G.R. (1987). The role of the instrumental contingency in the motivational control of performance. *Quarterly Journal of Experimental Psychology, 39,* 78–94.

Dietrich, A., & Kanso, R. (2010). A review of eEG, ERP, and neuroimaging studies of creativity and insight. *Psychological Bulletin, 138,* 822–848.

Dill, K.E., & Thill, K.P. (2007). Video game characters and the socialization of gender roles: Young people's perceptions mirror sexist media depictions. *Sex Roles, 57,* 851–864.

Dion, K.K., Berscheid, E., & Walster, E. (1972). What is beautiful is good. *Journal of Personality and Social Psychology, 24,* 285–290.

Dionne, G., Dale, P.S., Boivin, M., & Plomin, R. (2003). Genetic evidence for bidirectional effects of early lexical and grammatical development. *Child Development, 74,* 394–412.

Dishion, T.J., & Owen, L.D. (2002). A longitudinal analysis of friendships and substance use: Bidirectional influence from adolescence to adulthood. *Developmental Psychology, 38,* 480–491.

Dishion, T.J., Véronneau, M.-H., & Myers, M.W. (2010). Cascading peer dynamics underlying the progression from problem behavior to violence in early to late adolescence. *Development and Psychopathology, 22,* 603–619.

Distel, M.A., Trull, T.J., Willemsen, G., Vink, J.M., Derom, C.A., Lynsky, M., et al. (2009). The five-factor model of personality and borderline personality disorder: A genetic analysis of comorbidity. *Biological Psychiatry, 66,* 1131–1138.

Dixon, J.A., & Marchman, V.A. (2007). Grammar and the lexicon: Developmental ordering in language acquisition. *Child Development, 78,* 190–212.

Dockrell, J., & Messer, D.J. (1999). *Children's language and communication difficulties: Understanding, identification, and intervention.* London: Cassell.

Dollard, J., Doob, L.W., Miller, N.E., Mowrer, O.H., & Sears, R.R. (1939). *Frustration and aggression.* New Haven, CT: Yale University Press.

Domjan, M. (2005). Pavlovian conditioning: A functional perspective. *Annual Review of Psychology, 56,* 179–206.

Dovidio, J.F., Brigham, J.C., Johnson, B.T., & Gaertner, S. (1996). Stereotyping, prejudice, and discrimination: Another look. In C.N. Macrae, C. Stanger, & M. Hewstone (Eds.), *Stereotypes and stereotyping.* Guilford Press: New York.

Dovidio, J.F., ten Vergert, M., Stewart, T.L., Gaertner, S.L., Johnson, J.D., Esses, V.M., et al. (2004). Perspective and prejudice: Antecedents and mediating mechanisms. *Personality and Social Psychology Bulletin, 30,* 1537–1549.

Dunbar, K., & Blanchette, I. (2001). The in vivo/in vitro approach to cognition: The case of analogy. *Trends in Cognitive Sciences, 5,* 334–339.

Duncker, K. (1945). On problem solving. *Psychological Monographs, 58* (Whole No. 270).

Durkin, K. (1995). *Developmental social psychology: From infancy to old age.* Oxford, UK: Blackwell.

Dzewaltowski, D.A. (1989). Toward a model of exercise motivation. *Journal of Sport & Exercise Psychology, 11,* 251–269.

Eagly, A.H., & Steffen, V.J. (1986). Gender and aggressive behavior: A meta-analytic review of the social psychological literature. *Psychological Bulletin, 100,* 309–330.

Ebbinghaus, H. (1885/1913). *Über das Gedächtnis* (Leipzig: Dunker) [translated by H. Ruyer & C.E. Bussenius]. New York: Teacher College, Columbia University.

Egan, S.K., & Perry, D.G. (2001). Gender identity: A multidimensional analysis with implications for psychosocial adjustment. *Developmental Psychology, 8,* 25–37.

Ekman, P., Friesen, W.V., & Ellsworth, P. (1972). *Emotion in the human face: Guidelines for research and an integration of findings.* New York: Pergamon.

Ekman, P., Friesen, W.V., O'Sullivan, M., Chan, A., Diacoyanni-Tarlatzis, I., Heider, K., et al. (1987). Universals and cultural differences in the judgments of facial expressions of emotion. *Journal of Personality and Social Psychology, 53,* 712–717.

Elder, J.H., & Goldberg, R.M. (2002). Ecological statistics of Gestalt laws for the perceptual organization of contours. *Journal of Vision, 2,* 324–353.

Elicker, J, Englund, M., & Sroufe, L.A. (1992). Predicting peer competence and peer relationships in childhood from early parent–child relationships. In R.D. Parke & G.W. Ladd (Eds.), *Family–peer relationships: Modes of linkage.* Hillsdale, NJ: Lawrence Erlbaum Associates, Inc.

Else-Quest, N.M., Hyde, J.S., Goldsmith, H.H., & Van Hulle, C.A. (2006). Gender differences in temperament: A meta-analysis. *Psychological Bulletin, 132,* 33–72.

Else-Quest, N.M., Hyde, J.S., & Linn, M.C. (2010). Cross-national patterns of gender differences in mathematics: A meta-analysis. *Psychological Bulletin, 136*, 103–127.

Ember, M. (1981). *Statistical evidence for an ecological explanation of warfare*. Paper presented at the 10th annual meeting of the Society for Cross-Cultural Research, Syracuse, NY.

Erb, H-P., Bohner, G., Rank, S., & Einwiller, S. (2002). Processing minority and majority communications: The role of conflict with prior attitudes. *Personality and Social Psychology Bulletin, 28*, 1172–1182.

Erel, O., Oberman, Y., & Yirmiya, N. (2000). Maternal versus nonmaternal care and seven domains of children's development. *Psychological Bulletin, 126*, 727–747.

Ericsson, K.A. (1988). Analysis of memory performance in terms of memory skill. In R.J. Sternberg (Ed.), *Advances in the psychology of human intelligence, Vol. 4* (pp. 137–179). Hillsdale, NJ: Lawrence Erlbaum Associates.

Ericsson, K.A., & Chase, W.G. (1982). Exceptional memory. *American Scientist, 70*, 607–615.

Evans, N., & Levinson, S.C. (2009). The myth of language universals: Language diversity and its importance for cognitive science. *Behavioral and Brain Sciences, 32*, 429–448.

Eysenck, H.J. (1982). *Personality, genetics and behavior*. New York: Praeger.

Eysenck, H.J., & Eysenck, M.W. (1985). *Personality and individual differences*. New York: Plenum.

Eysenck, H.J., & Eysenck, S.B.G. (1975). *Manual of the Eysenck Personality Questionnaire*. London: Hodder and Stoughton.

Eysenck M.W. (1979). Depth, elaboration, and distinctiveness. In L.S. Cermak & F.I.M. Craik (Eds.), *Levels of processing in human memory*. Hillsdale, NJ: Lawrence Erlbaum Associates, Inc.

Eysenck, M.W. (1992). *Anxiety: The cognitive perspective*. Hove, UK: Psychology Press.

Eysenck, M.W. (1997). *Anxiety and cognition: A unified theory*. Hove, UK: Psychology Press.

Eysenck, M.W. (2009a). Anxiety disorders: phobias. In M.W. Eysenck (Ed.), *A2 level psychology*. Hove, UK: Psychology Press.

Eysenck, M.W. (2009b). *Fundamentals of psychology*. Hove, UK: Psychology Press.

Eysenck, M.W. (2012). *Fundamentals of cognition (2nd ed.)*. Hove, UK: Psychology Press.

Eysenck, M.W., Derakshan, N., Santos, R., & Calvo, M.G. (2007). Anxiety and cognitive performance: Attentional control theory. *Emotion, 7*, 336–353.

Eysenck, M.W., & Keane, M.T. (2010). *Cognitive psychology: A student's handbook (6th ed.)*. Hove, UK: Psychology Press.

Fagot, B.I., & Leinbach, M.D. (1989). The young child's gender schema: Environmental input, internal organization. *Child Development, 60*, 663–672.

Fahrenberg, J. (1992). Psychophysiology of neuroticism and anxiety. In A. Gale & M.W. Eysenck (Eds.), *Handbook of individual differences: Biological perspectives*. Chichester, UK: Wiley.

Fehr, E., & Fischbacher, U. (2003). The nature of human altruism. *Nature, 425*, 785–791.

Fehr, E., & Fischbacher, U. (2004). Third-party punishment and social norms. *Evolution and Human Behavior, 25*, 63–87.

Fein, S., Hilton, J.L., & Miller, D.T. (1990). Suspicion of ulterior motivation and the correspondence bias. *Journal of Personality and Social Psychology, 58*, 753–764.

Feingold, A. (1990). Gender differences in effects of physical attractiveness on romantic attraction: A comparison across five research paradigms. *Journal of Personality and Social Psychology, 59*, 981–993.

Feinstein, J.S., Adolphs, R., Damasio, A., & Tranel, D. (2011). The human amygdala and the induction and experience of fear. *Current Biology, 21*, 34–38.

Fellner, C.H., & Marshall, J.R. (1981). Kidney donors revisited. In J.P. Rushton & R.M. Sorrentino (Eds.), *Altruism and helping behavior*. Hillsdale, NJ: Lawrence Erlbaum Associates, Inc.

Fenson, L., Dale, P., Reznick, J., Bates, E., Thal, D., & Pethick, S. (1994). Variability in early communicative development. *Monographs of the Society for Research in Child Development, 59* (5, Serial No. 242).

Fenstermacher, S.K., & Saudino, K.J. (2007). Toddler see, toddler do? Genetic and environmental influences on laboratory-assessed elicited imitation. *Behavior Genetics, 37*, 639–647.

Fernandez-Duque, D., Grossi, G., Thornton, I.M., & Neville, H.J. (2003). Representations of change: Separate electrophysiological marks of attention, awareness, and implicit processing. *Journal of Cognitive Neuroscience, 15*, 491–507.

Fijneman, Y.A., Willemsen, M.E., & Poortinga, Y.H. (1996). Individualism–collectivism: An empirical study of a conceptual issue. *Journal of Cross-Cultural Psychology, 27*, 381–402.

Fischer, P., Krueger, J.I., Greitemeyer, T., Vogrincic, C., Kastenmuller, A., Frey, D., et al. (2011). The bystander effect: A meta-analytic review on bystander intervention in dangerous and non-dangerous emergences. *Psychological Bulletin, 137*, 517–537.

Fischhoff, B., & Beyth, R. (1975). "I knew it would happen" – Remembered probabilities of once-future things. *Organizational Behavior and Human Performance, 13*, 1–16.

Fiske, A.P. (2002). Using individualism and collectivism to compare cultures – A critique of the validity and measurement of the constructs: Comments on Oyserman et al. (2002). *Psychological Bulletin, 128,* 78–88.

Fiske, S.T. (2002). What we know now about bias and intergroup conflict, the problem of the century. *Current Directions in Psychological Science, 11,* 123–128.

Fleeson, W., & Gallagher, W. (2009). The implications of Big Five standing for the distribution of trait manifestation in behavior: Fifteen experience-sampling studies and a meta-analysis. *Journal of Personality and Social Psychology, 97,* 1097–1114.

Flett, G.L., Krames, L., & Vredenburg, K. (2009). Personality traits in clinical depression and remitted depression: An analysis of instrumental-agentic and expressive-communal traits. *Current Psychology, 28,* 240–248.

Flynn, J.R. (1987). Massive IQ gains in 14 nations – What IQ tests really measure. *Psychological Bulletin, 101,* 171–191.

Forsythe, C.J., & Compas, B.E. (1987). Interactions of cognitive appraisals of stressful events and coping: Testing the goodness-of-fit hypothesis. *Cognitive Therapy and Research, 11,* 473–485.

Fortin, M., Voss, P., Lord, C., Lassande, M., Pruessner, J., Saint-Arnour, D., Rainville, C., et al. (2008). Wayfinding in the blind: Large hippocampal volume and supranormal spatial navigation. *Brain, 131,* 2995–3005.

Fraley, R.C., & Spieker, S.J. (2003). Are infant attachment patterns continuously or categorically distributed? A taxometric analysis of Strange Situation behavior. *Developmental Psychology, 39,* 387–404.

Franz, C., Weinberger, J., Kremen, W., & Jacobs, R. (1996). *Childhood antecedents of dysphoria in adults: A 36-year longitudinal study.* Unpublished manuscript, Williams College.

Franzoi, S.L. (1996). *Social psychology.* Madison, WI: Brown & Benchmark.

Friedman, M., & Rosenman, R.H. (1959). Association of specific overt behavior pattern with blood and cardiovascular findings. *Journal of the American Medical Association, 96,* 1286–1296.

Frisén, A., Nordenström, H., Falhammar, H., Filipsson, G., Holmdahl, P.O, Janson, M., et al. (2009). Gender role behavior, sexuality, and psychosocial adaptation in women with congenital adrenal hyperplasia due to CYP21A2 deficiency. *Journal of Clinical Endocrinology and Metabolism, 94,* 3432–3439.

Fumagalli, M., Vergari, M., Pasqualetti, P., Marceglia, S., Mameli, F., Ferrucci, R., et al. (2010). Brain switches utilitarian behavior: Does gender make the difference? *Public Library of Science One,* Jan 25; 5(1): e8865.

Furnham, A. (1981). Personality and activity preference. *British Journal of Social and Clinical Psychology, 20,* 57–68.

Furnham, A. (1988). *Lay theories: Everyday understanding of problems in the social sciences.* Oxford, UK: Pergamon.

Gaab, J., Blatter, N., Menzi, T., Pabst, B., Stoyer, S., & Ehlert, U. (2003). Randomized controlled evaluation of the effects of cognitive-behavioral stress management on cortisol responses to acute stress in healthy subjects. *Psychoneuroendocrinology, 28,* 767–779.

Gaertner, S.L., Rust, M., Dovidio, J.F., Bachman, B., & Anastasio, P. (1994). The contact hypothesis: The role of a common ingroup identity on reducing intergroup bias. *Small Groups Research, 25*(2), 224–249.

Gaffan, E.A., Hansel, M.C., & Smith, L.E. (1983). Does reward depletion influence spatial memory performance? *Learning and Motivation, 14,* 58–74.

Gale, A. (1983). Electroencephalographic studies of extraversion-introversion: A case study in the psychophysiology of individual differences. *Personality and Individual Differences, 4,* 371–380.

Garcia, J., Ervin, F.R., & Koelling, R. (1966). Learning with prolonged delay of reinforcement. *Psychonomic Science, 5,* 121–122.

Gardner, H. (1983). *Frames of mind: The theory of multiple intelligences.* New York: Basic Books.

Gardner, H. (1993). *Creating minds: The anatomy of creativity as seen through Freud, Einstein, Picasso, Stravinsky, Eliot, Graham, and Gandhi.* New York: Basic Books.

Gardner, H., Kornhaber, M.L., & Wake, W.K. (1996). *Intelligence: Multiple perspectives.* Orlando, FL: Harcourt Brace.

Gardner, R.A., & Gardner, B.T. (1969). Teaching sign language to a chimpanzee. *Science, 165,* 664–672.

Gazzaniga, M.S., Ivry, R.B., & Mangun, G.R. (2009). *Cognitive neuroscience: The biology of the mind (2nd ed.).* New York: W.W. Norton.

Geher, G. (2004). *Measuring emotional intelligence: Common ground and controversy.* New York: Nova Science Publishing.

Gentile, D.A., Anderson, C.A., Yukawa, S., Ihori, N., Saleem, M., Ming, L.K., et al. (2009). The effects of prosocial video games on prosocial behaviors: International evidence from correlational, longitudinal, and experimental studies. *Personality and Social Psychology Bulletin, 35,* 752–763.

Geraerts, E., Schooler, J.W., Merckelbach, H., Jelicic, M., Hunter, B.J.A., & Ambadar, Z. (2007). Corroborating continuous and discontinuous memories of childhood sexual abuse. *Psychological Science, 18,* 564–568.

Gergely, G., Bekkering, H., & Kiraly, I. (2002). Rational imitation in preverbal infants. *Nature, 415,* 755.

Gershoff, E.T. (2002). Corporal punishment by parents and associated child behaviors and experiences: A meta-analytic and theoretical review. *Psychological Bulletin, 128,* 539–579.

Gershoff, E.T., Grogan-Kaylor, A., Lansford, J.E., Chang, L., Zelli, A., Deater-Deckard, K., et al. (2010). Parent discipline practices in an international sample: Associations with child behaviors and moderation by perceived normativeness. *Child Development, 81,* 487–502.

Gervain, J., & Mehler, J. (2010). Speech perception and language acquisition in the first year of life. *Annual Review of Psychology, 61,* 191–218.

Ghiselin, B. (1952). *The creative process.* New York: Mentor.

Gick, M.L., & Holyoak, K.J. (1980). Analogical problem solving. *Cognitive Psychology, 12,* 306–355.

Gilbert, D.T. (1995). Attribution and interpersonal perception. In A. Tesser (Ed.), *Advanced social psychology.* New York: McGraw-Hill.

Gilhooly, K.J., & Murphy, P. (2005). Differentiating insight from non-insight problems. *Thinking & Reasoning, 11,* 279–302.

Gilligan, C. (1977). In a different voice: Women's conception of the self and morality. *Harvard Educational Review, 47,* 481–517.

Gilligan, C. (1982). *In a different voice: Psychological theory and women's development.* Cambridge, MA: Harvard University Press.

Gilligan, C., & Wiggins, G. (1987). The origins of morality in early childhood relationships. In J. Kagan & S. Lamb (Eds.), *The emergence of morality in young children.* Chicago: University of Chicago Press.

Girbau, D. (2002). A sequential analysis of private and social speech in children's dyadic communication. *Spanish Journal of Psychology, 5,* 110–118.

Glennerster, A., Tscheang, L., Gilson, S.J., Fitzgibbon, A.W., & Parker, A.J. (2006). Humans ignore motion and stereo cues in favor of a fictional stable world. *Current Biology, 16,* 428–432.

Goldberg, L.R. (1990). An alternative "description of personality": The big-five factor structure. *Journal of Personality and Social Psychology, 59,* 1216–1229.

Goldfarb, W. (1947). Variations in adolescent adjustment of institutionally reared children. *American Journal of Orthopsychiatry, 17,* 499–557.

Goldstein, E.B. (2009). *Sensation and perception (8th ed.).* Belmont, CA: Thomson.

Gollwitzer, P.M. (1999). Implementation intentions. *American Psychologist, 54,* 493–503.

Gollwitzer, P.M., & Brandstätter, V. (1997). Implementation intentions and effective goal pursuit. *Journal of Personality and Social Psychology, 73,* 186–199.

Golombok, S., & Hines, M. (2002). Sex differences in social behavior. In P.K. Smith & C.H. Hart (Eds.), *Blackwell handbook of childhood social development.* Oxford, UK: Blackwell.

Graf, P., & Schacter, D.L. (1985). Implicit and explicit memory for new associations in normal and amnesic subjects. *Journal of Experimental Psychology: Learning, Memory, and Cognition, 11,* 501–518.

Gray, J. (1992). *Men are from Mars, women are from Venus.* New York: HarperCollins.

Greenberg, J.H. (1963). Some universals of grammar with particular reference to the order of meaningful elements. In J.H. Greenberg (Ed.), *Universals of language.* Cambridge, MA: MIT Press.

Greene, J.D., Nystrom, L.E., Engell, A.D., Darley, J.M., & Cohen, J.D. (2004). The neural bases of cognitive conflict and control in moral judgment. *Neuron, 44,* 389–400.

Gregory, R.L. (1970). *The intelligent eye.* New York: McGraw-Hill.

Greitemeyer, T., & Osswald, S. (2010). Effects of prosocial video games on prosocial behavior. *Journal of Personality and Social Psychology, 98,* 211–221.

Griffin, A.M., & Langlois, J.H. (2006). Stereotype directionality and attractiveness stereotyping: Is beauty good or is ugly bad? *Social Cognition, 24,* 187–206.

Grill-Spector, K., & Kanwisher, N. (2005). Visual recognition: As soon as you know it is there, you know what it is. *Psychological Science, 16,* 152–160.

Gross, R. (1996). *Psychology: The science of mind and behavior (3rd ed.).* London: Hodder & Stoughton.

Grossman, K., Grossman, K.E., Spangler, S., Suess, G., & Uzner, L. (1985). Maternal sensitivity and newborn responses as related to quality of attachment in Northern Germany. In J. Bretherton & E. Waters (Eds.), *Growing points of attachment theory. Monographs of the Society for Research in Child Development, 50,* No. 209.

Gudykunst, W.B., Gao, G., & Franklyn-Stokes, A. (1996). Self-monitoring and concern for social appropriateness in China and England. In J. Pandey, D. Sinha, & D.P.S. Bhawk (Eds.), *Asian contributions to cross-cultural psychology.* New Delhi: Sage.

Gueguen, N., Meineri, S., & Charles-Sire, V. (2010). Improving medication adherence by using practitioner nonverbal techniques: A field experiment on the effect of touch. *Journal of Behavioral Medicine, 33,* 466–473.

Guilford, J.P. (1967). *The nature of human intelligence.* New York: McGraw-Hill.

Gunter, B. (2008). Media violence: Is there a case for causality? *American Behavioral Scientist, 51,* 1061–1122.

Hackmann, A., Clark, D.M., & McManus, F. (2000). Recurrent images and early memories in social phobia. *Behaviour Research and Therapy, 38,* 601–610.

Hall, J.E., Sammons, P., Sylva, K., Melhuish, E., Taggart, B., Siraj-Blatchford, I., & Smees, R. (2010). Measuring the combined risk to young children's cognitive development: An alternative to cumulating indices. *British Journal of Developmental Psychology, 28,* 219–238.

Hamann, S.B., & Squire, L.R. (1997). Intact perceptual memory in the absence of conscious memory. *Behavioral Neuroscience, 111,* 850–854.

Haney, C., Banks, C., & Zimbardo, P. (1973). Study of prisoners and guards in a simulated prison. *Naval Research Reviews, 26,* 1–17.

Hardt, O., Einarsson, E.O., & Nader, K. (2010). A bridge over troubled water: Reconsolidation as a link between cognitive and neuroscientific memory research traditions. *Annual Review of Psychology, 61,* 141–167.

Harley, T.A. (2010). *Talking the talk: Language, psychology and science.* Hove, UK: Psychology Press.

Harrison, L.J., & Ungerer, J.A. (2002). Maternal employment and infant–mother attachment security at 12 months. *Developmental Psychology, 38,* 758–773.

Hart, D., Fegley, S., Chan, Y.H., & Mulvey, D. (1993). Judgments about personality identity in childhood and adolescence. *Social Development, 2,* 66–81.

Haslam, S.A., Ryan, M.K., Postmes, T., Spears, R., Jetten, J., & Webley, P. (2006). Sticking to your guns: Social identity as a basis for the maintenance of commitment to faltering organizational projects. *Journal of Organizational Behavior, 27,* 607–628.

Hearold, S. (1986). A synthesis of 1043 effects of television on social behavior. In G. Comstock (Ed.), *Public communication and behavior* (Vol. 1). Orlando, FL: Academic Press.

Heath, R.G. (1964). *The role of pleasure in behavior: A symposium by 22 authors.* New York: Hoeber Medical Division of Harper & Row.

Heider, F. (1958). *The psychology of interpersonal relations.* New York: Wiley.

Heine, S.J., & Buchtel, E.E. (2009). Personality: The universal and the culturally specific. *Annual Review of Psychology, 60,* 369–394.

Heine, S.J., Foster, J.A.B., & Spina, J.-A. (2009). Do birds of a feather flock together? Cultural variation in the similarity-attraction effect. *Asian Journal of Social Psychology, 12,* 247–258.

Heine, S.J., & Hamamura, T. (2007). In search of East Asian self-enhancement. *Personality and Social Psychology Review, 11,* 4–27.

Heine, S.J., Lehman, D.R., Markus, H.R., & Kitayama, S. (1999). Is there a universal need for positive self-regard? *Psychological Review, 106,* 766–794.

Hennessey, B.A., & Amabile, T.M. (2010). Creativity. *Annual Review of Psychology, 61,* 569–598.

Henrich, J., Heine, S.J., & Norenzayan, A. (2010). The weirdest people in the world. *Behavioral and Brain Sciences, 33,* 61–83.

Henrich, J., McElreath, R., Barr, A., Ensminger, J., Barrett, C., Bolyanatz, A., et al. (2006). Costly punishment across human societies. *Science, 312,* 1767–1770.

Hetherington, E.M., Cox, M., & Cox, R. (1982). Effects of divorce on parents and children. In M.E. Lamb (Ed.), *Nontraditional families.* Hillsdale, NJ: Lawrence Erlbaum Associates, Inc.

Hetherington, E.M., & Kelly, J. (2002). *For better or worse: Divorce reconsidered.* New York: W.W. Norton.

Hewstone, M., & Brown, R.J. (1986). *Contact is not enough: An intergroup perspective in intergroup encounters.* Oxford, UK: Blackwell.

Hines, D.A., & Saudino, K.J. (2008). Personality and intimate partner aggression in dating relationships: The role of the "Big Five". *Aggressive Behavior, 34,* 593–604.

Hockett, C.F. (1960). The origin of speech. *Scientific American, 203,* 89–96.

Hodges, B.H., & Geyer, A.L. (2006). A nonconformist account of the Asch experiments: Values, pragmatics, and moral dilemmas. *Personality and Social Psychology Review, 10,* 2–19.

Hodges, J., & Tizard, B. (1989). Social and family relationships of ex-institutional adolescents. *Journal of Child Psychology and Psychiatry, 30,* 53–75.

Hoffman, C., Lau, I., & Johnson, D.R. (1986). The linguistic relatively of person cognition. *Journal of Personality and Social Psychology, 51,* 1097–1105.

Hoffman, M.L. (1970). Moral development. In P.H. Mussen (Ed.), *Carmichael's manual of child psychology, Vol. 2.* New York: Wiley.

Hoffman, M.L. (2001). *Empathy and moral development: Implications for caring and justice.* Cambridge, UK: Cambridge University Press.

Hoffmann, H., Kessler, H., Eppel, T., Rukavina, S., & Traue, H.C. (2010). Expression intensity, gender and facial emotion recognition: Women recognize only subtle facial emotions better than men. *Acta Psychologica, 135,* 278–283.

Hofling, K.C., Brotzman, E., Dalrymple, S., Graves, N., & Pierce, C.M. (1966). An experimental study in the nurse–physician relationship. *Journal of Nervous and Mental Disorders, 143,* 171–180.

Hofstede, G. (1980). *Culture's consequences: International differences in work-related values.* Beverly Hills, CA: Sage.

Hogg, M.A., Turner, J.C., & Davidson, B. (1990). Polarized norms and social frames of reference: A test of the self-categorization theory of group polarization. *Basic and Applied Social Psychology, 11,* 77–100.

Hogg, M.A., & Vaughan, G.M. (2005). *Social psychology (4th ed.).* Harlow, UK: Prentice Hall.

Hohmann, G.W. (1966). Some effects of spinal cord lesions on experienced emotional feelings. *Psychophysiology, 3,* 143–156.

Hollingworth, A., & Henderson, J.M. (2002). Accurate visual memory for previously attended objects in natural scenes. *Journal of Experimental Psychology: Human Perception & Performance, 28,* 113–136.

Hollis, K.L., Pharr, V.L., Dumas, M.J., Britton, G.B., & Field, J. (1997). Classical conditioning provides paternity advantage for territorial male blue gouramis (*Trichogaster trichopterus*). *Journal of Comparative Psychology, 111,* 219–225.

Holmes, T.H., & Rahe, R.H. (1967). The Social Readjustment Rating Scale. *Journal of Psychosomatic Research, 11,* 213–218.

Hong, Y.-Y., Chiu, C.-Y., & Kung, T.M. (1997). Bringing culture out in front: Effects of cultural meaning system activation on social cognition. In K. Leung, Y. Kashinma, U. Kim, & S. Yamaguchi (Eds.), *Progress in Asian social psychology (Vol. 1).* Singapore: Wiley.

House, J.S., Umberson, D., & Landis, K.R. (1988). Structures and processes of social support. *Annual Review of Sociology, 14,* 293–318.

Howe, C.M.L., & Courage, M.L. (1997). The emergence and early development of autobiographical memory. *Psychological Review, 104,* 499–523.

Howe, C.M.L., Courage, M.L., & Edison, S.C. (2003). When autobiographical memory begins. *Developmental Review, 23,* 471–494.

Hughes, M. (1975). *Egocentrism in preschool children.* Unpublished PhD thesis, University of Edinburgh, UK.

Hunt, R.R. (2006). The concept of distinctiveness in memory research. In R.R. Hunt & J.E. Worthen (Eds.), *Distinctiveness and memory* (pp. 3–25). New York: Oxford University Press.

Hunt, R.R., & Smith, R.E. (1996). Accessing the particular from the general: The power of distinctiveness in the context of organization. *Memory & Cognition, 24,* 217–225.

Hunter, J.E. (1986). Cognitive ability, cognitive aptitudes, job knowledge, and job performance. *Journal of Vocational Behavior, 29,* 340–362.

Hupp, J.M., Smith, J.L., Coleman, J.M., & Brunell, A.B. (2010). That's a boy's toy: Gender-typed knowledge in toddlers as a function of mother's marital status. *Journal of Genetic Psychology, 171,* 389–401.

Huston, T.L., Ruggiero, M., Conner, R., & Geis, G. (1981). Bystander intervention into crime: A study based on naturally-occurring episodes. *Social Psychology Quarterly, 44,* 14–23.

Hyde, J.S. (2005). The gender similarities hypothesis. *American Psychologist, 60,* 581–592.

Hyman, I., Boss, S., Wise, B., McKenzie, K., & Caggiano, J. (2009). Did you see the unicycling clown? Inattentional blindness while walking and talking on a cell phone. *Applied Cognitive Psychology, 24,* 597–607.

Ibarra-Rovillard, M.S., & Kuiper, N.A. (2011). Social support and social negativity findings in depression: Perceived responsiveness to basic psychological needs. *Clinical Psychology Review, 31,* 342–352.

Ihlebaek, C., Love, T., Eilertsen, D.E., & Magnussen, S. (2003). Memory for a staged criminal event witnessed live and on video. *Memory, 11,* 310–327.

Imperato-McGinley, J., Guerro, L., Gautier, T., & Peterson, R.E. (1974). Steroid 5-reductase deficiency in man: An inherited form of male pseudohermaphroditism. *Science, 186,* 213–216.

Isenberg, D.J. (1986). Group polarization: A critical review and meta-analysis. *Journal of Personality and Social Psychology, 48,* 1413–1426.

Isurin, L., & McDonald, J.L. (2001). Retroactive interference from translation equivalents: Implications for first language forgetting. *Memory & Cognition, 29,* 312–319.

Jacobs, J. (1887). Experiments on 'prehension'. *Mind, 12,* 75–79.

Jacobs, R.A. (2002). What determines visual cue reliability? *Trends in Cognitive Sciences, 6,* 345–350.

Jacoby, L.L., Debner, J.A., & Hay, J.F. (2001). Proactive interference, accessibility bias, and process dissociations: Valid subjective reports of memory. *Journal of Experimental Psychology: Learning, Memory, and Cognition, 27,* 686–700.

Jaffee, S., & Hyde, J.S. (2000). Gender differences in moral orientation: A meta-analysis. *Psychological Bulletin, 126,* 703–726.

James, W. (1890). *Principles of psychology.* New York: Holt.

Janis, I.L. (1982). *Groupthink (2nd ed.).* Boston: Houghton Mifflin.

John, O.P., Naumann, L.P., & Soto, C.J. (2008). Paradigm shift in the integrative Big Five taxonomy: History, measurement, and conceptual issues. In O.P. John, R.W. Robins, & L.A. Pervin (Eds.), *Handbook of personality: Theory and research (3rd ed.).* New York: Guilford Press.

Johnson, J.G., & Sherman, M.F. (1997). Daily hassles mediate the relationship between major life events and psychiatric symptomatology: Longitudinal findings from an adolescent sample. *Journal of Social and Clinical Psychology, 16,* (4), 389–404.

Johnson, R.D., & Downing, L.L. (1979). Deindividuation and valence of cues: Effects on prosocial and antisocial behavior. *Journal of Personality and Social Psychology, 37,* 1532–1538.

Jones, P.E. (2007). From 'external speech' to 'inner speech' in Vygotsky: A critical appraisal and fresh perspectives. *Language & Communication, 29,* 166–181.

Judge, T.A., Jackson, C.L., Shaw, J.C., Scott, B.A., & Rich, B.L. (2007). Self-efficacy and work-related performance: The integral role of individual differences. *Journal of Applied Psychology, 92,* 10–127.

Kagan, J. (1984). *The nature of the child.* New York: Basic Books.

Kalakoski, V., & Saariluoma, P. (2001). Taxi drivers' exceptional memory of street names. *Memory & Cognition, 29,* 634–638.

Kalat, J.W. (1998). *Biological psychology (6th ed.).* Pacific Grove, CA: Brooks/Cole Publishing Co.

Kalavana, T.V., Maes, S., & De Gucht, V. (2010). Interpersonal and self-regulation determinants of healthy and unhealthy eating behavior in adolescents. *Journal of Health Psychology, 15,* 44–52.

Kamin, L.J. (1969). Predictability, surprise, attention and conditioning. In R. Campbell & R. Church (Eds.), *Punishment and aversive behavior.* New York: Appleton-Century-Crofts.

Kandel, D. (1973). Adolescent marijuana use: Role of parents and peers. *Science, 181,* 1067–1070.

Kanizsa, G. (1976). Subjective contours. *Scientific American, 234,* 48–52.

Karpicke, J.D., Butler, A.C., & Roediger, H.L. (2009). Metacognitive strategies in student learning: Do students practice retrieval when they study on their own? *Memory, 17,* 471–479.

Keane, M. (1987). On retrieving analogues when solving problems. *Quarterly Journal of Experimental Psychology, 39A,* 29–41.

Kelley, M.L., & Power, T.G. (1992). Children's moral understanding: Development and social contextual determinants. In L.T. Winegar & J. Valsiner (Eds.), *Children's development within social context: Vol. 2: Research and methodology.* Hillsdale, NJ: Lawrence Erlbaum Associates, Inc.

Kelly, A.E., & Rodriguez, R.R. (2006). Publicly committing oneself to an identity. *Basic and Applied Social Psychology, 28,* 185–191.

Keltner, D., & Gross, J.J. (1999). Functional accounts of emotions. *Cognition & Emotion, 13,* 467–480.

Kendler, K.S., Kuhn, J., & Prescott, C.A. (2004). The interrelationship of neuroticism, sex, and stressful life events in the prediction of episodes of major depression. *American Journal of Psychiatry, 161,* 631–636.

Kenrick, D.T., & Keefe, R.C. (1992). Age preferences in mates reflect sex-differences in reproductive strategies. *Behavioral and Brain Sciences, 15,* 75–133.

Keogh, E., Bond, F.W., & Flaxman, P.E. (2006). Improving academic performance and mental health through a stress management intervention: Outcomes and mediators of change. *Behaviour Research and Therapy, 44,* 339–357.

Kernis, M.H. (2003). Toward a conceptualization of optimal self-esteem. *Psychological Inquiry, 14,* 1–26.

Ketelaars, M.P., van Weerdenburg, M., Verhoeven, L., Cuperus, J.M., & Jansonius, K. (2010). Dynamics of the theory of mind construct: A developmental perspective. *European Journal of Developmental Psychology, 7,* 85–103.

Kistner, J., Counts-Allan, C., Dunkel, S., Drew, C.D., David-Ferdon, C., & Lopez, C. (2010). Sex differences in relational and overt aggression in the late elementary school years. *Aggressive Behavior, 36,* 282–291.

Kitsantas, A. (2000). The role of self-regulation strategies and self-efficacy perceptions in successful weight loss maintenance. *Psychology and Health, 15,* 811–820.

Klahr, D., & Simon, H.A. (2001). What have psychologists (and others) discovered about the process of scientific discovery? *Current Directions in Psychological Science, 10,* 75–79.

Klein, H.J., Wesson, M.J., Hollenbeck, J.R., & Alge, B.J. (1999). Goal commitment and the goal-setting process: Conceptual clarification and empirical synthesis. *Journal of Applied Psychology, 84,* 885–896.

Klein, J., Frie, K.G., Blum, K., Siegrist, J., & von dem Knesebeck, O. (2010). Effort–reward imbalance, job strain and burnout among clinicians in surgery. *Psychotherapie Psychosomatik Medizinische Psychologie, 60,* 374–379.

Knafo, A., Israel, S., & Ebstein, R.P. (2011). Heritability of children's prosocial behavior and differential sensitivity to parenting by variation in the dopamine receptor D4 gene. *Development and Psychopathology, 23,* 53–67.

Knafo, A., Zahn-Waxler, C., Van Hulle, C., Robinson, J.L., & Rhee, S.H. (2008). The developmental origins of a disposition toward empathy: Genetic and environmental contributions. *Emotion, 8,* 737–752.

Knappe, S., Beesdo, K., Fehm, L., Hofler, M., Lieb, R., & Wittchen, H.-U. (2009). Do parental psychopathology and unfavorable family environment predict the persistence of social phobia? *Journal of Anxiety Disorders, 23,* 986–994.

Knowles, E.D., Morris, M.W., Chiu, C.Y., & Hong, Y.Y. (2001). Culture and the process of person perception: Evidence for automaticity among East Asians in correcting for situational influences on behavior. *Personality and Social Psychology Bulletin, 27,* 1344–1356.

Knowlton, B.J., & Foerde, K. (2008). Neural representations of nondeclarative memories. *Current Directions in Psychological Science, 17,* 107–111.

Kochanska, G., Aksan, N., Prisco, T.R., & Adams, E.E. (2008). Mother–child and father–child mutually responsive orientation in the first 2 years and children's outcomes at preschool age: Mechanisms of influence. *Child Development, 79,* 30–44.

Kohlberg, L. (1963). Development of children's orientations toward a moral order. *Vita Humana, 6,* 11–36.

Kohlberg, L. (1966). A cognitive-development analysis of children's sex-role concepts and attitudes. In E.E. Maccoby (Ed.), *The development of sex differences.* Stanford, CA: Stanford University Press.

Kohlberg, L. (1975). The cognitive-developmental approach to moral education. *Phi Delta Kappa, June,* 670–677.

Kohlberg, L. (1981). *Essays on moral development: Vol. 1. The philosophy of moral development.* San Francisco: Harper & Row.

Koluchová, J. (1976). The further development of twins after severe and prolonged deprivation: A second report. *Journal of Child Psychology and Psychiatry, 50,* 441–469.

Koole, S. (2009). The psychology of emotion regulation: An integrative review. *Cognition & Emotion, 23,* 4–41.

Korchmaros, J.D., & Kenny, D.A. (2001). Emotional closeness as a mediator of the effect of genetic relatedness on altruism. *Psychological Science, 12,* 262–265.

Kosslyn, S.M. (1994). *Image and brain: The resolution of the imagery debate.* Cambridge, MA: MIT Press.

Kosslyn, S.M., & Thompson, W.L. (2003). When is early visual cortex activated during visual mental imagery? *Psychological Bulletin, 129,* 723–746.

Kotov, R., Gamez, W., Schmidt, F., & Watson, D. (2010). Linking "big" personality traits to anxiety, depressive, and substance use disorders: A meta-analysis. *Psychological Bulletin, 136,* 768–821.

Kowalski, K. (2007). The development of social identity and social intergroup attitudes in young children. In O.N. Saracho & B. Spodek (Eds.), *Contemporary perspectives in social learning in early childhood education* (pp. 51–84). Charlotte, NC: Inform Age Publ.

Krevans, J., & Gibbs, J.C. (1996). Parents' use of inductive discipline: Relations to children's empathy and prosocial behavior. *Child Development, 67,* 3263–3277.

Króliczak, G., Heard, P., Goodale, M.A., & Gregory, R.L. (2006). Dissociation of perception and action unmasked by the hollow-face illusion. *Brain Research, 1080,* 9–16.

Krueger, J., & Clement, R.W. (1994). The truly false consensus effect: An eradicable and egocentric bias in social perception. *Journal of Personality and Social Psychology, 67,* 596–610.

Krueger, R.F., Hicks, B.M., & McGue, M. (2001). Altruism and antisocial behavior: Independent tendencies, unique personality correlates, distinct etiologies. *Psychological Science, 12,* 397–402.

Krull, D.S., Seger, C.R., & Silvera, D.H. (2008). Smile when you say that: Effects of willingness on dispositional inferences. *Journal of Experimental Social Psychology, 44,* 735–742.

Kulkarni, D., & Simon, H.A. (1988). The processes of scientific discovery – The strategy of experimentation. *Cognitive Science, 12,* 139–175.

Kumsta, R., Kreppner, J., Rutter, M., Beckett, C., Castle, J., Stevens, S., et al. (2010). Deprivation-specific psychological patterns. *Monographs of the Society for Research in Child Development, 75,* 48–78.

Kuper, H., Singha-Manoux, A., Siegrist, J., et al. (2002). When reciprocity fails: Effort–reward imbalance in relation to coronary heart disease and health functioning within the Whitehall II study. *Occupational and Environmental Medicine, 59,* 777–784.

Kuppens, P., van Mechelen, I., Smits, D.J.M., & de Boeck, P. (2003). The appraisal basis of anger:

Specificity, necessity and sufficiency of components. *Emotion*, 3, 254–269.

Kurtz, K.J., & Loewenstein, J. (2007). Converging on a new role for analogy in problem solving and retrieval: When two problems are better than one. *Memory & Cognition*, 35, 334–341.

La Freniere, P.J., Strayer, F.F., & Gauthier, R. (1984). The emergence of same-sex affiliative preferences among preschool peers: A developmental/ethological perspective. *Child Development*, 55, 1958–1965.

Lamm, H., & Trommsdorff, G. (1973). Group versus individual performance on tasks requiring ideational proficiency (brainstorming) – Review. *European Journal of Social Psychology*, 3, 361–388.

Langlois, J.H., Kalakanis, L., Rubenstein, A.J., Larson, A., Hallam, M., & Smoot, M. (2000). Maxims or myths of beauty? A meta-analysis and theoretical review. *Psychological Review*, 126, 390–423.

Lansford, J.E. (2009). Parental divorce and children's adjustment. *Perspectives on Psychological Science*, 4, 140–152.

Larson, J.R., Foster-Fishman, P.G., & Keys, C.B. (1994). Discussion of shared and unshared information in decision-making groups. *Journal of Personality and Social Psychology*, 67, 446–461.

Latham, G.P. (2003). Toward a boundaryless psychology. *Canadian Psychologist*, 44, 216–217.

Latham, G.P., & Brown, T.C. (2006). The effect of learning vs. outcome goals on self-efficacy and satisfaction in an MBA program. *Applied Psychology: An International Review*, 55, 606–623.

Latham, G.P., & Locke, E.A. (2007). New developments in and directions for goal-setting research. *European Psychologist*, 12(4), 290–300.

Lavric, A., Forstmeier, S., & Rippon, G. (2000). Differences in working memory involvement in analytical and creative tasks: An ERP study. *Neuroreport*, 11, 1613–1618.

Lazarus, R.S. (1982). Thoughts on the relation between emotion and cognition. *American Psychologist*, 37, 1019–1024.

Leary, M.R., & Downs, D.L. (1995). Interpersonal functions of the self-esteem motive: The self-esteem system as a sociometer. In M.H. Kernis (Ed.), *Efficacy, agency, and self-esteem*. New York: Plenum.

Leary, M.R., Haupt, A.L., Strausser, K.S., & Chokel, J.T. (1998). Calibrating the sociometer: The relationship between interpersonal appraisals and state self-esteem. *Journal of Personality and Social Psychology*, 74, 1290–1299.

Le Bon, G. (1895). *The crowd*. London: Ernest Benn.

Lee, S.W.S., Oyserman, D., & Bond, M.H. (2010). Am I doing better than you? That depends on whether you ask me in English or Chinese: Self-enhancement effects of language as a cultural mindset prime. *Journal of Experimental Social Psychology*, 46, 785–791.

Lee, W.E., Wadsworth, M.E.J., & Hotop, M. (2006). The protective role of trait anxiety: A longitudinal cohort study. *Psychological Medicine*, 36, 345–351.

Lefkowitz, E.S., & Zeldow, P.B. (2006). Masculinity and femininity predict optimal mental health: A belated test of the androgyny hypothesis. *Journal of Personality Assessment*, 87, 95–101.

Lesar, T.S., Briceland, I., & Stein, D.S. (1997). Factors related to errors in medication prescribing. *Journal of the American Medical Association*, 277, 312–317.

Levenson, R.W. (1999). The intrapersonal functions of emotions. *Cognition & Emotion*, 13, 481–504.

Levenson, R.W., Ekman, P., & Friesen, W.V. (1990). Voluntary action generates emotion-specific autonomic nervous-system activity. *Psychophysiology*, 27, 363–384.

Levin, D.T., Drivdahl, S.B., Momen, N., & Beck, M.R. (2002). False predictions about the detectability of visual changes: The role of beliefs about attention, memory, and the continuity of attended objects in causing change blindness blindness. *Consciousness and Cognition*, 11, 507–527.

Levine, M. (2002). *Walk on by?* [Relational Justice Bulletin]. Cambridge, UK: Relationships Foundation.

Levine, M., & Crowther, S. (2008). The responsive bystander: How social group membership and group size can encourage as well as inhibit bystander intervention. *Journal of Personality and Social Psychology*, 95, 1429–1439.

Levy, J., Trevarthen, C., & Sperry, R.W. (1972). Perception of bilateral chimeric figures following hemispheric deconnection. *Brain*, 95, 61–78.

Lewis, M., & Brooks-Gunn, J. (1979). *Social cognition and the acquisition of self*. New York: Plenum Press.

Leyens, J.P., Camino, L., Parke, R.D., & Berkowitz, L. (1975). Effects of movie violence on aggression in a field setting as a function of group dominance and cohesion. *Journal of Personality and Social Psychology*, 32, 346–360.

Lief, H., & Fetkewicz, J. (1995). Retractors of false memories: The evolution of pseudo-memories. *The Journal of Psychiatry & Law*, 23, 411–436.

Lin, S., Keysar, B., & Epley, N. (2010). Reflexively mindblind: Using theory of mind to interpret behavior requires effortful attention. *Journal of Experimental Social Psychology*, 46, 551–556.

Lindquist, K.A., Wager, T.D., Kober, H., Bliss-Moreau, E., & Barrett, L.F. (2012). The brain basis of emotion: A meta-analytic review. *Behavioral and Brain Sciences*, 35, 121–202.

Lindsay, R.C.L., Ross, D.F., Read, J.D., & Toglia, M.P. (Eds.) (2007). *The handbook of eyewitness psychology: Volume II: Memory for people.* Mahwah, NJ: Lawrence Erlbaum Associates, Inc.

Lippa, R.A., Collaer, M.L., & Peters, M. (2010). Sex differences in mental rotation and line angle judgments are positively associated with gender equality and economic development across 53 nations. *Journal of Sexual Behavior, 39,* 990–997.

Lipset, S.M. (1996). *American exceptionalism: A double-edged sword.* New York: W.W. Norton.

Lisle, A.M. (2007). Assessing learning styles of adults with intellectual difficulties. *Journal of Intellectual Disabilities, 11,* 23–45.

Liu, L.L., Uttal, D.H., Marulis, L.M., & Newcombe, N.S. (2008). *Training spatial skills: What works, for whom, why and for how long?* Poster presented at the 20th annual meeting of the Association for Psychological Science, Chicago.

Lo, C., Helwig, C.C., Chen, S.X., Ohashi, M.M., & Cheng, C.M. (2011). The psychology of strengths and weaknesses: Assessing self-enhancing and self-critical tendencies in Eastern and Western cultures. *Self and Identity, 10,* 203–212.

Locke, E.A. (1968). Toward a theory of task motivation and incentives. *Organizational Behavior and Human Performance, 3,* 157–189.

Loehlin, J.C., McCrae, R.R., Costa, P.T., & John, O.P. (1998). Heritabilities of common and measure-specific components of the Big Five personality factors. *Journal of Research in Personality, 32,* 431–453.

Loehlin, J.C., & Nichols, R.C. (1976). *Heredity, environment, and personality: A study of 850 sets of twins.* Austin, TX: University of Texas Press.

Loftus, E.F., & Davis, D. (2006). Recovered memories. *Annual Review of Clinical Psychology, 2,* 469–498.

Loftus, E.F., Loftus, G.R., & Messo, J. (1987). Some facts about "weapons focus". *Law and Human Behavior, 11,* 55–62.

Loftus, E.F., & Palmer, J.C. (1974). Reconstruction of automobile destruction: An example of the interaction between language and memory. *Journal of Verbal Learning and Verbal Behavior, 13,* 585–589.

Loftus, E.F., & Zanni, G. (1975). Eyewitness testimony – Influence of wording of a question. *Bulletin of the Psychonomic Society, 5,* 86–88.

Lopes, P.N., Brackett, M.A., Nezlek, J.B., Schutz, A., Sellin, I., & Salovey, P. (2004). Emotional intelligence and social interaction. *Personality and Social Psychology Bulletin, 30,* 1018–1034.

Love, J.M., Harrison, L., Sagi-Schwartz, A, van IJzendoorn, M.H., Ross, C., Ungerer, J.A., et al.

(2003). Child care quality matters: How conclusions may vary with context. *Child Development, 74,* 1021–1033.

Lovibond, P.F. (2006). Fear and avoidance: An integrated expectancy model. In M.G. Craske, D. Hermans, & D. Vansteenwegen (Eds.), *Fear and learning: From basic processes to clinical implications.* Washington, DC: American Psychological Association.

Low, J., & Hollis, S. (2003). The eyes have it: Development of children's generative thinking. *International Journal of Behavioral Development, 27,* 97–108.

Lucas-Thompson, R.G., Goldberg, W.A., & Prause, J.A. (2010). Maternal work early in the lives of children and its distal associations with achievement and behavior problems: A meta-analysis. *Psychological Bulletin, 136,* 915–942.

Luchins, A.S. (1942). Mechanization in problem solving: The effect of Einstellung. *Psychological Monographs, 54,* 248.

Luckow, A., Reifman, A., & McIntosh, D.N. (1998). *Gender differences in caring: A meta-analysis.* Poster presented at 106th annual convention of the American Psychological Association, San Francisco.

Lundahl, B., Risser, H.J., & Lovejoy, M.C. (2006). A meta-analysis of parent training: Moderators and follow-up effects. *Clinical Psychology Review, 26,* 86–104.

Luo, S.H., & Zhang, G.J. (2009). What leads to romantic attraction: Similarity, reciprocity, security, or beauty? Evidence from a speed-dating study. *Journal of Personality, 77,* 933–964.

Lustig, C., Konkel, A., & Jacoby, L.L. (2004). Which route to recovery? Controlled retrieval and accessibility bias in retroactive interference. *Psychological Science, 15,* 729–735.

Lykken, D.T., & Tellegen, A. (1993). Is human mating adventitious or the result of lawful choice – A twin study of mate selection. *Journal of Personality and Social Psychology, 65,* 56–68.

Lyn, H. (2007). Mental representation of symbols as revealed by vocabulary errors in two bonobos (*Pan paniscus*). *Animal Cognition, 10,* 461–475.

Mackintosh, N.J. (1975). A theory of attention: Variations in the accessibility of stimuli with reinforcement. *Psychological Review, 82,* 276–298.

Mackintosh, N.J. (1998). *IQ and human intelligence.* Oxford: Oxford University Press.

Madsen, E.A., Tunney, R.J., Fieldman, G., Plotkin, H.C., Dunbar, R.I.M., Richardson, J.M., et al. (2007). Kinship and altruism: A cross-cultural experimental study. *British Journal of Psychology, 98,* 339–359.

Main, M., Kaplan, N., & Cassidy, J. (1985). Security in infancy, childhood, and adulthood: A move to the level of representation. In I. Bretherton & E. Waters (Eds.), Growing points of attachment theory and research. *Monographs of the Society for Research in Child Development, 50* (1–2).

Mainous, A.G., Everett, C.J., Diaz, V.A., Player, M.S., Gebregziabher, M., & Smith, D.W. (2010). Life stress and atheriosclerosis: A pathway through unhealthy lifestyle. *International Journal of Psychiatry in Medicine, 40,* 147–161.

Mann, L. (1981). The baiting crowd in episodes of threatened suicide. *Journal of Personality and Social Psychology, 41,* 703–709.

Mares, M.L., & Woodard, E. (2005). Positive effects of television on children's social interactions: A meta-analysis. *Media Psychology, 7,* 301–322.

Markus, H.R., & Kitayama, S. (1991). Culture and the self: Implications for cognition, emotion and motivation. *Psychological Review, 98,* 224–253.

Marlowe, F.W., & Berbesque, J.C. (2007). More 'altruistic' punishment in larger societies. *Proceedings of the Royal Society B, 275,* 587–590.

Marmot, M.G., Bosma, H., Hemingway, H., Brunner, E., & Stansfeld, S. (1997). Contribution of job control and other risk factors to social variations in coronary heart disease incidence. *Lancet, 350,* 235–239.

Marsh, E.J., & Tversky, B. (2004). Spinning the stories of our lives. *Applied Cognitive Psychology, 18,* 491–503.

Martin, C.L., & Halverson, C.F. (1987). The roles of cognition in sex role acquisition. In D.B. Carter (Ed.), *Current conceptions of sex roles and sex typing: Theory and research.* New York: Praeger.

Martin, C.L., & Ruble, D.N. (2009). Patterns of gender development. *Annual Review of Psychology, 61,* 353–381.

Martin, C.L., Ruble, D.N., & Szkrybalo, J. (2004). Recognizing the centrality of gender identity and stereotype knowledge in gender development and moving toward theoretical integration: Reply to Bandura and Bussey (2004). *Psychological Bulletin, 130,* 702–710.

Martin, C.L., Wood, C.H., & Little, J.K. (1990). The development of gender stereotype components. *Child Development, 61,* 1891–1904.

Martin, R.A. (1989). Techniques for data acquisition and analysis in field investigations of stress. In R.W.J. Neufeld (Ed.), *Advances in the investigation of psychological stress.* New York: Wiley.

Martinez, A., Anllo-Vento, L., Sereno, M.I., Frank, L.R., Buxton, R.B., Dubowitz, D.J., et al. (1999). Involvement of striate and extrastriate visual cortical areas in spatial attention. *Nature Neuroscience, 4,* 364–369.

Mason, J.W. (1975). A historical view of the stress field. *Journal of Human Stress, 1,* 22–36.

Massen, C., & Vaterrodt-Plünnecke, B. (2006). The role of proactive interference in mnemonic techniques. *Memory, 14,* 89–96.

Massen, C., Vaterrodt-Plünnecke, B., Krings, L., & Hilbig, B.E. (2009). Effects of instruction on learners' ability to generate an effective pathway in the method of loci. *Memory, 17,* 724–731.

Mather, G. (2009). *Foundations of sensation and perception (2nd ed.).* Hove, UK: Psychology Press.

Matsumoto, D. (2009). Facial expression of emotion. In D. Sander & K.R. Scherer (Eds.), *The Oxford companion to emotion and the affective states* (pp. 175–176). Oxford: Oxford University Press.

Matt, G.E., & Navarro, A.M. (1997). What meta-analyses have and have not taught us about psychotherapy effects: A review and future directions. *Clinical Psychology Review, 17,* 1–32.

Matthews, D., Lieven, E., Theakston, A., & Tomasello, M. (2005). The role of frequency in the acquisition of English word order. *Cognitive Development, 20,* 121–136.

Matthews, K.A. (1988). Coronary heart disease and Type A behavior: Update on an alternative to the Booth-Kewley and Friedman (1987) quantitative review. *Psychological Bulletin, 104,* 373–380.

Matthews, K.A., Glass, D.C., Rosenman, R.H., & Bortner, R.W. (1977). Competitive drive, Pattern A, and coronary heart disease: A further analysis of some data from the Western Collaborative Group. *Journal of Chronic Diseases, 30,* 489–498.

Mayer, J.D., Salovey, P., Caruso, D.R., & Sitarenios, G. (2003). Measuring emotional intelligence with the MSCEIT V2.0. *Emotion, 3,* 97–105.

Mayer, R.E. (1990). Problem solving. In M.W. Eysenck (Ed.), *The Blackwell dictionary of cognitive psychology.* Oxford: Blackwell.

McCartney, K., Harris, M.J., & Bernieri, F. (1990). Growing up and growing apart: A developmental meta-analysis of twin studies. *Psychological Bulletin, 107,* 226–237.

McCauley, C., & Stitt, C.L. (1978). An individual and quantitative measure of stereotypes. *Journal of Personality and Social Psychology, 36,* 929–940.

McCourt, K., Bouchard, T.J., Lykken, D.T., Tellegen, A., & Keyes, M. (1999). Authoritarianism revisited: Genetic and environmental influences examined in twins reared apart and together. *Personality and Individual Differences, 27,* 985–1014.

McCrae, R.R., & Costa, P.T. (1985). Updating Norman's "adequate taxonomy": Intelligence and personality dimensions in natural language and in questionnaires. *Journal of Personality and Social Psychology, 49*, 710–721.

McCrae, R.R., & Costa, P.T. (1990). *Personality in adulthood*. New York: Guilford Press.

McGarrigle, J., & Donaldson, M. (1974). Conservation accidents. *Cognition, 3*, 341–350.

McGuire, J. (2008). A review of effective interventions for reducing aggression and violence. *Philosophical Transactions of the Royal Society B, 363*, 2577–2597.

McPherson, F. (2004). *The memory key: Unlock the secrets to remembering*. New York: Barnes & Noble.

Mehta, P.H., & Beer, J. (2009). Neural mechanisms of the testosterone-aggression relation: The role of orbitofrontal cortex. *Journal of Cognitive Neuroscience, 22*, 2357–2368.

Meichenbaum, D. (1985). *Stress inoculation training*. New York: Pergamon.

Menzies, R.G., & Clarke, J.C. (1993). The etiology of childhood water phobia. *Behaviour Research and Therapy, 31*, 499–501.

Metcalfe, J., & Kornell, N. (2007). Principles of cognitive science in education: The effects of generation, errors, and feedback. *Psychonomic Bulletin & Review, 14*, 225–229.

Metcalfe, J., & Wiebe, D. (1987). Intuition in insight and noninsight problem solving. *Memory & Cognition, 15*, 238–246.

Mezulis, A.H., Abramson, L.Y., Hyde, J.S., & Hankin, B.L. (2004). Is there a universal positivity bias in attributions? A meta-analytic review of individual, developmental. and cultural differences in the self-serving attributional bias. *Psychological Bulletin, 130*, 711–747.

Mickelson, K., Kessler, R.C., & Shaver, P. (1997). Adult attachment in a nationally representative sample. *Journal of Personality and Social Psychology, 73*, 1092–1106.

Miele, F. (2002). *Intelligence, race, and genetics: Conversations with Arthur R. Jensen*. Boulder, CO: Westview.

Miles, D.R., & Carey, G. (1997). Genetic and environmental architecture of human aggression. *Journal of Personality and Social Psychology, 72*, 207–217.

Milgram, S. (1974). *Obedience to authority*. New York: Doubleday.

Miller, G.A. (1956). The magic number seven, plus or minus two: Some limits on our capacity for processing of information. *Psychological Review, 63*, 81–93.

Miller, N.E. (1941). The frustration-aggression hypothesis. *Psychological Review, 48*, 337–342.

Milner, A.D., & Goodale, M.A. (2008). Two visual systems re-viewed. *Neuropsychologia, 46*, 774–785.

Mols, F., & Denollet, J. (2010). Type D personality in the general population: A systematic review of health status, mechanisms of disease, and work-related problems. *Health and Quality of Life Outcomes, 8*, Article no. 9.

Monat, A., & Lazarus, R.S. (Eds.) (1991). *Stress and coping: An anthology (3rd ed.)*. New York: Columbia University Press.

Montoya, R.M., Horton, R.S., & Kirchner, J. (2008). Is actual similarity necessary for attraction? A meta-analysis of actual and perceived similarity. *Journal of Social and Personal Relationships, 25*, 889–922.

Morris, C.D., Bransford, J.D., & Franks, J.J. (1977). Levels of processing versus transfer appropriate processing. *Journal of Verbal Learning and Verbal Behavior, 16*, 519–533.

Morris, P.E., Jones, S., & Hampson, P. (1978). An imagery mnemonic for the learning of people's names. *British Journal of Psychology, 69*, 335–336.

Morris, P.E., Fritz, C.O., Jackson, L., Nichol, E., & Roberts, E. (2005). Strategies for learning proper names: Expanding retrieval practice, meaning and imagery. *Applied Cognitive Psychology, 19*, 779–798.

Morris, P.E., & Reid, R.L. (1970). Repeated use of mnemonic imagery. *Psychonomic Science, 20*, 337–338.

Moscovici, S. (1980). Toward a theory of conversion behavior. In L. Berkowitz (Ed.), *Advances in experimental social psychology, Vol. 13*. New York: Academic Press.

Moss, E. (1992). The socioaffective context of joint cognitive activity. In L.T. Winegar & J. Valsiner (Eds.), *Children's development within social context: Vol. 2*. Hillsdale, NJ: Lawrence Erlbaum Associates, Inc.

Mowrer, O.H. (1947). On the dual nature of learning: A reinterpretation of "conditioning" and "problem-solving". *Harvard Educational Review, 17*, 102–148.

Mullen, B., Brown, R., & Smith, C. (1992). Ingroup bias as a function of salience, relevance, and status: An integration. *European Journal of Social Psychology, 22*, 103–122.

Mutter, B., Alcorn, M.B., & Welsh, M. (2006). Theory of mind and executive function: Working-memory capacity and inhibitory control as predictors of false-belief performance. *Psychological Reports, 102*, 819–835.

Myrtek, M. (2001). Meta-analyses of prospective studies on coronary heart disease, type A personality, and hostility. *International Journal of Cardiology, 79*, 245–251.

National Institute of Child Health and Development (NICHD) Early Child Care Research Network (2003). Does quality of child care affect child outcomes at age 4½? *Developmental Psychology, 39*, 451–469.

Nemeth, C., Mayseless, O., Sherman, J., & Brown, Y. (1990). Exposure to dissent and recall of information. *Journal of Personality and Social Psychology, 58*, 429–437.

Newell, A., & Simon, H.A. (1972). *Human problem solving.* Englewood Cliffs, NJ: Prentice Hall.

Norton, M.I., Frost, J.H., & Ariely, D. (2011). Does familiarity breed contempt or liking? Comment on Reis, Maniaci, Caprariello, Eastwick, and Finkel (2011). *Journal of Personality and Social Psychology, 101*, 571–574.

Oakes, P.J., Haslam, S.A., & Turner, J.C. (1994). *Stereotyping and social reality.* Malden, MA: Blackwell.

Oatley, K., & Johnson-Laird, P.N. (1987). Towards a cognitive theory of emotions. *Cognition & Emotion, 1*, 29–50.

Ochs, E., & Schieffelin, B. (1995). The impact of language socialization on grammatical development. In P. Fletcher & B. MacWhinney (Eds.), *Handbook of child language* (pp. 73–94). Oxford: Blackwell.

Ochsner, K.N., & Gross, J.J. (2008). Cognitive emotion regulation: Insights from social cognitive and affective neuroscience. *Current Directions in Psychological Science, 17*, 153–158.

O'Connor, T.G., Caspi, A., DeFries, J.C., & Plomin, R. (2003). Genotype–environment interaction in children's adjustment to parental separation. *Journal of Child Psychology and Psychiatry, 44*, 849–856.

O'Connor, T.G., & Croft, C.M. (2001). A twin study of attachment in pre-school children. *Child Development, 72*, 1501–1511.

O'Connor, T.G., Rutter, M., Beckett, C., Keaveney, L., Kreppner, J.M., and the English and Romanian Adoptees Study Team (2000). The effects of global severe privation on cognitive competence: Extension and longitudinal follow-up. *Child Development, 71*, 376–390.

O'Connor, T.G., Thorpe, K., Dunn, J., & Golding, J. (1999). Parental divorce and adjustment in adulthood: Findings from a community sample. *Journal of Child Psychology and Psychiatry, 40*, 777–789.

Ohlsson, S. (1992). Information processing explanations of insight and related phenomena. In M.T. Keane & K.J. Gilhooly (Eds.), *Advances in the psychology of thinking.* London: Harvester Wheatsheaf.

Oishi, S., Diener, E., Scollon, C.N., & Biswas-Diener, R. (2004). Cross-situational consistency of affective experiences across cultures. *Journal of Personality and Social Psychology, 86*, 460–472.

Olds, J., & Milner, P. (1954). Positive reinforcement produced by electrical stimulation of septal areas and other regions of rat brains. *Journal of Comparative and Physiological Psychology, 47*, 419–427.

O'Neill, D.K. (1996). Two-year-old children's sensitivity to parent's knowledge state when making requests. *Child Development, 67*, 659–677.

Orne, M.T. (1962). On the social psychology of the psychological experiment: With particular reference to demand characteristics and their implications. *American Psychologist, 17*, 776–783.

Ortner, T.M., & Sieverding, M. (2008). Where are the gender differences? Male priming boosts spatial skills in women. *Sex Roles, 59*, 274–281.

Ostojic, P., & Phillips, J.G. (2009). Memorability of alternative password systems. *International Journal of Pattern Recognition and Artificial Intelligence, 23*, 987–1004.

Owusu-Bempah, P., & Howitt, D. (1994). Racism and the psychological textbook. *The Psychologist, 7*, 163–166.

Oyserman, D., Coon, H.M., & Kemmelmeier, M. (2002). Rethinking individualism and collectivism: Evaluation of theoretical assumptions and meta-analyses. *Psychological Bulletin, 128*, 3–72.

Panksepp, J. (2000). Emotions as natural kinds within the mammalian brain. In M. Lewis & J.M. Howland-Jones (Eds.), *Handbook of emotions (2nd ed.).* New York: Guilford Press.

Panksepp, J. (2007). Neurologizing the psychology of affects: How appraisal-based constructionism and basic emotion theory can coexist. *Perspectives on Psychological Science, 2*, 281–296.

Parke, R.D., & Slaby, R.G. (1983). The development of aggression. In P.H. Mussen (Ed.), *Handbook of child psychology, Vol. IV (4th ed.).* New York: Wiley.

Pass, J.A., Lindenberg, S.M., & Park, J.H. (2010). All you need is love: Is the sociometer especially sensitive to one's mating capacity? *European Journal of Social Psychology, 40*, 221–234.

Pasterski, M.E., Geffner, C., Brain, P., Hindmarsh, C., & Hines, M. (2005). Hormone-behavior associations in early infancy. *Hormones and Behavior, 56,* 498–502.

Pastore, N. (1952). The role of arbitrariness in the frustration-aggression hypothesis. *Journal of Abnormal and Social Psychology, 47,* 728–731.

Pasupathi, M., & Wainryb, C. (2010). On telling the whole story: Facts and interpretations in autobiographical memory narratives from childhood through mid-adolescence. *Developmental Psychology, 46,* 735–746.

Patenaude, J., Niyonsenga, T., & Fafard, D. (2003). Changes in students' moral development during medical school: A cohort study. *Canadian Medical Association Journal, 168,* 840–844.

Patterson, G.R. (1982). *Coercive family processes.* Eugene, OR: Castalia.

Patterson, G.R., DeBaryshe, B.D., & Ramsey, E. (1989). A developmental perspective on antisocial behavior. *American Psychologist, 44,* 329–335.

Patterson, G.R., Reid, J.B., & Dishion, T.J. (1992). *Antisocial boys.* Eugene, OR: Castalia Press.

Patterson, K., Nestor, P.J., & Rogers, T.T. (2007). Where do you know what you know? The representation of semantic knowledge in the human brain. *Nature Reviews Neuroscience, 8,* 976–987.

Paunonen, S.V. (2003). Big Five factors of personality and replicated predictions of behavior. *Journal of Personality and Social Psychology, 84,* 411–424.

Payne, B.K. (2001). Prejudice and perception: The role of automatic and controlled processes in misperceiving a weapon. *Journal of Personality and Social Psychology, 81,* 181–192.

Pedersen, N.L., Plomin, R., McClearn, G.E., & Friberg, L. (1988). Neuroticism, extraversion, and related traits in adult twins reared apart and reared together. *Journal of Personality and Social Psychology, 55,* 950–957.

Pegna, A.J., Khateb, A., Lazeyras, F., & Seghier, M.L. (2005). Discriminating emotional faces without primary visual cortices involves the right amygdala. *Nature Neuroscience, 8,* 24–25.

Peissig, J.J., & Tarr, M.J. (2007). Visual object recognition: Do we know more now than we did 20 years ago? *Annual Review of Psychology, 58,* 75–96.

Pellicano, E. (2010). Individual differences in executive function and central coherence predict developmental changes in theory of mind in autism. *Developmental Psychology, 46,* 530–544.

Penley, J.A., Tomaka, J., & Wiebe, J.S. (2002). The association of coping to physical and psychological health outcomes: A meta-analytic review. *Journal of Behavioral Medicine, 25,* 551–603.

Perry, D.G., & Bussey, K. (1979). The social learning theory of sex differences: Imitation is alive and well. *Journal of Personality and Social Psychology, 37,* 1699–1712.

Peterson, R.S., Owens, P.D., Tetlock, P.E., Fan, E.T., & Martorana, P. (1998). Group dynamics in top management teams: Groupthink, vigilance, and alternative models of organizational failure and success. *Organizational Behavior and Human Decision Processes, 73,* 272–305.

Pettigrew, T.F. (1958). Personality and sociocultural factors in intergroup attitudes: A cross-national comparison. *Journal of Conflict Resolution, 2,* 29–42.

Pettigrew, T.F., & Tropp, L.R. (2008). How does intergroup contact reduce prejudice? Meta-analytic tests of three mediators. *European Journal of Social Psychology, 38,* 922–934.

Phelps, J.A., Davis, J.O., & Schartz, K.M. (1997). Nature, nurture, and twin research strategies. *Current Directions in Psychological Science, 6,* 117–121.

Pickel, K.L. (2009). The weapon focus effect on memory for female versus male perpetrators. *Memory, 17,* 664–678.

Piliavin, I.M., Rodin, J., & Piliavin, J.A. (1969). Good samaritanism: An underground phenomenon? *Journal of Personality and Social Psychology, 13,* 289–299.

Piliavin, J.A., Dovidio, J.F., Gaertner, S.L., & Clark, R.D. (1981). *Emergency intervention.* New York: Academic Press.

Pinker, S. (1984). *Language learnability and language development.* Cambridge, MA: Harvard University Press.

Pinker, S. (1989). *Learnability and cognition.* Cambridge, MA: MIT Press.

Pinker, S. (2011*). The better angels of our nature: The decline of violence in history and its causes.* London: Allen Lane.

Plomin, R. (1988). The nature and nurture of cognitive abilities. In R.J. Sternberg (Ed.), *Advances in the psychology of human intelligence (Vol. 4).* Hillsdale, NJ: Lawrence Erlbaum Associates, Inc.

Plomin, R. (1990). The role of inheritance in behaviour. *Science, 248,* 183–188.

Plomin, R., DeFries, J.C., & McClearn, G.E. (1997). *Behavioral genetics: A primer (3rd ed.).* New York: Freeman.

Pohl, R.F., & Hell, W. (1996). No reduction in hindsight bias after complete information and repeated testing. *Organizational Behavior and Human Decision Processes, 67,* 49–58.

Poldrack, R.A., & Gabrieli, J.D.E. (2001). Characterizing the neural mechanisms of skill learning and repetition priming: Evidence from mirror reading. *Brain, 124,* 67–82.

Postmes, T., & Spears, R. (1998). Deindividuation and anti-normative behavior: A meta-analysis. *Psychological Bulletin, 123,* 238–259.

Price-Williams, D., Gordon, W., & Ramirez, M. (1969). Skill and conservation: A study of pottery-making children. *Developmental Psychology, 1,* 769.

Pylyshyn, Z.W. (2000). Situating vision in the world. *Trends in Cognitive Science, 4,* 197–207.

Rahe, R.H., & Arthur, R.J. (1977). Life changes patterns surrounding illness experience. In A. Monat & R.S. Lazarus (Eds.), *Stress and coping.* New York: Columbia University Press.

Rahe, R.H., Mahan, J., & Arthur, R. (1970). Prediction of near-future health-change from subjects' preceding life changes. *Journal of Psychosomatic Research, 14,* 401–406.

Ramachandran, V. (1988). Perception of shape from shading. *Nature, 331,*163–165.

Rank, S.G., & Jacobsen, C.K. (1977). Hospital nurses' compliance with medication overdose order: A failure to replicate. *Journal of Health and Social Psychology, 18,* 188–193.

Reali, F., & Christiansen, M.H. (2005). Uncovering the richness of the stimulus: Structure dependence and indirect statistical evidence. *Cognitive Science, 29,* 1007–1028.

Redding, G.M., & Vinson, D.W. (2010). Virtual and drawing structures for the Müller-Lyer illusions. *Attention, Perception & Psychophysics, 72,* 1350–1366.

Reicher, S.D. (1984). The St. Pauls' riot: An explanation of the limits of crowd action in terms of a social identity model. *European Journal of Social Psychology, 14,* 1–21.

Reicher, S., & Haslam, S.A. (2006). Rethinking the psychology of tyranny: The BBC prison study. *British Journal of Social Psychology, 45,* 1–40.

Reicher, S., Spears, R., & Postmes, T. (1995). A social identity model of deindividuation phenomena. In W. Stroebe & M. Hewstone (Eds.), *European review of social psychology* (Vol. 6). Chichester, UK: Wiley.

Reis, H.T., Maniaci, M.R., Capranello, P.A., Eastwick, P.W., & Finkel, E.J. (2011). Familiarity does indeed promote attraction in live interaction. *Journal of Personality and Social Psychology, 101,* 557–570.

Rensink, R.A., O'Regan, J.K., & Clark, J.J. (1997). To see or not to see: The need for attention to perceive changes in scenes. *Psychological Science, 8,* 245–277.

Richeson, J.A., & Nussbaum, R.J. (2004). The impact of multiculturalism versus color-blindness on racial bias. Journal of Experimental Social Psychology, *40,* 417–423.

Robbins, J.M., & Krueger, J.I. (2005). Social projection to ingroups and outgroups: A review and meta-analysis. *Personality and Social Psychology Review, 9,* 32–47.

Robertson, S.I. (2001). *Problem solving.* Hove, UK: Psychology Press.

Robinson, J.L., Zahn-Waxler, C., & Emde, R.N. (1994). Patterns of development in early empathic behavior: Environmental and child constitutional influences. *Social Development, 3,* 125–145.

Robinson, M.D. (2009). Self-report. In D. Sander & K.R. Scherer (Eds.), *The Oxford companion to emotion and the affective sciences* (pp. 359–360). Oxford: Oxford University Press.

Rochat, P., Dias, M.D.G., Guo, L.P., Broesch, T., Passos-Ferreira, C., Winning, A., & Berg, B. (2009). Fairness in distributive justice by 3- and 5-year-olds across seven cultures. *Journal of Cross-Cultural Psychology, 40,* 416–442.

Rock, I., & Palmer, S. (1990). The legacy of Gestalt psychology. *Scientific American* (December), 48–61.

Rode, J.C., Mooney, C.H., Arthaud-Day, M.L., Near, J.P., Baldwin, T.T., Rubin, R.S., et al. (2007). Emotional intelligence and individual performance: Evidence of direct and moderated effects. *Journal of Organizational Behavior, 28,* 399–421.

Roediger, H.L., & Karpicke, J.D. (2006). Test-enhanced learning: Taking memory tests improves long-term retention. *Psychological Science, 17,* 249–255.

Rogers, M.B., Loewenthal, K.M., Lewis, C.A., Amlot, R., Cinnirella, M., & Ansari, H. (2007). The role of religious fundamentalism in terrorist violence: A social psychological analysis. *International Review of Psychiatry, 19,* 253–262.

Rönnlund, M., Nyberg, L., Bäckman, L., & Nilsson, L.-G. (2005). Stability, growth, and decline in adult life span development of declarative memory: Cross-sectional and longitudinal data from a population-based study. *Psychology and Aging, 20,* 3–18.

Rortvedt, A.K., & Miltenberger, R.G. (1994). Analysis of a high-probability instructional sequence and time-out in the treatment of child noncompliance. *Journal of Applied Behavior Analysis, 27,* 327–330.

Rosenbaum, M.E. (1986). The repulsion hypothesis: On the non-development of relationships. *Journal of Personality and Social Psychology, 51,* 1156–1166.

Rosenman, R.H., Brand, R.J., Jenkins, C.D., Friedman, M., Straus, R., & Wurm, M. (1975). Coronary heart disease in the Western Collaborative Group Study: Final follow-up experience of 8½ years. *Journal of the American Medical Association, 22*, 872–877.

Rosenthal, R. (1966). *Experimenter effects in behavioral research*. New York: Appleton-Century-Crofts.

Ross, R.R., & Altmaier, E.M. (1994). *Intervention in occupational stress: A handbook of counselling for stress at work*. London: Sage.

Rossen, E., & Kranzler, J.H. (2009). Incremental validity of the Mayer-Salovey-Caruso Emotional Intelligence Test Version 2.0 (MSCEIT) after controlling for personality and intelligence. *Journal of Research in Personality, 43*, 60–65.

Rowe, M.L. (2008). Child-directed speech: Relation to socioeconomic status, knowledge of child development and child vocabulary skill. *Journal of Child Language, 35*, 185–205.

Rubinstein, S., & Caballero, B. (2000). Is Miss America an undernourished role model? *Journal of the American Medical Association, 283*, 1569–1569.

Runco, M.A. (2010). Creative thinking may be simultaneous as well as blind. Comment on "Creative thought as blind-variation and selective-retention: Combinatorial models of exceptional creativity" by Dean Keith Simonton. *Physics of Life Reviews, 7*, 184–185.

Rutter, M. (1970). *Education, health and behavior*. Harlow, UK: Longmans.

Rutter, M. (1981). *Maternal deprivation reassessed (2nd ed.)*. Harlow, UK: Penguin.

Rutter, M., Sonuga-Barke, E.J., & Castle, J. (2010). I. Investigating the impact of early institutional deprivation on development: Background and research strategy of the English and Romanian adoptees (ERA) study. *Monographs of the Society for Research in Child Development, 75*, 1–20.

Sagi, A., van IJzendoorn, M.H., & Koren-Karie, N. (1991). Primary appraisal of the Strange Situation: A cross-cultural analysis of the pre-separation episodes. *Develomental Psychology, 27*, 587–596.

Sagotsky, G., Wood-Schneider, M., & Konop, M. (1981). Learning to cooperate: Effects of modeling and direct instructions. *Child Development, 52*, 1037–1042.

Salovey, P., & Mayer, J.D. (1990). Emotional intelligence. *Imagination, Cognition, and Personality, 9*, 185–211.

Samson, D., & Apperly, I.A. (2010). There is more to mind reading than having theory of mind concdepts: New directions in theory of mind research. *Infant and Child Development, 19*, 443–454.

Sander, D. (2009). Amygdala. In D. Sander & K.R. Scherer (Eds.), *The Oxford companion to emotion and the affective sciences* (pp. 28–32). Oxford: Oxford University Press.

Sander, D., & Scherer, K.R. (2009) (Eds.). *The Oxford companion to emotion and the affective sciences*. Oxford: Oxford University Press.

Savage-Rumbaugh, E.S., McDonald, K., Sevcik, R.A., Hopkins, W.D., & Rupert, E. (1986). Spontaneous symbol acquisition and communicative use by pygmy chimpanzees (*Pan paniscus*). *Journal of Experimental Psychology: General, 115*, 211–235.

Saville, P., & Blinkhorn, S. (1976). *Undergraduate personality by factored scales*. NFER: London.

Saxton, M. (1997). The contrast theory of negative input. *Journal of Child Language, 24*, 139–161.

Sbarra, D.A., Law, R.W., & Portley, R.M. (2011). Divorce and death: A meta-analysis and research agenda for clinical, social, and health psychology. *Perspectives on Psychological Science, 5*, 454–474.

Scarpa, A., Haden, S.C., & Tanaka, A. (2010). Being hot-tempered: Autonomic, emotional, and behavioral distinctions between childhood reactive and proactive aggression. *Biological Psychology, 84*, 488–496.

Scarr, S. (1997). Why child care has little impact on most children's development. *Current Directions in Psychological Science, 6*, 143–148.

Schacter, D.L. (1999). The seven sins of memory – Insights from psychology and cognitive neuroscience. *American Psychologist, 54*, 182–203.

Schacter, D.L., & Addis, D.R. (2007). The cognitive neuroscience of constructive memory: Remembering the past and imagining the future. *Philosophical Transactions of the Royal Society B, 362*, 773–786.

Schacter, D.L., Guerin, S.A., & St. Jacques, P.L. (2011). Memory distortion: An adaptive perspective. *Trends in Cognitive Sciences, 15*, 467–474.

Schaefer, C., Coyne, J.C., & Lazarus, R.S. (1981). The health-related functions of social support. *Journal of Behavioral Medicine, 4*, 381–406.

Schaffer, H.R. (1996). *Social development*. Oxford, UK: Blackwell.

Schaffer, H.R., & Emerson, P.E. (1964). The development of social attachments in infancy. *Monographs of the Society for Research on Child Development* (Whole No. 29).

Scherer, K.R., & Ellsworth, P.C. (2009). Appraisal theories. In D. Sander & K.R. Scherer (Eds.), *The Oxford companion to emotion and the affective sciences*. Oxford: Oxford University Press.

Schieffelin, B.B. (1990). *The give and take of everyday life: Language socialization of Kaluli children*. Cambridge, UK: Cambridge University Press.

Schlaefli, A., Rest, J.R., & Thoma, S.J. (1985). Does moral education improve moral judgement? A meta-analysis of intervention studies using the Defining Issues Test. *Review of Educational Research, 55,* 319–352.

Schmitt, D.P., Realo, A., Voracek, M., & Allik, J. (2008). Why can't a man be more like a woman? Sex differences in Big Five personality traits across 55 cultures. *Journal of Personality and Social Psychology, 94,* 168–182.

Schoenborn, D.A. (1993). The Almeida Study 25 years on. In S. Maes, H. Leventhal, & M. Johnston (Eds.), *International review of health psychology.* Chichester: Wiley.

Schommer, N.C., Hellhammer, D.H., & Kirschbaum, C. (2003). Dissociation between reactivity of the hypothalamic-pituitary-adrenocortical axis and the sympathetic-adrenal-medullary system to repeated psychosocial stress. *Psychosomatic Medicine, 65,* 450–460.

Schonert-Reichl, K.A. (1999). Relations of peer acceptance, friendship adjustment, and social behavior to moral reasoning during early adolescence. *Journal of Early Adolescence, 19,* 249–279.

Schwartz, S.H., & Rubel, T. (2005). Sex differences in value priorities: Cross-cultural and multimethod studies. *Journal of Personality and Social Psychology, 89,* 1010–1028.

Schwarzkopf, D.S., Zhang, J.X., & Kourtzi, Z. (2009). Flexible learning of natural statistics in the human brain. *Journal of Neurophysiology, 102,* 1854–1867.

Segerstrom, S.C., & Miller, G.E. (2004). Psychological stress and the human immune system: A meta-analytic study of 30 years of inquiry. *Psychological Bulletin, 130,* 601–630.

Sekuler, R.W., & Blake, R. (2002). *Perception (4th ed.).* New York: McGraw-Hill.

Selye, H. (1950). *Stress.* Montreal: Acta.

Senghas, A., Kita, S., & Özyürek, A. (2004). Children creating core properties of language: Evidence from an emerging sign language in Nicaragua. *Science, 305,* 1779–1782.

Shackleford, T.K., Schmitt, D.P., & Buss, D.M. (2005). Universal dimensions of human mate preference. *Personality and Individual Differences, 39,* 447–458.

Shaffer, D.R. (1993). *Developmental psychology: Childhood and adolescence (3rd ed.).* Pacific Grove, CA: Brooks/Cole.

Shallice, T., & Warrington, E.K. (1974). The dissociation between long-term retention of meaningful sounds and verbal material. *Neuropsychologia, 12,* 553–555.

Shanks, D.R. (2010). Learning: From association to cognition. *Annual Review of Psychology, 61,* 273–301.

Shapira, N.A., Okun, M.S., Wint, D., Foote, K.D., Byars, J.A., Bowers, D., et al. (2006). Panic and fear induced by deep brain stimulation. *Journal of Neurology, Neurosurgery and Psychiatry, 77,* 410–412.

Sherif, M. (1966). *Group conflict and cooperation: Their social psychology.* London: Routledge & Kegan Paul.

Sherif, M., Harvey, O.J., White, B.J., Hood, W.R., & Sherif, C.W. (1961). *Intergroup conflict and cooperation: The Robbers Cave experiment.* Norman, OK: University of Oklahoma.

Sherman, J.W., Stroessner, S.J., Conrey, F.R., & Azam, O.A. (2005). Prejudice and stereotype maintenance processes: Attention, attribution, and individuation. *Journal of Personality and Social Psychology, 89,* 607–622.

Shotland, R.L., & Straw, M.K. (1976). Bystander response to an assault: When a man attacks a woman. *Journal of Personality and Social Psychology, 34,* 990–999.

Shriver, E.R., Young, S.G., Hugenberg, K., Bernstein, M.J., & Lanter, J.R. (2008). Class, race, and the face: Social context modulates the cross-race effect in face recognition. *Personality and Social Psychology Bulletin, 34,* 260–274.

Shuell, T.J. (1969). Clustering and organization in free recall. *Psychological Bulletin, 72,* 353–374.

Sieber, J.E., & Stanley, B. (1988). Ethical and professional dimensions of socially sensitive research. *American Psychologist, 43,* 49–55.

Siegler, R.S. (1998). *Children's thinking (3rd ed.).* Upper Saddle River, NJ: Prentice Hall.

Siegler, R.S. (2007). Cognitive variability. *Developmental Science, 10,* 104–109.

Siegler, R.S., & Jenkins, E.A. (1989). Strategy choices in children's time-telling. In I. Levin & D. Zakay (Eds.), *Time and human cognition: A life-span perspective.* Amsterdam: Elsevier Science.

Siegler, R.S., & McGilly, K. (1989). Strategy choices in children's time-telling. In I. Levin & D. Zakay (Eds.), *Time and human cognition: A life span perspective.* Amsterdam: Elsevier Science.

Siegler, R.S., & Munakata, Y. (1993). Beyond the immaculate transition: Advances in the understanding of change. *Society for Research in Child Development Newsletter, 36,* 10–13.

Siegler, R.S., & Shrager, J. (1984). Strategy choices in addition and subtraction: How do children know what to do? In C. Sophian (Ed.), *Origins of cognitive skills.* Hillsdale, NJ: Lawrence Erlbaum Associates, Inc.

Siegler, R.S., & Svetina, M. (2002). A microgenetic/cross-sectional study of matrix completions: Comparing short-term and long-term change. *Child Development, 73,* 793–809.

Siegrist, J., & Rodel, A. (2006). Work stress and health risk behavior. *Scandinavian Journal of Work Environment, 32,* 473–481.

Silverman, I., Choi, J., & Peters, M. (2007). The Hunter-Gatherer theory of sex differences in spatial abilities: Data from 40 countries. *Archives of Sexual Behavior, 36,* 261–268.

Silverman, K., Robles, E., Mudric, T., Bigelow, G.E., & Stitzer, M.L. (2004). A randomized trial of long-term reinforcement of cocaine abstinence in methadone-maintained patients who inject drugs. *Journal of Consulting and Clinical Psychology, 72,* 839–854.

Silvia, P.J. (2008). Another look at creativity and intelligence: Exploring higher-order models and probable confounds. *Personality and Individual Differences, 44,* 1012–1021.

Simon, H.A. (1966). Scientific discovery and the psychology of problem solving. In H.A. Simon (Ed.), *Mind and cosmos: Essays in contemporary science and philosophy.* Pittsburgh, PA: University of Pittsburgh Press.

Simon, H.A. (1974). How big is a chunk? *Science, 183,* 482–488.

Simons, D.J., & Chabris, F. (1999). Gorillas in our midst: Sustained inattentional blindness for dynamic events. *Perception, 28,* 1059–1074.

Simonton, D.K. (2010). Creative thought as blind-variation and selective-retention: Combinatorial models of exceptional creativity. *Physics of Life Reviews, 7,* 156–179.

Sio, U.N., & Ormerod, T.C. (2009). Does incubation enhance problem solving? A meta-analytic review. *Psychological Bulletin, 135,* 94–120.

Skinner, B.F. (1938). *The behavior of organisms.* New York: Appleton-Century-Crofts.

Skinner, E.A., Edge, K., Altman, J., & Sherwood, H. (2003). Searching for the structure of coping: A review and critique of category systems for classifying ways of coping. *Psychological Bulletin, 129,* 216–269.

Skoe, E.E.A. (1998). The ethic of care: Issues in moral development. In E.A.A. Skoe & A.L. van der Lippe (Eds.), *Personality development in adolescence: A cross-national and life span perspective.* London: Routledge.

Slaby, R.G., & Crowley, C.G. (1977). Modification of cooperation and aggression through teacher attention to children's speech. *Journal of Experimental Child Psychology, 23,* 442–458.

Slepian, M.L., Weisbuch, M., Rutchick, A.M., Newman, L.S., & Ambady, N. (2010). Shedding light on insight: Priming bright ideas. *Journal of Experimental Social Psychology, 46,* 696–700.

Smith, C.A., & Kirby, L.D. (2001). Toward delivering on the promise of appraisal theory. In K.R. Scherer, A. Schorr, & T. Johnstone (Eds.), *Appraisal processes in emotion: Theory, methods, research* (pp. 121–138). New York: Oxford University Press.

Smith, C.A., & Lazarus, R.S. (1993). Appraisal components, core relational themes, and the emotions. *Cognition & Emotion, 7,* 233–269.

Smith, E.R., & Mackie, D.M. (2000). *Social psychology (2nd ed.).* Philadelphia: Psychology Press.

Smith, L.A., Roman, A., Dollard, M.F., Winefield, A.H., & Siegrist, J. (2005). Effort–reward imbalance at work: The effects of work stress on anger and cardiovascular disease symptoms in a community sample. *Stress and Health, 21,* 113–128.

Smith, P.B., & Bond, M.H. (1993). *Social psychology across cultures: Analysis and perspectives.* New York: Prentice-Hall.

Snarey, J.R. (1985). Cross-cultural universality of social-moral development: A critical review of Kohlbergian research. *Psychological Bulletin, 97,* 202–232.

Solomon, R.L., & Wynne, L.C. (1953). Traumatic avoidance learning: Acquisition in normal dogs. *Psychological Monographs, 67* (Whole No. 354), 1–19.

Sorkin, A.R. (2009). *Too big to fail.* London: Penguin.

Spangler, G. (1990). Mother, child, and situational correlates of toddlers' social competence. *Infant Behavior and Development, 13,* 405–419.

Spangler, G., Johann, M., Ronai, Z., & Zimmermann, P. (2009). Genetic and environmental influence on attachment disorganization. *Journal of Child Psychology and Psychiatry, 50,* 952–961.

Spector, P.E., Dwyer, D.J., & Jex, S.M. (1988). Relation of job stressors to affective, health, and performance outcomes. A comparison of multiple data sources. *Journal of Applied Psychology, 73,* 11–19.

Spence, J.T., & Helmreich, R.L. (1978). *Masculinity and femininity: Their psychological dimensions, correlates, and antecedents.* Austin, TX: University of Texas Press.

Spence, J.T., Helmreich, R.L., & Stapp, J. (1974). The Personal Attributes Questionnaire: A measure of sex role stereotypes and masculinity-femininity, *JSAS Catalog of Selected Documents in Psychology, 4,* 43 (Np. 617).

Spiers, H.J., Maguire, E.A., & Burgess, N. (2001). Hippocampal amnesia. *Neurocase, 7,* 357–382.

Spitz, R.A. (1945). Hospitalism: An inquiry into the genesis of psychiatric conditions in early childhood. *Psychoanalytic Study of the Child, 1,* 113–117.

Sprecher, S. (1998). Insiders' perspectives on reasons for attraction to a close other. *Social Psychology Quarterly, 61,* 287–300.

Stajkovic, A.D., & Luthans, F. (1998). Self-efficacy and work-related performance: A meta-analysis. *Psychological Bulletin, 124,* 240–261.

Stams, G.J., Brugman, D., Dekovic, M., van Rosmalen, L., van der Laan, & Gibbs, J.C. (2006). The moral judgment of juvenile delinquents: A meta-analysis. *Psychological Bulletin, 124,* 240–261.

Stein, J.A., Newcomb, M.D., & Bentler, P.M. (1992). The effect of agency and communality on self-esteem: Gender differences in longitudinal data. *Sex Roles, 26,* 465–481.

Stephens, C.L., Christie, I.C., & Friedman, B.H. (2010). Autonomic specificity of basic emotions: Evidence from pattern classification and cluster analysis. *Biological Psychology, 84,* 463–473.

Sternberg, R.J. (1985). *Beyond IQ: A triarchic theory of human intelligence.* Cambridge, UK: Cambridge University Press.

Sternberg, R.J. (1995). *In search of the human mind.* New York: Harcourt Brace.

Sternberg, R.J. (2004). Intelligence. In R.L. Gregory (Ed.), *The Oxford companion to the mind.* Oxford, UK: Oxford University Press.

Sternberg, R.J., & Kaufman, J.C. (1998). Human abilities. *Annual Review of Psychology, 49,* 479–502.

Stevens, S., Hynan, M.T., & Allen, M. (2000). A meta-analysis of common factor and specific treatment effects across the outcome domains of the phase model of psychotherapy. *Clinical Psychology: Science and Practice, 7,* 273–290.

Stone, A.A., Reed, B.R., & Neale, J.M. (1987). Changes in daily life event frequency precede episodes of physical symptoms. *Journal of Human Stress, 134,* 70–74.

Subra, B., Muller, D., Bègue, L., Bushman, B.J., & Delmas, F. (2010). Automatic effects of alcohol and aggressive cues on aggressive thoughts and behaviors. *Personality and Social Psychology Bulletin, 36,* 1052–1057.

Sulin, R.A., & Dooling, D.J. (1974). Intrusion of a thematic idea in retention of prose. *Journal of Experimental Psychology, 103,* 255–262.

Svetlova, M., Nichols, S.R., & Brownell, C.A. (2010). Toddlers' prosocial behavior: From instrumental to empathic to altruistic helping. *Child Development, 81,* 1814–1827.

Sweller, J., & Levine, M. (1982). Effects of goal specificity on means–ends analysis and learning. *Journal of Experimental Psychology: Learning, Memory, and Cognition, 8,* 463–474.

Swim, J.K., Aikin, K.J., Hall, W.S., & Hunter, B.A. (1995). Sexism and racism: Old-fashioned and modern prejudices. *Journal of Personality and Social Psychology, 68,* 199–214.

Taglialatela, J.P., Savage-Rumbaugh, S., & Baker, L.A. (2003). Vocal production by a language-competent Pan paniscus. *International Journal of Primatology, 24,* 1–17.

Tajfel, H. (1981). *Human groups and social categories: Studies in social psychology.* Cambridge, UK: Cambridge University Press.

Tajfel, H., & Turner, J.C. (1979). *An integrative theory of intergroup conflict.* In W.G. Austin & S. Worchel (Eds.), *The social psychology of intergroup relations* (pp. 33–47). Monterey, CA: Brooks/Cole.

Tarr, M.J., Williams, P., Hayward, W.G., & Gauthier, I. (1998). Three-dimensional object recognition is viewpoint-dependent. *Nature Neuroscience, 1,* 195–206.

Taylor, S.E., Cousino-Klein, L., Lewisz, B.P., Grunewald, T.L., & Updegraff, J.A. (2000). Behavioral response to stress in females: Tend and befriend, not fight-or-flight. *Psychological Review, 107,* 411–429.

Tenenbaum, H.R., & Leaper, C. (2002). Are parents' schemas related to their children's gender-related cognitions? A meta-analysis. *Developmental Psychology, 38,* 615–630.

Teper, R., Inzlicht, M., & Page-Gould, E. (2011). Are we more moral than we think? Exploring the role of affect in moral behavior and moral forecasting. *Psychological Science, 22,* 553–558.

Terlecki, M.S., & Newcombe, N.S. (2005). How important is the digital divide? The relation of computer and videogame usage to gender differences in mental rotation ability. *Sex Roles, 53,* 433–441.

Terracciano, A., Abdel-Khalek, A.M., Adamovova, L., Ahan, C.k, Ahan, H.-n., Alansari, B.M., et al. (2005). National character does not reflect mean personality trait levels in 49 cultures. *Science, 310,* 96–100.

Terrace, H.S., Pettito, L.A., Sanders, D.J., & Bever, T.G. (1979). On the grammatical capacities of apes. In K. Nelson (Ed.), *Children's language, Vol. 2.* New York: Gardner Press.

Tetlock, P.E., Peterson, R.S., McGuire, C., Chang, S., & Feld, P. (1992). Assessing political group dynamics: A test of the groupthink model. *Journal of Personality and Social Psychology, 63,* 403–425.

Tilker, H.A. (1970). Socially responsible behavior as a function of observer responsibility and victim feedback. *Journal of Personality and Social Psychology, 49*, 420–428.

Tizard, B. (1977). *Adoption: A second chance*. London: Open Books.

Tollestrup, P.A., Turtle, J.W., & Yuilee, J.C. (1994). Actual victims and witnesses to robbery and fraud: An archival analysis. In D.F. Ross, J.D. Read, & M.P. Toglia (Eds.), *Adult eyewitness testimony: Current trends and developments*. New York: Wiley.

Tolman, E.C. (1959). Principles of purposive behavior. In S. Koch (Ed.), *Psychology: A study of a science: Vol. 2. General systematic formulations, learning, and special processes*. New York: McGraw-Hill.

Tomasello, M. (2005). Beyond formalities: The case of language acquisition. *Linguistic Review, 22*, 183–197.

Tomlinson-Keasey, C., & Keasey, C.B. (1974). The mediating role of cognitive development in moral judgment. *Child Development, 45*, 291–298.

Townsend, J.M., Kline, J., & Wasserman, T.H. (1995). Low-investment copulation – Sex differences in motivations and emotional reactions. *Ethology and Sociobiology, 16*, 25–51.

Trautner, H.M., Ruble, D.N., Cyphers, L., Kirsten, B., Behrendt, R., & Hartmann, P. (2005). Rigidity and flexibility of gender stereotypes in childhood: Developmental or differential? *Infant and Child Development, 14*, 365–381.

Triandis, H.C., Carnevale, P., Gelfand, M., Robert, C., Wasti, A., et al. (2001). Culture, personality and deception in intercultural management negotiations. *International Journal of Cross-Cultural Management, 1*, 73–90.

Triandis, H.C., McCusker, C., Betancourt, H., Iwao, S., Leung, K., et al. (1993). An etic-emic analysis of individualism and collectivism. *Journal of Cross-Cultural Psychology, 24*, 366–384.

Triandis, H.C., McCusker, C., & Hui, C.H. (1990). Multimethod probes of individualism and collectivism. *Journal of Personality and Social Psychology, 59*, 1006–1020.

Trickett, S.B., & Trafton, J.G. (2007). "What if …": The use of conceptual simulations in scientific reasoning. *Cognitive Science, 31*, 843–875.

Triesch, H., Ballard, D.H., & Jacobs, R.A. (2002). Fast temporal dynamics of visual cue integration. *Perception, 31*, 421–434.

Trivers, R.L. (1971). The evolution of reciprocal altruism. *Quarterly Review of Biology, 46*, 35–57.

Tropp, L.R., & Pettigrew, T.F. (2005). Relationships between intergroup conflict and prejudice among minority and majority status groups. *Psychological Science, 16*, 951–957.

Trzesniewski, K.H., Donnellan, M.B., Caspi, A., Moffitt, T.E., Robins, R.W., & Poultin, R. (2006). Adolescent low self-esteem is a risk factor for adult poor health, criminal behavior, and limited economic prospects. *Developmental Psychology, 42*, 381–390.

Tuckey, M.R., & Brewer, N. (2003a). How schema affect eyewitness memory over repeated retrieval attempts. *Applied Cognitive Psychology, 7*, 785–800.

Tuckey, M.R., & Brewer, N. (2003b). The influence of schemas, stimulus ambiguity, and interview schedule on eyewitness memory over time. *Journal of Experimental Psychology: Applied, 9*, 101–118.

Tulving, E., & Schacter, D.L. (1990). Priming and human-memory systems. *Science, 247*, 301–306.

Turkheimer, E., Haley, A., Waldron, M., D'Onofrio, B., & Gottesman, I.I. (2003). Socio-economic status modifies heritability of IQ in young children. *Psychological Science, 14*, 623–628.

Turner, R.N., & Crisp, R.J. (2010). Explaining the relationship between ingroup identification and intergroup identification and intergroup bias following recategorization: A self-regulation theory analysis. *Group Processes & Intergroup Relations, 13*, 251–261.

Turton, S., & Campbell, C. (2005). Tend and befriend versus fight or flight: Gender differences in behavioural response to stress among university students. *Journal of Applied Biobehavioral Research, 10*, 209–232.

Tuvblad, C., Raine, A., Zheng, M., & Baker, L.A. (2009). Genetic and environmental stability differs in reactive and proactive aggression. *Aggressive Behavior, 35*, 437–452.

Twenge, J.M. (2000). The age of anxiety? Birth cohort change in anxiety and neuroticism, 1952–1993. *Journal of Personality and Social Psychology, 70*, 1007–1021.

Twenge, J.M., Gentile, B., DeWall, C.N., Ma, D., Lacefield, K., & Schutz, D.R. (2010). Birth cohort increases in psychopathology among young Americans, 1938–2007: A cross-sectional meta-analysis of the MMPI. *Clinical Psychology Review, 30*, 145–154.

Tyerman, A., & Spencer, C. (1983). A critical test of the Sherifs' Robbers Cave experiment: Intergroup competition and cooperation between groups of well-acquainted individuals. *Small Group Behaviour, 14*, 515–531.

Tyrell, J.B., & Baxter, J.D. (1981). Glucocorticoid therapy. In P. Felig, J.D. Baxter, A.E. Broadus, & L.A. Frohman (Eds.), *Endocrinology and metabolism*. New York: McGraw-Hill.

Uchino, B.N. (2006). Social support and health: A review of psychological processes potentially underlying links to disease outcome. *Journal of Behavioral Medicine, 29*, 377–387.

Uchino, B.N., Cacioppo, J.T., & Kiecolt-Glaser, K.G. (1996). The relationships between social support and physiological processes: A review with emphasis on underlying mechanisms and implications for health. *Psychological Bulletin, 119*, 488–531.

Udry, J.R., & Chantala, K. (2004). Masculinity–femininity guides sexual union formation in adolescents. *Personality and Social Psychology Bulletin, 30*, 44–55.

Ũnal, B., Critchley, J.A., Fidan, D., & Capewell, S. (2005). Life years gained from modern cardiological treatments and population risk factor changes in England and Wales, 1981–2000. *American Journal of Public Health, 95*, 103–108.

Van Dellen, M.R., Campbell, W.K., Hoyle, R.H., & Bradfield, E.K. (2011). Compensating, resisting, and breaking: A meta-analytic examination of reactions to self-esteem threat. *Personality and Social Psychology Review, 15*, 51–74.

Van der Linden, D., te Nijenhuis, J., & Bakker, A.B. (2010). The general factor of personality: A meta-analysis of Big Five intercorrelations and a criterion-related validity study. *Journal of Research in Personality, 44*, 315–327.

Van IJzendoorn, M.H., & Kroonenberg, P.M. (1988). Cross-cultural patterns of attachment: A meta-analysis of the Strange Situation. *Child Development, 59*, 147–156.

Van Oudenhouven, J.P., Groenewoud, J.T., & Hewstone, M. (1996). Cooperation, ethnic salience and generalization of inter-ethnic attitudes. *European Journal of Social Psychology, 26*, 649–662.

Vargha-Khadem, F., Gadian, D.G., Watkins, K.E., Connelly, A., Van Paesschen, W., & Mishkin, M. (1997). Differential effects of early hippocampal pathology on episodic and semantic memory. *Science, 277*, 376–380.

Vazire, S., & Carlson, E.N. (2011). Others sometimes know us better than we know ourselves. *Current Directions in Psychological Science, 20*, 104–108.

Verkuyten, M., Drabbles, M., & van den Nieuwenhuijzen, K. (1999). Self-categorization and emotional reactions to ethnic minorities. *European Journal of Social Psychology, 29*, 605–619.

Viggiano, M.P., Giovannelli, F., Borgheresi, A., Feurra, M., Berardi, N., Pizzorusso, T., et al. (2008). Disruption of the prefrontal cortex by rTMS produces a category-specific enhancement of the reaction times during visual object identification. *Neuropsychologia, 46*, 2725–2731.

Viswesvaran, C., & Schmidt, F.L. (1992). A meta-analytic comparison of the effectiveness of smoking cessation methods. *Journal of Applied Psychology, 77*, 554–561.

Vögele, C., Ehlers, A., Meyer, A.H., Frank, M., Hahlweg, K., & Margrat, J. (2010). Cognitive mediation of clinical improvement after intensive exposure therapy of agoraphobia and social phobia. *Depression and Anxiety, 27*, 294–301.

Vul, E., & Pashler, H. (2007). Incubation benefits only after people have been misdirected. *Memory & Cognition, 35*, 701–710.

Wachtel, P.L. (1973). Psychodynamics, behavior therapy and the implacable experimenter: An inquiry into the consistency of personality. *Journal of Abnormal Psychology, 82*, 324–334.

Wagner, U., Gais, S., Haider, H., Verleger, R., & Born, J. (2004). Sleep inspires insight. *Nature, 427*, 352–355.

Walker, L.J. (2004). Progress and prospects in the psychology of moral development. *Merrill-Palmer Quarterly Journal of Developmental Psychology, 50*, 546–557.

Walker, L.J., Pitts, R.C., Hennig, K.H., & Matsuba, M.K. (1995). Reasoning about morality and real-life moral problems. In M. Killen & D. Hart (Eds.), *Morality in everyday life: Developmental perspectives*. Cambridge, UK: Cambridge University Press.

Wallas, G. (1926). *The art of thought*. London: Cape.

Wallerstein, J.S. (1984). Children of divorce: Preliminary report of a ten-year follow-up of young children. *American Journal of Orthopsychiatry, 54*, 444–458.

Wang, A.Y., & Thomas, M.H. (2000). Looking for long-term mnemonic effects on Serial recall: The legacy of Simonides. *American Journal of Psychology, 113*, 331–340.

Wang, K., Shu, Q., & Tu, Q. (2008). Technostress under different organizational environments: An empirical investigation. *Computers in Human Behavior, 24*, 3002–3013.

Warr, P. (1996). *Psychology at work (3rd ed.)*. Harmondsworth, UK: Penguin.

Watson, D., & Clark, L.A. (1992). Affects separable and inseparable: On the hierarchical arrangement of the negative affects. *Journal of Personality and Social Psychology, 62*, 489–505.

Watson, D., & Clark, L.A. (1994). *The PANAS-X: Manual for the Positive and Negative Affect Schedule – Expanded form*. Unpublished manuscript, University of Iowa, Iowa City.

Watson, J.B. (1913). Psychology as the behaviorist views it. *Psychological Review, 20*, 158–177.

Webb, T.L., & Sheeran, P. (2006). Does changing behavioral intentions engender behavior change? A meta-analysis of the experimental evidence. *Psychological Bulletin, 132,* 249–268.

Weisstein, N., & Wong, E. (1986). Figure-ground organization and the spatial and temporal responses of the visual system. In E.C. Schwab & H.C. Nusbaum (Eds.), *Pattern recognition by humans and machines, Vol. 2.* New York: Academic Press.

Weizman, Z.O., & Snow, C.E. (2001). Lexical input as related to children's vocabulary acquisition: Effects of sophisticated exposure and support for meaning. *Developmental Psychology, 37,* 265–279.

Wellman, H.M., Cross, D., & Watson, J. (2001). Meta-analysis of theory-of-mind development: The truth about false belief. *Child Development, 72,* 655–684.

Wellman, H.M., & Gelman, S.A. (1988). Children's understanding of the nonobvious. In R.J. Sternberg (Ed.), *Advances in the psychology of human intelligence, Vol. 4.* Hillsdale, NJ: Lawrence Erlbaum Associates.

West, T.V., Pearson, A.R., Dovidio, J.F., Shelton, J.N., & Trail, T. (2009). Superordinate identity and intergroup roommate friendship development. *Journal of Experimental Social Psychology, 45,* 1266–1272.

Westen, D. (1996). *Psychology: Mind, brain, and culture.* New York: Wiley.

Westen, D. (1998). The scientific legacy of Sigmund Freud: Toward a psychodynamically informed psychological science. *Psychological Bulletin, 124,* 333–371.

Weston, D.R., & Main, M. (1981). The quality of the toddler's relationship to mother and to father: Related to conflict behavior and the readiness to establish new relationships. *Child Development, 52,* 932–940.

Wetherell, M. (1982). Cross-cultural studies of minimal groups: Implications for the social identity theory of intergroup relations. In H. Tajfel (Ed.), *Social identity and intergroup relations.* Cambridge, UK: Cambridge University Press.

Wheeler, L.R. (1942). A comparative study of the intelligence of East Tennessee mountain children. *Journal of Educational Psychology, 33,* 321–334.

Wheldall, K., & Limbrick, L. (2010). Do more boys than girls have reading problems? *Journal of Learning Disabilities, 43,* 418–429.

Whiting, B.B., & Whiting, J.W.M. (1975). *Children of six cultures: A psychocultural analysis.* Cambridge, MA: Harvard University Press.

Whitley, B.E. (1985). Sex-role orientation and psychological well-being: Two meta-analyses. *Sex Roles, 12,* 207–225.

Williams, J.E., & Best, D.L. (1990). *Sex and psyche: Gender and self viewed cross-culturally.* Newbury Park, CA: Sage.

Wilson, S.J., Lipsey, M.W., & Derzon, J.H. (2003). The effects of school-based intervention programs on aggressive behavior: A meta-analysis. *Journal of Consulting and Clinical Psychology, 71,* 136–149.

Wimmer, H., & Perner, J. (1983). Beliefs about beliefs: Representation and the constraining function of wrong beliefs in young children's understanding of deception. *Cognition, 13,* 103–128.

Woike, B., Gershkovich, I., Piorkowski, R., & Polo, M. (1999). The role of motives in the content and structure of autobiographical memory. *Journal of Personality and Social Psychology, 76,* 600–612.

Wojciszke, B., Bazinska, R., & Jaworski, M. (1998). On the dominance of moral categories in impression formation. *Personality and Social Psychology Bulletin, 24,* 1245–1257.

Wood, R.E., Mento, A.J., & Locke, E.A. (1987). Task complexity as a moderator of goal effects: A meta-analysis. *Journal of Applied Psychology, 72,* 416–425.

Wood, W., & Eagly, A.H. (2002). A cross-cultural analysis of the behavior of women and men: Implications for the origins of sex differences. *Psychological Bulletin, 128,* 699–727.

Wood, W., Lundgren, S., Ouellette, J.A., Busceme, S., & Blackstone, T. (1994). Minority influence: A meta-analytic review of social influence processes. *Psychological Bulletin, 115,* 323–345.

Wood, W., Wong, F.Y., & Chachere, J.G. (1991). Effects of media violence on viewers' aggression in unconstrained social interaction. *Psychological Bulletin, 109,* 371–383.

Wu, A.W., Folkman, S., McPhee, S.J., & Lo, B. (1993). How house officers cope with their mistakes. *Western Journal of Medicine, 159,* 565–569.

Ybarra, O. (2001). When first impressions don't last: The role of isolation and adaptation processes in the revision of evaluative impressions. *Social Cognition, 19,* 491–520.

Yearta, S., Maitlis, S., & Briner, R.B. (1995). An exploratory study of goal setting in theory and practice: A motivational techniques that works? *Journal of Occupational and Organizational Psychology, 68,* 237–252.

Zahavi, S., & Asher, S.R. (1978). The effect of verbal instructions on preschool children's aggressive behavior. *Journal of School Psychology, 16,* 146–153.

Zahn-Waxler, C., Radke-Yarrow, M., & King, R.A. (1979). Child rearing and children's prosocial initiations toward victims of distress. *Child Development, 50,* 319–330.

Zahn-Waxler, C. Radke-Yarrow, M., Wagner, E., & Chapman, M. (1992). Development of concern for others. *Developmental Psychology, 28,* 1038–1047.

Zakowski, S.G., Hall, M.H., Klein, L.C., & Baum, A. (2001). Appraised group, coping, and stress in a community sample: A test of the goodness-of-fit hypothesis. *Annals of Behavioral Medicine, 23,* 158–165.

Zárate, M.A., Garcia, B., Garza, A.A., & Hitlan, R.T. (2004). Cultural threat and perceived realistic group conflict as dual predictors or prejudice. *Journal of Experimental Social Psychology, 40,* 99–105.

Zeidner, M., Matthews, G., & Roberts, R.D. (2009). *What we know about emotional intelligence.* Cambridge, MA: MIT Press.

Zeki, S. (1993). *A vision of the brain.* Oxford, UK: Blackwell.

Zelko, H., Zammar, G.R., Ferreira, A.P.B., Phadtare, A., Shah, J., & Pietrobon, R. (2010). Selection mechanisms underlying high impact biomedical research – A qualitative analysis and causal model. *Public Library of Science One, 5,* e10535.

Zhang, X., Norris, S.L., Gregg, E.W., & Beckles, G. (2007). Social support and mortality among older persons with diabetes. *Diabetes Educator, 33,* 273–281.

Zhu, Y.-S., & Imperato-McGinley, J. (2008). Male sexual differentiation disorder and 5a-reductase-2 deficiency. *Journal of the Global Library of Women's Medicine, (ISSN: 1756–2228).* DOI 10: 3843/GLOWM.10350.

Zihl, J., von Cramon, D., & Mai, N. (1983). Selective disturbance of movement vision after bilateral brain damage. *Brain, 106,* 313–340.

Zillmann, D., & Weaver, J.B. (1997). Psychoticism in the effect of prolonged exposure to gratuitous media violence: On the acceptance of violence as a preferred means of conflict resolution. *Personality and Individual Differences, 22,* 613–627.

Zimbardo, P.G. (1970). The human choice: Individuation, reason, and order versus deindividuation, impulse, and chaos. In W.J. Arnold & D. Levine (Eds.), *Nebraska symposium on motivation, 17,* 237–307. Lincoln, NE: University of Nebraska Press.

Zimbardo, P.G. (1989). *Quiet rage: The Stanford Prison Experiment video.* Stanford, CA: Stanford University.

Zosuls, K.M., Ruble, D.N., Tamis-LeMonda, C.S., Shrout, P.E., Bornstein, M.H., & Greulich, F.K. (2009). The acquisition of gender labels in infancy: Implications for gender-typed play. *Developmental Psychology, 45,* 688–701.

Index

Bold indicates where key terms are defined.

Accommodation (eye), **317**
Accommodation (Piagetian), **121**
Adjustment phase, **190**
Adoption studies, 268
Adrenaline, **53**
Adrenocorticotrophic hormone (ACTH), **54**
Affective blindsight, **77**
Aggression, 85–99
  biological approach, 93–94
  catharsis, 96–97
  child-based interventions, 97
  coercive cycle, **90**, 97
  cognitive factors, 89–90
  cultural differences, 86
  family processes, 90
  frustration–aggression hypothesis, 86–87
  gender differences, 93–94
  general aggression model, 94–96
  genetic factors, 93
  historical factors, 85–86
  media violence, 87–88
  parent training, 97–98
  proactive, **85**
  reactive, **85**
  reducing, 96–98
  situational factors, 86–90
  social learning, 91–93
  video games, 88–89
Altruism, **213**
  encouraging, 219–221
  explaining, 215–217
Ames room, **320–321**
Amnesia, **331**
Amygdala, **79–81**
Androgyny, **174**, 175
Animal language, 144–147
Anterior cingulate cortex, 79, 81
Anxiety, 10, 343–344
Appraisal theory, 76–77
Arousal: cost–reward model, 223–224
Artificiality of experiments, 20–21
Asch, Solomon, 230–232
Assimilation, **121**
Attachment, 181–185
  avoidant, **182**
  Bowlby's theory, 181
  cultural variations, 183–184
  definition, 181
  dimensions, 183

  disorganised and disoriented, 182
  gene–environment interaction, 185
  maternal sensitivity hypothesis, 184
  resistant, **182**
  secure, **182**
  Strange Situation, 182
  temperament hypothesis, 184–185
  theories, 185–186
  types of, 182–183
Attraction
  physical, 252–254
  romantic, 257–259
Attributions, 247–250
Authoritarian personality, **201**
Autism, **131–133**
Autobiographical memory, 299, 300–301, **335**
Autonomic nervous system, **39–40**
Avoidance learning, **111–112**
Avoidant attachment, **182**

Bandura, Albert, 91, 114, 290–291, 291
BBC prison study, 241
Behavioural interventions, aggression, 97
Behaviourism, **103**
Biederman, Irving, 318–319
Big Five model, 287–289
Binocular cues, **317**
Biological approach
  aggression, 93–94
  behaviour, 35–49
  gender development, 172–174
Blocking effect, **105**
Bobo doll, 91–92
Body mass index (BMI), 254
Bowlby, John, 181, 186
Brain
  cerebral cortex, **42–45**
  emotional systems, 73, 79–82
  hemispheric specialisation, **44–45**
  methods of studying, 45–47
  organisation, 41–42
  split-brain patients, 44–45
British Psychological Society (BPS) code of ethics, 30
Bystander intervention, **213**, 221–225

Case study, 27–28
Categorical clustering, **336**
Catharsis, **96–97**
Cattell, Raymond, 284–286
CCTV images, 342
Central coherence, **132**
Central executive, **332**
Central nervous system, **38**
Centration, **123**
Cerebellum, 42
Cerebral cortex, **42–45**
Cerebrum, **41**
Change blindness, 322–326, **322**
Change blindness blindness, **323**
Child-directed speech, **141**, 143
Chimpanzee language, 144–147
Chunks, **331–332**
Claparède, Edouard, 333–334
Classical conditioning, **103–107**
Clever Hans, 20
Clinical psychology, 9–11
Coercive cycle, **90**, 97
Cognitive appraisal, **76**
Cognitive-behavioural therapy, 10
Cognitive development, 121–135
  overlapping waves model, 129–131
  Piaget's theory, 121–127
  theory of mind, **131–133**
  Vygotsky's theory, 127–129
Cognitive-developmental theory (Kohlberg), 152–156
Cognitive factors, aggression, 89–90
Cognitive reappraisal, **78**
Collectivistic cultures, 8, 218, 249, 263, 279–280, 298, 301, 307–308
Common sense, 4–6
Compliance, **232**
Concrete operations stage, 125–126
Conditioned reflex, **104**
Conditioned response, **104**
Conditioned stimulus, **104**
Conditioning
  classical, **103–107**
  operant, 107–113, **108**
Confirmation bias, **343**
Conformity, 229–234
Confounding variables, **18–19**
Congenital adrenal hyperplasia, **173**
Congruence model, 174, 175

Conservation, **123**, 124
Conventional morality, **154**
Convergence, **317**
Convergent thinking, **356**
Conversion, **232**
Coping strategies, 63–64
Correlation, **26**
Correlational studies, 26–27
Cortisol, **54**
Cost–benefit analysis, 30
Counterbalancing, **23**
Creativity, **356–360**
Crisis phase, **190**
Critical period, **186**
Cross-cultural psychology,
    7–8, *see also* Cultural
    variations
Cross-race effect, 342–343
Cross-sectional method, **25**–26
Crowd behaviour, 241–243
Cued recall, **330**
Cultural mindset, **307**
Cultural variations
    aggression, 86
    attachment, 183–184
    fundamental attribution error,
        249
    implicit personality theory, 252
    personality, 279–280
    physical attractiveness, 254
    pro-social behaviour, 218–219
    self-concept, 298, 301–302
    self-esteem, 307–308
Culture, 7

Darwin, Charles, 35
Day care, 191–193
Decentration, **125**
Deception, 30
Declarative memory, **333–335**
Deindividuation, **242**
Demand characteristics, **21**
Dependent variable, **18**
Depression, 10
Deprivation, **186**–190
Depth perception, 316–318
Diffusion of responsibility, **222**
Direct tuition, **168**
Discrimination (behaviour), **197**
    reducing, 205–209
    stages, 197
Discrimination (conditioning), 105
Dispositional attribution, **248**
Distinctiveness, **366–367**
Divergent thinking, **356**
Divorce, 190–191
Dizygotic twins, **36**
DNA tests, 341
Dream analysis, 9

Eating, 12, 292–293
Ecological approach, 106
Ecological validity, **20**
Effort–reward imbalance, 58
Egocentric speech, 128
Egocentrism, **124**–125
Elaboration, 366
Emotion, 69–83
    appraisal theory, 76–77
    brain systems, 73, 79–82
    definition, 69
    facial expressions, 71–72
    functions, 70–71
    gender differences, 70
    James–Lange theory, 74–75
    moods and, **69**–70
    psychological theories, 74–78
    regulation, 77–78
    self-reported, 72–73
Emotion-focused coping, 63–64
Emotional intelligence, 274–275
Emotional Quotient Inventory
    (EQ-i), 274
Empathy, **213**, 215
Enactive experience, **168**
Encoding, 329
Environmental influences,
    intelligence, 266–270
Episodic buffer, **333**
Episodic memory, **334**
Equilibration, **122**
Equipotentiality, **110**
Ethical issues, 28–30
Event-related potentials, 46
Evolutionary psychology, 35–36,
    215
Executive processes, **131**
Expansions, 142–143
Experimental designs, 21–23
Experimental hypothesis, **17**–18
Experimental method, 17–24
Experimenter effect, **20**
Explicit memory, **333–335**
Exposure therapy, 11, **107**
Extinction, **105**
Extraversion, **286**
Eyewitness testimony, **341–344**
Eysenck, H.J., 286–287, 288

F (Fascism) Scale, 201
Face recognition, 319
Faces–goblet illusion, 314
Facial expressions, 71–72
Factor analysis, **270–271**
False belief tasks, 131
False consensus effect, 254
False uniqueness bias, **306**
Familiarity, 256–257
Family factors, aggression, 90

Femininity, 174–176
Field experiments, **23**
Figure–ground organisation, **314**,
    315
Fixation, **281–282**
Flynn effect, **269**
Forebrain, 41
Forgetting, 338–341
Formal operations stage, 126–127
Free association, 9
Free recall, **329**
Freud, Sigmund, 9–10, 27, 280–282
Frontal lobe, 42, 43
Frustration–aggression hypothesis,
    86–87
Functional fixedness, **352**
Functional magnetic resonance
    imaging (fMRI), 45–46
Fundamental attribution error,
    248–249
Fundamental lexical hypothesis, **284**

Gender, 165
Gender development, 167–174
    biological theories, 172–174
    self-socialisation theory, 170–172
    social cognitive theory, 168–169
Gender differences
    aggression, 93–94
    emotions, 70
    intelligence, 166
    personality, 167
    romantic attraction, 257–259
    self-concept, 301–302
    social support, 65–66
    spatial ability, 166–167
Gender identity, 165–166
Gender schemas, **170**
Gender similarities hypothesis, **165**
Gene–environment interaction, 185
General adaptation syndrome,
    52–53
General aggression model, 94–96
Generalisation, 104–105
Genetic factors, 36–38
    aggression, 93
    intelligence, 266–270
    pro-social behaviour, 215
Genovese, Kitty, 222
Geons, **318**
Gestaltists, 313–315
Gilligan, Carol, 157–159
Goal-setting theory, 375–376
Grammatical morphemes, **139**
Group, **125**
Group decision making, 238–240
Group polarisation, **238**
Groupthink, **238–239**
Guevedoces, 173

Hassles, 56
Health psychology, 11–12
Healthy eating, 12
Hemispheric specialisation, 44–45
Heredity, *see* Genetic factors
Heuristics, 354–355
Hierarchical theory, intelligence, 270–271
Hill climbing, **355**
Hindbrain, **42**
Hindsight bias, **6**
HM, 27
Hollow-face illusion, 322
Hormones, 93, 94, 172
Hypothalamic-pituitary-adrenocortical (HPA) axis, 53, 54–55
Hypothalamus, **41**
Hypotheses, **17**

"I", 298
Illness, stress-related, 59–61
Immune system, 59–60, 61
Implacable experimenter, **21**
Implementation intentions, 12, **376–377**
Implicit memory, 333–334, 335–336
Implicit personality theory, 250–252
Inattentional blindness, **322**
Inborn characteristics, 36–38
Incompatible-response technique, 97
Incubation, 357–358
Independent design, **21**
Independent self, **301–302**
Independent variable, **18**
Individualistic cultures, 8, 218, 249, 263, 279–280, 298, 301, 306
Informational influence, **231**
Ingroup bias, **204**
Inner speech, 128
Inside-out theories, 140–142
Insight, **350**
Instinctive drift, 110
Insula, 79, 81
Intelligence, 263–277
    creativity and, 356–357
    definition, 263–264
    emotional, **274–275**
    environmental influences, 266–270
    factor analysis, **270–271**
    gender differences, 166
    heredity, 266–270
    hierarchical theory, 270–271
    multiple, 271–273
    testing, 264–266
    types of, 270–275
Intelligence quotient (IQ), **264–265**
Interdependent self, **301–302**

Interference, 338–339
Intergroup contact hypothesis, 205–207
Inter-observer reliability, **25**
Interposition, **316**
Interpretive bias, **11**
IQ, **264–265**

James–Lange theory, 74–75
Job control, 58

Kanizsa's illusory square, 317
Kohlberg, Lawrence, 152–156

Language bioprogram hypothesis, 140
Language development, 137–149
    in animals, 144–147
    defining language, 137
    inside-out theories, 140–142
    outside-in theories 140, 142–144
    stages of, 138–139
Law of Prägnanz, 313–314
Law of reinforcement, **108**
Leading questions, 342
Learning
    levels-of-processing, 366–369
    memory and, 329
    by remembering, 373–374
Levels-of-processing, 366–369
Life events, **56**, 57
Lifestyle, 11–12, 60–61
Limbic system, 41
Linear perspective, **316**
Linguistic universals, **140**
Little Hans, 27
Lobes of brain, 42–43
Locationist theory, 79–81
Long-term memory, 330–331, 333–336
Longitudinal method, **25–26**
Looking-glass self, 297

Majority influence, 230–232
Masculinity, 174–176
Matched participants design, **21–22**
Maternal deprivation hypothesis, **186–188**
Maternal sensitivity hypothesis, 184
Maxi task, 131
Mayer-Salovey-Caruso Emotional Intelligence Test (MSCEIT), 274–275
"Me", 298
Means–end analysis, **354–355**
Means–end relationship, **110**
Media influence, 87–88, 220–221
Medulla oblongata, 42
Memory, 329–347

autobiographical, 299, **300–301**, **335**
chunks, **331–332**
cued recall, **330**
declarative (explicit), **333–335**
distinctiveness, 366–367
episodic, **334**
everyday, 341–344
eyewitness testimony, **341–344**
forgetting, 338–341
free recall, **329**
improving, 369–373
learning and, 329
long-term, 330–331, 333–336
multistore model, 330–331
non-declarative (implicit), **333–334**, 335–336
organisation, 336–338
recognition, **330**
recovered, 340
rehearsal, **330**
schemas, 336–338
semantic, 334–335
short-term, 330–333
span, **331–332**
stages, 329
working, **332–333**
Mental rotation, **167**
Mental set, **352–353**
Method of loci, 369–370
Methods of investigation, 17–28
    case study, **27–28**
    correlational studies, 26–27
    cross-sectional method, **25–26**
    experimental method, 17–24
    field experiments, **23**
    longitudinal method, **25–26**
    observational studies, 24–25
Microgenetic method, **129**
Midbrain, **41**
Milgram, Stanley, 5, 235–238
Minority influence, 232–234
Mirror self-recognition, 298–299
Mnemonics, **369–373**
Modern racism, 198
Molaison, Henry (HM), 27
Monocular cues, **316**
Monotropy hypothesis, **186**, 188
Monozygotic twins, **36**
Moods, 69–70
Moral development, 151–163
    cognitive-developmental theory (Kohlberg), 152–156
    components of morality, 151
    consistency of morality, 152
    Gilligan's theory, 157–158
    parental influence, 159–160
    peer influences, 160–161
Morality of care, **157**

Morality of justice, **157**
Moscovici, Serge, 232–234
Motion parallax, **316**
Motivation, 374–377
Müller-Lyer illusion, 320, 321, 322
Multiple intelligences, 271–273
Multistore model, 330–331

Names, remembering, 371
Nature–nurture issue, 36
Negative punishment, **111**
Negative reinforcers, **112**
Nervous system, 38–41
Neuroticism, **286**
Non-declarative memory, **333–334,**
    335–336
Noradrenaline, **53**
Normative influence, **231**
Norms, **242**
Null hypothesis, **18**

Obedience to authority, 5, 234–238
Object permanence, **122**
Object recognition, 318–320
Observational learning, **114–116,**
    168
Observational studies, 24–25
Occipital lobe, 42, 43
Occupational stress, 57–58
Oculomotor cues, **317**
Operant conditioning, 107–113,
    108
Opportunity sampling, **20**
Orbitofrontal cortex, 79, 81
Order effects, 22–23
Outside-in theories, 140, 142–144
Over-regularisation, **139**
Overlapping waves model, 129–130

Parasympathetic nervous system, **40**
Parental influence
    aggression, 90, 97–98
    moral development, 159–160
    pro-social behaviour, 219–220
Parietal lobe, 42, 43
Participant selection, 19–20
Pavlov, Ivan, 103–105
Peer influences, moral development,
    160–161
Pegword system, 370–371
Perception, **313**, *see also* Visual
    perception
Peripheral nervous system, 38–40
Personality, 279–295
    altruism, 217
    assessment, 282–284
    Big Five model, 287–289
    cultural variations, 279–280
    definition, 279

determinants, 280
Freud's psychoanalytic approach,
    280–282
gender differences, 167
implicit personality theory,
    250–252
prejudice, 201–202
questionnaires, 283–284
social cognitive theory, 289–293
stress, 55–56
trait theory, 284–289
Type A, **55**
Type D, **56**
Phobias, 106–107
    social phobia, 10–11
Phonological loop, **332**
Phonology, **138**
Physical attractiveness, 252–254
Piaget, Jean, 121–127
Pictorial cues, 316
Pidgin language, 141
Planning, 355–356
Pons, 42
Population, **19**
Positive and Negative Affect
    Schedule (PANAS-X), 72
Positive punishment, **111**
Post-conventional morality, **154**
Pragmatics, **138**
Pre-conventional morality, **154**
Prefrontal lobe, 43
Prejudice, **197**
    declining levels of, 197–198
    explanations of, 200–205
    intergroup contact hypothesis,
        205–207
    personality, 201–202
    realistic group conflict theory,
        203–204
    recategorisation, **208–209**
    reducing, 205–209
    salient categorisation, **207–208**
    social identity, 204–205
    stereotypes, **198–200**
Pre-operational stage, 122–126
Primacy effect, 250–251
Primary reinforcers, **108**
Priming, **335–336**
Privation, **186,** 188–189
Proactive aggression, **85**
Proactive interference, **338–339**
Problem-focused coping, 63–64
Problem solving, 349–356
    definition, 349
    heuristics, **354–355**
    ill-defined problems, 349
    insight vs. non-insight problems,
        350–351
    past experience, 351–354

planning, 355–356
    strategies, 354–356
    well-defined problems, 349
Productive language, **138**
Pro-social behaviour, **213–227**
    cultural variations, 218–219
    development, 214–215
    encouraging, 219–221
    individual differences, 215
    parental influence, 219–220
    television programs encouraging,
        220–221
    video games, 221
Psychoanalysis, 9–10
Psychoanalytic approach, 280–282
Psychology
    as common sense, 4–6
    defined, 3
    described, 3–4
    importance of, 9–12
    usefulness, 4–7
Psychosexual development, 281
Psychoticism, **286**
Public self-presentation, 302
Punishment, 111

Quota sampling, **19–20**

Racism, 197–198
Random sampling, **19**
Randomisation, **21**
Rationalisation, **337**
Reactive aggression, **85**
Realistic group conflict, 203–204
Recategorisation, **208–209**
Receptive language, **138**
Reciprocal altruism, **215**
Recognition, **330**
Recognition-by-components theory,
    318–320
Recovered memories, 340
Regression, **282**
Rehearsal, **330**
Reinforcement schedules, 108–109
Reliability, **265**
Repeated measures design, **21,**
    22–23
Replication, **23**
Representative sample, **19**
Repression, 340–341
Research methods, *see* Methods of
    investigation
Resistant attachment, **182**
Retrieval, 329
Retroactive interference, **338–339**
Reversibility, **123–124**
Robbers Cave study, 203
Romanian orphanage children, 189
Romantic attraction, 257–259

Salient categorisation, 207–208
Sample, **19**
Schedules of reinforcement, 108–109
Schemas, **336–338**
Scientific creativity, 358–360
Secondary reinforcers, **108**
Secure attachment, **182**
Selective placement, **268**
Self-concept, 297–309
    changing, 302–303
    cultural variations, 298, 301–302
    development, 298–301
    gender differences, 301–302
    "I", 298
    "me", 298
    public self-presentation, 302
    self-descriptions, 299–300
    self-esteem, **305–308**
    self-knowledge, 304–305
    self-recognition, 298–299
    social identity, 303
    three aspects, 297
Self-descriptions, 299–300
Self-disclosure, **257**
Self-efficacy, **290**
Self-esteem, **305–308**
Self-knowledge, 304–305
Self-recognition, 298–299
Self-regulation, **291–293**
Self-serving bias, **305–306**
Self-socialisation theory, 170–172
Semantic bootstrapping, 140
Semantic dementia, 43
Semantic memory, **334–335**
Semantics, **138**
Sensori-motor stage, 122
Sex, 165
Sex differences, *see* Gender differences
Sex-role stereotypes, **165**
Sex-typed behaviour, **165**
Shading, 316
Shaping, **109**
Shared attention, 131, 132
Short-term memory, 330–333
Siegler, Robert, 129
Similarity, 254–256, 259
Situational attribution, **248**
Situational factors, aggression, 86–90
Sixteen Personality Factor (16PF) test, 284–285
Skill learning, **335–336**
Skinner, Burrhus Fred, 108
Social cognitive theory
    gender development, 168–169
    personality, 290–293

Social competence training, 97
Social desirability bias, **283**
Social identity, 204–205, 303
Social influence, **229–245**
    conformity, **229–234**
    crowd behaviour, 241–243
    group decision making, 238–240
    majority influence, 230–232
    minority influence, 232–234
    obedience to authority, 5, 234–238
    social power, **240–241**
Social learning, aggression, 91–93
Social norms, **86**
Social perception, **247**
    attributions, 247–250
    familiarity, 256–257
    implicit personality theory, **250–252**
    physical attractiveness, 252–254
    romantic attraction, 257–259
    similarity, 254–256, 259
Social phobia, **10–11**
Social power, 240–241
Social Readjustment Rating Scale (SRRS), 57
Social support, 64–66
Socially sensitive research, 28
Sociometer theory, 305
Somatic nervous system, **39**
Spatial ability, 166–167
Split-brain patients, 44–45
Spontaneous recovery, **105**
Standardised procedures, 20
Standardised tests, **264**
Stanford prison experiment, 240–241
Stereopsis, **317**
Stereotypes, **198–200**
Storage, 329
Story method, 371–372
Strange Situation, 182
Stress, 51–67
    causes, 51, 55–59
    coping strategies, 63–64
    definition, 51
    effects of, 51–52
    general adaptation syndrome, 52–53
    hassles, 56
    hypothalamic-pituitary-adrenocortical (HPA) axis, 53, 54–55
    illness link, 59–61
    life events, 56, 57
    personality factors, 55–56
    physiology of, 52–55

    reducing, 61–66
    rising levels of, 52
    social support, 64–66
    sympathetic adrenal medullary (SAM) system, 53
    technostress, 58–59
    workplace, 57–58
Stress inoculation training (SIT), 61–62
Stressor, 51
Sympathetic adrenal medullary (SAM) system, 53
Sympathetic nervous system, **40**
Syntax, **138**

Technostress, 58–59
Telegraphic period, **138**
Television, 87–88, 220–221
Temperament hypothesis, 184–185
Temporal lobe, 42, 43
Testing effect, **373–374**
Testosterone, 93, 94, 172
Texture gradient, 316
Thalamus, **41**
Theory of mind, **130–133**
Third eye problem, 126–127
Third-party punishment, **216**, 217, 218
Three mountains task, 124–125
Time-out technique, 97, **111**
Token economy, **112–113**
Traits, **284–289**
Transfer-appropriate processing, 368
Twenty Statements Test, 279–280, 301
Twin studies, 36–38, 93, 201, 215, 267–268
Type A personality, **55**
Type D personality, **56**

Unconditioned reflex, **104**
Unconditioned response, **104**
Unconditioned stimulus, **104**
Uses of a Brick test, 356

Validity, **265–266**
    ecological, **20**
Variables
    confounding, **18–19**
    dependent, **18**
    independent, **18**
Verbal mnemonics, 371–372
Video games, 88–89, 221
Viewpoint-dependent perception, **319**
Viewpoint-invariant perception, 318

Vision-for-action system, 322
Vision-for-perception system, 321–322
Visual illusions, 314, 317, **320**–322
Visual imagery mnemonics, 369–371
Visual perception, 313–327
    change blindness, 322–326, **323**
    depth perception, 316–318

object recognition, 318–320
perceptual organisation, 313–315
visual illusions, 314, 317, **320**–322
Visuo-spatial sketchpad, **332**–333
Vocabulary, 139
Vygotsky, Lev, 127–129

Watson, John, 103
Weapon focus, **343**–344
Weapons effect, **89**–90
WEIRD societies, 7
Working memory, **332**–333
Workplace stress, 57–58

Zimbardo, Philip, 240–241
Zone of proximal development, **127**

Illustration credits

Chapter 1
Page 7: Shutterstock.com. Page 9: © adoc-photos / Corbis. Page 12: Paul Maguire / Shutterstock.com.

Chapter 2
Page 23: faberfoto / Shutterstock.com.

Chapter 3
Page 35: © adoc-photos / Corbis. Page 37: Shutterstock.com. Page 45: Shutterstock.com.

Chapter 4
Page 57: Chad McDermott / Shutterstock.com. Page 61: Nejron Photo / Shutterstock.com. Page 65: Galina Barskaya / Shutterstock.com.

Chapter 5
Page 71 (left): Shutterstock.com. Page 71 (right): Bruce Yeung / Shutterstock.com. Page 80 (top): From Lindquist et al., 2012. © Cambridge University Press 2012. Reproduced with permission. Page 80 (bottom): From Ward (2010) © Psychology Press.

Chapter 6
Page 89: Sean D / Shutterstock.com. Page 90: © Guy Cali / Corbis. Page 91: Reproduced by kind permission of Professor Albert Bandura.

Chapter 7
Page 103: © Underwood & Underwood / Corbis. Page 104 (top): © Bettmann / Corbis. Page 108: Time & Life Pictures / Getty Images. Page 109 (bottom): © Steve Allen / Brand X / Corbis.

Chapter 8
Page 121: © Farrell Grehan / CORBIS. Page 122: Pinkcandy / Shutterstock.com. Page 123: Photos by Peter Willetts. Reproduced with permission.

Chapter 9
Page 138: Photo supplied by Professor Michael W. Eysenck. Page 139: Reproduced with permission from the International Linguistic Association. Pages 145 & 146: From Savage-Rumbaugh & Lewin (1994). Used by permission of John Wiley & Sons Inc.

Chapter 10
Page 158: Losevsky Photo and Video / Shutterstock.com. Page 161: Joseph / Shutterstock.com.

Chapter 11
Page 171 (left): Shutterstock.com. Page 171 (right): Shutterstock.com.

Chapter 12
Page 189: © Bernard Bisson / Sygma / Corbis. Page 192: paulaphoto / Shutterstock.com.

Chapter 13
Page 198: © Bettmann / CORBIS. Page 199: © Image Source / Corbis. Page 201: © Hulton-Deutsch Collection / CORBIS.

Chapter 14
Page 214: © Image Source / Corbis. Page 215: Rene Jansa / Shutterstock.com. Page 220: Karen Struthers / Shutterstock.com. Page 224: © Science Photo Library / Corbis.

Chapter 15
Page 235: From the film Obedience © 1968 by Stanley Milgram. Copyright © renewed 1991 by Alexandra Milgram and distributed by Penn State Media Sales. Permission granted by Alexandra Milgram. Page 240: Reproduced with permission of P.G. Zimbardo Inc.

Chapter 16
Page 249: Lisa F. Young / Shutterstock.com. Page 253 (top left): © Rune Hellestad / Corbis. Page 253 (top right): courtyardpix / Shutterstock.com. Page 253 (bottom left): © Rune Hellestad / Corbis. Page 253 (bottom right): tikona / Shutterstock.com. Page 256: Monkey Business Images / Shutterstock.com.

Chapter 17
Page 263: paul prescott / Shutterstock.com.

Chapter 18
Page 283: © Ronnie Kaufman / Corbis. Page 287: © Sunset Boulevard / Corbis. Page 288: Dolly / Shutterstock.com. Page 291: Kzenon / Shutterstock.com.

Chapter 19
Page 298: Alison Williams / Shutterstock.com. Page 303: Nicholas Moore / Shutterstock.com.

Chapter 20
Page 316: © Momatiuk - Eastcott/Corbis. Page 324: From Rensink et al. (1997). Copyright © 1997 by SAGE. Reprinted by permission of SAGE Publications. Page 325: From Hollingworth & Henderson (2002). Copyright © 2002 American Psychological Association. Reproduced with permission.

Chapter 21
Page 336: Kristin Smith / Shutterstock.com. Page 343: From Bruce et al. (1999), Copyright © 1999 American Psychological Association. Reprinted with permission. Page 344: Daniel Wiedemann / Shutterstock.com.

Chapter 22
Page 356: Nejron Photo / Shutterstock.com.

Chapter 23
Page 371 (top): Pixsooz / Shutterstock.com. Page 371 (bottom): Stuart Jenner / Shutterstock.com. Page 373: Bikeworldtravel / Shutterstock.com. Page 374: From Roediger & Karpicke (2006). Copyright © Blackwell Publishing. Reproduced with permission. Page 376: From Klein et al. (1999). Copyright © American Psychological Association. Reproduced with permission.

All cartoons by Sean Longcroft www.longcroft.net/ © Psychology Press.